THE CAMBRIDGE HISTORY OF
AMERICAN LITERATURE

Volume 6
Prose Writing
1910–1950

The Cambridge History of American Literature addresses the broad spectrum of new and established directions in all branches of American writing and will include the work of scholars and critics who have shaped, and who continue to shape, what has become a major area of literary scholarship. The authors span four decades of achievement in American literary criticism, thereby speaking for the continuities as well as the disruptions sustained between generations of scholarship. Generously proportioned narratives allow at once for a broader vision and sweep of American literary history than has been possible previously, and while the voice of traditional criticism forms a background for these narratives, it joins forces with the diversity of interests that characterize contemporary literary studies.

The *History* offers wide-ranging, interdisciplinary accounts of American genres and periods. Generated partly by the recent unearthing of previously neglected texts, the expansion of material in American literature coincides with a dramatic increase in the number and variety of approaches to that material. The multifaceted scholarly and critical enterprise embodied in *The Cambridge History of American Literature* addresses these multiplicities – the social, the cultural, the intellectual, and the aesthetic – and demonstrates a richer concept of authority in literary studies than is found in earlier accounts.

THE CAMBRIDGE
HISTORY OF
AMERICAN LITERATURE

Volume 6
Prose Writing
1910–1950

General Editor

SACVAN BERCOVITCH
Harvard University

CAMBRIDGE
UNIVERSITY PRESS

PUBLISHED BY THE PRESS SYNDICATE OF THE UNIVERSITY OF CAMBRIDGE
The Pitt Building, Trumpington Street, Cambridge, United Kingdom

CAMBRIDGE UNIVERSITY PRESS
The Edinburgh Building, Cambridge CB2 2RU, UK
40 West 20th Street, New York, NY 10011-4211, USA
477 Williamstown Road, Port Melbourne, VIC 3207, Australia
Ruiz de Alarcón 13, 28014 Madrid, Spain
Dock House, The Waterfront, Cape Town 8001, South Africa

http://www.cambridge.org

First published 2002

Printed in the United Kingdom at the University Press, Cambridge

Typeface Garamond 3 11/13 pt   *System* LaTeX 2_ε [TB]

A catalog record for this book is available from the British Library

ISBN 0 521 49731 0 hardback

CONTENTS

Acknowledgments   *page* viii

Introduction   xiii

A CULTURAL HISTORY OF THE MODERN
AMERICAN NOVEL   1
David Minter, Rice University

Introduction   3

    1   A Dream City, Lyric Years, and a Great War   10

1. The Novel as Ironic Reflection   10
2. Confidence and Uncertainty in *The Portrait of a Lady*   15
3. Lines of Expansion   23
4. Four Contemporaries and the Closing of the West   34
5. Chicago's "Dream City"   37
6. Frederick Jackson Turner in the Dream City   43
7. Henry Adams's *Education* and the Grammar of Progress   48
8. Jack London's Career and Popular Discourse   57
9. Innocence and Revolt in the "Lyric Years": 1900–1916   63
10. The Armory Show of 1913 and the Decline of Innocence   71
11. The Play of Hope and Despair   77
12. The Great War and the Fate of Writing   89

    2   Fiction in a Time of Plenty   102

1. When the War Was Over: the Return of Detachment   102
2. The "Jazz Age" and the "Lost Generation" Revisited   108
3. The Perils of Plenty, or How the Twenties Acquired
   a Paranoid Tilt   125
4. Disenchantment, Flight, and the Rise of Professionalism
   in an Age of Plenty   134

5. Class, Power, and Violence in a New Age 142
6. The Fear of Feminization and the Logic of Modest Ambition 151
7. Marginality and Authority / Race, Gender, and Region 160
8. War as Metaphor: the Example of Ernest Hemingway 170

      3   *The Fate of Writing During the Great Depression* 184

1. The Discovery of Poverty and the Return of Commitment 184
2. The Search for "Culture" as a Form of Commitment 190
3. Three Responses: the Examples of Henry Miller,
   Djuna Barnes, and John Dos Passos 200
4. Residual Individualism and Hedged Commitments 208
5. The Search for Shared Purpose: Struggles on the Left 225
6. Documentary Literature and the Disarming of Dissent 241
7. The Southern Renaissance: Forms of Reaction and Innovation 250
8. History and Novels / Novels and History: the Example
   of William Faulkner 266

FICTIONS OF THE HARLEM RENAISSANCE 283
Rafia Zafar, Washington University in St. Louis

1. A New Negro? 285
2. Black Manhattan 289
3. Avatars and Manifestos 295
4. Harlem as a State of Mind: Hughes, McKay, Toomer 306
5. A New Negro, A New Woman: Larsen, Fauset, Bonner 317
6. "Dark-skinned Selves without Fear or Shame": Thurman
   and Nugent 326
7. Genre in the Renaissance: Fisher, Schuyler, Cullen,
   White, Bontemps 332
8. Southern Daughter, Native Son: Hurston and Wright 340
9. Black Modernism 348

ETHNIC MODERNISM 353
Werner Sollors, Harvard University

Introduction 355
1. Gertrude Stein and "Negro Sunshine" 368
2. Ethnic Lives and "Lifelets" 384
3. Ethnic Themes, Modern Themes 405
4. Mary Antin: Progressive Optimism against the Odds 411

5. Who is "American"?   422
6. American Languages   428
7. "All the Past We Leave Behind"? Ole E. Rölvaag
   and the Immigrant Trilogy   434
8. Modernism, Ethnic Labeling, and the Quest for Wholeness:
   Jean Toomer's New American Race   442
9. Freud, Marx, Hard-boiled   452
10. Hemingway Spoken Here   465
11. Henry Roth: Ethnicity, Modernity, and Modernism   475
12. The Clock, the Salesman and the Breast   490
13. Was Modernism Antitotalitarian?   512
14. Facing the Extreme   539
15. Grand Central Terminal   552

   Chronology   557
   Bibliography   597
   Index   605

ACKNOWLEDGMENTS

FROM THE GENERAL EDITOR

My thanks to Harvard University for its continuing support of this project. I am grateful for the cheerful assistance of Ray Ryan of Cambridge University Press and for the steady personal and professional support of Eytan Bercovitch and Susan L. Mizruchi. I would also like to express my gratitude to Jonathan Fortescue, an outstanding member of a new generation of Americanists, who composed the Chronology, compiled the Bibliography, and wrote most of the second part of the Introduction, summarizing the connections between the different parts of this volume.

Sacvan Bercovitch

A CULTURAL HISTORY OF THE MODERN AMERICAN NOVEL

I am indebted to Rice University for research support that enabled me to complete my contribution to this volume and to Emory University for support that enabled me to begin it.

Among several scholars who worked with me on the *Columbia Literary History of the United States*, I want especially to acknowledge those who wrote on the prose of the period covered by this book: Daniel Aaron, Quentin Anderson, James M. Cox, Donald M. Kartiganer, Donald McQuade, Elaine Showalter, Wendy Steiner, Robert Stepto, Linda Wagner, and Michael Wood. I learned from all of them. I am also indebted to my colleagues on *The Harper American Literature* – Robert Atwan, Martha Banta, Justin Kaplan, Donald McQuade, Robert Stepto, Cecelia Tichi, and Helen Vendler. Working with them was a privilege.

At an early stage, I presented parts of this work at Harvard University, where I benefited from the suggestions of several people, including Daniel Aaron, Frank Lentricchia, John T. Matthews, Werner Sollors, and Robert Stepto. At a later stage, Charles Altieri and Carolyn Porter read parts of the manuscript. I am grateful for their help and encouragement. Sacvan Bercovitch has offered suggestions and encouragement all along the way. I am deeply grateful to him.

Terry Munisteri of Rice University helped me in the last stages of this project, and I am grateful for her expert assistance.

Finally, I want to thank my large family, several generations deep, who have been with me as I wrote, including those now dead whose lives spanned part or all of the period that my contribution covers: my parents, Kenneth Cruse Minter (1889–1948) and Frances Hennessy Minter (1892–1948); my sisters Mary Frances Minter Wright (1917–67), Elizabeth Minter White (1919–99), and Anna Minter Froman (1922–98). To Caroline, my wife, who has talked with me about this work from its beginnings to its end, I owe more than I can possibly say. Together, we dedicate it to our children, Christopher and Frances, with good hope, gratitude, and love.

David Minter

FICTIONS OF THE HARLEM RENAISSANCE

For my mother, Elizabeth Meyers Zafar Havens, born in Indianapolis at the height of the Harlem Renaissance, who got herself to New York City just as fast as she could.

Many people supported me as I worked to write, then revise, then finish this project. First and foremost I would like to thank Sacvan Bercovitch, mentor, friend, and colleague, who convinced me to take on the daunting task of writing a narrative of Harlem Renaissance fiction; I hope my efforts come somewhere near the mark his own scholarship has set. Werner Sollors, another long-time inspiration, helped me over many a rough spot – by his example, through his advice, and with his encouragement. Had I not had the research assistance of Susan Hays Bussey, this project would have taken even longer to appear; Matt Calihman pitched in at the eleventh hour. Adele Tuchler and Raye Riggins provided a nonstop cheering section. Numerous faculty friends at Washington University, in English and in African and Afro-American Studies, put up with a sometimes distracted colleague. My husband, Bill Paul, and son, Nathan, provided love in abundance. Were it not for all of you, I might have given up long ago. The faults of the text are indisputably mine. Its successes I happily share with family, colleagues, and friends.

Rafia Zafar

ETHNIC MODERNISM

I am grateful to Sacvan Bercovitch for asking me to contribute to *The Cambridge History of American Literature*, for encouraging me along the way, for his helpful comments, and for his remarkable patience. The final writing was facilitated by a senior fellowship from the National Endowment for the Humanities. I am grateful to Jesse Matz for reading some sections and making excellent suggestions; and I profited enormously from presenting the introductory sections at a Harvard English Department faculty colloquium. I also wish to acknowledge the research assistance of Breda O'Keeffe, Jessica Hook, and, in the last stages of writing, Erica Michelstein – who also proofread the whole manuscript and made many valuable suggestions; Marques Redd assisted in putting together the Chronology; and Francesca Petrosini helped with loose ends and the double-checking of sources. More than a decade of teaching a course on "Ethnicity, Modernity, and Modernism" at Harvard University has helped me shape the argument that is developed here, and I am grateful to the graduate students who taught the sections as well as to the undergraduates who took the course and wrote many excellent term papers. I have also benefited from student work in many other courses, and I would like to acknowledge that my interest in Japanese American newspapers from the detention camps was first aroused by Karen Sekiguchi's 1977 term paper, "Perceptions of an Ethnic-American Identity," for a course at Columbia College.

Instead of aiming for "coverage," which would be a particularly complicated goal for the present section, I have chosen to place emphasis on certain works that were particularly important for the story of American ethnic prose literature from 1910 to 1950. Though occasionally plots are "summarized," there is a continued focus on single sentences and paragraphs as the representative units of prose works. Analogous developments in the visual arts are examined throughout, and a recurrent concern is for examples of modernity, in representations of means of transportation such as the trolley as well as in selected examples of secularization.

Werner Sollors

CHRONOLOGY

I owe thanks to the many colleagues and students at Harvard University who have made teaching, learning, and writing about literature and history a pleasure, particularly Tim McCarthy, Neal Dolan, and Charles Ruberto. For his sage, contrarian, and truly sympathetic advice, I thank Adam Weisman. More than anyone else, Sacvan Bercovitch has been instrumental in my progress as a scholar. I am grateful here for his help with the Chronology and especially for his collaboration on the Introduction. Most of all, I thank my wife, Elizabeth, for her constant support and companionship.

Jonathan Fortescue

A version of David Minter's contribution to this volume of the Cambridge History of American Literature was previously published as *A Cultural History of the American Novel, 1890–1940: Henry James to William Faulkner.*

INTRODUCTION

This multivolume history marks a new beginning in the study of American literature. The first *Cambridge History of American Literature* (1917) helped introduce a new branch of English writing. *The Literary History of the United States*, assembled thirty years later under the aegis of Robert E. Spiller, helped establish a new field of academic study. This *History* embodies the work of a generation of Americanists who have redrawn the boundaries of the field. Trained mainly in the 1960s and early 1970s, representing the broad spectrum of both new and established directions in all branches of American writing, these scholars and critics have shaped, and continue to shape, what has become a major area of modern literary scholarship.

Over the past three decades, Americanist literary criticism has expanded from a border province into a center of humanist studies. The vitality of the field is reflected in the rising interest in American literature nationally and globally, in the scope of scholarly activity, and in the polemical intensity of debate. Significantly, American texts have come to provide a major focus for inter- and cross-disciplinary investigation. Gender studies, ethnic studies, and popular-culture studies, among others, have penetrated to all corners of the profession, but perhaps their single largest base is American literature. The same is true with regard to controversies over multiculturalism and canon formation: the issues are transhistorical and transcultural, but the debates themselves have often turned on American books.

However we situate ourselves in these debates, it seems clear that the activity they have generated has provided a source of intellectual revitalization and new research, involving a massive recovery of neglected and undervalued bodies of writing. We know far more than ever about what some have termed (in the plural) *American literatures*, a term grounded in the persistence in the United States of different traditions, different kinds of aesthetics, even different notions of the literary.

These developments have enlarged the meanings as well as the materials of American literature. For this generation of critics and scholars, American literary history is no longer the history of a certain agreed-on group of American masterworks, nor is it any longer based on a certain agreed-on historical perspective on American writing. The quests for certainty and agreement continue, as they should, but they proceed now within a climate of critical decentralization – of controversy, sectarianism, and, at best, dialogue among different schools of explanation.

This scene of conflict signals a shift in structures of academic authority. The practice of all literary history hitherto, from its inception in the eighteenth century, has depended on an established consensus about the essence or nature of its subject. Today the invocation of consensus sounds rather like an appeal for compromise, or like nostalgia. The study of American literary history now defines itself in the plural, as a multivocal, multifaceted scholarly, critical, and pedagogic enterprise. Authority in this context is a function of disparate but connected bodies of knowledge. We might call it the authority of difference. It resides in part in the energies of heterogeneity: a variety of contending constituencies, bodies of materials, and sets of authorities. In part it resides in the critic's capacity to connect: to turn the particularity of his or her approach into a form of challenge and engagement, so that it actually gains substance and depth in relation to other, sometimes complementary, sometimes conflicting modes of explanation.

This new *Cambridge History of American Literature* claims authority on both counts, contentious and collaborative. In a sense, this makes it representative of the culture it describes. Our *History* is fundamentally pluralist – a federated histories of American literatures – but it is a pluralism divided against itself, the vivid expression of ongoing debates within the profession and the society at large about cultural values, beliefs, and patterns of thought. Some of these narratives may be termed celebratory, insofar as they uncover correlations between social and aesthetic achievement, between technological and stylistic innovation. Others are explicitly oppositional, sometimes to the point of turning literary analysis into a critique of (even attacks on) pluralism itself. Ironically, however, the oppositional outlook here marks the *History*'s most traditional aspect. The high moral stance it assumes – literary analysis as the occasion for resistance and alternative vision – is grounded in the romantic reverence of art and the genteel view of high literature. That view insisted on the universality of ideals embodied in great books. By implication, therefore, and often by direct assault on social norms and practices, especially those of Western capitalism, it fostered a broad ethical-aesthetic antinomianism. The result was a celebration of literature as a world of its own, a sphere of higher laws that thus provided (in Matthew Arnold's words) a standing criticism of life.

By mid-twentieth century, that approach had issued, on the one hand, in the New Critics' assault on industrial society, and, on the other hand, in the neo-Marxists' utopian theory of art. The new oppositionalism, including that of the counterculture critics, is inextricably bound up with these legacies.

The complex relationship this makes between advocacy and critique speaks directly to the problem of nationality. This has become a defining problem of our time, and it may be best to clarify what for earlier historians was too obvious to mention: that in these volumes, *America* designates the United States, or the territories that were to become part of the United States. Although several of our authors adopt a comparatist trans-Atlantic or pan-American framework, although several of them discuss works in other languages, and although still others argue for a postnational (even post-American) perspective, as a rule their concerns center on writing in English in the United States – "American literature" as it has been (and still is) commonly understood in its linguistic and national implications.

This restriction is a deliberate choice on our part. To some extent, no doubt, it reflects limitations of time, space, training, and available materials; but it must be added that our contributors have made the most of their limitations. They have taken advantage of time, space, training, and newly available materials to turn nationality itself into a *question* of literary history. Precisely because of their focus on English-language literatures in the United States, the term *America* for them is neither a narrative donnée – an assumed or inevitable or natural premise – nor an objective background (*the* national history). Quite the contrary: it is the contested site of many sorts of literary-historical inquiries. What had presented itself as a neutral territory, hospitable to all authorized parties, turns out on examination to be, and to have always been, a volatile combat zone.

America in these volumes is a historical entity, the United States of America. It is also a declaration of community, a people constituted and sustained by verbal fiat, a set of universal principles, a strategy of social cohesion, a summons to social protest, a prophecy, a dream, an aesthetic ideal, a trope of the modern (*progress, opportunity, the new*), a semiotics of inclusion (*melting pot, patchwork quilt, nation of nations*), and a semiotics of exclusion, closing out not only the Old World but all other countries of the Americas, North and South, as well as large groups within the United States. A nationality so conceived is a rhetorical battleground. *America* in these volumes is a shifting, many-sided focal point for exploring the historicity of the text and the textuality of history.

Not coincidentally, these are the two most vexed issues today in literary studies. At no time in literary studies has theorizing about history been more acute and pervasive. It is hardly too much to say that what joins all the special interests in the field, all factions in our current "dissensus," is an overriding interest in history: as the ground and texture of ideas, metaphors, and myths; as the substance of the texts we read and the spirit in which we interpret them. Even if we acknowledge that great books – a few configurations of language raised to an extraordinary pitch of intensity – have transcended their time and place (and even if we believe that their enduring power offers a recurrent source of opposition), it is evident on reflection that concepts of aesthetic transcendence are themselves time bound. Like other claims to the absolute, from the hermeneutics of faith to scientific objectivity, aesthetic claims about High Art are shaped by history. We grasp their particular forms of beyondness (the aesthetics of divine inspiration; the aesthetics of ambiguity, subversion, and indeterminacy) through an identifiably historical consciousness.

The same recognition of contingency extends to the writing of history. Some histories are truer than others; a few histories are invested for a time with the grandeur of being "definitive" and "comprehensive"; but all are narratives conditioned by their historical moments. So are these. Our intention here is to make limitations a source of open-endedness. All previous histories of American literature have been either totalizing or encyclopedic. They have offered either the magisterial sweep of a single vision or a multitude of terse accounts that come to seem just as totalizing, if only because the genre of the brief, expert synthesis precludes the development of authorial voice. Here, in contrast, American literary history unfolds through a polyphony of large-scale narratives. Because the number of contributors is limited, each of them has the scope to elaborate distinctive views (premises, arguments, analyses); each of their narratives, therefore, is persuasive by demonstration, rather than by assertion; and each is related to the others (in spite of difference) through themes and concerns, anxieties and aspirations, that are common to *this* generation of Americanists.

The authors were selected first for the excellence of their scholarship and then for the significance of the critical communities informing their work. Together, they demonstrate the achievements of Americanist literary criticism over the past three decades. Their contributions to these volumes show links as well as gaps between generations. They give voice to the extraordinary range of materials now subsumed under the heading of American literature. They express the distinctive sorts of excitement and commitment that have led to the remarkable expansion of the field. Finally, they reflect the diversity of interests that constitutes literary studies in our time as well as the ethnographic diversity that has come to characterize our universities, faculty and students alike, since World War II, and especially since the 1960s.

The same qualities inform this *History*'s organizational principles. Its flexibility of structure is meant to accommodate the varieties of American literary history. Some major writers appear in more than one volume because they belong to more than one age. Some texts are discussed in several narratives within a volume because they are important to different realms of cultural experience. Sometimes the story of a certain movement is retold from different perspectives because the story requires a plural focus: as pertaining, for example, to the margins as well as to the mainstream, or as being equally the culmination of one era and the beginning of another. Such overlap was not planned, but it was encouraged from the start, and the resulting diversity of perspectives corresponds to the sheer plenitude of literary and historical materials. It also makes for a richer, more intricate account of particulars (writers, texts, movements) than that available in any previous history of American literature.

Sacvan Bercovitch

Every volume in this *History* displays these strengths in its own way. This volume is notable for its focus on the intricate interweavings of text and context. The three authors – David Minter, Rafia Zafar, and Werner Sollors – demonstrate how social, political, economic, and technological transformations informed and embodied the emergence of aesthetic modernism in the United States. And at the same time they demonstrate how aesthetic modernism helped shape modern America. Broadly viewed, their narratives describe how the experience of rupture and fragmentation was fundamental to writers of the era. In all cases the story picks up with the disintegration of the slow, steady, typically uniform life of small-town America, and then proceeds to the shock of modernity: the invigorating yet unsettling influx of millions of immigrants; the massive internal migrations, from South to North and from rural to urban areas; and the excitement of a world where automobiles, airplanes, radio, and cinema meant that life was accelerating in every area of communication and representation. The authors relate all this to literary developments. They detail how the modernists' formalist innovations inhere in the changes in both public and private spheres, and vice versa. They reveal that modernism in America represented the conflict between, on the one hand, a nationalist nostalgia for the self-determining individual and, on the other hand, a broadening recognition – partly through the influence of such thinkers as Darwin, Marx, and

Freud – that natural forces, social factors, and family histories circumscribed personal agency. And from their different perspectives they capture the hopeful as well as the despairing efforts to champion the political promise of a democratic aesthetics.

Together, these narratives cover the full range of literary prose in the first half of the twentieth century. David Minter provides a cultural history of the American novel from the booming spectacle of the Lyric Years prior to World War I, through the postwar disillusionment of the Lost Generation, to the consolidation of the left in response to the mire of the Great Depression. Rafia Zafar tells the story of the Harlem Renaissance. Its astonishing creative energies, she shows, were not only one of the great triumphs of American literary modernism but also perhaps the most palpable metonym for the enormous national transformations of that time. Werner Sollors locates his narrative in a more international setting, drawing on intellectual as well as artistic crosscurrents. The story he tells parallels the slow, grudging, and then finally celebratory acceptance in mainstream America of the radical tenets of modernism with the concomitant assimilation of non Anglo-Saxon immigrants into the nation.

David Minter centers his discussion of the American novel on cultural dissonance. His history is episodic, building on analyses of texts and events as reciprocal expressions of a culture in conflict. Whether his subject is the ironic shape of Henry James's style, the construction of Chicago as the nation's representative city, the linguistic play of Gertrude Stein, the strategies of consumer capitalism, the hedonism of the Jazz Age, or the moral efforts to document economic corruption and collapse, he demonstrates how the writers he treats capture the contradictions and tensions in modern American life. What he reveals culturally is a network of imperfect communities whose unity and continual renewal depend upon precariously possessed, often painful, memories, along with internally contending values. His literary portrait of the period includes the crafted fiction of high society, hard-boiled novels of the mean streets, and darkly nostalgic accounts of a fading rural life. It also provides detailed examinations of the major novelists from Edith Wharton and F. Scott Fitzgerald to William Faulkner. Fusing text and context, Minter's readings illuminate simultaneously the achievement of the modern American literature and the dynamics of modernity in the United States.

Even a cursory view of the Chronology suggests the centrality to that literature of the Harlem Renaissance. It is almost as if in the 1920s and 1930s the national imagination migrated north along with the African American population. Rafia Zafar complicates this image with her account of how this movement arose out of self-conscious artifice, political motivation, and social engineering. Tracing the origins of the Harlem Renaissance back to the writings of major thinkers and political leaders (such as W. E. B. Du Bois, Marcus Garvey, and Alain Locke) and then describing the creative flowering of the movement in its major writers (among others, Zora Neale Hurston, Langston Hughes, Richard Wright, and Nella Larsen), Zafar tells of the complex effort to join artistic expression and the process of social and racial empowerment. Her story leads through the dramatic historical changes after World War I, when a series of racial crises – black veterans returning to claim their rights in the country for which they had fought, abused tenant farmers fleeing the failing agricultural regions, the increasing enforcement of segregation laws in the South – solidified the political commitments of black intellectuals and artists. In contrast to the writers of the Lost Generation, these African Americans, Zafar shows, came north to construct the proud figure of the "New Negro," a figure which, in its several guises, has had a lasting impact on the American mind and imagination.

The public reception of modernism is a main subject of Werner Sollors's narrative. For him, the early mainstream denigration of cubism and jazz, the banning of Joyce's *Ulysses*, and William Randolph Hearst's campaign against modernist art are examples of an intensifying conflict through the 1930s between "fascist realism" and "democratic modernism." In effect Sollors elucidates the connections between the struggle for control over what counts as art and who counts as the public for art. And he shows that at the heart of these connections lay what Henry James called "the ethnic question." His analysis thus centers on ethnic writers of the period, often fluent in "foreign languages" and comfortable with international currents of thought, who undertook the work of reimagining the United States as a multicultural country. Set against the background of widespread ethnic intolerance, the first half of his narrative brings together a diversity of literary-cultural themes: for example, the ethnic equanimity and formal experimentation in Gertrude Stein's *Three Lives*, the immigrant claim to authentic American identity in Mary Antin's *The Promised Land*, the stripped-down style of modern speech in Ernest Hemingway's *A Farewell to Arms*, and the effort to reintegrate the African experience within the definition of "American" in Jean Toomer's *Cane*. In Henry Roth's *Call It Sleep*, Sollors locates a fusion in ethnic modernism of all these elements; he then turns to provocatively different resolutions or resistant patterns in the work of Pietro di Donata, Jerre Mangione, and many others.

Sollors's narrative follows the progress of modernism through four stages: cosmopolitan and experimental from 1910 through World War I; self-reflexive and demotic in the twenties; realist and socially committed in the wake of the Great Depression; and then, with World War II and the Cold War, an

A CULTURAL HISTORY OF THE MODERN AMERICAN NOVEL

David Minter

INTRODUCTION

N EAR THE END of *The Rebel*, Albert Camus speaks, first, of the "procedures of beauty," which he defines as imaginative affirmations of "the
value and the dignity common" to all human beings, and, then, of
the "procedures of rebellion," which he associates with all forms of resistance
to injustice, as ways of contesting "reality while endowing it with unity."
Some of Camus's key terms – "beauty" and "rebellion," for example – may
strike us as being too extreme. But his words place both aesthetic creation
and political resistance within history and, then, implicitly define them as
ways of contesting established relations. In addition, almost surreptitiously,
his formulation reminds us that all of our contesting retains as one part of its
motive the restoration if not the preservation of "unity."

While celebrating itself as the land of the free, the United States has repeatedly demonstrated its willingness to deal harshly, as though in an emergency,
with those who violate the written and unwritten rules by which it seeks both
to authorize and to limit resistance. It tells us a great deal about the varied
means and the vigilance of our society in authorizing and policing freedom
that novelists as different in background, social status, and disposition as Jack
London, Edith Wharton, and William Faulkner have added protagonists as
different as Martin Eden, Lily Bart, and Joe Christmas to its list of victims.
Yet even when it has tilted toward the dream of perfect order – as it has in
crucial moments throughout its history, including the 1920s and the 1950s,
for example – the United States has continued to honor, however cautiously,
the counterdream of personal freedom and civil liberty, as though mindful
that no culture can survive by embracing one of these dreams and abandoning the other. To avoid desiccation, cultures committed principally to the
dream of order have found it necessary to tolerate some measure of change;
to avoid disintegration, those committed principally to the dream of freedom
have found it necessary to impose limits. Both the oscillation of the culture
of the United States in this regard and the changing roles of its literature in
this process are central to the story we can recover by examining, yet again,

the fiction of the late nineteenth and early twentieth centuries provided we examine that fiction with the intention of searching out reciprocities not only within and among novels but also between novels and cultural events. In such a venture, we must read novels as cultural events, mindful that history shapes our writing and our reading as well as other aspects of our lives; and we must also read cultural events as texts that differ in degree, but not in kind, from novels. When we use words to record, report, or interpret events, we turn them into scenes, spectacles, or stories. Whether this process is elaborate, as it tends to be in art, or more modest, as it tends to be in journalism or history, it does violence to events because, as actions, events do not make meaning; they take possession of time. They fill the minutes of our days, command our attention for their duration, and then disappear. Once we take possession of them as storytellers, with words arranged in a certain order, we transform them. Furthermore, although writing and reading play different roles in this process, they have crucial things in common, as Ralph Waldo Emerson suggests in "The American Scholar" when he pairs "creative reading" with "creative writing" as activities of "labor and invention," put to the task of making words on a page become "luminous with manifold allusion." Once we begin to trace reciprocities among novels and between novels and cultural events, we are likely to assume that we will be able to create a well-wrought narrative that follows a traditional, linear, logocentric line only to discover that, in order to discuss cultural events as different kinds of narratives and different kinds of narratives as cultural events without hypostatizing the events or idealizing the stories, we must give up such a model and trace instead interrelated yet discontinuous lines, engaging and reengaging novels in some moments, cultural events in others. What follows, therefore, is, in one of its aspects, an episodic cultural history that is built around discussions of a series of events and in part around a discussion of several novels that unfolds as an episodic cultural history. Put another way, it is a narrative in which cultural events provide a lens for reading novels, and novels provide a lens for reading cultural events.

In 1887 Matthew Arnold noted, with dismay, that the novel had become "the most popular and the most possible" form of imaginative literature. Between 1890 and 1940 the novel continued to rise both in popularity and in authority. Its means of dominance changed, however, pushed in part by Henry James's interest in refining it as an art form. With the work of the great historical sociologists of the nineteenth and early twentieth centuries – Karl Marx, Emile Durkheim, Ernst Troeltsch, and Max Weber, among others – came a new awareness of how history envelops human life. Even Troeltsch, whose greatest subject was the social teachings of the Christian churches, found envelopment easier to imagine than transcendence. With the rise of psychology came an awareness of the ways culture shapes consciousness, and consciousness shapes "experience" – a term that James defined, in his preface to *The Princess Casamassima*, as "our apprehension and our measure of what happens to us as social creatures," as though to remind us that language is one of our chief means of apprehending and measuring our experience. Acquiring more force, psychology changed our sense of the social scenes in which we live and the lives we live within them. Working with new forms of linguistics and anthropology, it also deepened our sense of how our modes of discourse as well as our institutions alter everything they touch. The rapid rise of cities ushered in a new recognition, as both Vachel Lindsay and Ezra Pound noted, that urban experience is more "cinematographic" than "narrative" in form and more fluid and "modern" than stable or "traditional."

Responding to these developments, novelists launched aggressive experiments in technique. They enlarged the range of dissonant noises they recorded, jeopardizing closure; they deepened our sense of the tension between lived time – the flow of human experience within the world – and words more or less fixed on the pages of a book; and they tilted the novel toward the formal self-consciousness and the open-ended improvisation that became in different moments the signature of the modern and the postmodern. Such moves kept the novel untamed. Recent novels embrace and resist the past; they also resist and embrace noises that defy closure and closure that tames noises. In *Sister Carrie*, Carrie Meeber is defined by a kind of deliberate forgetting of her past. She seldom thinks of her parents, her sister, Drouet, or Hurstwood once they pass from her range of vision. In *The Great Gatsby*, Jay Gatsby transforms his past by turning remembrance into aggressive mythmaking. In *My Ántonia*, forms of both of these activities take place. How such things mirror larger acts of cultural forgetting and remembering – why, for example, the twenties tilted more toward mythmaking as a form of remembering in which selective forgetting played a large role, and the thirties tilted toward remembering and reporting that merged surreptitiously with forms of mythmaking and its selective forgetting – constitutes parts of the story told here.

In order to teach us how both language and culture work, novels carry us up into the handsome drawing rooms of the very rich and down into the mean streets and slums of the very poor. They give us a sense of how lives lived in other times and places both resemble and differ from our own. They challenge us to register voices whose moral and cultural resonances – or gendered and racial resonances – differ from our own. By the range of our response, we reflect the range of our capacity for allowing fiction to call our own lives into question. One conviction that grew in me with the writing of this work is this: that despite the varied dreams and the many experiences of success that mark the culture of the United States, the burden of its history teaches us that its citizens should not speak of that success unless they are prepared to confront its costs by seeing it as its victims – those excluded from it or, more drastically, sacrificed for it – saw it. Under proper pressure, the novels of the late nineteenth and early twentieth centuries can, as I hope to show, make clear the slightly unusual logic of such a claim.

Novels also do other things than cut across the grain, of course. In the United States, for example, they have worked in countless ways to authorize what should or should not be honored as "American." The need to form a consensus about such things and to make visible the interlinked ideas, assumptions, and beliefs, the rhetoric, the rituals, and the symbols that undergird it, stems in part from the country's sense of belatedness vis-à-vis older – especially European, though also other – cultures that goes with its sense of being perpetually young. But it also stems in part from its sense of being deliberately created as a nation, which goes with its sense of vast purpose, and its sense of religious, moral, regional, racial, and ethnic diversity, which goes with its sense of being a new confederation as well as a nation. The urge to consolidate and the urge to resist consolidation by protecting and even celebrating regionalism remained strong throughout the late nineteenth and early twentieth centuries. "Dissensus" found expression within the shifting consensus, just as resistance to ideology found expression within the dominant ideology. Both the events and the novels of the time remain openly conflicted, championing things they criticize and criticizing things they champion.

In trying to understand the role that literature and literary history can play in the cultural process of consolidation and resistance, I have taken my lead from Hannah Arendt's "The Revolutionary Tradition and Its Lost Treasure" in *On Revolution* (1963). The United States has lost touch with its revolutionary tradition, Arendt argues, because it has failed "to remember" it, and it has failed to remember it because it has failed to talk about it. One sign of this, she says, is our fear of the revolutions of others. If it is true, she continues, "that all thought begins with remembrance, it is also true that no remembrance remains secure unless it is condensed and distilled" in language. What saves our affairs from futility is "incessant talk about them, which in turn remains futile unless . . . certain guideposts for future remembrance, and even for sheer reference, arise out of it." This process, Arendt asserts, is at once political, cultural, and literary. "How such guideposts for future reference and remembrance arise out of this incessant talk," she adds in a footnote, "may best be seen in the novels of William Faulkner, whose 'literary procedure,' built around 'incessant talk,' is 'highly political.'"

For Arendt, Faulkner remains "the only author to use" incessant talk for these purposes. It is more likely, I think, that Faulkner, an intensely modern and American as well as a deeply Southern writer, was in this practice representative as well as extreme. Faulkner had no need to break through to some wholly new "literary procedure." He had only to remain conflicted and enmeshed; and that, as it turned out, was for him unavoidable. Like many other writers of his time, he remained divided — skeptical as well as committed, committed as well as skeptical — even about the force of "literature." Beyond that he and his contemporaries had only to put their internal conflicts to the task of recovering lost themes and forgotten voices, while remembering, in Mikhail Bakhtin's words, that "to be means to communicate," and that "absolute death (non-being) is the state of being unheard, unrecognized, unremembered." To be "means to be for another, and through the other, for oneself," Bakhtin adds, before going on to remind us that "authentic human life" may best be conceived verbally as "open-ended dialogue."

Since the writers I engage and discuss see the things they value as threatened by cooptation as well as destruction and corruption, personal acts of recovery and catharsis lie for them near the heart of every act of creativity. But many of them, including Faulkner, also think of the individual as what Kenneth Burke, in *Attitudes Toward History* (1937), calls the "corporate we." To them isolation means being excluded from the ongoing dialogue in which acts of articulation become empowering as well as interdependent or, more radically, become empowering because interdependent. Furthermore, this recognition often came with another: that for people who remain voiceless, history exists only as an array of forces that impinge upon them. It is important to recognize that some novels of the early twentieth century helped to "socialize" readers in the sense of coopting them for purposes not their own. But it is also important to recognize that novels also helped to draw readers into culture as a dynamic process — or what Bakhtin calls "open-ended dialogue" — that made room for those we might call "opposing selves." Even novels that try to speak for the voiceless essentially cannot speak to them, since the voiceless do not read their words, as James Agee painfully came to recognize in writing *Let Us Now Praise Famous Men* (1941). But it does not follow that such novels failed to serve the voiceless. So long as reading texts and events remains for some of us a way of participating in incessant talking or open-ended dialogue, and so long as these activities play a part in helping us to form as well as discover our fears and our desires, it will remain true that by changing the books we read and the ways we read them we can change as well the things we fear and desire and our ways of fearing and desiring them. Contrary to the logic of much recent criticism — which (c)overtly valorizes itself by (c)overtly celebrating its prowess in forcing works of art back into the nexus of power relations from which they came, denying their status as "art" and exposing them as tools of the status quo – change is one lesson that the past persists in teaching us. Like those who think of themselves as rebels, those who think of themselves as champions of the status quo often serve ends that run counter to those they espouse. The considerable though limited hope that a history of American fiction of the early twentieth century can hope to capture and convey does not lie in pure lines of action in which one set of forces is good, the other bad, and one wins while the other loses the future. It lies in victories and defeats that are always more as well as less than those who experienced them expected them to be precisely because the opposing forces that define them do not merely engage in conflicts; they also embody contradictions. Insofar as reading and writing can play significant roles in changing the things we desire and our ways of desiring them, they do so by entering the historical process where, in their own modest ways, they help to change the world. It is in this sense that our knowledge, like our actions, as Elizabeth Bishop reminds us in her poem "At the Fishhouses," is so radically historical as to be "forever, flowing and drawn," and also forever "flowing, and flown."

Recent developments in criticism have helped to free us of reverential attitudes toward authors and texts that were neither necessary nor desirable; and they have made us aware of many ways in which as writers and readers we may be taken in and used by stereotypes or, on a larger scale, myths and ideologies – inflected by race, gender, and class, for example – that are hostile to our interests and thus to our lives. At their best, however, these developments also reiterate what we might call, borrowing another term from Kenneth Burke, the "spiritual motive" of the modern novel in the United States. For they serve the ongoing task of spontaneously creating imperfect communities, knit together by imperfectly possessed and even painful memories as well as imperfectly shared and practiced values. In this process our conflicted novels can still play important roles. Henry James's *The Portrait of a Lady* stops rather than concludes, with its author uncertain and its heroine still on the go; Theodore Dreiser leaves Carrie rocking in her chair as she gazes down from a hotel room onto an unfinished world; F. Scott Fitzgerald leaves Carraway still searching for lost words with which to clarify the significance of the faces and scenes he remembers; several of William Faulkner's best novels, from *The Sound and the Fury* to *Absalom, Absalom!* to *Go Down, Moses*, present themselves as stories still engaged in the process of their own formation. Even when such novels speak of the past, a spirit of contemporaneity infuses them; and even when they seem about to become narrowly self-involved, they continue to evoke the putative community they seek to serve.

In this work, I make considerable use of several discoveries of our new "hermeneutics of suspicion." But as much as possible I have followed the lead of Tzvetan Todorov in trying to avoid the special terms associated with many of these discoveries. Having acknowledged that there is a sense in which "one is always talking to oneself when one writes," Todorov goes on to pose a crucial question: "Must we really write exclusively for members of our own profession?" "Only physicists can read physicists," he adds, but in "the humanities and social sciences, including literary criticism," we write about people, and what we write will interest some of them if we make our "discourse accessible and interesting" by avoiding "jargon better adapted for conveying to our colleagues which army we belong to than for conveying to our readers what we are talking about" and follow instead the examples of the "writers" who furnish us our subject matter. Todorov's aim in this admonition is to remind us that communities are always in the process of becoming and that they depend upon ongoing dialogue – upon words spoken both for and against the "Law" that undergirds them, for and against both what is and is not permitted or privileged. To help my narrative's modest chances of contributing to that dialogue, I have followed the advice of a friendly reader and devised "a kind of Victorian contents list" which I hope will aid readers in coping with my unorthodox way of jumping and circling.

Finally, let me say a few words about my title. While writing this work, I began calling it "Heirs of Changing Promise." By "heirs" I meant to include both the novelists and the characters I discuss as well as their readers and mine. By "changing promise," I meant to include both the United States as a still unruly, shifting cultural scene and the novel as a still unruly, shifting genre. Implicit in my effort to reconstitute and juxtapose selected novels and events, I came to recognize, was the hope that this work might contribute to the ongoing process of defining who those changing heirs are and what those changing promises might and even should be. Convinced of the need for greater clarity, I have adjusted my title. But I still hold to the layered hopes of my earlier version of it.

A dream city, Lyric Years, and a Great War

THE NOVEL AS IRONIC REFLECTION

NOVELISTS AS different as Henry James and Theodore Dreiser began the twentieth century as they ended the nineteenth, torn by conflicting allegiances. On one side, their openness to what Henry James called the "strange irregular rhythm of life," and thought of as the "strenuous force" that kept fiction on its feet, drew them toward history and a shared story of conquest, the taming of a continent and the making of a new nation and a new people, as we see in a range of titles, including James's *The American* (1877), William Dean Howells's *A Modern Instance* (1882), Willa Cather's *O Pioneers!* (1913), Gertrude Stein's *The Making of Americans* (1925), Dreiser's *An American Tragedy* (1925), John Dos Passos's *U.S.A.* (1938), and Richard Wright's *Native Son* (1940). On another, they were drawn toward what James called the "romantic" and described as the "beautiful circuit and subterfuge of our thought and our desire" – things, he added, that "we never *can* directly know." Like Flaubert, James wanted to tidy up the loose, baggy traditions of the novel. Even more than Flaubert, he associated the novel's looseness with history. Simply by placing human thought and desire under the aspect of the "beautiful," defined in terms of order and subtle indirection ("circuit and subterfuge"), James evoked the lyrical tradition of the nineteenth century, in which self-examination became a prelude to self-transcendence and the journey toward the self's interior became a covert preparation for a journey up and out of time itself, for the solitary reader as well as the solitary singer. The move toward the interior provided the means but self-transcendence was the end of the lyric, the real work of which was to bring the solitary self's thought and desire into harmony with the timeless world of "great" poems and "noble" thoughts, the scattered notes of the "supreme" or "absolute" song, that had begun when human time began – or more drastically, into harmony with the timeless music of the spheres. All art "constantly aspires toward the condition of music," Walter Pater announced in *Studies in the History of the Renaissance*

(1873). "The thinker feels himself floating above the earth in an astral dome," Friedrich Nietzsche added in *Human, All-Too-Human* (1878), in discussing Beethoven's Ninth Symphony, "with the dream of immortality in his heart. All the stars seem to glimmer about him and the earth seems to sink ever further downward." In the hands of the Poet, Stéphane Mallarmé added, in "Crisis in Poetry" (1886–95), unlike those "of the mob," language "is turned, above all, to dream and song."

None of these writers – Pater, Nietzsche, Mallarmé – advocated traditional forms of spirituality. But it was not foolish error that led "upholders of culture," including religious leaders, who often turned cold eyes on the novel, to prefer lyric poetry, particularly as represented by the "Genteel" tradition and the "Fireside" poets, nor an accident that they did so the more ardently as the nineteenth century's assault on traditional religious beliefs intensified. However secular or even pagan the lyric's enterprise might seem at times, it retained its tilt toward the spiritual.

The novel, by contrast, remained the most terrestrial of literary forms. Even when it was drawn toward the voice of a single, solitary character caught in the act of flight – Huckleberry Finn's, for example – its own less sublime commitments to ordinary and even sordid aspects of human thought and desire and obdurate social realities held it. The novel's orientation flowed from its commitment to what James called the *real:* the world of actualities – the colloquial, the vernacular, and the regional; the daily rhythms of love and work and play; the pull of desire and the push of competition in the day-to-day tasks of getting and spending money as well as time – things, James added, that we can't not know sooner or later in one way or another and yet can never fully measure. If, furthermore, the first of these moves, toward a sordid or seamy consciousness, opened the novel to a fuller, less pretty psychology, the second move maintained the novel's commitment to the force of history – and that, as Robert Frost might have said, has made all the difference.

The modern novel might be epic in reach, but it had less interest than the epic in valorizing the past. Whatever role it might play in valorizing social authority, it could not, in Genteel terms, be lyric. Many of the ministers and priests who praised the lyric's devotion to spirituality and transcendence warned readers against the novel, fearing that its allegiance to the historical, material world it purported to represent would promote worldliness. Novelists might lament, as James did, the inadequate life and materialist values of the Gilded Age. Certainly they wrote more out of disenchantment than approbation. But they gave their deeper loyalty to what Walt Whitman – a reform-minded poet bent on claiming poetry for the same middle class that had claimed and been claimed by the novel – called, in *A Backward Glance o'er Travel'd Roads* (1888), "vivification" of contemporary facts and "common lives" and defined as "the true use for the imaginative faculty of modern times." The rising authority of the novel – which by the late nineteenth century posed so direct a challenge that William Dean Howells wondered aloud whether the lyric might not be dying – was thus grounded in its willingness to embrace an expanding "people," the middle class, and grapple with the force of history, even when such commitments meant confronting an incorporating, rampaging, ransacking business civilization, thundering "past with the rush of the express," as Andrew Carnegie put it in *Triumphant America* (1886) – and even when this willingness carried the risk of implicating it in the historical processes and materialist values of the class and culture it embraced.

As concept, history embraces both the natural world as primal and residual force and the social, cultural world as constituted of all the things that humans have done to nature, including the transformations they have worked on themselves in the process of doing that work. But it also embraces art – if by art we mean, as Henry James did, the "maximum of ironic reflections" that humans can bring to bear on the scenes and spectacles of life. At the turn of the century, a wide array of interactive events and developments – periods of prosperity and depression; new technologies; waves of immigration; rapid urbanization; a new, centralized form of corporate capitalism; a Great War; big labor; bigger and bigger government; the rise of the professions; the cult of the therapeutic; the cult of personal pleasure; rapid communications and rapid transit; rapid transformations in the lives of black Americans as they struggled up from bondage; and the emergence of the "new woman" as writer and protagonist, as well as object of poorly repressed male insecurities and anxieties – changed society. But they also changed fiction by deepening the alienation and the fascination that writers experienced as they confronted the nation's changing scene. Artists in general and novelists in particular became more self-conscious, self-absorbed, and self-referential between 1890 and 1940, in part because the pace of change seemed almost out of control and in part because, during what André Malraux called "the twilight of the absolute," the arts – and later the disciplines devoted to their study – were tending to become their own absolutes. Writers and artists began thinking of their works as autotelic at least in part because their age was so convincingly dominated by forces other than the arts.

Revisiting the United States in 1904, for the first time in twenty-five years, Henry James encountered a greater array of items than he had ever before seen – greater, he added in *The American Scene* (1907), than his "own pair of scales would ever weigh." The problem James faced – of whether the maximum of ironic reflection could match the "maximum of 'business' spectacle" then looming in the United States in a mass too large for any known language – lingered at least through the first several decades of the twentieth century as *the* problem of the novel. If Nietzsche also has lingered, especially for literary artists, along with Darwin, Marx, and Freud, as a major precursor, it is because the question of art also lingered, stubborn and obdurate, as a question not merely about the cultural role of art but, more ominously, about the adequacy of art to any cultural role it might care to claim.

One problem had to do with continuities or, more accurately, with their loss, which became a great theme of James, as well as of Gertrude Stein, Edith Wharton, Sherwood Anderson, Willa Cather, Theodore Dreiser, F. Scott Fitzgerald, Ernest Hemingway, and William Faulkner. For what loss of a sense of sequence threatened was narrative. In traditional village cultures, Ezra Pound observed, people acquired a sense of slow time and thus of sequence based on shared knowledge. Because they knew what they, their families, and neighbors had done before, during, and after "the Revolution," and because they regularly related what they knew in stories, their lives acquired historical meaning as parts of a larger cultural narrative, though it might be oral rather than written. As a result, their lives lent themselves to and even acquired a sense of formal fictional narrative. Cities, by contrast, like modern capitalist economies, celebrated the new and the present and thus the temporary. They bombarded consciousness with sensory impressions of changing objects and scenes that overlapped; they were, Pound said, "cinematographic." As a result, they threatened to defy narrative altogether. But it was not only the possibility of narrative that was at stake; it was also the adequacy of language. The spectacle of life seemed, as James put it in *The American Scene*, to be hanging there, suspended "in the vast American sky ... fantastic and abracadabrant, belonging to no known language."

Hoping to resist what he once called (in a letter to Daniel Cory) "the alienation of the intellect from the milieu," George Santayana used the role of the outsider-as-insider to gain insight into the persons and places of the land that from 1872 to 1912 he more or less called home. There were, to be sure, important things that Santayana only glimpsed, including the special role that economic abundance was playing in shaping his country's version of modernity and the peculiar way in which, having created and named itself as a nation and a people, and having built into its federal organization and its Constitution a set of provisions against both fragmentation and unionization, the United States had promptly set about testing, both in the Civil War and in unprecedented waves of immigration, whether it could resist the centrifugal forces working to fragment it without succumbing to the centripetal forces working to homogenize it. Still, what he saw, he saw clearly: that, given its tilt toward the future, unimpeded, as he put it, "by survivals of the past," the United States would embrace the modern, would become a modern instance, a window to the world's future. Offended by such hasty embrace, Santayana returned to Europe, where old traditions and institutions were slowing the march of time. But he stayed in the United States long enough to see, as though for the first time, how singularly marked it was by its openness to change.

What Santayana both exemplified and grasped as insight was the peculiar authority, moral as well as aesthetic, that a sense of marginality would confer on writers shrewd enough or lucky enough to control it, particularly in a country where changing facts were coming increasingly to loom as too numerous and novel for any one mouth to speak or any known language to convey. In 1903, a year before James's last trip to the United States and nine before Santayana's departure, W. E. B. Du Bois published *The Souls of Black Folk* (1903), announcing that there was "dogged strength" as well as pain in the predicament of a people who, robbed of "true self-consciousness," were permitted to see themselves – in anger, pity, fear, or amused contempt – only "through the eyes of others," and so were doomed to feel "their twoness." Du Bois thus joined Santayana in recognizing, first, the extraordinary pressures that the United States would exert on the people it marginalized and dispossessed and, second, the peculiar authority that the voices of such people would come increasingly to possess as the twentieth century unfolded. In considerable measure, the nation's fiction recounts the plights and adventures of deprived, betrayed, or battered people, often still young, like Huckleberry Finn, who are forced to enter the social fray when the twin tasks of redefining reality and shaping a new language adequate to ironic reflection in a new age are becoming the tasks of life as well as art. Seizing these tasks as art's challenge was Mark Twain's great achievement; living out their consequences became Huckleberry Finn's mixed fate. When Twain thought of writing a sequel to his masterpiece and saw Huckleberry Finn in middle age, standing on the edge of the twentieth century rather than on the edge of a boundless territory, he thought of him as having gone mad and fallen silent.

2

❦

CONFIDENCE AND UNCERTAINTY IN
THE PORTRAIT OF A LADY

THE FICTION of Henry James often features "passionate pilgrims" who leave home in search of "chance feasts" and then proceed through life as "wondering and dawdling and gaping" seekers. But it also features people who scheme and design pushed by economic competition and pulled by sexual desire as well as a desire for personal power. The discourse of imaginative contemplation, the discourse of profit and loss, and the discourse of sexual conquest merge in James's work, each converted, as it were, into the currency of the other. In *The Golden Bowl* (1904), Adam Verver's "majestic scheme" possesses "all the sanctions of civilization" and aims at meeting the needs of the "thirsty millions" who seek culture as people once sought faith. Behind his "strange scheme" lie two convictions: that "he had force" because "he had money" and that "acquisition of one sort" could become the "perfect preliminary to acquisition of another." Finally, we come to see both the majestic millions he has made and the majestic palace of art he envisages as products of his capitalistic gifts for "transcendent calculation and imaginative gambling" or, put another way, for "getting in" and "getting out" at the right times – in short, for the "creation of 'interests' that were the extinction of other interests."

In order to place Adam Verver's talent for accumulating money and power under the aspect of his talent for majestic scheming in the name of art and, conversely, his talent for majestic scheming in the name of art under the aspect of his acquisitive talents, James employs a language in which erotic, political, economic, and aesthetic desires intermingle. His cosmic strategists want to rid themselves of his passionate pilgrims, just as his passionate pilgrims want to free themselves of his cosmic strategists. In the end, however, each discovers a need for the other. If, furthermore, some of his characters, including Isabel Archer, long to be free of history, so also does history – if by history we mean human experience as shaped by political economies – want to be free of resistive, dissenting individuals in full possession of individual consciousnesses. Intolerant of many things in James's novels, history is especially intolerant of a desire for and the exercise of genuine independence – this being one of James's great themes, at least from *The Portrait of a Lady* (1881) to *The Golden Bowl* (1904). And it is aggressively intolerant of the desires of those that it most wants to control – namely, women, lower-class men, and all recent immigrants who belong to racial and religious minorities.

The Portrait of a Lady underwent a long gestation, during which James struggled to transform his story of "the mere slim shade of an intelligent but presumptuous girl" into a big subject. One way of accomplishing this task was by surrounding his heroine with a rich social context of people and events; another was by making her an heir of romanticism's long effort to discover and name a wide range of private, incommunicable things that we can never directly know, thus permitting her to emerge as an independent figure of consciousness. In theory, James honored the second of these more than the first; in practice, he used both: he added characters and events that enlarge Isabel Archer's world, and he endowed her with a personal consciousness that carries her toward a sense of personal destiny.

These two strategies for making a small subject large – the one by incorporating social history, the other by tracing the emergence of a personal consciousness capable of measuring history – were in fact becoming central to James's notion both of himself as artist and of the novel as literary form as he wrote *The Portrait of a Lady*. Like *Watch and Ward* and *The Bostonians*, *The Portrait of a Lady* reflects the lingering influence of female novelists James read in his youth, especially Louisa May Alcott and Anne Moncure Crane Seemuller, and the lingering influence of his father's confused yet forcibly articulated opinions about sex, marriage, and women. But *The Portrait of a Lady* enlarges the play of James's conflicted imagination in two related ways, and as a result it makes visible two strategies that have shaped the efforts of other novelists to cope with a world of rapidly expanding and changing facts. For James finds a way of doing justice to the pressure of history as overdetermining force while also exploring the fates of individuals who want and need to feel free. If abject failure was one possibility, unsuccess was another. Most of his passionate pilgrims begin, like Isabel Archer, as unsponsored children and then become isolated expatriates or marginalized observers of an alien world that they had little or no part in shaping.

The Portrait of a Lady begins with a description of a dense, palpable milieu that tends to incorporate everyone:

Under certain circumstances there are few hours in life more agreeable than the hour dedicated to the ceremony known as afternoon tea. There are circumstances in which, whether you partake of the tea or not – some people of course never do, – the situation is in itself delightful. Those that I have in mind in beginning to unfold this simple history offered an admirable setting to an innocent pastime.

James's emphasis here is on an imposing social order that has served as an effective medium of value. We see one token of its force in its ability to envelop people who prefer not to partake of it; another, in the presence of terms like "dedicated," "delightful," "admirable," and "innocent"; and yet another, in the self-assured voice of its narrator. As *The Portrait of a Lady* unfolds, however, it leaves this world behind. First, we encounter Isabel Archer, a child of promise, who comes from the still New World of the United States. Since she is open, unaffected, and wants to experience life firsthand, Isabel is perfectly suited to serve as an exemplary protagonist of a cautionary tale in which the heroine suffers in order to acquire if not wisdom at least a clearer sense of how her world works. Early in the novel, the narrator seems confident that society's lessons will turn out to be good as well as inevitable – as they are, more or less, for Jane Austen's Emma Woodhouse. Soon, however, we discover that the society undergirding England's tea parties suffers from some deep malaise: "There's something the matter with us all," Ralph Touchett says, reminding us that, although the gardens and drawing rooms of England and Europe demand accommodation and sometimes reward it, they no longer serve as a source of shared values. Only Mr. Touchett, a dying citizen of a dying age, conveys a sense of what conviction, connectedness, and loyalty might mean. Each of the other characters seems somehow already to have learned, without remembering when or how, the lesson that Ralph Touchett lifts to visibility with his gift to Isabel: that money is the foundation of their social order. Simply by accepting the imperial process by which Isabel, upon acquiring a large fortune, becomes the center of their lives, they acquiesce to the economic imperative on which their society is based – and thus commit themselves to confronting the large question of whether freedom is to be defined in spiritual or material terms, as freedom from earthly entanglements and restraints or as possession of money and power.

Madame Merle and Gilbert Osmond differ from other characters in *The Portrait of a Lady* primarily because, untroubled by what they know, they are prepared to make the most of it. Having noted that "the greatest invention of the nineteenth century was the invention of the method of invention," Alfred North Whitehead went on to describe the rise of the inventor as a fall into "disillusionment" or "at least anxiety." Having once thought of themselves "as a little lower than the angels," human beings had, with their discovery, become servants "of nature," he said. Fulfilling the prophecy of Francis Bacon, he added, this turnabout had undermined "the foundations of the old civilisation." Socialized almost beyond the point of being human, Merle and Osmond show little interest in nature. Their world is social, their style is imperial, and their aim is domination. In brief, in their attitude toward society they mirror the same curious dominance-as-subservience that Whitehead locates in modern science's attitude toward nature. Moved by a desire similar in this respect to modern science's, they follow a similar strategy. They are realists who submit to society in order to give the appearance of dominating it.

The confrontation between Isabel and Madame Merle, in chapter 19 of *The Portrait of a Lady*, turns for Isabel on the role of appearances – the trappings of class, including manners and accents, as well as the furnishings of life, teacups, gowns, and jewels – in representing the real thing: her unique, essential self. But it turns for Madame Merle on whether there is a self that precedes or even exists independent of its signs and the social conventions that govern them – the hope of semiautonomy as well as transcendence having already been surrendered. This debate, though of uncertain beginnings, is intensely modern, and Merle and Osmond are modern in nothing so much as this: that in them the line between being passive and being active dissolves. As master manipulators they stage and direct scenes; as servants if not slaves, attendant lords, in J. Alfred Prufrock's phrase, they play out their lives as overdetermined creatures in a world they never made. "It still remains to be seen," Whitehead concluded, "whether the same actor can play both" the part of the inventor and the part of the servant. Having once pictured himself as the detached lord of his own creations, James Joyce came full circle in *Finnegans Wake*: "My consumers, are they not my producers?" Merle and Osmond know how to manipulate money and status, conversations and conventions, words, paintings, and people, including themselves, for their own amusement. They treat everyone the same: as pawns in a game played out in the twilight of purposive existence. Passion and pleasure as well as joy and wonder lie somehow already behind them. Amusement, precariously based on a sense of dominance, is their only anodyne for malaise.

By making Isabel's world their world, James turns his cautionary tale of youthful folly into a tale of an evil fate. Born a child of promise, Isabel falls into history, only to find herself "ground in the very mill of the conventional." In this story, which James almost certainly conceived as a version of the story of the United States and the modern world, "our heroine" suffers out of all proportion to her folly, largely because she is cleverer at doing what she wills – at having her way – than she is at willing what she wills – that is, at clarifying, knowing, and naming her own desires. Isabel's problems have several sources, of course. Her money brings possessions that become something like a soft if not an iron cage; and since she is a child of an older United States, she assumes that money brings responsibility because it appears to bring power. In addition, she is surrounded by people who are expert manipulators of themselves and others.

But Isabel's deeper problems revolve around her own uncertain impulses. Her "visions of a completed consciousness" – like Ralph Touchett's dream of seeing her soar above her world – turn less on a narrative desire to enter her world and take hold of it than on a lyric desire to transcend it. Even after she falls into history, she finds surrendering her separatist, transcendent desires very difficult. Furthermore, as she begins to accept the fact of being enmeshed, her own consciousness emerges as strange, uncertain, and conflicted until it comes to resemble the ambiguous world in which she moves. In exploring what it means that humans in a technological age can more nearly do what they will than ever before yet cannot will what they will, the great physicist Werner Heisenberg quotes the Chinese sage Chang Tsu: "Whoever loses his simplicity becomes uncertain in the impulses of his spirit." And so it is with Isabel. Loss of simplicity not only changes her; it turns her story into a tragic story of the socialization of consciousness – a development that seems to thrust itself on James's narrator almost as harshly as on his reader, making *The Portrait of a Lady* a new novel.

Just after Isabel recognizes that Osmond's declaration of love is something she has invited as well as something that surprises her, James's narrative voice changes. Once sure of itself, it now finds itself moving over strange and threatening ground:

What had happened was something that for a week past her imagination had been going forward to meet; but here, when it came, she stopped – that sublime principle somehow broke down. The working of this young lady's spirit was strange, and I can only give it to you as I see it, not hoping to make it seem altogether natural. Her imagination, as I say, now hung back: there was a last vague space it couldn't cross – a dusky, uncertain tract which looked ambiguous and even slightly treacherous, like a moorland seen in the winter twilight. But she was to cross it yet.

With both the narrator's early assurance and our own as readers having suddenly become relics of the past, like teatime at Gardencourt, what is left – for Isabel, her narrator, and her readers alike – is a world in which the representative structure becomes Osmond's "house of darkness," where life and art, ground in the mill of the conventional, seem moribund. Isabel's limited triumph consists, first, in recognizing that her world is one in which all human values are threatened and, second, in sensing that in its own conflicts her consciousness resembles her world. Indeed, it is the shock of this double recognition that initiates a moment of "liminality" in which she realizes that her old dreams for herself in that world must be relinquished. In her midnight meditation – in chapter 42 – Isabel's internal life becomes the *other* side of a social scene that is slouching its way toward emptiness because it no longer understands its own desires. To salvage from that world and for it – and of herself and for it – all that can be salvaged, she must recognize, first, that she is entangled and encumbered, second, that selfhood is a social issue as well as a private concern, and, third, that to become a responsible social agent she must master words, customs, conventions, mores, and institutions that possess histories of their own that preclude their ever becoming wholly hers. Similarly, she must confront the "bitter" knowledge that she, too, has been used: "the dry staring fact that she had been an applied handled hung-up tool, as senseless and convenient as mere shaped wood and iron." These recognitions become an extension of her rereading of her life, and they carry her away from the lyric desire for transcendence toward a narrative desire for entanglement, not as "renunciation," but as a deep "sense that life would be her business for a long time to come." Rome, she has come to realize, is a "world of ruins" where "people have suffered." These interrelated recognitions possess, as James presents them, a "very modern quality" that detaches itself and becomes "objective," allowing Isabel to see her own disappointments in a new light. First, "in a world of ruins the ruin of her happiness" becomes a "less unnatural catastrophe"; second, surrounded by things that have "crumbled for centuries and yet still were upright," she discovers a "companionship in endurance" that reinforces and enlarges her commitment to herself by making it a commitment to doing all that she can to rescue Pansy, until toward the end she become something like Pansy's earthly "guardian angel."

In these interrelated discoveries and developments, we observe the return of several things that Isabel has denied. The staying power of the denied as well as of the past is part of what she learns for herself and teaches us about Osmond's world. In this way James reminds us that works of literature – especially novels – achieve one of their tasks by embracing the public thought of their time. This was not a new lesson, of course, but it was necessary, in part because it enabled James to remind us that a novel can expose the secret fears and hopes of an age even if it cannot resolve them. Only by confronting her own complicity and her own limitations can Isabel hope to find a way to counter Merle's duplicities and Osmond's manipulations and replace her own empty dream of the "infinite vista of a multiplied life" with possibilities open to an implicated, conflicted, and used self. What she thus inches her way toward resembles what James calls, in his preface to *The Lesson of the Master*, "the high and helpful public and, as it were, civic use of the imagination."

James was drawn to the drama of such discoveries because he felt the need of them. His sense of mounting technical confidence as a novelist finds expression in the brilliant manipulations of Merle and Osmond. His uncertainties and confusions, which were moral as well as aesthetic, find expression in Isabel's predicament. As Isabel sits by the fire rereading her life, her problem emerges as a problem of perception, of consciousness, and, by extension, a problem of language. But it is also a problem of Isabel's conception of herself as an autonomous agent. The moment James's development of her crisis draws our attention to the tools and processes of consciousness and recasts the self as neither coherent unity nor conflicted multiplicity but rather as the play among possibilities, Isabel becomes a modern protagonist. Our preference for her over Gilbert Osmond and Madame Merle can be put in several ways. But it turns, in part, on her refusal to let disappointments, or more drastically "ruins," rob her of her will and, in part, on her refusal to let proliferating ambiguities and uncertainties persuade her that moral judgments always mask self-interest – the cynical position that Merle and Osmond fix as one of the major temptations of the modern world.

In the world of *The Portrait of a Lady*, the lyric desire for transcendence makes itself felt in Isabel's longing to live the "infinite vista of a multiplied life" and in Ralph Touchett's desire to see her rise soaring above her world. But Isabel acquires and retains as well a narrative impulse toward entanglement that squares more fully both with living in the encumbered worlds of historical societies and with becoming the heroine of a novel in which the story of the United States becomes entangled with the story of the modern world. That story is scientific, technological, philosophical, political, aesthetic, and literary, in ways *The Portrait of a Lady* never directly engages. Like modern science and technology, literary modernism emerged as a fast-moving affair, fueled by dislocations and upheavals as well as innovations. It would be played out in major cities of Russia, middle Europe, Western Europe, England, and the United States, and also in villages in Minnesota, Mississippi, Mexico, and Argentina, in China, Korea, and Japan, to name a few. In the United States – a "half-savage country, out of date," to borrow Pound's words, populated by people from a hundred lands, uprooted and even rootless – two very different styles, both geared to ironic reflection in a new age, would dominate narrative expression. One was based on Mark Twain's discovery of the energy and cunning of vernacular English, particularly as expressed in the voice of Huckleberry Finn as he grapples with what it means to be enslaved or free, black or white, female or male, damned or saved. The other was based on James's grand style, which had its origins in Isabel's midnight vigil. In both of these, technical confidence would mingle with – and would serve both to counter and to stress – moral and spiritual confusions, evasions, and insights. We see them in the oblique confessions of Willa Cather's Jim Burden and F. Scott Fitzgerald's Nick Carraway; in the self-conscious fluidity of Gertrude Stein's prose and the self-conscious restraint of Ernest Hemingway's; and in the audacity of William Faulkner's, where concealment matches disclosure, mystification matches expression, and evasion vies with revelation. These and other acts of style acknowledge epistemological difficulties and imply that beauty has become almost impossible. They thus pay tribute to the dawning of an age, confident as never before of its technical powers and yet unsure of itself, too.

It is, then, a new and colder darkness – in which values begin to fade and the world seems to be speeding up as it runs down – that James forces upon us in *The Portrait of a Lady*. By situating his story of the modern self in a rich social context, James presents the problem of replacing lost values and countering spiritual impoverishment as society's problem and the novel's as well as the self's. The imagination's task of vivifying the facts of life becomes Isabel's no less than James's, and hers no more than her readers'. But Isabel is a model for us on another count, too. Back in New York, in a room whose only door to life's street has been sealed, she has read novels that filled her mind with impossible dreams. Yet we cannot say simply that that experience poorly prepares her for living in the only world given her. For what is it that she does, as she sits alone by the fire, if not to engage in reading and rereading both her life and her historical culture as historical novels that disclose and reveal as well as mislead and misguide. Between her midnight vigil and the last paragraph of the novel, she is able to reconcile for herself tension between freedom and consent. The freedom to defy her husband by turning away from him, she claims as her own. Having exercised her freedom once, however, she retains it as an option even when, at the end of her recorded story, she uses it as the basis for deciding not to turn away from Pansy, the stepdaughter who needs a "guardian angel" and has no hope of finding anyone else to play that role for her.

3

❦

LINES OF EXPANSION

TO GRASP the full authority of Isabel Archer's story, we must see behind it the force of history as felt in the interplay of two contrastive lines of expansion. The first of these lines carried people from Europe to the New World and its frontiers; the second carried immigrants to its cities and the children of farmers and ranchers back from its frontiers to its cities, or even across the Atlantic to England and Europe. Between 1820 and 1930, more than 62 million people uprooted themselves and resettled in "foreign" lands dwarfing the great *Volkerwanderung* of the Teutonic tribes during the last centuries of the Roman Empire. Of these, roughly 42 million settled in the United States, Europe's and then Asia's main frontier, making it not only the most diverse country in the world but also, as Santayana saw, the home of descendants of the most restless peoples in the world. Interacting with this migration was another – from the soil of farms and footpaths of villages, in Europe as well as the United States, to the sidewalks and streets of cities. If novels like Willa Cather's *My Ántonia* (1918) and O. E. Rölvaag's *Giants in the Earth* (1924–25 in Norwegian; 1927 in English) trace the first of these lines of expansion, Theodore Dreiser's *Sister Carrie* (1900) traces the second, toward the cities of the upper Midwest and the East – a line that James extended back across the Atlantic to Europe in scores of stories, including Isabel Archer's.

Political and economic as well as cultural, these lines of expansion yielded hundreds of stories in life as well as art: William Dean Howells's, Mark Twain's, Hamlin Garland's, and Edith Wharton's; F. Scott Fitzgerald's, Jay Gatsby's, and Nick Carraway's; Willa Cather's as well as Jim Burden's; Theodore Dreiser's as well as Carrie Meeber's; Henry James's as well as Isabel Archer's and Adam Verver's. In one way or another, furthermore, all of these lives were driven by dreams of possession – sexual, cultural, and economic. The "New World," early promoters promised, was a "*Paradise* with all her Virgin beauties," waiting to be claimed. The Scots Irish, as one formulation put it, landed on the Eastern shores of the New World and spread out across the continent, keeping the

Sabbath and everything else they could lay their hands on. "I take possession of the old world," says the protagonist of "The Passionate Pilgrim" (1871), one of James's early international tales, "I inhale it – I appropriate it!"

Adventure as taking possession and taking possession as adventure, and both of these as versions of living that can slide almost imperceptibly into versions of dying, became the nation's story, almost from the beginning. On his third voyage, having decided that the world was not round but pear-shaped and that he was standing near its highest point, Christopher Columbus wrote his sovereigns to report "that the Terrestrial Paradise" testified to in Holy Scriptures now lay before him like a dream – for him to explore and them to possess. "Your Highnesses have an Other World here," he wrote, one that would expand their dominion and wealth. Later, as English-speaking Protestants got into the act, the lines separating piety, patriotism, profit, and possession continued to blur. John Winthrop and his followers braved the "Vast Sea" of the North Atlantic on instructions from God in order "to possess" this "good land" and build there "a City upon a Hill" to serve as a beacon to the world. Later still, as the literature of exploration became a literature of settlement, and so became "American" as well as Spanish, French, Dutch, and English, connotations multiplied. Writing at the end of the sixteenth century, Sir Walter Raleigh described "the sweet embraces of ... Virginia," while another voyager depicted the New World as "a country that hath yet her maydenhead." Richard Hakluyt, the great collector of explorers' narratives, urged Sir Walter to persevere "a little longer" so that his "bride will shortly bring forth new and most abundant offspring," implicitly enlarging the role of male explorers and diminishing the role of women. Late in the nineteenth century, the daunting term "New World" and its cognates – "Wilderness," "Garden," "Virgin Land" – still carried connotations of some special sanction. What could such terms as "America" and "American" mean if they did not mean something special? The "mission" of the American people was twofold – to civilize the New World and in the process not only experience renewal but also become a model of it. That, as William Gilpin defined it, first, in 1846 and, then, in 1876 in *The Mission of the North American People*, was the great untransacted destiny of the American people.

Similar imperatives continued to echo in the literary and political discourse of the United States for generations: in Walt Whitman ("Seest thou not God's purpose from the first"), Hart Crane ("Terrific threshold of the prophet's pledge"), and Frederick Jackson Turner ("the richest gift ever spread before civilized man"), for example. Caught up in the Civil War's testing of the nation's survival, Congress passed the Homestead Act (1862), which granted free farms of 160 acres to all citizens and applicants for citizenship who occupied and

improved the land for five years, in part to reiterate the nation's commitment
to subduing and possessing the continent and in part to separate Thomas
Jefferson's agrarian vision of the New World from the institution of slavery.
And in the years following the Civil War, that double intent seemed about to
be realized. Between 1860 and 1890, the number of farms and ranches rose
from 2 million to 5,737,000, adding 430,900,000 acres of settled land, more
than had been claimed in all the decades before 1860 combined.

In fact, however, the increased pace of immigration did at least as much
to enlarge the cities as to settle the prairies, which is to say that it also fed
the nation's second line of development, from the plains back to Chicago and
the cities of the East. Between 1880 and 1890, Chicago tripled in size and
New York grew from less than 2 million to more than 3.5 million. Begun as
a nation of villages and farms, the country was becoming a nation of cities. In
1830 one of fifteen Americans lived in cities of 8,000 or more; by 1900 one of
three; by 1910 nearly half, and by 1920 more than half. In 1860 there were
141 cities of 8,000 or more; by 1910 there were 778, often located on the
sites of old mission churches, trading posts, frontier forts, or Indian battles.
With this concentration of people went another: by 1910, 1 percent of the
nation's business firms produced 45 percent of its manufactured goods. With
both kinds of concentration came a new kind of diversification. By 1890, after
two immense waves of immigration had brought millions of "strangers" to the
nation's shores, one fourth of the population of Philadelphia and one third of
the populations of Boston and Chicago were foreign-born, and four of five New
Yorkers were either foreign-born or the children of foreign-born parents. Soon
a third wave would swell to tidal proportions, bringing millions of people from
Southern and Eastern Europe – a development reflected in Alfred Stieglitz's
photograph "The Steerage, 1907." Following Stieglitz's lead, Henry Roth,
in the prologue to *Call It Sleep* (1934), describes 1907 as "the year that was
destined" to bring the greatest number of immigrants to the shores of the
United States. Actually, however, although each year between 1909 and 1914
matched 1906 and 1907 by bringing more than a million immigrants to the
United States, the peak year was 1913, when 1,285,349 arrived.

Each of these epic stories – the exploration and settlement of the West, the
new immigration, and the migration to cities – found literary expression time
and again. And each fed off the others. In Rölvaag's *Giants in the Earth* we follow
Beret and Per Hansa as they pack their possessions in a few trunks and begin
the great voyage from Norway, across an ocean so wide it seems to have no
end, to the "Promised Land." Docking in Quebec, they move through Detroit,
Milwaukee, Prairie du Chien ("Had that been in Wisconsin?"), Lansing, Iowa,
and Fillmore County, Minnesota, before they finally reach the Dakota Territory,

a "vast stretch of beautiful land." There, fifty-two miles from Sioux Falls and so far from the world of their births that they have lost track, they stake a claim, which Per Hansa records on June 6, 1873, eleven years after the Homestead Act:

This vast stretch of beautiful land was to be his – yes, *his* – and no ghost of a dead Indian would drive him away! . . . His heart began to expand with a mighty exaltation. An emotion he had never felt before filled him and made him walk erect . . . . "Good God!" he panted. "This kingdom is going to be *mine*!"

Per Hansa is not a brutal man. His story, as Rölvaag signals both in his subtitle – "A Saga of the Prairie" – and in his dedication – "To Those of My People Who Took Part in the Great Settling . . . " – evokes the earliest story of the United States. But it is a story in which women play subordinate roles and suffer, as Beret does, great loneliness; and it is a story in which the dispossession and the deaths of Native Americans seem to be sanctioned if not by God at least by history.

Willa Cather's *My Ántonia* (1918), written earlier but set several years later, follows two related journeys. Jim Burden is an orphan who travels from an old Virginia farm through Chicago, across so many rivers that he becomes "dull to them." Ántonia Shimerda is a member of the first Bohemian family to journey "across the water" through Chicago to Black Hawk, Nebraska. Later, Burden, who becomes the narrator of Ántonia's story, journeys from what was for a time the western edge of the New World through Chicago to New York. Later still, he goes back to visit Ántonia, in preparation for telling her story. Hamlin Garland wrote stories – *A Son of the Middle Border* (1920) and *A Daughter of the Middle Border* (1921) – that resemble Burden's and Ántonia's, and he lived a story that resembled Burden's. Born in Wisconsin, he moved to Boston, where he won the friendship of William Dean Howells, before going back to the Middle Border to write. Theodore Dreiser's *Sister Carrie* (1900) recounts the story of another child of immigrants who moves from the rural Midwest to Chicago, carrying her belongings in a small trunk and a satchel and her savings, four dollars, in a yellow leather snap purse. "It was in August, 1889. She was eighteen years of age, bright, timid, and full of the illusions of ignorance and youth."

As poorly equipped for the move she makes and the strange new world she encounters as Beret and Per Hansa are for theirs, or Ántonia is for hers, Carrie, too, must learn by going where she has to go. Full of yearning though she is, she remains so vague as to seem almost passive, "A Waif amid Forces." Drawn from Columbia City to Chicago and then to New York, she moves from one dry relationship to another. Even after she becomes a wealthy performer, she remains curiously blank. In one sense, life is something that happens to her; in another, it is something that is always about to happen. Early and late, we see her sitting in a rocking chair, moving yet going nowhere. On her first evening in Chicago, sitting in her sister's small flat on Van Buren Street, she feels "the drag of a lean and narrow life" and moves "the one small rocking-chair up to the open window," where she sits, "looking out upon the night and streets in silent wonder." Later we see her onstage, gazing out at audiences that gaze back at her, or sitting in other rocking chairs, observing the world's spectacles as they parade past her windows or through her mind's eye. In the novel's last scene, we see her in "her comfortable chambers at the Waldorf," reinforced by "her gowns and carriage, her furniture and bank account," still waiting for the "halcyon day when she should be led forth among dreams become real." During her performances, she goes down, into time and history, where she becomes a social creature and makes money. After or between performances, she moves up and out of the fray, protected by her jewels and furs and bank account, toward a kind of secular transcendence, where she can look down on the street life of her world and feel almost free of society and its requirements. Filled with yearnings that linger, she continues to move without going anywhere, as we see in the novel's last lines: "In your rocking-chair, by your window dreaming, shall you long, alone. In your rocking-chair, by your window, shall you dream such happiness as you may never feel."

Ántonia's story, like Per Hansa's, is the story of a family within a dispersed yet supportive community of families in which the family still functions as the basic economic unit of society. In 1787 it took nine farm families to feed one town or city family. By 1940 one farm family could sustain eight city families. In 1954, in *The Dollmaker*, Harriette Arnow described one part of what the loss of the farm family as an economic unit meant to women:

> It wasn't the way it used to be back home when she had done her share, maybe more than her share of feeding and fending for the family. Then with egg money, chicken money, a calf sold here, a pig sold there, she'd brought in almost every bit of food they didn't raise. Here everything, even the kindling wood, came from [her husband].

Ántonia lives a much harder life than Carrie lives. By the end of her story she seems worn and even battered by time. But she remains the central member of a definable unit that is larger than herself. Carrie, by contrast, lives as a single separate self in a large, almost limitless city of performers and observers. Neither Per Hansa nor Ántonia has anything we would call a "career," though their lives are filled with deeds done — marriages made and sustained, homes and barns built, children born and reared, crops planted, harvested, and laid by. Carrie lives in rented rooms, apartments, or hotels, and her life is filled with activities that we associate with theaters, music halls, and sports arenas – with rehearsals that possess meaning only as preparation for performances that are intense yet ephemeral, intimate yet distanced, personal yet stylized. Her career, clothes, and jewels are in the end all she possesses.

Behind these contrasts lie vast differences. Per Hansa and Ántonia live in a world of forces and rhythms not made by human hands. Both of them – as James Dickey once remarked of Theodore Roethke – are animal enough to feel themselves half into unthinking nature yet human enough to be uncomfortable there. Their homes are shelters built to protect their human mortalities. They travel great distances and live full lives, but they never travel far enough or live long enough to encounter a world like Carrie's cities, where life is shaped by human hands to mirror human desires.

In *Giants in the Earth*, *My Ántonia*, and *Sister Carrie* elements of what, following Henry James's lead, we might call the "real" and the "romantic" mingle, though it is probably fair to say that elements of "romantic" are more pronounced in *Giants in the Earth* and *My Ántonia* than in *Sister Carrie*. Yet in James's terms, these worlds divide in the opposite way. Ántonia and Per Hansa move amid forces that are real precisely because they do *not* conform to human desire, while Carrie inhabits a world that mirrors human longings. Insofar as her world remains *other*, it remains other despite being shaped by human hands. If her world fails her, as in some sense it surely does, it fails because it mirrors what Heisenberg calls uncertainties "in the impulses of the spirit." Having triumphed, Carrie becomes a woman of means who possesses to an unprecedented extent the capacity to do whatever she wills. Only her capacity for controlling or even understanding what she wills remains limited.

The sights and sounds of Carrie's world are products of the concerted efforts of people to manipulate their environment in the name of will and desire – which is to say, power and longing. Ántonia and Per Hansa live in a land of the big sky and the great plains, of dry winds and great blizzards. Above them the great ball of the sun rises, grows enormous, and then retreats "farther and farther into the empty reaches of the western sky." "At the moment when the sun" disappears, "the vastness of the plain seem[s] to rise up on every hand," filling "the silence . . . with terror," until the "spell of evening" crowds in and lays "hold of them" and the plain takes possession of those who would possess it.

Like Carrie, Ántonia and Per Hansa look to the future, filled with hope and fear. But all of the grand spectacles of their world belong to nature. For them, task follows task; there is always work to be done. They live hard, unillustrious lives, and time scars and carries them as it does all things. Having left home to be married, Ántonia is driven back, deserted and pregnant. Carrie, by contrast, carries on extended affairs with Drouet and Hurstwood without apparent concern about pregnancy, as though she can control what happens to her body by will alone. Per Hansa dies in a blizzard, trying to return home from an errand undertaken to help a sick neighbor. Yet there is a sense in which both Ántonia and Per Hansa feel themselves to be the masters of their days. Though often heavy, their steps are measured in ways that Carrie's are not. When Per Hansa dies on the open prairie, leaning against a haystack, with his "eyes . . . set toward the west," his mind is filled, not with vague dreams of the future, but, first, with memories of his wife and home as they "come, warm and tender," making him laugh softly, and then with hope for his son. Although Ántonia's life is no more illustrious than Per Hansa's, she too becomes one of the earth's giants. She leaves images in the mind, Jim Burden remarks near the novel's end, that grow stronger with time, because she lends

herself to immemorial human attitudes which we recognize by instinct as universal and true. I had not been mistaken. She was a battered woman now, not a lovely girl; but she still had that something which fires the imagination, could still stop one's breath for a moment by a look or gesture that somehow revealed the meaning in common things.

Embedded in Jim Burden's celebration of Ántonia, however, is an oblique confession of his own internal confusions as well as the empty marriage he has made and the sterile life he lives – of which both his frenetic travels and his way of coming accidentally to tell the only story that matters to him are signs. The strengths he celebrates in Ántonia emerge as the other side of his own weaknesses. His seeming loyalty to nature is in fact another part of his sentimental, nostalgic loyalty to the past. Insofar as his celebration of Ántonia lifts her out of time, it allows him to claim possession of her, as the novel's title suggests. And in doing this, it does violence to her earned relationship to the cyclical world of nature, from which he is already alienated, in order to claim her for the linear world represented by the trains he rides and serves. In his hands, Ántonia is judged by a code of conscience not her own, a fact that reinforces our sense of the wide, never completely traversable distances that separate many things in My Ántonia – including act from word, event from memory, pioneer settlers from inheritors, hired girls from bourgeois families, West from East, land from city, and above all female heroine from male narrator. My Ántonia explores all of these distances; in its many juxtapositions of them, it may even be said to make each explicit exploration of one an implicit exploration of the others. But its structure stresses the last of them and thus brings each of them under its controlling aspect.

Jim Burden, as it turns out, is as incapable of fathering children as Carrie is of bearing them. But Carrie fills her life not with stories out of her past but with performances. Time carries her, as it carries Jim and Ántonia, but with a difference, in part because few characters in the history of the literature of the United States carry so few active memories with them. Carrie rarely mentions her family and never looks back longingly toward anything we might call "home." Once they have dropped out of her life, she scarcely thinks about Drouet or Hurstwood. Between performances, she practices, looking to the future; between practices, she rocks and waits, filling her life with formless yearning.

To understand Carrie's characteristic moment as one in which living becomes yearning, we must understand her urban world as one made to reflect human desires – for pleasures, comforts, and diversions as well as power – that have become indiscriminate, mixed, and confused, and thus insatiable. And we must understand it as having in the process acquired a forward-looking, expansive logic of its own:

In 1889 Chicago had the peculiar qualifications of growth which made such adventuresome pilgrimages even on the part of young girls plausible. Its many and growing commercial opportunities gave it widespread fame, which made of it a giant magnet, drawing to itself, from all quarters, the hopeful and the hopeless – those who had their fortune yet to make and those whose fortunes and affairs had reached a disastrous climax elsewhere . . . . Its population was not so much thriving upon established commerce as upon the industries which prepared for the arrival of others. The sound of the hammer engaged upon the erection of new structures was everywhere heard. Great industries were moving in. The huge railroad corporations which had long before recognised the prospects of the place had seized upon vast tracts of land for transfer and shipping purposes. Street-car lines had been extended far out into the open country in anticipation of rapid growth. The city had laid miles and miles of streets and sewers through regions where, perhaps, one solitary house stood out alone – a pioneer of the populous ways to be. There were regions open to the sweeping winds and rain, which were yet lighted throughout the night with long, blinking lines of gas-lamps, fluttering in the wind. Narrow board walks extended out, passing here a house, and there a store, at far intervals, eventually ending on the open prairie.

Chicago, Carrie's first city, is most fully itself as an inspired outline of what it will be. We feel its force most deeply in its forward-leaning crunch – in industries designed to prepare for the arrival of new industries, and in buildings built to prepare for buildings yet to be built. It preempts because it is insatiable as well as unfinished. The reaching lines of streetcars and streetlights exist as lines of expanding force. They thrust into the open prairie and windy night "in anticipation of rapid growth." In this they recall *The Cliff Dwellers* (1893) by Henry Fuller, whom Dreiser called "the father of American realism," in part because he set his novel in a skyscraper; and they anticipate Alfred Stieglitz's photograph "From the Shelton Hotel" (1932) in which the most striking feature of the city's skyline is the scaffolding of an unfinished building reaching up into the sky. Carrie lives in a world of human making that thrusts up into the sky and out along the earth, driven by gathered forces of its own. People hurry to it in order to observe the ongoing works of human hands and read in them their human reasons for being. Yet in Carrie as well as in the novel that bears her name those reasons have become vague by virtue of becoming indiscriminate, unrestrained, and insatiable, in all of which they resemble the capitalism that dominated the United States in the late nineteenth and early twentieth centuries. The lines that thrust out into the open prairie and up into the sky have no known destinations and no recognized boundaries, not because they are sufficient ends in themselves but because they are fed by and feed the large engines that drive their world.

Carrie's intimate relation to her present context, the remarkable extent to which she emerges as a creature of the world around her, make her one of the most important characters in her nation's fiction. In one of her representative moments, she sits in her rocking chair, almost forlorn, dreaming and yearning yet going nowhere; in another she occupies a stage, where staring seems the only "proper and natural thing" to do. As a performer and celebrity who inhabits a "shiny plush-covered world" of things, she discovers both "the meaning of the applause which was for her" and "the delight of parading," of being seen and creating a stir, until her head is "so full of the wonder of it that she [has] time for nothing else."

In James's *The Portrait of a Lady*, when Isabel Archer sits through the night by the fire in her husband's "house of darkness" and discovers uncertain truths about herself, her husband, her marriage, and her world, we observe the power as well as the limitations of "motionless seeing." Isabel's "mere still lucidity" does little, perhaps nothing, to alter her world. It acquires such force as it acquires only by yielding insight. We never know to what extent effective action will flow from Isabel's vigil. In James's fiction, history as limiting force weighs heavily even on the lives of people born in the United States. But Isabel possesses an internal richness, a changing yet constituted life, that contrasts sharply with the rich, successful, yet attenuated life of Carrie, and there is a sense at least in which she also discovers her human connectedness.

Carrie, by contrast, comes to us as a largely vacant self – or, more drastically, as an object in a world of objects. She becomes "Carrie Madenda," a celebrity whose name blazes in incandescent lights at Broadway and 39th Street. She attains everything that had "seemed life's object" (gowns, a carriage, furniture, a bank account, success, applause, celebrity) only to have "once far off, essential things" become in possession "trivial and indifferent." Her longings and yearnings, like her sad discoveries, are neither symptoms nor signs. She becomes the deep figure both of the novel that bears her name and of the larger world whose indiscriminately incorporating self inspired Dreiser to create it precisely because her intimacies, privacies, and secrets of self find expression only in theatricalities that commercialize and trivialize them. After publishing *Sister Carrie*, Doubleday, Page & Company tried to limit its distribution, apparently because Carrie's "fall" from virtue is never properly punished. But Doubleday's concerns were misplaced. Carrie is a dangerous character not because she lets her erotic instincts run riot. She does not. She is dangerous because she so perfectly sublimates them.

Carrie begins her travels as a young woman who is already manipulated by the desires of men, as opposed to the desire for them. Women in *Sister Carrie* remain to a large extent figments or projections of male imaginations. They are sometimes (as with Hurstwood's wife) less than and sometimes (as with Carrie) all that men desire, but they are never more. Carrie's life is shaped by her sense of what those desires mean and her assumption (acquired we can only guess how) that they are what matter, as force always matters. She is controlled not by her own sexual desires – something Dreiser seems incapable of imagining – but by her society's definition of her as a beautiful young woman. She learns to make her sexuality an asset by using it to please the men who gaze at her with desire. To manipulate them, however, she must also manipulate herself. After she gets to New York and Hurstwood's energies begin to fail, she takes charge of her life and becomes a star. Having learned from her incorporating ethos both an aesthetics and an economics of desire, she discovers that in cities sex, desire, entertainment, and money go hand in hand. Hurstwood's fall and her rise, turning as they do on work, money, and social position, are indicators not of a world of limitless possibilities but rather of one where one person's fall balances another's rise. Furthermore, whereas Carrie's lower-class status enhances her appeal to Hurstwood – by emphasizing not only her youthful yearning but also her vulnerability and dependence, in short, her "femininity" – his fall accentuates the difference in their ages, undermining his "masculinity" and robbing him not only of appeal but also of clear sexual identity.

Having learned the imbalance of power implicit in being gazed upon and analyzed, Carrie also learns to protect her private life by living alone. She thus saves herself for prying eyes that are prepared to pay. When she performs, she watches and analyzes the crowd that watches and analyzes her. Gazing at those who gaze at her, what does she see? What Dreiser can safely leave us to imagine: herself as she exists for the crowd, as though in a mirror. For Carrie is at one and the same time the creator of an image and the image of her own creation. She thus becomes a savvy exploiter both of herself and of her capitalist, sexist society. Yet the more proficient she becomes in meeting the needs of her social and economic self, the more her private self regresses until it exists only as a neglected, exploited, still yearning child within her, crying, "Watch me, watch me!" not simply out of familiar egotism or insatiable appetite for attention but rather because, as a child of present sensation and yearning, she depends on admiring eyes and clapping hands to confirm her existence. They see me and love me, she seems to say. They will hold what I look like and what I do in their minds. They will remember it, and that will make it true.

Though attractive and, we sense, sensuous, Carrie never becomes a creature of sexual desire. In her merge three different senses of what a distinctively American self might be. She is a "performing" self, an "incorporating" and an "imperial" self: she lives in part to stir applause for herself, in part to take possession of things "for herself as recklessly as she dared," and in part to become preeminent. Yet in her rocking chair, surrounded by possessions and awaiting another performance, she seems beleaguered, as though afraid, as Tocqueville prophesied, that time is running out on her pursuit of happiness built on acquiring money, possessions, status, and power. Between performances, her face becomes almost blank in its beauty, with no expression because she has little to express, and her life becomes a weatherless one of waiting. In all of this – in her pastlessness; in her name, given her by a man; in her accidental discovery of herself as a performing self; in her desire for celebrity and her affinity with the city and the new century's changed form of capitalism; and in the curious blankness of her inner life when she is alone – she becomes the representative creature of her world and also, as its title suggests, a close relative to us all.

4

🌱

FOUR CONTEMPORARIES AND THE
CLOSING OF THE WEST

OTH THE PIONEERING MOVE into the lands of the West and the urbanizing move back into the cities of the upper Midwest and the East yielded stories in life as well as in fiction. To gauge the force of these contrasting lines of development, which were social, economic, and political as well as cultural, we need to keep three facts before us: first, that Henry Adams (1838–1918) and Henry James (1843–1916) were younger contemporaries of the great Sioux leader Sitting Bull (1834–90) and Buffalo Bill Cody (1846–1917), as well as older contemporaries of Isabel Archer, Ántonia Shimerda, Jim Burden, and Carrie Meeber; second, that the same Congress that devised Radical Reconstruction in order to secure the rights of black people of the South also enacted and funded a policy of radical subjugation and segregation of the original inhabitants of the West in order to conquer and dispossess them; and third, that the same group of Eastern industrial and banking interests that underwrote the cultural achievements of the Northeast became the chief beneficiaries of these policies as well as of the Homestead Act, which was rationalized as a reading and implementation of Thomas Jefferson's agrarian dream.

In the summer of 1868, three years and a few months after the Palm Sunday, April 9, 1865, on which Robert E. Lee and Ulysses S. Grant met in Appomattox to sign the agreement that ended the Civil War, the federal government launched a relentless campaign against Native Americans and appointed General William T. Sherman, one of the deliverers of the black slaves of the South, to head it. Some soldiers, like General George Crook, West Point '52, known among the Indians as the Gray Fox, continued to feel conflicted about the annihilation of Native Americans. "Yes, they are hard," he said of the wars. "But the hardest thing is to go out and fight against those who you know are in the right." Yet the policy of total war prevailed: "I will urge General Sheridan to push . . . for the utter destruction and subjugation" of all Indians of "hostile attitude" outside the reservations, Sherman wrote. "I propose that [Sheridan] shall prosecute the war with vindictive earnestness," until "all hostile

Indians . . . are obliterated or beg for mercy." "The only good Indians I ever saw," Sheridan later stated, "were dead" – a line that gave birth to an aphorism.

Soon the frontier was transformed into what Walt Whitman, in "A Death-Sonnet for Custer," called the "fatal environment": a scene of mortal conflict between people to whom the land belonged and people determined to seize it in the name of profit, piety, and progress. In the late 1870s, after two hundred battles and countless skirmishes – after the Red River War (1869–74), the Battle of Little Big Horn (June 1876), and Chief Joseph's Rebellion (1877) – resistance virtually ended. By the early 1880s, the great buffalo herds, numbering more than 13 million in 1865, had almost been annihilated, depriving Native Americans of the Plains of food, clothing, and shelter. "Kill every buffalo you can," the army instructed. "A buffalo dead is an Indian gone." The last act in a struggle that virtually ended in the late 1870s came in 1890 when, shortly after Sitting Bull died at Standing Rock, two hundred Dakota men, women, and children danced their last Ghost Dance and then were massacred by U.S. Army troops in the Battle of Wounded Knee. "Nits make lice," ran one justification for the killing of Native American women and children. "Kill the nits, and you'll get no lice."

Even before the West had been won, its herds destroyed, and its original inhabitants either killed or forced onto reservations, its story was being incorporated for profit. At age thirteen, William F. ("Buffalo Bill") Cody began working as a pony express rider. Later he worked as a buffalo hunter, a stage coach driver, and a prospector before joining the Union Army and winning the Congressional Medal of Honor. From 1868 to 1872, he was chief scout for the Fifth U.S. Cavalry. In 1869, the year in which he participated in the defeat of the Cheyenne, Edward Zane Carroll Judson, writing under the name of Ned Buntline, wrote the first of twenty dime novels that transformed Cody into a national hero. Lured by Buntline to appear in Chicago in a melodrama called "Buffalo Bill, King of Bordermen," Cody spent eleven years on the stage before he followed Buntline's example and began turning fictional versions of his experiences into a marketable narrative of his own.

In its first version, Cody's story featured a cast of cowboys, Indians, horses, and buffalo and was called "The Wild West, Rocky Mountain, and Prairie Exposition." After opening in Omaha, Nebraska, in 1883, it moved across the country to Coney Island, where it played to capacity crowds. A year later, dubbed "Buffalo Bill's Wild West Show," with a hundred more Indians, a hundred more horses, and an enlarged cast of cowboy stars (including Buck Taylor, "Mustang Jack," "Country Kid" Johnny Baker, "Squaw Man" John Belson, and Annie Oakley), Buffalo Bill opened in St. Louis, moved to Chicago and then east, playing to one sellout crowd after another. In 1887 he took his story to England, France, Spain, and Italy, on one of the most successful tours of Europe ever made by an American storyteller. During one remarkable recounting in London, at Queen Victoria's Jubilee, he loaded the kings of Belgium, Denmark, and Greece on the Deadwood Coach and drove them safely through an "Indian attack," with the Prince of Wales riding shotgun. Later, hoping to hold off a group of aggressive competitors, he added episodes from other frontiers, including the Battle of San Juan Hill and the Boer War. But the story of the West – a story of overt subjugation and covert incorporation – remained the core of his tale. By the time he died in 1917, he had left his mark on the circus and the movies and had made his name known over much of the world.

In Buffalo Bill's narrative, the West, once an expanse no eye could measure, acquired a different kind of eternalism. Though ostensibly historical, Cody's story recorded something like a human triumph over history and thus reminds us that historical narratives, like philosophy, religion, and literature, can serve submerged social, political ends. For it celebrated as a triumph for humankind both the virtual annihilation of Native Americans and the hardship of the pioneers. Looking back on himself as a boy still named Itshak Isaac Granich – before the Palmer Raids of 1921 forced him to change it – Mike Gold, author of *Jews Without Money* (1930) and editor of *New Masses*, described himself as "disappointed" that he could find no "Messiah who would look like Buffalo Bill." What Gold wanted, and may even be said to have needed, was a hero who could "save" his people and "annihilate" their enemies while bringing the hardships of the one and the destruction of the other under the aspect of righteousness.

5

&

CHICAGO'S "DREAM CITY"

TEN YEARS after his first tour of the United States and six after his first tour of Europe, Buffalo Bill brought his Wild West Show to the World's Columbian Exposition in Chicago in what turned out to be one of his last triumphant presentations. Once a small Indian village on the shores of Lake Michigan, Chicago pushed and promoted itself past older Eastern rivals who wanted to host the nation's Columbian celebration by recounting its quintessential American rise from meager beginnings to a bustling center of trade, commerce, stockyards, and railways, and by insisting that it was the nation's window to the future. Chicago might have no culture, one citizen remarked, but when it got some it would "make it hum."

Persuaded, Congress gave Chicago exclusive rights to official commemoration of the four hundredth anniversary of Columbus's discovery of the Americas, and then passed a bill authorizing the World's Columbian Exposition of "arts, industries, manufactures, and the products of the soil, mine, and sea," which President Benjamin Harrison signed in the spring of 1890, the first year in which the value of the nation's manufactured goods surpassed that of its agricultural commodities. A year later, six thousand workers were employed on projects sponsored by forty-four nations and twenty-six colonies and provinces. "Make no little plans," instructed Daniel Burnham, the Chicago architect charged with coordinating the mammoth effort to transform seven hundred acres of Jackson Park into a wonderland of promenades, canals, lagoons, plazas, parks, streets, and avenues as well as four hundred buildings.

To assist him in planning Chicago's "Dream City," Burnham assembled a group of advisers that included the park builder Frederick Law Olmsted, the painter Kenyon Cox, and the sculptor Augustus Saint-Gaudens. Do "you realize," Saint-Gaudens asked at a planning session, "that this is the greatest meeting of artists since the Fifteenth Century?" But the real business of the Exposition was competitive cultural politics, national and international. Burnham's planners took for granted that their exposition would surpass Philadelphia's Centennial celebration of 1876. Their serious competition was the great

Paris Exposition of 1889, and their aim was total victory. Theirs would be the best-planned, best-operated, most dazzling exposition ever.

On all counts, Burnham and his advisers succeeded. Replicas of scenes from around the world – a Parisian café, a Bohemian glass factory, a Moorish palace, a Cairo street, a Japanese bazaar – sprang up on the Exposition's clean, well-lighted grounds, illuminated, William Dean Howells reported, by "myriad incandescent bubbles" made possible by alternating-current electrical power. Miniature replicas of whole villages, complete with native inhabitants, including Germans, Turks, Chinese, and Dahomans, also found space. Above the grounds soared a conspicuous display of U.S. technological prowess, conceived by a young Chicago civil engineer, George Washington Gale Ferris, as a direct challenge to the Eiffel Tower: an enormous illuminated wheel that lifted its passengers high into the air to see the New World's newest city rising from the plains. "[Before] I had walked for two minutes," Owen Wister, author of *The Virginian*, wrote in his diary, "a bewilderment at the gloriousness of everything seized me . . . until my mind was dazzled to a standstill."

The Exposition's planners welcomed tourists in record numbers, proud that their endeavor had inspired Karl Baedeker of Leipzig to publish the first Baedeker's guide to the United States. Working from mixed motives, they viewed their exposition as another phase in the nation's plan for dominating and converting the world. They welcomed people like the Dahomans, whom they thought of as cruel and barbarous, in order to teach them how a people of energy, ingenuity, and discipline could transform, in Burnham's words, a "desolate wilderness" and a "dreary landscape" into a glittering world of technological wonders. Enlightened, the Dahomans could return to their primitive homes with new images of the "influences of civilization" etched in their minds.

Burnham and his colleagues thought of themselves as disciples of Matthew Arnold. A new alliance between business and government, on one side, and culture, on the other, was one of their avowed aims. But what could such an alliance mean to people who were as tradition-bound and backward-looking about art as they were present-minded and forward-looking about politics, business, and technology? Burnham had helped to establish Chicago as an architectural center. In the first stages of planning, he supported the innovative plans of his friend John Root for making architecture the principal cultural focus of the Exposition. But both men wanted national participation; and when they called in Richard Hunt, acknowledged dean of architecture in the United States, the firm of Peabody and Stearns from Boston, and that of McKim, Mead, and White of New York, Burnham and Root found themselves outnumbered. Before the end of the first conference, Burnham had abandoned

Root's hope for an eclectic, experimental approach in favor of celebrating
Eastern formalism, a triumph signaled when McKim lowered Saint-Gaudens's
twenty-foot Diana from atop New York's Madison Square Garden and raised
her above the Pantheonlike dome of his new building in Jackson Park.

To Burnham and his advisers the results were gratifying. The architectural
focus of the Exposition was the White City, and the center of the White City
was the reflection pool of the Court of Honor, surrounded by massive "Greek"
temples. The "Fair," Burnham boasted, "was what the Romans would have
wished to create, in permanent forms." To Louis Sullivan, whose Transportation
Building was the only nonclassical structure on the grounds, the results were
an "appalling calamity" and a "betrayal of trust": a "suavely presented" and
"cleverly plagiarized" but deeply "fraudulent . . . use of historical documents."

In correspondence, Henry Adams described the Exposition's buildings as
"fakes and frauds" that seemed mischievous in their deception of "our innocent
natives." Walking the grounds, he spent most of his time studying innovative
"dynamos and . . . steam-engines." Later, in his *Education*, he described the
Exposition as an astonishing "scenic display," more spectacular than anything
in Paris or North America, from Niagara Falls to the Yellowstone Geysers. But
its lessons came from its "industrial schools," where one acquired "the habit
of thinking a steam-engine or dynamo as natural as the sun." The questions
posed by its "half-thoughts and experimental outcries" were whether the new
creations "could be made to seem at home" on the shores of Lake Michigan
and whether their maker, the American, could be "made to seem at home
in it."

· To such questions, Burnham's creation had little directly to say. The dis-
sociation of art from history that Sullivan and Adams decried – "lesions" was
Sullivan's term; "rupture" was Adams's – was precisely what Burnham desired.
"The influence of the Exposition architecture will be to inspire a reversion to
the pure ideal of the ancients," he said, not in despair but in hope. Standing on
Burnham's grounds, Hamlin Garland delivered a lecture titled "Local Color in
Fiction." But for Burnham even architecture, the most terrestrial of the arts,
was decorative and ornamental except when it bodied forth the timeless, transcendent ideals of the ancients. If, furthermore, this was Burnham's problem
on one level, it was Chicago's on another, and the nation's on another. Vulgar
forms of art could serve vulgar ends. Dime novels, Horatio Alger's books, and
Buffalo Bill's story of the West, which Chicago's Dream City helped to promulgate, were useful both in justifying the nation's conquest of the continent
and in teaching its young boys manly aspirations. In its own way, even the
Dream City admitted that "art" could also serve crass ambitions. California's
strange contribution – a "knight on horseback" made entirely of California

prunes – was billed as a "unique departure in statuary." Descended from knights of the American Plains and chivalric knights of old, it evoked ideals of a near as well as distant past. But California's knight, the *Guide* to the Exposition makes clear, belonged to the future, by signaling that the United States was prepared to expand its markets abroad. California's prunes, it notes, were already being "introduced victoriously into all lands, to the discomfiture of the products of other countries." A few years later, the nation commenced, in Howells's haunting words, "to preach the blessings of [its] deeply incorporated civilization by the mouths of [its] eight-inch guns."

But in Chicago's Exposition, true "art" belonged to the Court of Honor, where "Greek" temples spoke of the past to the ages, without challenging the Exposition's aggressive nationalism, or its emphatic exclusion of the poor, or its emphatic control of Native Americans, women, and black Americans. Outside its gates, one hundred thousand victims of the panic of 1893, the nation's worst depression to that time, wandered the streets, searching for food and shelter. "What a spectacle!" the journalist Ray Stannard Baker exclaimed, observing the pitiful throng outside the fairgrounds. "What a downfall after the magnificence and prodigality of the World's Fair." In that same year, as though in ironic commemoration of the Exposition's grand opening, Stephen Crane published *Maggie: A Girl of the Streets*, a nightmare vision of the cruel consequences of urban poverty. Like London's *Martin Eden* (1909) – and, more obliquely, both Kate Chopin's *The Awakening* (1899) and Edith Wharton's *House of Mirth* (1905) – Crane's story ends in suicide. But Maggie's march to the river in which she dies is even more harrowing than Martin Eden's dive into the sea, or Edna Pontellier's long swim away from society's shore, or Lily Bart's drift into unconsciousness, in part because it comes to us as the logical outcome of a young woman's life in a world ruled by exploitation.

Thousands of laborers, of "half a score of nationalities and of as many trades," had built the Exposition, wrote Walter Wyckoff, who worked there as a road builder. But the Exposition's *Official Manual* saved its accolades for Burnham and the stout bankers, lawyers, and politicians who served as advisers and sponsors. In *Midway Types: A Book of Illustrated Lessons...* (1894), Native Americans appear as "well-known thorns in the side of Uncle Sam." Offended by the Dream City and the story it sought to tell, Chief Simon Pokagon walked the grounds, distributing a pamphlet called *Red Man's Greeting*, which reminded visitors that "the land on which Chicago and the Fair" stood still belonged to the Potawatomis, "as it has never been paid for." But the Exposition's official story, which defined American Indians as a nuisance finally eliminated, was reiterated in its "Ethnology Department," which presented them as representatives of "primitive" peoples destined to extinction in the name of progress. Less a vanishing than a vanished people, North America's first inhabitants were at last wholly *other*.

Having lost hope of achieving parity with men in planning the Exposition, women settled for a single building, adjoining the Children's Building and situated on the border between the exalted art of the White City and the varied amusements of the garish Midway. Although assigned to Sophia Hayden, the design of the building was controlled by a "Board of Lady Managers" – a designation set by the U.S. Congress and resented by its own members. Elizabeth Cady Stanton, Susan B. Anthony, and Jane Addams were among the many women who spoke there, backed by two large murals that were given equal status: Mary Fairchild MacMonnies's *Primitive Woman*, depicting women engaged in traditional tasks of service and nurturance, and Mary Cassatt's *Modern Woman*, depicting young women in a garden, enjoying the fruits of nature and the arts. The effect of the whole, said the artist Candace Wheeler, was to present "a man's ideal of woman – delicate, dignified, pure, and fair to look upon," terms that recall Burnham's notion of "culture." But these two images of women – as performers of domestic tasks and as guardians of culture and refinement – in fact represented assumptions and interests so deeply embedded in the culture at large that most men and many women came "naturally" to share them. In 1927 the writer Mary Austin (1868–1934) recalled the culture of her early years as one in which women were regarded as too refined to be driven by worldly ambitions or carnal desires. Focused on the immediate and the eternal, on the needs of hearth and home and the thought of heaven, women were taught to shun the push of competition and the pull of desire that both drove and entitled men to run the world.

Despite repeated petitions for a building, a department, or an exhibition, black Americans were forced to settle for a "day." In 1893 Scott Joplin, a native of Texarkana, Texas, moved from St. Louis to Chicago and organized his first band, launching a career that made him the "King of Ragtime." One year earlier, Anna Julia Cooper, a native of South Carolina living in Chicago, had published a book called *A Voice from the South*, comparing the fate of being a black woman to living with one eye bandaged and darkened. But the fathers of White City showed little interest in black men or black women, except as menials hired to work on the grounds and as cleanup crews; granting them a "day," which black Americans renamed "Darkies' Day," was for them a concession. Noting that the Exposition and the civilization it celebrated had been built by the labor of thousands of black men and women, Frederick Douglass used the occasion to rename Chicago's White City the "Whited Sepulcher." And in fact the Exposition's treatment of black Americans reiterated a theme that was implicit in its version of the "official" lineage of the nation's people. Speaking at the Exposition's World's Parliament of Religions, Lyman Abbott called Chicago "the most cosmopolitan city" and Americans "the most cosmopolitan race on the globe." But foreign peoples were given space only along the garish Midway, outside the Dream City itself, in a series of villages arranged in an order whose ethnic logic was clear: the exhibits of the Teutonic and Celtic races came first, then the Mohammedans, the West Asian peoples, the East Asian peoples, and the Africans of Dahomey. The continent's first settlers, Native Americans, came last. "Let no one fear," added John Henry Barrows, of the First Presbyterian Church of Chicago, "that the solar orb of Christianity is to be eclipsed by the lanterns and rush lights of other faiths" – sentiments that squared perfectly with the Exposition's clear definition of "American" culture and its subordination of other civilizations to its own.

6

ꙮ

FREDERICK JACKSON TURNER IN THE
DREAM CITY

S TANDING in the Dream City – within "the greatest city of modern
times: Chicago, the peerless," as John Flinn's *Official Guide to the World's
Columbian Exposition* (1893) called it – and speaking to members of the
American Historical Association, Frederick Jackson Turner, a young professor
from Wisconsin, delivered his famous address, "The Significance of the Frontier in American History." The dominant traits of the nation – strength and
inventiveness of mind, buoyancy and exuberance of spirit, "restless, nervous energy," and "dominant individualism" – Turner said, were "traits of the frontier,
or traits called out elsewhere because of the existence of the frontier." "The
true point of view" in U.S. history, therefore, was "not the Atlantic coast"
but the "Great West." Since the days when Columbus sailed, he added, in
a line that embraced the nation's emerging political economy as well as its
storied past, "America has been another name for opportunity, and the people
of the United States have taken their tone from the incessant expansion" virtually forced upon them by their environment. The "expansive character of
American life," he predicted, would go on demanding "a wider field for its
exercise."

At times, Turner seemed to be looking forward, anticipating the war that
would come in 1898, when, following President McKinley's "Open Door" policy, the nation started seeking "wider fields." When his gaze fixed on the past,
however, it almost stopped short, arrested by the sense of an ending: "Never
again will such gifts of free land offer themselves." Despite his exuberance,
Turner's tone is, as a result, often elegiac. Part discovery and part invention,
his "thesis" draws on words of earlier writers – from explorers and early settlers through Jefferson and Jackson to George Bancroft, Francis Parkman, and
William Gilpin – as well as on selected facts of history. It remains controversial
due in part to its active biases and in part to its convenient omissions. His
story of the United States revolves around white male explorers and settlers,
modeled on Daniel Boone and Leatherstocking, as we see when he describes
"the wilderness" mastering "the colonist" by stripping "off the garments of

43

civilization and array[ing] him in the hunting shirt and the moccasin." Women, black and brown Americans, the violent destruction of ancient civilizations, and the quick exploitation of the land and its resources play minor roles in his story, a fact that strikes with added force for being not only convenient but also consonant with the logic of Chicago's Exposition. Furthermore, although Turner speaks of the "composite nationality" of the people of the United States, he largely ignores new immigrants. He knew that the lessons of the West were mixed – that coarseness went with strength, expediency with inventiveness, and a lack of artistic sensibility with a "masterful grasp of material things." And he occasionally worried that frontier violence and exploitation might inculcate violence and greed. But he believed that his nation stood at a critical juncture and concluded that it needed its hard frontier virtues to meet new challenges. In speaking of the past, he in fact spoke to the present about the future. In this special sense, he was as much a moralist as a historian. His underlying and overriding purpose lay in creating a usable past for an uncertain future. In 1914 he was still reiterating what he had announced in 1893:

American democracy was born of no theorist's dream; it was not carried in the Susan Constant to Virginia, nor in the Mayflower to Plymouth. It came stark and strong and full of life out of the American forest, and it gained new strength each time it touched a new frontier.

The appeal of Turner's story owed something to its status as another declaration of independence from Europe and something to its assertion of a distinctive past. But it also owed something to its reassuring "modernity." From Chicago, Henry Adams returned to Washington in time to watch Congress repeal the Silver Act. Bankers and "dealers in exchange" supported a single gold standard, Adams reported, the silver minority opposed it, and "the people" continued, as they had for a hundred years, to vacillate, torn between "two ways of life": one, that of an agrarian republic based on a dispersed form of entrepreneurial capitalism, to which Chicago had been a gateway; and the other, that of an urban, industrialized nation based on a centralized form of corporate capitalism, "with all its necessary machinery," to which the Dream City was a window. But Adams knew where the future lay, and so, as we shall see, did Turner. He knew that, despite the trust-busting reforms of the late nineteenth and early twentieth centuries, the future belonged to a world dominated by the means and ends of corporate capitalism, as the strange fate of the Homestead Act had already made clear.

After the Civil War, advertisements of "free land for the landless" spread around the world. But few landless families could finance long journeys, and of those that could, few were prepared to cope with the ecology of the Great Plains, where the bulk of public lands lay. Nearly two thirds of all homesteaders who filed claims between 1870 and 1890 later lost their farms. Meanwhile, the bulk of public lands dispersed served other interests. Of 3,737,000 farms and ranches established between 1860 and 1900, fewer than 600,000 (roughly 16 percent) came from homestead patents, accounting for only 80 million of 430,900,000 acres (less than 19 percent) of new land claimed. The rest went to ranchers set on expanding their empires or to rail companies set on expanding theirs – results that fit perfectly the aims of Eastern bankers and industrialists who opposed the Jeffersonian ends of the Homestead Act.

Major parts of the United States remained rural and agricultural well into the twentieth century, and many farming communities as well as most of the South remained poor. But a new way of life was emerging, and it was urban, industrial, commercial, affluent, and secular. Dominant first in the East, it spread across the upper Midwest and then incorporated the nation's heartland. Eventually, it triumphed even in the South. Chicago, "or rather the World's Fair City," Howells wrote, "was after all only a Newer York, an ultimated Manhattan, the realized ideal of that largeness, loudness, and fastness, which New York has persuaded the Americans is metropolitan."

Having begun her career by writing stories about frontier Nebraska, where she had moved at age nine, after a journey that took her through Chicago, Willa Cather later turned to stories – *A Lost Lady* (1923), *The Professor's House* (1925), and *Death Comes for the Archbishop* (1927) – that trace the decline and fall not simply of the "frontier" but of the preurban, preindustrial, premodern world to which Chicago was saying goodbye. Writing as one fearful that the early days of the United States might also have been its best, Cather presents her novels as archeological digs that unearth the shards, rituals, folkways, and memories of worlds almost lost. In them, customs, mores, manners, and accents as well as turns of speech vary, but other things, including the sense of being in tune with nature and inheritors of traditional wisdom, do not. In them culture comes to us through inarticulate artisans who know their tools and inarticulate farmers who know their fields and animals. Or it comes in rituals preserved in the inherited phrases of ancient languages, which remain authentic because they convey an interpretive framework, a way of organizing reality, that endows both communal existence and individual existences with purpose and meaning.

To people like Adams and Cather, "progress" seemed little more than an honorific term for change. For Turner, as for Chicago's Dream City, its validity as concept seemed self-evident. What Turner sought was a new mode of discourse with which to save what he saw as valuable lessons of the nation's past, and he found it in Darwinian thought:

The buffalo trail became the Indian trail, and this became the trader's "trace"; the trails widened to roads, and the roads into turnpikes, and these in turn were transformed into railroads . . . until at last the slender paths of aboriginal intercourse have been broadened and interwoven into the complex mazes of modern commercial lines; the wilderness has been interpenetrated by lines of civilization growing ever more numerous. It is like the steady growth of a complex nervous system for the originally simple, inert continent.

Turner's story fit, on one side, the story told by Buffalo Bill in his Wild West Show and, on the other, the story told by Burnham and his advisers in their Dream City. Turner knew that growth was only one part of the story because he knew that the nation was already working its way free of its religious and political moorings. He sensed, moreover, what Emile Durkheim saw: that interests can connect people, but that they "can only give rise to transient relations and passing associations," not to a sense of community. Turner's larger aim was to preserve a sense of community, grounded in history and made manifest in cultural practices, so that his people could go forward, thinking and acting in consort. His thesis is programmatic as well as explanatory.

Like Chicago's Exposition and Buffalo Bill's show, however, Turner's thesis reminds us that the forging of national identities always involves a process of exclusion, negation, and suppression as well as inclusion and affirmation. In saying what the United States willed to be, what it willed to give its name to and incorporate, Turner virtually shouted what it willed to control, exclude, or suppress. He thus added his words to the mixed discourse of self-confidence and self-doubt that continued to echo through the early decades of the twentieth century, as the nation continued its search for an adequate identity. To Buffalo Bill's language of showmanship and Chicago's of technology, he added his own, taken in part from words and deeds of the past and in part from Darwin and biology, and put it to the purpose of propounding the pertinence of frontier virtues to the new order signaled by Chicago. His thesis promises a way of reconciling the natural and the civil, individualism and egalitarianism, separatism and civic-mindedness, secession and union – without altering the power structure of his world, except by enlarging his country's share of it. When he reaches back to evoke a lost world, to celebrate pioneer sturdiness and frontier independence, he laments the passing of an era, and his tone becomes elegiac, evoking the era of the early republic. But when he fixes his gaze on the scene emerging around him and then begins to speak of progress, he moves from the nation's earlier modes of discourse toward a discourse informed by the sciences, especially Darwin, and the social sciences, including that of the American Association, at whose meeting he delivered his most celebrated address. Armed in this way, he invented an image of his country as still a New World, whose future lay before it like a dream and whose people remained heirs according to divine promise.

For Turner, therefore, the answers to Adams's questions – whether the scenic display of the Dream City could be made to seem at home in Chicago and whether "the American" could be made "to seem at home in it" – were clear and reassuring. Adams's sense of the past left him believing in accelerating change but confident of little else. Turner's version of it enabled him to face the future with contained alarm, sustained by faith in the grammar of progress – from simplicity to complexity, from frontier to society, from wilderness to civilization, from the "slender paths of aboriginal intercourse" to the "complex images of modern commercial lines." It was, therefore, stunningly appropriate that he should deliver his first great address when and where he did. Chicago's Dream City, which helped to launch his spectacular career, not only gave him a platform; it also reinforced his themes with its celebrations and endorsed his omissions with its exclusions. In the decades that followed, the interests bodied forth in the World's Columbian Exposition continued to sponsor him and his thesis.

7

❦

HENRY ADAMS'S *EDUCATION* AND
THE GRAMMAR OF PROGRESS

Adams might well have conceded Turner special authority, for he thought of people like Turner as allied with the future. He may even have felt some sympathy for Turner's purpose: few episodes in the search for some "form of religious hope" or "promise of ultimate perfection" left him wholly unmoved. Still, in his own reflections he remained ambivalent about the consolidated forces that were shaping the modern world and skeptical about the several theories – "formulas," "arranged sequences," and "convenient fictions," he called them at various times – that proposed to explain them. In a chapter of *The Education* called "The Grammar of Science" (the title of a book by Karl Pearson published in 1899), he follows Pearson in contrasting the precision of our knowledge of the world made available through sensory experience to science with the uncertainty of our knowledge of all relations between our deepest human needs and the world we inhabit:

> Pearson shut out of science everything which the nineteenth century had brought into it. He told his scholars that they must put up with a fraction of the universe, and a very small fraction at that – the circle reached by the senses, where sequence could be taken for granted.... "Order and reason, beauty and benevolence, are characteristics and conceptions which we find solely associated with the mind of man."

In his sense of the allure and the threat of dissociation between nature and culture, in which nature becomes an object of analysis, manipulation, and exploitation, while culture becomes the creation of human hands directed by "characteristics and conceptions... solely associated with the mind of man," Adams locates the origin of the "modern" mind – including "American" versions of it. It was at virtually this same moment that pragmatism was emerging in the United States as a philosophical movement charged by the demand that philosophy continue to meet our deepest needs as human beings, even if that meant placing the process of knowing within the process of conduct and replacing the search for ultimates with a search for effective means of coping with the present. In Adams's context, even Lyell and Darwin are more premodern than modern in the problems they address because, unlike Pearson, they attribute to nature not change but evolution, not accidental collocations of atoms but meaningful selection – or, more precisely, selection that corresponds to human conceptions of what meaningful selection might mean. In one of his most telling depictions of himself – "a child of the seventeenth and eighteenth centuries" forced "to play the game of the twentieth" – his most striking act is to treat the century in which he was born and lived most of his life as an interim between an old world in which people could believe that the earth had been created for their habitation and a new world in which they recognized that order, reason, beauty, and benevolence – as characteristics and conceptions associated only with their own minds – were as doomed to extinction as they.

The "modern" movement, if by that we mean the artistic, literary, and philosophic "modernisms" that emerged in the late nineteenth and early twentieth centuries, thus arose not only in the great cities of Europe, but also along the ragged edges of the New World. And it found different forms of expression, including efforts to hold traditional values, customs, and forms in mind while modifying or abandoning them in practice. Such contradictions enter novels by Edith Wharton and Jack London as well as Willa Cather and Theodore Dreiser, and they dominate Buffalo Bill's tale and Turner's thesis. They even lie behind Burnham's separation of art from life, which served the dual purpose of protecting "interests" from exposure to what James called the "maximum of ironic reflection" and of protecting art from being exposed as another elaborate, disguised, or even sinister expression of mere "interests." These and other versions of "modernism" arose, furthermore, only in part because energy abounded; they also arose because interests abounded. No single version of the "modern," as it turned out, could meet all of the needs at hand.

Despite the popularity of Darwinism, the deeper implications of evolutionary theory for understanding ties between human thought and human culture, on one side, and human origins in nature, on the other, would be decades unfolding. Despite the power of Marxist thought to inspire critiques of culture, its implications for understanding the conflicted relations between history and culture as expressions of human will and history and culture as shapers of human will were only beginning to emerge. Finally, despite the growing popularity of Freudian thought, its implications for understanding the haunting discrepancy between the ability of the human will to do what it willed and its ability to will what it willed had scarcely been glimpsed. Such fundamental tensions as these the "modern" movement addressed: including a tension between nature as a realm from which human life had evolved and culture as a product of human hands doing the work of human minds and so giving expression to needs associated with those minds alone; and then between culture as the product of peculiarly human needs and culture as a historical scene that was unlike anything humans ever much wanted to see. One result, present in poetry as well as fiction, took shape as a separation of literature from history as well as from nature and even from the personal voice and self of the writer. In theory at least, "literature" began separating itself from history, culture, and self as well as from nature by declaring itself a special realm of detached, impersonal, and even transcendent discourse, hoping, strange as it may seem, to name itself the peculiar realm of everything distinctive in the human spirit.

Behind the pathos of the present that lies so deep in Adams's thought as to constitute its mysterious armature lay his conviction that "The Grammar of Science" had forever divided human beings against themselves by defining them as human animals whose deepest needs, though met for a time by human inventions, must in the end be forfeited. Having suddenly become inventors of all formulas having to do with "order and reason, beauty and benevolence," humans might fancy themselves exalted inventors of all the gods, and authors of all their words. But the price paid for such exaltation struck Adams as severe, if only because purely human formulas, lacking divine or even natural sanctions, were certain to fail in meeting the human needs that inspired them. "Our nada who art in nada," one of the characters in Hemingway's "A Clean, Well-Lighted Place" (1933) says to himself, as he begins to turn out the lights in a café, "nada be thy name thy kingdom nada thy will be nada in nada as it is in nada.... Hail nothing full of nothing, nothing is with thee."

Adams's anxiety was, then, no less "American" than Turner's, but it was more fully "modern," and it made his sense of the critical juncture at which the United States stood more inclusive as well as different. Like Turner, Adams saw the nation moving from the dispersed, agrarian world toward an urbanized, centralized, and mechanized world. He, too, realized that this new world would be driven by "the capitalistic system with all its necessary machinery." In addition, however, he saw the emerging culture as one in which faith in purpose was becoming more difficult and skepticism was becoming more preemptive.

In his sense of the implications of a dissociation between the sensory world of nature and the motions of human minds (and, by extension, the tools, instruments, and formulas devised by them to meet their needs), Adams glimpsed what Werner Heisenberg later saw clearly. In picturing for ourselves the nature of the existence of elementary particles, Heisenberg said, "we may no longer ignore the physical processes by which we obtain information about them" since "every process of observation" causes disturbances in the field of observation. "In consequence," he continued, "we are finally led to believe that the laws of nature which we formulate mathematically in quantum theory deal" not "with the particles themselves but with our knowledge of" them. In short, Adams sensed about the science of Lyell and Darwin what Heisenberg observed about science generally: "In science, also, the object of research is no longer nature in itself," Heisenberg says, "but rather nature exposed to man's questioning, and to this extent man here also meets himself." To some extent, then, even in the study of nature, "one sees what one brings." Adams understood, however, that working hypotheses can meet the needs of science far more satisfactorily than they can meet those of philosophy. Where philosophical inquiry was concerned, he had little interest in partial success or workable solutions, including those promised by pragmatism.

In 1917, a year before Adams died, Bertrand Russell reiterated the harsh implications of modern skepticism he had first articulated in 1902:

Such, in outline, but even more purposeless, more void of meaning, is the world which Science presents for our belief. Amid such a world, if anywhere, our ideals henceforth must find a home. That Man is the product of causes which had no prevision of the end they were achieving; that his origin, his growth, his hopes and fears, his loves and his beliefs, are but the outcome of accidental collocations of atoms; that no fire, no heroism, no intensity of thought and feeling, can preserve an individual life beyond the grave; that all the labours of the ages, all the devotion, all the inspiration, all the noonday brightness of human genius, are destined to extinction in the vast death of the solar system, and that the whole temple of Man's achievement must inevitably be buried beneath the debris of a universe in ruins – all these things, if not quite beyond dispute, are yet so nearly certain, that no philosophy which rejects them can hope to stand. Only within the scaffolding of these truths, only on the firm foundation of unyielding despair, can the soul's habitation henceforth be safely built.

Two years later, Joseph Conrad wrote to Russell describing his own "deep-seated sense of fatality governing this man-inhabited world," a sentiment later echoed in Hemingway's revision of the Lord's Prayer. Toward the end of *The Education*, especially in the chapter called "The Grammar of Science," Adams describes the modern self in terms even bleaker than Russell's because he saw darknesses within the modern self that matched those without. Like Russell, Adams presents life as coming "inexplicably out of some unknown and unimaginable void" into which it is doomed to disappear. But other constraints haunt his "tired student," who feels so pushed by the force of history and the work of culture ("external suggestion") and so driven by the force of nature ("nature's compulsion") that nothing – not his art, his philosophy, or even his internal dream world – can be called his own. More than most writers of his time, Adams realized that the interactions between biology and culture, or nature and history, in shaping individual human lives and determining the fate of humankind were something people had only begun to understand. He took some consolation in thinking that what Lionel Trilling later called a "hard, irreducible, stubborn core of biological urgency, and biological necessity, and biological reason" might in some measure place us beyond culture's powers to control us with enticements and threats. But the self as scene of balancing compulsions, some welling up from within, others felt from without, seemed to Adams cold consolation. He persisted in his effort "to invent a formula of his own for his universe" because he thought the effort deeply human. But he worked knowing that the contours of human hope had forever changed.

In 1868 Adams had landed in New York to see "American society as a long caravan stretching out towards the plains." In 1904 he again landed in New York to find an urban world of almost frantic energy:

Power seemed to have outgrown its servitude and to have asserted its freedom. The cylinder had exploded, and thrown great masses of stone and steam against the sky. The city had the air and movement of hysteria, and the citizens were crying, in every accent of anger and alarm, that the new forces must at any cost be brought under control. Prosperity never before imagined, power never yet wielded by man, speed never reached by anything but a meteor, had made the world irritable, nervous, querulous, unreasonable and afraid. All New York was demanding new men, and all the new forces, condensed into corporations, were demanding a new type of man.

Like Chicago's Dream City, Adams's New York is a product shaped by human hands to meet human needs. But since it is also driven by forces and interests that have outgrown their servitude, it threatens to turn its makers into servants shaped to its requirements. In 1921 Ezra Pound described city life as "cinematographic." A few years earlier, Vachel Lindsay had predicted that city life would give unprecedented authority to visual media – to images, signs, and symbols, to drawings, cartoons, illustrations, and photographs – that were creating a "hieroglyphic civilization." Earlier, cities had undergone explosive growth that both required and generated concentrations of capital that could fuel industrial growth and the creation of new technologies. New York, like Chicago's Dream City, expressed the human desire to dominate space and master natural forces. But control accompanied expansion. Country clubs, landscaped city parks, amusement parks, and wilder, more expansive national parks further extended social control over human contact with nature and human use of leisure. As modern cities became more coextensive with human activities, they also became more authoritative in shaping and even creating human desires, as we see in Adams's New York – and much earlier in Poe's "The Man of the Crowd" (1840).

Natural science presupposes human beings, Niels Bohr once noted, as both spectators and participants on the stage of life. The city, as represented by Poe's almost anonymous and interchangeable London, is so preemptive along these lines that the distinction between being an observer and being a participant virtually dissolves. By surrendering concern for things inside him in order to observe the "scene without," Poe's nameless protagonist emerges as a model of the evacuation and objectification of the modern self. The external world of the city, its street life, provides the only life he knows. Having studied people in groups, he begins examining details of their clothes, gaits, faces, and expressions. Although he possesses considerable learning, some of it arcane, he remains internally impoverished. Finally, having studied the crowd, he fixes his attention on one stranger – a worn man of searing countenance. And from this drama depicting the interaction of spectator and participant comes a moment of recognition in which the two figures merge as related versions of a single, almost anonymous figure: the "man of the crowd."

The "man of the crowd" – both as narrator-spectator and as participant-actor – is a modern, urban hero. His contacts with other people are brief, impersonal, and superficial; and since interests alone create them, they remain external and transient. Though intimacy is sometimes insinuated, none is conceivable. Personal commitments, together with the claims and expectations that go with them, no longer exist. Social life consists of a succession of unrelated yet almost interchangeable scenes. Poe's London, like Adams's New York and Baudelaire's Paris, is unreal yet vivid – ever shifting yet almost predictable, crowded yet lonely, diseased yet energetic, splendid yet squalid. It is in Adams's terms a scene "from which every trace of organic existence had been erased." To speak of what Poe's protagonist is, we must speak of the roles he plays. He is part spectator-as-participant and part participant-as-spectator. In one sense his seeing is narcissistic: everywhere he looks, he finds images of his own empty self. In another, it is imperial: hounded by his own internal blankness, he incorporates other figures. All of his surviving needs are thus fed by what Vachel Lindsay called "crowd splendor." In him the forlornness and the bravado of the modern city merge.

Turner sought to salvage the story of the frontier as a set of experiences and a set of words that people might use in confronting the novel demands of the nation's emerging cities. A bit earlier, Buffalo Bill had begun telling his version of that story for his profit and the world's edification. In *The Virginian* (1902), Owen Wister presents as a model citizen a socialized frontiersman whom both Turner and Cody would have recognized on the spot. Wister's hero, another hero without a name, is at once traditional and modern – traditional in his personal code, modern in his social ethic. He heroically faces danger not simply because he is brave but also because he is free of internal conflicts: even under maximum pressure, he never doubts that his code is right. He values his honor and his reputation neither less nor more than he values the institution of personal property, which he accepts as essential to the social order. In the early scene in which he confronts Trampas, he is prepared to kill a man who insults him. Later he leads a group of men in hanging an old friend named Steve, who has become a cowboy-rustler, proving that he is willing to kill in order to protect his employer's property, or more broadly the institution of property. If in his personal code he holds fast to an old sense of honor, in his social ethic he defends a conception of society bluntly spelled out by Paul Elmer More, who taught at Harvard, alma mater of both Owen Wister and Theodore Roosevelt, to whom Wister rather elaborately dedicated *The Virginian*. Looking "at the larger good of society," More asserts in *Aristocracy and Justice* (1915), "we may say that rightly understood the dollar is more than the man" and that "the rights of property are more important than the right to life." Earlier, such thinking had been used to justify slavery. But once the Virginian commits himself to it and then marries Molly Wood, a native of Vermont and a descendant of heroes of the American Revolution, he is ready to become one of Wyoming's leading citizens, a member of a new elite whose task – of continuing to make manifest the destiny of the United States – flows directly from shared interests.

In fact, however, the world for which Cody, Turner, and Wister sought to save the story of the frontier was only in part a presupposition and consequence of a certain conception of the importance of property and capital. It was also a world shaped by the grammar of science and the logic of technology, which, as Heisenberg noted, were forever changing the relation between nature and man by holding "incessantly and inescapably ... the scientific aspect of the world before his eyes." The engineer emerged as one of the heroes of Chicago's Columbian Exposition because of his crucial role in transforming a "desolate wilderness" and "dreary landscape" into a "Dream City." From one angle, technology may be defined as a step-by-step process by which people impose their desires on their environment. With each technical advance, people enlarge their material power over their lives and their world. Max Weber once spoke of material possessions as an "iron cage," and F. Scott Fitzgerald later suggested that possessions might become possessors: "The Victor belongs to the Spoils," he wrote. But at the century's turn, the goal of technological advance remained almost unchallenged, except by inconstant mavericks like Adams.

Adams knew that the modern city made manifest the desire of human beings to imprint versions of themselves on the world. But in describing New York of 1904 as "unlike anything man had ever seen – and like nothing he had ever much cared to see," he identified what Heisenberg later defined as the moment when technology ceases to be "the product of conscious human effort for the spreading of material power" and begins to outgrow its servitude and assert its freedom. Having become a process driven by forces of its own, technology reminds us, Heisenberg notes, that large forces attract large forces and that human beings remain limited in nothing so much as this: that, even when they can do what they will, they cannot perfectly control what they will. In developing this notion, Heisenberg quotes the Chinese sage Chang Tsu:

When a man uses a machine he carries on all his business in a machine-like manner. Whoever does his business in the manner of a machine develops a machine heart. Whoever has a machine heart in his breast loses his simplicity. Whoever loses his simplicity becomes uncertain in the impulses of his spirit. Uncertainty in the impulses of the spirit is something that is incompatible with truth.

Adams knew that machines were here to stay and that technology was not the only source of uncertain impulses. But he remained unconvinced that even Turner's continent-striding nineteenth-century American could control the massed forces of the modern world.

Writers of the twentieth century – from Frank Norris and Jack London to Ernest Hemingway and Ken Kesey – have gone on looking to the nation's early frontiers for models. The frontier, Norris said, is an "integral part of our conception of things." Jay Gatsby owns a library full of books he has never read. But Fitzgerald lets us know that he has read both Benjamin Franklin's *Autobiography* and a book called *Hopalong Cassidy*. In *One Flew over the Cuckoo's Nest*, Kesey evokes loggers, trail hands, and wagon masters – figures of frontier folklore – as heroic models. And in moments of maximum pressure, with life as well as freedom at stake, his protagonist, Randall Patrick McMurphy, rubs his nose with his index finger, then thrusts his thumbs into the pockets of his jeans, imitating the character that the actor John Wayne became. First in Chicago and later in New York, Adams observed a "breach of continuity," a rupture in historical sequence, so profound that it left the world demanding a new type of man, "born of contact between the new and the old energies." Opening the last chapter of his *Education*, he defines this new man as the "sole object of his interest and sympathy." But he also pictures him as almost disappearing ("the longer one watched, the less could be seen of him"), as though to explain why the task of seeing him required the play of imagination as well as the work of observation.

Adams's search for a new protagonist for the modern world was in part – like Gatsby's search and McMurphy's – a search for a new code of conduct. In *The Sun Also Rises*, Jake Barnes suggests that modern codes must follow experience: "I did not care what it was all about," Jake says." All I wanted to know was how to live in it. Maybe if you found out how to live in it you learned from that what it was all about." But traditional philosophy, not pragmatism, still held Adams's loyalty, and he knew that commitment to it meant trying to get to the ground of truth itself, even if that ground was shifting. In presenting the mind engaged in that endeavor, and thus in the act of creating meaning, Adams anticipated the general blurring of generic lines in literature that has characterized the twentieth century. His *Education* is part philosophy, part intellectual and cultural history, and part autobiography, and it makes wholesale use of novelistic techniques. In the process it sets the discovery of some new kind of self-originating discourse as the task of literary art in the twentieth century.

8

❦

JACK LONDON'S CAREER AND
POPULAR DISCOURSE

I N OUTLOOK, Jack London was closer to Cather and Dreiser than to James and closer to Turner than to Adams. But in his talent for turning personal adventures into remunerative art and culturally illuminating narrative, he resembles Buffalo Bill. Born in San Francisco on January 12, 1876, the illegitimate son of William Henry Chancy, an itinerant astrologer, and Flora Wellman, a spiritualist, London was named for his stepfather, John London. In 1886 his stepfather's farm failed, and the family moved to Oakland, the workingman's city of which another Oakland artist, Gertrude Stein, later said, "There is no there there." But Stein had lived in Pennsylvania and Europe before her family moved to Oakland, and her privileged life had given her very different standards. The vacancies of Oakland were the closest thing to home that London ever found. At age fourteen, he quit public school and began spending his days working in a laundry and then a cannery, and his nights frequenting libraries and saloons or working in San Francisco Bay as an oyster pirate. Later, older and tougher, he signed on as an able-bodied seaman on the *Sophie Sutherland*, a sealer bound for the Siberian coast and Japan, and began a life of remarkable adventures. Later still, in 1901 and 1905, he tried to become Oakland's first socialist mayor.

In 1894, one year after Adams's trip to Chicago and Stein's matriculation at Radcliffe College, London joined Kelley's Industrial Army, a group of unemployed workers that marched with Coxey's Army on Washington, hoping to force the government to help the unemployed. Back in Oakland, he studied briefly at the University of California, Berkeley, as a special student and then left to go prospecting for gold in the Klondike. Back in Oakland again, his pockets still empty, he began the adventure of writing about his adventures. His first book, a collection of stories called *The Son of the Wolf* (1900), catapulted him to fame. By the time he died sixteen years later, he had published forty-three books and made several small fortunes as one of the most popular, highly paid writers of his time.

One explanation for London's emergence as a writer-hero of the years before World War I lies in his talent, like that of Herman Melville, for transmuting his adventures into fiction. He worked as a sailor, an oyster pirate, and Klondike prospector. He was arrested for vagrancy in Buffalo and again in Niagara Falls, where he spent thirty days in jail. Preparing to write *The People of the Abyss* (1903), he lived for several months as a tramp in the East End of London. During years of national adventurism and imperialism, he kept on finding new frontiers to write about. Not even great success stilled his restlessness. After *The Call of the Wild* (1903) and *The Sea Wolf* (1904) had made him famous and earned him large sums of money, he left for Japan and Korea to cover the Russo-Japanese War for the Hearst newspapers. When the Mexican Revolution broke out in 1914, he headed for Veracruz to cover the war for *Collier's* magazine.

When London began writing, he intended simply to recount his adventures. But he soon found himself caught up in a remarkable unfolding in which his desultory reading played an obtrusive role. Traces of his reading – in Hobbes, Bacon, Locke, Kant, Laplace, and Freud, as well as in Swinburne, Shaw, Conrad, and Kipling – are scattered throughout his writings. In addition, he relied heavily on popularizers like Ernst Haeckel, whose *The Riddle of the Universe* (1899) applied the doctrine of evolution to philosophy and religion, and Herbert Spencer, who saw evolutionary thought as the key to understanding all change in the knowable universe, including ethics and social organization. But Darwin, Marx, and Nietzsche were his great heroes. From his readings of and about their works, he emerged with ideas, often reductive, that shaped his sense of everything he had experienced. His writings thus inscribe three adventures: his effort to make money by recounting his experiences, his effort to find meaning in his experiences, and the struggle among three giants to shape his interpretive venture.

To true disciples of any one of London's intellectual heroes, his appropriations are sure to seem unsatisfactory. His desire for social justice and his sympathy for society's outcasts reinforced the influence of Marx. But nothing could displace his fascination with nature as a scene of the struggle for survival, or with human beings as animals shaped by primal forces that can never be obliterated. In his repeated attempts to enter the consciousness of animals, his fascination with the human urge to recapture elemental, ecstatic forms of consciousness, through moments of struggle with primal forces, survived. Believing that such moments belonged to an elite company of the truly courageous who were willing to risk everything, he continued celebrating them, despite their clash with his politics.

In the "blood longing" that Buck feels in *The Call of the Wild*, we see traces of Nietzsche as well as Darwin. Having come to embody the skills and traits of his primal animal community, Buck becomes its leader because, as a courageous, skilled killer, he knows how to survive "triumphantly in a hostile environment where only the strong survived." Buck is a natural aristocrat who commands the life around him by virtue of his superiority. Even Nietzsche's notion of racial superiority had a lasting impact on London's mind: "I am first of all a white man," he wrote, "and only then a socialist." Given the basic thrust of his writings, in which women remain as subordinate as they do in Turner's, it is important to feel the narrow, exclusionary sense of the second of his operative terms ("man") as well as the first ("white").

As a result, mixed and even contradictory elements entered virtually everything London wrote. In *The People of the Abyss*, the modern city's slum becomes a frontier of savagery that stands as an indictment of the money-based, class-ridden society promoted by modern capitalism. There are a half-million or more human beings "dying miserably at the bottom of the social pit called London," he reports. Yet in writing about society's victims, he presents himself as a heroic superman. *The Call of the Wild* traces the reprimitivization of Buck, a "civilized" and thus partially denatured aristocrat among dogs. By obeying the call of the wild and surrendering his civilized restraints, Buck becomes again a primal animal who survives "triumphantly in a hostile environment." In *White Fang* (1905), the sequel to *The Call of the Wild*, London reverses this process. While Buck's journey carries him toward nature, White Fang's carries him toward civilization.

"I love the wild not less than the good," Thoreau says in *Walden*. "What really happened to" the people and the children of people "who left civilization and traveled the wilderness road?" asks T. K. Whipple in *Study Out the Land*. "All America lies at the end of the wilderness road, and our past is not a dead past but still lives in us," he adds; "thus the question is momentous. Our forebears had civilization inside themselves, the wild outside. We live in the civilization they created, but within us the wilderness still lingers. What they dreamed, we live; and what they lived, we dream." London believed that the wilderness still lived within people like himself, and he thought of this as representative rather than exceptional. For, like Thoreau, he regarded the savage and the civilized as contending principles, not as fixed scenes or as fixed states of being. He valued both the capacity to be changed by "socialization" in the name of the "good" and the capacity to remain "natural" by retaining one's affinity for the "wild." More than Thoreau, however, he thought of the wild, in the city of London no less than in the Yukon, as a truly savage realm where there was "no law but the law of the club and the fang" – a phrase in which the distance between nature and its weapons ("the fang") and civilization and its weapons ("the club") almost vanishes. In fiction and nonfiction, he presents life in frontier terms, as a struggle of instincts and wills as well as weapons. Society mirrors nature in his writings because it is dominated by elemental struggle. He thus locates in societies of the modern world disguised versions of the tangled skein of conflicting impulses and desires that lie observed in nature.

London wrote plain prose that makes a direct appeal to experience, and he possessed a gift for narrative. But his works owed some of their popular appeal to the way in which they served the cult of the "strenuous life" that arose as a counter to the fear of "gentility" and "femininity," which increased around the turn of the century. In short, though London thought of himself as a rebel, and in some ways was one, he served the culture of which he was a critic in ways that he never fully understood – except imaginatively in *Martin Eden*, where such knowledge leads to despair. And he served it by constructing stories beneath whose simple surface lurked confused, destabilizing issues that neither he nor his society could tame.

Given the almost magisterial control of his later novels, Henry James is sometimes thought of as epitomizing the lessons and virtues of form, or even those of transcendent art. Given the exposed seams and sheer noisiness of his work, London is often thought of as epitomizing the culture-bound artist. Yet in different ways both writers remind us that social and economic forces play shaping roles even in art. James's novels depend on a language of interests and investments, of power, manipulations, and economic status, and thus on a specific political economy that seems almost to flaunt its capacity for shaping modes of understanding and habits of expression as well as habits of the heart; habits of desire, aspiration, and wonder as well as habits of industry; and thus social, moral, and aesthetic as well as intellectual reflexes. There are, of course, several explanations for James's reiterated, self-aware relinquishing of the sense of fixed meaning and unambiguous tone that faith in the possibility of absolute truth demands. Some of these explanations are philosophical, others aesthetic. But James's insistence on knowing every mind through another mind, and his habit of treating even the pretense of knowing clearly and directly as dangerous, illicit, or vampirish, had social as well as epistemological and aesthetic roots. He avoided primal social and economic scenes as well as primal sexual scenes, not simply out of reticence or because he was unfamiliar with them, but also because he thought of language and sensibility as always already too deeply conditioned by and implicated in them. What was lost in advance was the possibility of their serving as anything more than radically imperfect tools for gaining the perspective that full understanding required. From *The Portrait of a Lady* on, language and sensibility were for him at once necessary and unreliable – the locus of illumination and understanding, and the locus of error and deceit. In his style, in which engagement and evasion coexist, he enacts the predicament of a writer who recognizes that his most essential tools are potentially deceitful and destructive as well as creative. And since he saw his predicament as modern rather than merely personal, he learned to confront it by sharing it with characters like Isabel Archer. The language of power and the power of language merge in his fiction. But his is also a world in which control as power and control as impotence coexist, drawing sublime triumph and abject failure closer together than they had ever been before.

Not understanding himself or his predicament as well, London approached nature both as a scene of adventure and as a haven. He identified with the wild, and especially with his wolflike dogs, by signing letters to close friends "Wolf" and by building a home he named "Wolf House." Ideas, by contrast, he approached as he approached society: in wary confrontation. Yet his novels owe their popularity in part to the ideas he never fully mastered. Even the novels (*The Call of the Wild*, *The Sea Wolf*, *White Fang*) and stories ("To Build a Fire") that struck readers as "pure" adventure are filled with crudely interpreted action. Where ideas were concerned, London remained an amateur in the double sense of being unprofessional and enamored. Yet he became a teacher to his nation more easily than James, in part because he was less disciplined and less concerted, a fact we must understand if we are to understand his success and the culture that made it possible.

The Call of the Wild begins by forcing us out of our anthropocentrism. "Buck did not read the newspapers," runs its first line. Through Buck, his St. Bernard-German shepherd hero, London reconnects us with the natural world from which we are descended and to which we still belong. London's cause is in a sense primitivistic: he wants to reawaken our ties to unthinking nature. "There is an ecstasy that marks the summit of life, and beyond which life cannot rise. And such is the paradox of living, this ecstasy comes when one is most alive, and it comes as a complete forgetfulness that one is alive." Behind his primitivism, or vitalism, lay a conviction that, in their effort to conquer nature, modern industrial-commercial-bourgeois societies have created a false relation between humans and nature, and thus between humans and themselves. Crudely yet tellingly, he insists that the underlying motives for the creation of such societies are economic, as we see early in *The Call of the Wild* when Buck is sold into captivity for profit. In *White Fang*, Beauty Smith is "a monstrosity," "the weakest of weak-kneed and sniveling cowards," who, seeing the strength and beauty of White Fang, the wolf-dog for whom the book is named, "desired to possess him" – in order to beat him for pleasure and exploit him for profit: "Beauty Smith enjoyed the task. He delighted in it. He gloated."

London tried, after his fashion, to be faithful to all of his heroes – Darwin, Marx, and Nietzsche – because he felt that he and his society needed them. As a result, there was something in his writings for admirers of people as different as Theodore Roosevelt, Eugene Debs, and Herbert Spencer. He traced and retraced actions that evoked the frontier myth in the hope of fostering moral and spiritual renewal. In his own forays into "virgin" territories, he found what earlier explorers had found in theirs: an economic as well as heroic potential. For, in the process of launching an amazingly remunerative career, he discovered a discourse that blends heroic self-dramatizations, clear evocations of his culture's frontier experiences and frontier myths, authentic political concerns, and self-taught (if also half-digested) ideas about nature and society.

9

❦

INNOCENCE AND REVOLT IN THE "LYRIC YEARS": 1900–1916

LONDON WROTE during a period of rapid, uneven economic recovery. Between 1900 and 1910, the nation's population jumped from 67 million to 92 million, with much of the gain coming in cities, where the rate of growth was three times faster than that in rural areas. Both average per capita wealth and average personal income increased, as did the unevenness of their distribution: in a period of strong economic expansion, the average real income of laborers fell. Investors, even those with modest capital to invest, were the winners, as both expansion and consolidation of industries pushed profits up – especially in railways, iron and steel, copper, meat-packing, milling, tobacco, and petroleum. By 1910, the men in charge of the nation's largest business firms possessed enormous political as well as economic power. "We have no word to express government by moneyed corporations," Charles Francis Adams, Jr., noted in 1869. Forty years later, the nation was still looking for words to describe its new political economy, which was dominated, Henry James observed, by the "new remorseless monopolies." Meanwhile, the poor were becoming poorer and more hopeless – "oxlike, limp, and lead-eyed," as the poet Vachel Lindsay put it. Some skilled laborers prospered, but others suffered, especially the new immigrants from Asia and Southern and Eastern Europe. In the North and the South, black Americans continued to be victimized by inferior schools, poor housing, and segregation that was vigilantly enforced in schools, churches, unions, and workplaces, as well as society at large.

Such contrasts quickly spawned a literature of protest. Having begun his career as a writer of adventure stories for boys' magazines, Upton Sinclair turned to reform fiction in 1906, in a novel called *The Jungle*, set in the bars, tenements, and packinghouses of a Chicago ghetto, where death hangs in the air like a "subtle poison." "What *Uncle Tom's Cabin* did for the black slaves," Jack London declared, *The Jungle* had a chance of doing "for the white slaves of today." On one side, Sinclair's fiction resembles social exposés like Lincoln Steffens's *The Shame of the Cities* (1904), John Spargo's *The Bitter Cry of the Children* (1906),

63

and Ida Tarbell's *History of the Standard Oil Company* (1904). On another, it resembles novels like Stephen Crane's "two experiments in misery," *Maggie: A Girl of the Streets* (1893) and *George's Mother* (1896), Abraham Cahan's *Yekl: A Tale of the New York Ghetto* (1896) and *The Rise of David Levinsky* (1917), Paul Laurence Dunbar's *The Uncalled* (1898) and *The Sport of the Gods* (1902), James Weldon Johnson's *The Autobiography of an Ex-Colored Man* (1912), and Anzia Yezierska's *Bread Givers* (1925). Similarly motivated, the painter John Sloan and other members of the "Ash Can school" and the "Revolutionary Black Gang" – Everett Shinn, William Glockens, and George Luks – sought to make painting "unconsciously social conscious." To genteel critics, Sloan and his associates were "apostles of ugliness." But urban life, not ugliness, was their subject, vernacular honesty their aim, as they scouted the dark alleys, dank saloons, and squalid tenements of New York in search of thieves, drunkards, and slatterns.

In fact, however, even as they studied the harsh world of the nation's cities, writers like Sinclair and painters like Sloan were lifted by hopeful winds of change. By 1912, when Woodrow Wilson announced his "New Freedom," *new* had again become a talismanic word, as it had off and on for several centuries, beginning with the early explorers of the "New World." The nation's tilt toward the dreamer and the tinkerer reflected its sense of itself as an unfinished scene; and in the first two decades of the twentieth century, an aggressive experimental mood, conscious of itself as revisionary, took hold. Spawning a "New Poetry," a "New Theater," a "New Art," and a "New Woman," it fractured the cultural scene. On one side stood devotees of the "Genteel Tradition," a term coined in 1911 by George Santayana. On the other stood young rebels imbued by a sense of urgency and high calling. Men in colorful clothing joined "smoking women" in flaunting the younger generation's victory "over the prostrate body of puritanism." Working "with knives in their brains," they examined the prejudices and inhibitions of their parents, determined to cast off everything that seemed to them petty, provincial, timid, or bland.

Mabel Dodge Luhan, author of *Movers and Shakers* (1936) and leader of the "rebel rich," as the novelist and journalist Floyd Dell called them, knew that some of the "Genteel Custodians" were tough-minded on some issues and of two minds on others. Several of them had enlisted in the mixed army of men and women fighting for women's suffrage; others worried about the diverse problems that had placed every "human relation," as Walter Lippmann wrote in the *New Republic* in 1914, "whether of parent and child, husband and wife, worker and employer," in a "strange situation." A few were even trying to address what Ludwig Lewisohn, in *Upstream* (1922), called the silent conflict between the interests of the established classes and "the sense of life and scale of values brought by the yet inarticulate masses of immigrants." But Luhan and the rebels could not help thinking of the Genteel Custodians as timid people bent on using their drawing rooms, private clubs, and country estates to shield them from the energy and problems of the new United States. Not only were the Custodians too fastidious; they had lost their nerve. They shrank from the poor, industrial working classes, the new immigrants, and black Americans, fearful of what their stirrings might mean. Their talk about "invasions of the darker types" hid two interconnected fears: fear that their racial "purity" might be lost if the new "strangers" were assimilated and fear that the "strangers," left unassimilated, might become dominant, displacing their privileged descendants. As a result, they evinced fear of every person or idea that had, as H. L. Mencken put it, an "alien smell" about it, lest they, the chief beneficiaries of the nation's abundance, should lose status and power as others gained them.

During the nineteenth century, the parents and grandparents of the Genteel Custodians had placed their interests and concerns at the top of the nation's official list of priorities. Having achieved a more or less coherent rationalization and justification of their ascendancy, they had become expert in using both descent relations, defined by blood, and consent relations, defined by marriage, partnership, or other agreements under law, to consolidate and enlarge the wealth and secure the privileges that, in their eyes, they had earned and, having earned, possessed the right to bequeath. Some of them admired the uses to which the energetic, aspiring young protagonists of Horatio Alger put consensual relationships; others realized that much of the nation's energy depended on its ability to inspire people with great expectations. But having arrived, they wanted to tilt their society and its political economy away from openness toward stability and privilege. Some of them enjoyed watching the antics of the rebels and even helped finance them. But in doing so, they were following a strategy familiar at least since France in the heyday of Voltaire and Rousseau: the upper-class strategy, described by Talleyrand, of taking delight in one's critics, confident of one's ability to tame their words and pictures with applause, money, and kisses. Recognition of the power of that strategy gave Jack London the story of *Martin Eden*; exploring it as he wrote filled him with despair.

At stake were the rights, privileges, and spoils that the Custodians thought of as theirs. At stake, too, was their ability to coopt the rebels and subvert the subversives. Their insistence that art remain aloof from local desecrations meant, first, that Beauty and Truth must be respected, and with them Tradition; second, that reticence and "good taste" must govern human relations; and third, as Henry Van Dyke put it, that the "spiritual rootage of art" must be preserved. In short, like Burnham and his advisers, they wanted to make lyric poetry, as the Genteel Tradition had defined it, normative for all art – a move that reflected deep commitments and protected clear interests, the extent of which can best be judged by the rebels' targets. It is, however, both ironic and telling that rebels like Floyd Dell and Genevieve Taggard, looking back, would call the heyday of their rebellion the "Lyric Years," without wondering what kind of independence they had achieved. For the "Lyric Years" – when the word *new* became almost talismanic and it seemed that the whole culture was about to be re-formed – proved in fact to be fleeting.

For a brief time, the assault appeared to be frontal. In 1911 Frederick Winslow Taylor, the "father" of "systematic management," published *The Principles of Scientific Management*, celebrating efficiency as an ideal that should be "applied with equal force to all social activities: to the management of our homes; the management of our farms; the management of the business of our tradesmen, large and small; of our churches, our philanthropic institutions, our universities, and our governmental departments." Twenty-five years later, John Dos Passos included a portrait of Taylor in *The Big Money* (1936), called his plan "The American Plan," and ended with Taylor lying "dead with his watch in his hand," as though to signal what worship of efficiency might lead to. In fact, however, the ideas associated with Taylor's name were widespread before Taylor systematized them, just as the critique of them was widespread before Dos Passos satirized them, and even before D. H. Lawrence, in *Studies in Classic American Literature* (1923), attributed them to Benjamin Franklin, as the nation's first secularized Puritan. In 1917 Randolph Bourne, in "The Puritan's Will to Power," framed one of several indictments that described industrial capitalists as descendants of a life-denying Puritanism and its dream of total control. Other diagnosticians named the Puritan as the chief carrier of repression, and repression as the nation's most enervating disease. In "Puritanism," James G. Huneker announced, "the entire man ended at his collarbone." By teaching themselves to refer to all natural acts euphemistically, to enclose all personal and especially all sexual relations in arduous formalities, and to make all social relations instrumental and exploitative, disciples of gentility and efficiency had turned maturation into a process of desiccation and made themselves victims of life-denying formulas. They were Puritans, and Puritans were money-hungry, life-denying neurotics who had forgotten how to laugh, feel wonder, or trust pleasure: "and down they forgot as up they grew," E. E. Cummings later wrote, in "anyone lived in a prettyhow town."

Meanwhile, in her salon on Fifth Avenue, Mabel Dodge Luhan was staging "Evenings" where writers as different as Edwin Arlington Robinson, Lincoln Steffens, Mary Austin, and Carl Van Vechten encountered journalists like

Walter Lippmann and political radicals like John Reed, Emma Goldman, and Bill Haywood. One thing Luhan's guests shared was a sense of the immediate past as what Joseph Freeman called a "dark age" across which the "meteors of Nietzsche, Whitman, Darwin, and Marx" had flashed; and another was the sense of the Lyric Years as a period in which barriers were going down and people were reaching out to communicate new thoughts in new ways. Gone forever was the world of the "vanished village" where God's commandments reigned with such authority that rebels who broke them assumed they had sinned. Now, Freeman said, you "had to make up your own right and wrong; you had to decide everything for yourself" – especially about sex but also about honoring your parents and accepting their authority. Gone, too, was the sense that the system of corporate capitalism must not be changed.

At times, the new art, the new sexuality, and the new politics seemed to go hand in hand. In Chicago, Van Wyck Brooks reported, "splendidly pagan" refugees of the drab farms, dried-up villages, and stagnant towns of the Midwest were gathering to discuss "art and socialism and the finer emotional forces that were to prevail in the future." The Midwest, Ford Madox Ford later reported from Paris, "was seething with literary impulse." Meanwhile, back in New York, Isadora Duncan – "what genius is," Luhan wrote – had become the high priestess of a sexual revolution that rebels assumed would sweep the land. Following her triumphant appearance in Carnegie Hall, Duncan's admirers hatched a scheme for having her dance in Harvard Stadium or the Yale Bowl before crowds of children too young to have been corrupted by Puritanical repression. Duncan was more than the "greatest living dancer" and more than the "symbol of the body's liberation" from outdated mores. She was a "sublime cult" that looked toward an era ever-more-about-to-be when life would be "frank and free" and people would believe in the "beauty of [their] own nature." "To die happy," the rebels said, one had to glimpse the future by seeing Isadora Duncan dance.

In fact, of course, the rebels were less liberated than they thought. A mix of pagans, aesthetes, and reformers – "earnest naive anarchists . . . labor leaders, poets, journalists, editors, and actors," as Luhan described them – they were also less unified than their enemies. It was very confusing, Luhan confessed; though the rebels "were all part of one picture," they were also "jumbled and scattered." One split set those who valued politics more than art against those who valued art more than politics. Another set those more concerned with social justice against those more concerned with personal freedom. Both anarchism and vagabondage were popular and both "spat indiscriminately upon all group life." Writers who saw the poet-artist under the aspect of the orphan, the wanderer, the outcast, and even the derelict favored those who chose the solitary way and rejected the "doom of being a joiner." Some settled for leading what Freeman called a dual life, supporting art with one hand, political reform with the other; others, including Freeman and Dell, turned to *Masses* in the hope of reconciling their "warring selves" and "connecting literature with revolution." Other magazines – including the *New Republic*, founded in 1914 by Herbert Croly and edited by Walter Lippmann, and *Seven Arts*, founded in 1916 and edited by James Oppenheim – sprang up to promote other versions of unity. Even established magazines – including *Smart Set*, edited after 1914 by H. L. Mencken with George Jean Nathan, and *Masses*, edited from 1913 to 1917 by Max Eastman – sought to make unity their cause. But in practice unity proved to be difficult.

Mencken was an early champion of the "crude" art of Dreiser, and he had written a controversial book on Nietzsche, adding his voice to the chorus fomenting revolt against the "denatured Brahmins," who seemed to him blind and deaf to everything "honest, interesting, imaginative, and enterprising" in life as well as art. But he had limited use for the complex if not deliberately obscure "modernist" works of writers like Ezra Pound, and even less for the reformers he called "birth controllers, jittery Socialists, and other such vermin." James Oppenheimer started *Seven Arts* in part because *New Republic* seemed to him, in its two short years, to have become one-sided in its concern for the "values of life" as opposed to art's concern with form and technique. The problem with Dreiser, Dell insisted, was the "Passive Attitude" he inculcated by presenting life in Darwinian terms. Louis Smith preferred the reformers Mencken called "vermin" to aesthetes who refused to make art socially responsible. Hutchins Hapgood, author of *The Spirit of the Ghetto* (1902), thought Stein and Pound as well as postimpressionists irresponsible in their abandonment of the idea that art should represent the "real" world.

What prevailed, when unity failed, was a more or less good-spirited truce. Although Mencken preferred his own accessible essays to obscure poems, he occasionally published Pound and Joyce. And he preferred even "vermin" to "Brahmins." Smith and Hapgood remained skeptical of those they called "aesthetes" and critical of nondoctrinaire radicals like Max Eastman. Eastman was a "half-ass intellectual," Smith said, "not a real revolutionary socialist." But like Hapgood, he preferred mild iconoclasts and even hedonists to the Genteel Custodians on grounds that any disturbance was a good one. Disturbances shake foundations, Hapgood wrote, and lead to new life, "whether the programs and ideas have permanent validity or not."

The result was what Pound called an "American Risorgimento," by which he meant a "whole volley of liberations" directed in more or less the same direction – against the Genteel Tradition. For years, rumors had been drifting across the Atlantic about a panoply of uprisings against authority. At stake were not only fundamental aesthetic values but also social traditions and ethical conventions, including, for Tristan Tzara and dadaism, the value of "art" and the idea of achieved culture as transmitted by what W. B. Yeats called "Monuments of unageing intellect." Caught up in their "volley of liberations," the rebels of the Lyric Years concentrated on the enemies they had named and, in a sense, created – "the denatured Brahmins," "the Puritan," "the Genteel Custodians" – and avoided the issues that divided them. American provincialism was one of their pet peeves, especially when it took the virulent form of fearing anything that had an alien look or smell about it. In the manners and dress displayed in their enclaves, as well as in the books they carried around and read, they were self-consciously cosmopolitan. One of their goals was recognition of what Randolph Bourne called "transnationality" – "a weaving back and forth, with other lands, of many threads of all sizes and colors."

At the same time, however, virtually all of them wanted to contribute to the creation of a distinctly "American" culture. Van Wyck Brooks, an editor of *Seven Arts* and author of *America's Coming of Age* (1915), spoke for many when he insisted that there could be no true revolution until native writers had brought their readers "face to face with [their] own experience." Brooks's indictments of the Puritanism and materialism of culture in the United States owed much to European thinkers. Yet he remained convinced that a "world of poetry" lay "hidden away" in the nation's past and that it might yet "serve, as the poetry of life should serve," to bring about the reconstruction of the nation's life. With this largely unexamined hope before them, he and his friends spent much of their time reading their precursors and reading one another: Brooks read Dell, Dell read Brooks, both read Bourne, and Bourne read both. They read the fiction of Norris, Sinclair, London, and Dreiser as well as Cather, Wharton, and Stein. And they read the verse, to cite Freeman's list, of "Robert Frost, Edgar Lee Masters, Vachel Lindsay, James Oppenheim, Amy Lowell, Ezra Pound, T. S. Eliot, [and] . . . Carl Sandburg," as well as "Walt Whitman, whose revolutionary message was expressing itself in the new freedom of our literature."

Caught up in the possibilities of renewal, the rebels skirted problems they could find no way to resolve, including the tension between identifying a national culture and creating a transnational culture. And they assumed, as Floyd Dell put it, with what now seems stunning innocence, that the "new spirit" abroad, generated by the "search for new values in life and art," would "logically . . . lead to a socialist society," accomplishing "Great Change" through "gradual conversion." For a time, particularly between 1913 and 1917, when Max Eastman edited it, *Masses* presided over radicalism in the United States

10

❦

THE ARMORY SHOW OF 1913 AND THE DECLINE OF INNOCENCE

NO EVENT more fully captures the rebellion, the divisions, and the evasions of the Lyric Years than the Armory Show that opened in New York on the evening of February 17, 1913, shortly before the Woolworth Building, standing 792 feet high, became the tallest building in the world. In *Movers and Shakers*, the third part of her four-part autobiography, *Intimate Memoirs* (1933–37), Luhan discusses several "Revolutions in Art" – and also reprints her own piece, "Speculations, or Post-Impressions in Prose," written on the occasion of the Armory Show, in which she asserts that "Gertrude Stein is doing with words what Picasso is doing with paint" – "impelling language to induce new states of consciousness." Luhan thus reinforces her broader claim: that the spirit that inspired the era's artists also imbued the planners of the Armory Show. Frederick James Gregg and Arthur Davies were co-conspirators with Stein and Picasso in a plot to open the eyes of "the great, blind, dumb New York Public" to art that is "really modern." Planning the exhibition, they talked "with creepy feelings of terror and delight" about their plan to "dynamite America." "Revolution – that was what they felt they were destined to provide for these States – and one saw them shuddering and giggling like high-spirited boys daring each other." The show itself, Luhan concluded, was the most important event of its kind "that ever happened in America" precisely because it had touched the "unawakened consciousness" of people, allowing artists to set them free.

In some respects, including the furor it created, the Armory Show almost matched the dreams of its makers. Some art critics, including Frank Mather for *Nation*, reassured readers that the hullabaloo would die down and sanity prevail, keeping art pure and society safe. Others followed Norman Hapgood in the *Globe*, who described the New Art's wanton violations of "ideal forms" and "noble subjects" as morally and aesthetically offensive, and Duchamp's *Nude Descending a Staircase* as a barbaric deformation of the human body. Kenyon Cox, adviser to Burnham in the building of Chicago's Dream City, described Cézanne as "absolutely without talent and absolutely cut off from tradition."

But the most important denouncements came from Royal Cortissoz, a man with close ties to such formidable institutions as the Century Club, the National Academy of Design, and the American Academy in Rome.

Cortissoz was a biographer of Augustus Saint-Gaudens (1907), another of Burnham's advisers, and John La Farge (1911). In 1913 his attacks on the Ash Can school and the Revolutionary Black Gang had established him as the most effective enemy of the new "barbarism." Following the Armory Show, he described Cézanne as ignorant, Van Gogh as incompetent, and "Picasso the Spaniard" as the creator "of a kind of Barnumism." Behind his message about the dangers of "Picasso the Spaniard," Gauguin "the stupid Frenchman," and Van Gogh the "tormented" Dutchman lie poorly repressed ethnic anxieties, the logic of which surfaces in his reference to the imminent threat that "foreign influences" pose to "American" society as well as "American" art. What "Post Impressionism" attacks, Cortissoz insists, is the notion of art as a timeless "manifestation of the eternal ideal" – in defense of which he names "Mr. Roger Fry, an English critic," and John S. Sargent as his allies. As it turns out, furthermore, the most invidious enemies of art – so-called artists who display technical "incompetence suffused with egotism" in subjects that are "dirty," styles that are "brutal," and results that are "obscure" – are also the most invidious enemies of "America."

Aided by notoriety, the Armory Show became a boisterous success. People rushed to see it. After it closed in New York, major parts of it moved to Chicago, where, attacked by the Law and Order League, it held its own in head-to-head competition for crowds with Lillie Langtry in vaudeville and George M. Cohan in *Broadway Jones*. From Chicago it moved to Boston. Back in New York, Gregg, Davies, and their co-conspirators staged a victory celebration. They marched through the halls where the show had opened to the music of fife and drum, raising their glasses in toast after toast. "Don't cheer, boys," John Quinn said, repeating the words of Captain Philip at Santiago as he and his crew watched a disabled Spanish ship sink, "The poor devils are dying."

The repercussions of the Armory Show lasted years. Impressionist and postimpressionist works had been shown earlier by Alfred Stieglitz in his gallery at 291 Fifth Avenue – "the largest small room of its kind in the world," Marsden Hartley called it. Although Bill Haywood thought Stieglitz narrow, artists thought him broad: having no narrow program of his own, he made convention his enemy and artists who defied it in interesting ways his friends. In 1908, 1910, 1911, and 1912 he had presented Rodin's drawings, Matisse's nudes, Toulouse-Lautrec's color lithographs, Cézanne's lithographs, and Picasso's drawings. But the Armory Show marked a turning point in lifting fauvist, cubist, and early futurist works to visibility. Of the several hundred paintings sold during its run, one was Cézanne's *The Poor House on the Hill*, purchased by the Metropolitan Museum. It was the first Cézanne acquired by a public institution in the United States.

Another set of repercussions came, however, from within the ranks of the rebels. To those who shared Brooks's commitment to native traditions, the show's concentration on Europe was disturbing. But the deeper issue had to do with the purpose of art. To Luhan, the paintings of Picasso were no more dangerous than the prose of Stein. What one was doing with painting the other was doing with words: using art "to induce new states of consciousness." But when Luhan went on to say what this meant – for Stein, Luhan observed, language becomes "a creative art rather than a mirror of history" – not even the talismanic word "new" could save her from offending socialists who insisted that art have social purpose or writers who regarded mimesis as an indispensable part of art's legacy. Formalists might be content to see individual artists like Stein dedicate themselves to reshaping the perception, sensibility, and thought of an elite group of *aficionados*. But to young idealists who hoped to fuse art and politics, the separation of art from social and economic actualities, and thus from "the people," spelled defeat. The failure of *Masses* to reach the masses was already an open secret. One wit wrote:

> They draw fat women for *The Masses*
> Denuded, fat, ungainly lasses –
> How does that help the working classes?

But the ideal of unity persisted. To surrender it was unthinkable not only to the editors of *Masses* but also to scores of rebels who remained committed to the idea of social reform, however uncritical they remained about the political implications of their own aesthetics or the aesthetic implications of their own politics.

Ezra Pound sat out the Armory Show in rural England and in general showed little interest in cultural disturbances masterminded by people like Gregg and Davies. To writers like Mencken and Lippmann as well as revolutionaries like Louis Smith and social critics like Hutchins Hapgood, Pound had all the markings – in costume, manner, and style – of an aesthete who cared little about material culture, let alone political realities and the plight of the masses. But Pound's concerns were more inclusive than most people thought, as his later career made clear, however sadly.

In his early years, Pound's concerns converged on the possibilities, problems, and powers of language. Later, after the Great War began killing off some of his friends, including the sculptor Henri Gaudier-Brzeska, his interest in politics and economics became more overt. In "Hugh Selwyn Mauberley" – which he described as "a study in form, an attempt to condense the James novel" – his enterprise embraces the task of saving culture as well as language not only from politicians, bankers, and warmongers but also from decadent aesthetes and hyperrefined literati. Later still, looking back from his confinement in Pisa at the end of World War II to his own version of the Lyric Years – the years he spent between 1913 and 1916 living with W. B. Yeats at Stone Cottage near Coleman's Hatch in Sussex – he thought of them as an innocent age, "before the world was given over to wars," when life seemed fresh and politics had not yet been born.

But Pound's eye for cultural politics in fact dated back to early disappoint-ments with the commercial magazines and publishing houses that dominated literature in Western democracies, including the United States. The survival of art mattered, as Pound saw it, because art's fate was inseparable from the fate of *all* forms of originality, freedom, and individuality. The seamlessness of culture convinced him that the forms of discipline dictated by commercial civ-ilization (maximum efficiency, standardized products, interchangeable parts and interchangeable workers, repetitive processes, and systematic manage-ment) were inimical to life as well as art. Sensing that the broader economic process – in which corporate capitalism inspired "systematic management" and "systematic management" reinforced corporate capitalism – he identified a threat to individuality that was also a threat to artistic creativity and so made resistance the center of his life. Unable to resolve the issue of how politics and art might be conjoined not only in fact, which at some level they were, but also in conception and intent, which they were not, Pound worked in fits and starts. His public persona as an aesthete, which was only partially true to his writings, triumphed over them, because it was easier both for him to communicate and for the public to grasp. But he knew what he desired, and it was not that art be separated from politics or that the United States try to turn back the clock. It was that the United States seize the artistic as well as the political promise of its democracy before its incorporating economy fur-ther diminished them, as his little book, *Patria Mia*, written in 1913, makes clear.

Pound's unsuccess, like that of the editors of the *Masses*, whose choice ran in the opposite direction in search of the same end, was prepared by his own fail-ure of will. But it was sealed by the coming of World War I. The outbreak of a general war in Europe was the fruit of decades of competition for markets and colonies. Fueled by industrial growth that it in turn fueled, that competition gave rise to frustrated as well as triumphant nationalism and spurred a mounting arms race. Within the United States, antiwar feelings ran highest among German Americans and Irish Americans, to whom fighting on the side of allies that included France and England was repugnant. The virulent antisemitism of the czarist empire made Jewish Americans reluctant to do anything that might help Russia. But many people in the United States, including most of the young idealistic rebels, watched Europe with shocked disbelief. Keeping a safe distance seemed the only wise course of action, lest their "Joyous Season" become a fool's paradise. As conflict led to conflict and atrocity to atrocity, however, hope of keeping Europe's madness at a safe distance died. In the end, most of the rebels accepted what Henry James expressed in a letter: that the war, "this abyss of blood and horror," and not the Lyric Years of good hope, was what the treacherous nineteenth century had all along been working toward.

The United States entered the Great War reluctantly, it entered late, and it remained uncertain of its motives almost to the end. "The world must be made safe for democracy," President Wilson said. "We are going to war upon the command of gold," countered Senator George Norris of Nebraska. Still, by the time Congress voted (the Senate on April 4, 1917, and the House, two days later, on a bleak Good Friday morning), most people supported the decision: the vote on the resolution to recognize the existence of a state of war with Germany was 82 to 6 in the Senate, 373 to 50 in the House. Americans remained divided about the origins of the war. "I voted for Woodrow Wilson," John Reed said in the summer of 1917, "mainly because Wall Street was against him. But Wall Street is for him now. This is Woodrow Wilson's and Wall Street's war." But such skepticism was more than balanced by enlistments in Wilson's "great crusade."

The full costs of waging what Wilson called "the most terrible and disastrous of all wars" emerged slowly. But one cost, anticipated by Wilson, surfaced early. War, he told a confidant in 1917, as though foreseeing the witch-hunts, spy scares, and kangaroo courts that lay ahead, will "overturn the world" we know; it will impose "illiberalism at home," instilling a "spirit of ruthless brutality" in the very "fibre of our national life." A year earlier, the government had banned *Masses* from the mails; a year later, in April and again in October 1918, it prosecuted, without success, Max Eastman, Floyd Dell, and Art Young for "conspiracy against the government." As late as 1916, when he launched *Seven Arts*, James Oppenheim still held to the faith of the Lyric Years: that "the lost soul among the nations, America, could be regenerated by art" or, as Van Wyck Brooks put it, that "a warm, humane, concerted and more or less revolutionary protest" could free the country of "whatever incubuses of crabbed age, paralysis, tyranny, stupidity, sloth, commercialism, lay most heavily upon the people's life." But such innocence faded. Within a year, the government had driven *Seven Arts* out of circulation, primarily because it opposed the war, and the Lyric Years – also called the "Little Renaissance," the "Confident Years," and the "Joyous Season" – had died, killing the hope shared by people like Luhan, Oppenheim, Brooks, Taggard, and Dell of bringing about "Great Change" through "gradual conversion."

THE PLAY OF HOPE AND DESPAIR

L IKE POETRY AND ART, fiction of the Lyric Years also got caught up in the play of hope and despair. In his early correspondence, describing his day-by-day struggles to get his fiction published in Eastern Coast magazines and by Eastern Coast publishers, Jack London complains, as Pound had, about the cost of postage as well as rejections. Later he began to flaunt his great success with macho swagger and then to analyze it with growing ambivalence, fearful that he had paid for it in the coin of corrupting compromise. In *Martin Eden* (1909), he confronts his writer-hero's confused ambitions and locates ties between them and the ambitions of his nation: "In the moment of that thought," he says of Martin Eden, "the desperateness of his situation dawned upon him. He saw, clear eyed, that he was in the Valley of the Shadow. All the life that was in him was fading, fainting, making toward death."

Martin Eden is the story of a writer whose life bears striking resemblances to London's own. One part of the significance of *Martin Eden* lies in the persistence with which it suggests that, despite its doctrine of impersonality, modern art often revolves around the interplay between artist and protagonist and between artist and work. Like London in his fiction, Gertrude Stein in hers, and Ernest Hemingway in his, Martin Eden treats everything that happens to him – poverty and wealth, obscurity and fame, neglect and celebrity, adventure and boredom, injury and good fortune, health and disease – as things that are somehow alien to him and yet are his own idea. He thus makes acts of attention acts of possession as well as creation. Through Nietzschean striving, he becomes a lionized and wealthy writer, forcing his materialistic, class-conscious society to acknowledge his superiority. In a sense, he appropriates the Horatio Alger plot: his is a story of a young man who rises from obscurity to fame, from rags to riches, from slum streets to fancy hotel suites. But he turns this familiar plot against the society that gave it birth and then made both its creators and its protagonists enormously successful by making his hero a social critic as well as an artist. The more his society honors and rewards Martin Eden, the more he despises it.

London clearly took delight in making the story he was writing resemble the one he had lived. He also took delight in posing as a lonely rebel who exposes society (both his own and Martin's) as having neither soul nor integrity left to lose. As a young man, full of passionate hope, Martin Eden becomes a writer and falls in love with a young woman named Ruth Morse, whose upper-middle-class parents are anxious about their own social standing and, therefore, about their daughter's suitors. Because he has neither money nor status – not even "a job" let alone "a position," as Ruth's parents teach her to put it – Ruth rejects him. Embittered, Martin takes consolation in believing that "Nietzsche was right," that the "world belongs to the strong" who are too noble to "wallow in the swine-trough of trade and exchange." When success comes to him, and money and fame pour in and he flashes, "comet-like, through the world of literature," he is amused. Like Rousseau, he learns how to market his bad manners and angry words. Having learned how to market so much, however, he begins to realize that the value of his achievements has been established by the world that publishes, buys, and praises them. Soon he stops writing and starts selling the yellowing manuscripts of discarded work that he no longer believes in; feeding his bank account, he also feeds his contempt for the publishers who print his work and the readers who buy it.

When Ruth and her family change their minds about his value, Eden's despair deepens. In the Morse family's first overture, Mrs. Morse sends Mr. Morse to Martin with a dinner invitation. When Martin rejects it, they send Ruth to his hotel room to persuade him of her love. What Martin already believes, he now sees clearly: that Ruth and her family are bereft of values. It "makes me question love, sacred love," he says to Ruth. "Is love so gross a thing that it must feed upon publication and public notice?" Finally, however, it is not simply the crassness of the Morse family that offends him; it is the power of society to shape human lives and human values, including his own. Nothing Ruth has "done requires forgiveness," he concludes, because she has always acted in accord with what society has taught her, "and more than that one cannot" ask. When he also recognizes that it was an idealized Ruth that "he had loved," one made beautiful in part by the glamour of her "station" and in part by the "bright and luminous spirit of his love-poems," he loses everything. "It is too late," he says, "I am a sick man . . . . I seem to have lost all values."

Unable to find any means of rereading his life, Eden sinks further into despair that eventually swallows everything. "I'm done with philosophy. I want never to hear another word of it," he says, not long before he sees that art, too, is duplicitous, presenting a false face of hope to the poor and a smug face of security to the rich. Finally, so emptied of belief that he loses "any desire for anything," he drifts toward death as desire and fulfillment: "All the life that was in him was fading, fainting, making toward death." Overcoming a natural, atavistic "will to live" that aborts his first suicide attempt, he succeeds in his second.

London wrote *Martin Eden* in 1908–9 while sailing his homemade yacht the *Snark* from California to the South Seas. In it he depicts a direct confrontation between two very different conceptions of culture – one built on the dream of interests powerful enough to impose virtual order and to absorb or coopt minor disturbances, which is the dream of the Morse family; the other built around the dream of values pure and noble enough to achieve expression and force recognition on their own, which is Martin's early dream. London's hope clearly lay with his protagonist, but his experience spoke to him in different terms. And it underwrote both the strategies of cooptation that the Morse family practice and the strategies of despair that engulf Eden. On the morning of November 22, 1916, seven years after he finished his most important novel, London died at the age of forty, apparently of a self-injected overdose of morphine. During the sixteen years between his first book and his death, he published forty-three books and piled up manuscripts from which editors and publishers fashioned seven more. He wrote as he lived, we may fairly conclude, as a man pursued. And he wrote as he thought, as a man grasping for hope as well as ideas: "Tell me," he seems to ask again and again with Laurel and Hardy, "why can't *we* ever get ahead?" His was an old man's rage even when he was still young. By the time he died, his body, once so beautiful that he described himself as being "proud as the devil of it," was a map of devastation: in his last years, he suffered from gonorrhea, insomnia (probably related to his heavy drinking), a severe skin condition, probably psoriasis, a syphiliticlike condition known as "Solomon sores," pyorrhea that forced him to have all his teeth removed, recurring dysentery, and chronic uremia. To cope with his maladies, he regularly took both arsenic (apparently to ease the pain in his bowels) and morphine. Yet he continued to eat raw fish and meat, which he loved, and, despite repeated warnings, to drink heavily – in obedience to something he once called, in *John Barleycorn* (1913), the "White Logic" of a "long sickness." In its pathos as well as its contours, dotted with excesses, in its desperate search for some accomplishment or idea that would suffice, and above all in its poverty and its riches and the telling way in which its poverty gave rise to hope and its riches to despair, London's life found expression in the story of Martin Eden. Like all good stories (including the story of the garden from which Martin got his name), Eden's story is many stories. But at bottom it is the story of a man who, having lost a home he can scarcely be said ever to have possessed, discovers that he can find no place he wants to call his own.

It is a long way from the world of Jack London to that of Edith Wharton, and from the story of Martin Eden to that of Lily Bart in *The House of Mirth*. But London's struggle, like Wharton's, was a struggle with form rather than for it. And it was troubled because it seemed to him that form and structure, in their striving to reconcile and integrate, were always already conservative. Art celebrated Dionysus but worshiped Apollo; it praised unruly eloquence but desired closure; it played at breaking forms but worked at creating them. London's art, like his identity as a writer, was troubled by his sense that literature was dedicated to suppressing both the social classes and the natural realities to which he was devoted. This is, of course, another way of saying that his identity crisis as a writer remained unresolved. And it is probably worth noting that his great commercial success, reflecting as it did national confusions that mirrored his personal confusions, had the effect of redoubling rather than resolving that crisis, as *Martin Eden* suggests. London remained a homeless child who wanted to claim art as well as life for dispossessed people. But he could find no way of succeeding as an artist without betraying his causes. His significance lies in the stark way in which the experience of feeling excluded drove him to seek inclusion that he could purchase only in the coin of betrayal.

If in London's life and art we observe the perils, for a man, of being born outside the nation's privileged circle, in Wharton's we see the perils, for a woman, of being born inside even the most privileged of circles. If, furthermore, London speaks as a man for whom inclusion held out the compromising promise of power, Wharton speaks as a woman for whom inclusion necessarily meant confinement. Born in 1862 into an elite family that counted itself among New York's "Four Hundred" – a number set by the size of Mrs. William Astor's new ballroom – Wharton had all the advantages that position and education could provide. Yet because she was a woman bent on becoming a writer, she was no less self-made than London, though for her self-making meant trying to slough off cultural baggage while his meant trying to acquire some. It tells us much about London that "home" was a concept whose weight he felt precisely because he had never experienced it, and much about Wharton that her earliest recorded memory was familial. Wharton's respectable family was a web of aunts, uncles, and cousins reinforced by a larger web of friends. The only cloud hanging over it came from a late, unsubstantiated rumor that she was the daughter not of her businessman father but of a young Englishman who had tutored her two brothers. That Wharton chose to take the rumor seriously points to her need to legitimize her felt marginality.

Reared as a well-bred daughter of a well-established family, Wharton came to a life of privilege that was also a life of constraints, several of which took the form of expectations. Wharton's family was prepared for many things, including her decision to come out into society at age eighteen and to make a suitable marriage at age twenty-three. But it was not prepared to see her act withdrawn in her youth (when she was in fact writing surreptitiously) or later to see her make her energies, conflicts, and ambitions public as a writer. The wealth of Wharton's world intensified its force. At no level of society was the proper role of women more clearly defined, and in none did terms like "proper" and "lady" carry more weight. For those able to accept and master propriety, her society allowed some play, even to women. But for those tilted toward resistance, it meant trouble, especially if they were women. Though Wharton knew her society well, she was never on easy terms with it, especially after she decided to become a maker as well as a consumer of culture. Her social world resembled the one that had given Henry James his great "international" theme and then authorized him to explore and exploit it. And it readily gave Wharton the right to live versions of some of the actions that James's novels trace. Once she had determined to be a writer, however, her world gave her the theme of women trapped between an established order and an emerging order. On one side stood a fading world that offered women place – as daughters, wives, mothers, and readers – but denied them voice, especially voice raised to an active social pitch. On the other stood a new order, too amorphous to provide her place, yet palpable enough to call forth her voice.

The cost of Wharton's career lay, therefore, less in the large effort of writing her books than in the perilous effort of forging a self that necessarily constituted an act against family and society. The repeated periods of debilitating self-doubt that Wharton experienced in her thirties resulted at least in part from the conflict between her residual loyalty to her heritage and her emerging loyalty to herself as a woman determined to become a writer. Her decision to live abroad was less crucial for the distance it put between her and New York than for the distance it put between her and her family, though both were necessary to her effort to see and expose the falseness of the rich and sometimes elegant society that she saw Americans devising for themselves as a prisonhouse.

In *The House of Mirth*, in the "malice of fortune" that shapes Lily Bart's fate, we see an analogue to Wharton's own predicament. For it is a historical as well as familial malice that Lily Bart points to – one that takes several forms, the most inclusive being a fatal disjunction between her needs as an individual and the logic of the social world in which she tries to make her way by following the teachings of her mother. Like Edna Pontellier in Chopin's

The Awakening (1894), Thea in Cather's *Song of the Lark* (1915), Dorinda in Glasgow's *Barren Ground* (1925), and Anna Leath in Wharton's *The Reef* (1912), Lily is a descendant of Hawthorne's Hester. She, too, is torn by tensions between what Chopin calls the "outward existence which conforms" and the "inward life which questions." But when she fails to find any place for herself – as a lover, a wife, a prophet, or a witness – she ends as Martin Eden ends, with the discovery that there is no place for her to go. She thus becomes a model of how hard effective resistance to one's milieu can be.

Lily Bart is, to be sure, much more likable than Martin Eden, in part because her requirements of life are more recognizably human. She wants genuine intimacy, yet she values her independence; she wants a full life, but she wants it as a consenting party and partner, not as an invited guest or an indulged wife. And since she is thoroughly modern, she also expects some adventure, excitement, comfort, and pleasure. Her dream includes a "day of plighting," we are told, and also a "haze of material well-being." Lily's world offers her the plighting and the comfort she seeks by holding out to her a woman's traditional role in the "house of mirth," as a proper wife of an appropriate man. But in making this offer, it insists that all her requests come either as pleas to be "spoken for" by a properly empowered man or as pleas to be "spoken about" by properly empowered women – alternatives that rule out intimacy as well as independence by implicitly insisting that Lily accept herself as a desirable object rather than a desiring subject.

The social class whose interests dominate Lily's world demonstrates its powers of enforcement repeatedly. It controls marriages in order to concentrate property and wealth. Against minor dissenters such as Lawrence Selden and Gerty Farish, it follows a policy of tolerant marginalization. Once it is clear that Rosedale's fortune is going to continue to grow, not even his being a Jew can deter its policy of shrewd cooptation. But when Lily persists in resisting the pressure to play the part assigned her in its rigid, arid social narrative by undermining her chances of making the kind of marriage expected of her, it connives in a plot designed to discredit and ostracize her. At times Lawrence Selden seems to stand above the interests of the class to which he belongs. But in fact he remains timid and inconstant both in resisting his moneyed world and in advocating his rarefied "republic of the spirit," whose trademark is freedom from all pressures and entanglements: "from money, from poverty, from ease and anxiety, from all the material accidents" of life.

By spoiling her chances of making a proper marriage, Lily in effect declines her ticket of admission into the "house of mirth." Her resistance to that world centers on a vague sense that it turns everything, including human beings – especially attractive women – into commodities. About Selden's more ethereal "republic of the spirit," she remains of two minds – in part, we may assume, because it offers her no language of female mastery and growth and so cannot empower her either to understand herself or to insist that she be understood, and in part because it seems too genteel and rarefied to meet her human needs. Left to make her way in a world in which her own best inclinations and desires go against everything that her parents as well as her society – her father by abnegation, her mother by indelible instruction – have taught her, she becomes internally conflicted and makes one self-defeating mistake after another. At no point does she discover a language free enough of the money- and status-conscious world of the house of mirth to enable her to review and recast her life. Toward the end she begins to suffer from neurasthenia, a condition that troubled Wharton herself off and on throughout the 1890s. Finally, drifting toward death, carried by a "physical craving for sleep," which becomes "her only sustained sensation," she carelessly consumes a lethal dose of sleeping drops. To the end we cannot be certain whether her act, like that of Edna Pontellier in *The Awakening*, stems from an impulse of the self to find affirmation beyond society's reach, even at the expense of death, or more simply from some assent to dismissal from a world she cannot accept, though both novels tilt toward the latter.

Theodore Dreiser possessed disaffections of his own, including several that ally him with London and a few that ally him with Wharton, and like them, he remained committed to fiction as a form of cultural criticism. But he possessed in abundance an ability that Wharton and London possessed only in measure: the ability to accept on its own terms the society into which he was born. As a result, he spent little time trying to reform society and less rejecting it. He saw the suffering that surrounded him and did not like it. But necessity seemed to him to rule life, and he saw no point in pretending it did not. While Adams continued to write as one convinced that the force of nature ("nature's compulsion") and the force of history ("external suggestion") were things humans had been put on earth to overcome, Dreiser wrote as one convinced that nature would get you even if history did not. Such knowledge pushes Martin Eden toward despair. But Dreiser drew different lessons and few morals from his experiences and readings. In a world in which "nothing is proved," he said, "all is permitted." History, whatever else it was, was not principled. People were simply caught, or "caged" as Adams had put it, like "frightened birds." "We suffer," Dreiser wrote, "for our temperaments, which we did not make, and for our weaknesses and lacks, which are no part of our willing or doing."

Born into a family of fifteen, Dreiser pulled away from both his rigid, dogmatic German Roman Catholic father, whom he learned to dislike, and his kind, ineffectual mother, whom he learned to pity. Dogged by poverty, the family moved from one small Indiana town to the next. To Booth Tarkington (1869–1946), rural Indiana was the "Valley of Democracy." To Dreiser (1871–1945) and, so far as we can judge, several of his siblings as well, rural Indiana was a slough of despond. Two of his brothers became alcoholics and two of his sisters "fell" early from virtue into scandal – including one whose story Dreiser transmuted into the story of Carrie Meeber, as the "sister" of his title, *Sister Carrie*, suggests.

Sister Carrie (1900) begins where youth ends, with Carrie on the road and on her own. In the early chapters of *An American Tragedy* (1925), we feel the pain of Dreiser's own childhood and youth more directly. Running from the poverty of his youth, Clyde Griffiths spends the whole of his short life acquiring the values of the successful people who inhabit the glamorous world he hopes to enter, which means that he learns to fear failure and worship success. Yet will plays a surprisingly small role in his life, in part because a harsh sense of necessity hovers over it. In the end, he drifts toward murder as Lily Bart drifts toward suicide. In a deep sense, both Lily and Clyde have always already done the one big thing – the one by embracing, the other by inflicting death – that neither of them ever quite does, which means, among other things, that their stories resemble Jack London's even more than they resemble Martin Eden's.

Dreiser tumbled into writing *Sister Carrie* in the summer of 1899 – after a decade of newspaper experience in Chicago, St. Louis, Toledo, Pittsburgh, and New York – when his friend Arthur Henry decided to try his hand at writing a novel and asked Dreiser to keep him company. On one side, Dreiser worked from within the "realist" tradition that had served as one of the principal means of assimilating and transmitting the family-centered, morally ordered social world that Henry Adams associated with Thomas Jefferson and John Adams. On the other, he drew on the "naturalist" tradition that informed both journalism's effort and the novel's to adjust determinist elements present in Darwin's view of nature and in Marx's view of history to the poverty and squalor of modern cities. Although he accepted these traditions as grounded in capitalist political economies, Dreiser associated realism with a dispersed, entrepreneurial, and largely agrarian capitalism, and naturalism with the new urban, corporate capitalism. The process of painful transition from one of these to the other is a part of what *The House of Mirth* may be said to chart. It is a "breach of continuity" or "rupture in historical sequence" (to use Adams's terms) that leaves Lily Bart with no place to go. To the fading world of gentility, Lily Bart appears too "modern" – particularly in her concern for physical comfort and pleasure and in her careless disregard for propriety. To the world emerging around her, however, her moral sensibility seems too concerned with candor and especially independence. If Lily Bart's needs and desires may be said to mirror Wharton's discontent with the world into which she was born, her fate may be said to mirror Wharton's residual loyalty to that world – a conflict out of which Wharton made fiction again, first in *The Custom of the Country* (1913) and then in *The Age of Innocence* (1920).

Dreiser, by contrast, fit the United States emerging on the near side of the historic shift that Adams located in 1893, and that Wharton limned, as perfectly as any writer of his time. His America is industrial and commercial, it is centralized, and it is affluent enough to make poverty all the more painful to those trapped in it. Above all, it is urban, and it is fast becoming secular. "We are unsettled," Lippmann observed in the *New Republic* in 1914, "to the very roots of our being. There isn't a human relation...that doesn't move in a strange situation." Having made "personal growth" its byword and "self-realization" its end, Dreiser's America imposes large burdens, especially on the young. Recalling his own youth during the first two decades of the twentieth century, Joseph Freeman spelled out that confusion clearly:

All this was very complicated. In the vanished village you knew where you stood. There were God's commandments and you obeyed or broke them; but at least you knew what was right and what was wrong. Now nobody knew. You had to make up your own right and wrong; you had to decide everything for yourself.

In Freeman's vanished village, organized religion played a crucial role in promulgating constructions of reality and authorizing codes and rituals that gave meaning to life and provided practical instructions about how to live it. Such formulas claimed divine authority on the basis of their origins, and they had become culturally sanctioned. In the new world Freeman describes, however, in which individuals are free to construct their own formulas and choose their own ways, they feel both empowered and burdened, both liberated and dispossessed. Like London's and Dreiser's protagonists, Wharton's and Stein's inhabit such a world and inherit its problems. In *The Custom of the Country*, Wharton's heroine, Undine Spragg, makes peace with this new world. Spragg is more openly erotic than Lily Bart, and she also sees her commodified world more clearly, which means that she accepts herself as possessing a clear trading value and a definite "trading capacity." In short, she knows what her resources are and learns how to use them. Accordingly, she succeeds where Lily fails. Yet having worked her value out successfully, acquiring money, rank, and power, she remains haunted by her longing for some "more delicate kind of pleasure" and even for "beauty."

With *Three Lives* (1909), Gertrude Stein began her long effort to adjust the structure and rhythm of prose to the fluid world emerging around her, in which everything seemed suddenly cut loose. Set against the backdrop of realist and naturalist prose, her fluid prose – full of participles and verb-nouns – provides a countertext. By focusing on the individual consciousnesses of two poor immigrant servant women and one sensitive young black woman, *Three Lives* also helped to announce an age in which the points of view of marginalized people would become increasingly important, in part because the risks of self-realization would vary inversely with society's authorization of the self. Stein works to capture the rhythms and intonations of almost silenced or lost voices. And she also works from a deep rapport with the cinematographic quality of modern life – its interplay of beginnings, repetitions, and endings – that anticipated several developments of the twenties. A sobering distance remains, however, between Stein's delight in finding new ways of conveying the fluid rhythms of the modern world, which can be appealing in their variety even when they are baffling in their slipperiness, and her protagonists' pain in trying to find ways of living among them.

Dreiser, by contrast, punctuated the early decades of the twentieth century with novels about the determined efforts of men and women to realize themselves within the new urban secular world of corporate capitalism. His novels belong to a nation scaled more to openness and change than to defined roles or fixed places. His men and women show little interest in family life. Pulled hither and yon by sexual desire or social ambition, they change apartments, partners, jobs, and cities. Physical as well as social mobility fascinates them, along with a love of the new and the novel – the romance of invention and change – even when fluidity and temporality threaten to engulf them. They live unsettled lives, moving up and down the social ladder, surrounded by buildings that are erected only to be razed. They live in boardinghouses, rented flats, or hotel rooms rather than homes; they have affairs rather than make marriages; they hold jobs or positions rather than pursue vocations; and they play roles rather than fashion identities. In short, they feel at home in the world we see emerging in *Martin Eden*, *The House of Mirth*, and *Three Lives*, a world in which "personality" is rapidly replacing "character" as the keyword to the only kind of selfhood that seems possible.

Dreiser's "trilogy of desire," especially *The Financier* (1912) and *The Titan* (1914), traces Frank Cowperwood's rise to wealth and power. In Cowperwood's story, Dreiser turns the Horatio Alger plot into the ultimate expression of an acquisitive affluent society. Twenty-five years earlier, in *Looking Backward* (1888), Edward Bellamy had imagined Boston in the year 2000 as a society in which people devoted themselves to possessing "the good things of the world which they helped to create." In the secular world of Cowperwood's Philadelphia and New York, the desire to possess things and the gratification of possession already signify more than galloping materialism because the accumulation of objects and especially of money – or, more abstractly, of "stocks and bonds" – has become the only way of keeping score in the only game that matters – the center, William Carlos Williams later observed, of this country's "whole conception of reality."

Cowperwood despoils the jungle world in which he lives, running through wives, friends, and rivals remorselessly and tirelessly. Yet he is not alone in embodying the United States that T. S. Eliot described as a nation in which "the acquisitive, rather than the creative and spiritual, instincts are encouraged." Even those whom Cowperwood exploits, defeats, or victimizes envy his brutal energy for the simplest of reasons: because it works. His rivals share his goal of dominance, without remembering when they absorbed it. They live in cities, made worlds of made objects, where life is so dominated by *things* that the desire to possess crowds out the desire to share and the desire to control crowds out the desire to protect. Early in Norris's *McTeague* (1899) we see McTeague respond to the sight of Trina lying helplessly in the dental chair in his office after he has given her gas. "Suddenly," Norris writes, "the animal stirred" in McTeague and the desire for total possession possessed him. In Trina as well as McTeague, furthermore, desire always circles back to possession. In both Norris's and Dreiser's novels, sex and money rule, and in their rule they become confounded. Late in *McTeague* we see Trina, caught up in her own merged desires, wildly pressing gold coins to her body.

Even as he worked to transmute the United States in which he lived into fiction, Dreiser also worked to remind his readers of what both he and they were doing. The Cowperwood stories are based on the spectacular career of Charles T. Yerkes (1837–1905), who became one of the most dazzling financiers of his day by seizing control of Chicago's street-railway system. *An American Tragedy* is based on the case of Chester Gillette, which Dreiser studied with care. A lesser novelist might have disguised his historical sources. Dreiser's openness confirms what the way he tumbled into the writing of fiction suggests: that, remarkably unencumbered with theories about it, he felt at home with fiction. He had done considerable reading, of Nietzsche, Darwin, Freud, and Spencer, as well as Dickens and Zola. But he was less hounded by his reading than London was and probably had done less of it than Wharton, Stein, Cather, or Rölvaag. Certainly, his encounters with the decentered world in which he lived seem less mediated than theirs. He felt the great shift that had overtaken the United States not as some "malice of fortune" but as a fact. Most of what he knew about the old ways he had learned from his parents, and he found neither the harshness of his failed father nor the weakness of his failed mother appealing. His newspaper experiences, as he moved through Chicago,

St. Louis, Toledo, and Pittsburgh to New York, had taught him much about the poverty, corruption, and slippery ethics of the nation's communities. But nothing he learned caused him to look back nostalgically on the string of small Indiana towns where he had lived as a young boy. Cities had come to him as a deliverance. Their ruthlessness bothered him, but their crassness scarcely fazed him, and he reveled in their hope, energy, and expansiveness. The ambivalence he felt toward life in the United States ran deep, but his openness to it ran deeper still, as the spilled-out clumsiness of his prose shows. As the country he labored to understand becomes ever more cautious, calculating, and self-protective, his openness may well come to seem more and more valuable.

12

❦

THE GREAT WAR AND THE FATE
OF WRITING

"IT IS THE GLORY of the present age that in it one can be young," Randolph
Bourne wrote in 1913, four years before World War I engulfed the United
States and five before he died at age thirty-two. Scarred and disfigured at birth
by a botched delivery, then crippled by spinal tuberculosis that deformed his
back and stunted his growth, Bourne learned early to think of himself as too
"cruelly blasted" to live a full life. Yet he wrote – *Youth and Life* (1913) and
Education and Living (1917) and a series of essays for *New Republic*, *Masses*,
Seven Arts, and *Dial* – as a fully engaged critic about the major concerns of
the Lyric Years: youth, rebellion, education, politics, literature, and the arts.
When it happened that he did not survive his age (he died in December 1918
of influenza), his friends came to regard him as the writer who best embodied
its lost hope. After his death, both James Oppenheim and Van Wyck Brooks
edited collections of his essays – *Untimely Papers* (1919) and *The History of a
Literary Radical* (1920) – in order to help establish him as its representative
cultural critic.

Had Bourne written about himself, as several critics of his time did, such
a development might seem less odd. In fact, however, though he took Walt
Whitman as one of his prophets, Bourne avoided himself as subject. He focused
instead on the aspirations and anxieties of his age, as though hoping vicariously
to live them, and so made its yearnings his yearnings, its despair his despair.
For him values are always social as well as personal. Even his passion for truth
remains overtly historical and so manifests itself as an effort to speak both of
and to a particular historical people. He writes not as a prophet speaking to
the ages but as a citizen speaking to citizens. Only in 1918, with his world
so mired in "Mr. Wilson's War" that the possibility of formulating a viable
political aesthetic seemed lost, did he veer toward the kind of separatism that
was for him the form of despair: "The enhancement of life, the education of
man and the use of the intelligence to realize reason and beauty in the nation's
communal living," he said, "are alien to our traditional ideal of the State,"
which "is intimately connected with war."

The Great War was, of course, one thing for a man like Bourne, who essentially could not enter it, and another for those who entered it as a grand crusade or great adventure. It was one thing for men and another for women, one thing for whites and another for blacks, one thing for volunteers and another for conscripts. But it engaged and provoked almost everyone, especially the thoughtful young, for many of whom it became either a life-shattering or a life-shaping experience. In 1914 Howells predicted that war would mean "death to all the arts." But Americans started writing about the war before their country officially began fighting it, and they haven't stopped yet, in part because Bourne's sense of it as the death knell of the Lyric Years of good hope has prevailed.

Half a century earlier, a large number of literate men had fought as officers and as common soldiers in the Civil War, and many literate women had been engulfed by it. During the Great War, numerous literate and even literary men and women either opposed the war or served near or in its battle zones. As the war became the crucial issue in the cultural debate between the Genteel Custodians and the "League of Youth," new voices arose – some, like that of John Dos Passos (b. 1896), on the side of the League, and others, like that of Richard Norton, on the side of tradition. But the Great War united the children of tradition, in part by giving them another tradition to draw on, while it divided the rebels. The suppression of *Masses* and *Seven Arts* retarded public dissent. Several rebels – including Alexander Berkman and Emma Goldman – were arrested and convicted under the Espionage Act (June 1917). Still others were intimidated by private threats and public lynchings, or "patriotic murders" as they came to be called. In Missouri in April 1918 a young German American named Robert Prager, whom the navy had rejected as physically unfit, was stripped, beaten, and then lynched while five hundred "patriots" cheered. Such acts, the *Washington Post* observed, in words that remain appalling, were signs of "a healthy and wholesome awakening in the interior of the country." With "a hideous apathy, the country has acquiesced," John Reed reported, "in a regime of judicial tyranny, bureaucratic suppression and industrial barbarism."

In the face of such pressure, divisions among the rebels deepened. Many rebels thought of war as the "curse of mankind," a sign that the disease of nationalism was not "confined to Germany." But such views lost credibility in a world in which almost everyone – traditionalists, anarchists, and socialists alike – began to act like "trained soldiers," as Freeman put it. Some rebels followed Wilson from his peace campaign into his crusade; others advocated some form of accommodation; and a few, including Upton Sinclair, turned about completely by joining the "hate the huns" campaign. "One after another," Freeman noted, the same people who had opposed the war started supporting it, sometimes in terms so hysterical that they "made reactionaries like Elihu Root appear sober and logical."

Heartened by the rebels' disarray, the Genteel Custodians promptly reclaimed the moral high ground that they had always assumed was properly theirs. Evoking an old tradition of glorious self-sacrifice, they started dispatching volunteers to France even before the nation entered the war. Founded in 1914 by Richard Norton, son of Charles Eliot Norton of Harvard, the Norton-Harjes Ambulance Service and other such organizations drew volunteers from universities as far away as Stanford. James Harold Doolittle, of World War II fame, left the University of California, Berkeley, to join the Lafayette Escadrille, an air unit financed by private funds from the United States but led by French officers. Other young patriots found their way into regular British or French fighting units.

Like John Reed, Walter Lippmann, and T. S. Eliot, Alan Seeger was a member of the Harvard class of 1910. Fresh out of Harvard, Seeger went to Greenwich Village, donned a long black opera cloak, and became, in Reed's words, an "eager / Keats–Shelley–Swinburne Mediaeval Seeger." From there he moved to Paris, planning to live the life of a poet. But in 1914 he volunteered for the French Foreign Legion and two years later was killed in action, by which time he had already become the voice of young men drawn by duty into the Great War. "It is for glory alone that I am engaged," he wrote, speaking for countless young men who went forth believing that they knew what honor, glory, and duty meant and hoping that Wilson's grand crusade would save their country from its drift toward ruin. The "sense of being the instrument of Destiny" was what he sought, Seeger said, adding that he pitied "poor civilians" who would never see or know the "things that we have seen and known" and so would miss the "supreme experience."

Seeger and his friends, many of them "young acquaintances" of such elder statesmen as Theodore Roosevelt and Oliver Wendell Holmes, Jr., left early for the field of battle because they were convinced of the heroic grandeur of war. In exclusive prep schools and venerable colleges, they had learned a code of honor that they thought of as reaching back beyond Sir Walter Scott and the Crusades to the glory and grandeur of Rome and Greece. One of the characters in Edith Wharton's *The Marne* (1918) turns specifically to ponder Horace's famous phrase, "Dulce et decorum est pro patria mori," as though to remind us of one of the ways in which tradition can work. The Civil War had come not only as a great ordeal but also as a "great good fortune" to young men of his generation, Oliver Wendell Holmes, Jr., observed, precisely because it had quickened their sense of life as a "profound and passionate thing." Even "in the midst of doubt, in the collapse of creeds," Holmes said, "there is one thing I do not doubt," the sublime beauty of a soldier who surrenders his life in the name of "a cause." Seeger wanted, he said, "to be present where the pulsations are liveliest" – and that meant facing war and even death, "the largest movement, the planet allows . . . a companionship to the stars." "I have a rendezvous with Death," he wrote in his most famous poem, in which traditional verse serves traditional ideas:

> I have a rendezvous with Death
> At some disputed barricade,
> When spring comes back with rustling shade
> And apple-blossoms fill the air.
> I have a rendezvous with Death
> When spring brings back blue days and fair.

"And I to my pledged word am true – " Seeger ends his poem, "I shall not fail that rendezvous."

Such sentiments led many Americans, women and men, to see the war principally in terms of its heroic potential. Even if it failed to free the world of tyranny and make it safe for democracy, it could still reinvigorate a culture that had grown soft, confused, artificial, and "unmanly." Devotion to a great cause, H. W. Boynton wrote in *The Bookman* (April 1916), had a "purifying influence." Anguish and suffering, Robert Herrick predicted in "Recantation of a Pacifist," in *New Republic* (October 1915), would bring about a "resurrection of nobility." Movies like *Pershing's Crusaders* and books like *The Glory of the Trenches* (1918) and *My Home in the Field of Honor* (1916) presented the war as a great adventure made noble by patriotism. Such sentiments spread through the culture as though history had prepared the way. "No kind of greatness is more pleasing to the imagination of a democratic people," Alexis de Tocqueville had noted, "than military greatness, a greatness of vivid and sudden luster, obtained without toil, by nothing but the risk of life." Richard Harding Davis's story "The Deserter" (1916) promotes commitment to the war on similar grounds, as does Mary Brecht Pulver's "The Path to Glory" (published in the *Saturday Evening Post* in March 1917), in which a poor family wins a community's respect when a son dies driving an ambulance in France. Ellen Glasgow's *The Builders* (1919) presents another brief on behalf of the war, though rather more in Wilson's terms than in Holmes's. Edith Wharton had already demonstrated – in *The House of Mirth* (1905), *Ethan Frome* (1911), *The Custom of the Country* (1913) – literary talents that included a gift for satire. When World War I came, however, Wharton made France's cause her own by organizing large relief programs and writing pro-war novels in terms inculcated by the class whose expectations had once stifled her own deepest needs. It is as though the soldiers' "great experience had purged them of pettiness, meanness, and frivolity," she writes in *Fighting France* (1917), echoing Herrick and Holmes, "burning them down to the bare bones of character, the fundamental substance of the soul."

In *Patriotic Gore* (1962), Edmund Wilson, a Princeton graduate who volunteered for the ambulance corps, looked back to find in the Civil War what he had observed firsthand in World War I: the rapid conversion of a divided nation into an "obedient flood of energy" that could "carry the young to destruction and overpower any effort to stem it." Some rebels protested to the end; a few followed Mike Gold to Mexico to avoid the draft. But as patriotic sentiments spread, more and more young men rushed to volunteer. "What was war like? We wanted to see with our own eyes," said John Dos Passos, another of Harvard's sons. "We flocked into the volunteer services. I respected the conscientious objectors, and occasionally felt I should take that course myself, but hell, I wanted to see the show." Soon the propaganda campaign took aim at women as well as men. One poster showed European women beseeching women of the United States to send their husbands and sons "to save our children"; another urged women to fulfill themselves by working in munition plants; and another, aimed at those still young at heart, featured a sexy, scantily clad young woman riding orgiastically across the skies on a large projectile. By late 1917, there were 175,000 troops in France. Six or seven months later, in the summer of 1918, nearly 10,000 per day were boarding troop transports bound for Europe. By November 11, 1918, when the Great War ended, 4 million Americans were in uniform, nearly half of them in France, and roughly 1.3 million had come under fire. Hundreds of others saw duty in combat zones as members of Norton-Harjes or the American Ambulance Field Service. Together they shifted the balance of power significantly, hastening an Allied victory.

Books like Wharton's *The Marne*, movies like *The Glory of the Trenches*, and verse like Seeger's, as well as other best-sellers, such as Robert W. Service's *Rhymes of a Red Cross Man* (1916) and Arthur Guy Empey's *"Over the Top"* (1917), offended some returning veterans, including Ernest Hemingway, another of those who joined the volunteer services. But patriotic works continued to come after the Great War had ended and disillusionment had begun. In Wharton's *A Son at the Front* (1923), a son teaches his father to see the war as a "precious responsibility" offered by Destiny to his generation: "If France went," his son says, "Western civilization went with her; and then all they had believed in and been guided by would perish." "The German menace must be met," the father adds, and "chance willed that theirs should be the generation to meet it." Later, quickened by the death of his son, the father is born anew as an artist. In Willa Cather's *One of Ours* (1922), Claude Wheeler, a successful yet unfulfilled son of the West, looks at a "statue of Kit Carson on horseback . . . pointed Westward" and mourns the loss of a life of adventure that he has been born too late to experience. Disappointed by his sense of being left to live in a diminished world where "there was no West, in that sense, any more," and convinced that adventures essentially never happen to those who stay at home, he heads for the trenches of France, where he finds fulfillment when he "falls" still holding to his "beautiful beliefs." "For him," his mother says, "the call was clear, the cause glorious."

As both the terrible toll of the Great War – 1.8 million killed for Germany; 1.7 million for Russia; 1.4 million for France; 1.2 million for Austria-Hungary; 947,000 for Britain; 48,000 killed, 2,900 missing, and 56,000 dead from disease for the United States – and its fruits – not the renewal prophesied by people as different as Woodrow Wilson and H. G. Wells, in *The War That Will End War* (1914), but a botched peace, continued turmoil in Europe, and renewed isolationism in the United States – became clear, however, a new disillusionment set in, especially among writers. Europe had emerged so decimated, depleted, exhausted, and debt-ridden, so torn by inflation and political unrest, that it was hard to see what the sacrifices had been for. Still reeling from their losses, the victors faced embarrassing disclosures of the atrocities they had committed in the name of "saving" civilization. Here is a list, jotted down in 1922 by Winston Churchill, then secretary of state for war for Great Britain:

All the honors of all the ages were brought together, and not only armies but whole populations were thrust into the midst of them . . . . Neither peoples nor rulers drew the line at any deed which they thought could help them to win. Germany, having let Hell loose, kept well in the van of terror; but she was followed step by step by the desperate and ultimately avenging nations she had assailed . . . . The wounded died between the lines: the dead mouldered into the soil. Merchant ships and neutral ships and hospital ships were sunk on the seas and all on board left to their fate, or killed as they swam. Every effort was made to starve whole nations into submission without regard to age or sex. Cities and monuments were smashed by artillery. Bombs from the air were cast down indiscriminately. Poison gas in many forms stifled or seared the soldiers. Liquid fire was projected upon their bodies . . . . When all was over, Torture and Cannibalism were the only two expedients that the civilized, scientific, Christian States had been able to deny themselves: and they were of doubtful utility.

Having emerged as a new world leader, blessed with an expanding economy and the prospect of unmatched prosperity, the United States decided to protect what it had by turning its back on the rest of the world, and so refused both to sign the Treaty of Versailles and to join the League of Nations, the only hope the world had for a new order.

At home, furthermore, the "obedient flood of energy" that had turned a divided nation into a concerted force had in fact been bought at a considerable price, including many betrayals of principles. Once the aristocrats of recent immigrants, German Americans had become the targets of "strident rant," to use Bourne's phrase. Sauerkraut and pretzels were declared "un-American"; coleslaw was renamed "liberty salad"; orchestras stopped playing German music; schools stopped teaching German language and literature; and the Metropolitan Opera House dropped all German operas from its repertoire. By the war's end, virtually every immigrant group had felt the impact of propaganda and abuse – spy scares, witch-hunts, kangaroo courts, and even lynchings. President Wilson talked loosely of foreign-born Americans as "creatures of passion, disloyalty, and anarchy" who "must be crushed out." The National Security League, originally formed to lobby for national defense provisions, aimed a barrage of name-calling and accusation at "imported people" and "hyphenated-Americans," imploring "100 percent Americans" to defend national security – an effort joined by such organizations as the American Protection League, the American Defense Society, the Boy Spies of America, and the Sedition Slammers. The result was an assault on foreign influences that rippled through the decade of the twenties, sometimes with terrible results.

Drawn into the war effort in record numbers, women assumed that an era of rapid progress had dawned. A few prominent leaders of the prewar years, notably Jane Addams, held firmly to their pacifist convictions, but most struck compromises that allowed them to support the war. The National American Woman Suffrage Association endorsed Wilson's initiatives even before the nation declared itself at war. Later, with the war under way, Carrie Chapman Cott, president of the association, declared women "opposed to anything that will bring a peace which does not forever and forever make it impossible that such sufferings shall again be inflicted on the world." Giving the vote to women, Wilson promptly told Congress, was "vital to the winning of the war." Some women served abroad in the American Expeditionary Force as nurses or telephone operators. Nearly a million took up war work, fueling hopes that a new day of employment as well as emancipation had come. Some, including Wharton, had the heady experience of making major contributions to what Wharton called "the greatest need the world has ever known." Others, including Cather, made writing about the war a way of making contact with it.

With such experiences behind them, women greeted passage of the Nineteenth Amendment as the culmination of a century of struggle that signaled a new era. What followed, however, was neither the reconstitution of society that supporters of suffrage had prophesied nor the disintegration that its enemies had predicted. Suffrage had little discernible influence on the nation's politics, and less on its economy. In 1923 the National Women's Party, led by Alice Paul, proposed the nation's first Equal Rights Amendment as a logical next step after suffrage. But far from becoming a new, unifying cause, the proposal drew fire from men and divided women. It set upper-class women against working-class women, and radical leaders, who scorned the jobs traditionally assigned to women, against moderates, whose first priority was to improve the pay and working conditions of women in jobs they already held. Both the new sexuality and the new technology proved to be mixed blessings – the first by pressuring women to be more physically appealing to men, the second by pressuring them to be more efficient in running their houses so that they could give more time to charity.

For a time, women had felt "no longer caged and penned up." Through the sacred glamor of nursing, they had gained self-esteem and had learned things about men that "reduced their inhibitions." In factories, they had "stepped into the shoes" of absent men and even "worn their pants" for a time, gaining access to new jobs at fair wages. When the war ended, however, the patriotism used to call them into factories was used to send them back home so that veterans could take their jobs. In 1920 women constituted a smaller percentage of the labor force than they had in 1910. As disillusionment mounted, suspicion spread – among women of men, and among men of women. In literary circles gender-based fear increased after the war.

Early in the war, advocates insisted that the war would do quickly what peace would take years to accomplish: not only would it advance women's rights, it would dehyphenate the "hyphenated-Americans." "The military tent where they all sleep side by side," Theodore Roosevelt announced, "will rank next to the public school among the great agents of democratization." Conscription and compulsory military training (estimates hold that roughly one of five draftees was foreign-born) were widely defended on grounds that they would transform the many peoples of the country into one "new nation." In fact, however, drafting new immigrants severely tested the fairness of military leaders, while the drafting of black Americans completely outstripped it. Strict racial segregation remained the unexamined rule, despite Roosevelt's description of the military tent, and proper training of black soldiers by white officers presented problems that no one was prepared to address. Several brutal courts martial and executions resulted, in Houston, Texas, and elsewhere. Those black soldiers who survived training were quickly assigned menial tasks. W. E. B. Du Bois and other leaders had hoped that the war would give black men a chance to earn advancement, first in the military and then in the labor market. Instead, new versions of old patterns prevailed. Abroad, black soldiers were discriminated against and even brutalized by other U.S. troops and some Allies as well as the enemy. When they returned home, they found that the Deep South remained the Deep South and that the industrial North, the new "Land of Hope," was still torn by white fear and black frustration.

Coupled with the carnage, atrocities, and betrayals that took place during the Great War, both the botched peace conference in Versailles and the Senate's rejection of the League of Nations compounded disillusionment. In Cather's *One of Ours*, Claude Wheeler dies believing the war a noble cause. But in his mother's mind, a window of doubt soon opens. "He died believing his own country better than it is, and France better than any country can ever be," she says, before adding words that present her son's faith as illusion and her wisdom as disillusionment: "Perhaps it was well to see that vision, and then see no more." Like Cather, Dorothy Canfield Fisher supported the war, but in her novel *The Deepening Stream* (1930), we encounter a young American woman who, having struggled to save her beloved France, is left walking the streets of Paris, her head filled with reports of behind-the-scenes deals that are aborting the peace talks. In the world being born, she realizes, she will always be a "refugee."

As their disillusionment deepened, survivors of the Great War took to writers like Bourne as their guides. But they also found support in unexpected places. Ellen La Motte was born in 1873 in Louisville, Kentucky. In 1915, shortly before Seeger joined the French Foreign Legion, she went to France to serve as a nurse with the French army. A year later she filed her report – *The Backwash of War: The Human Wreckage of the Battlefield as Witnessed by an American Hospital Nurse* – which focuses on the pain and slime she encounters in the backwash behind the lines. Her "Heroes" are soldiers who face the bitter realization that they are anonymous parts of a '"collective physical strength" dedicated to a Pyrrhic advance of "Progress and Civilization." This knowledge makes some of them contemptuous of life, including their own; and it turns others into lonely victims. La Motte tells, for example, of a young aviator who, a few days after being decorated for destroying a zeppelin, kills himself flying drunk. In "A Citation," she recounts the last terrible days of a young soldier who holds on to life, waiting for a general to come to honor his heroism with medals, only to die "after a long pull, just twenty minutes before the General arrived with his medals." War, she observes, in direct contradiction to the discourse of glorious self-sacrifice, is not a filtering process "by which men and nations may be purified." It is lonely, senseless dying in the "backwash" of the world.

During the twenties, literature dealing with the Great War followed La Motte's lead more than Seeger's; setting terrible losses against dubious gains, it countered the discourse of honor with a discourse of disillusionment. "There died a myriad," Pound wrote in "Hugh Selwyn Mauberley" (1920),

> And of the best, among them,
> For an old bitch gone in the teeth,
> For a botched civilization,
> Charm, smiling at the good mouth,
> Quick eyes gone under earth's lid,
> For two gross of broken statues,
> For a few thousand battered books.

Behind such words lay a suspicion that the Great War had finally laid bare a secret about modern technological societies: that they depend on economies that in turn depend both on the preparation of war to stimulate invention and production and on the execution of war to stimulate consumption, including the heightened form of consumption called destruction. The Great War was not merely another episode in an endless conflict; it was a sign that sooner or later nations will do whatever their weapons make possible. Pound knew that "civilized" nations had used "old men's lies" to attract young recruits. Writing years later, echoing Robert Graves's reminder that patriotism died in the trenches, William March, a Marine from Alabama who won the Distinguished Service Cross, the Navy Cross, and the Croix de Guerre, filed another brief against the Great War, in a novel called *Company K* (1933), that included a brutal parody of a commanding officer's letter to a bereaved parent:

Dear Madam: Your son, Francis, died needlessly in Belleau Wood. You will be interested to hear that at the time of his death he was crawling with vermin and weak from diarrhea. His feet were swollen and rotten and they stank. He lived like a frightened animal, cold and hungry. Then, on June 6th, a piece of shrapnel hit him and he died in agony, slowly.... He lived three full hours screaming and cursing by turns. He had nothing to hold on to, you see: He had learned long ago that what he had been taught to believe by you, his mother, who loved him, under the meaningless names of honor, courage and patriotism, were all lies.

Such total bleakness descended on relatively few Americans, of course. Most Norton-Harjes and American Ambulance Field Service volunteers and most combat troops held fast to the set of beliefs that led them to volunteer. Some of them dismissed the works of writers like Pound, Dos Passos, and Hemingway as unrepresentative. But there were widespread signs of disillusionment in the culture at large. One came in 1920, when the Senate turned its back on Europe, repudiating the nation's avowed purposes for entering the war and forfeiting its chance of claiming world leadership on the basis of vision rather than power. Another came with the rapid repudiation of the reform spirit and the progressive faith of the Lyric Years. People like H. L. Mencken and

George Jean Nathan were soon bragging about being self-absorbed rather than high-minded. "The great problems of the world – social, political, economic and theological – do not concern me in the slightest," Nathan wrote. "What concerns me alone is myself, and the interests of a few close friends. For all I care the rest of the world may go to hell at today's sunset." At the same time, overtly sexist and racist discourse began to spread, while toleration, even as a laudable idea, lost ground.

Writing in 1936, Cather remarked that "the world had broken in two in 1922, or thereabouts," naming the year in which *One of Ours* was published. In *A Lost Lady* (1923), her affection for an already vanished America, and her disillusionment with the United States of the twenties, emerged in a portrait of Ivy Peters as the perfect bourgeois real-estate developer of the emerging nation. Having followed "dreamers" and "adventurers," Peters has learned how to get "splendid land from the Indians some way, for next to nothing," and then develop it for profit:

Now all this vast territory . . . was to be at the mercy of men like Ivy Peters, who had never dared anything, never risked anything. They would drink up the mirage, dispel the morning freshness, root out the great brooding spirit of freedom . . . . The space, the color, the princely carelessness of the pioneer they would destroy and cut up into profitable bits, as the match factory splinters the primeval forest. All the way from Missouri to the mountains this generation of shrewd young men, trained to petty economics by hard times, would do exactly what Ivy Peters had done.

For Cather, the lost world that had come earliest in her own life, as well as that of her nation, suddenly seemed almost blessed. But there is more than nostalgia in her evocations. She reminds us of the power of places and of landscapes that are not of human making, just as Dos Passos reminds us of the power of those that are. Stein, living in Europe, dated the breaking point in 1914. Several writers favored 1919, the year for which Dos Passos named one of his novels. But even those who resisted the bleak term "Waste Land" agreed that the Great War had changed the landscape of life. In *Death Comes for the Archbishop* (1927), Cather describes the Southwest of the early nineteenth century as a place where "death had a solemn social importance," not as "a moment when certain bodily organs" of an isolated individual "cease to function, but as a dramatic climax" to a life lived in a community. "Among the watchers," she adds, "there was always hope that the dying man might reveal something of what he alone could see." For Cather as for many other writers, war had made injury and death more terrible by making them so completely personal that no discourse could convincingly tie them to purpose or insight. The turnabout that Cather limns makes the mass anonymous deaths of the Great War's trenches a perfect introduction, if not to life in the twentieth century, at least to the literature of the twenties.

The *War Letters* (1932) of Harry Crosby are considerably more direct. In them we follow the transformation of another son of Harvard – a nephew of J. Pierpont Morgan – who became an ambulance driver. Convinced that God had "ordained the war" in order to make the world a "finer, cleaner, and squarer place," Crosby's early reports are good-spirited. Gradually, however, he begins to describe, with obsessive and even perverse delight, landscapes ravaged by war, the surreal horror of nighttime warfare, and horrific images of the dead and dying. Having survived the war, Crosby was decorated by France and the United States for his heroism. But having lost his hold on the old world he associated with St. Mark's and Harvard, he had become, his wife Caresse remarked, "electric with rebellion." In June 1927, at a Four Arts Ball in Paris, he turned ten live snakes loose during a wild dance and then stepped back to watch the show. "I remember," he wrote in his diary,

two strong young men stark naked wrestling on the floor for the honor of dancing with a young girl...and I remember a mad student drinking champagne out of a skull which he had pilfered from my Library as I had pilfered it a year ago from the Catacombs...and in a corner I watched two savages making love...and beside me sitting on the floor a plump woman with bare breasts absorbed in the passion of giving milk to one of the snakes!

Two years later, on December 10, 1929, in a hotel room in New York, Crosby shot and killed himself. Having already left, in his letters and diary, a record of how the Great War had emptied him of beliefs, leaving him with nothing but a hunger for exotic visual stimulation and a deeply spectatorial disposition, which he used to manipulate his fascination with danger and death, he left no further note of explanation.

One part of the story of the twenties would be played out in the lives and deaths of people like Harry Crosby. Hart Crane would become a casualty of the times, and so would Zelda Fitzgerald. The mood of the decade would cultivate a tone and style so ironic and haunted as to seem almost paranoid: "At the start of the winter came the permanent rain and with the rain came the cholera," Hemingway writes in *A Farewell to Arms* (1929). "But it was checked and in the end only seven thousand died of it in the army." Nothing any longer seemed sacred, least of all the platitudes of official patriotism. "I was always embarrassed," Frederic Henry remarks in *A Farewell to Arms*,

by the words sacred, glorious, and sacrifice and the expression in vain. We had heard them...and we had read them and I had seen nothing sacred, and the things that were glorious had no glory and the sacrifices were like the stockyards at Chicago if nothing was done with the meat except to bury it. There were many words that you could not stand to hear and finally only the names of places had dignity.

People emptied of beliefs remained rare, of course, even in the aftermath of the Great War. Soon a spirit of energy and exuberance, quite different from that of the Lyric Years, began reaching out to embrace writers as old as Gertrude Stein (1874–1946) and as young as Langston Hughes (1902–67) in what seemed for a time a single "younger generation," united by the sense of being survivors, exiles, and refugees as well as geniuses together. Their brief engagement in the Great War had taken them a long way from the moment during the Lyric Years when the world seemed just to have begun and the promise of transforming society and reinventing the United States seemed at hand. And it had taught them to regard big, hallowed words and the social uses to which they could be put with suspicion. But in the process it had also deepened their belief in the power of words – a belief that the wholly disillusioned can never know. If language possessed force, everything lay open to inspection – not only myths of heroism and old customs and mores but the force of history and the authority of fiction. In addition the war had given them a new sense of parity with Europe. Europe lay devastated with many of its great writers dead or shattered. The United States had been catapulted into a position of international prominence that promised finally to free it of lingering cultural colonialism. Writers continued to regard their culture with mixed fascination and disappointment, but they assumed that the future belonged to the United States, and by extension to them as well. "The war ... or American promise!" Bourne had said. "One must choose.... For the effect of the war will be to impoverish American promise." And much of the promise of the Lyric Years had in fact died during World War I. In particular, few writers of the twenties spoke with confidence about the possibility of reforming their society. But another task – that of cutting their ties with the past in order to invent the future of their literature – still seemed to them bright with possibility. To it, as well as the pursuit of pleasure, they were ready to give themselves with rare exuberance.

2

Fiction in a time of plenty

I

❦

WHEN THE WAR WAS OVER: THE RETURN
OF DETACHMENT

H ENRY ADAMS died in Washington, DC, on March 27, 1918, less
than eight months before World War I ended. Two years earlier
he had authorized a posthumous edition of *The Education of Henry
Adams*, one hundred copies of which had been printed privately in 1907.
As it happened, then, *The Education* was published on September 28, 1918,
one day after President Woodrow Wilson opened the Fourth Liberty Loan
campaign with a stirring speech to a crowd of five thousand at the Metropolitan
Opera House in New York. "At every turn . . . we gain a fresh consciousness
of what we mean to accomplish," Wilson asserted. The war must end with
the "final triumph of justice and fair dealing," and the League of Nations
must be established as an integral part "of the peace settlement itself." The
next morning, the *New York Times* urged people, "Back the Right and Might
of Wilson and Pershing with the Dollars of Democracy!" Six weeks later, on
November 11, the armistice was signed in a railroad car in Compiègne Forest.
"By a kind of irony, just at the greatest moment in history," the *North American
Review* announced in its December 1918 review of *The Education*, "appears this
prodigy of a book."

Widely reviewed, *The Education* became a best-seller. For twenty-five years,
Adams had been writing his friends bleak letters, predicting that the United
States would follow Europe's drift toward catastrophe. Early in 1914 Henry
James responded to one such letter by describing it as a melancholy outpour-
ing of "unmitigated blackness." Still Adams persisted. "When one cares for
nothing in particular," he said, even disaster "becomes almost entertaining."
A great show is about to begin, he wrote John Hay, "the *fin-de-siècle* circus."
What he wanted was the best possible seat for seeing the show whether it be
in Washington, New York, London, Paris, Berlin, or Calcutta. "To me it is
amusing," he said, "because I said and printed it all ten years ago."

In one sense, it was appropriate that Adams should die so near the end of the war that struck him as the final gasp of the world into which he had been born – "the past that was our lives," as James put it, paraphrasing Adams's "melancholy outpouring." In his early years, he had hoped to help reform that world. What we need, he wrote his brother Charles at age twenty-five, is new energy and vision "not only in politics, but in literature, in law, society, and throughout the whole social organism of our country." Gradually, however, and then emphatically with the election of Ulysses S. Grant – who made the theory of evolution ludicrous, he said – history had rejected his ambition. "We have lived to see the end of a republican form of government," he observed shortly before he died. But it was also appropriate that his voice should survive the war. For while grieving "the past that was our lives," he had continued to wonder what the world replacing it would yield. "A great many things interested Adams," T. S. Eliot told readers of the *Atheneum*, in a review of *The Education*, "but he could believe in nothing."

The divisions that found expression in Adams's bleak outpourings also shaped his efforts to present himself as a detached observer of his world. *Mont-Saint-Michel and Chartres* (1904) enacts, among other things, a lyric aesthetic of flight. For us, Adams says, "the poetry is history, and the facts are false." But his retreat into the past also became a covert preparation for his examination of the world emerging around him. In *The Education*, his companion piece to *Mont-Saint-Michel and Chartres*, he uses another distancing device – that of telling the story of his own life in the third person – in order to make it the story of his age. In *The Education*, he becomes a disinterested interpreter – a theatergoer, a traveler, or, more radically, a posthumous observer – recounting the spectacle of his life and times. Having placed failed versions of his social self at his story's center, he places surviving, reflective versions of himself on its periphery.

As a social self, Adams acts as a "realist" bent on analyzing society and finding new ways of influencing it. He wants to be a "statesman" rather than a "politician" – that is, a principled servant of society rather than an opportunistic exploiter of it. But he also wants to be a man of affairs, and in this role he acts as an enlightened positivist. He knows that culture is grounded in profane history, but he wants moral purpose to inform it. In this endeavor he fails repeatedly, in part because his world no longer shares his concern with moral purpose and in part because he possesses little talent for mastering the language of power. The power of language imaginatively employed becomes his principal resource. As a social creature or man of affairs directly engaged in shaping history as event, he fails repeatedly. Only as a disembodied voice engaged in acts of style does he become a creature of force: a self-sufficient, surprisingly resourceful master of words.

During the thirties, as a way of looking back on the twenties, Malcolm Cowley and Bernard Smith edited a collection of essays titled *Books That Changed Our Minds*. George Soule wrote on Sigmund Freud's *The Interpretation of Dreams*; Charles Beard on Frederick Jackson Turner's *The Frontier in American History*; John Chamberlain on William Graham Sumner's *Folkways*; R. G. Tugwell on Thorstein Veblen's *Business Enterprise*; C. F. Ayres on John Dewey's *Studies in Logical Theory*; Paul Radin on Franz Boas's *The Mind of Primitive Man*; Max Lerner on Charles Beard's *Economic Interpretation of the Constitution*; David Daiches on I. A. Richards's *The Principles of Literary Criticism*; Bernard Smith on V. L. Parrington's *Main Currents in American Thought*; Max Lerner on Nikolai Lenin's *The State and the Revolution*; and Lewis Mumford on Oswald Spengler's *The Decline of the West*. The second essay of the book, behind Soule on Freud, is Louis Kronenberger's on *The Education*.

To "intellectuals of the twenties," Kronenberger reports, *The Education* was "a perfectly *conscious* study of frustration and deflected purpose" by a writer equipped to disclose to them "the plight of the modern world." Born an heir to power, Adams had given up "being a participant," choosing "instead, a place on the sidelines," where he could turn the story of his life into a story of and for his age. *The Education* recounted "personal weakness" as well as "social disorder." What set it apart was Adams's ability to make language serve several purposes simultaneously. "Henry Adams, who lived life in a minor key, took every precaution to write about it in a major one. *The Education* is a completely full-dress performance," Kronenberger asserts. It belongs among "the textbooks . . . of American experience."

The tensions with which *The Education* grapples – between humans as social, pragmatic, analytical, interdependent, consensus-seeking creatures, on one side, and private, idealistic, intuitive, imaginative, self-sufficient, mythmaking creatures, on the other; and between language as referential, demystifying, authenticating, discrete, analytic tool, on one side, and as self-referential, merging, blurring, generative, contriving, unruly, synthetic medium, on the other – remained broadly cultural as well as deeply literary through the twenties and beyond. By juxtaposing two versions of himself, by simultaneously acknowledging and then blurring the lines between (auto)biography, cultural history, and fiction, and between social documents and personal narrative, and by employing language as itself several changing things, Adams introduced himself into the culture of the twenties as a member of the first generation of modernists. *Mont-Saint-Michel and Chartres* was, among other things, his way of ransacking culture – shoring fragments against his ruins, to borrow a phrase from Eliot's *The Waste Land* – and his way of writing a prose "poem including history," to borrow from Pound's description of *The Cantos*. In *The Education*, he pieces together fragments of failed dreams that are social and familial as well as personal. In one motion, he depicts the present as shaped by the past; in another, he shows how we reshape the past to meet the needs of the present. On behalf of himself and his society, he creates a sense of the present and its possibilities by inscribing the present's sense of the past and its thrust. At the same time, he adds to art's social, mimetic commitment both a psychological and an epistemological commitment. In the first of these moves, he makes art's processes an imitation of the processes of the external world; in the second, he traces the processes of consciousness as it engages in the act of knowing that world. He thus blends his effort to reach an adequate understanding of the processes of the world with his effort to reach an understanding of the processes of his own consciousness.

The Education arrived on the public scene at a time when the self's efforts to find some free space – independent of the great determinants of nature as defined by Darwin, of family as reconstituted by Freud, and of society, culture, and history as reconceived by Marx – were becoming more and more problematical. This development proved particularly troublesome in the United States, where confidence in the simple, solitary self as free – bolstered by a Renaissance confidence in the modern self's powers of self-fashioning and by an enlightened confidence in the modern self's freedom from fealty to emperors and kings as well as its freedom to dominate nature through science – had gone largely uncontested, especially among white males. In democracies, where the fixed relations of aristocracies are broken, people "acquire the habit of always considering themselves as standing alone," Alexis de Tocqueville remarked,

and they are apt to imagine that their whole destiny is in their hands.

Thus not only does democracy make every man forget his ancestors, but it hides his descendants and separates his contemporaries from him; it throws him back forever upon himself alone and threatens in the end to confine him entirely within the solitude of his own heart.

For Tocqueville, isolation and freedom go hand in hand. But for Henry Adams, who had never been able to decide whether his prominent family had marked him more deeply by branding him as a youth or by deserting him as a young man, solitude came from other sources and took different forms, and so did his hedged sense of freedom. As a result, his life became a search for other possibilities.

In that search, Adams made three interrelated discoveries: first as Albert Einstein later put it, that the "history of an epoch" is the "history of its instruments"; second, that institutions like the church and icons like the "Virgin," or even presidents and first ladies, no less than dynamos, must be numbered among a culture's instruments; and third, that our instruments not only empower but also control us. Madeleine "found herself," he wrote in *Democracy* (1880),

> before two seemingly mechanical figures, which might be wood or wax, for any sign they showed of life. These two figures were the President and his wife; they stood stiff and awkward by the door, both their faces stripped of every sign of intelligence, while the right hands of both extended themselves to the column of visitors with the mechanical action of toy dolls. . . . There they stood, automata, representatives of the society which streamed past them. . . .
> What a strange and solemn spectacle it was. . . . She felt a sudden conviction that this was to be the end of American society, its realization and its dream at once. She groaned in spirit.

In *The Education*, Adams's sense of his social predicament, like Madeleine's, is complicated by his sense of nature, family, and history as shaping and misshaping forces, and by his sense that the loss of religious faith has deprived consciousness of its moorings. No one can find an object worthy of worship, Madeleine notes. There "will be no other," she adds. "It is worse than anything in the 'Inferno.'"

By 1918, the rapid shift from a discourse of patriotism to one of disillusionment, reinforced by an increasingly intrusive advertising industry, was making virtually every reflective American more alert to culture's manipulative force. In *The Education*, Adams's life unfolds both as an effort to find some margin of freedom and as a record of the erosion of his confidence in that venture. Eventually his story calls into doubt virtually everything except the force of nature and culture in shaping individual and collective existence. Even playfulness of the kind that he practices in attributing his "Editor's Preface" to Henry Cabot Lodge and in dating his "Preface" on his birthday, February 16, 1907, seems strained. At last, he had written his brother Brooks in 1899, "life becomes . . . a mere piece of acting" in which one goes on behaving as if seeing, talking, acting, and writing really matter. In the form he gives *The Education*, he inscribes the moment when the performer as hero of action and the spectator as heir of consciousness become representative figures of modern culture. By positioning active versions of his "self" at the center of his story, as its ostensible subject, and contemplative versions of his "self" on its periphery, as observer or reporter, and then presenting the life of the first through the consciousness of the second, he prefigures novels that juxtapose performers and spectators, actors and critics, the doers of deeds and their interpreters, in works as different as E. E. Cummings's *The Enormous Room*, F. Scott Fitzgerald's *The Great Gatsby*, and William Faulkner's *Absalom, Absalom!* In *U.S.A.* (1938) John Dos Passos combines the writer's role with aspects of the spectator-manager-director that we have learned to associate with architects, engineers, and movie directors. Having created this several-sided spectatorial role for himself, he balances it with episodes in the "Camera Eye" sections in which he becomes an actor in the spectacle he has designed, structured, and directed. Like Adams, he modifies the hyperrefined aloofness of the observer-spectator by acknowledging complicity and seeking involvement in a culture that he knew he could not escape.

2

❦

THE "JAZZ AGE" AND THE
"LOST GENERATION" REVISITED

OF SEVERAL DESCRIPTIONS of the culture of the twenties, two – F. Scott Fitzgerald's "Jazz Age" and Gertrude Stein's "Lost Generation," the one stressing involvement, the other detachment – have proved most durable, and both have paid a price for their durability: they have lost much of their power to spark recognition. In the letters, diaries, and journals of the era as well as the published memoirs – Margaret Anderson's *My Thirty Years' War* (1930), Edith Wharton's *A Backward Glance* (1934), Joseph Freeman's *An American Testament* (1936), Mabel Dodge Luhan's *Movers and Shakers* (1936), Robert McAlmon's *Being Geniuses Together* (1938), Sylvia Beach's *Shakespeare and Company* (1959), Janet Flanner's *An American in Paris* (1940), Harold Loeb's *The Way It Was* (1959), Matthew Josephson's *Life Among the Surrealists* (1962), Ernest Hemingway's *A Moveable Feast* (1964), and Malcolm Cowley's *Exile's Return* (1934) and *A Second Flowering* (1973), to name a few – anecdotes abound: of the lost "exiles" who shared Paris as a "moveable feast"; of Pound's efforts to make things new; of Sherwood Anderson's rejection of business for art; of Stein's, Anderson's, and Hemingway's struggles to perfect their style; of Hemingway's and Stein's divisive competitiveness; of John Freeman's, Dos Passos's, and Genevieve Taggard's lonely efforts to sustain the spirit of social reform by broadening the special disillusionment of the postwar years into a general disillusionment with the cultures of corporate capitalism; of the stunning effulgence, particularly in music and literature, in the flats, pubs, speakeasies, and cabarets of Harlem; of the rise that Zelda and Scott Fitzgerald shared and the crack-ups that divided them; of the suicides of writers as different as Dorothea and Gladys Cromwell, Harry Crosby, and Hart Crane; and of William Faulkner's singular decision to return to the place of his birth, as a kind of resident exile who would always feel "at home" there, "yet at the same time . . . not at home."

If, however, we attend the ways in which Stein's and Fitzgerald's terms reinforce each other, they acquire fresh meaning. The Jazz Age, Fitzgerald said, "had no interest in politics at all." It "was an age of miracles, it was

an age of art, it was an age of excess, and it was an age of satire." "That's
what you all are.... You are a lost generation," Stein said to Hemingway,
referring specifically to the young people who had survived the war. Used by
Fitzgerald in the title of his fourth book, *Tales of the Jazz Age* (1922), the
term "Jazz Age" caught the exuberance of the era's wild parties. But even for
Fitzgerald, who had not seen the killing and dying in France, disillusionment
preceded exuberance. In his first book, *This Side of Paradise* (1920), he depicts
his generation as doomed to shout old cries without meaning them and to fear
poverty and worship success with a new, naked intensity, as though possessing
money might somehow help to stave off disillusionment and keep alive a
sense of beauty. For Hemingway, who had seen some of the killing and dying,
the term "Lost Generation," used as an epigraph for *The Sun Also Rises* (1926),
carried special authority because it conveyed a sense of how indelibly the Great
War had marked the young who survived it. Both Fitzgerald and Hemingway
knew, however, as Malcolm Cowley later observed, that the "Lost Generation"
also felt "wrenched away from . . . attachment to any region or tradition" by the
colleges they attended and the cities they flocked to as well as the publishing
houses they relied on, which, "like finance and the theater," were cutting
regional ties and "becoming centralized after 1900." Determined to make
the most of their predicament, writers began thinking of themselves as the
nation's first generation to be wholly unsponsored disciples of the new. They
were both branded and free, forsaken and chosen. They were refugees of a
general wreck, yet their prospects as artists were boundless. In describing
their predicament, they characteristically combined remarkable self-pity with
grandiose self-consciousness. It "was given to Hawthorne to dramatize the
human soul," John Peale Bishop announced. "In our time, Hemingway wrote
the drama of its disappearance."

In claiming for themselves the special charm – to borrow another of
Fitzgerald's titles – of the beautifully damned, they named themselves prophets
of their age, a role most of them clearly preferred to that of social reformers.
They were by turns sentimental, fun-loving, and almost carefree, stricken,
proud, stoic, and defiant. But they realized that the national habit of feeling
special meant nothing if it did not include doing something special. To take
possession of their predicament, they wrote stories they thought of as disclosing the secret truth about the century with which they had been born and
with which they identified. "After the war we had the twentieth century," said
Gertrude Stein, who also suggested that she (born in 1874) had belonged to
the twentieth century years before it officially began. Many aspects of life in
their new century offended them, but others fascinated them, including its
speed and technology. They practiced and even promoted some of the excesses

they condemned. But they remained disappointed that world leaders, especially those in the United States, were more adept at corrupting language than enlarging human happiness; and they found in their divisions, doubts, and estrangement the ground for declaring themselves prophets, explorers, and mappers of the modern world.

At the heart of their project lay the task of restoring freshness to a much-abused language. Stein became a teacher of writers as different as Sherwood Anderson, Ernest Hemingway, Carl Van Vechten, and Richard Wright precisely because she saw clearly that the task of renewing language was certain to become a ground theme of literature in the twentieth century. We see similar awareness in *U.S.A.*, where Dos Passos uses several strategies – juxtaposition, collage, the splicing of sketches, and the splicing of different narrative modes – in order to make words behave like forms on a cubist surface; we see it in *The Great Gatsby* (1925), where Fitzgerald uses Nick Carraway's voice to evoke tunes of the twenties and fragments of words heard long ago; and we see it in *The Sound and the Fury* (1929), *As I Lay Dying* (1930), and *Absalom, Absalom!* (1936), where Faulkner juxtaposes, splices, and even overlays voice on voice and style on style.

E. E. Cummings's *The Enormous Room* (1922) grew directly out of his experience in the Great War, which began when he volunteered to serve in France as an ambulance driver and culminated when be was wrongfully incarcerated for six months in the Camp de Triage de la Ferté Macé on suspicion of treasonable correspondence. In Cummings's mind, that experience, initiated and administered by bureaucratic paranoia and incompetence, became yet another sign of a world botched almost beyond recognition. In response, he wrote letters and then a book. But the first models for his response, in which playfulness mingles with near hopelessness, he locates on the walls of the first cell in which he is confined. There, in semidarkness, he discovers a "cubist wilderness" created by artists and writers who have covered the cell's walls "with designs, mottoes, pictures," as well as selections from Goethe; "a satiric landscape"; an "exquisite portrait"; a drawing of a "beloved boat"; and a strange picture, masterful in its "crudity," of "a doughnut-bodied rider" on a "totally transparent sausage-shaped horse who was moving simultaneously in five directions." Later, with the example of the imprisoned John Bunyan before him, Cummings lifts his eyes and sees the bars of his cell as his "own harp." More immediately, he resolves "to ask for a pencil at the first opportunity," in the hope of finding new ways of using old words so that he can turn the deprivations and intimate violations of his imprisonment into art.

In his effort to appropriate experiences forced upon him and make them his own, Cummings draws words and phrases from several languages ("My *cellule* was cool, and I fell asleep easily"); allegorizes foes ("Turnkey-creature," for example, which he then cuts to "T-c") and friends alike ("The Delectable Mountains," as he calls three heroes "cursed with a talent for thinking"); and borrows most of the structural apparatus of his narrative from Bunyan's *Pilgrim's Progress.* Yet he writes with mounting confidence that his words can make alien experiences his own and that his experiences can renew borrowed words.

On November 11, 1921, the third anniversary of the armistice, a few months before the publication of *The Enormous Room,* President Harding led a group of cabinet members, Supreme Court justices, members of Congress, and military leaders into Arlington Cemetery to bury an unknown soldier in his "native soil garlanded by love and covered with the decorations that only nations can bestow." Years before, Henry James had termed Theodore Roosevelt's patriotic pronouncements "crude and barbaric." But Harding's assumption that he could ensure that a soldier's "sacrifice, and that of the millions dead, shall not be in vain," combined with his curious celebration of the state – as an entity capable of feeling love, powerful enough to survive wars, and wise enough to select those whom it should decorate – seemed to many writers to push the abuse of words to a new low. Earlier, in *One Man's Initiation: 1917* (1920), his first response to the Great War, Dos Passos had decried "the lies, the lies, the lies, the lies that life is smothered in," calling on people to "rise and show at least that we are not taken in." Later, he ended *1919* (1932) – the second volume of his trilogy *U.S.A.* – by revisiting Harding's burial of the unknown soldier, "in the memorialamphitheatreofthenationalcemeteryatarlingtonvirginia," with a defiant act of style:

> In the tarpaper morgue at Chalon-sur-Marne in the
> reek of chloride of lime and the dead, they picked
> out the pine box that held all that was left of
>   enie menie minie moe plenty other pine boxes
> stacked up there containing what they'd scraped up
> of Richard Roe
>   and other person or persons unknown. Only
> one can go. How did they pick John Doe?
>   Make sure he aint a dinge, boys,
>   make sure he aint a guinea or a kike,
>   how can you tell a guy's a hundredpercent
> when all you've got's a gunnysack of bones, bronze
> buttons stamped with the screaming eagle and a pair
> of roll puttees?

Writers of the twenties, including Cummings and Dos Passos, felt betrayed by the political leaders who presumed to represent them. They also felt cut off from older writers who had not shared their adventures or suffered their disillusionment. They were, they proclaimed, members of a "Lost Generation," citizens of an era that had begun when the war ended. T. S. Eliot's *The Waste Land* (1922) was scarcely published before writers adopted it as the only possible name for the scarred world left to them. The 1890s and the Lyric Years had in fact anticipated many things that writers of the twenties claimed as peculiarly theirs, including their sense that all the significant things that had happened to them were unique and their assumption that their art therefore could be wholly new. A "new classic," Hemingway announced almost casually in *Green Hills of Africa* (1935), "does not bear any resemblance to the classics that have preceded it." The drawings of John Held, Jr., which helped to make the Flapper and the College Joe of Fitzgerald's novels trademarks of the era, were widely regarded as radically new – despite the fact that they owed almost as much to drawings on pre-Columbian sculpture and Greek vases as to the fine-line drawings of the richly illustrated French weekly *La Vie parisienne.* Yet the Lost Generation's feeling of being at once branded and abandoned touched so much that it acquired authority of its own, despite its simplifications and omissions.

Jazz, certainly among the most distinctive artistic creations of the era, embodied the contradictions of the age in instructive ways. Its harmonies were drawn from old hymns, marches, and work songs, while its varied rhythms and changing beat depended on improvisation. Its aim was the creation of spontaneous communities of listeners and performers – or, more radically, of performers willing to become listeners and listeners able to become performers – who engage simultaneously in active remembering and deliberate forgetting. Jazz is sensuous and even sinuous; it is illicit, spontaneous, and unpredictable; it is ungenteel and uninhibited; it scorns pretense, endorses protest, and celebrates change. Offended by its sexuality, A. C. Ward called it a "dance of death" for Europe as well as the United States. Yet even as it celebrates the present moment of new creation, jazz evokes and echoes old words and rhythms that it treats as almost sacred. This doubleness made jazz the appropriate music of the twenties. In one mood it exemplifies a radical principle of origination. Like the United States and modernism, it is obsessed with the possibility of wholly new beginnings. It defines true artists as those able to shake themselves free of history long enough to engage in pure improvisation, and it therefore defines true art as work in which anteriority seems almost to vanish. And yet, like other forms of modernism, it works subtly to call into question the possibility of the modern so construed. In celebrating its generative powers, it acknowledges its own historicity, founding itself in contradiction: it declares its independence of the past, claiming the present as its own, but in doing so it defines its predicament as the historical one of trying to make a wholly new start in a world so old that everything that can happen has happened.

People heard jazz everywhere: from orchestras on boats and in ballrooms; from bands in speakeasies, dance halls, and high-school gymnasiums; on radios and wind-up phonographs at home; over loudspeakers in stores and at work. Jazz's harmonies, born of contradictions, were one thing, however, while contradictions actually lived were another, as the strained and even tortured lives of scores of jazz musicians remind us. Compared with the exuberance of the Lyric Years – which was buoyed by a sense that old barriers were falling, that workers were marching, and that geniuses were sprouting while Isadora Duncan danced – the exuberance of the Jazz Age seems forced. In some moods, it reflects the sadness of a world already black and blue; in others, it reflects the anxiety of people so uncertain of what lies ahead that they are afraid to let the party end.

Similar strains and contradictions showed even in the witty proclamations of older writers like H. L. Mencken and his disciple George Jean Nathan, who shared a poorly controlled need to sound outrageous: love, Mencken said, is a "minimum of disgusts"; "If I am convinced by anything, it is that Doing Good is in bad taste"; the "ignorant should be permitted to spawn *ad libitum*," to provide a "steady supply of slaves" for talented people like him and his friends. Mencken, Nathan, and other survivors of the Lyric Years kept alive the Puritan as scapegoat. When he published *A Gallery of Women* (1924), Dreiser announced that it would make "the ghosts of the Puritans rise and gibber in the streets." But *A Gallery of Women* presents a far more male-dominated view of female sexuality than Dreiser supposed, and a bleaker one as well. Similarly, Mencken and Nathan remained secret agents of things they despised. In their balancing act, important elements never quite balanced. Mencken's most ambitious work, *The American Language* (1919), is a brilliant as well as eccentric historical analysis of the origins and growth of the second of two major "streams of English." As such, it is a celebration of the new. Yet as Mencken continued to correct, enlarge, and rewrite *The American Language*, adding several supplementary volumes, it became clear that his desire to celebrate the new was matched by his desire to control it. His working assumption that he and his friends were entitled to money, power, and pleasure often made him sound like an ad man of the self-absorbed, consumer-oriented bourgeois culture that he criticized. Compared with Fitzgerald's downward spirals into darkness – from fame and fortune into alcoholism, depression, and neglect; from *Flappers and Philosophers* (1920) to *Tales of the Jazz Age* (1922) to *All the Sad Young Men* (1926) to *Taps at Reveille* (1935) – both Mencken's mocking essays and much of the satiric fiction he most admired, such as James Branch Cabell's *Jurgen* (1919), now seem shallow.

An amateur sociologist and anthropologist, Sinclair Lewis displayed an almost inexhaustible enthusiasm for recording the surfaces of modern American life. The many catalogues and lists that he made helped him win Mencken's praise as a collector of examples of the venality, hypocrisy, demagoguery, and vulgarity that Mencken called "Americana." Lewis, Mencken announced, was "the one real anatomist" of "American Kulture" of the "booboisie." Neither as polished nor as sophisticated as *Jurgen*, *Main Street* and especially *Babbitt* are finally more important examples of what Matthew Josephson, in *Portrait of the Artist as American* (1930), called "resistance to the milieu" epitomized by Harding. In them, Lewis mixes satire, parody, and caricature with yearning that is cultural rather than merely personal; and he presents them in prose that tilts the novel toward the kind of sociology practiced by people like Robert and Helen Lynd in *Middletown, U.S.A.* (1929). Even tensions that Lewis never fully controls prove to be telling, in part because he recreates the sadness of having to choose between alternatives as inadequate as Wilson's high-sounding idealism and Harding's crass appeal to selfishness and greed. "Stabilize America first, prosper America first, think of America first, exalt America first," Harding said in 1920 – the same year in which he coined the term "normalcy." "Not nostrums, but normalcy," he said, launching a splurge of self-indulgence that lent itself to easy satire.

Published in 1920, with the inauguration of "normalcy," *Main Street* focuses on a small Midwestern town called Gopher Prairie. Published in 1922, two years after the first U.S. census to report that a majority of the population lived in cities, *Babbitt* is set in a growing Midwestern city of 250,000 to 300,000 named Zenith, "the Zip City – Zeal, Zest and Zowie – 1,000,000 in 1935." In *Main Street* the principal conflict is between its protagonist, Carol Kennicott, and the dull, intolerant townspeople of Gopher Prairie, who seem determined, as Edith Wharton observed, to expose the poverty of the nation's life in the midst of plenty. But *Babbitt* is divided against itself, just as its protagonist, George Babbitt, is divided against himself. Its weaknesses as a novel shadow Babbitt's as a man. Finally, however, it possesses the force of its flaws and so becomes most compelling, not in the satire that made it famous, but in the tensions it never fully controls.

Lewis pokes fun at almost everything about the people of Zenith; their slang ("everything zips" "Oh, by gee, by gosh, by jingo" "Gotta hustle" "Service & Boosterism"); their fascination with new possessions – cars, gadgets, clothes, and furniture; their tastelessness, as seen, for example, in Zenith's "Athletic Club," which features a gothic lobby, a Roman Imperial washroom, a Spanish Mission lounge, and a Chinese Chippendale reading room; their "Romantic Hero," not "the knight, the wandering poet, the cowpuncher, the aviator, nor the brave young district attorney, but the great sales-manager" who keeps "an Analysis of Merchandising Problems on his glass-topped desk"; their churches, private clubs, and civic organizations; and their values – habits of mind and heart.

Here's the specifications of the Standardized American Citizen! Here's the new generation of Americans: fellows with hair on their chests and smiles in their eyes and adding machines in their offices. We're not doing any boasting, but we like ourselves first-rate, and if you don't like us, look out – better get under cover before the cyclone hits town.

Zenith's citizens give new meaning to Chicagoans' promise to make culture hum once they got some; and they also reiterate the prejudices of the "Dream City." Among the advantages they claim for Zenith over older, more sophisticated Eastern cities, one is the preponderance of "Ideal Citizens" ("first and foremost," Babbitt says, "busier than a bird-dog") and "Regular Guys" ("whooping it up for national prosperity!"), as opposed to long-haired types who call themselves "liberals," "radicals," or "intelligentsia," and "foreign-born" types with their "foreign ideas and communism." Inspired by such thoughts, Babbitt and his "Regular Guys" look forward to a civilization that has finally rid itself of all the wrong types, leaving "Regular Guys" free to live in a paradise of shiny gadgets and private clubs, as hollow as the world Waldo Frank later described in *The Re-Discovery of America* (1929), one of several important jeremiads of the twenties:

Our success does not make us happy, our loyalty to State or Corporation does not enlarge, our cult of sport does not invigorate, our cult of crime does not release; our education does not educate, our politicians do not govern, our arts do not recreate, our beauty does not nourish, our religions do not make whole. Yet it is our energy that feeds these practices and cults. With our spirit we give them life and blood, in order that they should fulfill us. *And they do not touch us.*

Babbitt reminds us that in fact such things can touch people without fulfilling them. Yearning born of emptiness inflects Lewis's satire from the start. At night Babbitt dreams of a "fairy child" who sees him as "gay and valiant" and who waits for him "in the darkness beyond mysterious groves." Even during the day, when pressures to conform burden him, he protects his friendship with Paul Riesling, whose name "sounds foreign" and whose discontent shows itself in daylight. Paul sits apart from the Regular Guys and encourages Babbitt to question their boosterism. Babbitt remains a middle-aged, middle-class American, but side by side with his materialism, boosterism, and vulgarity, his poverty of mind and spirit, he retains a capacity for affection and loyalty, a desire for affiliation, a gift for hope, and an almost sacred discontent with life devoid of such things. Moved by the affection he feels for Paul and his own son – inspired by the example of one and the promise of the other – he tries to rebel: he flouts the mores of his society, chooses the bohemian Bunch over the Regular Guys, publicly supports his unpopular friend Seneca Doane, and defends a group of strikers.

There is, of course, something pathetic about Babbitt's rebellion. His clichéd dreams, particularly those revolving around his "fairy child," belong to a male preserve, and even in rebellion, he remains timid. He and Zenith's other rebels are almost as culturally deprived as its conformists. Possessing little strength and no independent imagination, he is from the outset overmatched by his world. Still, his weaknesses coexist with yearning and discontent that Lewis never completely discredits. Babbitt mouths precepts he cannot believe. He fears the power of his administered society, which offers rewards (security, position, gadgets, property, slogans, and clubs) for conformity and threatens punishment (being ostracized "from the Clan of Good Fellows" who enjoy and control society's spoils) for resistance. "The independence seeped out of him," we read, "and he walked the streets alone, afraid of men's cynical eyes and the incessant hiss of whispering." Putting "his late discontent" behind him, he becomes a parody of the "Good Fellow": he joins the "Good Citizens' League," which is spreading "through the country," and gets "fired up" about "the wickedness of Seneca Doane, the crimes of labor unions, the perils of immigration, and the delights of golf, morality, and bank accounts." Still, having reclaimed his place among "the best-loved men in the Boosters' Club," he continues to feel trapped. "They've licked me; licked me to a finish!" he says to himself, as he sees the pathos of his life reaching out into the future: "I'm going to run things and figure out things to suit myself," he says, "when I retire." "But I've never – . . . I've never done a single thing I've wanted to in my whole life!" he admits to his son, in a speech that tries to turn confession into moral imperative. "I don't know's I've accomplished anything except just get along," he says, as his voice fades out. "Well, maybe you'll carry things on further," he adds, with no apparent awareness of the haunting ambiguity hidden in the word "further."

In *Babbitt*, as in much of the fiction of the twenties, the century is still young, particularly in its confused efforts to cope with new attitudes toward human sexuality and new techniques of manipulation used by its culture. Yet at times it also seems too old to hope with conviction. Assuming, as it were, Freud's discoveries, on one side, and Marx's, on the other, Lewis subjects both family and society to overt suspicion by depicting them as institutions that divide people against themselves. Babbitt desires union yet fears it, longs for intimacy yet shuns it, wants adventure yet dares not seek it. Sick with desire and sick with fear, he oscillates, failing to resolve anything. His dreams of a "fairy child" are clichés before they enter his consciousness, just as his hopes for his son are clichés before they touch his lips. Having rebelled against his society, he shrinks back, accepting the protection it offers him against the perils of intimacy and adventure. Both his vague yet obdurate discontent and his vague yet obdurate hope become signs not of life lived but of life deferred to the next generation, despite the likelihood that deferral will mean carrying his abnegations rather than his resistance "further."

Babbitt's story remains his own, but his story bears his name, which has become a part of American English, as a continuing reminder of just how insecure and anxious the nation's middle class is, poised between the threat of falling and the hope of rising. Babbitt puts everything be can find – alcohol and drugs, enclaves and clubs, the feel of new gadgets and the thrill of power and speed, a rhetoric of union and a rhetoric of resistance, a rhetoric of love and a rhetoric of outrage – to the task of controlling the contradictory longings that leave him internally conflicted. As his will to resist yields to his will to survive, his life bends toward resignation and deferred hope.

It was business and businessmen, not rebels or dissenters, who ruled the twenties, as Lewis makes clear. Calvin Coolidge differed from Warren Harding in several important respects, but he changed the nation's priorities only by making them more respectable. Harding's regime (1920–23) was noted for the cronyism of its own "Clan of Good Fellows" and "Regular Guys," even before conspicuous corruption tumbled it into disgrace. Charles R. Forbes, head of the Veterans Bureau, was tried, convicted, and sentenced to prison for malfeasance; Jesse Smith, a close associate of Henry Dougherty, the attorney general, killed himself to avoid a similar fate; Thomas W. Miller, Harding's alien property custodian, went to jail for accepting a bribe; and Albert Fall, secretary of the interior, was both fined and sentenced to jail for bribery. Only death, on August 2, 1923, following a heart attack, saved Harding from sharing disgrace with his friends. Coolidge, by contrast, was noted for asceticism and personal integrity both as Harding's vice-president and during his own administration (1923–29). But he shared Harding's deep faith in the nation's business civilization. He had spent years working hard, saving his money and currying the favor of people in positions of wealth and power, waiting for his big chance. When it came with Harding's sudden death, he seized it as something both ordained and earned.

"The business of America is business," Coolidge announced. "The man who builds a factory builds a temple. . . . The man who works there worships there." He was, William Allen White observed, "sincerely, genuinely, terribly crazy" about wealthy men like Andrew Mellon, in part because he believed, like the Episcopal bishop William Lawrence, that "godliness [was] in league with riches." The wealthy deserved their wealth, the poor, their poverty. If money and power were visible signs of virtue, however hidden, and poverty and powerlessness visible signs of slothfulness, however disguised, it followed as night the day that the nation's important affairs should be entrusted to men who respected wealth even if they did not possess it.

Even more than Harding, Coolidge presided over an era of unprecedented prosperity. Led by him, the nation became so single-minded in its desire to establish a "businessman's government" and a "businessman's culture" that little else seemed to interest it. Here, for example, is the world according to Edward Earl Purinton, who sounds like one of Babbitt's or Coolidge's friends:

What is the finest game? Business. The soundest science? Business. The truest art? Business. The fullest education? Business. The fairest opportunity? Business. The cleanest philanthropy? Business. The sanest religion? Business.

Reinforced by prosperity, such thinking gained credibility. Major portions of the United States remained rural and agricultural throughout the twenties, and the South remained so poor that it later came to think of itself as having been ahead of the rest of the nation, waiting for it, when the Great Depression hit. But under Harding and Coolidge, the nation's new pattern of life – urban, industrial, commercial, affluent, and secular – swept across the land, powered by success. Tensions between the affluent and the poor, the house of have and the house of want, persisted. But the power and authority of the affluent, and their mounting skill in marketing hope, executed by an increasingly sophisticated advertising industry, muted protest during the twenties. Between 1920 and 1929, the population grew from 106,466,000 to 121,770,000 (+14.35 percent) and the gross national product jumped from $73 billion to $104 billion (+42.5 percent). More striking, however, was a drastic redistribution of wealth spurred by significant changes in the tax structure. In 1920 the top 5 percent of the population controlled 23.96 percent of the nation's wealth; in 1929 the top 5 percent controlled 33.49 percent of the wealth and their taxes had dropped from approximately 11.5 percent of their income to 3.5 percent.

As the drive to make and spend money accelerated, "conspicuous consumption" and "pecuniary emulation" flourished. Freedom of choice meant the freedom to choose from an expanding range of goods, commodities, and activities, and the freedom to pay for them on installment plans. Soon a new "consumer ethic" and "leisure ethic" that stressed immediate gratification began to displace an older "work ethic" that stressed working and saving and the importance of self-discipline and self-restraint. Slowly and then more quickly, the value of restraint, which Coolidge continued personally to practice, began to lose its hold as a principle allied with success and respectability. Acting on impulse, doing whatever one wanted, began to gain acceptance as a "natural" and therefore desirable way of achieving self-fulfillment. In the challenged ethos, self-denial preceded self-realization. In the emergent ethos, with the promise of plenty eroding the authority of asceticism, self-assertion, self-realization, and even self-indulgence established themselves as respectable goals. A burgeoning advertising industry and a whole set of therapeutic enterprises catered to the notion that certain people were entitled to prosperity as well as psychic and physical well-being. One sign of this shift was the rapid rise of the term "personality," modified by such words as "fascinating," "attractive," "magnetic," "charismatic," "sweet," "charming," "dominant," "impressive," and "forceful." For unlike the word "character," "personality" claims no intrinsic value. It exists to be noticed, named, judged, and rewarded. At once modern and public, it centers on display and performance.

Several aspects of the nation's changing ethos, already dominant in *Babbitt*, were surveyed by Robert and Helen Lynd in *Middletown, U.S.A.*, which sets the vanishing culture of independent citizens who retained strong traditional restraints against the rising culture of new business types who believed in utilitarian individualism. Both corporate capitalism, as it came increasingly to dominate the political economy, and proliferating bureaucracies, as they came increasingly to dominate a broad range of professional organizations and social clubs, including those devoted to the study of history and literature, as well as local, state, and federal governments, became effective instruments of the "New America." The tasks associated with controlling the vast resources of the nation, as well as legitimizing the new ethos, were formidable. With bureaucracy went a new managerial style and a new professionalism that extended tentacles of control, making every profession or craft more thoroughly regulated and administered. New marketing and advertising techniques began to focus on the process of manipulating – of stimulating and creating as well as directing – consumer "needs" for movies, magazines, and books as well as radios, automobiles, appliances, bathtubs, clothes, jewelry, cosmetics, and deodorants.

Implicit in this large-scale transformation was the analytical model that science and technology presented as defining the individual's relation to nature, and it made the new century increasingly an age of analysis. "The utilitarians," Irving Babbitt wrote in *Rousseau and Romanticism* (1919), have "been able to stamp their efforts on the very face of the landscape." The people of the United States remained restless, always on the move; and they had long since announced that they no longer had a king. But they were also becoming increasingly conscious both of their power for science and technology and of their power through them. Science's claim of being able to reach "out into the whole cosmos" with its analytical method of classifying phenomena made itself felt with mounting authority because it worked. As science went "forward from relationship to relationship" and from scene to scene, Heisenberg noted, so also did technology go forward, step by step, transforming the environment by impressing "our [human] image upon it." By enlarging the "material power of man," science and technology reinforced human confidence in human power. At the same time, however, they increased human dependence upon it, creating new problems. "In earlier times," Heisenberg notes, man

> was endangered by wild animals, disease, hunger, cold, and other forces of nature, and in this strife every extension of technology represented a strengthening of his position and therefore progress. In our time, when the earth is becoming ever more densely settled, the narrowing of the possibilities of life and thus the threat to man's existence originates above all from other people, who also assert their claim to the goods of the earth. In such a confrontation, the extension of technology need no longer be an indication of progress.
>
> The statement that in our time man confronts only himself is valid in the age of technology in a still wider sense. In earlier epochs man saw himself opposite nature. Nature, in which dwelt all sorts of living beings, was a realm existing according to its own laws, and into it man somehow had to fit himself. We, on the other hand, live in a world so completely transformed by man that, whether we are using the machines of our daily life, taking food prepared by machines, or striding through landscapes transformed by man, we invariably encounter structures created by man, so that in a sense we always meet only ourselves.

If one secret to understanding the culture of the twenties lies in recognizing the difficulties people faced in adjusting to new technologies and a changing ethos, another lies in understanding the ways in which delight gave way to dismay when people saw their desires more and more clearly stamped on their world. George Babbitt's world is homemade; it is made by humans to reflect human desires. Nature scarcely exists for Babbitt. Yet whether he stands inside the invisible walls of his social world in compliance or outside them in resistance, his world remains *alien*. In this respect he becomes an extreme extension of certain traits we see in Sister Carrie; in him, her curious blankness, her passivity, and her endless vague yearning lead to a life that is either intermittent or largely deferred.

Although Lewis's art is often crude, Babbitt's confusions are not shallow. His experience is mixed not merely because his homemade world remains imperfect, or because it seems imperfect in unexpected ways, but also because the old familiar bipolar characterizations of his world – into subject and object, inner and outer world, body and soul – somehow no longer apply. As subject, Babbitt merges with his world as object. In looking at it, he sees himself; in looking at himself, he sees it. In addition, he sees both in people around him – in fellow members of the Good Citizens' League and the Boosters' Club – and in his own conflicted self what his forgotten ancestors had seen principally in nature or in historical enemies: the hostile, adversarial, imperfectly repressed or suppressed *other.* Viewed in this light, his confusions become both earned and modern.

Triumphant first in the East, Babbitt's new America spread easily across the upper Midwest. Then, following lines of trade, travel, and communication, it crossed the Great Plains and converted the vagrant West. During the twenties it gained ground even in the recalcitrant if not backward South. In the brief span between the beginning of the Civil War and the end of World War I, the erosion of the authority of the church and family had accelerated, as had the growth of cities and the expansion of the nation's most successful businesses into national or international markets – first in cities, the easier targets, and then, as canals, railways, and telegraphs extended their networks, in towns and villages. After World War I, the national economy, once again stimulated by wartime production, moved through a period of brief adjustment toward one of unprecedented boom. Cosmetics and cigarettes, refrigerators and porcelain bathtubs, along with scores of gadgets designed to reduce drudgery and provide entertainment began to appear and disappear. In addition, concoctions advertised as prolonging youth, promoting health, and ensuring social acceptability (by curing bad breath, poor complexion, or body odors, for example) crowded the market. Having entered World War I as a debtor nation, the United States emerged as the world's largest creditor nation. Over the next ten years, national income as well as the gross national product soared, giving the country the highest standard of living the world had ever known. Between 1900 and 1930, the number of telephones installed rose from 1.4 million to 20.2 million and the number of automobiles produced soared from 4,000 to 4.8 million. By 1929 the United States accounted for 34.4 percent of total world production, compared with 39.6 for Great Britain, France, Germany, Russia, and Japan combined.

As the nation's economic growth gained momentum, two infatuations that the world's poor essentially cannot know took hold – a fascination with new possessions, from autos and gadgets to trinkets and jewels, and a fascination with the future. In 1909 Americans purchased 2 million horse-drawn carriages and 80,000 automobiles. In 1923 they bought 10,000 horse-drawn carriages and 4 million automobiles. Soon a frenzy of speculation began lifting the new age of corporate capitalism to unheard-of heights. In 1923 new capital issues totaled 3.2 billion dollars, and shares traded totaled 236 million. In 1927, after Congress helped the rich by cutting the real-estate tax in half and reducing the surcharge on individual income, new capital issues exceeded

10 billion dollars and total shares traded reached 1,125 million. With the promise of prosperity before them, more and more people made the dream of becoming rich their way of reaching out to touch the future.

Sooner or later, the cultural shift touched everything. It shaped the detachment, the self-satisfaction, and the arrogance of remote manufacturers and stockholders who were shielded from the actual scenes of labor and production, as well as the attitudes of laborers who were separated from the objects they made. And it touched consumers not only by shielding them from the human costs of production but also by making them dependent on transient, depersonalized forms of possession. Writing in 1925 to his Polish translator, Witold von Hulewicz, Rainer Maria Rilke noted that "the Great War [had] completely interrupted" his writing of the *Duino Elegies.* Begun in 1912, resumed in 1914, and then taken up again in 1922, the *Elegies* had undergone a shift. "The 'Elegies' show us" engaged, Rilke wrote, in the "continual conversion" of our fragile and transient earth. When possessions were few and change was slow, the transformations worked by human hands acquired a certain seemliness; they created "not only intensities of a spiritual kind, but – who knows? new substances, metals, nebulae and stars." Now, Rilke said, the nature of such conversions had been altered. To shared objects such as houses, wells, and towers, as well as personal possessions, including books and clothes, our forebears added something of their shared humanity, making them signs of hope and meditation. "We are perhaps the last" generation to have "known such things," he added. For now "empty, indifferent things, pseudo-things," crowd "over from America."

Rilke's nostalgia turns in part on a break between the nineteenth century and the twentieth. But it also possesses spatial connotations. Empty, indifferent, anonymous objects are for him American. In fact, of course, the shift that he describes (from objects made authentic by "the hope and the meditation" of those who made and possessed them to objects mass-produced anonymously and then casually and even fleetingly possessed) originated in Europe, not the United States. It is peculiarly American only insofar as this country is peculiarly modern. "America has become the wonder of the world," Kenneth Burke noted in an essay in *Vanity Fair* in 1923, simply because it "is the purest concentration point of the vices and vulgarities of the [modern] world."

To judge the importance of the correlation between the United States and the "modern," and between the modern and the rush of new mass-produced objects, we must recognize that the parts of life most deeply touched by mass production had little to do with the cheap, vulgar imitations, the "empty, indifferent things" that Rilke deplores. They had to do with work and play and love – with the conditions of life and the rhythm of living it – for those who made things as well as those who bought them. Traditional craftspeople made objects from start to finish, one or two at a time. Modern workers assemble them by repeating segmented tasks. Their goal is standardization – which, in its deepest logic, makes workers replaceable, parts interchangeable, and products identical. In its dream of perfect efficiency, the moment to which it aspires, mass production does to work what trench warfare did to fighting and dying: it robs it of meaning by making it anonymous.

For consumers, mass buying, the synergistic partner of mass production, also changed everything – from clothes and houses, to travel and communication, to games and vacations. One "industry" after another experienced a "revolution" that in turn spawned revolutionary changes in fashion and taste. And with each succeeding revolution came an acceleration in both the economics and the psychology of change. The need to see new techniques and new products displace old ways and old possessions touched everything, including literature, music, and painting, where tradition had once counted heavily. The characteristic claim of every avant-garde movement of the twenties was that it made some earlier technique, genre, or theory "old-fashioned" if not obsolete. In short, the modern valued what it depended on – not permanence but change. It privileged the "new" or "new-fangled" over the old or "old-fashioned." It counted on the unspoken promise of the "new" – that is, the stunning promise that nothing lasts.

People of the twenties – ordinary people as well as the thoughtful young – felt the impact of modernity's infatuation with impermanence, and many of them felt it with unprotected intensity. Like Babbitt, they felt more hurried as well as more confused, as though time might run out on them before it ran out on their newest gadgets. In *A Backward Glance*, Edith Wharton describes her writing of *The Age of Innocence* (1920) as a "momentary escape," a "going back to . . . childish memories of a long vanished America," by which she meant New York of the 1870s. In *French Ways and Their Meaning* (1919), she pictures the world since 1914 as "like a house on fire," with the lodgers standing on the stairs in disarray, their doors wide open, their furniture exposed, and their habits revealed. In her images of haste and loss and her image of the world's residents as lodgers, as temporary residents of changing quarters, Wharton captures the sense of the modern that reaches back to Sister Carrie and forward to Daisy and Tom Buchanan, who buy and sell mansions as well as rent flats in apartment buildings or suites in hotels. For it follows from the logic of what Wharton called the "roaring and discontinuous universe" inaugurated by the Great War that what matters most is changing possessions, preferably by increasing their number, but if necessary simply by changing their arrangement. One response, seen more in Lewis than in Wharton, was to expose the emotional poverty of such plenty. A second, closer to Rilke's letter and to Wharton's practice in *The Custom of the Country* (1913), was to decry the "invading races" of vulgarians who were displacing the rightful heirs, the "vanishing denizens," of the world or, as Wharton does in *A Backward Glance*, to bemoan the ways in which vulgar immigrants are soiling the hitherto unnoticed "purity" of North American English. A third, close to Cather's practice in *Death Comes for the Archbishop* (1927), was to explore or celebrate lost worlds where tradition still mattered. And a fourth was to confront the discontinuous world directly by focusing on crippled or even ghostlike creatures who drift through attenuated lives, speaking a language like Babbitt's, which blends archaic phrases with strained slang and empty slogans.

3

❦

THE PERILS OF PLENTY, OR HOW THE
TWENTIES ACQUIRED A PARANOID TILT

AS THE TWENTIES lurched back and forth between salvaging the old and embracing the new, a series of interrelated developments – including the rise of the Ku Klux Klan, the long, divisive trial of Nicola Sacco and Bartolomeo Vanzetti (1920–27), and the passage of the National Origins Act of 1924 – exposed conflicts that gave the era a paranoid tilt. In the Black Sox scandal of 1919, the greed of gamblers and of Charles A. Cominskey, owner of the Chicago White Sox, merged with the resentments of the players to besmirch baseball, the "national pastime," and ruin the careers of innocent as well as guilty players. A. Mitchell Palmer, Hoover's attorney general, once a devout Quaker and prewar Progressive, took the lead in promoting postwar hysteria by accusing recent immigrants of bringing the nation to the edge of "internal revolution." In his campaign, Palmer attracted a group of unlikely supporters, including avid nativists, resurgent fundamentalists, and men bearing distinguished names and occupying high offices. "The Nordic race" must fight "against the dangerous foreign races," wrote Madison Grant, the patrician New Yorker who headed the Museum of Natural History, in *The Passing of the Great Race* (1916). Other socially prominent sorts, including Senator Henry Cabot Lodge, President F. A. Walker of MIT, Professor John W. Burgess of Columbia, and Professor N. S. Shaler of Harvard, voiced similar sentiments. An "alien usually remains an alien no matter what is done to him," the less polished Hiram Wesley Evans wrote shortly after the war, no matter "what veneer of education he gets, what oaths he takes." In "instincts, character, thought and interests . . . – in his soul – an alien remains fixedly alien to America and all it means." Amplified by people like Palmer, such fears spread quickly. Both the Red Scare of 1919 and the Palmer Raids of 1919–20, which were authorized by and named for Hoover's attorney general, led to wholesale violations of civil liberties, including widespread harassment, unjustified arrests, and illegal deportations, of "dark," "foreign" threats. Soon *they*," Palmer said, soldiers of the "alien invasion," will "outnumber us." "Out of the sly and crafty eyes of many of them," he added, "leap cupidity, cruelty, insanity, and crime; from their lopsided faces, sloping brows, and misshapen features may be recognized the unmistakable criminal types." A "stream of alien blood" has diluted our power "to maintain our cherished institutions," added Congressman Albert Johnson, chair of the House Committee on Immigration.

Alarmed by people like Palmer, Evans, and Grant, as well as Lothrop Stoddard's *The Rising Tide of Color Against White World-Supremacy* (1924) and Shane Leslie's *The Celt and the War* (1917) (which Fitzgerald reviewed for *Nassau Literary Magazine* in May 1917), some concerned citizens began speaking out. In January 1920, one such group – including reformers like Helen Keller, Norman Thomas, and Jane Addams, ethicists like Harry Ward of Union Theological Seminary, pacifists like Jeanette Rankin, labor leaders like Duncan MacDonald and Julia O'Connor, publishers like B. F. Huebsch of Viking Press, and lawyers like Felix Frankfurter – gathered to form the American Civil Liberties Union (ACLU). But while the ACLU grew slowly, thousands flocked to the Ku Klux Klan, a white-hooded army of night riders dedicated to obliterating what Evans called "radicalism, cosmopolitanism, and alienism of all kinds." Between 1919 and 1925, the Klan's membership rose from 5,000 to 5 million.

Among thousands of people who were ridiculed or terrorized for not being native-born, white, gentile, Protestant "Americans," two – Nicola Sacco and Bartolomeo Vanzetti – became the most famous. Arrested in May 1920 on charges of murdering a paymaster and a guard while committing a payroll robbery at a shoe factory in South Braintree, Massachusetts, Sacco and Vanzetti endured a long series of hearings, trials, and appeals. By the time they were finally executed, on August 23, 1927, they had become national symbols – for some, of the threat posed by dark, sly aliens intent on fomenting an "internal revolution" and, for others, of the threat posed by a society determined to persecute and control those who threatened its ruling classes.

Both Sacco and Vanzetti – the one a "good shoemaker," the other a "poor fish peddler," in Vanzetti's words – were Italian immigrants, and both were convinced anarchists whose radical affiliations reached back through the Lyric Years of Emma Goldman's *Mother Earth* and Bill Heyward's Industrial Workers of the World (IWW) to a deep-seated distrust of government acquired in their peasant homes in Italy. During World War I, they fled to Mexico, hoping for the day when Italy would finally be free of the tyranny of government. Back in Massachusetts, their hopes for Italy's reclamation dashed, they joined other immigrant anarchists in planning and executing demonstrations and bombings aimed at keeping alive the impossible ideal of what they called the "beautiful Idea" of a world free of government. They were, however, almost certainly innocent of the South Braintree robbery and murder; and they

were certainly denied a fair trial. While sitting as judge on the case, Webster
Thayer worked with other government officials to orchestrate sustained, systematic violations of their constitutionally guaranteed rights – by withhold-
ing and suppressing evidence and by conniving with the district attorney,
Frederick G. Katzmann, to exploit their "alien blood," their broken English,
their opposition to the war, and their unpopular social philosophy – in order
to arouse against them what Felix Frankfurter described as a riot of "political
passion and patriotic sentiment." By 1927, when Sacco and Vanzetti were
finally executed, most of the Italian Americans who shared their devotion to
their "beautiful Idea" were deported, jailed, or dead, victims of a formidable
campaign waged by native-born men and women, including Attorney General
Palmer, Judge Thayer ("those anarchist bastards," he privately called them,
while still conducting their trial), Katzmann, the governor of Massachusetts,
the presidents of Harvard and MIT, and many members of the best old families
of Massachusetts. Observing the spectacle, Edmund Wilson concluded that it
"raised almost every fundamental question of our political and social system."

Another result of the widespread campaign was the splintering of reformers into small, ineffective groups. United, radical reformers would have remained a marginal force; divided, they possessed virtually no power. For a
time the Sacco-Vanzetti case – the most famous of its kind in the history of the
United States – almost pulled reformers, writers, artists, and prewar suffragists
into a concerted political force. Abroad, sympathetic workers rioted in Lyons,
marched in London, and burned U.S. flags in Casablanca. At home, Mike Gold
tried to place Sacco and Vanzetti at the center of a larger class struggle. To
become martyrs in that struggle – "a legend for millions of fishermen, coolies,
peasants, miners, steel workers . . . war cripples, bonded girl prostitutes, prisoners, negro slaves, poets, Einstein, Barbusse, able-bodied seamen and Jewish
tailors" – was a "beautiful fate," he told readers of *New Masses* in October 1927.

But the trial and execution of Sacco and Vanzetti produced as much art as
action, and most of both are now forgotten. On the evening of their execution,
Edna St. Vincent Millay, Lola Ridge, John Dos Passos, and Powers Hapgood
joined a motley group of other writers, artists, laborers, and friends in a vigil at
Charlestown Prison. Later, Cowley, Dos Passos, Babette Deutsch, and Witter
Bynner wrote poems; Millay wrote both the best-known poem about the case,
"Justice Denied in Massachusetts," and an impressive poetic essay, "Fear";
Upton Sinclair wrote *Boston* (1928), a careful historical record of the case; and
Maxwell Anderson collaborated with Harold Hickerson in writing the play
Gods of the Lightning (1928) and wrote the play *Winterset* (1935).

In May 1929 in *New Masses*, Gold published a "worker's Recitation" based
on the public speeches and letters of Vanzetti, including the famous words

Vanzetti spoke to Philip D. Strong, a reporter for the North American Newspaper Alliance, in late April 1927:

If it has not been for these things, I might have live out my life, talking at street corners to scorning men. I might have die, unmarked, unknown, a failure. Now we are not a failure. This is our career and our triumph. Never in our full life can we hope to do such work for tolerance, for joostice, for man's understanding of man, as now we do by an accident.

Our words – our lives – pains – nothing! The taking of our lives – lives of a good shoemaker and a poor fish peddler – all! That last moment belong to us – that agony is our triumph.

Not long after the execution of Sacco and Vanzetti, Dos Passos began writing *The 42nd Parallel* (1930), the first volume of *U.S.A.*, his panoramic, three-volume chronicle of the country from the turn of the century into the 1930s. In the second volume, *1919* (1932), he extends his chronicle, and in the third and final volume, *The Big Money* (1936), he brings his long work full circle, back to the shoemaker and the fish peddler, through a character named Mary French, who joins in the vigil at the prison where the two martyrs are executed. In one of the "Camera Eye" sections of *The Big Money*, Dos Passos seems to speak in his own voice of having watched as his nation split into two conflicting camps:

they have clubbed us off the streets they are stronger they are rich they hire and fire the politicians the newspapereditors the old judges the small men with reputations the collegepresidents the ward heelers (listen businessmen collegepresidents judges America will not forget her betrayers). . . .

all right you have won you will kill the brave men our friends tonight. . . .

America our nation has been beaten by strangers who have turned our language inside out who have taken the clean words our fathers spoke and made them slimy and foul. . . .

all right we are two nations

In the twenties, however, about which Dos Passos wrote these words, as opposed to the thirties, in which he wrote them, reformers remained so demoralized and divided that nothing, not even the trial and execution of Sacco and Vanzetti, could unify them.

In 1919, when Congress extended wartime Prohibition by passing the Volstead Act over Wilson's veto, the nation found itself divided along very different lines. Prohibition intensified tensions between the "highbrows" and the evangelical Protestants. It also set law-enforcement officers against many citizens who suddenly became casual lawbreakers, both in the countryside, where they associated bootlegging with old-fashioned self-reliance, and in the cities, where they thought of it as a new way to get rich. Soon stills, bootleggers, and speakeasies were feeding big money into organized crime, and gangsters were fighting openly on country roads and city streets to see who would control the profits of vice. In Washington, DC, three hundred licensed saloons gave way to seven hundred speakeasies supplied by four thousand bootleggers. Boston had more than four thousand speakeasies and Detroit more than twenty thousand, as millions of Americans, including regular churchgoers, began breaking the law. In Chicago, where "Scarface" Al Capone headed a 60-million-dollar empire and an army of nearly one thousand, unsolved murders became commonplace: in 1926 and 1927 there were no convictions in 130 gangland killings. In many instances cheap liquor – bearing names like Jackass Brandy, Panther Whiskey, and Yack Yack Bourbon – crippled or poisoned drinkers. Observing the spectacle, E. B. White proposed that the government nationalize speakeasies in order to provide citizens with "liquor of a uniformly high quality" and Congress with enough money to enforce Prohibition.

Prohibition began, of course, as another crusade to make the world safe by ensuring, to borrow one of Nick Carraway's lines in *The Great Gatsby*, that people would stand "at a sort of moral attention forever." Carried away by their own ardent rhetoric, leaders of the temperance movement tied "demon rum" to horrors ranging from venereal and hereditary diseases to the crimes and licentiousness that their listeners associated with dark foreigners. But their larger defeat came after victory, when Prohibition did more to increase lawlessness than it did to promote moral restraint.

Prohibition was in part a story about the awkwardness of a people trying to cope with rapidly changing rules, and it marked the end of an era in which local institutions like the family and church felt they could ensure moral restraint with little or no help from the federal government. But Prohibition also demonstrated how effective forces of change would be in converting victories by parties of the past to its own ends. And in this sense, it was simply another story coming out of 1919 reiterating the triumph of the new. It promoted new forms of lawlessness and new ways of getting rich quick, as Fitzgerald makes clear in *The Great Gatsby*. Currents of energy seemed to be "breaking out everywhere," Dos Passos wrote in *Three Soldiers* (1921), "as young guys climbed out of their uniforms . . . ready for anything turbulent and new." Veterans used their "separation checks" as civilians used proceeds from their "Liberty" bonds: to launch a record-breaking party and buying spree. The year 1919 struck many people, including Dos Passos, who returned to it in the second volume of his trilogy *U.S.A.*, as marking a shift from a politics of reform (now become "nostrums") to a politics of splurge (now become "normalcy"), a turn from a kind of residual innocence toward new fears and prejudices, and the dominance of an advertising industry that increasingly manipulated needs and stimulated desires. Taken together, the results inflected life in the twenties with artificial intensity and frenetic pace. Looking back on his own meteoric rise, Fitzgerald called it "unnatural, unnatural as the boom itself" – a comment that reminds us again of just how inextricably "life" and "art" are interlaced.

As the country moved with scarcely a blink from the scandals of Harding's regime to the excesses of Coolidge's, more and more writers began to feel "like aliens in a commercial world," Cowley wrote in *Exile's Return* (1934). They were "restless, uneasy, and disaffected," Walter Lippmann added, "world-weary at the age of twenty-two." Some took refuge in enclaves in Memphis, New Orleans, Chicago, or New York. Others, following the examples of James, Wharton, Stein, Eliot, H. D., and Pound, left the United States for Europe as soon as they had enough money to buy steamer tickets. Still others, most conspicuously Fitzgerald, joined extravagant parties on both sides of the Atlantic. Even those who prospered tended to identify with writers bent on saying "No!" to what Lippmann called the "diffused prosperity" of the "New Capitalism" and what Dos Passos called the "bastard culture" of Henry Ford and Andrew Mellon. Among several exemplary tales of the era, a favorite focused on the day November 27, 1912 – when a thirty-six-year-old man named Sherwood "Jobby" Anderson walked out of his paint factory in Elyria, Ohio, and headed for Chicago, turning his back on his successful business and his bourgeois family in order to devote his "life" to "art." "I hardly know what I can teach," Anderson wrote his brother Karl, "except anti-success."

Standing near the end of the long transformation of romanticism into modernism, Anderson made authenticity and sincerity the twin pillars of his conception of himself as an artist. Sensing that the story of his conversion might serve as a model for others, he tidied up some parts of it and dramatized others. His break with business was among other things a nervous breakdown that his marriage, in fact, survived; and, after arriving in Chicago, he began writing advertising copy in order to make a living. But the pattern he needed was there, and it enabled him to present himself as the prototype of the vulnerable yet resilient citizen who values his aesthetic sensibility, and thus his immortal soul, enough to avoid settling for the inadequate fate of mere success.

In the letters he wrote, the tales he told about himself, and his autobiographical writings – *A Story-Teller's Story* (1928), *Tar: A Midwest Childhood* (1926), and the posthumous *Sherwood Anderson's Memoirs* (1942) – Anderson mixed memory and desire by adjusting the facts of his life to the requirements of his self-appointed role. His autobiographical narratives bear some resemblance to novels like *Babbitt*, where the protagonist tries and fails to break away, and considerable resemblance to novels like Zona Gale's *Preface to a Life* (1926), which focuses on a businessman who discovers the emptiness of everything he has desired – success, a family, admiring friends – before escaping "into something real." Such parallels help us both to understand how close Anderson came to creating himself as a fictional character for the edification of his contemporaries and to recognize that his deeper motives were social and didactic as well as personal and literary. His story of dropping out and breaking away not only demonstrates the value of "anti-success." It also defines art as an act of resistance that combines intrusion and embrace and so becomes an act of love that "forces us out of ourselves and into the lives of others." "In the end," Anderson said, as he neared the end of his own life, "the real writer becomes a lover."

Anderson's dramatic conversion found expression in *Windy McPherson's Son* (1916), his first published novel, where he recasts memories of his father in light of his own disillusionment with the world of business. His second novel, *Marching Men* (1917), celebrates the militant brotherhood of industrial workers in ways that veer disturbingly toward totalitarianism. But in *Winesburg, Ohio* (1919), he turned toward something he had experienced more directly: the lonely half-life of a small Midwestern town. Though small, Winesburg is no longer a community. Its people are divided by competing interests rather than knit together by shared purposes; they have nothing to look backward to with pride or forward to with hope. The feeling of being trapped in a cultural wasteland and of being isolated haunts and even cripples them. What they share is being grouped together by their maker as "grotesques."

Stylistically, Anderson was indebted to Gertrude Stein's *Three Lives* (1909). "She is making new, strange and to my ears sweet combinations of words," he said of Stein – whose reliance on simple diction and whose experiments with different forms of repetition and juxtaposition proved particularly helpful to him in his own fumbling search for new ways of rendering the shrunken lives of his inarticulate characters. Such breakthroughs as he records belong more to him than to his characters. In their struggles to express themselves verbally, as in their struggle to cope with their unfocused feelings and forbidden desires, most of his characters, including Wing Biddlebaum, remain locked in timid failure. Blighted speech, awkward silences, and compulsive gestures dominate their efforts to express themselves and establish relationships. Such hope as survives lies with the young who, like George Willard, summon enough energy to break away.

Formally, *Winesburg, Ohio* reflects the influence of Ivan Turgenev's *A Sportsman's Sketches* (1852), James Joyce's *Dubliners* (1914), and Edgar Lee Masters's *Spoon River Anthology* (1915). Anderson uses a version of literary collage to give form to his discontinuous narrative. Several of his stories and characters, "The Tales and the Persons" of *Winesburg, Ohio*, create smaller patterns of their own; together, they contribute to the larger framework of

Anderson's "Book of the Grotesque," which gradually becomes more than the sum of its parts. By permitting jumps and gaps, Anderson's discontinuous narrative allows him – as it later allowed Ernest Hemingway in *In Our Time* (1924), Jean Toomer in *Cane* (1923), and William Faulkner in *Go Down, Moses* (1942) – to omit some things and avoid others. In this sense, it simplifies his tasks in advance. In addition, it anticipates the more drastic jumps and shifts as well as the fragmentation and collage that, on a different scale, dominate Dos Passos's *U.S.A.*

In Anderson's hands, however, discontinuous narrative serves primarily to reinforce the theme of isolation. Repressed needs, thwarted desires, failed communications, and misshapen lives fill his work. His characters are not only cut off from one another; they are at odds with themselves and their own bodies. Wing Biddlebaum, for example, Anderson's "obscure poet," is represented by his "Hands," which seem to live a life of their own. Like many of Anderson's stories, "Hands" begins and ends abruptly, as though it has been amputated. The principle of fragmentation that pulls toward disintegration works against the principle of integration that is essential if *Winesburg, Ohio* is finally to become the story of a town. Reinforcing this tension as he goes, Anderson creates an enlarged role for his readers, of whom he remains acutely conscious. As his part in the literary transaction, he creates a sense of fragmented simultaneity before he begins the move toward continuity, or sustained narrative, by foregrounding the story of George Willard and by making his tales interactive. But he assigns much of the task of continuity to his readers, whose role he also foregrounds. Having observed that relations stop nowhere, Henry James went on to say that the artist's task was to make them appear to do so. In Anderson's world – of severed ends, dangling lives, deferred words – relations are imperiled. "It's just as well," says one character, thinking of a speech not made. "Whatever I told him would have been a lie." To read *Winesburg, Ohio* on its own terms, as the narrative of a town, the reader must discern relations, finish communications, and fashion connections out of hints and suggestions that lie impacted in awkward silences and blighted speech. And in this sense, the reader becomes another version of the artist as lover, or at least as matchmaker and healer, and thus comes to share the roles that Anderson creates for himself as a writer.

As much as any writer of his time, Anderson combined the fate of remaining a flawed writer ("For all my egotism," he remarked late in his life, "I know I am but a minor figure") and becoming a major force ("He was the father of my generation of American writers," William Faulkner said, "and the tradition of American writing which our successors will carry on"). One explanation for this tension lies in his origins. During the years in which New York was replacing Boston as the cultural center of the United States, the center of literary creativity was also shifting. The East was still home to many critics and readers and most of the major publishing houses, but many important writers were coming from the provinces, from the South and especially from the Midwest. Margaret Anderson and Janet Flanner came from Indianapolis; Dorothy Canfield Fisher from Lawrence, Kansas; Zona Gale from Portage, Wisconsin; Josephine Herbst from Sioux City, Iowa; Harriet Monroe and John Dos Passos from Chicago; Fitzgerald from St. Paul; Hemingway from Oak Park, Illinois, near Chicago; Lewis from Sauk Center, Minnesota; Ruth Suckow from Howarden, Iowa; and Langston Hughes from Joplin, Missouri – to name a few. Soon even Van Wyck Brooks, whose work as literary historian presented New England's literature as "American literature," was convinced "that the heart of America lay in the West" and that Sherwood Anderson, who came from Camden, Ohio, "was the essence of his West."

Anderson opened up a large part of that essence, including the human ordinariness of the tender yet jealous sexual lives of children and of the touching yet grotesque sexual lives of repressed adults, in *Winesburg* and then passed it on to writers like Hemingway, Fitzgerald, Faulkner, and Thomas Wolfe. Related to this, the legacy of Freud's great work, was Anderson's exploration of the loneliness of the modern world as manifested in the social, cultural, and spiritual desiccation of small twentieth-century towns. The isolation that cripples his characters is social as well as psychological, and it possesses an economic history as well as an erotic one. His characters want to touch other lives and explore other worlds because they long for a sense of purpose and a sense of human connectedness. For Anderson, all acts of reaching out – even efforts to speak and hear – are also acts of reaching back, undertaken in hope of reestablishing ties with some lost or forfeited self as well as some lost or forfeited community.

4

❦

DISENCHANTMENT, FLIGHT, AND
THE RISE OF PROFESSIONALISM
IN AN AGE OF PLENTY

S OME OF THE writers and artists who sailed for France or joined enclaves
back home had read enough of Henri Murger's *Scènes de la vie de bohème* to
think of themselves as bohemian artists. Others, inspired by the example
of Flaubert, longed to make the "quaint mania of passing one's life wearing
oneself out over words" their own. Joseph Hergesheimer, to take one example,
became so enamored of Flaubert's admonitions that he wrote, Edmund Wilson
remarked, nearly as badly in a studied way "as Dreiser did in a crude one."
Others drifted from place to place, experimenting, or like Babbitt, moved in
and out of bohemian enclaves as troubled or merely curious visitors. Lacking political edge, their discontent sometimes seems shallow. Even among
those who shunned possessions and traveled light, serious commitment to reform politics remained rare. Cultural critics like Brooks, Cowley, and Wilson
thought of themselves as "men of letters," not academic critics. During the
twenties, they remained for the most part present-minded, caught up in the
literary scenes they wrote about. When they turned toward the past, they
looked for writers who spoke to the stranded condition of their generation.
By a "useable past," they meant one useful to writers who wanted to continue
culture. What held them together, beyond the abandonment of old restraints
and a glamorization of new indulgences involving sex and alcohol as well as
lavish parties, was a sense of shared predicament and common endeavor: their
feeling that, paradoxically, they had been left alone together to experiment
"in a void."

In addition, they remained young professionals on the make. The inadequacy
of mere success and society's hostility to art, or more generally to the needs of
the human spirit, coalesce in the story of Anderson. But Anderson's version
of "anti-success" included large ambitions built around his effort to become a
professional writer. Immortality was one aim they shared. "I want to be one
of the greatest writers who ever lived, don't you?" a young Fitzgerald said to
a young Wilson. Recognition and money were others. Several of the writers
we remember, including Fitzgerald, Hemingway, and Dos Passos, and several

we have almost forgotten, like Louis Bromfield, built substantial reputations before they were thirty, and a few made substantial sums of money doing it. Even those who lagged behind in reputation or fortune were for the most part able to make a living in jobs connected with writing, without having to give their energies to alien pursuits.

They worked for magazines or presses or in bookstores, in London, Paris, or New York, Chicago, Memphis, or New Orleans; and they sold their work to presses as well as magazines, a few of which, like the *Dial*, offered prestigious annual prizes. Some "little magazines" lasted for years. Others were launched with a splash only to lead shrinking lives. But even those that were short-lived – *Double Dealer, Broom, Transition, Fire, Harlem, The Messenger*, to name a few – played important roles not only by publishing the work of little-known writers side by side with experimental work of well-known writers but also by paying the writers who edited them modest salaries and helping to re-form the taste and reading skills of the nation's most adventuresome readers, including emerging writers.

At the opposite end of the spectrum was the *Saturday Evening Post*. Having achieved an average weekly circulation of 2,500,000 during the twenties, the *Post* commanded large advertising fees and paid large publication fees – as much as $6,000 per story or $60,000 for a serial. By 1928 most of its issues were running over 200 pages, with roughly half devoted to advertisements. Shunning ads for alcohol and cigarettes, the *Post* welcomed ads for automobiles and household items – Premier Duplex vacuum cleaners, Kohler plumbing fixtures, Victor radios, Singer sewing machines, Kelvinator refrigerators, and Toastmasters. Like the *Post*, the *Ladies' Home Journal* promoted and profited from the nation's affluence and consumerism. When the Lynds surveyed Muncie, Indiana, in 1924, as *Middletown, U.S.A.*, they found that the aggregate circulation of the *Post* and the *Journal* was sixty times greater than that of *Harper's* and *Atlantic*. Both the slogans of the *Post* – "soberness of living" and "evenness of mentality" – and the preoccupations of the *Journal* – domestic efficiency and civic virtue – interacted with two prominent themes: gossip about wealthy people and advice about how to join their ranks. What the *Post* celebrated – businessmen and engineers as creators of wealth and as shapers of the new world – the *Journal* endorsed; and what the *Journal* celebrated – attractive yet genteel women as servants of society and guardians of virtue – the *Post* endorsed. In addition, both offered "free" advice, implicit and explicit, on a range of themes prominent in Henri Laurent's *Personality: How to Build It* (1916): how to be aggressive and original without forfeiting "the esteem of others"; how to widen acquaintances and make connections; how to acquire poise and style while making and spending money. In short, they helped to define what being a successful man or woman meant by catering to an audience that increasingly depended on the advice of strangers about everything from morals and mores to hygiene and manners. And in their advertisements they began making wholesale use of the fluid, nonlinear, nonrepresentational techniques that were beginning to dominate fiction. In 1915 Vachel Lindsay had announced, in a book titled *The Art of Motion Pictures*, that the civilization of the United States was growing "more hieroglyphic every day." The fast-paced life of the city as well as the art of the motion picture had something to do with the transformation that was under way. But so, too, did the young, rapidly growing, advertising industry.

"Modernism offered the opportunity of expressing the inexpressible," said the advertising executive Ernest Elmo Calkins, "of suggesting [and selling] not so much a motor car as speed, not so much a gown as style, not so much a compact as beauty." In a whole range of books (*More Power to You*, *It's a Good Old World*, *What Can a Man Believe?*, *On the Up and Up*, and especially *The Man Nobody Knows*, the remarkable best-seller that presents Jesus Christ as the "founder of modern business"), Bruce Barton used advertising to press the claims of a culture in which consumerism and self-realization went hand in hand. What was involved in advertising, however, as a tool for marketing products, including Jesus Christ, was the crucial dissociation of words and concepts from specific or clear referents that the French sociologist Henri Lefebvre has described as "the decline of the referentials."

One sign of the power, sophistication, and opportunism of the young advertising industry came with the move of John B. Watson, author of *Behaviorism* (1924), after he had lost his position as professor of psychology at the Johns Hopkins University, following a scandal involving one of his graduate students, to an executive position with the J. Walter Thompson Company, a large and still powerful advertising firm. Watson thought of "consciousness" as a vague abstraction. Tangible stimuli and measurable responses – "observed facts" – he believed in. Properly studied, such things could lead to the "prediction and control of behavior," he wrote. Advertising enabled him to bring two decades of basic research in behavioral psychology to bear on problems "connected with markets, salesmanship, public resistances, types of appeal, etc."

Popular culture of the twenties – the stories and advertisements found in the *Post* and the *Journal*, big-time spectator sports, radio programs, and picture shows – challenged serious literature by providing competing diversions. But popular culture also enhanced the prospects of professional writers. Following the formation of Alfred A. Knopf in 1915, Boni & Liveright in 1917, and Harcourt, Brace in 1919 came Viking in 1925 and Random House in 1926, the same year in which the Book of the Month Club and the Literary Guild were established. Advertising not only manipulated buyers; it attracted readers and helped to train them. Big-time sports made heroes of Jack Dempsey, Babe Ruth, Bill Tilden, Bobby Jones, and Red Grange, and movies created a series of idols: Gloria Swanson in *Male and Female*; Douglas Fairbanks in *The Mark of Zorro*; John Gilbert and Greta Garbo in *Flesh and the Devil*; Rudolph Valentino in *The Son of the Sheik*. Furthermore, all of these – radio broadcasts, sports contests, and movies alike – bathed the minds of the nation's people in stories and serials that had discernible beginnings, middles, and endings and yet made wholesale use of jumps and shifts as well as blurred, coalescing images in order to tell stories of dramatic discoveries that promoted the idea that instant stardom was the truly modern way of achieving fame and fortune.

In 1922, 40 million people bought tickets to see movies; by 1930, an average of 100 million were buying tickets each week, making the movie theater, in Glenway Wescott's phrase, the "imagination's chapel in the town." The new dream of instant stardom – of being singled out, renamed, and transformed into a star – began to rival the older dream of attaining wealth by working hard and saving money. Stardom was something that happened to people, like war and disease, as the careers of characters as different as Buntline's Buffalo Bill and Dreiser's Carrie Madenda remind us. And like the dust and the dew, it was known to fall on thistles as well as roses – on the profligate Babe Ruth as well as the upright Lou Gehrig – which meant that virtue and hard work were but one route to fame. Once discovered or created, furthermore, stars existed to be seen and emulated. They entertained by exemplifying success and its rewards and by inspiring hope. In literature as well as in movies and sports, stardom was something that could happen to anyone, anywhere, at any time, and it could happen to writers as well as to their characters. Even those too old or battered to hope for it themselves could share in it vicariously for the price of a ticket to the local chapel of the imagination.

Few writers made fortunes, but few felt hounded by dollars. "The Jazz Age," Fitzgerald said, seemed to race "along under its own power, served by great filling stations full of money. . . . Even when you were broke, you didn't worry about money, because it was in such profusion around you." Many writers, including some of those who longed for prosperity and attained it, remained ambivalent about what Joseph Freeman, who had come of age during the Lyric Years, called the nation's "money culture." Hoping to free themselves from the habits it instilled by visible and invisible means, of judging yourself and everyone else by a single standard, "your income," they tried to make their enclaves counterworlds where "rhymes were more precious than dollars" and creativity counted more than greed. Yet on this score as on others, they met with mixed success, in part because, having appropriated the nation's old belief that individuals could reinvent themselves and so become anything they wanted to be, they simplified their task in advance.

Even Fitzgerald, whose interest in enclaves was limited and whose faith in new beginnings was tempered by an imagination tilted toward disaster, found himself drawn to stories of fresh starts and dramas of self-fashioning, as we see in *The Great Gatsby*. He also found himself fascinated by a spectacle he wanted to explore rather than reform:

The uncertainties of 1919 were over – there seemed little doubt about what was going to happen – America was going on the greatest, gaudiest spree in history and there was going to be plenty to tell about it. The whole golden boom was in the air – its splendid generosities, its outrageous corruptions and the tortuous death struggle of the old America in Prohibition. All the stories that came into my head had a touch of disaster in them.

Fitzgerald's proprietary instincts centered less on a world than on a generation: "my contemporaries," he called them. The same paths that no longer connected young people to anything, even one another, seemed to Fitzgerald to lead to him and his contemporaries. Their task, and their fate, to borrow a phrase from his story "The Scandal Detectives," consisted of "experimenting in a void," using "the first tentative combinations of the [new] ideas and materials they found ready at their hands." Since most writers of the twenties came from middle-class homes, they found it hard to judge success without regard to money. The more they exaggerated the distance between the world into which they had been born and the one in which they lived, the more their dream of success became the principal thing they had to fall back on. Nostalgia, a harking back to some lost, remembered place or some warm feeling, marks their words. But so, too, does the thrill and even the terror of embracing the future. Loss, whatever else it might be, was a spur to experimenting in life and art. Here, again, is Fitzgerald in "The Scandal Detectives":

Some generations are close to those that succeed them; between others the gulf is infinite and unbridgeable. Mrs. Buckner – a woman of character, a member of Society in a large Middle-Western city – carrying a pitcher of fruit lemonade through her own spacious back yard, was progressing across a hundred years. Her own thoughts would have been comprehensible to her great-grandmother; what was happening in a room above the stable would have been entirely unintelligible to them both. In what had once served as the coachman's sleeping apartment, her son and a friend were not behaving in a normal manner, but were, so to speak, experimenting in a void. They were making the first tentative combinations of the ideas and materials they found ready at their hand – ideas destined to become, in future years, first articulate, then startling and finally commonplace. At the moment when she called up to them they were sitting with disarming quiet upon the still unhatched eggs of the mid-twentieth century.

Contrary to the subversive connotations of this passage, what Mrs. Buckner's son and his friend are doing has more to do with books than with bombs or bodies, and as much to do with preparing for careers and getting money, if not exactly earning it. They are behaving scandalously by collecting data on local scandals. "Ripley Buckner, Jr., and Basil D. Lee, Scandal Detectives" are working on "THE BOOK OF SCANDAL," in which they have "set down such deviations from rectitude on the part of their fellow citizens" as they have been able to unearth. Some of these deviations – or "false steps," as they are also called – have been authored by grizzled old men and have become part of the community's folk literature. Other "more exciting sins," based on everything from confirmed reports to mere rumors, would bewilder or anger the town's caretakers; still others, based on "contemporary reports," would, if known, fill "the parents of the involved children with horror or despair."

The book is Basil's idea, and reading it requires "the aid of the imagination," for it is written in ink that becomes visible only when it is held close to a fire. Both boys are preoccupied with desirable girls and dangerous rivals, and they delight in pranks that require careful planning and clever disguises. Like Tom Sawyer and Jay Gatsby, they have read a few books and have drawn models as well as ideas from them. Basil's favorite character is Arsène Lupin, "a romantic phenomenon lately imported from Europe," who has inspired Basil's dream of going to Yale and becoming a great athlete in preparation for following Lupin's example as "a gentleman burglar." Fitzgerald thus creates a more illicit version of a story he clearly knew, Owen Johnson's *Stover at Yale* (1912), in which Ricky Ricketts, sitting in Mory's, entertains Dink Stover by explaining his scheme for becoming "a millionaire in ten years": find "something all the fools love and enjoy," convince "them that it's wrong," concoct a substitute, patent and advertise it, then "sit back, chuckle, and shovel away the ducats."

Like Ricky Ricketts's imagination, Basil's moves back and forth between the familiar and the scandalous – between life governed by accepted rules and life as illicit adventure directed by the imagination toward success that is to be measured in terms of style and dollars rather than rectitude. If an older, ceremonious life has prepared Mrs. Buckner for crossing spacious lawns and serving lemonade on soft summer afternoons, another, still tentative and unhatched, is carrying her son and his friend away from home as she knows it. Fitzgerald juxtaposes these possibilities, knowing in advance, as the reader does, what the boys' choice must be. But there is irony, humor, and even pathos in their predicament. Although the town needs shaking up, the boys' dreams and methods are shallow as well as illicit. Their only real gain – learning what it is like to feel "morally alone" – is cloaked in loss. At the end of the story, Basil is left with little more than callow confidence in the "boundless possibilities of summer," which holds out the promise of easy sex and even easy love as well as easy adventure, easy money, and easy fulfillment.

Fitzgerald set out, like several of his contemporaries, hoping to live with intensity, have a grand time, and become a successful writer. By 1925, with the publication of *The Great Gatsby*, he stood on the edge of doing just that. By 1928, when he wrote "The Scandal Detectives," he was already showing signs of feeling battered and disillusioned. Yet in many respects he remained an aging boy. Buoyed by his residual innocence, he still took delight in acting out, in part because he was convinced that most artists, like most art, are allied with the illicit. To his indignant perception, modern culture was at odds with human fulfillment, especially in the repressive mores with which it governed pleasure in general and sexual pleasure in particular. He took pride in believing that his generation had emerged from the war steeped in disillusionment and schooled, in the "mobile privacy" of the automobile, in what he called acts of "sweet and casual dalliance." What followed, he later reported, was an "intensive education" designed to make the members of his generation devotees of pleasure. "Let me trace some of the revelations," he wrote, looking back on the twenties from November 1931.

We begin with the suggestion that Don Juan leads an interesting life (*Jurgen*, 1919); then we learn that there's a lot of sex around if we only knew it (*Winesburg, Ohio*, 1920), that adolescents lead very amorous lives (*This Side of Paradise*, 1920), that there are a lot of neglected Anglo-Saxon words (*Ulysses*, 1921), that older people don't always resist sudden temptations (*Cytherea*, 1922), that girls are sometimes seduced without being ruined (*Flaming Youth*, 1922), that even rape often turns out well (*The Sheik*, 1922), that glamorous English ladies are often promiscuous (*The Green Hat*, 1924), that in fact they devote most of their time to it (*The Vortex*, 1926), that it's a damn good thing too (*Lady Chatterly's* [sic] *Lover*, 1928), and finally that there are abnormal variations (*The Well of Loneliness*, 1928, and *Sodome and Gomorrhe*, 1929).

Alarmed by the spectacle that delighted Fitzgerald, Joseph Wood Krutch, who was only three years older than Fitzgerald, complained that the new barbarians had come as "barbarians have always come, absorbed in the processes of life for their own sake . . . begetting children without asking why they should beget them, and conquering without asking for what purpose they conquer." But Fitzgerald's problem was of a different kind. Beginning with the publication of his first novel, *This Side of Paradise*, (1920), he fancied himself ringleader of a revolt that embraced music and literature as well as sex and alcohol and that was laden with social and moral as well as aesthetic implications. Yet he continued to think of his art and his career as apolitical. The crucial ties that undergirded the money culture of the twenties – or that "diffused prosperity of the 'New Capitalism,'" as Lippmann put it – he grasped only subliminally and disclosed only in his finest fiction: namely, that the splurge of the young, their unleashing of the erotic will in the pursuit of pleasure, was part of a larger national splurge in which their parents and political leaders were unleashing their political will in pursuit of power and their economic will in pursuit of money. This recognition gave him the core story of the rise and fall of Jay Gatsby, a self-made, self-named "star" who learns to trust power and possession more than pleasure even before he falls victim to the cynical manipulations of the chief beneficiaries of his world's political economy, the very rich. But Fitzgerald's art – and in this, too, it is representative – played a reinforcing as well as a countering role in the process that it exposes to view – a fact Fitzgerald discloses in Nick Carraway's curious combination of hesitation and readiness, diffidence and arrogance, guilt and smugness, and then more fully explored in his only other enduring novel, *Tender is the Night* (1934).

5

❧

CLASS, POWER, AND VIOLENCE
IN A NEW AGE

N *Workers: An Experiment in Reality – The West* (1899), Walter Wyckoff
surveys the harsh consequences of being poor in a land of plenty, particularly when poverty begins to close in as something remorseless and final,
enforcing a sense that one is a "superfluous human being" for whom "there is
no part in the play of the world's activity." Dreiser glimpsed such moments as
a boy and never forgot them. The diaries he kept between *Sister Carrie* (1900)
and *An American Tragedy* (1925) show little sympathy for blacks and Jews and
less interest in the plight of the poor than in his own string of sexual conquests.
But memories of his own painful childhood stayed with him. "Any form of
distress," he once remarked – "a wretched, down-at-heels neighborhood, a
poor farm, an asylum, a jail," or people without "means of subsistence" – was
sufficient to provoke something close to actual "physical pain."

Dreiser begins *An American Tragedy*, his first commercial success, with Clyde
Griffiths, a young boy full of yearning, enclosed by "the tall walls of the
commercial heart of an American city." He then traces Clyde's brief rise to no
great height and ends with him locked in a prison cell, waiting to be executed.
Enticed by his society's major inducements – not only wealth, status, and
power, but also meretricious glamor and beauty – Clyde becomes an easy
victim of its failure to provide him any values by which to live, other than hope
of entering, as a member rather than as a hired hand or guest, the world of the
very rich. His money-conscious, pleasure-seeking world teaches him to admire
people above him and use those below him. Part victim and part victimizer,
he resembles both a doomed Carrie Madenda and a failed Frank Cowperwood,
the protagonist of Dreiser's "trilogy of desire": *The Financier* (1912), *The Titan*
(1914), and *The Stoic* (1947). His most representative moment is one in which
he so little knows his own heart's desire that he can neither act nor stop
acting, as he wavers and hesitates before clumsily and almost unintentionally
completing a murder he has carefully planned.

An American Tragedy, which was banned in Boston, among other places, but
celebrated in Russia, makes an interesting comparison with another ironic and

haunting story about the fate of the American dream that was also published in 1925 – Fitzgerald's *The Great Gatsby* – in part because the latter has worn better. In one respect, Fitzgerald mirrored his nation's new attitude toward money: he was even more interested in making and spending it than in accumulating it. Even when he made large sums by selling stories to the *Post*, he and his wife, Zelda Sayre Fitzgerald, author of *Save Me the Waltz*, found ways to spend it on glamorous parties and extravagant sprees held in hotels, rented houses, or flats. Yet long before the crack-ups that began the last chapter of their lives, strong undertones of sadness began to run through Fitzgerald's stories, as though the temporariness of things and his own uncertainties about himself, his life, and his world haunted him. What sustained him, enabling him to go on "experimenting," beyond his ambition and his gift for hope, was a belief in work: "I'm a workman of letters," he said in one of his most telling self-characterizations, "a professional."

Jay Gatsby wants, as it turns out, much of what Scott and Zelda wanted – not mere success (a mansion, fabulous millions, and a beautiful life), but success enlarged and even sanctified by a dream that could give it purpose. Clyde Griffiths lives in a bleak rented room; Carrie Madenda lives in a suite in the Waldorf, Jay Gatsby lives in a mansion on Long Island. The work of a failed "plan to Found a Family," Gatsby's mansion fits both the history he has invented for himself and the dream he hopes to live. As it turns out, however, his newly purchased "ancestral home" is another temporary address. For he lives in a world whose secret logic Dreiser glimpsed in *Sister Carrie*: of waifs caught in a field of forces – or, put another way, of lives that are at once self-invented and overdetermined. Bearing assumed names (call me Carrie Madenda, call me Jay Gatsby, they seem to say), they live lives that are not so much careers as performances filled with words, gestures, and yearnings that just miss being absurd.

In some moments Gatsby stands under a "wafer of a moon" amid "blue gardens," breathing air in which "yellow cocktail music" and the sounds of "chatter and laughter" seem almost like an "opera." Wild rumors circulate about him, lifting him into a kind of celebrity as well as notoriety. In other moments, he moves in the "unquiet darkness" of a world best represented by a desolate "valley of ashes" that is shaped by driving winds and so remains fluid and insubstantial: "a fantastic farm where ashes grow like wheat into ridges and hills and grotesque gardens; where ashes take the forms of houses and chimneys and rising smoke and, finally, with a transcendent effort, of men who move dimly and already crumbling through the powdery air." On both the first and last times that we see him, isolation and silence enclose him, setting him apart. Toward the end, he reminds us that silence can be a shield of the defeated as well as the burden of the suppressed. But when he speaks, as in his striking remark that Daisy Buchanan's voice "sounds like money," he reiterates his isolation by speaking as a self-fashioned creature who wants language to serve less as a medium of social exchange than as a means of evoking essences that he alone recognizes, validates by his attention, and names – to which we, like Carraway, can only assent. In his love for Daisy, he evokes the love of a serf for a fair and beautiful princess, or of a poor man for the "golden girl." Money and class are linked in *The Great Gatsby*, as they are in *An American Tragedy*; and in both novels they serve as effective barriers to the fulfillment of desire, and also as strong intensifiers of it. In a curious way, they even elevate Gatsby's love of Daisy and, while it lasts, Daisy's love of Gatsby.

More than any of his contemporaries with the exception of Faulkner, Fitzgerald made the history and myths of the United States – promises kept and betrayed – his own. Even late in his life, amid mounting despair, he could write words such as these:

France was a land, England a people, but America, having about it still that quality of the idea, was harder to utter – it was the graves at Shiloh and the tired, drawn, nervous faces of its great men, and the country boys dying in the Argonne for a phrase that was empty before their bodies withered. It was a willingness of the heart.

One source of exuberance that comes through in his fiction, especially his short fiction, flowed from the satisfaction he took in knowing that some people who had been excluded had finally got into the money, the excitement, and the spotlight of celebrity. Fitzgerald became the voice of the "Jazz Age" and the poet of the big, conspicuously expensive party. Yet he retained what he called a "presentiment of disaster" that had several sources, including his sense that his partylike world was too mercurial to last, that its boom, like his own rise, was "unnatural."

During the Great War, Fitzgerald served a stint in the army at a base in Kansas, where Dwight D. Eisenhower was his commanding officer, and one in Alabama, where he met Zelda Sayre. But the war, which was for him more a lark than an ordeal, hovers over his fiction. "All my beautiful lovely safe world blew itself up here with a great gust of high explosive love," Dick Diver says to Rosemary Hoyt during a tour of Europe's battlefields in *Tender is the Night* (1934). "This land here cost twenty lives a foot that summer," he says a bit earlier.

See that little stream – we could walk to it in two minutes. It took the British a month to walk to it – a whole empire walking very slowly, dying in front and pushing forward behind. And another empire walked very slowly backward a few inches a day, leaving the dead like a million bloody rugs.

In *The Great Gatsby*, the war enters as a moment of recognition between Gatsby and Carraway. But the desperation that Fitzgerald directly knew finds expression in frenetic parties that are built around the desire to say yes to money and pleasure and no to moral restraints. He and Zelda were by turn romantic lovers, glamorous dreamers, and rootless, world-weary lost souls. Their extravagances were told and retold in the gossip columns of the magazines and newspapers as well as the memoirs and fiction of their era, including Carl Van Vechten's *Parties* (1930). It was a part of their mystique that they always said no to the mores of the past and never said no to a party, a drink, or a dalliance. Yet both of them were too sensitive and vulnerable, and in ironic ways too old-fashioned, not to sense that they might have to pay a high price for their extravagant goings-on. By 1930, when Fitzgerald said we have "no ground under our feet," their presentiments had become facts.

Jay Gatsby, a veteran of the Great War, lives in a "gross, materialistic, careless society of coarse wealth spread on top of a sterile world," to borrow a line from *Tales of the Jazz Age*. And it is a world where almost all values seem to be dying. What sets him slightly apart from other characters – the Buchanans, the Wilsons, Jordan Baker, Nick Carraway, and Meyer Wolfsheim, a co-conspirator in fixing the 1919 World Series – is his "heightened sensitivity to the promises of life," a "romantic readiness," a "gift for hope." Gatsby springs, we learn, not from his poor immigrant parents named Gatz and his lowly birth in the Midwest, but from his Platonic conception of himself. In his commitment to self-invention, he makes contact with a tradition, dating back to the Renaissance, that has helped to shape modern lives in history as well as fiction. "In any real sense of the word," the British drama critic Kenneth Tynan once remarked, turning his back on his birth in Birmingham, April 2, 1927, "I was born at Oxford." "I have no more connection with my early life and Birmingham than I have with Timbuctoo."

Although Jay Gatsby is almost an "Oxford man," he takes his own practical methods of self-fashioning from Benjamin Franklin's *Autobiography*, as seen in his "SCHEDULE" of self-improvement, dated September 12, 1906, that as a boy he copied on the flyleaf of a "ragged old copy of a book called Hopalong Cassidy." "'I came across this book by accident,'" Gatsby's father says to Nick Carraway, holding it, not wanting to close it. "'Jimmy was bound to get ahead. He always had some resolves like this or something.'" But Gatsby takes his romantic self-conception, as opposed to his social, pragmatic one, from versions of national dreams that owe as much to Hopalong Cassidy as to Benjamin Franklin. Born James Gatz, son of "shiftless and unsuccessful farm people" from the Midwest, he becomes Jay Gatsby, heir of the nation's promise. Unlike Carrie Madenda, who recounts nothing of her past,

Jay Gatsby recalls his only as he has fabricated it. The vagueness with which he presents himself leaves us as well as Carraway to imagine most of his history. Yet his restraint reinforces the strange kind of authenticity that defines him – in which he pays homage to high culture without falsely claiming it. "'They're real,'" says the little owl-eyed man of the books in Gatsby's library. "'See!' he cried triumphantly. 'It's a bonafide piece of printed matter. It fooled me. This fella's a regular Belasco. It's a triumph. What thoroughness! What realism! Knew when to stop too – didn't cut the pages.'" Near the end of one of his parties we see Gatsby the perfect "figure of the host," standing with his hand lifted "in a formal gesture of farewell" that he has picked up somewhere along the way. He remains vague about how he amassed his fortune in part because it is a quintessential American fortune: money got no matter how for the purpose of rising in a society that worships it. But he also remains secretive about the larger dream that he has pieced together from his nation's past. From moment to moment, he reflects the blend of confidence and insecurity that marks him as a "nobody" who has become a "star."

When Nick Carraway first realizes that Gatsby's mansion is situated across the bay from Daisy's home not by "strange coincidence" but by design, Gatsby's life takes on new shape. "He came alive to me," Carraway says, "delivered suddenly from the womb of his purposeless splendor." Both an "appalling sentimentality," associated with his romantic side, and an appalling materialism, born of his utilitarian individualism, touch almost everything Gatsby says and does. Yet we also hear in his words echoes of "an elusive rhythm, a fragment of lost words" heard long ago, that date back to the dreams and letters of the original discoverers and settlers of the New World. Like the silence in which he often moves, his sentimentality and his materialism evoke a dream to which his plan – to make millions, buy a mansion, and win Daisy Buchanan away from Tom Buchanan – remains an inadequate correlative. The secret to Gatsby's failure lies, however, only in part in the inadequacy of his dream and his plan for realizing it, both of which, like him, always just miss "being absurd." It also lies in the fact that his world, which pretends to be receptive to dreamers, in fact protects those who have been born to riches and power.

The Great Gatsby is in part a regional story of displaced Midwesterners who come East, where the action is, and then discover a world so corrupt that it kills Gatsby, among others, and sends Carraway back home, hoping to find a world that still stands at moral attention. But it is also a story of class conflict between "little" people who yearn to enter the privileged world of wealth, power, and status, and "big" people like Daisy and Tom Buchanan who have been born into that world and have no intention of relinquishing their hold on it. The "very rich . . . are different from you and me," Fitzgerald had written in "The Rich Boy." "Yes," Hemingway replied snidely, "they have more money." But Fitzgerald was right. The very rich of the twenties were set apart by their determination to claim as their own the right of casual indifference to the consequences of their actions. Having made themselves models to be emulated, they became expert in protecting themselves from the competition of those who tried it. As members of the first generation to have grown up with what Caspar W. Whitney called (in 1894) "the blessings of the country club," that "really American institution," Tom, Daisy, and their golfing friend Jordan Baker assume that they have a right to spend vast sums of money without even pretending to make any. And if wealth is one of their entitlements, power is another. Nick Carraway, who has been born into a privileged class but has been left no real money and so must work, is marginal by fate as well as disposition. He is related to Daisy and, like Tom, is "a Yale man." But he lives in a small house on the edge of Gatsby's estate and is employed handling the stocks and bonds of the very rich.

As poorly born, we may assume, as James Gatz, Myrtle and George Wilson live and work in the "valley of ashes," in an apartment above their garage: "Repairs. George B. Wilson. Cars bought and sold. – " Unlike her already defeated husband, Myrtle still hopes to enter the rich, exciting world of the Buchanans. Though she differs from Gatsby on many counts, she too is full of yearning; and she too learns that the glamorous world she longs to enter knows how to exploit her but remains indifferent to her. Gatsby seeks to reconstitute his life by bringing it into accord with a dream he possesses in haunting if degraded form. Myrtle Wilson simply wants to enter the heedless, selfish world of the very rich. As it turns out, however, the two things she and Gatsby share (their impoverished beginnings and their acquired hopes) are larger determinants of life, and thus of fate, than the different textures of their dreams. Gatsby's dream comes more from his culture's past, Myrtle's from its present. But they pay the same high price for being presumptuous – for wanting, as Daisy Buchanan says of Gatsby, "too much." Myrtle dies as the hit-and-run victim of Daisy's careless driving; Gatsby dies as the victim of George Wilson's mistaken revenge after Tom and Daisy conspire to protect Daisy by telling Wilson "the truth": that Gatsby is the owner of the car that killed Myrtle.

Nick Carraway, another privileged survivor, remains marginal to the end, and then returns to the Midwest with a story to tell. The Buchanans, however, walk away unscathed, Daisy looking for another party, Tom for another polo match:

It was all very careless and confused. They were careless people, Tom and Daisy – they smashed up things and creatures and then retreated back into their money or their vast carelessness, or whatever it was that kept them together, and let other people clean up the mess they had made.

Tom epitomizes an aristocracy of such wealth and power that it can afford to be careless as well as narrowly self-interested. When he disappears from our sight, both his string of polo ponies and his prejudices, which involve gender and race as well as class, remain intact – and so too does his not quite articulated assumption that people like Jay Gatsby and Myrtle Wilson have been put on earth to entertain him, and people like George Wilson, to run his errands. "That fellow had it coming to him," he says to Carraway about Gatsby. "He threw dust into your eyes just like he did in Daisy's" – trying to convince Carraway that as a threat to their status and power Gatsby had to be taken care of. Daisy, though far more winning than Tom, rediscovers her dependence on him and so moves inevitably toward the moment when she imitates his carelessness and then becomes his willing co-conspirator in self-protective deceit and crime. In killing Gatsby, Wilson betrays Myrtle, to whom he wants to remain loyal, and serves Tom and Daisy, his own and his wife's twin destroyers. He remains to the end a bland, ineffectual, nondescript, almost ghostlike creature who acts decisively only when he acts as a tool of the rich. He thus suffers an extreme version of the fate that Sherwood Anderson rejected and that George Babbitt halfheartedly resists.

The Great Gatsby owes some of its staying power to the way in which it presents the twenties as a deeply "American" decade. In addition, it draws on the texture and plot of a story – that of the young man from the provinces – which, as Lionel Trilling observed, has figured prominently both in history and in the novel since the late eighteenth century. By presenting Gatsby's story through the mind and voice of Nick Carraway, however, Fitzgerald distances himself from his novel and also establishes several sets of tensions: between the East and the Midwest; between a world of grim, ashen poverty and one of careless, ruthless wealth; between Gatsby's dream and Myrtle's yearning; between a past in which the United States inspired the poor to dream and then gave them space in which to live their dreams and a present in which it manipulates the hope-driven energies of the poor while offering them little or no chance of sharing its rewards; and, thus, between an era in which the American dream remained an enabling myth and one in which it often functioned as a cultural lie. Carraway possesses the special self-consciousness of one who is aware that history, however lost or forgotten it may be, continues to shape the present. At scattered points within the novel, and especially in the frame provided by its first two pages and its last page, he evokes a historical context for his readers, or more precisely, as if for his readers, as a surrogate historian who is also a surrogate artist. He thus brings imagination into the novel as a faculty that is always moral and historical as well as aesthetic, complicit as well as provisionally independent, and shared as well as personal. Jay Gatsby is a failure who dies, but *The Great Gatsby* remains his story in part because his effort to recreate himself in an overdetermined world allies him with both the narrator and the author of his story. Gatsby knows that it is meaning he seeks, not mere facts. He senses, too, that society should function as a repository of noncoercive codes and models that transform facts into meaning. He even senses that no simple sequence, taxonomy, or hierarchy for arranging facts will suffice to meet his needs for meaning. And so he fashions a dream — made up of models, charts, and lost fragments of words — on the basis of which he tries to fashion a life.

For Gatsby and Carraway, *The Great Gatsby* accordingly becomes a story about several forms of resistance. For Tom Buchanan, a truly modern, nomadic ex-Midwesterner, it is a story about power. Though obtuse about many things, Tom possesses a bone-deep understanding of the centripetal forces that dominate his world. Power-smart as well as power-hungry, he focuses his resistance on those — Gatsby and the Wilsons, and now and again Carraway and Daisy — who threaten his domination either by trying to turn back the clock ("Of course, you can," Gatsby says, hoping to undo events that have made Tom triumphant) or by trying to wrest control from him. Despite occasional setbacks, furthermore, Tom wins every contest he enters, including the one for Daisy. As a result, the hope held out to us in *The Great Gatsby* is hauntingly limited. It is aesthetic, insofar as Carraway learns imperfectly how to make something of an inadequate past and present; and, to a lesser degree, it is moral, as we see in Carraway's mixed efforts to wrestle with moral issues. But the novel's hope is not in any larger sense historical. The possibility that Daisy might claim independent control of her own life never enters the picture. She and Tom move on as though Jay Gatsby and Myrtle and George Wilson had never existed, without even attending their funerals.

Jay Gatsby is not, however, a victim of Tom Buchanan alone. We may think of Franklin's *Autobiography* as in part a story of how one man learned to protect himself from his culture by running away from his home in Boston and by learning to keep his own counsel, protect his privacy, and make his way without accepting either his society's sexual mores, stressing monogamy, or its economic imperative, stressing the need of men to go on making more and more money. Similarly, we may think of Hopalong Cassidy, Gatsby's other model, as a modern knight of the plains whose life is informed by a romantic code of honor and gallantry. But the chief cultural work of these models – one a social pragmatist, the other a romantic idealist – as played out in Gatsby's life, is to make him vulnerable to the machinations of the rich. In particular, they make him an easy victim of Tom Buchanan, which is to say that they serve the nation's moneyed classes. Myrtle's dream, of marrying into wealth and power, is no less literary than Gatsby's; its origins are less specific only because they are newer. It serves the same class that Gatsby's serves, and it leads to the same end.

Virtually ignoring Myrtle Wilson, whose manner, dress, speech, and dreams continue to reflect her lower-class origins, Nick Carraway overcomes his snobbish scorn for Jay Gatsby and "takes care" of him by trying to elevate his story. In the process, however, he simplifies it, in part because he wants to contain as well as celebrate Gatsby. As Carraway's voice becomes more intrusive, particularly in the novel's first and last pages, Gatsby's resistance becomes more a grand gesture. Only by altering Carraway's voice do Gatsby's subversive hopes survive. At times his story also seems used by his cultural models – Franklin's schedule, Hopalong Cassidy's code, and his mentor's (Dan Cody by resonant name) example. Finally, however, Gatsby's story uses them as it uses Carraway's voice. To the end, Jay Gatsby goes on struggling for, as well as with, James Gatz and the cultural models given him, and for, as well as with, Daisy and Nick, in a never completely lost contest with Tom Buchanan, in which a part of Fitzgerald's art, and almost silently, Myrtle and George Wilson's lives, are also joined.

6

❦

THE FEAR OF FEMINIZATION AND THE
LOGIC OF MODEST AMBITION

AT TIMES Fitzgerald and his contemporaries gained enough perspective on their sense of feeling dispossessed to recognize it as an old story – as we see, for example, in Glenway Wescott's *Goodbye, Wisconsin* (1928), where displaced Midwesterners become "a sort of vagrant chosen race like the Jews." But for the most part they left such ties unexplored. Rather than reach out to recent immigrants, women, or African Americans, they remained almost as jealous of their status and control as Tom Buchanan is of his. Cowley notes, for example, that "the admired writers of the generation were men in the great majority" and adds that they were also "white, middle-class, mostly Protestant by upbringing, and mostly English and Scottish by descent," without stopping to wonder whether such a configuration was more created than given and, if created, by whom and in whose interests and, further, why, once created, it gained such easy acceptance in the United States during Coolidge's presidency. In the process, he ignores issues that now leap out at us.

Cowley's "admired writers" thought of themselves as rejecting the prejudices and provincialisms of their day. They bemoaned the Senate's acts in the aftermath of the war; denounced the KKK, the Red Scare, and the persecution of Sacco and Vanzetti; and condemned the vulgar materialism and ruthless profiteering of businessmen. Such pronouncements fit their sense of themselves as an oppressed minority of cultural loyalists. Yet many writers, including some Cowley admired, harbored and even expressed versions of the ambitions and prejudices they thought of themselves as rebelling against, a fact that may help to explain why their society rewarded them in ways that it did not reward black writers of Harlem, Jewish writers of New York's East Side, or women writers anywhere, from New Orleans to Chicago to New York to Paris, many of whom it pushed into the marginalized tasks of running bookstores, editing small journals, and writing diaries.

In *The New Negro: An Interpretation* (1925), Alain Locke and his collaborators – including Jean Toomer, Zora Neale Hurston, Countee Cullen, Claude McKay, James Weldon Johnson, Langston Hughes, W. E. B. Du Bois, and

Jessie Fauset – declare the language of race to be a part of the nation's strategy of subjugation, and then they work to overturn it by exploring the moral authority and aesthetic possibilities of imposed marginality. In Harlem, a growing number of artists were working to make the diversity of African American life visible. Important political organizations, such as Marcus Garvey's Universal Negro Improvement Association, flourished side by side with writers like Cullen, Hughes, Hurston, Johnson, Toomer, and Nella Larsen. But most white writers who ventured into Harlem regarded the lives and the culture of people of color as exotic, if not comic, profligate, or primitive. The language of race thrived in the twenties, and it worked to denigrate as well as marginalize recent immigrants as well as black writers.

In "The American Sense of Humor" (1910), Katherine Roof articulates a set of propositions that found an expanding audience in the twenties, and she does so by locating another threat. The "American mind," Roof said, was becoming "more forceful perhaps in certain ways, but of coarser grain" because of "the tremendous influx of Continental foreigners," who represent "the raw and often the waste material of the countries they came from" and who possess "minds of a different color." Such people remain "essentially un-American" even after a generation or two, she notes, in terms that bear striking resemblance to statements made by prominent leaders like Madison Grant, Lothrop Stoddard, Hiram Wesley Evans, and A. Mitchell Palmer. In such discourse, immigrants, whom Santayana had praised as the most restless, energetic, and adventuresome people in the world, come to us as the world's refuse.

Civilization in the United States (1923), edited by Harold Stearns, consists of thirty-three essays that variously decry the "emotional and aesthetic starvation" of the nation. In an effort to call people back to their historic destiny, writers like Van Wyck Brooks, Lewis Mumford, H. L. Mencken, John Macy, and George Jean Nathan exhort and blame, warning their readers that the nation's materialism, cultural incoherence, and anti-intellectualism must be overcome. What is most remarkable about *Civilization in the United States*, however, aside from the exuberance of its disappointment, are the two scapegoats it singles out. One is the Puritan: the repressed pioneer gobbling up land now transformed into a repressed businessman gobbling up money and power. The other is woman, as we see especially in Stearns's indictment of the intellectual life of the United States, where women are depicted as feminizing social life:

When Professor Einstein roused the ire of the women's clubs by stating that "women dominate the entire life of America," and that "there are cities with a million population, but cities suffering from terrible poverty – the poverty of intellectual things," he was but repeating a criticism of our life now old enough to be almost a *cliché*. Hardly any intelligent foreigner has failed to observe and comment upon the extraordinary feminization of American social life, and oftenest he has coupled this observation with a few biting remarks concerning the intellectual anaemia or torpor that seems to accompany it.

Elsewhere in *Civilization in the United States*, in an essay on sex, Elsie Clews Parsons notes "the commonly observed spirit of isolation or antagonism between the sexes" and urges better understanding. But Stearns's sense of the debilitating influence of women on culture, and his corresponding distress before the sad plight of the male intellectual in the United States, rules out rapprochement. Men have finally realized, he asserts, that what women seek is total domination: "Where men and women in America to-day share their intellectual life on terms of equality and perfect understanding, closer examination reveals that the phenomenon is not a sharing but a capitulation. The men have been feminized."

The consequences are, of course, terrible, both for men and for culture. "I have by implication rather than direct statement contrasted genuine interest in intellectual things with the kind of intellectual life led by women," Stearns writes. Women, he concludes, are too preoccupied with "one's enlarged social self" to resonate to the "mystery of life," too self-involved to be disinterested, and too utilitarian to be metaphysical. As a result, they diminish everything they touch. They turn intellectual life into an "instrument of moral reform," leaving culture "crippled and sterile," and men repressed and debilitated. Hope lies, accordingly, not in the liberation of women but in the liberation of culture from women and the "dull standardization" that they force upon it, turning it into a "spiritual prison."

If the anxieties present in Stearns's essay had been his alone, they would require little comment. But the language of male anxiety was almost as widespread as the language of race; and among intellectuals, it was more respectable. It found expression, furthermore, not only in books but also in the limited roles that women were allowed to play in professional organizations, on college campuses, and in literary circles. A woman who did not know how to cook, announced Edward Bok, editor of *Ladies' Home Journal*, simply lacked the "real knowledge that every normal woman should possess." Women who sought "Higher Education," said Charles William Eliot, president of Harvard, should be content with learning things that contributed to the "improvement of family life." American literature is being "strangled with a petticoat," Joseph Hergesheimer announced in 1921 in the *Yale Review*, in an essay titled "The Feminine Nuisance in American Literature." Echoing Stearns and Hergesheimer, Robert Herrick wrote three essays in *Bookman* (in December

1928, March 1929, and July 1929), urging men to resist "the feminization of our literature" and reassert the values of masculine culture. The "penalty" of feminization, he concluded in his third essay, "in art as in nature is sterility, extinction." The protagonist of Edmund Wilson's *I Thought of Daisy* (1929) thinks of himself as a literary rebel who wants "to leave behind the constraints" of middle-class society and the "shame of not making money." But he also conceives his "whole life" as a protest against "those forces of conservatism and inertia" that women epitomize. Seven years later, John Crowe Ransom wrote a piece called "The Poet as Woman," later reprinted in *The World's Body* (1938), echoing Stearns. Since women are "indifferent to intellectuality," he asserts, they are "safer as a biological organism."

Before the war, suffrage had become a rallying cry for men as well as women. With the war and suffrage won, many women hoped to move from success to success in reconstituting society. But they quickly found themselves reassigned to traditional roles as defined by people like Bok and Eliot. Dorothy Canfield Fisher's novel *The Home-Maker* (1924) is built around the difficulties that Evangeline and Lester Knapp face – and the lies they must tell and try to shape their lives by – in order to defy tradition: the notion that men have been put "in the world to get possessions, to create material things, to see them, to buy them, to transport them" and that women have been put in it to nurture children and take care of their homes and husbands. But defiance of the sort practiced by the Knapps – in which Lester becomes a happy, competent housekeeper and homemaker, and Evangeline becomes an ambitious, successful, and fulfilled businesswoman – remained rare in art as well as life. And when it occurred, it sometimes drew fire from women as well as men. Some younger women advocated sexual freedom and even practiced it. But most older women opposed it, and some, especially those accustomed to thinking of women as purer than men – not so much repressed as blessed in being less passionately endowed – regarded the new sexuality, epitomized by the flapper, as a betrayal of a trust sanctioned by nature, culture, and God. Even efforts to find common ground in a war to obliterate prostitution and poverty proved disappointing. "I know of no woman who has a following of other women," said Democratic committeewoman Emily Newell Blair, nor any "politician who is afraid of the woman vote on any question under the sun."

In 1792, responding to Rousseau, Mary Wollstonecraft wrote *A Vindication of the Rights of Women*. Her aim, she said, was to give women power "over themselves," not "power over men." But male fear of being engulfed and displaced, having declined during the Lyric Years, flourished in the twenties. In James Branch Cabell's *Jurgen* (1919), a failed poet is carried back to youth with his middle-aged frustrations intact. For Jurgen shares not only the era's infatuation with youth but also its conviction that women enforce taboos invented by their mothers for the purpose of manipulating or even crippling men. The only women interested in recognizing and meeting Jurgen's deepest needs are figments of his aging, lecherous imagination. His story, which is clearly allied with pornography, displays throughout a thinly veiled hostility toward women. In 1932 the implications of that convergence gained further clarity in Nathanael West's *Miss Lonelyhearts.* The "lady" writers that West's male writers complain about bear such suggestive names as Mary Roberts Wilcox and Ella Wheeler Catheter. What they need, the reporters agree, is a "good rape."

What writers of the twenties feared in any further move of women into the world of literature and art, especially as makers of major novels and poems, was both social displacement and renewed impugning of their besieged masculinity. For two hundred years, since the day in Boston when Benjamin Franklin's father "saved" him from being a poet, business and politics had been generally regarded as proper work for men in the United States, culture and family as the proper concerns of women. Even in London, Ford Madox Ford remarked, "a man of letters [was] regarded as something less than a man." Such breathing room as existed in an increasingly materialistic society required that men retain their status as makers of art and that women content themselves with being helpmates, caretakers, and consumers of it. As pressure from women mounted, resistance in men deepened. "I was never a member of [the] 'lost generation,' " Louise Bogan observed, looking back on the twenties from the thirties. Soon women like Bogan found themselves forming enclaves within enclaves, in Paris as well as New York. In her Paris letters, Janet Flanner, Paris correspondent for the *New Yorker*, writes more as a sojourner or guest in the republic of letters than as a citizen, and more as an interested yet detached observer of the literary scene than as a full-fledged participant in it.

During the twenties, no black writer and no recent immigrant made it into Cowley's group of "admired writers." But one woman, Gertrude Stein, did, as one of the least conventional, most experimental writers of her time. Unlike her unconventional and experimental precursor Emily Dickinson, who never left home, Stein left the United States for Europe, as did Djuna Barnes, Natalie Barney, Sylvia Beach, Caresse Crosby, H. D., Janet Flanner, Jane Heap, Mina Loy, and Anaïs Nin, to name a few. What links many women writers of the twenties, however, in addition to the drift of their lives, is a haunting discrepancy between their very considerable creative talents and their stifled as well as neglected talents. Those who managed to break through to expression tended, like Nin and Flanner, to excel in marginal genres or, like H. D. and Stein, to become self-consciously and even aggressively experimental.

Gertrude Stein knew one big thing: that the twentieth century differed radically from the nineteenth less because of its discoveries and the things it knew to be new than because of its losses – the things it no longer knew or had decided deliberately to forget. She found her own voice by perfecting her role as enthusiastic anarchist. A champion of the new, she remained clear that the only forms of stability that her world permitted were contrived and, indeed, provisional, which is to say illusory. "Let no one think that anything has come to stay," she said. A restless searcher, she persisted in trying to reshape everything she could find – from strange, erotic, and forbidden experiences to "the language of dishes and daylight" – into sentences that are sometimes abstract and hermetic and sometimes simple and lucid. Her barbed opinions about food and parties, paintings and painters, writing and writers made her famous. A year after she published *The Autobiography of Alice B. Toklas* (1933), which is filled with witty and sometimes scathing judgments, a group of Parisian writers and artists countered with *Testimony Against Gertrude Stein.* But Stein recognized her opinions for what they were – temporary, improvised certainties – and so attributed real but limited value to them. "You see why they talk to me," she said, explaining her success in conducting a seminar at the University of Chicago in 1934, "is that I am like them I do not know the answer. . . . I do not even know whether there is a question let alone having answers for a question." "What is the answer?" she asked on her deathbed, just before her remarkable energies failed completely, and hearing no answer murmured, "In that case, what is the question?"

Stein's world is full of clauses and phrases strung together one after another without coordinating or subordinating connectives for the same reason that it is full of gerunds: because it is a world in which nothing – neither things perceived nor the consciousness that apprehends them, neither the moment of apprehension nor the fluid words in which an apprehension is rendered – stands still. Using various abstract ideas and hermetic codes, she makes art a celebration of the "thing seen at the moment it is seen" in order to force us to examine relations not simply between things and words but also among the processes of the world, the processes of consciousness, and the processes of composition. One result was a radical redefinition of the relation between the writing-speaking subject and the absorbing-transforming reader by making the process of reading, as another process of consciousness, a process of recomposition. "I had in hundreds of ways related words, then sentences then paragraphs to the thing at which I was looking," she said, without adding that she had also broken most known rules governing punctuation and syntax and many governing diction, both as a part of her effort to make things new and as a part of her effort to draw readers into the process of renewal. The playfulness of her mind comes through in everything from her subtle ways of interlacing sexuality and writing to her aggressive ways of making us pay close attention to even the simplest words.

The verbal dexterity of Stein's art – which enables her to move back and forth between the familiar and the strange, and between a rage for order and a love of fluidity – is characteristically devoted to locating what she calls the "bottom nature" of our shifting identities as human beings. She uses familiar and often monosyllabic words to confront us with fundamental distinctions, between being and remembering, for example, or between consciousness and self-consciousness, or between both of these and the process of fashioning a self. We see this when she invites us to add commas to lines like this one from *What Are Masterpieces* (1940) – "At any moment when you are you[,] you are you without the memory of yourself because[,] if you remember yourself while you are you[,] you are not for the purpose of creating you" – and then reminds us that what we have done is arbitrary as well as plausible.

It is probably not too much to say of such sentences, first, that no other writer of Stein's time could have written them, though many learned from them, sometimes by writing poorly disguised imitations; and second, that a battery of marginalizing forces – being a Jew, being an American in Paris, being a lesbian, and, especially, being a woman – helped to shape the mind and imagination that formed these words, but that none of these was more important than being a female artist in a world dominated by male artists. In Stein's work, as in that of Edith Wharton and Ellen Glasgow, two versions of the self – a voluntarist self devoted to working in culture and creating it, and a determinist self concerned with its status as a victim of a rigidly gendered society – contend with one another. In her stylistic idiosyncrasies, Stein plays with her sense of herself and her work as, paradoxically, at once marginal and central. In a similar move, she plays with a notion crucial to modernism, where surface complexity vies with formal coherence, tentatively endorsing and directly challenging a notion that later found expression in the New Criticism – namely, that the reader's proper task is to ensure that coherence triumphs over complexity.

Juggling words in ways that defied conventions which, among other things, gendered them in advance, Stein fashioned an art whose dialectical dexterity embraced its own predicament and processes. From *Three Lives* (1909), where we see "realism" and "naturalism" in a process of decomposition, through the verbal collage of *Tender Buttons* (1914) and *The Making of Americans* (1925) to *What Are Masterpieces* and *Wars I Have Seen* (1945), no writer remained more persistent and few were more inventive in finding ways of displaying the determined efforts of an impacted consciousness to achieve a liberating understanding of itself. In *The Geological History of America* (1936), Stein insists that in the modern world "the important literary thinking is done by a woman" because she believed that, as a woman writer who was both Jewish and lesbian and who had lived in exile, she understood both the forces that affected freedom and the costs of being determined to achieve it. In her art, she authorizes the eye and the conscious mind to dominate the ear and the unconscious mind because she regarded control as essential to the freedom that remained her cause. Similarly she celebrates our human need for invention by inventing in ways that call attention both to the process of invention and especially to her activity as an artist engaged, playfully and seriously, in the act of inventing. In her hands invention as consciousness's imposition of meaning becomes, clandestinely, an invitation extended to the reader to join in the act of invention which for her always begins with an act of consciousness. She knew, furthermore, that the act of invention, or at least the illusion of it, was a necessary fiction to the reader-critic-interpreter as well as the writer. In this, her world resembles the one Jorge Luis Borges locates in a fragment of Heraclitus: "You shall not go down twice to the same river." We admire the dexterity of this line, Borges observes, "because the ease with which we accept the first meaning ('The river is different') clandestinely imposes upon us the second ('I am different') and grants us the illusion of having invented it."

In *Wars I Have Seen*, Stein uses what she called the "continuous present" to replace the notion of history as a story of decline or advance. She rejects these views, however, not simply in order to incorporate the past into the present, though there is an imperial aspect to what she does, nor merely in order to remind us that the past is always with us and that it is always being modified by the actions of the living, though she clearly wants to do this too, but also in order to free us from all nostalgic, determinist, and utopian views of history. Her mythmaking cannot be nostalgic, if only because as a woman she does not think of herself as possessing a golden age to look backward to with longing; and she remains skeptical of great conquests, the stuff of progress, because she sees women as always lined up among the dispossessed. In brief, she remains skeptical of all familiar orderings of history. Yet she rejects historical determinism because she wants to preserve the possibility that art can be transformational, if not revolutionary.

The expectations – literary as well as social – that enwrapped women of the twenties were no less confining for being the opposite of great, as Stein clearly understood. One expectation, the more sinister for being unexamined, was that women should write, as they should live, in a minor key, by keeping journals or writing "sentimental" novels or "sweet" lyrics about "domestic" affairs. "She is feminine," Robert Spiller's *Literary History of the United States*

(1948) later reported of Marianne Moore, "in a very rewarding sense, in that she makes no effort to be major" – a formulation that perpetuates attitudes that flourished in the twenties. Women who modestly conformed to such expectations, or at least appeared to do so, could safely be praised as authors of minor masterpieces; those who refused, like Stein, were likely to be thought of as strange aberrations, roles some of them took delight, and others refuge, in playing. In Anaïs Nin's *Diaries* (1966–74), we witness an unresolved tension between the desire to express herself in a major key, by establishing herself as subject, which men as different as James Joyce and Henry Miller were able to do in their fiction, and the pressure to meet social expectations by giving up any attempt to be major and, thus, any attempt to be a subject. Nin clearly understands which of these alternatives is culturally sanctioned for women. She also recognizes that conformity holds out the promise of acceptance as well as limited recognition – rewards that are psychological, social, and economic. The alternative, of seeking independent status and recognition as an artist and colleague among artists and colleagues, she clearly recognizes as culturally off-limits, as she signaled by showing only selected portions of her diaries to men. "There is not much future in men being friends with great women," Hemingway later remarked in *A Moveable Feast* (1964), reiterating his version of male anxiety as though it were a law of nature; "and there is usually even less future with truly ambitious women writers."

7

MARGINALITY AND AUTHORITY / RACE, GENDER, AND REGION

THE RESEMBLANCES that might have fostered recognitions among writers of the twenties – white of black and male of female – worked more often to divide them. Cowley's group of "admired writers" coveted the power that accompanied recognition, and once they had achieved it, they held tightly to it. But they also wanted to claim as their own the sense of being marginalized. "That was always my experience," Fitzgerald observed in 1938: "a poor boy in a rich town; a poor boy in a rich boy's school; a poor boy in a rich man's club at Princeton. . . . I have never been able to forgive the rich for being rich, and it has colored my entire life and works." Ten years earlier, T. S. Eliot had written Herbert Read, giving his twist to the experience of being an outsider:

Some day I want to write an essay about the point of view of an American who wasn't an American, because he was born in the South and went to school in New England as a small boy with a nigger drawl, but wasn't a southerner in the South because his people were northerners in a border state and looked down on all southerners and Virginians, and who so was never anything anywhere and who therefore felt himself to be more a Frenchman than an American and more an Englishman than a Frenchman and yet felt that the U.S.A. up to a hundred years ago was a family extension.

Several things leap out of Fitzgerald's and, especially, Eliot's words, including a whole range of exclusionary principles – money and position; gender, race, region, and dialect; and a sense of moral, cultural, and racial superiority and condescension. Submerged in all of them, however, for both writers, is recognition that marginal voices possess special authority. Eliot, who was at least as patrician by heritage and experience as a writer like Fitzgerald wanted to be, nevertheless claims for himself the experience of being excluded: of being looked down on and even, if we take full measure of his racial slur, of feeling despised and of being forced to see himself, as W. E. B. Du Bois had put it, in anger, pity, fear, and contempt, "only through the eyes of others" who possess some inherited, unearned cultural authority.

Behind the persistence with which writers like Fitzgerald and Eliot exaggerated their own marginalizing pressures lay more than the familiar desire to think of themselves as self-made or, more radically, as self-originating. Grave differences in personal experience separated them from black women writers like Nella Larsen, Jessie Fauset, and Zora Neale Hurston. But Fitzgerald and Eliot claimed the experience of being excluded because they thought it charged with creative potential. In this move, their mood was more imperial than conciliatory. Actually feeling despised might be painful and even humiliating, but claiming it could spur creative response, based on recognizing oneself in despised others, and despised others in oneself.

Like the boundaries governing race and gender, the regional boundaries that continued to divide the nation – putting the Midwest in competition with the East and the South at odds with the North, which from the South's vantage point included the upper Midwest as an already incorporated extension of the East – correlated with privilege and subjugation. After the Civil War, sectionalism had dissolved into competition among regions because, as William Dean Howells saw, in losing the political power to declare themselves separate nations, New England and the Midwest as well as the South had forfeited the hope of perpetuating distinctive cultures. "New England has ceased to be a nation unto itself," Howells wrote, in *Literary Friends and Acquaintances* (1900), and so has lost the chance of having "anything like a national literature." For a time, the South, stubborn as well as abject in defeat, tried to hold on to its identity; even the distinction of being defeated, it decided, was better than no distinction at all. And New England – hoping to claim the spoils of victory without succumbing to the centripetal forces that had made victory possible – tried vainly to cling to a sense of itself as distinctive. But eventually both regions discovered that the nation's new political economy would eventually mean the end of their cultural independence as distinct regions.

During the late nineteenth and early twentieth centuries, writers of the South and the Midwest as well as New England continued to draw on fading regional folkways, hoping to delay homogenization. New England tended to look down on other regions of the United States as England had once looked down on it – as a dependent colony. Culturally, it remained toward them more imperial than conciliatory. While Sarah Orne Jewett worked to preserve the region's "local color," Van Wyck Brooks launched a massive effort to establish New England's literature as "American literature." Like New York, New England continued to function as a cultural magnet. Many writers moved from the Midwest or South to Boston or New York; few moved from Boston or New York to Minnesota or Mississippi. Yet as they became modern cities, Boston became less and less New England's provincial capital; New York, less and less its commercial outlet. New lines of transportation and communication muted regional differences even as they incorporated new territories.

In an era increasingly dominated by cities, New York quickly became the symbol of everything that was new, exciting, alluring, troubling, and confusing. Its skyscrapers, like those of Chicago, became temples to the growing power of people to impose themselves and imprint their will on their world. At some point in its growth, however, scarcely discernible until after it had been passed, New York became not a community but a collection of communities. "London is like a newspaper," Walter Bagehot remarked in 1858, "everything is there, and everything is disconnected" – a remark that fit both New York in the twenties and the magazine it inspired.

Henry Luce (1898–1967) and Briton Hadden (1898–1929), classmates at Yale, first planned to call their magazine *Facts* and then decided on *Time*. *Time* would be adapted to the "TIME" that "BUSY MEN" could give to keeping themselves "INFORMED." No "article will be written to prove any special case," Luce and Hadden announced in 1923: "This magazine is not founded to promulgate prejudices, liberal or conservative." In practice, however, *Time* became a collection of unsigned, disconnected essays – "National Affairs" (later "The Nation"), "Foreign News" (later "The World"), "Books," "Art," "The Theater," "Cinema," "Music," "Education," "Religion," "Medicine," "Law," "Science," "Finance" (later divided into "U.S. Business" and "World Business"), "Sport," "The Press," and "Milestones," which featured information about births, marriages, divorces, and deaths of the rich and famous. These diverse elements were held together less by an announced consistency in style ("curt, concise, and complete" was the slogan of *Time*, though not always its practice) than by an unacknowledged ideology. Here, to take one example, is the curt, concise, unprejudiced description in *Time* of one of President Coolidge's trips, complete with echoes of *Hiawatha* (August 29, 1927): "To his haughty redskin brothers, to the haughty strong Sioux nation, with his wife and son beside him, with big medicine in his pocket, came the pale Wamblee-Tokaha, New White Chief and High Protector – otherwise Calvin Coolidge, 29th U.S. President, but first President ever to visit any Amerindians on one of the reservations set aside for them by their Caucasian conquerors."

Like the city of busy men for whom it was designed, *Time* was held together, from section to section and issue to issue, not by human bonds but by a remarkably productive economy and the interests it generated. It gave expression to a people who were morally confused, economically at odds, and yet increasingly interdependent and crowded. If the barrage of overlapping yet competing sights, sounds, and smells of New York intensified one's awareness of oneself as a sentient receiver of impressions, the sheer mass of other people gathered there intensified awareness of oneself as an object of observation, scrutiny, and analysis. At the end of Cummings's *The Enormous Room* (1922), the New York on which the protagonist looks out is filled with "tall, impossibly tall, incomparably tall" buildings that shoulder their way "upward into hard sunlight" and lean "a little through the octaves of its parallel edges"; emitting "noises of America," they throb "with smokes and hurrying dots which are men and which are women and which are things new and curious and hard and strange and vibrant and immense." Writing in Paris in the thirties but drawing on earlier experiences in Berlin as well as on the poetry of Baudelaire, Walter Benjamin noted that cities were teaching people new ways of seeing – reflected not only in impressionist paintings and the movies but also in the avid yet anxious ways in which people hurried about, gazing at the scenes of life. Other very different responses to the barrage of confusing yet exciting, discontinuous yet overlapping impressions and temptations included the rush to receive anonymous advice – in newspaper and magazine columns, for example – and the desire to take refuge in the long, willed sleep, or psychic anesthesia, that we encounter in novels as different as Nathanael West's *Miss Lonelyhearts* (1933) and Robert Penn Warren's *All the King's Men* (1946). By contrast, the second form of new self-consciousness that urban realities fostered – consciousness of oneself as an object of gazing – produced two contrasting results: the hope of being discovered as a star, of movies or sports, for example, and then transformed into a celebrity; and the fear of being exposed as a dangerous rival, an enemy, or a nobody.

In the concise brilliance of *The Great Gatsby*, Fitzgerald traces each of these possibilities: while Jay Gatsby's rise tracks the curve of modern hope, his murder at the hands of a virtual stranger tracks the curve of modern danger. Similarly, if in Sister Carrie's rise we see an early realization of that hope, in her careful retreat from view, when she sits alone, sheltering her life, we sense her recognition of her world's peculiar danger as one in which success and exploitation merge. Thus, in these two characters we observe the matched hopes and fears of the modern world: the hope of discovery and celebrity that inspires a willingness to perform conspicuously, to project oneself forcefully, to make an entrance and become a "somebody" whom strangers whisper about; and the danger of being exposed or recognized not only as a rival or enemy but also as an exploitable resource or commodity, both of which foster the desire to protect one's privacy or, more drastically, to remain anonymous by wearing nondescript and even unisexual uniforms of the day, to go incognito or travel in disguise, in short, to reverse the process of becoming a star and become a nameless, voiceless "nobody." What we observe in the fiction of Fitzgerald no less than in the poetry of Eliot is the sense that urban, mass society calls forth increasingly calculated, self-conscious responses that include both Gatsby's extravagant, audacious performances and Prufrock's painful diffidence and self-abnegation. Gatsby throws grand parties, poses as "the host," seeks to marry the golden princess, and dares to challenge the power of his world; Prufrock wears the uniforms of his class, worries about the appropriateness of his words and the fit of his trousers, fears women, and tries to avoid disturbing his world.

Another innovation owed something to the sheer mass of the city and more to the burgeoning "productive process" that undergirded it. Advertising was spawned as a new industry by a productive process that needed new ways of making itself and its products desirable or even indispensable. "I am in advertising because I believe in business and advertising is the voice of business," Bruce Barton (1886–1967) said. Born in rural Tennessee, where his father was a Congregational minister, Barton acquired in his youth a need to excel and a need to clothe his life with moral purpose. Having thought briefly of becoming a history professor, he drifted into advertising in Chicago, where quick success earned him a trip to New York, the advertising capital of the world. There he wrote advertising copy for Collier's Five-Foot Shelf of Harvard's Classics designed to convince people that Dr. Charles William Eliot, president of Harvard, could give them "the essentials of a liberal education in only 15 minutes a day." Later he wrote several series of inspirational articles for *American Magazine* that became books called *More Power to You* (1917), *Better Days* (1924), and *On the Up and Up* (1929). In addition, he served in Congress, ran for the Senate, and was discussed as a possible presidential candidate. But his genius lay in understanding the role advertising would play in the modern world. "He came as close as anyone will," Alistair Cooke wrote at the time of Barton's death (1967), "to achieving a philosophy of advertising, because he saw the whole of human history as an exercise in persuasion."

Discourse was history for Barton, and history, as we see in his story of the life of Jesus, *The Man Nobody Knows* (1925), was discourse. In *Babbitt* (1922), Lewis presents a parody of a Protestant minister bent on revitalizing religion by allying it with "masculinity" and "business" in editorials called "The Manly Man's Religion" and "The Dollars and Sense Values of Christianity." In this way, "the Reverend John Jemmison Drew, M.A., D.D., LL.D.," hopes to keep "old Satan" from monopolizing "all the pep and punch" of the modern businessman. Earlier, around the time of Barton's birth in 1886, the nineteenth century's long quest for the historical Jesus had culminated in popular interpretations that depicted Him as everything from a bourgeois moralist and a preacher of unforgettable sermons to a peace-loving social democrat and a revolutionary spokesman for the proletariat. In Barton's hands Jesus becomes a Progressive businessman – not a "killjoy" but the world's finest conversationalist and a model interlocutor, and thus "the most popular dinner guest in Jerusalem." Far from being a weak "failure" who must die, Jesus emerges as a practical-minded leader who "picked up twelve men from the bottom ranks of business and forged them into an organization that conquered the world."

First published in serial form in the *Woman's Home Companion*, *The Man Nobody Knows* became a best-seller. Barton was in advertising, he said, because he believed that "the larger development of business and the gradual evolution of its ideals" constituted "the best hope of the world." "Advertising sustains a system that has made us leaders of the free world," he added: "The American Way of Life." Such thinking made Barton a champion of most of the things Lewis satirized, including business and businessmen, promoters and salesmen. For generations, Protestant sons, among others, had been taught that men who produced goods and saved money were culture's true heroes. Barton became a heroic figure by recognizing that the new age of abundance and consumption belonged to the persuasive manner of the salesman and even more the persuasive voice and pen of the ad man. Yet his piety – which he employed in persuading people that Jesus wanted them to enjoy the products of the production system that was drawing them to its cities – was no less fervent for being secular. What he spoke with his mouth and wrote with his pen he witnessed to with his life. He became the persuading "voice of business."

Expansive, unsettled, and dynamic, truly "cinematographic" in its style, New York was prepared to play its role as the new capital of the nation's literature precisely because it was the deregionalized home of Barton's reified message. It drew aspiring writers from across the country, as settlers had once been drawn to the United States, and it gave them temporary homes. It was a world of flats, apartments, and hotels, and it felt as comfortable with change – the flow of the strange and the spectacular, the "tradition of the new" – as it did with its unchallenged position as the seat of capital investment and the center of burgeoning publications and communications industries. In one way or another, virtually every writer of the country had to come to grips with it, not because it nurtured them but because it published them and, even more, because, as a window to the future, it seemed to hold within itself signs of everything that was to be in the century with which they identified.

John Dos Passos was born in a Chicago hotel on January 14, 1896, the illegitimate son of Lucy Addison Sprigg Madison and John Randolph Dos Passos, a wealthy Chicago attorney. Raised by his mother with his father's generous support, Dos Passos lived a comfortable "hotel childhood" that included long stays in Europe. Having prepared in private schools in England and Connecticut, he attended Harvard, where he read Veblen and Dreiser as well as Pater and Flaubert and wrote reviews for the *Harvard Advocate* of John Reed's

Insurgent Mexico as well as the early poetry of Pound and Eliot. By the time he graduated in 1916, he had cultivated three interests – experimental art, history, and reform politics – that gave focus to the rest of his life.

Having opposed the entrance of the United States into World War I, Dos Passos remained skeptical of the "mountain of lies" produced to support it. But the war drew him both as an adventure and as an introduction to the "senseless agony of destruction." "I want to be able to express, later – all of this – all the tragedy and hideous excitement of it. I have experienced so little I must experience more of it, & more. The gray crooked fingers of the dead, the dark look of dirty, mangled bodies." First in *One Man's Initiation: 1917* (1920), then in *Three Soldiers* (1921), and again in *1919* (1932), the second volume of his trilogy *U.S.A.*, Dos Passos focused on "Mr. Wilson's War" with bitter fascination.

In *Manhattan Transfer* (1925), Dos Passos places the impact of World War I against the transformation of the United States from a predominantly rural, agricultural, republican, traditional culture into an increasingly urban, industrial, commercial, centralized, secular, and diverse one. This story, of a changing nation, became the backbone of his best fiction. Sinclair Lewis said of *Manhattan Transfer* that its composition was based on the "technique of the movie, in its flashes, its cut-backs, its speed." And in fact Dos Passos's art bears many traces of the movie, particularly the collage techniques of Sergei Eisenstein and D. W. Griffith, as well as the modern painting to which he was exposed early in life and the modern poetry he began reading in college. The narrative shifts and the absence of transitions, combined with varied engagements with history, which became his trademarks, also have much in common with Pound's *Cantos* (1915–70), Eliot's *The Waste Land* (1922), and Hart Crane's *The Bridge* (1930). In his overwhelmingly urban world, made for and by people, the strange and the familiar intermingle until the distance between the imaginary and the real begins to close, as it does in Freud's theory of the uncanny, where the fulfillment of things wished for becomes terrifying. Later, in *The Culture of Cities* (1938), Lewis Mumford wrote of human desires being transformed into patterns of conduct and systems of control as well as of "signs and symbols" of these things. In Dos Passos's novels, the city consists not only of patterns and systems – marvels of architectural design, civil engineering, social planning, and human governance – but also of noisy, disordered, congested, conflicted scenes in which repressed anxieties and animosities return to insist on being recognized and lawlessness flourishes. The uncanny thus becomes more terrible, and curiously more alien, because it is at once old and new – familiar as well as strange, personal as well as public. Its shock is redoubled – as are all of our encounters with extreme forms of human madness and cruelty – precisely because it comes to us as recognition of something we somehow already know.

The uncanny is, of course, one thing in fiction and another in life, as Freud observed, in part because "a great deal that is not uncanny in fiction would be so if it happened in life" and in part because we have better means of controlling or distancing the uncanny in fiction. Like Baudelaire and Zola, however, Dos Passos reminds us that encounters with the uncanny increase and intensify in the homemade world of cities, where the gap between imagination and reality has already begun to narrow. Dos Passos narrows that gap further by making the processes of his fiction mirror the processes of the external, urban world. He features people engaged in making and remaking their world, as well as people engaged in perceiving and interpreting it. In an effort to work his way out of the dead end at which "realism" and "naturalism" seemed to him to have arrived, he employs new techniques for conveying the scenic speed – the rapid pace, the sharp contrasts, and the abrupt shifts – of urban life. Skyscrapers serve as signs of society's determination to assert its domination, whereas subways serve as signs of subterranean forces that seem about to erupt. In countless places, in unfamiliar voices as well as in machines, he locates strange sounds. In "Experimental Music" (1958), John Cage speaks of the efforts of composers to open "the doors of music to the sounds that happen to be in the environment," their aim being not disorder but "a harmony to which many of us are unaccustomed." Charles Ives, one of the composers Cage refers to, blends new sounds with rhythms taken from old hymns or, in the case of his *Scherzo for String Quartet*, from a song called "The Streets of Cairo" that was first performed at the 1893 Columbian Exposition, which Ives attended with his uncle Lyman Brewster. A comparable desire – that of opening literature to new sounds that happen to be in the environment – informs Stein's work from at least *Three Lives* on. Humans, Kenneth Burke once remarked, are "rotten with perfection," before adding that language is "in its distinctive ways" as "intrinsically perfectionist" as its maker. The special quality of Dos Passos's art lies in this: that it remains "intrinsically perfectionist" even as it seeks to incorporate harsh and alien sounds, including mechanical and industrial noises as well as strange accents that float through the air of his city. Like Ives, Dos Passos wants to incorporate and amplify new sounds; and like Ives, he also wants to endow them with something resembling order, if only by bringing them into the presence of remembered refrains drawn from the nation's past.

Offended by Dos Passos's picture of life, Paul Elmer More, philosopher-author of *Shelburne Essays* (1904–21) and an architect of the "New Humanism," likened *Manhattan Transfer* to an "explosion in a cesspool." But *Manhattan Transfer* is in fact incurably romantic as well as emphatically modern. In

The 42nd Parallel (1930), the first volume of *U.S.A.*, Dos Passos continued
to adjust his fiction to the nation's rapid transformation of itself from a "story-
book democracy" into a "mass society" by finding new ways of making it reflect the processes of the external world as people were coming to know it.
He weaves the scenes of his narrative together in ways that "expand in the
reader's mind," as the poet Delmore Schwartz once observed, to "include the
whole context of experience." He thus gives a new twist both to Henry James's
remark that the novelist would succeed "to the sacred office of the historian"
and to Wyndham Lewis's remark that artists are "always engaged in writing
a detailed history of the future" out of their awareness "of the nature of the
present." *U.S.A.* reflects this double ambition. It is, as Dos Passos put it, a
"collective" novel about "the march of history," made up mostly of "the speech
of the people." Diverse in style and panoramic in scope, it reaches from the
prewar years into the thirties and stretches from New York to California, from
Chicago to Mexico, from the United States to Europe. In some moments, it
moves with dizzying speed – which Dos Passos likened to "the trembling joy
that is akin to [the] terror" one experiences in constant travel. In others, it stops
abruptly to provide close-ups of imagined faces and scenes or offer biographies
of famous lives. *The 42nd Parallel* focuses on the story of a new generation
in a new and hopeful century in a "New America." *1919* follows a trail of
carelessness and deceit to the ceremonial burial of the Unknown Soldier, the
nation's representative of all the faceless, nameless dead of its wars – except,
of course, certain outsiders: "'Make sure he aint a dinge, boys, / make sure he
aint a guinea or a kike.'" *Big Money* presents an increasingly manipulative and
materialistic society in which banality, hypocrisy, corruption, violence, and
injustice punctuate history. *U.S.A.* thus traces a declining history, from an age
of hope (1910–17) through a war and stacks of betrayals to the deaths of Sacco
and Vanzetti. In one sense it is a national epic; in another, it recalls the Puritan
jeremiads of the late seventeenth and early eighteenth centuries that decry the
declension of a world that is no longer new.

Lewis, Fitzgerald, and Hemingway, among others, also wrote social fiction.
But Dos Passos's works – from his early war novels on, but especially from
Manhattan Transfer on – anticipate the social fiction of the thirties in ways
matched by few works of the twenties. In Dos Passos's novels, the lingering
hope of the Lyric Years fades but never completely disappears. Like other
writers of his time, Dos Passos knew that history and society work on and
in people in unfathomable ways, shaping and misshaping their lives. But for
him, that awareness possessed an edge felt by few other writers. His artists,
even those who think of themselves as possessing a spectatorial attitude and
achieving an almost mountainous detachment, are implicated, entangled, and

sometimes complicit in the society they observe, especially as it becomes more centralized in its control and more sophisticated in its use of the mass media and advertising. Having studied the new media, Dos Passos incorporated them in his art because he realized that they were instruments of power that could be put to the purpose of producing and manipulating a "mountain of lies." Yet he held to the conviction that the United States – and by extension, the modern world – could be reformed, if rebel artists and social reformers would again unite in directing human energies toward something other than the process and satisfaction of making and spending money. His spectatorial "I" was his stronghold against total incorporation into a society that insisted upon naming each individual either a "failure" (the victim as victim) or a "success" (the victim as victimizer, often of oneself as well as others).

   U.S.A. confronts class conflict, and it examines the trauma inflicted by rapid modernization on both the fabric of social life and individual human psyches. But it also explores the intellectual and aesthetic implications of rapid incorporation and commercialization. In it the act of living for art and literature emerges as a process of constructing new paradigms, models, and theories about almost everything from "consciousness" and "reality" to "psychic needs" and "biological urges" to "social forces" and "natural laws." Few novels in history have done as much to survey the varied, ingenious ways in which human beings have used their minds and imaginations to impose their wills on one another: through the stories they tell, the advertisements they create, and the propaganda they generate as well as the wars they wage. It is in this inclusive sense that *U.S.A.* is a political novel. In confronting several very different faces of power, it brings everything, including art, under the aspect of the political. Committed though he is, furthermore, to the claims of the community, Dos Passos reserves his deeper sympathy for the beleaguered, individual self. His circle of life is more urban than natural, this being a part of the large cultural transformation that he thought of as having taken place between the age of Emerson and the twenties. But Emerson remained one of his heroes, and even when Dos Passos's faith in reform and his belief in human progress were most deeply threatened, Emerson helped him to sustain his faith in the self's ability to protect its integrity and maintain the semi-independence of its soul, even against the sometimes subtle and sometimes crude pressures of an increasingly administered society.

8

❦

WAR AS METAPHOR: THE EXAMPLE
OF ERNEST HEMINGWAY

W RITERS WHOSE ART drew more from the customs and dialects of
a region – as, for example, Jewett's and Frost's did from New
England, Anderson's and Lewis's did from the Midwest, and
Faulkner's did from the South – had their own reasons for resisting New York.
Even those who came to regard New York as a second home – as both Fitzgerald,
born in St. Paul, Minnesota, and Langston Hughes, born in Joplin, Missouri,
did at times, and as Anzia Yezierska, born in Plinsk, Poland, did more completely – continued to draw sustenance from their memories of the provincial
cultures that they carried with them. Writers from the South carried the additional burden of a history haunted by slavery, guilt, poverty, and defeat, and
nothing that happened in the twenties lightened their load. To Mencken, who
made infrequent use of understatement, the Midwest was a "forlorn country"
of yokels and hypocrites. The "truths" that Carol Kennicott, protagonist
of *Main Street* (1920), discovers were, Mencken reported, simply the truth:
"the contentment" of the Midwest *was* "the enchantment of the quite dead."
The Midwest was "negation," "prohibition," and "slavery": it was "dullness
made God." But Mencken spoke for the nation in making the South his favorite
target of ridicule. The South epitomized the "idiocies of the Bible Belt," he
said, surpassing in hypocrisy and benightedness every civilization in history.

The Midwest's advantages over the South, which were considerable, derived ironically from the middle-class prosperity and ethos that Mencken had
been born into and then spent his life trying to escape. As a result, despite
Mencken, the Midwest retained a political and economic as well as moral self-
assurance that the South's aristocratic pretensions ruled out. "What we call the
middle classes are for the most part the church-going classes," John Dewey
observed. "The 'Middle West,' the prairie country, has been the center of active
social philanthropies and political progressivism," he added, "because it is the
chief home of this folk." The Midwest retained a sense of cultural inferiority
toward the East, played on by Mencken, to which writers were especially sensitive. It also felt some latent guilt for having transformed Turner's "great

American West" into another scene of production that fed big business. But it also retained the self-confidence reflected in Dewey's statement. And that self-confidence was sometimes employed in resisting its own ethos, as Dreiser, Anderson, and Fitzgerald made clear in their ways, and several women made clear in theirs. Now and then, for example, in stories and novels by Fitzgerald and Hemingway, or more concertedly in a long string of novels by Zane Grey, the old strategy of trying to overcome isolation by both eroticizing and spiritualizing the landscape reappears in the fiction of the twenties. But in the works of Willa Cather and Zona Gale, we encounter subtle subversions of the male strategy of celebrating male protagonists engaged in conquering natural scenes that are associated, in thought and language, with female beauty and fecundity. And in this, the novels of Cather and Gale parallel the paintings of Georgia O'Keeffe, which throughout the twenties and thirties associated nature's resistance to such mastery with the presence in it of charged images of obdurate female sexuality.

For the most part, however, other modes of resistance dominated fiction in the twenties, particularly among writers of the Midwest, who resented the authority of the past as much as or even more than they resented Eastern domination. By a "generation," Fitzgerald wrote, speaking for Cowley's group of "admired writers,"

I mean that reaction against the fathers which seems to occur about three times a century. It is distinguished by a set of ideas, inherited in moderated form from the madmen and outlaws of the generation before; if it is a real generation it has its own leaders and spokesmen, and it draws into its orbit those born just before it and just after, whose ideas are less clear-cut and defiant.

Fitzgerald liked the notion that he and his generation had rejected the funny-looking clothes and outmoded social concerns of "those born just before" them and the notion that they had preempted those born "just after" by reaching back and selectively claiming certain "madmen and outlaws" of the past as the true progenitors of the modern. One result was another reinvention of the literary history of the United States. At times, writers of the twenties merely reiterated what Randolph Bourne and others had stated before the war. "Puritanism," for example, remained a scapegoat for most known forms of provincialism, greed, and repression. One purpose of the historical and critical works of the twenties – including both broad-gauged studies, such as D. H. Lawrence's *Studies in Classic American Literature* (1922), Lewis Mumford's *The Golden Day* (1926) and *The Brown Decades* (1931), and William Carlos Williams's *In the American Grain* (1925), and works on individual writers, such as Van Wyck Brooks's *The Ordeal of Mark Twain* (1920) – was to identify prophetic dissenters of the past. In Claude Bowers's *The Tragic Era* (1929), for example, the period following the Civil War was identified as an analogue of the twenties. But most writers of the twenties showed less interest in identifying a dominant tradition than in finding precursors of the disenchantment and the spectatorial attitude that the Great War had endowed with special authority.

The sense of a world already deeply wounded yet in some sense still at war hovers over the fiction of the twenties. Hemingway and Dos Passos were among those who had seen some fighting. Fitzgerald and Faulkner were among those who had volunteered for service only to be left behind. Faulkner's bitterness at the inadequate fate of being one on whom "they had stopped the war" found direct expression in several of his early stories and his first novel, *Soldiers' Pay* (1926). In addition, it entered several extravagant inventions – tales of daring training-camp escapades and even of heroic combat ordeals – through which he tried to correct the clumsy work of "the sorry jade, circumstance" (another phrase from *Soldiers' Pay*) that had robbed him of his chance at glory. "Like most of my generation, I was obsessed with the idea of 'War' as the test of your courage, your maturity, of your sexual powers," Christopher Isherwood (b. 1904) later remarked, in words that help us to gauge what Faulkner and others were trying to claim for themselves in the heroic tales they concocted. Even Hemingway, who volunteered for ambulance service and then stretched its boundaries to the point of becoming a decorated hero, felt driven to improve on his adventures.

Spectatorial attitudes possess remarkable elasticity, of course, as we see in novels like *Sister Carrie*; and they had roots in cultural changes that had begun long before the Great War, as we see in Poe's "A Man of the Crowd" (1840). But the war altered and reinforced them – by penning people in trenches for long days and nights or putting them in ambulances, where waiting, watching, and cleaning up seemed to exhaust possible responses. Spectatorial attitudes were also reinforced by the rapid rise of movies, spectator sports, and even radio broadcasts, which turned people into audiences for reports on labor disputes, race riots, and gangland wars. For many survivors, however, the basic sense of being a more or less terrified yet helpless observer went back to the war. Scarred by that experience, the protagonist of Dorothy Canfield Fisher's *The Deepening Stream* (1930) thinks of herself as a permanent refugee. *Children of Fate* (1917), by Marice Rutledge, pseudonym for Marie Louise Gibson Hale, recounts the experiences of a woman who, realizing that she has been duped by "governments and capitalists" into supporting the war, feels sickened with shame and declares something like a "separate peace" of her own. In Dos Passos's *Three Soldiers* (1921), we enter the "heroic fantasies" of a character named Fusselli shortly before he encounters the "reality of war," only to realize that his false expectations have been shaped by "long movie reels of heroism." In E. E. Cummings's *The Enormous Room* (1922), traditional heroic fantasies dissolve and then re-form as paranoid nightmares. In Dos Passos's *1919* (1932), Fred Summers describes the war as a tour gone awry. "Fellows," he keeps saying, "this ain't a war, it's a goddam madhouse . . . it's a goddam Cook's tour." Gone, as though forever, we learn in Hemingway's *A Farewell to Arms* (1929), is a world where words like "sacred, glorious, and sacrifice, and the expression in vain" could be spoken without embarrassment. Gone, too, are places like the barn Frederic Henry remembers playing in as a boy, where adventure and security coexist. "You could not go back," Henry says, shortly before realizing that he will have to go forward with trepidation, knowing that the next may be his final inch.

In Thomas Boyd's *Through the Wheat* (1923), that preview features a world as strange, surreal, and deathlike as T. S. Eliot's "Unreal City," where crowds of people shuffle about "under the brown fog of a winter dawn." Boyd's protagonist, William Hicks, begins with the familiar hope of seeing "some real action" and becoming a real hero. But his first encounter is with the unglamorous odors of military latrines, and his next is with a war zone from which all signs of order, coherent authority, and clear purpose have vanished. Overwhelmed by the spectral quality of the world around him, in which he must perform tasks without discernible purposes or clear consequences, he begins to suffer from a form of neurasthenia, a recoil as it were, in which the self becomes numb and the scenes of what is left of life become weightless, insubstantial, unreal. Objects appear and disappear, as images might, without rhyme, reason, or explanation. At the end of *Through the Wheat* we see Hicks in "No Man's Land," tramping

on through the field, dimly sensing the dead, the odors, the scene. He found his knife where he had thrown it. As he picked it up, the ridge swarmed with small gray figures, ever growing nearer. He turned and walked toward his platoon. The breath from his nostrils felt cool. He raised his chin a little. The action seemed to draw his feet from the earth. No longer did anything matter, neither the bayonets, the bullets, the barbed wire, the dead, nor the living. The soul of Hicks was numb.

From Paris to London to the American Midwest, people wrote letters, journals, and diaries about the war that now seem like prefaces to the chronicles of disillusionment written after it. Even writers of the Lyric Years like Genevieve Taggard and Joseph Freeman, who continued to hope that a collective effort of will might change society, shared the sense of being "refugees" and "exiles." War, Bourne had observed, was "not a relation between men, but between powers." For many writers of the twenties, the Great War seemed to have changed the fabric of social life by defining social existence as a set of relations among powers rather than among people. What they sought in response were ways of distancing or protecting themselves from governments, bureaucracies, businesses, and even advertisements. Their enclaves were less advances than retreats, where they could try in some motions to force some pleasure out of life and in others to turn their negative experiences into art.

"The peace intensified that moral and intellectual nihilism which the war had generated," Freeman observed. Some writers took refuge in an aesthetic cult that extolled the "Fleeting Moment" of intense experience, of which Pierrot – the clown-lover of Italian opera and pantomime whom French writers like Charles Baudelaire and Jules Laforgue had claimed for modern literature – became the "tragic symbol." For them, all delight became "a poignant sorrow, all beauty a snare to the flesh and a thorn in the spirit, all success at best a not ignoble failure." Faulkner, among others, appropriated the figure of Pierrot early and carried it with him through the twenties and beyond. But aestheticism made its appeal side by side with a desire to become an active public figure. What Freeman called the "dualism between poetry and politics," as a version of the "dualism which pervaded all Western civilization," intensified. To many writers the hope of being both a citizen in "The Republic of Letters," devoted to the arts, and a citizen of society, active in social and political life, seemed to exist only as a lost possibility. Almost everywhere they looked – to the reclusive Emily Dickinson, the public Walt Whitman and Mark Twain, and the detached Henry Adams – they found precursors who had been willing to pursue that possibility even though they knew that a not ignoble failure was as much as they could hope for in wrestling with tensions they had no way of resolving.

Hemingway built his life and his art around that effort as conspicuously as any other writer of the twenties. Many people have commented on Hemingway's egotism, in part because no other writer – not Whitman, Stein, or Fitzgerald, not even Norman Mailer – tried with more success to thrust his life upon the reading and even the nonreading public. Creating a public persona was central to his effort to become a force in the larger social world. In his last painful years, he was haunted by fear that time, age, illness, and injuries had robbed him of his powers as a writer. But he was also troubled by the recognition that he could no longer bear the weight of the public image he had created for himself. Much has also been made of his competitiveness, in part because few writers have matched the rancor he expressed toward other writers. His attacks in *A Moveable Feast* (1964) are tame compared with remarks he made in letters to his editor, Maxwell Perkins. Even in *A Moveable Feast*, where his skills as a memoirist are displayed with penetrating wit, he reveals a sad need to get even with Gertrude Stein for the jabs she directed at him in *The Autobiography of Alice B. Toklas* (1933) and an even sadder need to persuade the world that Fitzgerald was inferior to him as a man as well as a writer.

In truth, Hemingway saw virtually every situation and relationship as a contest waged with some threatening *other* who was bent on destroying him as a man and as an artist. Nature, with its scenes of beauty and terror; society, with its rituals of work, play, and love, of striving, courting, and mating, as well as its scenes of open warfare; and the in-between worlds of hunting, fishing, and bullfighting: all of these were populated with creatures, including human creatures, male and female, who harbored – or, as it sometimes seemed to Hemingway, flaunted – needs and desires that made them rivals he had been put on earth to test himself against and overcome. Reared in a proper bourgeois home that often seemed on the edge of war, in the proper bourgeois suburb of Oak Park, Illinois, just west of Chicago, where according to its slogan "the saloons end and the churches begin," Hemingway began early to depend upon excursions into nature that sooner or later either skirted, as in "Big Two-Hearted River," or gave way, as in "Indian Camp," to violence.

In 1951, more than twenty years after his father's suicide and two days after his mother's death, Hemingway wrote Carlos Baker, his biographer, about how happy he and his siblings had been as very young children, before "everything went to hell in the family." But for him that early fall had been so decisive that memories of the brief period of happiness preceding it gradually lost their force and, therefore, existed more as a lost possibility than as an enabling memory. He characteristically thought of families as destructive scenes. "Sometimes you can go quite a long time before you criticize families," he notes in *A Moveable Feast*, "your own or those by marriage." But families do such "terrible things" and inflict such "intimate harm," he adds, that no one can escape their force forever: "Even when you have learned not to look at families nor listen to them and have learned not to answer letters, families have many ways of being dangerous."

Hemingway retained his sense of moving in harm's way for as long as he lived, and in this as in much else his art measured his life. In *The Autobiography of Alice B. Toklas*, Stein taunts Hemingway, noting that for a tough man he seemed to get hurt a lot. In a similar vein, Dos Passos added that for a virile lover he seemed to spend most of his time in bed recovering from injuries. But Hemingway's injuries and wounds were no less real because he occasionally went out of his way to suffer them, and his tough public persona was no less telling for being so contrived. Without ever being a soldier, he managed to serve in World War I, the Spanish Civil War, and World War II, in the first of which, as a Red Cross worker, he was badly wounded by shrapnel. What can we conclude from this except that he was driven to prove himself to himself as well as to others? "Wounds don't matter," he wrote his family from a Milan hospital. "I wouldn't mind being wounded again so much because I know just what it is like." He was in fact driven to test himself, and he was also remarkably accident-prone. In 1953 he crash-landed in Africa, only to have the rescue plane crash and burn shortly after it picked him up. When he got to Nairobi for treatment, he was suffering from severe injuries to his spine and several internal organs and was bleeding from his ears, nose, mouth, and anus. Yet this was one episode among many. Everywhere he went – Italy, Spain, France, Africa, Wyoming, Montana, the Florida Keys, Cuba – something happened to him. By the time he killed himself in Idaho in 1961, his body was a personal geography of wounds.

Among the most intense of Hemingway's early experiences, to judge from the memories he carried with him, were those that centered on the hunting and fishing he did near the family's cottage on the upper peninsula of Michigan, where he learned the ritual of the hunt and the code of the hunter. His father, an accomplished marksman, fisherman, and woodsman, was a tough teacher who insisted that his children – his daughters as well as his sons – learn to hunt and then to eat what they killed, even if it was muskrat. Violations of his code meant punishment, and serious violations meant punishment with a razor strop, after which his children were expected to kneel and ask God for His forgiveness. Hemingway's mother preferred churches to saloons, sidewalks to running streams, suburbs to woods, and almost anything that seemed feminine to anything that seemed masculine – except memories of her father and a favorite uncle, which she could control. Having named her first son Ernest for her father and Miller for the favored uncle, her father's brother, she began to play with her son's sense of himself as male. At times she seemed pleased by his already conspicuous efforts to demonstrate his masculinity. On other occasions, she dressed him in dresses and fancy hats.

Pressured to choose between his father's rigid clarity and his mother's mer-curialness, Hemingway drew closer to his sisters, especially one named Ursula, who became the model for both Littless in "The Last Good Company" and the sister whom Nick Adams refers to in "Fathers and Sons" as the only member of his family "he liked the smell of; one sister." Littless and Nick "loved each other," we read in "The Last Good Company," "and they did not love the others. They always thought of everyone else in the family as the others." Led by the more adventuresome Littless, Nick enters a series of conversations about sex that culminate, first, in talk about their becoming common-law husband and wife and, second, in talk about androgyny. "It's very exciting," Littless says, after she has cut her hair so short that she looks "like a wild boy of Borneo." "Now I'm your sister but I'm a boy."

In both the music room at home and at a friend's house, Hemingway sought his own kind of clarity by setting up boxing rings in which, with his sisters watching, he practiced the manly art of self-defense. Later he bragged of having pitted himself against several well-known boxers. In fact, he preferred opponents he knew he could beat. For there was already within him not only a reservoir of poorly repressed hostility and an insatiable need for dominance, which his easy smile masked, but also a drive to display the hostility he felt and to gain the supremacy he craved. As a result, he developed a genuinely histrionic sensibility: he liked to perform and wanted to be watched, as though by proving himself to others he could convince himself as well. As one part of this, he acquired a flair for conspicuous heroism. At Oak Park High, he saved three girls, the Oak Park newspaper reported, from "flying to destruction" down the shaft of the lunchroom dumbwaiter, by grabbing the rope and holding on, blocking it at the top of the pulley with his bare hands, until other boys could help pull the girls to safety.

World War I confirmed Hemingway's darkest suspicions: that violence and terror are parts of nature and parts of us, and parts of us not only as societies and nations but as individuals. On one level, he saw these things within people, goading, pushing, and dividing them. In his deepest self, Hemingway was at war. "As to Ernest as a boy . . . ," Fitzgerald wrote in his *Notebooks*, "it is undeniable that the dark was peopled for him" – and, we might add, the silences, too. In World War I, the shaping political as well as military drama of his generation, he located a scene that corresponded to his sense of the conflicts he saw around him, pitting a single, vulnerable, solitary self against the world. Whether this correspondence was a discovery or a projection is, of course, a vexed issue. For Hemingway's art, however, as well as for his life, the balance between discovery and projection scarcely matters. He was at war, and he saw a world at war. Of what he felt and what he saw, he wrote novels and stories in which death and danger – found in scenes of hunting, fishing, and bullfighting, of boxing and war, and between different genders, classes, and races, and thus on streets and in bars and bedrooms everywhere – push themselves on us as disclosures of what in our secret selves we are and what in our public performances we secretly want to become. His art was thus born of deep reciprocities as well as deep conflicts in which the several faces of fear loom large. He not only succeeded in making varied scenes of violent conflict visible to us. He also made his capacity for pain, injury, and recovery the world's, and the world's his. Someday, Fitzgerald remarked, Hemingway will be read "for his great studies in fear." Even the wit and nostalgia of *A Moveable Feast* coexist with darknesses born of fear. Virtually nothing Hemingway ever wrote wholly escapes that note.

In the structure of *In Our Time* (1925), we move back and forth between interchapters that are public and stories that are private. In "Chapter I," we see a "whole battery" going along a road "in the dark . . . to the Champagne." In "Indian Camp," the first story in the book, Nick Adams holds the basin while his father uses a jackknife to perform, without anesthesia, a cesarean on a frightened young Indian woman and then closes the incision with nine-foot, tapered gut leaders. Horrified, Nick turns his head away, so as not to see what his father is doing. Once the ordeal is over, they discover that the woman's husband, who has been in the bunk above her, listening to her cries, has cut his throat from ear to ear.

> "Why did he kill himself, Daddy?"
> "I don't know, Nick. He couldn't stand things, I guess."
> "Do many men kill themselves, Daddy?"
> "Not very many, Nick."
> "Do many women?"
> "Hardly ever."
> "Don't they ever?"
> "Oh, yes. They do sometimes."

In December 1928, Hemingway's father shot himself in the right temple with a Civil War "Long John" revolver that he had inherited from his father. During Hemingway's last years, as the voices that filled the darknesses of his life became more and more real and uncontrolled, his behavior became markedly paranoid. On July 2, 1961, he loaded both barrels of a double-barreled shotgun and obliterated his cranial vault. In the fall of 1966, Ursula, his favorite sister, poisoned herself. In 1982, his only brother, Leicester, killed himself with a single shot to the head.

After World War I, Hemingway exaggerated his war experiences, including the combat he had seen, the wounds he had suffered, and the heroism he had displayed – in part, perhaps, because no heroism could match his needs and in part because like Krebs, the protagonist of "Soldier's Home," he felt driven to lie to people who had heard so much propaganda that truth, even about genuine heroism, no longer interested them. It seems likely, too, that having lied Hemingway felt what Krebs feels, a distaste for the things "that had happened to him in the war," including "the times so long back when he had done the one thing, the only thing for a man to do, easily and naturally, when he might have done something else." And this at least is clear: that he was seriously wounded by shrapnel from enemy fire and that, in the words of the citation of the Italian government, which awarded him, among several medals, its Silver Medal of Military Valor, he showed "courage and self-sacrifice" in assisting Italian soldiers before allowing himself to be evacuated from the scene of battle. Subject though it was to later exaggeration, furthermore, what he felt then almost certainly deepened the prophetic sense growing in him that for people deprived of any belief in God fear of dying would hang like a dark cloud over life. Finally, however, what haunted him was not only fear that in an age of disbelief people would be unable to find anything to believe; it was fear that when they became truly desperate they would believe in anything, including vain words and empty promises.

We cannot finally separate Hemingway's success as a writer from his success in imposing on us as readers his fascination with intimate harms as well as dramatic ones – as things private and public, inherited and invented, discovered and projected. Nor is there any way to separate this from his success in forging a prose style, still widely imitated and parodied, that became one of the most recognizable literary "trademarks" in modern literature. Hemingway began to master the immediacy we associate with representational realism, to which modern reporting aspires, while working on the *Kansas City Star*, fresh out of high school, under the direction of C. G. (Pete) Wellington, who insisted that reporters write fresh, direct prose in short, forceful sentences, free of adjectives and jargon. Later, under the tutelage of Anderson, Pound, and Stein, he read widely in modern writers – James Joyce, for example, as well as Stephen Crane, Joseph Conrad, and Henry James – and began to join what he had learned from Wellington with qualities that run contrary to conventional "realism." But his originality also lay in forging relations, between writer and work and between reader and writer, in which care and restraint become necessary to the preservation of a shared sense of humanity. Style was for him a stronghold against formidable forces that threatened to inculcate a sense of disillusionment and cynicism and obliterate a sense of hope and purpose. The issue of words and how we use them became for him a test of how we face living and dying.

"In writing for a newspaper," he reported in *Death in the Afternoon*,

you told what happened and, with one trick or another, you communicated the emotion aided by the element of timeliness . . . ; but the real thing, the sequence of motion and fact which made the emotion and which would be as valid in a year or ten years or, with luck and if you stated it purely enough, always, was beyond me and I was working very hard to get it.

Hunting, fishing, and bullfighting were subjects that lent themselves to orderly movement from one detail to the next. Writing about them, Hemingway found a way of renewing and even purifying language. If a part of his commitment was to putting "down what really happened," another was to "knowing truly what you really felt," however selfish or ugly it might be, "rather than what you were supposed to feel" or had been taught to feel. He was drawn to the "simplest things" because they were fundamental; and in a violent world "one of the simplest things of all and the most fundamental," he said, "is violent death."

In Hemingway's self-conscious style, including his practice of using simple words in economical ways, we also should recognize a passion, both American and modern, for technique. Hemingway treats language as a tool or an instrument. He calls attention to new ways of using familiar words, much as modern painters call attention to their brush-strokes and colors. In a 1958 interview, he described his sense of how a writer makes things new: "From things that have happened and from things as they exist and from all the things that you know and all those that you cannot know, you make something through your own invention that is not a representation but a whole new thing truer than any thing true and alive." "Big Two-Hearted River," to take an example, is grounded in Hemingway's knowledge of fishing the Fox River north of Seney, Michigan. But in writing the story, he told Stein, he was "trying to do [his] country like Cezanne" had done Provence in paintings that helped shape cubism.

Convinced that his wounds were necessary preparations for serious writing, Hemingway assumed that in one way or another wounds were necessary to others, too. We are all wounded "from the start," he wrote Fitzgerald in 1934. "But when you get the damned hurt use it – don't cheat with it. Be as faithful to it as a scientist." Faithfulness in Hemingway's case meant bringing style as technique to bear on fear. His deepest subject turned on the analogy he created between the performance of a writer and that of a person – soldier, hunter, bullfighter – facing danger and even death. "Writing, at its best, is a lonely life," he observed in a letter accepting the Nobel Prize. For a writer "does his work alone and if he is a good enough writer he must face eternity, or the lack of it, each day." The bullfight, as we see in *Death in the Afternoon*, epitomized this fundamental life-and-death predicament for him because he thought it the only art "in which the artist is [literally] in danger of death and in which the degree of brilliance in the performance is left to the fighter's honor." In the bullring, style ("purity of line") and courage ("grace under pressure") become inseparable. But similar control is also necessary for good writing because writing always tests the limits of the writer's courage and integrity. Hemingway stripped his style bare because he believed that beauty required control and knew that control was difficult. In *In Our Time*, and especially in "Big Two-Hearted River," we become aware that Nick is holding tight to details of the landscape and the rules that govern such simple activities as making a camp and building a fire in order to cope with the darknesses welling up within as well as around him. As his taut actions find expression in sharp, clear, precise prose, we feel the encroachment of a legacy of losses so severe that life has become a killing field in which a single slip spells disaster.

Hemingway considered naming *The Sun Also Rises* (1926) "The Lost Generation." And the novel quickly became, as Edmund Wilson observed, both the era's favorite expression of romantic disillusion and the source of several of its favorite poses, including stoic heartbreak, grim, nonchalant banter, and heroic dissipation. In bars from New Orleans and Memphis to Chicago, New York, and Paris, young people tried to sound like Hemingway's characters as they drank evenings away, hoping somehow to force more pleasure, or at least gratification, out of life. But *The Sun Also Rises* does not trace the advent of a new era of pleasure. It modifies the disillusionment of the twenties by introducing a depth of feeling and sentimentality that are almost wholly absent in *In Our Time*. The stoicism that Hemingway adopts in one sense and that his protagonists adopt in another serves as the last shield of truly vulnerable people who feel more than their confidence in themselves and their world will permit them to express. Brett Ashley and Jacob Barnes know themselves to be living in a world that has lost its way. Personal desires and public rituals are all they have left to fall back on, and they are less than they need. Behind them lies a sense of a better life that is always somehow already lost. "Could we but live at will upon this perfect height . . . ," said the Irish poet Lionel Johnson, "then we were all divine." But fleeting glimpses of such moments are all that any of Hemingway's characters can hope for, and only few can hope for that. Even the luckiest move from one approximation to the next, trying to find a way adequately to comport themselves in a harsh world. The style they seek to master provides them a way of carrying on, the hope that life lived under proper pressure will yield them some understanding of themselves and their world.

The ending of *A Farewell to Arms*, of which Hemingway wrote more than thirty versions, takes us back toward the war, and it is even more crippled than the ending of *The Sun Also Rises*. It leaves Frederic Henry alone, in the grip of an advanced form of neurasthenia, in which, as Anaïs Nin observed, life and art seem to be slipping away, leaving people alone, drifting with time and fighting with shadows. Overmatched, Henry declares a separate peace of his own, hoping to make withdrawal and disengagement the center of his life. When he first meets Catherine Barkley, a beautiful young English nurse whose manner bears some resemblance to Brett Ashley's, he sees her merely as a substitute for going out "every evening to the house for officers where the girls climbed all over you and put your cap on backwards as a sign of affection between their trips upstairs with brother officers." When he finally realizes that Catherine is drawing him out of his protective shell, everything turns over inside him. "We could be close," he says, "when we were together, alone against the others." In the end, however, after Catherine and their child die, he is left alone again, completely cut off. Sitting in the darkened room with Catherine's body, he tries to feel something yet cannot. The closest he comes to real emotion is envy for the child that has died at birth, choked by its own umbilical cord. In short, he is even farther gone than Krebs, the protagonist of "Soldier's Home."

> He [Krebs] would have liked to have a girl but he did not want to have to spend a long time getting her. He did not want to get into the intrigue and the politics. He did not want to have to do any courting. He did not want to tell any more lies. It wasn't worth it.
>   He did not want any consequences. He did not want any consequences ever again. He wanted to live alone without consequences. Besides he did not really need a girl. The army had taught him that.

Isolation and death, not life and connectedness, became Hemingway's true subjects, and they brought with them a consuming desire for release that becomes a consuming desire for peace. Style became his means of confronting isolation and death as well as his means of holding out against them because it offered him the possibility of controlling even moments of maximum desire and maximum pressure.

In the introduction to *Paris Was Yesterday: 1925–1939*, Janet Flanner recounts a conversation with Hemingway in which the two of them shared the fact that their fathers had committed suicide:

> Our talk ended with the mutual declaration that if either of us ever killed ourself, the other was not to grieve but to remember that liberty could be as important in the act of dying as in the acts of living. So, years later, I ... had automatically recognized that fatal gunshot as his mortal act of gaining liberty. But I grieved deeply when the pitiful facts of his final bondage were made public ... At Ernest's death, I grieved most because he died in a state of ruin.

At the end of *For Whom the Bell Tolls* (1940), Hemingway pictures Robert Jordan alone, badly injured, waiting for the enemy to come, hoping that his wait will not last long because he does not know how much pain he can bear. "Oh, let them come, he said. I don't want to do that business that my father did." Later, thinking again about suicide, he says that perhaps it would "be all right" to get "the whole thing ... over with." Still he waits, trying to think about other things – about his comrades, or about Montana or Madrid – hoping to blot out the mounting pain. It would be all right, he says, to end it, but waiting, holding out is better as long as there is something one can do that may make a difference: "*One thing well done can make –* " he thinks, as he holds on. At the book's end we see him, "his heart beating against the pine needle floor of the forest," waiting with his submachine gun in the crook of his arm, as nameless and almost faceless enemies come up the trail toward him, knowing that when he fires, they will fire, and then it will all be over.

By the time he died, Hemingway was ravaged more by disease, injuries, and weariness than by age, and he had lost control of his art as well as his life. His career, having suffered a decline, had undergone a revival with the publication of *The Old Man and the Sea* (1952), in part, as Delmore Schwartz observed, because people found just enough in it to remind them of what a great writer he had been at his best. In fact, however, he published few works after the twenties that were as good as *In Our Time*, *The Sun Also Rises*, *Men Without Women* (1927), and *A Farewell to Arms*, and all of them were short stories: some of those in *Winner Take Nothing* (1933), for example, and later still "The Snows of Kilimanjaro" and "The Short, Happy Life of Francis Macomber." In them we see again his effort to reclaim simple, spare, disciplined prose for art – and his effort to make the act of writing a model of how a truly vulnerable self can make its way against great odds, long enough to do something worthwhile. "I know you don't like the sort of thing I write," he wrote his father in 1927, recalling the hurt he had felt when his mother condemned *The Sun Also Rises*. But "I *know* that I am not disgracing you in my writing but rather doing something that some day you will be proud of ... you cannot know how it makes me feel for Mother to be ashamed of what I know as sure as you know that there is a God in heaven is *not to be ashamed of.*" "Suicide is prepared within the silence of the heart," Albert Camus wrote, "as is a great work of art." In books punctuated by violence, loss, death, and disillusionment, Hemingway not only enriched and illumined his world; he also held out against the final act of destruction that drew him, sustained by faith, not in art's power to redeem social life in his time, but more modestly in the power of writing to provide models of effective resistance for writers like himself and for readers like the sister he called "Littless," in their uneven contests to protect their shared humanity.

3

The fate of writing during
the Great Depression

I

❦

THE DISCOVERY OF POVERTY AND
THE RETURN OF COMMITMENT

W HEN THE Crash of October 1929 ended the biggest speculative
binge in the nation's history, it brought the Roaring Twenties to
a close. Scary economic indicators had been gathering for years.
Farm income and industrial wages remained low throughout the twenties,
and by 1929, with 35 percent of all personal income going into the pockets of 5 percent of the population, even the middle class was showing signs
of stress. Residential construction, consumer spending, industrial production, commodity prices, and employment were going down while business
inventories were going up. Looking back on the late twenties from the vantage point of the early thirties, F. Scott Fitzgerald located signs of anxiety in
everything from the "nervous beating of feet" and the sudden "popularity of
cross-word puzzles" to the remembered faces of Princeton classmates who had
disappeared "into the dark maw of violence" before the Crash, including one
who had jumped from a skyscraper and another who had "crawled home"
to die at the high-toned Princeton Club after being beaten in a Manhattan
speakeasy. But it took a crash to counter what Zelda Fitzgerald called "the
infinite promises of American advertising." Borrow to spend was one message,
borrow to invest, another. Bankers, brokers, and political leaders directed
the campaign; newspapers, magazines, and radios reinforced it. McNeel's of
Boston was one of countless "financial service" operations that specialized in
persuading people they could get rich on borrowed money – a message many
politicians in Washington endorsed. On December 4, 1928, in his last address
to Congress, President Coolidge assured the nation that it could "regard the
present with satisfaction and anticipate the future with optimism."

In terms of technical training, business experience, and public service, Herbert Hoover was better prepared to be president than Coolidge. But he believed in the alliance forged between business and government during the twenties and saw no reason to change anything. "We in America," he said during his campaign, "are nearer the final triumph over poverty than ever before in the history of any land.... Given a chance to go forward with the policies of the last eight years, we shall soon with the help of God be in the sight of the day when poverty will be banished from this nation." "I have no fears for the future of our country," he added in his inaugural address, echoing Coolidge again. "It is bright with hope." And so the nation splurged and the market soared. On September 11, 1929, with signs of trouble spreading, the *Wall Street Journal* gave the nation this "thought for the day," borrowed from Mark Twain: "Don't part with your illusions; when they are gone you may still exist, but you have ceased to live."

During the Lyric Years, the nation's citizens – "the almost chosen people," as Lincoln called them not long before he died – had assumed that peace and prosperity would last. Following the tainted peace of Versailles, they cut foreign entanglements in order to concentrate on becoming history's heirs. Caught up in speculation and self-indulgence, they began making, spending, and investing money at a record pace. In 1923 the volume of sales on the New York Stock Exchange topped 236 million shares for the first time. In 1928 it exceeded 1.1 billion shares. Through the early fall of 1929, the market continued to rise, as droves of new investors entered the fray, many of them on money borrowed in a tight credit market. Meanwhile, millions followed the market as spectators, dreaming of the day when they, too, would get rich. In the first eight months of Hoover's administration, the *New York Times* average of selected industrial stocks jumped from 250 to 450.

Late in September and again in mid-October, the market shuddered, and on the 23rd it began a slide that neither the bankers and brokers in New York nor the politicians in Washington could halt. Within two weeks, the *New York Times* average of selected industrial stocks fell 228 points, from 452 to 224, triggering a fall in which securities listed on the New York Stock Exchange lost more than 40 percent of their total value. Words of assurance continued to float out of President Hoover's mouth. "America is sound," he insisted. But his words had lost credibility. "Yes, America is sound," replied Gilbert Seldes. "The sound is hollow."

By 1932, after years of decline, it seemed that everyone was either in trouble or threatened by it and that no one – neither the president and his secretary of the treasury, Andrew Mellon, nor the governors and mayors – knew what to do. In three years following the Crash, national income fell from $81 billion to $41 billion; new capital issues fell from $10 billion to $1 billion; 85,000 businesses, with liabilities of more than $4.5 billion, failed; and 5,000 banks closed, wiping out more than 9 million savings accounts. In 1931 alone, 2,294 banks failed, an average of 45 per week. Between 1930 and 1934, unemployment tripled, leaving between 13 and 16 million people out of work. Farm income, already low, fell 65 percent and the value of stocks traded on the New York Stock Exchange fell 78 percent.

By the winter of 1932–3, the nation was mired in the deepest crisis it had faced since the Civil War. As unemployment rose, social and economic mobility plummeted, particularly for women, the urban poor, and all people of color. Meanwhile, two shifts in population began reversing themselves. In 1932 emigrants fleeing the "land of opportunity" outnumbered immigrants entering it three to one. Similarly, the migration of people from farms to cities, which had been spurred for six decades by the nation's rapid incorporation of itself, slowed and then reversed, as people lost faith in the promise of their new urban, industrial civilization and turned back toward the land. In literature, a revival of agrarian utopianism gained in popularity in the North as well as the South, the Midwest, and the West. Meanwhile, in breadlines, soup kitchens, and shantytowns, called "Hoovervilles," people who had grown accustomed to thinking of themselves as proud and self-reliant learned to beg for assistance.

Spurred by anger and despair, hundreds of thousands of men and teenage boys as well as thousands of women left their homes to ride the rails, seeking release in motion. Some of those who stayed at home gathered around radios purchased in better days to hear the latest antics of Amos 'n' Andy or the smooth sounds of Duke Ellington and Benny Goodman; others sought relief in the darkness of local picture shows. "Motion pictures offered several avenues of escape" from the burdens of "hard times" and "daily woes," the *New York Times* reported in December 1935: Clark Gable in *Mutiny on the Bounty*, Errol Flynn in *Captain Blood*, Gary Cooper in *Lives of a Bengal Lancer*, Greta Garbo in *Anna Karenina*, Marlene Dietrich in *The Devil Is a Woman*, Bette Davis in *Dangerous*, and the Marx Brothers in *A Night at the Opera*. Meanwhile, readers made bestsellers of novels like Hervey Allen's *Anthony Adverse* (1933), which entertained them with the glamorous adventures of a hero in Napoleonic Europe, and Kenneth Roberts's *Northwest Passage* (1937), which carried them back to a time when the nation's sense of shared purpose had been rising rather than falling.

By contrast, confidence in the future plummeted: during the thirties, the marriage rate fell sharply, the birthrate plunged to its lowest level in the nation's history, and the suicide rate rose. Soon ordinary people began to fear that the whole political economy might collapse, while those who were more radical, or more skeptical, began to suspect that something was fundamentally wrong with the nation's way of life. In 1932, 15,000 veterans joined a protest march on Washington, more than 1 million voters cast votes for candidates on the radical fringes of the political spectrum, and ordinary citizens had begun listening to drastic solutions. Some followed political leaders like Huey Long. Some followed religious leaders like Father Charles Coughlin. Others listened to leaders of the Communist Party. "I wish we might double the number of Communists in the country," said Father John Ryan, "to put the fear, if not of God, then . . . of something else, into the hearts of our leaders." In cities, hunger marches sprang up; in the country, farmers banded together to protect their homes and farms from foreclosures. Bankers and businessmen, objects of adulation in the twenties, became objects of scorn. People challenged their right to collect bills, denounced their high-sounding ideals as self-serving, and repudiated their claims to be the nation's rightful leaders.

Given their ebullience and considerable cultural achievements, the twenties, once gone, were sure to evoke nostalgia of the kind we hear in Fitzgerald's "Echoes of the Jazz Age" (1931). Yet writers as different as Frederick Lewis Allen, Malcolm Cowley, Josephine Herbst, Genevieve Taggard, and James Thurber soon expressed a sense of relief that the long splurge had come to an end. Not having shared the booming prosperity of the United States, England and Europe were spared the startling reversal that inspired wry signs of the kind Thurber spotted in a small shop on 14th Street: "Busted & Disgusted." But George Orwell located in England a shift that bears a striking resemblance to the one that took place in the United States, from "the twilight of the gods into a sort of Boy Scout atmosphere of bare knees and community singing." Soon writers were acting more like eager-minded schoolchildren bent on studying the past and organizing reform movements than like cultural refugees left with nothing to fall back on except the lonely discipline of writing and the shared pursuit of pleasure and prosperity: "If the keynote of the writers of the 'twenties is 'tragic sense of life,'" Orwell noted, "the keynote of the new writers is 'serious purpose.'"

Stark economic realities and new political intensities distanced the twenties from the thirties. But the abrupt shift also spurred efforts to examine the past as a way of understanding the present. With the sense that a dramatic break had occurred came the sense that the lost world lay close by – *Only Yesterday*, as Frederick Lewis Allen put it in a book published in 1931. As heirs of a bloodless tradition that drained literature of social responsibility, "palefaced aesthetes" quickly fell into bad repute. Refugees of the twenties apologized for having thought of art as above politics, and many of them actively sought what writers of the twenties had shunned: a sense of continuity with the immediate past. Looking backward, Herbst saw the twenties, not as a unified period of parties, miracles, satire, jazz, and art, but as a jumble in which unfashionable ideas like social service had continued to attract champions. She found, in other words, a world that resembled, beneath its surface, the "soul-shattering" world of the thirties, "which had come in like a hurricane," sweeping a whole generation into "violent protest." Dos Passos's *U.S.A.* reaches back through the twenties to the Lyric Years in order to set the loss that the Crash inflicted against the gains it opened up, by making the carelessness that prevailed in the twenties the only possible starting point for understanding the different kinds of commitment that arose during the thirties.

That commitment remains difficult to gauge, however, in terms of both its depth and its ideological grounding. Shortly after writing "Echoes of the Jazz Age," describing the twenties as having "no interest in politics at all," Fitzgerald began what he thought of as a serious study of the writings of Karl Marx. "To bring about the revolution," he observed in his *Notebooks*, "it may be necessary to work inside the communist party." Hoping to infuse his fiction with his new politics, he wrote a note to himself describing Dick Diver of *Tender is the Night* as "a communist-liberal-idealist, a moralist in revolt." Fitzgerald had in fact always thought of himself as a "liberal-idealist"; even in the twenties he occasionally called himself a "socialist." In the changed world of the early thirties, the call for political commitment appealed to him. But he remained both ill-suited for party work of any kind and ill-equipped for critical engagement with ideologically based theory. By 1934, when he finished his elegiac story of Dick Diver's decline in *Tender is the Night*, he had decided to give up politics once again, leaving it, as he had in the twenties, to people like Edmund Wilson, whom he called his "intellectual conscience" – first, because worrying about politics drained his waning energies; second, because he found it impossible to infuse his fiction with any explicit ideology; and third, because he had begun to suspect that the "Great Change" he believed in conflicted with his "allegiance to the class" that he was "part of."

The speed of Fitzgerald's conversion and recantation was extreme even in a decade characterized by quick moves. But it is telling on several counts, not least because it reminds us that in terms of relations between politics and literature the thirties differed in significant degree but not in kind from the twenties. Looking back on the twenties, Herbst saw "crumbs and pieces which completely contradict each other." "It was all flux and change," she concluded, where even "ideas of social service, justice, and religious reaction had their special spokesman." Such words suggest what Herbst believed: that the novels of writers like Anderson, Cummings, Dos Passos, Fitzgerald, Hemingway, Lewis, and Stein remain deeply political even when they are not overtly political.

And her insight should also warn us to be skeptical of such familiar terms as "the Red Decade" and "the Angry Decade."

Many writers of the thirties made conscious moves toward the political left, and they often stayed there longer than Fitzgerald. Ideology played a far more conspicuous role in their fiction than it had in the fiction of the preceding decade. But few if any writers of the thirties – Kenneth Burke, who was, of course, also a writer of the twenties, being a possible exception – made significant contributions to radical theory. And most of the representative works of the period, including those identified with the radical left, are more deeply infused with fervent feeling – the sense of working together in the name of some loosely defined yet fervently held ideas and beliefs; the sense, in Cowley's words, of "being not leader, but just one in the ranks of the great army that was marching toward a new dawn" – than with any clear revolutionary commitment or specific political strategy. For a time, they helped to tilt the country away from its fascination with material possessions and its habit of judging human worth as well as success in terms of money. The nation became less materialistic and more community-minded during the thirties than in any other decade of the twentieth century. But strong countercurrents, individualistic and even antinomian, continued to find expression in the thirties, and so did a kind of nativism or nationalism. Even writers whose work was most revisionary – writers who managed to reconceive the nature of culture and rethink the issue of how it worked and who it served – retained a fascination with the nation's culture that was at bottom a form of loyalty to it. The drastic change they hoped to accomplish they thought of as rooted in native soil. Pressing forward "toward a new dawn," they looked to the past – to the Lyric Years, especially, but also to abolitionists and other dissenters – Emerson, Whitman, and Thomas Paine among them – for guides who could help them decide what "serious purpose" might mean in the thirties.

2

❦

THE SEARCH FOR "CULTURE" AS A FORM
OF COMMITMENT

POLITICAL COMMITMENT found expression in explorations of the national mood such as Louis Adamic's *My America* (1938), Sherwood Anderson's *Puzzled America* (1935), Nathan Asch's *The Road: In Search of America* (1939), Theodore Dreiser's *Tragic America* (1932), and Edmund Wilson's *American Jitters* (1932). It found expression in explicitly proletarian writing that Granville Hicks and others collected in *Proletarian Literature in the United States* (1935). It found expression in numerous "radical" novels – many of them auto-biographical and all of them more fervently felt than rigorously "proletarian" – including Nelson Algren's *Somebody in Boots* (1935), Thomas Bell's *Out of This Furnace* (1941), Robert Cantwell's *Land of Plenty* (1934), Jack Conroy's *The Disinherited* (1933), Edward Dahlberg's *Bottom Dogs* (1930), Daniel Fuchs's *Summer in Williamsburg* (1934), Mike Gold's *Jews Without Money* (1930), Albert Maltz's *The Underground Stream* (1940), Tess Slesinger's *The Unpossessed* (1934), and Clara Weatherman's *Marching! Marching!* (1935). And it found expression in a vast "documentary literature": films, recordings, and paintings as well as books about the lives, mores, and values of "the people" that culminated in a series of striking collaborations between writers and photographers, including James Agee and Walker Evans's *Let Us Now Praise Famous Men* (1941); Sherwood Anderson's *Home Town* (1940), for which Edwin Rosskam selected Farm Security Administration photographs; Erskine Caldwell and Margaret Bourke-White's *You Have Seen Their Faces* (1937); Dorothea Lange and Paul S. Taylor's *An American Exodus* (1939); Archibald MacLeish's *Land of the Free* (1938), which used FSA photographs; and Richard Wright's *Twelve Million Black Voices* (1941), for which Edwin Rosskam again selected FSA photographs.

The vast documentary movement of the thirties extended the boundaries of "literature" and also exposed the problematics embedded in U.S. radicalism. Documentary works vary in quality. None of them, not even Agee's, is highly sophisticated ideologically. Indeed, at times they move toward a kind of agrarian utopianism that runs so contrary to the basic urban thrust of modern history as to seem nostalgic as well as anti-ideological. Much of their considerable power derives from a fascination with the culture they inscribe. They look to the future by locating grounds of hope in the painful present and the failed past. In brief, each of them is in this deep sense an act of critical loyalty. They are "revisionary" primarily because they redefine "culture" so as to reclaim it for "the people." Having queried, judged, and dismissed the distinction between "high" and "low" culture, they go on to make a discovery that alters the meaning of "culture" itself. Implicit in Nick Carraway's tone, as well as in Sinclair Lewis's and H. L. Mencken's, is an elitist notion of "culture" that often echoes some of Matthew Arnold's famous definitions – of "criticism," for example, as a "disinterested endeavour to learn and propagate the best that is known and thought in the world," and of "Culture" as consisting of the "best that has been known and said in the world, and thus with the history of the human spirit." What writers of the thirties move toward is a sense of the interrelatedness – or seamlessness – of culture as the interactive play of all the institutions and organizations that make up the political economy of a society and all the mores, manners, and customs, all the rules and regulations, both legal and moral, all the tools and gadgets, all the games and dreams as well as the art, music, philosophy, and literature that shape and express the work, play, and love of a people. In different ways, two terms that gained currency during the thirties – "the American way of life" and "the American dream," for example, reinforced this sense of the seamlessness of culture. But documentary works also performed, more or less surreptitiously, another set of tasks. They defined the process of building a culture as a quest for value and meaning, they assumed that quest to be collective, and they pointed to haunting discrepancies between the promises and the realities of life in the United States. Ironically, however, even in the process of documenting the failures of the nation's industrial civilization, they reiterated its promise.

One part of the broad, eclectic reassessment of the New World as no longer new unfolded as a search for rhetorical ties with the past. This search – which found expression in novels by Herbst, Dos Passos, and scores of others, as well as in travel writings, autobiographies, biographies, and histories – is a tribute both to how scary the thirties were and to how resourceful its writers became. Biographies, particularly of people forced to grapple with crises, multiplied – of John Brown by Robert Penn Warren, of Jefferson Davis and Stonewall Jackson by Allen Tate, of Abraham Lincoln by Carl Sandburg, and of Mark Twain by Bernard De Voto, to name a few. In looking toward the past, writers of the twenties had specialized in finding stories of frustrated or deflected purpose. Their novels trace the adventures of people who voluntarily uproot themselves and become nomadic exiles. Writers of the thirties, feeling more threatened as well as more entangled, wrote less as spectators and observers armed with irony than as citizens committed to telling the stories of heroes who had learned to deal successfully, or at least gallantly, with social crises. When they turned to stories of marginal people, as they frequently did, they focused on the truly marginal – that is, on people who are aware of their lack of status and of their vulnerability. Protagonists of the thirties do not move from place to place voluntarily, pulled by hope – as Isabel Archer, Carrie Meeber, Jim Burden, George Willard, Jay Gatsby, and Nick Carraway do; they move involuntarily, driven by privation, anger, or despair, or pursued by the same law that lets Tom and Daisy Buchanan go free. As the thirties lengthened and the grip of the Depression held, Van Wyck Brooks, in *The Flowering of New England, 1815–1865* (1936) and *New England: Indian Summer* (1940), turned his ransacking of the past into a search for both obscure and well-known heroes of difficult hope. Summing up a many-faceted effort in *The Ground We Stand On* (1941), Dos Passos found words that assert a hope that many books of the thirties either proclaim or enact. "In times of change and danger," he wrote, "when there is a quicksand of fear under men's reasoning, a sense of continuity with generations gone before can stretch like a lifeline across the scary present."

With the Great War behind them, political leaders like Harding and Coolidge had begun talking as though both the idea of prosperity and an economy of plenty were their own inventions, and neither of them paid much attention either to the debts their ideas owed to the nation's past or the debts the prosperity they administered owed to the Progressive era and the post-war economy. Practicing their own form of willed forgetfulness, writers of the twenties declared themselves cut off from everything except a few madmen and prophets of the past, largely ignoring the roots their remarkable stylistic and formal experiments had in the prewar poetry of Frost, Eliot, and Pound and the prewar prose of James, Cather, Dreiser, and Stein. Feeling bereft was, indeed, critical to their identity. In fact, however, the real if sometimes shaky confidence that sustained them possessed cultural roots as well as generational ties. Fitzgerald and his contemporaries assumed that the literature of the United States was coming of age, and they knew that the United States was rapidly becoming a nation of immense power and prosperity. Yet they continued to write "jeremiads," lamenting almost to the point of strange ecstasy their nation's failings. And in doing so they brought success under the aspect of failure, failure under the aspect of success, and both under the aspect of restless yearning, the emotion most deeply embedded in the country's sense of itself as a land of tinkerers, inventors, and dreamers. Even writers who stayed in Europe long enough to draw sustenance from it – Stein and Hemingway, to take very different examples, or Eliot and Pound – tended to think of Europe as a world of endings and of the United States as a world of beginnings. In *The Making of Americans*, Stein presents her family's move from Europe to the United States as a move from the world's old center to its new center, which is to say, from the past toward the future. Her story, she says, is not simply hers or her family's or her nation's; it is "everybody's history."

The literary potential of the cultural predicament that writers of the twenties claimed as their own took many forms, including John Peale Bishop's assertion that Hemingway had written the drama of the disappearance of the human soul "in our time." Bishop assumes that dramatic cultural events require imaginative works strong enough to trace them. More surreptitiously, he assumes that imaginative works require critical discourse strong enough to make visible their tracings. And in the process, he signals both the coming of age of literature in the United States and the professionalization of its study. "In opulent and commercial societies," Adam Smith predicted, thinking and writing will become "like every other employment, a particular business, which is carried out by a very few people, who furnish the public with all the thought and reason possessed by the vast multitudes that labour." In the decade following the Great War, that process accelerated. The production of novels, for example, like the production of thought and reason, increasingly became a specialized function. Novels spread as the institution of commercial publishing spread to produce and distribute them as commodities. In 1928 Paul Rosenfeld left the prestigious *Dial*, which was devoted to international modernism, to become editor of *American Caravan*, which was dedicated to publishing new young American writers. A year later, after nearly five years of planning, Jay B. Hubbell and others announced the establishment of *American Literature: A Journal of Literary History, Criticism, and Bibliography*.

Both of these developments were signs that writers of the thirties wanted to reorient the tasks of producing and distributing creative and critical texts, first, by making more explicit the ties between cultural events and imaginative discoveries and, second, by using critical discourse to make visible the social logic of literary discoveries. At their best, they also sought to clarify the ties between literature's social logic and the imaginative discoveries that accompanied them by rooting the present in the past and by tying literature to the culture of which it was a part. Cowley's work changed in the thirties, and so did Edmund Wilson's, who moved from *Axel's Castle* (1931) through *The American Jitters* (1932) and *Travels in Two Democracies* (1936), based on his visit in Russia, toward *To the Finland Station* (1940). Kenneth Burke's work not only changed; in its deep concern for the social, political power of rhetoric, symbol, and myth, it found its proper home in the thirties. In her path-breaking work,

American Humor: A Study of the National Character (1931), Constance Rourke sought to discover the roots of the nation's culture not in a few great, isolated figures of the past but in the larger cultural patterns in which ordinary people lived their lives and from which writers drew their material.

"Change the world" became a slogan of the thirties, Herbst observed, because "the world had changed." Joseph Freeman, heir of the Lyric Years, continued to talk as he always had. Hope for him still lay in calling on the working class of the United States to resume its revolutionary "path toward the New World." But "the great knife of the depression," as Robert and Helen Lynd observed in their update of *Middletown*, *Middletown in Transition* (1937), had cut through "the entire population cleaving open lives and hopes of rich as well as poor." And for a time, especially in 1932 and 1933, the world seemed to tremble with possibility. "I'm afraid, every man is afraid," said Charles Schwab of U.S. Steel. It was, Edmund Wilson announced in the *New Republic* in January 1931, as if life had come suddenly under a shadow so dark that the nation's "whole money-making and -spending psychology" had finally become discredited, leading people to "put their idealism and their genius for organization behind a radical social experiment."

In the large cultural task that was involved in placing the call for social experimentation, literature broadly defined – historical studies, personal reminiscences, and critical discourse as well as poetry, drama, and fiction – played several crucial roles. Movements sprang up on the right as well as the left. For a time, many writers, old as well as young, followed the advice of Mike Gold in an editorial in *New Masses* in 1929: "Go Left, Young Writers." By 1932, with hunger and bankruptcy spreading as though by invisible means, leaving millions of once-proud people desperate, "communism" loosely defined was on the rise. To a few, including Lincoln Steffens, Russia was a model of the kind of "faith, hope, liberty, a living" that the United States had once advocated and ought to copy. To others – John Dos Passos and James T. Farrell, for example – Marxist thought seemed valuable primarily as an analytic tool. In 1932 Cowley and Wilson joined Waldo Frank, Mary Heaton Vorse, and others in supporting Kentucky's striking coal-miners. What they saw – several miners shot and several supporters, including Waldo Frank, beaten – pushed them farther to the left. That same year, Cowley, Herbst, and Wilson joined fifty other writers, Sherwood Anderson, Dos Passos, Langston Hughes, and Steffens among them, in issuing a pamphlet, *Culture and Crisis*, that described the nation as "a house rotting away."

For many people, however, communism was more attractive as a secular religion, preaching an old morality of self-denial and sacrifice in service to a noble cause, than as a call to revolution or even a program for action. People who joined the Party, Cowley later remarked, were listened to, even by people like himself, who did not join, "as if they had received advice straight from God." To a considerable degree, however, their authority depended on their vagueness. Recognizing the psychological as well as the social impact of the Depression, Party leaders welcomed almost anyone committed to reform, whether or not they understood or endorsed the Party's tenets. Political tracts, manifestos, and petitions proliferated, but few of them were rigorous in theory or clear about strategy. Specific issues of real import tended to divide the Party, and clearly stated positions on tough issues regularly led to defections from it.

Franklin Delano Roosevelt was born in 1882 and began his study of politics during the Progressive era when the written word and traditional discourse, not the radio or newsreel, dominated political campaigns. In his speeches of 1932, Roosevelt anticipated several programs that became parts of the "New Deal." He sketched plans for the Civilian Conservation Corps and advocated both social welfare legislation and government regulation of utilities. There was considerable vagueness in what he said, however, and some contradiction. Still, he carried forty-two of forty-eight states, including every state west and south of Pennsylvania, which is to say, those farthest from his own center of activity. The vote, though clearly a rejection of Hoover, became a triumph for Roosevelt. And it anticipated others to come by demonstrating his skill as a rhetorician who could dominate the radio as a medium.

Roosevelt not only recognized the possibilities of the radio and its networks in a new era of sound; he also understood the importance of using actions and words as symbols. "Let it be symbolic," be told the cheering convention that had nominated him, "that I broke the tradition," calling attention to his unprecedented decision to fly to Chicago to accept the nomination in person. Henceforth, he added, let it be the "task of our Party to break foolish traditions." Later, both in his inaugural address and in his famous "fireside chats," he entered the "homes" of "the people" to make them feel that he was speaking specifically to them of their hopes and fears, and that he was mindful of their places in and their dependence upon the land he was pledged to renew. In the process, he created a new kind of presidency, of unprecedented political and social power, based on his ability to persuade the people that, in pledging to discard the foolish, reform the outmoded, save the essential, and create the new, his voice was theirs. In the crucial campaign of 1932, in calling for a new era of bold experimentation, he showed himself to be more rhetorically and more historically minded than either Coolidge or Hoover. The urge to tinker and experiment – the desire to foster change and embrace the new – lay, he insisted, at the heart of the nation's great historic tradition. In his only use of the keyword "revolution," in the crucial year of 1932, he stayed within that tradition: "the right kind, the only kind of revolution this nation can stand for," he said, was a "revolution at the ballot box." Once elected, his New Deal emerged slowly as a mix of humanitarianism, realistic politics, and economic common sense. But with the help of the radio, it found a name, taken from a throwaway line in an early speech, that was consistent with the spirit of the "bold, persistent experimentation" that he had rediscovered for and reawakened in "the people."

The New Deal was neither as radical as some have charged nor as timid as others have claimed. Given time to emerge and work, it saved the country's capitalist political economy by modifying it, and it created new social arrangements by redefining what democracy might mean. Part of this it owed to Roosevelt's ability to conceive government defining ends and taking actions that Hoover could not imagine. But much of it depended on his genius for finding words that rooted his reforms in the nation's past and then using the radio to dispatch those words into homes across the land. "Every man has a right to life," he said in September 1932, "and this means that he has also a right to make a comfortable living. . . . Our government, formal and informal, political and economic, owes to everyone an avenue to possess himself of a portion of the plenty" created by our society "sufficient for his needs, through his work." "Republican leaders not only failed in material things, they have failed in national vision, because in disaster they had held out no hope," he told cheering delegates at the Democratic Convention in Chicago. "Let me assert my firm belief," he said, in the most famous line in his inaugural address, "that the only thing we have to fear is fear itself."

At first, Walter Lippmann, author of *The New Imperative* (1935) and *The Good Society* (1937), was skeptical of Roosevelt. Roosevelt was pleasant, Lippmann wrote in 1932, but he was highly impressionable, lacked strong convictions, and possessed no important qualifications for the office he aspired to hold. Shortly after Roosevelt's inauguration, however, Lippmann sensed a turnabout that struck him as earned. "At the beginning of March," Lippmann wrote, "the country was in . . . a state of confused desperation." By June it was regaining "confidence in the government and in itself." Broad restoration of confidence came slowly, of course, and complete economic recovery took years. Even after 1935, when some of the worst signs of the Depression had vanished, apprehension continued to run high. But the reforms that became the New Deal began quickly, with legislation designed to put agriculture and industry on a sounder footing and to bring relief to hard-pressed home owners (the Home Owners Loan Act) and unemployed workers (the Civilian Conservation Corps). As radios continued to carry Roosevelt's voice into homes throughout the country – not only in his own news conferences and "fireside chats" but also in Henry Luce's "March of Time," founded in 1931 as a radio program and then changed to a newsreel in 1935 – more and more people identified his ameliorating reforms with what "American" radicalism meant.

As the New Deal gained support, literary radicalism began to function more as a mode of cultural criticism than as a means of promoting radical action. One sign of this unfolded as something we might call the Americanization of Karl Marx, or, more broadly, of Marxist thought. "I can only welcome Communism by converting it into my own vocabulary. I am, in the deepest sense, a translator," Kenneth Burke wrote. "I go on translating, even if I must but translate English into English." A brilliant student of rhetoric, Burke knew that some things get lost in translation. But he also believed that many were saved and a few discovered. At the famous American Writers' Congress in April 1935, he examined the social function of revolutionary symbols and myths as tools that enabled carpenters and welders to discover "a sense of interrelationship by which, . . . though differently occupied, [they] can work together for a common social end." By 1935, however, Roosevelt was proving himself more effective in using symbols and myths than the Party was, and his aim was ameliorative, not revolutionary.

On this count, as on several others, literature followed politics more than it led. As signs of recovery increased, writers began drawing on "native" traditions and idioms – "translating," as it were – with curious results. "I felt myself to be a radical, not an ideologue," Alfred Kazin later recalled in *Starting Out in the Thirties* (1965). "I was proud of the revolutionary yet wholly literary tradition in American writing to which I knew that I belonged," he adds, assuming that a revolutionary tradition can remain wholly literary. In short, several forms of innocence survived the battering thirties just as they had the disillusioning twenties, and they inspired writers to try odd things. "What young writers of the thirties wanted," Kazin wrote, "was to prove the literary value of our own experience, to recognize the possibility of art in our own lives, to feel we had moved the streets, the stockyards, the hiring halls into literature – to show that our radical strength could carry on the experimental impulse of modern literature." Versions of what Kazin called a literature of "strong social argument, intellectual power, [and] human liberation" turned up repeatedly. In their expressed desire to embrace previously nonliterary scenes and subjects, writers changed "realist" fiction and contributed to the emergence of documentary literature. But Kazin's statement is also notable for tensions it leaves unresolved, and these too are representative – particularly those between personal experience and ambition, on one side, and social realities and responsibilities, on the other. Ultimately, Kazin locates his hope for deliverance in words employed, not as Burke advocated or as Roosevelt practiced, but as poets were thought always to have used them. Power was not what came out of the barrel of a gun or even from the threat of its use; it was not even control of the complex bartering that went on among businessmen, government agents, and union leaders in their efforts to control the flow of products, manipulate demand, and distribute profits. Power was the word, somehow "American" and yet "wholly literary," "modern" and yet timeless – which is to say, enriched by overlapping histories yet free of all historical contaminations. "Salvation would come by the word, the long-awaited and fatefully exact word that only the true writer would speak," Kazin concluded.

How to square nonelitist, revisionary aims with elitist assumptions was not a question the thirties successfully addressed. In declaring his faith in the power of *writers* to *speak* with fateful precision, Kazin appeals to Edmund Wilson, and through him to Marcel Proust, as Wilson describes Proust in *Axel's Castle* (1931): "the little man with the sad appealing voice, the metaphysician's mind, the Saracen's beak, the ill-fitting dress-shirt and the great eyes that seem to see" everything. For Kazin, Proust represented the power of art, or more precisely the power of the novel, to provide searching accounts of "the loves, the society, the intelligence, the diplomacy, the literature and the art of the Heartbreak House of capitalist culture." Yet the problem of how to bridge the gap that separated the lives of Proust's characters from those of people who worked in the streets, stockyards, and hiring halls of the Great Depression remained largely unanswered. Westerns, which flourished in the thirties, turned back toward a world divided along different lines. Detective novels, which came of age in this decade, redirected an individualistic, separatist, antinomian tradition, which Henry Miller's fiction put to very different ends. "Proletarian" fiction used "class" as a lens for measuring that distance, often by insisting that the obliteration of "class" was the key to closing it. Documentary literature recorded and dramatized the fact of it and also examined its human costs. The most self-consciously experimental works of the era – Henry Miller's *Tropic of Capricorn* (1939); Djuna Barnes's *Nightwood* (1936); Dos Passos's *U.S.A.* (1930–6); Faulkner's *The Sound and the Fury* (1929), *As I Lay Dying* (1930), *Light in August* (1932), *Absalom, Absalom!* (1936), and *Go Down, Moses* (1942); Nathanael West's *Miss Lonelyhearts* (1933) and *The Day of the Locust* (1939); James Agee's *Let Us Now Praise Famous Men* (1941); Richard Wright's *Uncle Tom's Children* (1938); Zora Neale Hurston's *Their Eyes Were Watching God* (1937), to name a few – directly engage poverty, race, gender, sex, caste, and class as critical social problems that are also crucial correlates of personal identity. Formal experiments of the thirties regularly embrace political and social themes. When they focus on the past, their authors work as amateur historians. When they examine the present, they often work, as Sinclair Lewis had, as amateur sociologists. Yet much of the explicitly political writing of the time, including political fiction, remained loyal to the reform spirit – the tradition of "good hope" – that reached back to the Lyric Years and beyond. And this loyalty, to what Kazin called the "revolutionary yet wholly literary tradition in American writing," often had the effect of taming if not blunting their protest, though it remains possible that their protests gained influence as a result.

Novels of the thirties remain divided in their depictions of the nation's culture. Protest dominates their mood. Silence plays an even larger role in the literature of the thirties than it does in *Winesburg, Ohio*, in part because it serves as a sign of blighted lives and of a grim resolve that sometimes bears striking resemblance to resignation. Having become less dependent on clever satire and irony, humor, like scorn, became a means of mastering bleak, inadequate fates. In one way or another, it helps to shore up the lives even of the most damaged and threatened human beings – Djuna Barnes's women, Henry Miller's antiheroes, William Faulkner's forgotten people, black and white, James Agee's sharecroppers, Richard Wright's angry rebels, and Zora Neale Hurston's resilient black women. But humor also helped to deflect the anger and despair such characters express, muting protest and making acquiescence bearable.

At times, of course, art, like life, seemed merely to be going on. For some writers, including Hemingway and Fitzgerald, the bleakness of the thirties was more personal than historical. Hemingway "is quite as nervously broken down as I am," Fitzgerald remarked shortly after he published "The Crack-Up," adding that Hemingway's breakdown inclined itself "toward megalomania" while his own tilted "toward melancholy." In what remained of their best writing – for Hemingway stories like "The Snows of Kilimanjaro" and "The Short, Happy Life of Francis Macomber" and for Fitzgerald *Tender is the Night* – they wrote of endings with such resonance that sooner or later we realize that they, like Proust, are writing about the end of an era, or perhaps a way of life, more or less clearly situated in "the Heartbreak House of capitalist culture." Other writers of the twenties – Dos Passos and Herbst, for example – found their social concerns affirmed by the thirties. And others – including Katherine Anne Porter (b. 1890), Henry Miller and Zora Neale Hurston (b. 1891), Djuna Barnes (b. 1892), and William Faulkner (b. 1897) – who were slower to develop than Hemingway and Fitzgerald, discovered that the search for culture fit their imaginations as well as it fit those of younger writers like James Agee (b. 1909), Henry Roth (b. 1906), and Nathanael West (b. 1903), and so made the thirties, bounded on one side by the Great Crash and on the other by the century's second great war, another distinctive multigenerational literary era.

3

❦

THREE RESPONSES: THE EXAMPLES
OF HENRY MILLER, DJUNA BARNES,
AND JOHN DOS PASSOS

By 1930, when he left New York for Paris, Henry Miller thought of
himself as one of the last heirs of the Lyric Years' commitment to
the value of childlike innocence and unmediated feelings. Bored with
literary works like Spenser's *Faerie Queene*, he had exchanged studies at City
College for a series of dreary jobs that included brief stints with a cement
company and his father's tailoring business and five years as supervisor of
Western Union's messenger service. But it was New York's street life that
engaged him, and its burlesque shows and dance halls, in one of which he met
a hostess named June Smith, who became the subject of much of his writing.
Later, gaining confidence, he denounced bookishness in favor of experience,
spontaneity, and instinct. But his writings – from his early studies of outcasts,
derelicts, and prostitutes to the series of novels that made him famous, *Tropic of
Cancer* (1934), *Black Spring* (1936), and *Tropic of Capricorn* (1939) – are in fact
highly self-conscious performances. They are shaped as much by the books
he had read – of Walter Pater and Henry James as well as Whitman, Dreiser,
Norris, and London, whom he more or less owned up to – as by the things he had
done and seen. And they demonstrate what his carefully constructed persona,
introduced in New York, perfected in Paris, then transported to California,
at once denied and suggested: that for him the doctrines of spontaneity and
instinctivism and his celebrations of unmediated experience coexisted with an
active, irrepressible aestheticism.

Less apparent but no less pervasive than the aestheticism that tied Miller
to the twenties were a set of social concerns, also rooted in the Lyric Years,
that blossomed in the thirties. Before leaving New York for Paris, he had
seen the country slide into an economic slough that matched his sense of its
dismal spiritual state. Over the next several years, living in exile, he wrote a
series of novels designed to smash the middle-class mores and the false dreams
promulgated by the Horatio Alger stories. That, as it turned out, was the extent
of Miller's social commitment. He believed, as George Orwell noted in 1940,
"in the impending ruin of Western Civilization," but he had no intention

of trying to stop it. Irresponsibility, an extreme form of antinomianism – a celebration of the single, solitary, pleasure-seeking, self-aggrandizing self against a society that seemed to him corrupt and enslaved as well as corrupting and enslaving – became his cause. No group and no cultural tradition, except the one that authorized his resistance to traditions, elicited his loyalty. His only commitment was to himself as a refugee, and as the refugee-hero of his books.

Working as an employment supervisor for the Cosmodemonic/Cosmococcic Telegraph Company of New York, the actual Henry Miller's fictitious Henry Miller acts as the first-person narrator of *Tropic of Capricorn*. Having launched a plan for improving the lives of the messengers he supervises, he is thwarted by a vice-president whose concerns are fixed by the narrow interests of a market economy. If you want to help the messengers, the vice-president says to Miller, write a Horatio Alger story for them. "I'll give you an Horatio Alger book," Miller thinks to himself. "I will give you Horatio Alger as he looks the day after the Apocalypse, when all the stink has cleared away" – a line that captures as fully as any one line can both the temporal setting and the harsh humor of fiction of the thirties. After requesting a leave, Miller's protagonist spends three weeks writing:

I sat riveted to my desk and I traveled around the world at lightning speed, and I learned that everywhere it is the same – hunger, humiliation, ignorance, vice, greed, extortion, chicanery, torture, despotism: the inhumanity of man to man: the fetters, the harness, the halter, the bridle, the whip, the spurs.

Armed with this knowledge, Miller's protagonist discovers a personal vocation that takes him as close as he ever comes to a social mission – namely, that of writing, as he put it in *Tropic of Cancer*, antibooks that record "all that which is omitted in books." Having quit his job with the Cosmodemonic/Cosmococcic Telegraph Company, he goes to Paris to become an undersider and outsider and write books that will "wipe Horatio Alger" and his cultural lies "out of the North American consciousness" forever.

Tropic of Capricorn earned Miller an outsized reputation for sexual explicitness. Although there had been a discernible increase in sexual explicitness in the twenties, there had also been much disguise, as we see in Stein's *Three Lives* (1909), much disgust and violence, as we see in Dos Passos's *Manhattan Transfer* (1925), and much shallow irony and titillation, as we see in James Branch Cabell's *Jurgen* (1919). Coming later, Miller's novels stretched the limits of the forbidden to the breaking point; they were frequently banned, especially in English-speaking countries, and were not published legally in the United States until the 1960s. But his novels are not merely full of often repetitious sex.

They are also full of ugly, poorly repressed anxieties and hostilities, including antisemitism and racism as well as sexism.

Miller presents himself both as a bohemian, devil-may-care artist who scorns worldly success and as a neglected, impoverished genius who settles scores. There is, however, a kind of self-criticism at work in his novels, as well as self-promotion. In *Tropic of Cancer* he launches a deliberate assault on the whole set of middle-class values built around the celebration of hard work and the fear of sex. But he also attacks all forms of transcendent hope, including aestheticism: "a gob of spit in the face of Art, a kick in the pants to God, Man, Destiny, Time, Love, Beauty . . . what you will" is a part of what he has in mind. He thus reminds us that radical novels can attack almost any target, including political responsibility, social allegiance, revolutionary ardor, bourgeois guilt, and aesthetic commitment. In part an epitaph, as Edmund Wilson observed, to all the writers and artists who left the United States for Europe, saying that they wanted to "experience" life and "serve" art, *Tropic of Cancer* provides a sad yet playful report that focuses on people, including Miller's self-protagonist, whose long bouts of drinking, eating, talking, and fornicating are broken by brief interludes devoted to reading books or visiting exhibitions. Still, a kind of truth-seeking emerges from Miller's exaggerations, just as a kind of comic irony emerges from his "confessions." And both of these things help to define his notion of what art should do. His celebration of his ego, which is full of distortions disguised as disclosures, constitutes a means of countering the alienation fostered by modern mass society, just as his wildly incorporating, self-aggrandizing ego constitutes a way of countering the modern world's diminution of the self.

Miller's "divine stuttering," as he calls it in "The Third and Fourth Day of Spring," is the work of an imagination that is given to repetition and allusional density as well as irony and humor, including three forms of these things — self-reflexivity, intertextuality, and authorial anxiety — that make Miller a forerunner of "postmodernism." His novels are megalomaniacal in their self-involvement and self-absorption. They affront, assault, and offend. Together, however, *Tropic of Cancer*, *Black Spring*, and *Tropic of Capricorn* form one large interreflexive assault on the bureaucratized, overdetermining modern world by celebrating a new kind of defiant if still imperial self: "For me the book is the man and my book is the man I am, the confused man, the negligent man, the reckless man, the lusty, obscene, boisterous, thoughtful, scrupulous, lying, diabolically truthful man that I am."

Miller's iconoclastic "truthfulness" frees sex of all romance. It treats most other people – all women and many men – as interchangeable parts, differenti-ated only by the names and the acts that he assigns them. Disappointments and anxieties tilt even his most lyrical prose toward ugliness: "O world, strangled and collapsed, where are the strong white teeth? O world, sinking with the silver balls and the corks and the life-preservers, where are the rosy scalps? O glab and glairy, O glabrous world now chewed to a frazzle, under what dead moon do you lie cold and gleaming?" But Miller's antipoetic poetry, like his antiheroic hero, reflects a sense of personal urgency that stems from the threat of personal annihilation. Experience and words, together with the books that preserve them, are all that he, as a doomed body and beleaguered imagination, has left. His experiences and his words, soiled by repetition, fit the beleaguered protagonist who knows that he is not and never was autonomous, knows in fact that even with the bravest and most cunning of struggles, a diluted form of semiautonomy is the most he can hope to achieve. His protagonists use words as they use acts of sex: to protect themselves by asserting themselves. They survive only as damaged goods or suspect commodities, to which terrible things have always already happened.

Miller's novels are, in short, Depression novels: they are written out of as well as about economic deprivation, political corruption, and historic catastrophe. The force of the large, gangrenous world enters his novels in two large ways. It enters as an alienating force that culminates in a hard-won detachment that enables him not only to write about his world as though it were both an apocalyptic fantasy and a dark comedy of earthly despair and about himself in the first person as though he were a visitor from another planet; and it also enters as a force that has transformed the purpose of art and sex by making them the last possible strongholds of the self and its imagination against the forces of domination and control. Since assimilation always means annihilation of the individual for Miller, and since the historical forces marshaled in its behalf, like the economic interests they serve, include almost everything – government and the manipulative media of the world; countless false notions about sex, perpetuated by culture, including literary culture, as epitomized in all romantic notions about it; and most art, as epitomized in the Horatio Alger stories – the odds against the individual's marginal survival become almost insurmountable. The darkness and savagery of Miller's humor fit the darkness and savagery of the world he renders. His characters move under dead moons that lie "cold and gleaming," and they spend most of their time picking either the scabs that dot their own bodies and souls or those that dot the bodies and souls of people around them. Those who succeed in the world's terms, even as writers, lose their mortal bodies in relinquished sex and their mortal souls in reading and writing false stories – and so do most of those who fail. Miller speaks, therefore, both for and to a remnant who battle long odds and more or less survive by remaining suspicious of the conquests they cannot live with or without.

Like other important writers of the thirties, including Dos Passos, Barnes, West, Agee, and Faulkner, Miller sought to adjust the special preoccupations of the twenties to a world darkened by the Depression. He flaunted his irreverence for the doctrines of the impersonality and the transcendent powers of art, as epitomized by its so-called triumph over history. Other important possibilities lay embedded, however, in the notion of art as iconoclastic counterstatement, or what Miller called "divine stuttering," and two of them meet a curious fate in his fiction.

The dominant culture that Miller faced as adversary not only celebrated self-reliance, privileging self-realization and diminishing the claims of community; it also assumed its representative individual to be white and male, not black or brown and not female. In short, it implicitly based privilege on race and gender. And in these crucial ways – in its celebration of the single, solitary, self-aggrandizing self; in its embrace of absolute individual rights as essential to the individual's resistance to assimilation and, therefore, annihilation; in its wholesale reduction of all claims of community as intrusive and abusive; and in its casual assumption that the only self that matters is gentile, white, and male, not Jewish, not black, and not female – Miller's fiction reiterates the dominant culture it presents itself as attacking. Despite their self-proclaimed iconoclasm, his novels both repeat crucial prejudices of the culture they attack and reiterate its fear of all efforts to defend individualism as socially desirable. As a result, much of their significance lies hidden in what they ignore. To read them fully, we must read them for their elisions.

The two crucial elisions that give Miller's trilogy, written between 1934 and 1939, its special importance also play central roles in two very different novels – Djuna Barnes's *Nightwood* (1936), which is so oblique and private as to seem subterranean, and John Dos Passos's *U.S.A.* (1930–36), one of the most open, inclusive, public novels ever written. If Barnes may be said obliquely to confront the consequences of female subjugation and repression by using enforced obliqueness as one sign of those consequences, Dos Passos may be said to make the fragmented, mixed form of his novel a sign of the absence of community in the land whose story he tries to tell.

Nightwood centers on a group of expatriates in Paris and Berlin. Through Felix Volkbein, it evokes the search for history and family; through Dr. Matthew O'Connor, an unlicensed Irish American gynecologist, it parodies the rise of modern therapeutic culture. O'Connor's alcoholic, melancholic, apocalyptic monologues on war, the modern world, and the bodies and minds of women and men are scattered throughout the novel. But the action of the novel centers on the relations between Robin Vote, who is married to Volkbein, and

Nora Flood, who becomes Robin's lover, and Jenny Petherbridge, for whom Robin leaves Nora. Like Robin, however, the novel's action remains shrouded, in part because Robin's beauty makes her vulnerable to the women as well as the men who look upon her with desire, letting their needs define her. Desire, depravity, and violence hover over *Nightwood*. As we become implicated in trying to read it, furthermore, we begin, like Dr. O'Connor and Nora Flood, to fix our gaze on Robin, as though determined to know and possess her. Yet the harder we push that endeavor, the more Robin, as though sensing her vulnerability, recedes before our eyes, leaving signs and traces that we can scarcely help misconstruing.

Finally, no one in the novel escapes the sexual politics of a world ruled by possession and suppression. Sexual acts are everywhere desired, feared, anticipated, and alluded to, but none is ever seen. What we see are the consequences, in the lives of men and women, of the suppression of women and the repression – indeed, the denial – of female desire. Juxtaposed to the aggressive, assaultive male sexuality of *Tropic of Capricorn*, the oblique, thwarted sexuality of *Nightwood* becomes even more clearly a story about the fate of women in a world in which only white males are authorized to express, in actions and words, or even feel the full range of their desires. If Miller's novel is a testament to authorized expression and aggression, Barnes's is a testament to enforced evasion, denial, and obliqueness. Together they make clear the dual logic of performance as it comes to bear on men who feel required to express and women who feel required to suppress desire. Both novels are filled with characters who function as actors, some of whom become skilled quick-change artists or experts in cross-dressing, changing accents, and switching languages. "Henry Miller's" performance is the virtuoso performance of a character who assumes that he is linear and stable despite his internal contradictions. *Nightwood*, by contrast, focuses on the oblique gestures, hidden acts, and reticent performances of women who remain conscious of themselves as too tentative, hesitating, provisional, multiple, and fluid even to be called "selves." In 1939, shortly after finishing his first trilogy, Miller left Paris for Greece, and in 1940 he returned to the United States, where he went on telling and retelling versions of his story for forty years, eventually in another self-celebrating trilogy, *Sexus* (1949), *Plexus* (1953), and *Nexus* (1960), collectively entitled *The Rosy Crucifixion*. Five years after finishing *Nightwood*, Barnes left Paris for New York, where she lived alone, maintaining herself in silence, as a last resort of the oppressed, until she died in 1982.

If *Nightwood* exposes one set of elisions that alter the cultural significance of Miller's fiction, *U.S.A.*, which includes three novels – *The 42nd Parallel* (1930), *1919* (1932), and *The Big Money* (1936) – exposes another by making scattered particulars of the social life and the patchwork culture of the United States visible. In *The Big Money* we see women singing out of lost love,

> I hate to see de evenin sun go down
> Hate to see de evenin sun go down
> Cause my baby he done lef' dis town

men singing out of uncertainty,

> Oh tell me how long
> I'll have to wait
> . . . .
> Do I get it now
> Or must I hesitate
> . . . .
> Oh tell me how long

and workers singing out of pain,

> While we slave for the bosses
> Our children scream an' cry.

At times Dos Passos seems to speak in his own voice about a nation hopelessly divided ("all right we are two nations") or hopelessly lost ("we stand defeated America"). Yet neither he as a narrator possessed of a discrete voice nor any of his characters succeeds in mastering the entangled historical forces that we encounter in *U.S.A.* Historical figures interact with fictional characters, blurring the line between history and fiction – and with it, the line between documentary reports and imaginative stories. Dos Passos refuses to separate history and fiction or to privilege one over the other, and he resists the temptation to view life as objectively determined yet subjectively free. Dialectical play among contrastive principles and contradictory wills is what he explores and, in his own way, celebrates. *U.S.A.* thus absorbs in its juxtapositional form several concerns of the twenties and most concerns of the thirties by recasting the large-scale cultural shift of the United States – from a predominantly agrarian, traditional society toward an increasingly urban, industrial, commercial, and secular society – into a story that culminates in open conflicts between a small group of rich, powerful people who know how to manipulate the economic forces that shape history and a large group of poor, almost powerless people who know what it feels like to be buffeted by them. A dispiriting story, *U.S.A.* reports on a nation in decline. At its end, we see an almost nameless young man called "Vag" standing by a road, trying to hitch a ride, and recognize in him the wreckage of broken promises and self-betrayals, so interlinked as to be inseparable, that was left in the wake of the Great Depression.

Upton Sinclair thought that Dos Passos's technical innovations diluted his political message; Hemingway thought that the message got in the way of the fiction. But Jean-Paul Sartre, whose sympathies included both reform politics and aesthetic innovations, called Dos Passos one of the century's greatest novelists and named *U.S.A.* his supreme achievement – in part, we may assume, because he recognized the significance of Dos Passos's efforts to acknowledge the force of history while celebrating the authority of fiction, and in part because he recognized the significance of Dos Passos's concern for the fate of communities as well as individuals in a secular world where money becomes the only countervailing force to helplessness that people really believe in.

4

❦

RESIDUAL INDIVIDUALISM AND
HEDGED COMMITMENTS

THE ELITISM that found expression in T. S. Eliot's famous description of himself as a "classicist in literature, royalist in politics, and anglo-catholic in religion" survived in the thirties. Worldly in its wit and reach, as it gathers fragments in different languages from different times and places, and world-weary in its tone, as it laments the loss of artistic tradition and religious faith, Eliot's style largely defined literature for shapers of the New Criticism. Art should be cosmopolitan yet imperial in its claims (meaning that it should claim everything high-up and good) and aristocratic in its exclusions (meaning that it should condemn everything middle-class, mean, or vulgar). But the thirties witnessed the revival of three overlapping forms of populism that had flourished during the Lyric Years and then languished in the twenties. One of these, more or less Marxist in tendency, descended from writers like Upton Sinclair, Randolph Bourne, Floyd Dell, John Reed, and Jack London. A second came from some of the same writers, especially London, and was primitivistic in logic. And a third, more "realist" than "naturalist," found expression in the heirs of William Dean Howells – writers like Willa Cather and Sherwood Anderson, who made fiction out of the manners and foibles, the aspirations and hypocrisies, the symbols and myths of the frequently maligned middle class. During the twenties, when the vocabulary of idealism fell into disrepute, the untested truce between populist and elitist tendencies fell apart. Mencken became almost typical in treating the "Middle Class" with contempt and all politics, including reform politics, as a farce.

In the thirties, fiction moved – backward or forward, depending on one's persuasions – toward "realism," not as a slice of life but as an organized selection of observed reality, and in the process it moved toward a reassessment of life as always political. Writers like Mike Gold spoke of formalists and aesthetes – "escapists, abstractionists, Freudians, and mystics of art, foggy symbolists, clowns and trained seals and sex-mad pygmies of the pen" – with undisguised contempt. But many writers of the thirties worked the same tension that writers of the twenties had worked: the tension between the principle that implicated the novel in history by defining it as a genre created to account for social phenomena and historical existence and the principle that freed it from history by defining it as a genre devoted to free imaginative play and semiautonomy, if not transcendence. What changed was the balance between these principles, which tilted toward the first during the thirties.

In sweeping away the affluence of the twenties, the Crash temporarily derailed the hopes of the nation's middle class – of buying radios, refrigerators, fashionable clothes, and Fords today, shares of stock and who-knew-what tomorrow, in pursuit of the good life. But it also dashed a related hope shared by many writers – of securing without crippling compromise a life of comfortable bohemian sufficiency, if not glamorous affluence, while writing for themselves. Gone, too, as though in the same motion, was the sense that writers could ignore, or even take pride in ignoring, the widening gap between their concerns and those of ordinary people. Within prose fiction, "realism," with its ties to social and historical phenomena, pulled fiction toward a larger if still somewhat specialized audience, while "surrealism," with its links to myth and symbol, to dreams and the unconscious, and thus to the unpredictable terrain of subjectivity, pulled it toward a smaller group of elite *aficionados*, educated, as it were, by people like Eliot. Gold's gifts for mixed metaphors occasionally got out of hand when he was debunking literary elitism as a sign of bourgeois decadence: "Even at their best, in the supreme expression of the bourgeois individualist, in a James Joyce or T. S. Eliot, defeat follows them like a mangy cur. They are up a historic blind alley and have no future." But such statements remind us of at least three things: that writers of the twenties worked in an economy that allowed waste and encouraged privatization as well as specialization; that waste, privatization, and specialization shaped lives lived as well as words written; and that ties between the literature and the dominant culture of the twenties can be observed in literary celebrations of the claims of the individual against the community as well as the widespread acceptance of still largely unexamined assumptions about genderized sexuality as well as class and race.

During the twenties, social irresponsibility was condoned in the few places where it was not in vogue. People wasted time and energy as well as money, and some of them wasted lives, on the ultimate privatistic assumption that one's life is wholly one's own, even to throw away. In the very different economy of the thirties, writers continued to take risks. They smoked, drank, made love, had sex, and traveled; they stayed up late and boasted of burning their candles at both ends. But given the scarcity of money and jobs, everyone – especially young people who were starting out – had to be more careful, a burden that differed markedly from that of being sophisticated, which in the twenties often seemed almost synonymous with sounding cynical. Merely being clever, amusing, or novel was no longer enough. By 1932 works of art and even casual remarks were checked regularly for the range of social concern they reflected.

Vigorous forms of aestheticism continued to flourish in the work of writers as different as Kenneth Burke, Wallace Stevens, and William Faulkner, as well as in music and movies. But they flourished side by side with new political intensities. In brief, writing of the thirties bears the marks of "strangers" and "outsiders" – Southerners, Jews, blacks, and women – for whom writing was necessarily a way of testing and transgressing boundaries. Dos Passos found the peculiar intensities of the thirties more congenial than he had ever found the privatism of the twenties. Slower to mature as a writer, Faulkner emerged as a major literary figure in the thirties, in part because the history of his family and his region had put him on familiar terms with poverty, failure, fear, and defeat and in part because his own experience had taught him that a sense of entanglement could coexist with and even support a sense of estrangement.

Writing for the *New Yorker* late in 1930, Robert Benchley announced that sex was "as tiresome as the Old Mortgage" and should not be "mentioned ever again." He was bored by rebellious youths and Victorian parents and gave not a hang whether all the young women in the country got ruined, wanted to get ruined, or kept from getting ruined. All he asked was an end to plays recounting their dilemmas. But such humor belonged more to the twenties than the thirties. Even when it focused on sex, the new humor was likely to be darker, like that of Nathanael West or Henry Miller. Self-conscious sophistication like James Branch Cabell's seemed almost as dated as Sinclair Lewis's scorn for rampant materialism. Amid a spreading threat of privation, worldliness seemed as shallow as world-weariness. "We prefer crude vigor to polished banality," Jack Conroy announced in *Anvil*, one of the era's better proletarian magazines. "It ain't a fit night for man or beast," W. C. Fields remarks in *The Fatal Glass of Beer*. "The time has come to take the bull by the tail and face the situation," he adds, evoking the comic tradition, shared with Groucho Marx, of turning confusion, ineptitude, failure, and pain into laughter.

Even lives thrown away were likely to be regarded more as public statements than as private acts. In April 1932, Hart Crane walked to the stern of the steamship *Orizobe*, which was bound from Mexico for New York by way of Havana. Standing there, he removed and folded his coat and then climbed to the ship's rail, where he balanced for a moment before diving into the sea. For years Crane had inveighed against the repressive, commercial society that had wounded him, at least in part by defining his sexuality as perversion. And he had also gone on drinking hard – sometimes to evoke the visions that he could turn into poetry and sometimes to blot out what he had done the night before with the sailors he sought out as homosexual partners. He was, he told his friends repeatedly, "caught like a rat in a trap." Who knows what he thought at the end – that he had squandered his gifts, that he had done all things he could do, that only the sea could deliver him from the intimate harms he had suffered during the broken intervals that constituted his life? He left no message, and his body was never recovered. Still, his death, like his life, came almost immediately to seem rhetorical, a final act as word, and so reached across the thirties – as we see in David Wolff's poem, "Remembering Hart Crane" (1935), and years later in John T. Irwin's "The Verbal Emblem" (1976), where Crane becomes the epitome of the poet-hero hurt by the incorporation of culture – first into poetry and then into the oblivion of the "smooth imperial Caribbean" to die.

Even more typical were acts of violence that were public from the start. In 1931, roughly a year before Crane's death, nine black teenagers, ranging in age from thirteen to nineteen, were arrested in Scottsboro, Alabama, and charged with raping two white women. Both the black teenagers and the white women were drifters, out riding the rails, searching for who knows what. They were people, as Kay Boyle put it, "that no one had use for, had nothing to / give to, no place to offer." The series of trials, appeals, and retrials set off by the Scottsboro arrests, along with the protests that accompanied them, stretched across the thirties as a long reminder of what Richard Wright called the "'plight of black folk'" as well as of the destructive insecurities of white folk. "Freedom don't mean a thing to me," one of the defendants said; life outside is "no different than prison." In 1934, while the Scottsboro tragedy was still unfolding, gangster violence reached a peak: on the afternoon of May 23, on a little-traveled road outside Shreveport, Louisiana, a posse of Texas Rangers pumped more than fifty bullets into the bodies of Bonnie and Clyde Parker; on the evening of July 22, in front of a Chicago movie theater, featuring Clark Gable in a gangster movie, federal agents gunned down John Dillinger; on the morning of October 22, on a farm in Ohio, federal agents shouted "Halt" and then filled the body of Charles "Pretty Boy" Floyd with bullets from machine guns and pistols; on November 28, following a gun battle in rural Illinois in which two federal agents died, the bullet-riddled body of George "Baby Face" Nelson was found abandoned in a ditch outside Chicago.

Different forms of violence run through documentary works, self-consciously "proletarian" novels, "radical" strike novels, and historical novels of the thirties, and the threat or fact of it dominates two of the period's most popular forms of fiction, Westerns and detective stories. Like writers of the ancient world, Milton and Shakespeare borrowed plots from history, including several that had already been turned into art. Both sin and the idea of sin, as encoding the story of the human fall into time, mortality, and exile, were familiar to Milton's readers. But Milton assumed that he could surprise his readers all over again. More recent formula stories, including detective stories and Westerns, owe their existence to modern publishing, modern circulation, and modern marketing. We find them in magazines and we read them on trains, subways, buses, and airplanes, in barbershops and beauty parlors, or in the waiting-rooms of doctors and dentists. Like older writers, however, their authors begin with received formulas and then surprise us with some distinctive twist in a familiar plot or some distinctive act of style that sets writer and protagonist apart. Yet their works differ from earlier formula stories in ways that expose one of the crucial secrets of the twentieth century: our fear that both authentic community and authentic individualism, far from coming to us as gifts of culture, come into existence only in scattered instances and against great odds – the first as an act of human contrivance, the second as an act of human will.

On the near side, as it were, of formula stories (including historical romances) stand isolated readers who feel trapped in routine, regimented lives. During the thirties, the sense of entrapment was compounded by economic circumstances that robbed people of the saving hope of the twenties: the hope that they might somehow gain entrance into the house of have. From one point of view, we may say that Westerns and detective stories exploited the need that Depression readers felt for "escapist" entertainment. But we may also say – neither more nor less neutrally – that they presented imaginatively constructed alternative worlds. Writers of Westerns go back in time, as Cody and Turner had, to reinforce a modern assumption, embedded in the nation's formative myths, that adventures essentially don't happen to people who stay at home. They take us out of our familiar worlds into adventure's or even harm's way, but they do so, as Cody had, at safe remove. In seclusion and comparative safety, we identify with characters who confront mystery, peril, and even death, or a failure of nerve that is a form of death. At the same time, however, Westerns deliver us from ultimate terror – first, by presenting a world that yields to outsized courage and skill and, second, by telling a story that works variations on a familiar formula, without finally disorienting us. Having taken us on an adventure, they deliver us from it.

There is, however, another cultural task that detective stories as well as Westerns perform. Drawing on several traditions, including classical political

theory and biblical religion, their protagonists reiterate the right and responsibility of individuals to judge everything for themselves. In them civil
community, or more broadly culture itself, depends for its survival not on
civic-minded citizens but on individualists who live by codes of their own.
The cowboy-drifters and outsiders of Zane Grey (a dentist who "fell in love
with the West") and the estranged detective-heroes of Dashiell Hammett and
Raymond Chandler serve society reluctantly because, though they honor community as an ideal, they reject it in its actual, fallen state in which both the
threat of punishment and the lure of money, power, and pleasure inculcate
"false" (sometimes "capitalist" and sometimes "feminine") values. If "false"
society serves as the villain of Westerns and detective stories, "true" culture
persists in them only as an unrealized dream.

Long before Dos Passos wrote *Big Money* (1936) – "they are stronger they
are rich they hire and fire the politicians . . . all right we are two nations" – the
popular fiction of the nation was virtually shouting about a crippling division
between men and women. "Domestic" novels were written primarily by, for,
and about women. Women are their main characters, and young women, frequently orphans, are their protagonists. Their settings favor enclosed, private
spaces such as kitchens and sitting rooms. When nature makes an appearance,
it typically enters as a pastoral landscape or a quiet garden. In short, the real
struggles of "domestic" novels are internal. Instruction designed to dispel internal confusion plays an important role in them and so, therefore, do reading
books, singing hymns, and saying prayers. Introspection, we learn, lies near the
heart of young female life as it gropes its way toward maturity. Whether one
will or will not marry or, more painfully, will or will not become wise – first, by
learning to remain chaste in thought as well as word and deed and, second, by
learning to subordinate oneself to an appropriate husband – become life's big issues. Religion and culture are inseparable, and women are the principal bearers
of both. In service to them, and thus to family, lies perfect "female" freedom.

Westerns, following Owen Wister's *The Virginian*, were generally written
for and about men. They, too, stress proper devotion as the test of all things.
But in them religious moorings are loose. Even in the late nineteenth and early
twentieth centuries, British novelists, especially women novelists, continued to
present ministers as heroes and to use them as authorial voices. Novels in the
United States, going back to Nathaniel Hawthorne, often subject them to harsh
scrutiny. When characters of spiritual force appear, they are usually women.
B. M. Bower, pseudonym for B. M. Sinclair, a woman who wrote stories about
the Flying U Ranch, is a notable exception to the tendency for Westerns to be
written by men. She is also an exception in that she concentrates on an almost

prefallen community,

[a] peaceful . . . little world tucked away in its hills, with its own little triumphs and defeats, its own heartaches and rejoicings; a lucky little world, because its triumphs had been satisfying, its defeats small, its heartaches brief, and its rejoicings untainted with harassment or guilt.

Bowers's Flying U stories anticipate the agrarian utopianism that flourished in the thirties. By contrast, Zane Grey's social world is fallen. Though it remains largely preindustrial, it is not quite premodern. For it is already deeply conflicted about the "progress" of industrial civilization and sometimes about religion. In Grey's novels, devout women remain spiritually strong and retain religious authority. But most men, including men of the cloth, tend to use religion as they use everything else – to enlarge their fortunes and increase their power, as we see especially in *Riders of the Purple Sage* (1912) in the contrast between Jane Withersteen and Elder Tull. Grey's heroes are drawn toward action rather than introspection, and they value integrity more than power, or even their own lives. In town, they prefer secular public spaces – livery stables, land offices, courthouses, railroad stations, or saloons – to homes and churches. But they give their deeper loyalty to a still almost untouched and, therefore, uncorrupted nature. Restlessness is one of their trademarks, isolation another. Taciturn and stoic in manner, they rarely feel desire, let alone reverence, for anything except "pure" women and unspoiled natural scenes – wide rivers, open prairies, majestic mountains, or the big sky – which they sometimes think of as vaguely feminine. Their own lives they govern by a stern code of honor they think of as masculine.

In *Riders of the Purple Sage*, ruthless Mormon elders control almost everything. In *Nevada* (1928) and *West of the Pecos* (1931), officers of the law are in cahoots with crooked, land-grabbing ranchers. In *Code of the West* (1934), a young Eastern woman named Georgiana Stockwell goes west, reeking of "modern" opinions: that traditional standards of conduct are "back numbers" and that "our sisters and mothers and grandmothers have been buncoed by the lords of creation. By men!" Determined to dress, talk, and act as she pleases, Stockwell advocates liberation and encourages Eastern jazz dancing whenever she gets a chance. Some of the conflict in *Code of the West* comes from old-style rustling and land-grabbing. The rest Georgiana stirs up – until, of course, she learns the valuable lessons of a fading but not yet lost frontier and so puts behind her "her pitiful little vanity of person, her absorption of the modern freedom, with its feminine rant about equality with men," and starts "longing to make amends." Thus chastened, she becomes a perfect wife – attractive and seemingly spirited yet cowed.

In typical Grey novels, male identity is (re)asserted and male hegemony is (re)established in a less overt and less strained way than in *Code of the West*. But even in them society rarely appears in an admirable light: the more developed it becomes, the more rotten it is apt to be. In novels like *Nevada* and *West of the Pecos*, society's rottenness is a secret that must be exposed. Grey's heroes belong to no community, if by community we mean a society possessed of a remembered past, knit together by shared commitments and hopes, and ordered by social justification of individual rights. Such memories and loyalties as they carry with them are their own, and so in a curious way is their seemingly timeless code of honor. By the time Grey picks up their stories, they are usually grown, and they are always already courageous and resourceful enough to perform any deeds circumstances require. Their hard pasts, often known through rumors, are etched in their faces. Despair threatens them more than fear because it threatens the resolve that keeps them from sliding into criminality. Only a personal code of honor and a lingering desire to help good people build simple homes and establish nuclear families keep them going straight. The hope that somehow they may yet share such things remains faint because, preferring loneliness to compromise, they will accept wife, home, and family only on their own terms. Deeper than the threat of loneliness or even death is the threat of losing their hard, manly virtues, of which their guns often serve as signs. "Give me my guns," Venters says to Jane Withersteen in *Riders of the Purple Sage*, as she talks to him of forbearance, mercy, and forgiveness. "I'll die a man! . . . Give me my guns." Those who affirm Christian beliefs do so selectively, refusing to let gentle persuasion threaten their masculinity. The codes they live by – and with which they hope to save society for "real" men, "pure" women, and other "good" people – they think of as allied with nature and, therefore, as older than the religions that hyperrefined women espouse and greedy men exploit. They want to save society from the greed of men gone bad and from the misguided softness of women because they want to enter it, if not as gods at least as gods might be, virile as some savage source.

Nevada begins with its hero in flight from the law, knowing that he has saved the lives of his best friend and the woman he loves: "Whatever might be the loneliness and bitterness of the future, nothing could change or mitigate the sweetness and glory of the service he had rendered." Later, Nevada saves his friend and his beloved once again, and with them an entire community, by defeating a conspiracy of killers, thieves, and crooked law officers. But this time he is permitted to join the life he has secured. Unlike the humble lives to which domestic novels characteristically commit their heroines, however, Nevada's leads him to something like an apotheosis: "'Arizona is smilin' down on us,'"

Nevada says in the book's closing lines, as he gazes "down at the sunset glow upon [the] rapt face" of the woman who loves him. "'Nevada is smiling down upon me,' she replie[s], dreamily."

Detective stories have several things in common with Westerns, including their habit of taking us for a walk on the wild side where we meet both gangster-outlaws and a variety of outsiders who are almost outlaws. In detective stories it is merely a matter of time before we discover that society is rotten from top to bottom. Although the lines that separate victims from victimizers and aveng-ing angels from hired gunmen are often blurred, they remain crucial, as does the line that separates the strict code of the detective-hero from the slippery ethics of virtually everyone around him, including a fair share of prominent cit-izens, civic leaders, and public servants who often turn out to be venal, greedy exploiters of the society they pretend to serve. Often failures in conventional terms – failed policemen, for example – detective-heroes are not only wily, tough, resourceful, and dependable; they are also lonely "separatists" at heart.

Though thoroughly urban, detectives, like cowboys, are social minimalists. They hark back to a culture that valued the young and the masculine more than the polished and the sophisticated. As amateur historians, however, detectives know that every present has a secret past. And since they remain, in one important respect, distant descendants of traditional Christians, including the early Puritans of New England, they think of that hidden past as evil and assume that it will provide clues to uncovering evil in the present. Unlike the early Puritans, however, cynicism and despair threaten them because they believe in sin without having much faith in redemption. "Man is conceived in sin and born in corruption," says Willie Stark, in Robert Penn Warren's *All the King's Men* (1946), to his reluctant detective Jack Burden; "and he passeth from the stink of the didie to the stench of the shroud. There is always something" – by which he means that evil reaches up into respectable society as surely as it reaches down into the rapacious criminal underworld and that everyone is entangled in it.

Like cowboy-heroes, detective-heroes must work against long odds. A life of hardship marks their faces and their bearing. They know that society un-dermines integrity with specious promises of happiness and fulfillment, and that sooner or later it destroys those it fails to corrupt. Money and sex are chief among its false lures. With sex goes the promise of pleasure, or possibly of love, intimacy, and even marriage. With money goes the promise of luxury, power, and status. From one or another of these, detectives are always under siege. Only their code and their sense of integrity protect them. The more determined and resourceful they prove to be, the further they are drawn into the darkness of a world that breaks most of those it cannot buy.

Detectives work in societies that are far more advanced in their capitalism than those Western heroes face. Most of the people they encounter are entrepreneurs on the make. As city folk, they live without the solace of space or the consolation of nature's beauties. Yet they too speak with the special authority of the truly marginal, and they too reassert masculine identity and hegemony as counters to feminine invasions of public spheres. Since women often mix the lure of pleasure and comfort with the lure of money and security, detectives regard them with redoubled suspicion. As modern knights, however, they display a special fondness for women in distress, along with other almost lost causes. Since experience has taught them that money is corrupting, they bring an especially hard eye to bear on modern capitalism. In their world, money and guilt go hand in hand, iterating and reiterating the fear that, given the intensity with which Americans worship success and fear failure and the readiness with which they measure everything by money, they will do anything to get it.

Despite their cynicism, however, detective-heroes retain a commitment to the idea of urban society and the possibility that the right kind of resourceful male individualists may somehow save it. Like Sister Carrie, they divide their lives between public performances and private retreats. A terse, taciturn lot, they specialize in the discourse of individualism, and the self-reliance that goes with it, rigorously controlling all emotions, needs, and desires that it leaves unexpressed. Only their sentimentality about good women and men of integrity, another trait they share with cowboys, attests to the large reservoir of needs that that discourse leaves unexpressed. Yet it too is crucial to the balancing act that defines their lives. If irony hardens their sentimentality, pushing them toward isolation, sentimentality softens their irony, carrying them toward community and the causes that sustain them, of rescuing the not-yet-corrupt and saving the not-yet-wholly-lost.

Striking a balance between the irony that keeps them detached and the sentimentality that keeps them humanly involved is, as it turns out, crucial to everything detectives do. Rationality, another legacy of their nineteenth-century origins, is one of their tools. But their rationality is tempered by experience, as we see in the scars that mark their bodies and the shadows that haunt their minds, reminding them of corruption and death. With them as our guides, we travel down into the underworld and up into high society, to see life as it really is. And with them, as with Henry Miller, we learn "that everywhere it is the same – hunger, humiliation, ignorance, vice, greed, extortion, torture, despotism." Detectives resist the temptations having to do with sex, money, and fear by accepting loneliness and meagerness, and by facing death; and they resist the temptation posed by cynicism in order to go on fighting the corruption that surrounds them and the doubt that lurks within them. "I've got a hard skin all over what's left of my soul," says the Continental Op, detective-hero of Dashiell Hammett's *Red Harvest* (1929), whose purity and detachment extend even to his name, "and after twenty years of messing around with crime I can look at any sort of murder without seeing anything in it but my bread and butter, the day's work. But this . . . is not natural to me. It's what this place has done to me." Detectives persevere primarily for the satisfaction of knowing that they have refused to sell out or give in. "What did it matter where you lay once you were dead?" we read at the end of *The Big Sleep* (1939), a title Raymond Chandler coins as a synonym for death. "You were dead, you were sleeping the big sleep, you were not bothered by things like that. Oil and water were the same as wind and air to you. You just slept the big sleep, not caring about the nastiness of how you died or where you fell."

Heroes of such knowledge rely principally on courage, resourcefulness, and a hard code of justice. Feared and even grudgingly respected by men, and desired by women, they need determination to keep them going straight and a tough skin to keep their souls alive. Sometimes, like cowboys, they live almost celibate lives. The women of Hammett's *The Maltese Falcon* (1930) can be taken as representative: Iva Archer is a selfish bitch; Brigid O'Shaughnessy is a beautiful, tempting murderess; and Effie Perine is a good woman or, as Sam Spade puts it, in paying her the ultimate compliment, "a damned good man, sister." Having ticked off six or seven reasons for deciding to send Brigid over to the law, turning his back on what might have been – "the fact that maybe you love me and maybe I love you" – Sam Spade remains faithful to the special code by which he lives, silently assuming that Brigid will silently endorse both what he is doing and his reasons for doing it – an assumption his author makes about us as his readers. Like Grey's cowboy-heroes, Spade clings to the idea of romantic love as a necessary fiction, without which cynicism might engulf him. But he is even more reluctant than Grey's Nevada to test that fiction by trying to live it. In the end, he finds himself not merely alone but lonely and almost dead to feeling. "I don't believe in anything," says his successor, Ned Beaumont in Hammett's *The Glass Key* (1931), "but I'm too much of a gambler not to be affected by a lot of things."

Raymond Chandler's style, basically ironic and often bitter, resembles the mood of his hero, Philip Marlowe, who moves back and forth, trying to balance the need to be tough against the need to remain vulnerable. Tempted by the lure of money and power, he protects himself. "To hell with the rich," he says, "they make me sick." Tempted by pleasure, his response is similar. "This was the room I had to live in," he says, as he throws the naked Carmen Sternwood out of his bed. "It was all I had in the way of a home. In it was everything that was mine, that had any association with me, any past, anything that took the place of a family." Marlowe thus reminds us that for him family is less a dream than a memory. And so, as it turns out, is being a knight. Life's not a "game for knights," he says. He commits himself to saving women who, however fair and beautiful, are almost always already corrupt, because he is determined to cling at least to the *idea* of romantic love. With similar irony, he remains loyal not only to himself and his code but also, after his fashion, to society as an idea, not because society deserves his loyalty but because he deserves something to which he can be loyal. He knows that the corrupt society around him is committed to practices that turn people against one another. But he clings to the hope that the sacrifices of the select company of the tough and vulnerable may somehow create a culture that enlarges human happiness because it is the only thing that keeps him going.

The magazine *Black Mask* was announced in 1919 and began publication in 1920 for the purpose of featuring "mystery, detective, adventure, western, horror, and novelty" stories. By the mid-twenties, the "private eye" had emerged as the new savior of society, and so had the ability of *Black Mask* to find and foster talent. Beginning in 1929, Hammett published four important novels – *Red Harvest*, *The Dain Curse*, *The Maltese Falcon*, and *The Glass Key* – each of which was serialized in *Black Mask*. Detective novels, like Westerns, blossomed in the thirties. They owed much to writers like Jack London, who used a violence of principle to offset and even defeat a violence of greed; and to writers like Ernest Hemingway, who early in his career, in *In Our Time* (1925) and *The Sun Also Rises* (1926), gave new authority to vulnerable, battered heroes who become tough in order to cope with the ugly world around them. Stories like "The Killers," "Fifty Grand," "After the Storm," and "In Another Country" pushed the emergence of Hemingway's "tough-guy" protagonists. One alternative to resistance was a steady carving away at life until there was little left to lose. A man "must not marry," runs a line from "In Another Country," a story in which life becomes the art of avoiding entanglements. "He cannot marry. . . . He should not place himself in a position to lose. He should find things he cannot lose," Hemingway's protagonist says. Another possibility was becoming tough enough to survive even crippling losses. During the thirties, as Hemingway's hold on his art slipped, he began taking more risks in life and fewer in fiction, with mostly sad results. But he continued to take some risks of both kinds. *To Have and Have Not* (1937), he joked a few years after its publication, was a "frail volume . . . devoted to adultery, sodomy, masturbation, rape, mayhem, mass murder, frigidity, alcoholism, prostitution, impotency, anarchy, rum-running, chink-smuggling, nymphomania and abortion." But its real subject, he told Maxwell Perkins, was the "decline of the individual."

Later, following his involvement in the Spanish Civil War as a pro-Loyalist reporter, he wrote *For Whom the Bell Tolls* (1940), a long, uneven work that marked his reaffirmation of faith both in the possibility of human solidarity and in the worthiness of some social causes. In *To Have and Have Not*, however, his only Depression novel and his only novel set in the United States, his bleakness seems almost total, as though, having lost faith in the discourse of radical individualism, he could find nothing to replace it. His protagonist, Harry Morgan, who has tried and failed to earn an honest living, becomes an outlaw and starts smuggling rum and illegal aliens into Cuba, only to discover that, in his dying words, "[o]ne man alone ain't got no bloody f—ing chance." Looking around after Harry's death, Maria, the novel's main female character, sees nothing but "this god-damned life."

Similar sentiments found expression in the hard-boiled fiction of James M. Cain and Horace McCoy, who lived and worked on the fringes of Hollywood, where scores of writers – Fitzgerald, Dorothy Parker, Stephen Vincent Benét, Dos Passos, and Faulkner, to name a few – worked on and off, primarily because Hollywood paid well even during the Depression. "Excess of sorrow laughs," Blake wrote, or seeks other relief, as Hollywood understood. Maxwell Anderson, Robert Sherwood, and Thornton Wilder all found Hollywood money too good to pass up, though none of them was ever hounded by dollars in the way that Fitzgerald was in the thirties or Faulkner was in and beyond them. Most writers, even minor ones earning outsized salaries, either found Hollywood offputting or at least felt obliged to say they did, in part because screenplays, like movies, were collaborative as well as mercenary ventures in which individual writers played limited as well as more or less invisible roles. Stories were not stories in Hollywood, Benét remarked; they were conferences. "Imagination is free or it is not free," Cain said, simplifying a bit, "and here it is not free." Writers mattered to some directors and producers, but there was a limit to how much any of them could matter because the industry's task was to make money for the parent corporations that owned the studios.

Cut off from almost everything except sick fictions about women and society, Cain's protagonists slouch their way through their commercialized worlds toward death. Cain's novels – particularly *The Postman Always Rings Twice* (1934) – enjoyed considerable popularity. And since they are bleak reports on the destruction of virtually all values, we must ask why so many people liked to read them. Cain's protagonists, including the self-conflicted artist John Howard Sharp in *Serenade* (1937), are not so much tough as ruthless. His female characters tend to be either seductive or infantile or both. Greed, lust, and boredom dominate their lives, until the desire for adventure triggers something like free play. Intrusions – unexpected visitors who drop in and stir things up – play crucial roles in Cain's novels, and so do emotional explosions, acts of passion in which violence and desire merge. A "drop of fear," Huff says in *Double Indemnity* (1936), is all it takes '"to curdle love into hate."

Cain's novels turn on three basic relationships, male–female, artist–society, individual–society, in each of which the *other* promises fulfillment yet poses a mortal threat. Cain's characters strain toward relationships that fall apart largely because his men fear that any relation they do not completely control will entrap and destroy them. As genuine possibility – as a larger wholeness in which the self is fully expressed, and yet more than the self is expressed – relationships do not exist. Dramas of arrested development are all we have: people who act out adolescent or even infantile obsessions in an adult world that has become cynical without having attained maturity. The representative agents of society are as familiar, anonymous, and predictable as the uniformed postman who always rings twice. Cain's characters, outsiders who hope to get into the world of meretricious glitter, are driven by greed and lust in lethal combination with boredom. Even those who try for very little stand convicted of wanting too much and so must be punished, if not by society's uniformed agents then by one another.

Finally, however, society is not only alien to Cain's characters; it is also a dark twin. In his preface to *The Butterfly* (1947), Cain speaks of himself as the poet of the "wish that comes true" – "for some reason," he adds, "a terrifying concept, at least to my imagination." Many of his women and most of his men are more at odds with themselves than with society – society having in a sense already won. In *Butterfly*, a father's incestuous love for his daughter awakens in her an incestuous desire for him. The novel's force is both abstract and corrupting. Although we suspect from the beginning that the characters cannot survive the acting out of their desires, we cannot help wanting to see what will happen when they try. In *The Postman Always Rings Twice* we encounter – in Nick, the dark-skinned alien *other*; in Frank, the "American" as outsider and finally outlaw; and in Cora, a woman who feels and expresses more desire and ambition than any woman is expected to feel or express – one of the most clearly doomed triangles in the literature of the United States. Nick, Frank, and Cora fight losing battles with their own unconscious desires as well as with one another. The forms of destruction toward which they move, even when they remain unexpected, also seem inevitable because they emanate from the premises of Cain's text, which succeeds in making fatalism entertaining. In *Serenade*, John Howard Sharp, the Artist, is afraid of what people may see in him: "There would be something horrible mixed up in it, and I didn't want to know what it was." "It," as it turns out, is double: both a homosexual attraction to a man named Winston who is socialized almost beyond the point of seeming human and a fearful desire to have his wish known, ostensibly in the hope that someone may be able to exorcise it.

The deepest truths about Cain's world, and the conflicted hopes that drive it, emerge in the resolution of Sharp's predicament, which is cultural as well as private. In a bullfighting scene, Juana, a primitive, archetypal female, saves Sharp by killing Winston. Making Sharp's hidden wish her own, Juana flees civilization with him and takes him as her lover – only to be destroyed with him by mundane developments: they grow old, their love dries up, and their lives run down. Sharp's eyes weaken, and his body turns to fat; Juana becomes a fat old hag and dies.

Horace McCoy (1897–1955), another "poet of the tabloid murders," to borrow Edmund Wilson's phrase for Cain, was less popular than Cain. But on one occasion he became a more effective artist – in part because he felt less threatened by the "feminization" of culture than by its political economy. *No Pockets for a Shroud* (1937) grew out of his work as a crusading journalist in Texas in the twenties and early thirties. From Texas he went to Hollywood, hoping to make money writing screenplays while also writing serious fiction. A successful screenwriter, he continued calling himself a "Hollywood hack" and his work a kind of "whoring." Of his four novels – *They Shoot Horses, Don't They?* (1935), *No Pockets for a Shroud* (1937), *I Should Have Stayed at Home* (1938), and *Kiss Tomorrow Goodbye* (1948) – the first is the strongest. Now largely forgotten except as a movie, it remains important, in part because some of its evasions can be traced in McCoy's revisions.

Recalling the background of *They Shoot Horses, Don't They?* McCoy said, "There were decadence and evil in the old walkathons – and violence. The evil, of course, as evil always has and always will, fascinated the customer and the violence possessed a peculiar lyricism that elevated the thing into the realm of high art." Gloria and Robert, the two principal characters of the novel, enter a danceathon to win money. Gloria comes from West Texas, "a hell of a place," as she calls it. Having read about Hollywood in movie magazines, she has moved west, hoping to live a glamorous life on the edge of the Pacific. Being "discovered" is one possibility; "getting married" is another. If such dreams are one gift of her inadequate culture, her passive strategy of waiting for the right man to discover her or propose to her is another. Filled with yearning, she follows the kind of advice offered young women by Marjorie Hillis in *Live Alone and Like It: A Guide for the Extra Woman* (1936). Women can be delivered from loneliness and insecurity, Hillis instructs, if they first assemble a proper wardrobe – including "at least two negligees" – and then learn how to wear makeup and mix martinis and manhattans the way men like them and then wait until the right man comes along.

Made vulnerable by her yearning and desirable by her beauty, Gloria becomes an easy target for the unscrupulous men who rule Hollywood. In an early draft of the novel, she relates a "laughable" fact about her love life: "I've never been laid on a bed in my life," she tells Robert. Later, in a line McCoy kept in the final version, she stands, anticipating her death, knowing that her life is already over: "This motion picture business is a lousy business . . . . I'm glad I'm through with it," she says. "I never paid any attention to her remark then," Robert says later, as he listens to the judge sentence him to die, "but now I realize it was the most significant thing she had ever said."

Gloria's hard-earned knowledge gives her voice authority for Robert and for the reader. The weight of the many things that have happened to her is felt in virtually every word she utters. As a result, she becomes the big thing that happens to Robert, a confused boy from Arkansas, who remains surprised by "how it all started" and mystified by how it ends. It "seems very strange," he says, adding that he still can't "understand it all." By being ruthless about herself as well as her world, Gloria earns her bitterness. "The whole thing is a merry-go-round. When we get out of here we're right back where we started." More specifically, she speaks to Robert as a woman seared by the experience of living in a world run by men. Robert feels compelled to listen to her, he remarks in an unpublished short story from which the novel came, "because she talked to me the way I would talk to a boy if I were a girl." This remarkable line helps to make clear why Gloria becomes Robert's great teacher. She pits her bitterness and her inverted egotism against his shallow optimism and conventional egotism. "Now I know how Jonah felt when he looked at the whale," Robert says, as Gloria's lessons begin to unfold. Within a few hours she has convinced him that the grand abstractions he clings to – hope and truth and justice – are empty; that the few parts of life, including his and hers, that are not obviously ugly are "just showmanship"; that he, a chance acquaintance, has become "her very best friend . . . her only friend," because he has listened to her story and heard her voice; and that he, therefore, must do her the favor of shooting her, because, as he says to the officers who arrest him, "They shoot horses, don't they?" meaning hopelessly crippled ones.

Marathon dances were a zany fad of the twenties that became a cruel racket in the thirties. Yet McCoy deleted from his novel a number of references to breadlines and other signs of the Depression in order to expose the deeper logic of a political economy that seemed to him to regard the right to property and profit as more important than the right to life, let alone what Roosevelt called the right to a "decent living." The entangling of public context with private lives comes through in *They Shoot Horses, Don't They?* both in the marathon dance that provides the structure of the central narrative of the novel and in the trial of Robert for the murder of Gloria. Each of the novel's thirteen chapters is preceded by words of the judge as he pronounces Robert guilty and sentences him to die. By depriving Gloria's fate and Robert's fate of suspense, McCoy focuses his novel on the implicit trial of modern society as one in which all worthy people are vulnerable and all vulnerable people sooner or later fall in love with death. Gloria's decision to go west to Hollywood, she tells Robert, came from reading movie magazines while she was in a hospital recovering from an attempt to poison herself. Thinking of her in the moment of her death, "in that black night on the edge of the Pacific," Robert remembers her as relaxed and comfortable and smiling: "It was the first time I had ever seen her smile," he says.

Like Cain's *Serenade*, McCoy's *They Shoot Horses, Don't They?* is built around characters who speak to us from the grave. In two executions – Robert's of Gloria and the court's of Robert – we witness the threatened end of the vulnerable, yearning, young American. Together, Gloria and Robert remind us that to be sustained one's hopes must be sanctioned by one's culture. And they also remind us that we should never speak of a historical culture without trying to see it through the eyes of its unendorsed victims as well as its victors.

5

THE SEARCH FOR SHARED PURPOSE:
STRUGGLES ON THE LEFT

NOVELS EMANATING from the radical left shared some of the detective novel's cynicism and most of Horace McCoy's bitterness. Behind them lay a native tradition that reached back at least to I. K. Friedman's *By Bread Alone* (1901) and *The Radical* (1907), Upton Sinclair's *The Jungle* (1906), Charlotte Teller's *The Cage* (1907), and Jack London's *The Iron Heel* (1908). But reform was what held the left together, and reform depended on hope. In 1937 – two years after Kenneth Burke urged the American Writers' Congress to make "the people" rather than "the worker" their "basic symbol of exhortation and allegiance" – Nathan Asch published *The Road: In Search of America*. Both parts of Asch's double adventure, of seeing "America" and then writing a book about it, unfold as a search for "the people," representations of whom he finds in a young Mexican couple in Denver, Colorado, who live lives of resigned desperation; in a middle-aged man in Eureka, California, who hopes to become sick enough to qualify for charity before he and his wife starve to death; in Henry John Zorn, who has been left to rot away "underneath Montana"; and in a black family in Lost Prairie, Arkansas, who live "in a sieve-like empty house amid a world of cotton." Such people, Asch insists, are not "exceptional" cases but "usual and everyday and common." Trapped in misery and dispossession, they resemble the residents of a flophouse that Sherwood Anderson describes in *Puzzled America* (1935), where people lie breathing "in and out together" in "one gigantic sigh." They are average in their suffering and average in their resistance to it, and they are victims of common enemies they have not yet learned how to name: the "very rich and very smart" people who live in Washington and New York and run the country for their own personal pleasure and profit. Unable to name their enemies, Asch's victims have no chance of mapping effective strategies for opposing them. But Asch also stops short by deferring active resistance to a putative future, a "someday," in which "the people" will unite in naming and resisting their enemies.

Like Asch's *The Road* and Russell Lee's photographs of "homesteaders," Jack Conroy's novel *The Disinherited* (1933) shuns self-conscious artifice. Its protagonist, a worker named Larry Donovan, moves from job to job, spurred less by hope of finding meaningful work that can restore his sense of purpose than by fear of unemployment that will sap his dwindling reserve of self-respect. Separated from the objects that his labor produces and the profits they yield, he is left to measure his efforts entirely in terms of falling wages. In some moments, Donovan treats real adventures as trivial games, a bit like Tom Sawyer. Finally, however, he is closer in spirit to Huck Finn, not because his life leads him to a grand flight west, away from civilization, civilization now being everywhere, but because he locates his proper home in his beginnings, among the "disinherited and dispossessed of the world."

There is, however, a basic confusion at work in *The Disinherited*. While capitalism remains Donovan's avowed enemy, Conroy's tone slips back and forth between angry protest and wide-eyed wonder. One explanation for this almost certainly lies in Conroy's divided loyalties. He thought of himself as a Marxist, but simply looking "at *Das Kapital* on the shelf gave" him a "headache," he once remarked. His own writings he thought of as belonging to a native tradition of radicalism, associated with "Whitman's injunction to vivify the contemporary fact," in which a strong strain of hopeful individualism survived. In a scene between a widowed mother and her son, who becomes Conroy's protagonist, age is set against youth, work against play, duty against freedom, and social organization against the single, solitary self. "You've got to be a man now. You're the only man I've got left," says the mother – to which her son responds by running out to play a game that begins with a familiar chant: "Bushel o' wheat / Bushel o' rye; / All not ready / Holler 'I.'"

Hollering "I" survived during the thirties both as an old tradition and as a principle of resistance to assimilation, including assimilation by the organization that advocated Marxist thought. James T. Farrell's troubled relations with the radical left became a familiar story. Studs Lonigan, Farrell's strongest protagonist, lives a life of swaggering individualism. Through his own brand of social realism – particularly and most forcibly in *Young Lonigan* (1932), *The Young Manhood of Studs Lonigan* (1934), and *Judgment Day* (1935) – Farrell preserved the novel as a source of information about the harsh realities of urban life. Torn between old neighborhood institutions – family, home, church, and school – and new neighborhood institutions – the playground, the poolhall, and street gangs – Studs Lonigan becomes part disappointed romantic and part tough-minded realist. From family, church, and Father Gilhooley, he acquires a graphic sense of evil, but he has been born too late to share the church's hope of redemption. Truly buffeted, his life seems virtually foreclosed. Both the romantic possibilities that he associates with Lucy Scanlon and the religious possibilities that his mother associates with the priesthood seem to him empty compared with the gang speech and gang adventures that transform antisocial behavior into a social organization.

Since the impoverishment of Studs's world is imaginative and moral as well as economic, emptiness is as much his enemy as want. The countless trivial, mundane things that happen to him are iterated and reiterated in a life that traces in its descending action the sad story of what Farrell calls "American destiny in our time." Finally, his descent seems neither better nor worse than the rise of Farrell's Danny O'Neill. The protagonist of *A World I Never Made* (1936), *No Star Is Lost* (1938), *Father and Son* (1940), and *My Days of Anger* (1943), O'Neill becomes more successful than Studs. Yet he is not so much better as merely different. The characteristic bleakness of Farrell's fiction comes through in both series, which, despite their overdependence on the massing of details, create a sense of indignation that is moral as well as social, as we see especially in Studs's yearning for what Emerson called "a world elsewhere" and Studs calls "something else."

In the early thirties, the Communist Party recruited many people. But some of the conversions were halfhearted and faded rapidly. Even Lincoln Steffens's *Autobiography* – published in 1931, when the house of want was becoming more and more crowded – is divided in its allegiance: dogged in its adherence to the major tenets of the Party it also tries to remain loyal to a native tradition of protest exemplified by Jack London and Randolph Bourne. Looking back, Ben Hagglund saw the "collective spirit" winning a temporary victory in the early thirties. But then, "when things eased up a bit, the old individualistic spirit got us again, and we were right back at each other's throats," he said. Proletarian "literature" also suffered, as Nelson Algren noted, because it was dominated by intellectuals like Mike Gold and Lincoln Steffens rather than by artists. Most novelists remained on the blurred borders of the Party, some closer than Farrell, others farther away. Daniel Fuchs's trilogy – *Summer in Williamsburg* (1934), *Homage to Blenholt* (1936), and *Low Company* (1937) – sets the shaping and misshaping force of place and circumstances, as they bear down on the lives of young people to teach them their limitations, against the residual hope that somehow the earth's poor may still "reign as consuls of the earth." Robert Cantwell's *Land of Plenty* (1934) focuses on young people who are trapped in a brutal strike and so must move from one darkness – "Suddenly the lights went out" runs the novel's first line – to the next, until at the novel's end three of them huddle together, "their faces dark with misery and anger, ... waiting for the darkness to come like a friend and set them free." In Ira Wolfert's *Tucker's People* (1943), poverty that kills hope in some people makes others "frantic for money and frantic to hunt it down." Once Wolfert's people have joined in the "game of marauding for profits," which seems to them to hold the "whole earth" in its grip, the line between legal and illegal capitalistic ventures blurs and then vanishes, making each a version of the other. In his trilogy about the Stecher family, which began with *White Mule* (1937), William Carlos Williams keeps the large-scale corruption that drew Wolfert in the background in order to focus on the subtle ways in which the pursuit of money, power, and status makes people "become callow and selfish," starting them "down the road of rationalizations and self-justifications," until countless small compromises finally leave them without any firm principles to live by.

The strengths that set Henry Roth's *Call It Sleep* (1934) apart from most novels of the thirties derive in part from Roth's gift for evoking the sights, sounds, and smells of Lower East Side Manhattan. The sense of place and the impinging force of environment, including the force of poverty, come through with considerable power in *Call It Sleep*. But Roth's novel is focused in another way, too: it recounts three years in the childhood of David Searle, a small, vulnerable, and very human animal. In one sense, it is a story of the emerging consciousness of a physical, social creature who must learn what it means to live in a gigantic and confusing world "created without thought of him." Although *Call It Sleep* confronts pain and suffering, it remains free of self-pity and is rich in the tenderness and terror that the wonder of childhood makes possible. Its deeper richness comes, however, from Roth's skill in depicting the forces and voices within David that emerge to contest external forces.

To the editors of *New Masses*, Roth's concern with David's consciousness was a sign of decadent bourgeois individualism. *Call It Sleep*, they declared, was both "introspective and febrile." But *Call It Sleep* is a social novel about a young boy's effort to survive in a world littered with broken promises. Written during the thirties, it takes us back to the Lyric Years just before World War I, when the national dream seemed to embrace almost everyone, except recent immigrants like David Searle's dislocated, divided, and self-conflicted parents. Roth's own Marxist sympathies are everywhere present – in his treatment of debased sexuality and David's violent, frustrated father, and in his rendering of the kind of bleak, brutal scenes we associate with urban naturalism. But his concern with David's uneven effort to become a force among forces dominates his story.

Power, as Roth renders it, comes from the play of an unfolding self as it interacts with other selves. The characters of *Call It Sleep* feel controlled by external forces, which they try to control. But the crucial political question that Roth confronts is whether the idea of agency – or of the self as independent agent – makes sense in a world where people come to consciousness by becoming aware of the myriad forces impacting them. David's awakening consciousness knows itself only in its contingencies, as something impinged upon by a conflicted family past that is not its own and a violent social world that it can never hope to measure.

In *Call It Sleep*, the emergence of a self and the emergence of the self's voice become interrelated, interactive developments. David's world is not only one of overlapping urban sounds; it is a world of speech, part polyglot and part pidgin, that has been damaged by loss of tradition and by a trail of broken promises. The early words David hears emanate from an already conflicted world. Those he acquires convey vague intimations of his yearnings and desires because they fit neither his experiences nor his needs. The silence into which he slips at the novel's end seems promising primarily because his young consciousness is still trying to gather the sights and sounds of his days. The "glint on tilted beards...the tapering glitter of rails...the glow of thin blond hair...the shrill cry, the hoarse voice, the scream of fear, the bells" exist for him as things "to cull again and reassemble" in a new state of mind – lying somewhere between willfulness and submission, assertion and acquiescence, the sheer fabrication of details and the mere recording of impressions – that we have no adequate word for and so "might as well call sleep." David's struggle to improvise a temporary, evolving self, like Roth's struggle to create an unfolding narrative, thus comes to us as an act of compromise as well as resistance.

Novels like Roth's, which begins by recalling the small steamers that brought millions of uprooted immigrants from Europe to the United States in the late nineteenth and early twentieth centuries, look at the past in light of a present in which something has gone drastically wrong. One theme that personal writings – memoirs, letters, and personal essays – of the thirties shared with public writings was a sense of astonishment that the country's money culture, having promoted the belief that everything depended on money, had suddenly stopped producing any. Mike Gold disapproved of *Call It Sleep*. But in his own writings he grappled in a more formulaic way with many of the same tensions that drove Roth. In *Jews Without Money* (1930), he stacks one brutal experience on top of another and then concludes with a formulaic celebration of the great revolution that will finally set all the East Sides of the world free from poverty, exploitation, and misery. As editor of *New Masses*, he sentimentalized writers who seemed determined to bear witness to life's hard facts. "A first book like yours, of a young working-class author, cannot be regarded as merely literature," Gold wrote Edward Dahlberg about *Bottom Dogs* (1930). "To me it is a significant class portent. It is a victory against capitalism," he continued, unperturbed by the issue of agency. "Out of the despair, mindlessness and violence of the proletarian life, thinkers and leaders arise. Each time one appears it is a revolutionary miracle."

The key words in Gold's tribute – "working-class," "proletarian life," "revolutionary miracle" – often produced crude critical judgments that privileged the "realism" of the articulate victim. One unexpected result, exemplified by Gold, was a blurring of the line that separated autobiography, with its focus on the individual, from social fiction, with its focus on social forces. To locate the point at which a witness intersects social history, both Conroy's *The Disinherited* and Gold's *Jews Without Money* combine autobiographically based fiction with autobiographically informed journalism. Lorry and Lizzie Lewis, the chief protagonists of Dahlberg's early fiction, are also the subject of his late, more openly autobiographical *Because I Was Flesh* (1964).

By privileging social-minded writing based on personal experience above other kinds of writing, writers of the thirties sought to adjust the social tenets of Marxism to the circumstances and traditions of the United States. But leaders of the left often construed that possibility rigidly. What the United States needed, Gold argued in "Go Left, Young Writers" (1929), were writers toughened by life – "a wild youth of about twenty-two, the son of working-class parents, who himself works in the lumber camp, coal mines, and steel mills, harvest fields and mountain camps of America." Where in Mr. Thornton Wilder's fiction, Gold later asked rhetorically, in "Prophet of the Genteel Christ" (1930), are the city streets, the cotton mills, "the child slaves of the beet fields," and "the passion and death of the coal miners"? Such questions reinforced the authority of tough-guy, bottom-dog male writers at the expense of men like Wilder and, almost casually, of virtually all women writers. In *Heaven's My Destination* (1934), Wilder traced the journey of George Brush across the much-mixed world of the thirties – its trailer camps, shantytowns, and bawdyhouses, its courtrooms and trains, its countryside and small towns. *Heaven's My Destination* bears interesting comparison with Dahlberg's exploration of the bottom-dog world of freight cars, hobo jungles, and flophouses; and it deserved more attention than it received from readers like Gold, if only because it explores, with considerable style and wit, the fate of goodness in a corrupt as well as depressed world. But George Brush's work as a traveling textbook salesman failed to interest Gold. And since less than 25 percent of women and only 15 percent of married women worked outside homes during the thirties, most of what women knew about poverty, pain, fear, and indignity struck him as narrow.

As though mindful of Gold's advice, Josephine Herbst made a conscious effort to write social fiction, only to discover that it was harder to write social fiction about women. Conroy could write, she observed, about "the feel of what it's like to work, how you handle a machine," and "how it feels to be without work, and with the imminent fear of starving," confident that his account of such ordeals would be accepted as socially significant. She could write of women who were willing to take chances and "be guilty of folly." But she could not write as a "witness of the times" who had seen firsthand "the passion and the death of the coal miners." Herbst, Meridel Le Sueur, Martha Gellhorn, Tillie Olsen, Mary Heaton Vorse, and scores of other women were welcomed to the ranks of the politically engaged. But leaders of the left, including the editors of journals, possessed a clear image of what wild poets should look like, and no woman resembled it. Unlike *Anvil* and *New Masses*, *Partisan Review* tried to blend political concerns of the thirties with aesthetic concerns of the twenties. Acknowledging that literature is always political, it also insisted, as its editor William Phillips put it, that the imagination cannot "be constrained within any orthodoxy." But *Partisan Review* helped to keep literary radicalism a largely male preserve. Looking back on her position as the drama critic of the *Partisan*, Mary McCarthy remembered herself as "a sort of gay, good-time girl" whose position reflected the sense that "the theater was of absolutely no consequence." Serious writing by women, including fiction that dealt with what Gold had called "the despair, mindlessness and violence of the proletarian life," usually seemed "narrow," "narcissistic," and "defeatist" to male readers, simply because it featured the private spaces that their female contemporaries knew best. Looking back, trying to account for the strange fate of her long-deferred novel called *Silences* (1978), which she began in the thirties, Tillie Olsen recalled the pressure exerted on her by the Young Communist League to submerge her "writing self" by turning her interests from fiction to journalism. Herbst and Le Sueur felt similar pressures, as did Tess Slesinger and Ruth McKenney, author of a careful investigation of social and economic conditions in Akron, Ohio, called *Industrial Valley* (1939).

Assured that their experience possessed social significance, men wrote count-less narratives – memoirs that resemble novels and novels that resemble mem-oirs – confident that their works would be greeted as revolutionary miracles. Dahlberg's *Bottom Dogs* is about coal-miners; Thomas Bell's *Out of This Furnace* (1941) is about steelworkers; Pietro di Donato's *Christ in Concrete* (1939) is about bricklayers; Conroy's *The Disinherited* moves from coal mines to railroad shops to rubber plants. But each of them is the story of a witness who has seen up close the wounded, damaged lives they recount. They rely heavily on the accumulation of brutal scenes, a literary equivalent of stockpiling, calcu-lated to make readers pity the victims of a brutal political economy. Their language, which comes from ghetto streets, slums, mine shafts, and factories, seems almost as misshapen as the lives of the people who speak it, and in them the Great Depression threatens to engulf everything except the counterforce of angry protest that they exemplify. During the thirties, that protest found expression in many unexpected places – on the sides of freight cars ("HOOVER – CAPLIST Dog"), in store windows ("Coolidge Blew the Whistle / Mellon rang the bell / Hoover pulled the throttle / And the country went to hell"), on placards carried by striking workers ("This is your country dont let the big men take it away from you"), and in songs sung by people like Sarah Ogan, the "Girl of Constant Sorrow," from Elys Branch, Kentucky:

> They take our very life blood, they take our children's lives,
> Take fathers away from children and husbands away from wives.
> Coal miners won't you organize, wherever you may be,
> And make this a land of freedom for workers like you and me.
> Dear miners, they will slave you till you can't work no more.
> And what will you get for your labor but a dollar in the company store?
> A tumble-down shack to live in, snow and rain pouring through the top,
> You'll have to pay the company rent, your payments never stop.
> I am a coal miner's wife, I'm sure I wish you well.
> Let's sink this capitalist system in the darkest pits of hell.

Eventually, the Communist Party gained strength even in hard-to-reach areas of the rural South. After 1933, however, as the New Deal gained momentum, defections increased. Some people were pulled by Roosevelt's appeal to native roots; others were pushed by the Party's early denunciation of the New Deal as "social fascism." A few, including Ruth McKenney, were kicked out of the Party for "deviationism." Realizing that their strategy was backfiring, Party leaders tried to claim Tom Paine and John Brown as precursors and to endorse Conroy's celebration of Whitman. Communism, they said, was "twentieth-century Americanism." But the Party continued to lose ground even after it blurred its message. Some writers who had supported William Z. Foster and his running mate James Ford in the election of 1932 never voted for Roosevelt. As late as 1936, a majority of the American Writers' Congress supported Earl Browder, the Communist Party candidate, while others supported Norman Thomas, the Socialist Party candidate. But the drift toward accommodation was strong. In 1937 the Communist Party itself officially endorsed Roosevelt's reforms.

Three important developments influenced this turnabout. First, despite the spread of proletarian sentiment and fiction, many writers recognized that the United States was of all places, as Herbst put it, "the least likely to produce" an organized proletariat. Its uneven affluence and mobility were deterrents, and so was its tradition of individualism and self-reliance. Second, they recognized that the nation was benefiting from the programs of a president they did not completely trust. "Preserving capitalism," wrote Leslie Fiedler, another writer who started out in the thirties, "the New Deal also preserved us who had been predicting its death and our own." Third, the drift of international events – especially the rise of Hitler's Germany and the surprising moves of Stalin's Russia – forced reappraisal. For a brief time, the first American Writers' Congress (April 1935) and the League of American Writers benefited from Hitler's presence as a common enemy, as Kenneth Burke later stated directly. With Stalin's atrocities still hidden, people who remained divided on many issues were united against Hitler, especially after reports of the staggering persecution of Jews began to drift across the Atlantic and as thousands of people, some of them writers, musicians, artists, scientists, and philosophers – people like Hannah Arendt and Thomas Mann – arrived, seeking refuge. But the fall of the Spanish Republic (March 1939) and the signing of the Hitler-Stalin pact (August 1939) left many radicals, as Fiedler put it, feeling like casualties of a "failed apocalypse."

By the late thirties, defections from the Party and its fringes were almost commonplace. Nelson Algren and James Gould Cozzens moved on to become commercially successful writers. Robert Cantwell, author of *Land of Plenty* (1934), joined the editorial boards of *Time*, *Life*, and *Fortune* and later became the first managing editor of *Sports Illustrated*. Saul Bellow, Bernard Malamud, and Arthur Miller began forging links among urban writers of the thirties and those of the forties, fifties, and sixties. Premature death saved a few writers, including Nathanael West, from having to carry on after the prophecies had failed. Haunted by personal problems, the contours of which remain obscure, Henry Roth lapsed into silent hibernation and waited for a later generation to rediscover him. By the early forties, Dos Passos and Farrell had begun sounding like garrulous, complaining shadows of their former radical selves.

John Steinbeck suffered a similar fate, though with less rancor, in part because he had less to feel disappointed about. Though aligned with the left, he had always worked primarily out of a native tradition of protest, different parts of which have since been traced in books like Louis Hartz's *The Liberal Tradition in America* (1955), Alice Felt Tyler's *Freedom's Ferment* (1944), Richard Hofstadter's *Age of Reform* (1955), Daniel Aaron's *Men of Good Hope* (1951) and *Writers on the Left* (1961). Starting out in the thirties, Steinbeck had persisted in drawing on his own sense of history, which was dominated by the nation's westering impulse, and he often presents "the people" whose stories he tells as history's heirs. Sharing the angry decade's sense of itself as having suffered a terrible reversal of fortune, he presents capitalism as a perverting force that violates the heavenly valleys of California – the Old World's as well as the New World's last Eden – as we see not only in his "strike" novel *In Dubious Battle* (1936) but also in *The Grapes of Wrath* (1939). Yet to read Steinbeck as a realist, a naturalist, or a proletarian novelist is to misread him.

Having acquired an early suspicion of realism ("I never had much ability for nor faith nor belief in realism," he remarked. "It is just a form of fantasy as nearly as I can figure"), Steinbeck remained a deeply literary writer. He borrowed titles from Milton (*In Dubious Battle*), as well as from hymns and the Bible. In *Tortilla Flat* (1935), he engages in an extended evocation of Malory's tales of King Arthur and the Knights of the Round Table. *The Grapes of Wrath* is full of literary evocations – of Jefferson, Emerson, and Whitman, among others – some of them so obvious as to seem crude. In short, Steinbeck wrote out of conflicts as well as about them. If some of his loyalties came from his reading of Emerson, whom he thought of as having unified man and nature as soul, others came from the influence of Edward F. Ricketts, a marine biologist and naturalist whom he met in 1930 and from whom he learned an early version of sociobiology that changed his sense of relations between individuals and groups. For Steinbeck it was as though Ricketts had disclosed something he had always known: "I have written this theme over and over and did not know what I was writing." "Group-men are always getting some kind of infection," says the doctor in *In Dubious Battle*. "Every man wanted something for himself," says the pioneer grandfather, "The Leader of the People," in *The Long Valley* (1938), before he goes on to depict "a whole bunch of people" who collectively want "only westering" as transformed "into one big crawling beast."

A poet of sorts, Steinbeck wanted to search out the sociobiological determinants of human behavior while also celebrating his belief in "the people." In some moments, the perils of individualism seem to dominate his range of vision; in others, all forms of collectivism seem to strike him as poisonous. Thus divided, he became for a brief time one of the most prominent writers in the United States. Like his fellow Californian Jack London, he was drawn to portrayals of people of reduced states of consciousness because he wanted to situate the human spirit within nature and to locate nature's force within human animals. Animal imagery pervades his novels, from the pirate in *Tortilla Flat*, who lives in a kennel with his dogs, through "The Leader of the People," to the famous description of a turtle crossing a highway in *The Grapes of Wrath*, where we see life both as a biological process that has always been historical and as a historical process that has always been biological.

The Grapes of Wrath became one of the most influential and controversial novels of the thirties. It was banned by libraries and denounced by schools and churches as well as U.S. senators; and it was extravagantly praised by Mike Gold in *New Masses* as proof that the "proletarian spirit had battered down the barricades set up by the bourgeois monopolists of literature." At the heart of its story lies the journey – the exodus or odyssey – of the Joad family from the dust bowl of Oklahoma through camp after camp, seeking California's heavenly valleys. Left without jobs and clear roles to shore up their sense of dominance, Steinbeck's men become bewildered and baffled. Challenged, his women – especially Ma Joad – become more assertive. At his most searching, Steinbeck senses, as Roth had, links between class oppression and gender oppression. But he consistently hesitates in the presence of his own insights and, then, begins to resist them. His female characters become empowered only when his male characters falter; they exercise power only in order to save the family as a patriarchal institution; and they therefore surrender power as soon as the men of the family are ready to resume their roles as protectors and providers. In short, Steinbeck brings the central problematic of his novel, which has to do with the distribution of power, under the aspect of gender, only to retreat, in part by feminizing nature in a way that allies women with passive dependence. The fate of the land emerges as a crucial issue in *The Grapes of Wrath*. But for Steinbeck, the issue is whether it is to be raped for profit by large impersonal, conglomerate, male-dominated agricultural corporations or tilled with loving care by individual, humane male farmers. Given such alternatives, neither Steinbeck nor we have much choice. But in saying that, what have we said if not that Steinbeck betrays his own insights? After celebrating Ma Joad's strength and allowing her to become the center of her abused, dislocated family, he confines her again to the nurturing role that he has temporarily permitted her to transcend. The "naturalness" of that role, set up by his depiction of nature, he reiterates in the novel's last scene, where Rose of Sharon, Ma Joad's daughter, nurses a starving man with milk meant for her stillborn child.

Steinbeck was at his most awkward when he engaged in self-conscious symbolism (featuring overburdened turtles, tractors, and crosses) and large gestures (such as the one with which *The Grapes of Wrath* ends). His strength lay in describing natural scenes that are imbued with human qualities and in depicting characters who feel more than they understand about the natural forces and social institutions that, bound together, shape their lives. At his best, he is more clinical than sentimental about people because his most telling loyalty was to the processes of life. He values social movements, including strikes and protests in the name of social justice, but he values them even more in the name of loyalty to life. In his fiction, however, that loyalty, which opened his eyes to some things, closed them to others. It allowed him to picture men behaving like natural animals, as Lennie does in *Of Mice and Men* (1937); like social animals, as the "group-man" does in *In Dubious Battle*; and like "natural" leaders, as Tom Joad and Jim Casy do in *The Grapes of Wrath*. But where women are concerned, his focus on the processes of life, featuring cycles of death and rebirth, extinction and renewal, reiterates confinement.

Unlike Dos Passos, Farrell, and Steinbeck, all of whom lived to write weaker novels in another era, Nathanael West died in 1940, just before the Great Depression began to disappear in the economic growth spurred by the century's second great war. Born in New York City in 1903, the son of prosperous Lithuanian Jewish immigrants, Nathan Weinstein began early to dash his parents' hopes. He preferred baseball to synagogue, and books by writers like J. K. Huysmans, Friedrich Nietzsche, and Feodor Dostoyevsky – or even out-of-the-way medieval Catholic mystics – to the Torah and homework. Having left high school without a diploma, he gained admission to Tufts University with forged documents and then withdrew with failing grades, before entering Brown University on the borrowed credentials of another student named Nathan Weinstein. Freed from onerous requirements in science and math, which the other Nathan Weinstein had satisfied, West finished at Brown, took his degree, and left for Paris, where he spent two years reading and trying to write. Back in New York, he continued to fend off parental attempts to draw him into his father's construction company, choosing instead to clerk in small hotels, where he cadged free rooms for writers like Caldwell, Farrell, and Hammett. Set free when the Depression destroyed his father's business, he followed Horace Greeley's advice – "Go west, young man" – by renaming himself. By 1931, when he published his first novel, *The Dream Life of Balso Snell*, he was Nathanael West.

West thus began a short career that established him as a virtuoso of what he called the "peculiar half-world" of dreams and nightmares. His world includes people who have been made grotesque by nature, like the girl in *Miss Lonelyhearts* (1933) who is born without a nose, and people whose weaknesses are exploited for profit, like Peter Doyle, the crippled man in *Miss Lonelyhearts*. At his best, however, West charges the pathos of his fiction with two kinds of political meaning. He contextualizes it by surrounding it with a sick, money-mad society in which the exploitation of nature for profit goes hand in hand with the exploitation of human beings for profit; and he internalizes it by presenting his characters as victims who harbor hidden affinities, learned from a confused as well as a corrupt world, with the secret causes of their own predicaments. As a result, West's is a world in which the most basic of all commitments – the commitment to life itself – is under siege.

The Dream Life of Balso Snell is a deeply parodic comedy built around the adventures of a poet who enters the belly of the Trojan horse through its anus and discovers a strange new world populated by writers searching for audiences. An act of apprenticeship, a declaration of independence, and a confession of guilt, *Balso Snell* launched West on a career dedicated to exploring the fate of art as well as life on a morning after the apocalypse, when artistic conventions and social precepts survive only in fragments, in broken, disfigured bodies, or in maimed memories. In *Miss Lonelyhearts* virtually everything in life – travel, art, philosophy, and religion; the primitive and the decadent; urban life and agrarian utopianism; good hope and cynicism; hedonism and stoicism, a fondness for the pleasures afforded by food, drink, and sex, as well as willed abstinence from them – comes to us either as an escapist activity, an addiction, or a sign of disease. For, in West's fiction, the country's whole therapeutic culture, rather than signaling a love of life, serves as a sign of fear and anxiety or, more drastically, a symptom of some fundamental dis-ease with life.

The newspaperman who agrees to write the paper's "Miss Lonelyhearts" column, hoping to advance his career, is transformed and then destroyed by a fatal conjunction between his paper's desire to exploit the pain and suffering of its readers, his desire to rise in his profession, and his readers' desires to find quick fixes to their problems or, failing that, a well of pity in which to drown themselves. West thus turns several of the nation's favorite dreams – of becoming wealthy, becoming self-reliant, or finding some way to get well quick – upside down and inside out. Part newspaper gimmick, part clichéd device, and part comic-strip character, Miss Lonelyhearts is destroyed by the role he agrees to play and becomes both a fool of pain and a mad, ludicrously inadequate Christ whose only work is to expose as false the myths that inform his life and the life around him.

A Cool Million (1934), West's third novel, exposes the American dream in general and the Horatio Alger myth to further mockery by tracing the sad misadventures of Lemuel Pitkin. A poor honest farm boy, Pitkin begins life confident that with energy, talent, and hard work he can become anything he wants to be. But in exploring the land that seems to lie before him like a dream he discovers a nightmare world of exploitation. An anachronistic threat to that world, Pitkin is robbed, wrongly imprisoned, and then slowly dismembered. Having lost his teeth, one eye, one thumb, one leg, and his scalp, he is finally shot, whereupon a false version of the story of his life and death is cynically used by the forces that have destroyed him in order to persuade others to try living the dream he has tried to live so that his society can go on being itself.

The Day of the Locust (1939), West's best work, has been compared to Fitzgerald's *The Last Tycoon* (1941) because they were written in and about Hollywood at roughly the same time. But *The Day of the Locust* has more in common with Horace McCoy's *They Shoot Horses, Don't They?* (1935) and even John O'Hara's *Hope of Heaven* (1938), Paul Cain's *Fast One* (1933), and Raoul Whitfield's *Death in a Bowl* (1930). For, like them, it focuses not on Hollywood's rich moguls but on its bitter lost dreamers who discover that their marketed love affair with stardom has become a love affair with death.

In it Hollywood is a land of illusions that promote self-deception as well as false dreams. Their characters are crippled and destroyed either by the things they dare to do or by those they are afraid to try. In them, audacity leads to lives that are short and violent, diffidence to lives that are empty. Rather than liberating people, their nation's new sexuality increases anxieties and manipulation. Jardin, the protagonist of Whitfield's *Death in a Bowl*, lives alone because he sees his world for what it is. Time and again, he arrests his feelings before they can become words, let alone deeds, in part at least because he does not want to become entangled in a world that seems to him to be drifting toward death. Resistance becomes the dominant principle of his life, isolation, the dominant strategy.

Early in West's *The Day of the Locust*, Tod Hackett begins to think of himself as the appointed artist of Hollywood's failed dreams and botched lives. At times he is tempted to become an active hero or lover. Occasionally, he even wishes he could set society straight. But learning to see and render his world are the tasks he sets for himself. Offended by the deception, decadence, and crime that surround him, he spends most of his time studying his world and trying to capture it on canvas. West himself was drawn to active participation in organized politics, and his writings sometimes reflect a tendency that marks other books of the thirties, where the caboose of literature follows the engine of social events. The gap between event and expression had closed during the Great War. Convinced that they were witnessing history as well as living it, young people started taking notes while the shells were still falling. During the twenties, the gap between event and expression widened, but during the thirties, it closed once again, as we see in writers like Clifford Odets, whose political sympathies were close to West's. Odets's plays were occasional in a special sense. Most of the things that happened to him – what he saw in the streets of New York and what he read in newspapers and magazines about events in Europe as well as other parts of the United States – fed his sense of urgency. *Waiting for Lefty* (1935) was a direct response to the New York taxi drivers' strike of 1934. In 1935, on the night after he read a report on Hitler's Germany published in *New Masses*, he started and finished *Till the Day I Die*.

For several years after moving to Hollywood, West concentrated on writing screenplays. When he took up fiction again, he brought the scenes he was witnessing under the aspect of a full-scale apocalypse, as his title, *The Day of the Locust*, which comes from the Bible, clearly suggests: "And in those days men will seek death and will not find it; they will long to die, and death will fly from them." Like McCoy's characters, West's come from the margins of Hollywood. They include a dilapidated comedian who ekes out a living selling shoe polish while trying to market his daughter for a fortune; his daughter, a film-struck beauty who shuffles through a stack of old dreams while waiting to be discovered; a forlorn, middle-aged hotel clerk from Iowa who has left his meager life behind, hoping to find happiness in Hollywood before time runs out; a screenwriter from Mississippi who lives in "an exact reproduction of the Old Dupuy mansion near Biloxi"; a feisty, irascible dwarf; a cock-fighting Mexican; a Hollywood cowboy; a Hollywood Indian; and, as narrator, Tod Hackett, a young Yale graduate, who studies the bizarre life of Hollywood in hope of becoming its painter.

West's Hollywood emerges as a quintessential expression of a political economy that depends on its ability to promise more than it can deliver. It thus raises to visibility the nation's will to disguise and exploit for profit its two deepest secrets: a fatal entangling of sex and violence and a fatal fascination with money as the measure of all things. Neither the nation's new eroticism, built around free expression, nor its old romanticized sexuality, built around enticing restraint on the part of women and licensed aggressiveness on the part of men, escapes the web in which sexual desire merges with the will to dominate, making it a commodity. What is lost, the hope of intimacy, resonates in an emptiness that haunts West's world, where all life is reduced to mean-spirited contests. Some of these games are subtle; some, such as cock-fights, are crude. But a fatal confluence of sex, violence, money, and power lurks in all of them. In the novel's last scene West's pathetic, repressed, almost wholly ineffectual former hotel clerk commits a senseless act that provokes mob hysteria and riot.

Shortly after he arrives in Hollywood to study set and costume design, Tod Hackett begins to focus on a few people who masquerade as victors and on several whose failure is as obvious as the cheap clothes they buy from mail-order houses. But his main interest focuses on the disenchanted who have come to the land of dreams hoping to find happiness before they die: "They were the people he felt he must paint." In the bedlam of the novel's last scene, when poorly repressed frustrations erupt, people begin to act out their dream-nightmares in an orgy in which inflicting death and suffering it become almost interchangeable experiences. Observing the scene around him, Hackett thinks of his masterpiece, *The Burning of Los Angeles*, which is based on the innumerable sketches he has "made of the people who come to California to die."

West's own subject – the United States at the end of the road – brings the novel as near as it can come to an apocalypse. In it, several important distinctions begin to dissolve, including those between dream and nightmare, living and dying, life and art. California in general and Hollywood in particular – the places Americans dream of going and go to dream – become the places they go to kill or die. *The Burning of Los Angeles*, Hackett's drawing of a surreal land of lies, begins to merge with the "actual" scenes of his life, just as he, West's designated artist, begins to merge with his world. As he is being carried off in a police car, Hackett remembers his painting and then sees it all around him in the bedlam he is actually living. Hearing the car's siren, he thinks that he is making the noise he hears. Feeling his lips with his hands, he discovers that they are clamped tight, then begins to laugh hysterically, and then begins to imitate the sound of the siren as loud as he can.

In April 1940, shortly after *The Day of the Locust* was published, Nathanael West and Eileen McKenney, subject of Ruth McKenney's *My Sister Eileen* (1938), were married and began a short, happy marriage that ended in December when they died in an automobile accident near El Centro, California. *The Day of the Locust* earned good reviews and poor sales and then dropped from sight, in part because the surreal strangeness that it brought to bear on the nation's last fairyland seemed too savage to people who were still trying to recover from the Depression. But West's art reminds us that grim awareness means nothing without matching comprehension. His best novels, *Miss Lonelyhearts* and *The Day of the Locust*, are guidebooks of a sort. They flaunt their freedom from the detachment we associate with photographs while also insisting on their reportorial accuracy. They enable us to confront the despair that fills the lives of people, even those with money, who know that they are truly homeless, as well as the violence that feeling lost and hopeless can provoke. And they surprise us with the consequences of ordinary emptiness. Horrors run amok in them. But their deepest horror derives from West's insistence that the despair that drives people toward death can also drive them to commit any atrocities they are capable of conceiving, including those that center on the pursuit and the deferral, the deferral and the pursuit, of inflicting death and suffering it.

6

❦

DOCUMENTARY LITERATURE AND
THE DISARMING OF DISSENT

PHOTOGRAPHY began acquiring documentary authority in the nineteenth century, when the daguerreotype first appeared. Later, as equipment improved, it began to assert itself as an art form that tied artistic fidelity to passivity. Later still, having joined forces with literary realism and naturalism, it reinforced aesthetic doctrines of direct presentation and authorial impersonality. During the thirties, it allied itself with history, as a recording instrument, and to a lesser extent with sociology, as an analytic tool. Large-scale efforts, including several funded by such government agencies as the Farm Security Administration, were launched to create photographic records of faces and scenes. In a related move, with the example of the camera in mind, writers began using words to record and preserve objects, faces, and scenes. Like Asch's *The Road* (1937), Louis Adamic's *My America* (1938) reports without photographs, but the recording instinct of the social reporter informs his work, and so does the example of the camera. In books like Margaret Bourke-White and Erskine Caldwell's *You Have Seen Their Faces* (1937), Dorothea Lange and Paul S. Taylor's *An American Exodus: A Record of Human Erosion in the Thirties* (1939), Archibald MacLeish's *Land of the Free* (1938), and Richard Wright and Edwin Rosskam's *Twelve Million Black Voices* (1941), words and photographs comment on one another. In each of these books, however, the text tends to become subordinate to the photographs, as MacLeish acknowledged by saying that, having begun as "a book of poems illustrated by photographs," his project had become "a book of photographs illustrated by a poem." Lange and Taylor in particular celebrate an aesthetic built on the clear, vivid, and seemingly detached art of photography.

Documentary literature in the thirties used the camera as an instrument, invoking the authority of its nascent aesthetic, in order to preserve a fading past and tame a threatening present. Like the new social sciences, including new forms of history, art and journalism joined the effort to preserve "the American way of life." In the process, often unwittingly, they contributed to the success of Roosevelt's New Deal. For Roosevelt's style of leadership, featuring experimentation, or "statesmanship as adjustment," depended on his ability to learn as he groped. But it also depended on his ability to persuade "the people" to learn as they groped by persuading them, in large part rhetorically, that by groping he and they were doing three things at once: continuing traditions of the past, saving the present, and shaping the future. Most of the "alphabet agencies" of the New Deal, including the FSA (Farm Security Administration), the CCC (Civilian Conservation Corps), and the WPA (Works Progress Administration), which included the FWP (Federal Writers' Project) and the FTP (Federal Theater Project), were parts of a large campaign in which action and persuasion reinforced each other. In them the line between agency and message – or propaganda – blurred.

The quality of the outpourings that resulted from the nation's large push to preserve its story, like the motives behind the government's initiatives, was mixed, and it remains difficult to assess. Recalling his own debt to the FWP (1935–42), Saul Bellow described it as belonging to a "day before gratitude became obsolete," when writers unexpectedly became beneficiaries of federally sponsored programs. Other writers viewed the government's programs as more or less subtle cooptive moves, and grateful artists as willing or not so willing dupes. Though some works produced were of marginal value, others were important. Richard Wright's *Uncle Tom's Children* (1938) won a prize from *Story* magazine for the best work by an FWP writer, and Pare Lorentz's documentary *The River*, which influenced both Steinbeck and Faulkner, was produced by the FSA. Certainly, the scope of government-sponsored projects was impressive. During its four-year existence, the FTP employed nearly 13,000 people and presented more than 42,000 performances, with a repertoire that ranged from *Macbeth* to *Hansel and Gretel*; from a folklore-based ballet of "Frankie and Johnnie," which featured pirouetting pimps and prostitutes, to scores of new plays by FTP writers – including Paul Green's *Hymn to the Rising Sun*, George Sklar's *Stevedore*, Theodore Brown's *Lysistrata*, Elmer Rice's *Prologue to Glory* (a play about Lincoln), and W. E. B. Du Bois's *Haiti* (about a revolt against Napoleon) – several of which were condemned by Martin Dies's House Un-American Activities Committee. Conrad Aiken, Arna Bontemps, Erskine Caldwell, Ralph Ellison, Margaret Walker, Eudora Welty, Edmund Wilson, Richard Wright, and Frank Yerby were among hundreds of writers employed on federal projects, some of whom worked in cooperation with teams of photographers to produce guidebooks that surveyed the people, land, history, and culture of each of the forty-eight states and Alaska. Simply in terms of accumulated data, the results were impressive. But in addition to the guidebooks, on which nearly 12,000 researchers, writers, and coordinators worked, hundreds of biographies, histories, compilations of folksongs and folkstories, accounts of expeditions and explorations, and a variety of documentary reports were produced.

The documentary enterprise sponsored by the New Deal reinforced an impression with which it may fairly be said to have begun: that the nation's culture had done and was doing too little for "the people." But it also enlarged the need it set out to meet – the need to recover, in Alfred Kazin's words, a sense of "America *as an idea*." As a result, it helped to stimulate a remarkable outpouring of creative energies. In its conjoining of words and photographs, furthermore, it encouraged further examination of the complex relations between scenes of life, on one side, and forms of human perception, feeling, and expression, on the other. Having brought the desire to recover the past into contact with efforts to record images of the nation's spaces, it gave new weight to a notion dating back to Plato – that human creativity begins with a sense of place. In addition, it recalled moments when empty spaces had become named places, including one when an expanse of land so large no wanderer could think the end of it, under a sky that seemed as big as time itself, had become the "Great Plains."

Following a visit in 1926, the Dutch historian Johan Huizinga observed, in "Life and Thought in America," that in this country serious fiction (Cather, Wharton, Dreiser, and Lewis are among the writers he mentions) exposes the cheap optimism and boosterism of the nation's society and protests its puritanical prohibitions and crass materialism. But he also noted that its culture tended to reassert its power by assimilating and neutralizing even its most acidic critics, often by making their roles ornamental. London, whom Huizinga does not mention, has this in common with Wharton, Dreiser, Cather, and Lewis, whom he does mention: that he became read and rewarded only to find in large popularity what they had experienced in more modest success – that the United States was surprisingly resourceful in resisting the implications of what he wrote.

The documentary movement of the thirties, though in part an effort to recover "America *as an idea*," was also an effort to make art – image and word – more than ornamental, first, by making it more responsible to social realities and, second, by making it an integral part of the effort to survive. In this way it sought to counter the process by which art loses force as it earns praise. By deciding to make *Land of the Free* "a book of photographs illustrated by a poem" rather than "a book of poems illustrated by photographs," MacLeish came close to making it another version of the reiterative art practiced by writers like Farrell – that is, a work that relies heavily on the quantitative piling up of similar scenes. Two books for which Edwin Rosskam selected FSA photographs – Sherwood Anderson's *Home Town* (1940) and Richard Wright's

Twelve Million Black Voices – also present verbal texts that illustrate visual texts. They, too, depend less on juxtaposition and progression than on the accumulation of discrete images. But other works – notably Lange and Taylor's *An American Exodus* and Bourke-White and Caldwell's *You Have Seen Their Faces* – accomplish more by remaining divided and even conflicted.

Both Lange and Bourke-White thought of the camera as the perfect instrument of documentary art because they believed in its directness and its passivity. "With a camera," Bourke-White said, "the shutter opens and closes and the only rays that come in to be registered come directly from the object in front of you." The "truth of the times," as the phrase went, could emerge through a camera, untainted by bias that no writer could escape, even by taking the camera as a model: "I am a camera with its shutter wide open," Christopher Isherwood said, "quite passive, not thinking." But Lange and Bourke-White accomplished more than their theory suggested possible, often by violating it. They began with the aim of recording the crippling effects of poverty on the suddenly visible poor: those who were "burned out, blowed out, eat out, tractored out," as one farmer interviewed by Lange and Taylor put it. The Great Depression was a leveling experience as well as a harsh one. It left a fair number of bankers and large landholders trapped in milder versions of the same hopeless, moneyless mess that robbed farmers of land and laborers of jobs. The results proved wrenchingly divisive. Several months after the Historical Section of the Resettlement Administration published a photograph made by Walker Evans in Bethlehem, Pennsylvania, in 1935 – of a cemetery against a backdrop of tenement houses, with a large steel mill looming in the background – a woman appeared at the Washington office of the Resettlement Administration and asked for a copy of the photograph so that she could send it to her brother, a steel executive in Pennsylvania, bearing a message: "*Your* cemeteries, *your* streets, *your* buildings, *your* steel mills. But *our* souls, God damn you."

Photographers like Lange, Bourke-White, and Evans played major roles in recording the faces of the Great Depression, and they did so in part by allowing their practice to outstrip the theory. Among the several large lessons of the Depression, one of the largest is this: that even in near disaster people find unexpected ways of refusing to be reduced to silence or passivity. In the thirties, photography and documentary literature helped to make these lessons visible, and they also enacted art's versions of them. They recorded the faces of weather-beaten, almost vanquished people – urban and rural, black, brown, and white – whom hunger, fear, and anger had taught how not to smile. They celebrated the resilience of former "hyphenated-Americans" and former slaves side by side with once-"native sons" and once-proud farmers. They recorded the personal narratives of former slaves and the folkmusic – songs of protest, drinking songs, and gospel songs – of people from the hills of Kentucky, Tennessee, North Carolina, and Georgia to the streets of New York, Detroit, Chicago, and San Francisco. In this vast undertaking, they made words and photographs work together in ways that have little to do with objectivity.

Like Bourke-White, Lange associated her art with passivity. But her famous "Migrant Mother," one of several photos she took of Florence Thompson on a wet March afternoon in 1936, in a migrant labor camp in Nipomo, California, gathers power from several sources, including its central figure, a mother weary of consideration and worn by privation, sheltering her shy, frightened, and almost helpless children. Both nature's force, which is felt directly, and society's indifference, which is felt as abnegation, come to bear on the lives of vulnerable human beings. But Lange's photograph also confronts its always more comfortable viewer with the suffering of people who ask, in all but words, what if anything they can make of their diminished lives. The children convey a sense of vulnerable yearning that privation has not yet extinguished; the mother, a strength and faithfulness that worry and weariness have not yet destroyed. At the same time, Lange's photograph depends on and even registers the vulnerability and faithfulness of an artist who refuses to let privilege drain her of compassion or near helplessness drain her of resolve. There is a felt correspondence, a reciprocity, between the Migrant Mother and Lange, as we see even more clearly when the most famous of the photographs is viewed in the context of the six that she made on that rainy afternoon. This dimension of Lange's art – its quiet celebration of art's engagement with life as the form that art's faithfulness to life and to itself must take – runs counter to the notion that photography's force depends on objectivity. And in this, it discloses the deeper significance of the documentary impulse: its determination that art be more than ornament.

Some documentary works – Ruth McKenney's *Industrial Valley* (1939) and George Leighton's *Five Cities* (1939), for example – as well as some more overtly imaginative works – including Albert Maltz's *The Underground Stream* (1940), a novel about automobile factories, and Thomas Bell's *Out of This Furnace* (1941), a novel about steelworkers in Pennsylvania – leave us with the sense of writers who feel almost overwhelmed by their tasks. "I, for one, considered myself a witness to the times rather than a novelist," said Jack Conroy. Under the double pressure of a "radical world view" and the "urgency of the times," imaginative acts seemed almost futile, Herbst remarked. Some writers tended, D. H. Lawrence noted, in speaking of Dahlberg, to be content with dramatizing their own defeat, as though they were in love with themselves in their "defeated role." But in the era's more remarkable collaborations – of Lange and Taylor,

Bourke-White and Caldwell, Wright and Rosskam, and especially Walker Evans and James Agee – the pressures against passive objectivity mount. Both Evans and Agee wanted, as Agee put it, "to perceive simply the cruel radiance of what is." But each of them also wanted to know it, as though for the first and last time, as artists working with and through their different media. One sign of this is Evans's curious mix of clearly posed and seemingly unposed photographs. Another is Agee's strained and even painful effort to integrate every nuance of all the motives as well as the means of his perceiving and recording into the story he tells. The result, *Let Us Now Praise Famous Men* (1941), constitutes one of the most remarkable encounters with the United States in crisis yet written. Agee analyzes the shame and pitiableness even more than the anger and fear of the Ricketts and the Gudger families of Alabama. He exposes the sexual desire that he feels for and attributes to the people he writes about. Gender, class, and race as facts of life and as social constructions also come into play, as does the force of privation. Yet Agee also celebrates the endurance and even the obdurate privacy of the families into whose lives he intrudes. Having anticipated the deprivation he encounters he finds himself surprised by the dignity of those deprived.

Like several other writers of the thirties, Agee preferred native traditions of radicalism, in part because he wanted to subordinate both the aesthetic concerns of the twenties and the political concerns of the thirties to a new kind of reporting in which the lines between history and art and between nonfiction and fiction blur. In one sense, the meaning of the sharecroppers' lives resides in the bare facts of their existence; in another, it is discovered as well as preserved through the intrusive acts that record them. Agee could and did describe his art as a teasing out of the "cruel radiance of what is," as though the radiance in question were prior to the act of writing – which is to say, were already wholly present in the object described. But he remained an almost painfully self-conscious artist who could and did speak of his art in very different terms; and in practice he worked through a far more complicated predicament.

Agee's effort to transform the invisible struggles "of an undefended and appallingly damaged group of human beings," first, into visible and, then, into "famous" lives draws on lessons gathered from several sources, including Whitman's injunction to vivify the facts, Dos Passos's insistence on the disjunctions between human lives and human scenes, and a range of rhetorical traditions of the South. As a result, he violates facile notions about the objectivity of documentary literature from the first page of his book to the last. His text not only interacts with Evans's photographs. It employs a wide range of discourses – ethnographic, sociological, phenomenological, theological, historical, autobiographical, poetic, novelistic – and utilizes an astonishing range of styles – realist, naturalist, impressionist, expressionist, surrealist, cubist, and visionary. He takes the radiance of the real seriously by taking the reconstitutive power of art seriously.

Power in fact emerges as one of Agee's great themes. We witness and thus become complicit in the power of words and of photographs to invade and impose themselves on human lives as well as to represent, fix, and transform them. The power of words and photographs to represent and construct are a part of what *Let Us Now Praise Famous Men* critiques. The book depends on those powers, and on the willingness of the poet and the photographer to use them in representing those who cannot represent themselves – cannot speak in their own voices or name their own enemies, cannot defend their interests or assert their rights, and certainly cannot impose their needs and desires upon their world. Agee discovers and confronts the presumption implicit in his effort to represent the unrepresented. He exposes, in a language of implicit confession, his own mixed needs – in which sexual desire, economic and professional ambition, and social condescension mingle – and acknowledges that he cannot hope faithfully to do all that needs to be done. He realizes that he belongs to the privileged world that has sentenced to silence and privation those whose lives he presumes to invade and condescends to honor. But like Lange and Evans, he persists in doing his work while making his confession because he believes that what he is doing is better done than not done.

Agee assumes that words become images and images, words; and he assumes that the world to which he belongs depends upon the power of words and images to shape as well as represent life. He knows, in short, the power of words like "art" and "artist" as well as "sharecropper," "tenant farmer," and "red-neck," just as he knows what interests profit from such words. When his manuscript, which was commissioned and then rejected by *Fortune* magazine, was first submitted to Harper Brothers in late August 1938, its title was *Cotton Tenants: Three Families*. But as Nazi armies swept across Poland, preempting the world's attention, Harper Brothers lost interest in the book. When it finally appeared, published by Houghton Mifflin in 1941, Agee had exchanged its descriptive title for a poetic one, and he had also given up hope of having the book produced in newsprint so that tenant farmers could afford to buy it. The first of these changes reflects his growing awareness of the oddity and power of his work; the second reflects his awareness of the gulf that separated him and his readers from the people about whom he had written and for whom he wanted to write. *Let Us Now Praise Famous Men* is, in short, a deeply self-conscious work. It is both a meditation on the cruel radiance of what we see and a meditation on the cruel fact that with all the goodwill we can muster we can never recognize and acknowledge more than a part of what we see. Beyond that, however, it is also a meditation on the limits of what, among the things we see and recognize, we can directly record or indirectly evoke with images and words. In it, even omission and silence come under inspection. What objects do to subjects, and subjects do to objects – the Rickettses and the Gudgers to Evans and Agee, as well as Evans and Agee to the Rickettses and the Gudgers – emerge as twin themes. Agee's narrative becomes confessional and autobiographical because under pressure it must: the objects of his observations – of his snoopings, spyings, and pryings – invade him, calling him and his vocation into question, forcing him to present both himself and his work for inspection and examination. One set of tensions he plays with has to do with social and economic class; another has to do with race and caste; another set of tensions has to do with sexual desires, his own as well as those he discerns or attributes to the Rickettses and Gudgers, both as they exist and as he renders them; and a fourth set of tensions has to do with journalism and art, even "honest" journalism and "selfless" art, for Agee knew that the struggle for money and fame is never for very long very far even from an artist's view.

Among prose works of the thirties and early forties, only Faulkner's greatest novels are as unrelenting as *Let Us Now Praise Famous Men* in scrutinizing the social and vocational predicament of literature and the writer. The guilt that Agee carries through his story is in part the guilt of a survivor. But it is also the guilt of that privileged creature, the artist, for whom suffering and loss become, among other things, art's occasion and subject: if the Rickettses and Gudgers *had* life – had expressive voices, decent spaces, and decent livings of their own – Agee seems to say, they should have no need of art or artists. Agee's irony constantly turns back on the self and work of the artist by positing indirectly an ideal state in which the Gudgers and Rickettses of the world so fully possess life – and with it, force – that they possess the only radiance worth having and so have no need of Evans or Agee and their arts of image and word. There is, as a result, deep ambivalence in *Let Us Now Praise Famous Men*; and there is also a hovering silence. The self-reflexivity fostered by Agee's double commitment – to the limited radiance of life itself and to the limited radiance of what art can do with and for broken, stunted lives – alters the boundaries between nonfiction and fiction by clouding them and so invites and challenges those who read his book to question themselves and their motives.

Agee and Evans opened the documentary tradition to directions that are still being explored. In doing this, however, they also defined the limits within which radical thought tended to work in the thirties. The widening web of suspicion that we associate with Marx and Freud – of social institutions and of personal and family relations – threatened at times to silence Agee. Privilege of the kind he had known at Phillips Exeter and Harvard became suspect to him, along with many familiar human motives, including those of artists and reformers. Not even loyalty and valor, human feeling and truth-seeking wholly escaped the web of his suspicion. He remained a sojourner everywhere he lived. But despite his doubts, he went on trying to enter the lives, hear the voices, and speak the language of those among whom he moved; and despite his desire for privacy and his fear of exposure, he went on inviting others to examine his. He found his finest moments both as a human being and as a writer in *Let Us Now Praise Famous Men* because he found in it a way of holding on to diminished life and imperfect art by making diminished life serve imperfect art and imperfect art enhance diminished life.

7

❧

THE SOUTHERN RENAISSANCE: FORMS
OF REACTION AND INNOVATION

ACING A WORLD that seemed in danger of losing its way, shapers of the documentary movement in the thirties brought to culmination the most extensive literary and artistic effort ever launched in the United States to search out, record, examine, and alter the life and values of the people of the United States. The guidebooks sponsored by the WPA present the thirties as a casualty of the past. They focus on dusty, windblown streets and peeling storefronts; on dried-up towns and eroded farms; on segregated water fountains and segregated restrooms; on houses whose windows and doors are shut; and on faces that are gaunt, blank, or even battered. Reiterating the messages conveyed by the titles of books like Dreiser's *Tragic America* (1931), Wilson's *American Jitters* (1932), and Anderson's *Puzzled America* (1935), they provide correctives, as Robert Cantwell noted, "to the success stories that dominate our literature." At the same time, they exemplify energy and resolve. By bringing photography into innovative conjunctions with new modes of reporting, Bourke-White and Caldwell, Wright and Rosskam, Lange and Taylor, and Agee and Evans added a literary dimension to the "bold, persistent experimentation" that was the trademark of the New Deal. In the process, they helped to salvage and rehabilitate both "America" and "the People" as ideas of genuine force.

Moved by a similar sense of crisis, historical novelists like Kenneth Roberts searched through the nation's past, looking for heroes. Documentary works of the thirties focus on the average suffering of the neglected and voiceless poor – and, if only as putative presences, on the intent, inquiring faces of writers and photographers jerked to attention by that suffering. Historical novels focus on the triumphs of heroic men, or occasionally a heroic woman, who command our attention by virtue of superior status or achievement. As putative presences, historical novelists sometimes lapse into the role of distracted dreamers born out of season, turned toward some distant home of the mind. But the role they covet blends the talents of a detective with the motives of a moralist who wants to make giants of the past serve as models for the present. In a series of novels – *Arundel* (1930), *Rabble in Arms* (1933), *Northwest Passage* (1937), and

Oliver Wiswell (1940) – Kenneth Roberts presents heroes who turn turmoil and trial into triumph. His books helped the nation retain a sense of itself as young during the first decade in which it felt old.

In the mid-thirties, as conditions began to ease some, several writers launched a counterattack against the negative reports that Cantwell thought of as needed correctives. Disaffected intellectuals who persisted in depicting the nation as puzzled, jittery, and tragic were labeled "misleaders" by Van Wyck Brooks. During the Lyric Years, Brooks had launched his career with *The Wine of the Puritans* (1908) and *America's Coming of Age* (1915), in which he used past failings to point American culture toward its true destiny. During the thirties, with the nation mired in disillusionment, he began writing success stories. Shortly after writing *The Life of Emerson* (1932), his first tale of literary triumph, he launched a five-volume series on "Finders and Makers" with *The Flowering of New England, 1815–1865* (1936) and *New England: Indian Summer, 1865–1915* (1940). The "goldenrod rises again in its season, and the folk-poem recovers its meaning, when the nation, grown old, returns to its youth," we read in *New England: Indian Summer*, in a line that captures almost perfectly a theme – of hope rooted in memories – that nudged its way into books like Louis Adamic's *My America* (1938). People are free, Brooks wrote in *The Flowering of New England*, sounding another shared theme, when "they belong to a living, organic, believing community, active in fulfilling some unfulfilled, perhaps unrealized purpose" rooted in the past. Dos Passos remained more skeptical than Brooks. But by 1937, a year after completing *The Big Money* (1936), he too decided to turn his long-standing fascination with the nation's past to the task of defining its "hope for the future." *The Living Thoughts of Thomas Paine* (1940) was one result, and *The Ground We Stand On* (1941) another. We "must never forget," he wrote in the latter, "that we are heirs to one of the grandest and most nearly realized world-pictures in all history."

It remained, almost by default, the task of the South to keep alive the darker view of history with which the thirties – buried in failed banks, dried-up farms, and blighted lives – had begun. World War I had changed the region. Thousands of young Northerners, including Fitzgerald, had taken basic training there, and thousands of Southerners, including one of Faulkner's brothers, had traveled north en route to France. At the Great War's end, a large migration from the depleted soil of the South to the streets of the North was still under way, particularly among African Americans. But the region's lingering resistance to the incorporating Union – typified by its persistence in voting Democratic while Republicans were running the country – preserved its isolation, and in 1920 the collapse of the agricultural market pushed it deeper in debt. As affluence and rumors of affluence continued to spread across the land, the South began to crack under the strain of being the only poor region in the world's richest nation. Hoping to make belated peace, a new generation of leaders intensified their efforts to attract industries from the North, particularly textile factories from New England. But nothing seemed to go right. In 1927 the heavens opened up, devastating the richest farmlands the South had left with a record-breaking flood, and then closed in a widespread, three-year drought that lasted through 1930, intensifying the impact of the Depression.

Merging as they did with the military build-up of World War II, the federally administered economic reforms of the New Deal changed every section of the United States. But they changed the South most because the South had farther to go. To be fully incorporated into the Union, the South had to change its values as well as its political economy. Agencies such as the Agricultural Adjustment Administration, the Civilian Conservation Corps, the Federal Emergency Relief Administration, and the Tennessee Valley Authority, to name a few, helped to keep the South solidly Democratic. They also accelerated its integration into the country's version of the modern world. Some Southerners thought of Roosevelt as a "prophetic figure"; others, resistant to the end, rejected everything he stood for. Most federal programs fell short of their goals. Others failed badly, especially among those most in need of help. Black Southerners called the NRA (National Recovery Act) the "Negro Run Around" or "Negroes Ruined Again." But the New Deal accelerated a transformation, tilting the South farther away from its old, dispersed, agriculturally based form of capitalism toward a new industrial, commercial, and centralized political economy administered from urban centers of communication and transportation as well as political, economic, and commercial exchange, such as Atlanta, Georgia. This rapid transformation contributed both to the sense of betrayal and the sense of hope that informed the emergence of the South's new literature.

The Southern Renaissance – the most striking literary development of the thirties – arose from an improbable confluence of events. On one side, the Crash brought the United States closer to the experience of the South, which had all along been closer to the experience of the world at large, making Southern experience suddenly more pertinent. On the other, it sped the South's integration into the Union, triggering dislocations and ambivalences in the South that were similar to those found in literary modernism. Looking back on his own beginnings as an experimental painter, Robert Motherwell noted that he and his colleagues had been "formed by the Depression, when the American Dream lay in pieces on the floor," making the "possibility of making money . . . inconceivable to us." What he and his friends had sought instead, he added, was "to use the standards of international modernism as a gauge" in order "to make painting that would stand up under international scrutiny." In many respects, Motherwell's aim was shared by Faulkner and several of the Southern Agrarians, including the early editors of the *Southern Review*. But it was shared with differences that can be accounted for only when we recognize that local history shapes literature, particularly fiction, far more directly than it shapes painting.

When the Crash came, bringing the nation down almost into the dust, it found the South waiting there, already on familiar terms with history's great negative lessons of poverty, failure, defeat, and guilt. Beneath the surface of the nation's official history lay thousands of brutal stories – of people captured and enslaved; of people robbed of their land and herded onto reservations; of pioneers whose backbreaking labors did little more than scar the plains; of women ignored, belittled, dominated, and abused; of working masses huddled in ghettos; of gaunt tenant farmers and itinerant day laborers. "It is not till you live in America, and go a little under the surface," D. H. Lawrence observed, "that you begin to see how terrible and brutal is the mass of failure that nourishes the roots of the gigantic tree of dollars." Yet "when we think of America," he noted, we think first of "her huge success" and "never realize how many failures have gone, and still go to build up that success."

When people thought of the South, by contrast, especially in the thirties and forties, they thought first of failure and defeat. In the days of the Revolution and the early republic, the South's story had been almost one with the nation's official story. It was a story of westward expansion, and it was a story of success piled on success. During the age of George Mason, George Washington, James Madison, and Thomas Jefferson, the South had been rich even in letters. Edgar Allan Poe and Mark Twain possessed ties to the South; and T. S. Eliot seems at times to have thought he did, particularly when he was writing about Mark Twain or was searching for a cultural explanation of the tensions that divided him and the sense of dispossession that haunted him – when, in short, he wanted to understand why he felt central by family heritage yet marginal by temperament. In fact, however, unlike Eliot's family, the South had begun living an almost separate history even before its fateful decisions that led it into secession. Its dream of an agrarian society built on the backs of black slaves and crowned by a white landed aristocracy ran contrary both to the nation's egalitarian rhetoric and to its headlong rush to transform itself into a model of corporate capitalism built on the backs of laborers and crowned by an aristocracy of wealth.

The South's decision to declare itself separate and commit itself to the institution of slavery intensified its regional differences. Four years of decimating war followed by twelve years of occupation left it sequestered in shame and resentment and poor in everything except subregions, dialects, and the great negative lessons of history, all of which both cut across and sharpened divisions based on class, caste, race, and gender. What the South dreamed was one thing, but what it directly knew was another. In 1929, despite several decades of slow recovery, the South remained guilt-ridden yet defiant. But it also remained internally conflicted, in part because its experience of defeat seemed inseparable from the only claims to distinction it had left.

During the late nineteenth and early twentieth centuries, when for the nation at large being an "almost chosen people" seemed clearly to mean being chosen for wealth and power, the South made small gains but fell farther behind. In 1929 it was in considerable part a land of sharecroppers and subsistence farmers, moonshine whiskey and feuding clans, and it was widely associated with cultural backwardness as well as a strict and often brutal system of racial segregation. When, infrequently, the larger nation paused to think about the subject, it regarded the South as an embarrassment. H. L. Mencken fancied himself an iconoclastic deflator of his nation's self-deceptions. Yet in virtually every word he uttered about the South, even in asides, he reinforced one of the North's deepest assumptions: namely, that Northern industry went with virtue and Southern backwardness with vice, or, put another way, that the South's failure had been moral before it became military and economic. Such assumptions carried weight in the South as well as the North, furthermore, because one thing the North and South shared was a religious tradition that had never been able to decide whether salvation was a reward for good works or a gift of grace.

The South's deepest fear derived from its share in this basic confusion. Neither its religious fundamentalism (another of its trademarks) nor its almost separate history had wholly separated it from the nation's dream of innocence and wealth. Yet to a region whose identity revolved around lessons of loss, what could that dream yield except redoubled self-doubt? In posing repeatedly the question Miss Rosa Coldfield raises in Faulkner's *Absalom, Absalom!* (1936), of why God let the South lose the war, the South raised repeatedly the half-repressed question that haunted it even more than losing the war itself: of whether in a nation that thought of itself as commissioned by God to become a model of confidence, industry, and prosperity, it had been chosen to stand as an antitype of guilt, sloth, and poverty. The deep alienation that stands at the heart of Southern writing in the thirties has several sources, including the ambivalence the South felt about the nation's headlong rush toward secularism, progress, prosperity, and power. At its best, however, especially the fiction of Faulkner, it also includes other kinds of ambivalence, one of which was generated by recognition that its mixed history contained literary possibilities that were waiting to be explored and exploited.

The result was a literature of divisions that are intensely if not peculiarly modern: stories about the hope of being chosen and the pain of being excluded; stories about being, and being doomed to remain, *other*; and stories in which defeat – both as a kind of death and as a principle of exclusion – spurs the imagination. These stories were nothing if not commodious. They made room for crucial questions about language and forms of storytelling and the ties of both of these to place or region. They made room for issues of class, caste, race, and gender, and thus for the language of power as well as the power of language. As a result, with the thirties as backdrop, the South was able to create a literature that laid claim to the future in part by studying out its past and in part by examining the moment to which that past had somehow led.

In 1922 a group of professors and students at Vanderbilt, led by John Crowe Ransom, a Tennessean educated at Oxford, founded a magazine called the *Fugitive* and began publishing verse characterized by wit, irony, restraint, impersonality, and formal precision – which is to say, verse that was as "modern" in style and form as it was "Southern" in origin and theme. As a result, by 1929 the Fugitives were prepared to join in a remarkable flowering that adjusted "modern" preoccupations to "regional" concerns. In that year – in which Hemingway published *A Farewell to Arms* and Lewis published *Dodsworth* – Joseph Wood Krutch of Tennessee published *The Modern Temper*, Ellen Glasgow of Virginia published *They Stooped to Folly*, Evelyn Scott of Tennessee published *The Wave*, Allen Tate of Kentucky published *Jefferson Davis: His Rise and Fall*, Robert Penn Warren of Kentucky published *John Brown: The Making of a Martyr*, Thomas Wolfe of North Carolina published *Look Homeward, Angel*, T. S. Stribling of Tennessee published *Strange Moon*, and William Faulkner of Mississippi published both *Sartoris*, a shortened version of *Flags in the Dust* (1973), and *The Sound and the Fury*. The decade that followed – which witnessed the continued work of Ransom, Scott, and Glasgow, the maturation of Stribling, Grace Lumpkin, Donald Davidson, Erskine Caldwell, Andrew Lytle, Katherine Anne Porter, Margaret Mitchell, and Zora Neale Hurston, as well as Warren and Young, and the emergence of writers like James Agee, Lillian Smith, Eudora Welty, and Richard Wright, as well as historians and sociologists like W. J. Cash, Frank Owsley, Howard Odum, John Ballard, David Potter, and C. Vann Woodward, together with several great novels by Faulkner – belonged to the South as no decade before or since has. Many novels of the thirties – not only strike novels, detective novels, and hard-boiled fiction, but novels by writers as different as Djuna Barnes, Henry Miller, James T. Farrell, John Dos Passos, and Nathanael West – are angry in mood. Yet most of them also remain interrogative in mood. Despite their bluster and surface confidence, they remain tentative even when, borrowing from documentaries, they are most concrete or, following early modernists, they strive for great formal control. "Why, why is God letting this happen to us?" they ask in a thousand ways.

It was, strangely, on such questions, which in a sense can never be answered, that Southern writers suddenly began to think of themselves as expert witnesses. In villages, where the South still lived in 1929, they had observed people who lived in slow time and acquired a sense of sequence and shared knowledge. But they had also seen history batter people with failures and defeats, leaving them with the sense of being entangled in messy stories whose beginnings and endings were hazy and whose meanings, like their margins, were blurred.

By 1929 more and more Southerners were beginning to buy into the dream of becoming rich and powerful enough to impose their wills on their environment. Having lost hold on an older sense of living in a world made for them, they began grabbing at the possibility of making one for themselves. The considerable ambivalence provoked by this effort can be observed in novels as different as Erskine Caldwell's *God's Little Acre* (1933) and Ellen Glasgow's *Barren Ground* (1925). It can also be seen in Faulkner's novels, where backward-looking ghosts vie with forward-looking parvenus for our attention. Many Southerners drawn toward the great project of bending the world to fit human desire still felt the pull of a world of which they could say what Faulkner said of North Mississippi – that its glory lay in the fact that God had done more for it than man had yet done to it. And when, having opted for the Union's way, they saw the nation's economy fall apart, their ambivalence was deepened by frustration. Faulkner became the most inventive of the nation's novelists of the twentieth century in part because, like Wallace Stevens, he learned to make expression the subject of expression and invention the subject of invention. In the process, he gave space to oppressed lives and expression to submerged voices, including occasionally those of people born poor, female, or black. But the South's ambivalence also triggered reaction. In 1930 a group of Southern Agrarians denounced the great technological project of the United States in a manifesto called *I'll Take My Stand*, which includes contributions by Davidson, Ransom, Tate, Warren, and Young, bearing titles like "Reconstructed but Unregenerate."

I'll Take My Stand is reactionary on several counts, including its denial of voice and space to black, female, and lower-class Southerners, as well as its strong preference for the agrarian way over the industrial-commercial way, for "high" culture over "low," for privileged classes over the dispossessed, and for timeless "literature" over mere writing. Only in "art" – and cautiously there – is innovation praised. Yet, by recoil, as it were, Davidson, Ransom, Tate, Warren, and Young clarify their moment. Where life is concerned, slow time is their aim. Having helped to invent a past in which a landed, educated, and sternly self-disciplined aristocracy ruled – as opposed to a merely landed one, though a merely landed one seemed to them superior to one dominated by industrialists and bankers – they propose that we turn back the clock, or at least slow it down, by funneling all human inventiveness into art. Even then, furthermore, they wanted to subject it to a hard and, as it seemed to them, masculine rationality. As a result, they tended to prefer Donne to Shakespeare, clean, clear poetry to noisy, messy fiction, and any number of inferior writers to William Faulkner.

With time, of course, the Agrarians changed: Ransom more than Davidson, Tate more than Ransom, and Warren more than Tate. But as young men writing in an old country and a dry season, recoil dominated their modes of expression.

Try as they might, however, they discovered that they could not master the South's negative heritage simply by declaring it a cultural model. Tate's and Warren's writing improved when they realized that the South's most useful literary resource was its negative identity: that the authority, moral as well as aesthetic, of marginality, failure, guilt, and shame was about all the South had to offer as imaginative capital, and that, in this fate, it had much in common with other peoples of the earth, including in the thirties many Americans. This unexpected overlap made it appropriate that the South should become the nation's dominant literary scene for the first time during the Great Depression. As scenes of publishing and marketing writing, Memphis, Nashville, New Orleans, Atlanta, Chapel Hill, Baton Rouge, and Charlottesville remained small, provincial capitals, and Oxford, Mississippi, and Eatonville, Florida, mere frontier outposts of Boston, New York, and Chicago. But as scenes of writing and as settings for stories, they became dominant.

The South's literary task was complicated, however, by its desire to find some way of continuing to honor its lost causes even as it began chasing prominence, prosperity, and power. It wanted, in short, to live out of its past in the double sense of claiming ties to it while working itself free of it. From 1935 to 1942 Robert Penn Warren and Cleanth Brooks edited the *Southern Review* out of Baton Rouge and made it an example of what the new literary South, as an extension of the New South, aspired to be. They published the work of several of the Fugitives – Ransom, Tate, Davidson – as well as other Southern writers, including Andrew Lytle and Eudora Welty. Some of the work they published harks back to the kinds of resistance celebrated in

I'll Take My Stand, and its appeal remained largely regional. But some of it points to enlarged ambitions that are reflected in the six fine stories by Welty published there between 1937 and 1939. Welty's stories are grounded in a strong sense of place. But they focus primarily on the South's little people – its traveling salesmen and its hairdressers – rather than on members of old families burdened with memories and aristocratic pretensions. And they are also written out of the formalist tradition that we associate with international modernism, and thus they mirror the larger literary ambitions of the *Southern Review*. Despite its regional ties and name, the *Southern Review* of the thirties was not provincial; it was imperial. Kenneth Burke, R. P. Blackmur, and F. O. Matthiessen, whose audiences were broadly American, published there, and so did Ford Madox Ford, Herbert Read, Aldous Huxley, Mario Praz, and Paul Valéry, whose audiences were international. The *Southern Review* thus mirrored the new aspirations of the region whose name it claimed. Despite its talk about aristocracy, the South had always been a preponderantly middle-class society, like the world of Welty's fiction and, for that matter, the rest of the United States. Although it wanted to honor its past as myth as well as fact, with words and monuments, it also wanted to collapse into a few short decades a process of industrialization that, by 1929, was a century old in New England and at least half again as old as that in England: it wanted to move from the old-style agrarian capitalism it had built on the backs of slaves living on plantations to a new-style capitalism built around banks, railroads, factories, and industrial corporations. It wanted to turn its preindustrial republic into a modern, incorporating political economy, so that the future could at last be *now*.

One set of consequences of this shift in allegiance from the Old and toward the New South can be seen in the dislocations, discontinuities, and confusions that directly enter its fiction – in, for example, the trilogy of T. S. Stribling called *The Forge* (1931), *The Store* (1932), and *Unfinished Cathedral* (1934); in the Snopes trilogy of Faulkner, *The Hamlet* (1940), *The Town* (1957), and *The Mansion* (1959); and in virtually all of the fiction of writers like Thomas Wolfe and Erskine Caldwell. Having written essays and documentary works as well as stories, Erskine Caldwell made his mark with *Tobacco Road* (1932) and *God's Little Acre*, both of which are set in the brutalizing countryside of the Piedmont, previously more ignored than forgotten. Caldwell's Piedmont remains oblivious to the South's preoccupation with cultural distinctiveness. Its history is felt in entrenched meagerness rather than haunting memories of lost elegance. And its present includes the New South's hope that industrialism may yet pave the way to greater wealth – and even to a fairer distribution of it. A traveler and a listener, Caldwell writes of despised and oppressed people, with as little adornment as possible and with almost no sense of mannered style. His land is a land of worn-out soil and new industry, including textile mills lured away from a declining New England; and it is a land of exploited, misshapen people who characteristically act with a minimum of reflection and a maximum of yearning and desire, whether they seek gold or sexual pleasure, respectability or justice. None of them fully understands either the cultural and economic deprivations of their lives or the inadequacies of their dreams. They claim our attention because, despite everything, they are not yet wholly inured to privation. Although they lead meager lives and have almost no education, they hold fast to some waning aspiration (in *Tobacco Road*, Jeter Lester's dream of a good tobacco crop; in *God's Little Acre*, Ty Ty Walden's dream of finding gold on a worn-out piece of ground, Will Thompson's dream of securing a fair wage, and Jim Leslie's pitiful dream of becoming respectable) as though to one last, fading dream. Simply by holding out against long odds, they give meager meaning to their lives.

Unlike Caldwell, many Southern writers found themselves in a double bind: they wanted to pay homage to the South's past while also deserting it, a tension that enters Southern fiction of the thirties in many ways. In Margaret Mitchell's *Gone with the Wind* (1936), it emerges as a struggle between what we might call a poetry of the past and a poetry of the future, and it makes Mitchell's novel considerably more interesting than its popularity has encouraged us to believe. Mitchell's poetry of the past emanates from the historical struggle about which she writes – the Civil War – and it remains the ostensible subject of her novel. Her poetry of the future emanates from the historical struggle out of which she wrote, which in her own day had entered a new phase and was nearing a decisive moment. That struggle, which Mitchell surreptitiously seizes as a sequel to the old war, makes itself felt in two very different ways – one an act of recognition, the other an act of suppression.

The recognition enters through the tension (which occasionally comes close to open conflict) between the unconventional, untraditional, pragmatic, self-involved, forward-looking, sentimental yet tough-minded, heroine-protagonist, Scarlett O'Hara, on one side, and the South's conception of itself, on the other. Scarlett's sentimentality surfaces in her regressive love for Ashley Wilkes and her nostalgia for Tara. But there is a sense in which Scarlett belongs more to the novel's future – which is to say, Mitchell's present – than she does to its ostensible present. She begins as a spunky, vain, willful young woman. But socialized by her changing world, she becomes not the woman the Old South would have her be, "a lady," but the opportunistic creature whom Mitchell presents the South as needing and secretly wanting: one who takes any quarter she can get but never gives any. Scarlett thus tilts *Gone with the Wind* toward Mitchell's present, when the South was emerging as a region anxious to make its way in the world but anxious, too, about the political and social emergence of blacks. And, on this count, *Gone with the Wind* remains an emphatically white novel, which is to say an emphatically reactionary one. It suppresses blacks not only as political agents but as independent agents of any kind – this being Mitchell's way of turning the clock back and then slowing it down.

Mitchell's persistence in making Scarlett respond unconventionally to familial and personal pressures as well as large social forces makes more striking her persistence in having Scarlett share the South's determination to keep black people in subordinate, subservient roles. Mitchell thinks of Scarlett, and sometimes has Scarlett think of herself, as a rebel, and so in some ways she is. She breaks several rules governing the behavior of women in her society. But she remains an ardent defender of her confused society, which thinks of itself as aristocratic and traditional even when it acts like the middle class on the make. Scarlett loves the land, but she's willing to leave it if by doing so she can enhance her chance of becoming affluent. She pays lip service to the forbearance and self-denial of women like Melanie, but it is her father's willfulness that she adapts to changing circumstances, in the name not of mere survival but of dominance. The Yankees are right about one thing, she remarks: it takes "money to be a lady," with which admission she embraces the New South emerging around her and turns her back on the Old South, in which money, like sexual desire, was something a "lady" did not talk about.

Like Mitchell's Atlanta, Scarlett is young, headstrong, and ambitious. Tara belongs to an older, agrarian world, where land was the only thing that counted because, allied as it was with family, class, and continuity, as well as the South's concept of "lady," it was the only thing that could be counted on. But Atlanta, where Margaret Mitchell in fact lived not as a lady, is the scene Scarlett makes her own, and it gives her special ties both to the new world rising out of the ashes of the old and to its poet, Margaret Mitchell. *Gone with the Wind* thus engages the story of the South in the extended moment that began with the South's defiance of the North and ended with its full incorporation by it. That moment embraces both the crisis of the Civil War and the crisis of its long aftermath, in which crucial questions of race, gender, and justice, as well as unbridled ambition, the fear of poverty, and the worship of success, came into play. On these questions, *Gone with the Wind* combines remarkable recognitions with remarkable evasions and suppressions, for Mitchell, like her region and even her nation, was not prepared to face them.

In discussing Dorinda Oakley, the heroine of *Barren Ground*, Ellen Glasgow praised the old-fashioned virtue of fortitude. Dorinda "exists wherever a human

being has learned to live without joy, where the spirit of fortitude has triumphed over the sense of futility." Dorinda's hard choice – to limit and control
all personal relationships with men and women in order to avenge and assert
herself by reclaiming unproductive land from proliferating broomsedge –
comes after she has been betrayed by a wealthy young man named Jason
Greylock; and it is apt to strike some of us as more surprising and troubling in
a woman than in a man. If that is our problem, however, Dorinda's is this: that
for her, as for men, it leads to a strikingly truncated life. Having disciplined
herself to go without many things, she becomes strong yet cold and even hard.
The other side of her self-determination and self-assertion is ruthless self-
denial – in all of which she resembles Faulkner's Thomas Sutpen in *Absalom,
Absalom!* Disappointed in love, she snaps back to triumph in life and so wins
our sympathy, just as she won Ellen Glasgow's. She is a model of resilience as
well as iron will. But it tells us much about the logic of Glasgow's art – and
by implication Dorinda's life – that as it moved toward *They Stooped to Folly*
(1929) and *The Sheltered Life* (1938) it became more distrustful of youthful
unrest, and more committed to fortitude – and the resignation that fortitude
makes possible – than to pleasure or joy. Glasgow's heroines and heroes form
purposes and sustain culture, together with its institutions and its values, despite the buffeting they receive from nature and history. But as Dorinda puts
it, they triumph by keeping themselves "untouched and untouchable." What
matters most is a vein of iron called *will*, which teaches the yearning self that
denial is the route to self-realization.

Transformed if not reinvented by her own needs in conjunction with the
exigencies of a great cultural crisis, Scarlett O'Hara becomes at least as ruthless
as Dorinda Oakley. But she never willingly practices resignation. She wants
and is determined to try for everything, including pleasures and comforts, if
not intimacies, that Dorinda forgoes. Like Dreiser's Carrie, she is sustained
by the hope of tomorrow even when everything goes wrong. The clearest
embodiment of self-willed energy in her world, she emerges as the only hope
the South has of beating the North at its own game. In some moments, she
comes to us as an old-fashioned character who acts as a force by making choices,
charting her own course, and trying to change her world. In others, she comes
to us as a newfangled personality, buffeted by the forces that surround and in
a sense shape her. Too hurried to be reflective, she assumes that playing well
the only game she's been given is better than choosing, like Ashley, to play no
game at all simply because the one he prefers has been taken away from him.

In brief, *Gone with the Wind* is "romantic," not "realistic." But it shares
important ground with the great historical novels written in the nineteenth
century by Stendhal, Tolstoy, Balzac, Trollope, Dickens, and others. For it,

too, gains power by tapping the political force of nationalism. In part because it is so accessible, and with the help of Hollywood has become so popular, it has endured as a vehicle for claiming and defining something like a *national* identity for the only despised region of a rich and powerful nation. Mitchell went on living in the New South, of course, even while she was thinking and writing about the Old South, a fact that helps to account for Scarlett's being the strongest part of *Gone with the Wind* and its history's being the weakest. Yet even as history *Gone with the Wind* is in one way more accurate than Allen Tate's *The Fathers* (1938). Tate studied history and wrote biographies. But he was finally more a moralist than a historian. What he valued were aristocratic forms of feeling that he thought of as having been crushed by change in continental Europe and England during the late eighteenth and early nineteenth centuries. For him the South's hope lay in trying to recreate them. Faith, tradition, and order lent dignity to life by creating high culture and making poetry possible. Although Tate settled for a position in a university, what he wanted for all good writers was a place in society. In his dream, economic sufficiency was enough, so long as literature was accorded a place of honor that recognized its sacred task of preserving a sense of the past and preparing the hearts and minds of men – and to a lesser extent, those of women – for the proper work of the future: the perpetuation of high culture. The South that Tate called into existence in his writings had committed itself to these things, only to abandon them. Betrayal haunted his mind even more than defeat. But the South he evoked in his essays and poems as well as in *The Fathers* had never been fully achieved even by the most blessed of Virginia's plantation owners. It was a necessary invention of a moralist searching for some adequate means of scolding both the South and the modern world into a program of conservative restoration.

Thomas Wolfe's struggle with the South was more tortured than Mitchell's and less historical than Tate's. For Wolfe was, to borrow the title of an openly autobiographical essay that he wrote and rewrote, "God's Lonely Man." Eugene Gant, the protagonist of *Look Homeward, Angel* (1929), traces his roots back to a scene in which as a small boy his father had watched Southern soldiers marching toward Gettysburg. But Gant's deeper wounds are more recent, and they resemble Wolfe's in being familial, personal, and mortal. Like Wolfe, Gant is an expert on the intimate harms done to children by parents and on the ingenious ways wounded children find of settling scores with their parents. Wolfe wrestled all of his life (he died in September 1938, not quite thirty-eight) and in all of his fiction with the pain of his youth, unable to make peace with it. Like Wolfe, Gant carries his grievances with him, and when they surface, they pour forth in a flood of poetic prose filled with adolescent yearnings as well as old grievances. At odds with his world, Gant is also self-conflicted. Union, the thing he most wants, is denied him as though by some smudge of fortune. Yearnings fill his attenuated life both as a prelude to extravagant spendings of his words and as a hedge against exhausting them.

If in Gant's story we seek Wolfe's image of the South or, more broadly, his image of the United States, we don't have far to go. The United States existed for Wolfe both as something present in the "forms we see on every hand of fear, hatred, slavery, cruelty, poverty, and need" and as an idea of free fulfillment too long deferred. Recognizing the *otherness* of the past, and the way in which it is always already lost, Wolfe tried to create voices that could incorporate old refrains in cadences that belonged to the present: "I believe we are lost here in America, but I believe we shall be found," he wrote in his last letter to "Foxhall Edwards" in *You Can't Go Home Again* (1940).

And this belief, which mounts now to the catharsis of knowledge and conviction, is for me – and I think for all of us – not only our own hope, but America's ever-lasting, living dream. I think the life which we have fashioned in America, and which has fashioned us – the forms we have made, the cells that grew . . . – was self-destructive in its nature, and must be destroyed. I think these forms are dying, and must die, just as I know that America and the people in it are deathless, undiscovered, and immortal, and must live.

I think the true discovery of America is before us. I think the true fulfillment of our spirit, of our people, of our mighty and immortal land, is yet to come. I think the true discovery of our own democracy is still before us. And I think that all of these things are as certain as the morning, as inevitable as noon.

Wolfe's books fit together as parts of one long, ragged story written by a person convinced that, by some miracle of election, he is both privileged and doomed to seek words for the lost meanings of his world. His various narrators speak in voices that resemble one another, and they echo his favorite poets. Together they help us locate Wolfe's overarching theme in a conflicted self whose paradoxical fate it is to be the center of a world – a family and community – from which he feels almost hopelessly cut off.

Wolfe characteristically begins his stories as he began his life, in a traditional world of small communities where people remember their ancestors, live textured lives in extended families, and accept the past as a guide to the future. But he and his protagonists quickly move away from home into a boardinghouse, out of an old, warm world into the modern world of open and endless seeking, yearning, and experimenting. Easy surrender to alienation as well as flight and death play familiar roles in his novels, as we see in Ben and Helen in *Look Homeward, Angel*, and so does the routine, vengeful seeking of recompense, as we see in Luke's mad pursuit of money and position. Wolfe's own version of this was a tortured search for a lost home and a lost father: "We are so lost, so naked and so lonely in America," he wrote. "Immense and cruel skies bend over us, and all of us are driven on forever and we have no home." "And which of us shall find his father, know his face, and in what place, and in what time, and in what land? Where?" These possibilities, the only ones that matter for Wolfe, exist primarily as ideas and are felt primarily in rhetoric – this being another sign of what being cut off means. Wolfe wrote on and on, retracing his loss and his hope again and again.

From one angle, we may say that the profligate quality of Wolfe's fiction, his rhetorical and poetic responses to want born of loss, resembles deficit financing. But his fiction, like Whitman's poetry, centers on his effort to locate and exploit correlations between his story and the nation's story. And his sense of that story brought the United States and his own life under the aspect of the South and the Great Depression into a tale informed, as he once put it in a letter, by an "intolerable memory" of "violence, savagery, immensity, beauty, ugliness, and glory," on one side, and an unfinished quest for wisdom and strength, on the other. Wolfe's art lacks the historical depth and the social reach of Faulkner's, and it misses these things both as enriching resources and as principles of order. But his transitory world still manages to remind us of the fate of regions in the United States. By the time Wolfe wrote, his South was fading as a distinct region. What had happened to New England, the Midwest, and the West was happening to the South, which had committed itself to being incorporated. If, furthermore, the ever-expanding Union, driven by its logic of incorporation, presents one problem, the South's ambivalence presents another. Wolfe's South, like Mitchell's, wants the Union, which is to say the modern, as much as the Union wants it, and so is prepared to leave to art both its distinctive and largely negative heritage of failure and its prized if largely imagined heritage of glory.

Several of Katherine Anne Porter's better stories – "Flowering Judas" and "Noon Wine," for example – trace the descent of people into erotic willfulness and economic opportunism and confront the effects of privation on the lives of marginalized farmers as they erupt into violence. Others, including "The Old Order," "The Grave," and "Old Mortality," are "Southern" in their attention to family, tradition, land, and the past. But their focus is on the creation and preservation of a sense of these things, not on the remembered possession of them. Throughout her life, Porter spread misrepresentations about her family and childhood, evoking family traditions that bore little relation except as compensatory strategies to the uprooted life she began in 1890 in a small L-shaped log cabin in Indian Creek, Texas. In its restraint, clarity, and control, her art is closer in style to Fitzgerald's, Hemingway's, and Cather's than to Wolfe's. Her South is not in transition; it is preserved in fabrications disguised as memories of an era of merriment and style that neither she nor her family had ever directly known.

8

❦

HISTORY AND NOVELS / NOVELS
AND HISTORY: THE EXAMPLE
OF WILLIAM FAULKNER

S PEAKING IN 1964, Ralph Ellison described William Faulkner as the
novelist who had brought "the impelling moral function of the novel
and . . . the moral seriousness of the form . . . into explicit statement
again." On one level, Ellison described this move as consonant with what the
"American novel at its best" (Melville, Twain, James, Fitzgerald, Hemingway
are among those he mentions) had always done. On another, he described it
as consonant with the "specific concerns of literature," including explorations
of "new possibilities of language." But he also described it as a move that was
natural and even necessary for Faulkner because he had "lived close to moral
and political problems which would not stay put underground."

Faulkner's fiction owes something to his powers of observation and his ear
for dialect, and something to his sense that human lives are always shaped by
natural and social forces, which is to say, by instinct, and preconscious needs
and desires, as well as by culture. His stories are rooted in history as both
natural scene and cultural construct. In addition, his fiction owes much to
stories and poems be had read and tales he had heard, some of them about
the adventures of his own prominent family in North Mississippi. As stories
based on direct observation, his novels come to us as more or less organized
reports on observed realities. As stories rooted in history, they remind us of
the historicity of all deeds done and all words spoken. As stories anchored in
individual consciousnesses – the memories and imaginations of narrators of
diverse needs and desires as well as mixed strengths and weaknesses – his novels
seem necessary and revealing in some moments, tricky and even deceitful in
others.

Faulkner thus engaged, obliquely in some moments, more openly in others,
the varied formal preoccupations of international modernism in the late moment of its turning back on itself in skepticism and critique as well as continuing celebration. In his fiction, as opposed to his early poetry and sketches,
his concern with his own expressive drive manifests itself in his willingness to
examine expressive acts. By repeating different versions of the same story and

proliferating different narrative voices, he extends and explores the old tales and talking, the core stories and the language – the dialects and the voices – on which his novels depend. His fascination with human creativity culminates in examinations of the need and occasion of human inventions. What sets his fiction apart, however, as the most remarkable of its time and place, are the varied ways in which it brings technical sophistication, often centered on what Hannah Arendt has called "incessant talking," to bear on grave social and moral problems – such as poverty and violence, race, gender, caste, and class – that are deeply but not peculiarly Southern. Indeed it is in this way that Faulkner is able to make visible to us what Ellison calls the "moral function of the novel" and the "moral seriousness of the form."

Looking back on the trilogy she began in 1933 with *Pity Is Not Enough*, Josephine Herbst thought of it as damaged by the "urgency of the times," which had deflected and even discredited the interests ("crumpled" is her term) with which she had begun, including language and the idioms in which she was writing. More isolated than Herbst, Faulkner retained the complex set of interests with which he began. By the end of World War II, Sherwood Anderson, F. Scott Fitzgerald, Ellen Glasgow, Nathanael West, and Thomas Wolfe were dead, and so were W. B. Yeats, James Joyce, and Virginia Woolf. The fifties belonged to a new generation of writers, including several – Welty among them – who had started out in the thirties. But Faulkner's great novels, which began with *The Sound and the Fury* (1929) and ended with *Go Down, Moses* (1942), coincided with the Great Depression, and in their own way gave expression to it.

Faulkner was an amateur historian, genealogist, and folklorist as well as a "failed poet" before he became a novelist. English poetry of the Renaissance and English and French poetry of the nineteenth and early twentieth centuries strongly influenced him, as did English and European novels from Cervantes's *Don Quixote* to Joyce's *Ulysses*. In addition to a remarkably retentive mind, he possessed an ear for dialect and an eye for folkways. He studied the history, geography, vegetation, and wildlife of North Mississippi, in part by collecting from oral traditions different and even contradictory versions of tales about his family and region. In the process, he came to think of literary culture as regional in its origins and historical in its thrust. He remained a weak poet in part because he remained dependent on words, rhythms, and even themes borrowed from distant poets. He became a strong novelist when he turned from the shared scenes and themes of *Soldiers' Pay* (1926) and *Mosquitoes* (1927) toward the largely unexplored territory of North Mississippi, where his need to think of himself as a radical originator, another sign of the "modern," was more easily sustained. Neither his great-grandfather, the "Old Colonel," W. C. Falkner, author of *The White Rose of Memphis* (1880), nor Stark Young, contributor to *I'll Take My Stand* (1930) and author of *So Red the Rose* (1934), a popular romance set in Mississippi during the Civil War, posed a serious threat to a writer who was prepared to create, name, and populate an imaginary county – Yoknapatawpha – as a correlate to the world he understood too well to love or hate.

Provincial shyness contributed to the uneasiness Faulkner felt in New York's literary salons; even the French Quarter in New Orleans got on his nerves after several months. So for the most part he stayed in Oxford, without feeling at home there, as though convinced that his art depended on his ability to achieve intimacy without being drawn into any union he did not largely control. His art is broad in its allusions, analogues, and reach. It brings the culture, society, and political economy of one imaginary North Mississippi county into the broad sweep of U.S. history, which he had studied in much the way Stein, Dos Passos, Herbst, and Warren had. The smaller worlds of his extended families, disfigured as they are by exploitation, privilege, and subjugation, are tied to larger worlds that are similarly disfigured. The logic of virtually every entangling word he wrote reiterates, then qualifies, and even disavows both the peculiarity, or regional *otherness*, of his fictional world and the dominance that he claimed for himself, on his hand-drawn map of Yoknapatawpha, as its "Sole Owner & Proprietor." Faulkner draws us into his major novels – *The Sound and the Fury*, *As I Lay Dying* (1930), *Light in August* (1932), *Absalom, Absalom!* (1936), *The Hamlet* (1940), and *Go Down, Moses* – with acts of style that seem simultaneously to assume that human experience is accessible to words imaginatively employed and to acknowledge that human experience remains incommensurate with words and resistive to imaginations. Words "go straight up in a thin line, quick and harmless," Addie Bundren insists in *As I Lay Dying*, while doing moves "terribly ... along the earth, clinging to it, so that after a while the two lines are too far apart for the same person to straddle from one to the other." Yet Addie remains a creature of memories and words as well as deeds done. She remembers and re-remembers, trying to make words serve her needs. That effort, of seeking words that are commensurate with a life lived, a faithful record of emotions felt and deeds done, remains for her as much a part of what it means to be human as feeling and doing.

Faulkner knew, however, as Addie insists, that words follow a line and lead a life of their own. And with some trepidation, he wanted them to do just that because he wanted them to serve not only as a record or critique of life but also as an enhancement of it or, more radically, as a supplement to it. Readers familiar with Faulkner's fiction know that he felt a special affinity for young, white, Southern males born, as he had been, into families whose best days lay behind them. Privileging such people seemed natural to him. Yet few writers have set so varied a cast of characters – rich and poor; illiterate, literate, and even literary; female and male; white and black; old and young – loose in search of words to fit their varied and often more or less desperate needs; and few have shared with so many characters his sense that our search for words is a part of our wisdom and a sign of our humanity – a critical part of living as well as the heart of our art. His characters struggle – like Addie and with him – to confess their mixed success in achieving some triumph over the limits of language as well as the limits of life.

We might begin with *The Sound and the Fury*, which forces us to surrender our most basic categories of understanding – space, time, and causality – in order to confront us with the relinquished, almost vanquished lives of four children named Compson: Benjy, Caddy, Quentin, and Jason. Looking back, Faulkner described his novel as an effort, several times repeated, to match his "dream of perfection." "It's not the sum of a lot of scribbling," he said; it's the dream of writing "one perfect book" that drives an artist. Yet in its first two sections *The Sound and the Fury* ignores every requirement of a well-told, logocentric, linear story. Its words seem not so much to follow a line of their own as to move in several directions at once. Even its familiar title, evoking Macbeth's sense of life – as "a tale / Told by an idiot, full of sound and fury, / Signifying nothing" – turns out to be disorienting. For it not only leads us into a world where our most familiar categories of understanding no longer apply; it also leads us into a world in which art becomes entangled with life rather than rising above it as a corrective to it. Having defied our desire for a well-told tale, it goes on to defy our sense of one well concluded: closure, the sense of a well-wrought ending, is another of the things Faulkner fails to provide. Imperfect success – in which stories divide and propagate, as one telling leads to another – emerges as the end of a novel whose striking means consist of fleeting glimpses, partial knowledge, and flawed expression. *The Sound and the Fury* seems at times to flaunt its willfulness in refusing to establish its coherence. It circles and repeats in one motion, and avoids and evades in another. And this is especially true where its missing center, Caddy – the only character who combines sexual energy and a spirit of adventure with a capacity for nurturing love and a spirit of caring – is concerned.

For Caddy is given little space of her own and less voice. She comes to us primarily through the felt needs of her three brothers – Benjy's need for shelter or, more broadly, for *home* as a place he does not have to earn; Quentin's need for deliverance from the desperation of a young man whose several hallucinations spring, on one side, from his rage for order and, on the other, from his rage for ecstasy, which is to say, his need to find both a principle of love and a person to love; and Jason's need to find someone to blame and punish for the dirty tricks that he thinks life has played on him. Otherwise, the novel approaches Caddy only to pull back, reenacting as well as rendering a process by which a male author conspires with his male characters to marginalize black servants descended of black slaves and also white women. Yet there is gain as well as loss in Faulkner's decision to give Caddy privacy rather than full expression. Faulkner's refusal of full disclosure in *The Sound and the Fury*, like his refusal of perfect coherence, is essential to the novel's freedom, just as its freedom is essential to its generosity. Few novelists have given readers larger roles in literary transactions and none has shared more fully the process of creation with them. By approaching Caddy and then avoiding her, disclosing her and then concealing her, Faulkner draws his readers into his own imaginative processes, making his art an art of conjecture and surmise and making his reader his hidden double.

Unlike *The Sound and the Fury*, *As I Lay Dying* begins as a straightforward linear tale. In the book's opening lines, we follow Darl and Jewel as they walk a dirt path "straight as a plumb-line, worn smooth by feet and baked brick-hard by July, between the green rows of laid-by cotton," toward the place where a brother named Cash is building a coffin for their mother, Addie Bundren. Focused on a single family, the novel traces a continuous action that begins at twilight, on a country farm, just before Addie dies, and then takes us on a bizarre journey through fire and flood to Jefferson, where it ends shortly after Addie has finally been buried and Anse, her husband, has bought a new set of teeth and found a new wife.

If, however, the action is in one sense continuous, in another it is fragmented. For it comes to us in fifty-nine sections recounted by fifteen different narrators, including friends and passing acquaintances as well as all seven members of the Bundren family. Together, its various narrators engage in, and occasionally parody, every possible activity of consciousness – intuitive, rational, and imaginative, primitive, conventional, and idiosyncratic. And though each narrator helps to advance the action, several also delay it in order to take us back into the past where, for example, we resee enough of the strange courtship and marriage of Addie and Anse and glimpse enough of Addie's buried life to see that private histories have worked both with and against entrenched poverty and rigid class and gender lines to lead to the variously rigid, truncated, confused, and diffuse lives of Anse, Addie, and their wounded children: Cash, Jewel, Darl, Dewey Dell, and Vardaman.

Like *As I Lay Dying*, *Light in August* begins in the "hot still pinewiney silence" of rural Mississippi, as another traditional, straightforward, linear, logocentric tale. "I have come from Alabama: a fur piece," Lena Grove says in the book's opening line as she sits by a country road leading to Jefferson, having traveled for almost four weeks across the slow, deliberate world of the still largely rural and partially traditional South, carrying her unborn child and looking for its runaway father. Lena is never "for one moment confused, frightened, alarmed," Faulkner later remarked. So confident is she of her own resourcefulness that pity never enters her mind even as something she does not need. Having reached Jefferson, she finds help, first, from an un-Byronic lover named Byron Bunch, who immediately falls in love with her – an obviously un-wed pregnant woman – "contrary to all the tradition of his austere and jealous country . . . which demands in the object physical inviolability"; and then from a failed minister and failed husband named Gail Hightower, D. D. – which means, the (always already ironic) townspeople tell Byron, "Done Damned." With Byron as a self-appointed protector and Hightower as a midwife, Lena gives birth to her illegitimate son and then sets out traveling again. "My, my. A body does get around," she says in the novel's last lines. "Here we aint been coming from Alabama but two months, and now it's already Tennessee."

In fact, however, *Light in August* had its own beginnings in a manuscript called "Dark House," home of the outcast minister, Gail Hightower, who is so crippled by his obsessions with his family's history that he has failed his calling, his congregation, and his wife. As an unwed pregnant woman who becomes an unwed mother, Lena too is something of an outcast. And Joanna Burden and Joe Christmas, toward whom the novel moves with a strong sense of fatality, are not only the most emphatic and compelling strangers in all of Faulkner's fiction; they are also among the most divided and doomed.

The last member of a family of stern, self-righteous, life-denying New England Puritans, Joanna Burden is descended, on one side, from almost invisible women and, on the other, from violent, domineering men, bearing names like Calvin and Nathaniel, who have come to the South to save it from the sins of sloth and pleasure-seeking as well as the evils of slavery. "I'm not ready to pray yet," Joanna says, after she and Joe Christmas have begun one of the strangest love-affairs in all of fiction. "Dont make me have to pray yet. Dear God, let me be damned a little longer, a little while."

Drawn into an affair with each other, Joanna Burden and Joe Christmas begin all over again to feel fated and doomed. Joe shares some of Joanna's sense of sex as fascinating and repugnant, irresistible and forbidden. But he is self-conflicted and unsure of himself on other grounds, including the crucial question – unresolvable in his case – of whether he is or is not part black. Abused, pursued, and finally mutilated by men, drawn to, befriended, and yet offended by women, fearful of progeny, Joe Christmas travels country roads that turn out to be more deadly than the "thousand savage and lonely streets" he has already traveled, where "memory believes before knowing remembers. Believes longer than recollects, longer than knowing even wonders." Toward the end, we see him carrying his fragile life with him "like it was a basket of eggs." Years later, referring to the fact that Joe Christmas's racial identity remains unresolved, Faulkner described Joe's story as the tragedy of a man who "didn't know what he was" and had "no possible way in life . . . to find out."

Faulkner's concern with race had emerged in earlier works, and it would emerge again, especially in *Absalom, Absalom!* and *Go Down, Moses*. But it was in *Light in August* that Faulkner first directly confronted his sense that a racist society magnifies race as a crucial correlate of identity simply by being racist. By defining black people as the dark, forbidden *other* and then seeking complete control of them, Faulkner's South not only makes race a crucial personal problem, the central correlate of personal identity; it also institutionalizes race as a crucial social problem and then contrives, as an elaborate rationalization, a historical justification for what it has done that reaches back through the Bible to the beginning of human time. In Joanna Burden, we see inscribed a similar process with regard to gender. On this count, however, which comes to us through Joanna Burden's family history, the North and the South are one. Both regions fear female desire, and both map strategies for ensuring male domination of it. The women of Joanna Burden's family are almost as male-dominated as the wives of Doc Hines and Mr. McEachern, Joe's grandfather and stepfather. Joanna Burden is a descendant of New England abolitionists who have come to the South to save it from its sins. When in middle age she takes a lover for the first time, she breaks every rule of propriety she has been taught: she takes someone she thinks of as younger in age, lower in class, and forbidden by caste. When she is finally destroyed, it is not because she holds unpopular views on race. It is because, despite deep internal conflicts, she has insisted on expressing as well as feeling sexual desire and on trying to control her own life.

The work of culture in inculcating attitudes about age, class, and caste visibly touches every character in *Light in August*, especially Joe and Joanna. In language, thought, and feeling, Joe and Joanna internalize attitudes about race, gender, and human sexuality that are so inimical to their lives that they figure directly in their destruction. In different ways, each of them tries to escape the web of associations that holds them. But they fail, in part because, as another sign of culture's work, they display a crippling fear of ambiguity and a matching desire for clarity, which we see especially in their dependence on bipolar distinctions (white–black, man–woman, salvation–damnation) that they cannot live with or without.

These destructive traits, as it turns out, including the deadly preference for clarity over truth, run deeper in the men of Yoknapatawpha than in the women. One sign of this is the way in which Joanna seems almost manlike when she displays them. Another is the way in which she seems so exclusively the child of her visible male forebears. And another is the fact that it is especially in Joe Christmas – in his responses to men and women and their responses to him – that the full force of Faulkner's novel is felt. The moment Joe chooses the hard, ruthless clarity of his stepfather, McEachern, over the tender concern of his stepmother – accepts the one as harsh yet reliable, the other as soft, insidious, and unpredictable – we come to see fully the crucial relation Faulkner sensed between a man's attitude toward women and his disposition toward life. For that moment tilts Joe toward the two fatal moments that mark the end of his life, in the first of which he kills Joanna Burden and in the second of which he is murdered and mutilated by Percy Grimm, a deputized as well as self-appointed defender of purity and clarity.

Joe Christmas and Joanna Burden are paired in *Light in August* as lovers and as victims. But while Joe is the novel's only male victim, Joanna Burden is one of several female victims – Joe's mother, his maternal grandmother, his stepmother, and Gail Hightower's wife being others – all of whom are victims of men: husbands, fathers, stepfathers, ministers, and deputy sheriffs. Lena Grove's triumph can be described in various ways, and since she is a limited heroine, it remains a limited triumph. But it is not negligible. It depends upon her steady refusal to permit anything – hardship and privation, elderly parents who die too soon, a harsh brother, a worthless lover who deserts her, a rigid, judgmental society, or condescending readers – to turn her into a victim. And there is a sense in which it sets her free. Her journey, which begins and ends the novel, takes her into and out of Yoknapatawpha, an escape few characters in Faulkner's fiction ever manage. And though it, too, can be variously described, there are clear signs, especially in her treatment of Byron Bunch, that it includes two things of importance – a youthful desire to get around and see her world before she settles down and a stubborn resolve to make a home unlike any she has ever seen.

Like the worlds of *The Sound and the Fury*, *As I Lay Dying*, and *Light in August*, those of *Absalom, Absalom!* and *Go Down, Moses* are in debt from the beginning. Their principal inheritance – of loss, defeat, guilt, and poverty, as seen in dark, dilapidated mansions, disintegrating families, weathered tombstones, shadows, and ghosts – haunts the lives of Faulkner's characters in a thousand ways. Neither Marcel Proust nor James Joyce nor Thomas Mann gives a larger role to crippling memories than Faulkner. The strange sentences with which

Absalom begins move in fits and starts, looking back in one moment, pressing forward in another:

From a little after two oclock until almost sundown of the long still hot weary dead September afternoon they sat in what Miss Coldfield still called the office because her father had called it that – a dim hot airless room with the blinds all closed and fastened for forty-three summers.

The force of place and of nature's rhythms, the weight of tradition, the burden of names, and the authority of naming mingle with dangling facts – "forty-three summers" – that the reader must work to understand. Hemingway, too, had started out in the twenties. But by the middle of that careless decade, he had mastered the spare, lean, cut-to-the-bone style that made him famous. Faulkner's distinctive style was slower to emerge, and when it appeared in *Sartoris* (1929) – later published in its original, uncut form as *Flags in the Dust* (1973) – and, more decisively, in *The Sound and the Fury*, published on October 7, 1929, on the eve of the Great Depression, its rhetorical extravagances came as a counterresponse to the hard, dried-up South of the thirties. Faulkner spends his words freely, as though determined somehow to reclaim his almost vanquished world and its bound, unfree descendants and their dead yet restless progenitors.

Absalom, Absalom! is, on one side, the story of the rise and fall of Thomas Sutpen, who was born in 1807 in the mountains of West Virginia and died in 1869 at Sutpen's Hundred, northwest of Jefferson. Born into a poor white family, in a primitive mountain community where the concept of property does not even exist, Sutpen, still a boy, has tumbled with his family down the mountainside into Tidewater, Virginia, where property is the foundation on which society is built and the measure by which the worth of all human beings is determined. There, where black people are property and poor, propertyless white people are serfs, Sutpen learns to see himself and his family as the landed gentry see them: as underclass people, evacuated into a world "without hope or purpose" for them, where they are expected to perform work that is "brutish and stupidly out of proportion to its reward." Affronted, Sutpen decides to acquire all of the things that give the people who possess them the political and economic power to exploit and the social right to despise those who do not. On one side, he wants to endow the lives of his ancestors with purpose; on the other, he wants to ensure that his and their descendants will be set forever free from "brutehood." In the process of working toward this, however – in acquiring a plantation, a mansion, and slaves and establishing a family – Sutpen becomes even more ruthless and arrogant than the Virginia plantation lord who first hurt him into action. He becomes, in short, an extender of the same patriarchal, slave society that has victimized him, his family, and his ancestors. A radical individualist, he affronts and insults not only his slaves and the children he has by them but also his wives and his legitimate children, sons and daughters alike, though in very different ways. Then, having abused everyone else, he betrays the trust of a poor, propertyless white man named Wash Jones, whose life recalls his own beginnings, by seducing and then casually discarding his granddaughter, Milly. Whereupon, Wash Jones, himself at last outraged, cuts Sutpen down with a rusty scythe.

At one point, with defeat staring him in the face, Sutpen recapitulates the basic facts of his life, hoping to understand where his plan went wrong. But telling his story belongs primarily to other people in *Absalom, Absalom!* It belongs to Miss Rosa Coldfield, his sister-in-law, who is herself one of the insulted and injured people left in the wake of his fatally flawed project. It belongs to Mr. Compson, son of General Compson, Sutpen's contemporary and friend. It belongs to Quentin Compson, suicidal brother of Caddy in *The Sound and the Fury*, whom Faulkner recruits to serve, first, as audience and interlocutor to Miss Rosa and his father and, then, as a tutor on Southern history and culture to Shreve, who becomes Quentin's audience and interlocutor and then begins to tell the story himself. And it belongs to Sutpen's daughter Judith, a woman of few words, who makes her plotting of the Sutpen family cemetery another commentary on the human consequences of Sutpen's scheme for giving meaning to his life.

The proliferation of interlocutors – of characters who listen and query, then comment and narrate – enlarges as well as enriches *Absalom, Absalom!*, which becomes a novel about storytelling as interpretation. Miss Rosa's account is a demonology in which Sutpen ("man-horse-demon") "abrupts" upon a peaceful world that he proceeds to savage and ruin. On one level, Sutpen's ruthlessness gives Miss Rosa a way of understanding the fate of her lost South, but her motives are personal as well as cultural. And on another level, Sutpen's ruthless hurry gives her a way of understanding the forces that have blighted her life. Through her demonology, she wins sympathy and achieves revenge. What she cannot do is reconstitute her life. From the novel's first scene on, we think of her as sitting in a too-tall chair like a "crucified child," wearing "eternal black," as though in anticipation of her own funeral, going over and over Sutpen's story, unable either to resolve it or to let it go.

To Mr. Compson, a source of considerable information, Sutpen's story belongs in part to the aborted hopes of the South and in part to the ages. Soured by his empty life, his declining family, and the declining South, Mr. Compson is too cynical and self-pitying to seek understanding. Drawn to Sutpen's story, he protects himself from its implications by presenting it as another tale of "misfortune and folly": "a horrible and bloody mischancing of human affairs." In his hands, the search for meaning and the effort to assess responsibility seem futile, and interpretive storytelling becomes another empty game: "Perhaps that's it," he says; things don't add up, "and we are not supposed to know."

Like Miss Rosa, Quentin and Shreve go over and over Sutpen's story, and like Mr. Compson, they often feel like giving up. "*Yes, too much, too long,*" Quentin thinks, just before he begins to listen again, this time to Shreve, whose ironic tone seems at times to resemble Mr. Compson's: "*but I had to hear it and now I am having to hear it all over again because he sounds just like father.*" It is, however, with Quentin and Shreve and the "happy marriage of speaking and hearing" they achieve that *Absalom, Absalom!* begins to yield plausible explanations for the devastation Sutpen has wrought in the story that he has lived – a story of a succession of wives and not-wives affronted; of children so neglected, abandoned, and ruthlessly manipulated that one kills another; of slaves conquered, abused, and betrayed; of friends used and discarded. Together Quentin and Shreve rewrite Sutpen's story into a tale of ruthless, self-involved ambition that leads to terrible violence both before and after it leads to desertion, fratricide, and consuming guilt.

Quentin's and Shreve's accounts of Sutpen's story are in some ways as biblical and personal as Miss Rosa's, particularly as they reach out to resonate with Quentin's agonized attachment to Caddy in *The Sound and the Fury*; and they are in some ways as classical and even literary as Mr. Compson's, particularly when they become stories about two brothers who are doomed to destroy each other and two sisters who are doomed to lives of love and faithfulness that are never returned. Finally, however, they become more daring and more plausible. They are more daring because they make imaginative leaps that tie stories of the past to those of the present and so confront dark truths that are, as Faulkner later suggested, "probably true enough." They are more plausible, first, because they seem less compromised by Miss Rosa's need to avenge and Mr. Compson's desire to escape responsibility; second, because they make better sense of the fragmentary and sometimes contradictory stories they inherit, especially about what drove one of Sutpen's sons to kill the other; and, third, because they acknowledge and even celebrate, as signs of shared humanity, the surmise, conjecture, and fabrication that enable them to extend the stories they inherit toward meaning. Such community as exists in *Absalom, Absalom!* is constituted of tales and talking that overlap one another, in which individual acts of style and voice, which tend toward isolation, are preserved but also softened. In *Absalom, Absalom!* language – or, more specifically, incessant talking – becomes the constitutive ground of community.

Quentin is a student of many things, including cemeteries. Midway through *Absalom*, we see him remembering a visit to the cemetery where Thomas Sutpen and Ellen Coldfield Sutpen lie buried in graves marked by "heavy vaulted slabs" ordered from Italy, "the best, the finest to be had," paid for by Thomas. But there are three other "identical headstones with their faint identical lettering, slanted a little in the soft loamy decay of accumulated cedar needles," which Judith Sutpen has arranged and paid for: one for Charles Bon, the part-black son whom Sutpen has denied repeatedly; one for Charles Etienne de Saint Valery Bon, son of Charles and grandson of Thomas; and one for Judith herself. Judith's action, of including and providing in death for two descendants Thomas Sutpen denied in life, comes to us as a commentary, a counterstatement, that she completes with her own grave. Having leaned down to examine Charles Bon's grave and to ponder it, Quentin moves on to brush the cedar needles away from the second, "smoothing with his hand into legibility" its "faint lettering" and "graved words." But it is the third that transfixes him – first, because it is separated from the others, "at the opposite side of the enclosure, as far from the other four as the enclosure would permit"; second, because it has been placed there on instructions written by Judith "when she knew that she was going to die," as another counterstatement to Sutpen's life; and third, because of what it says and does not say:

He had to brush the clinging cedar needles from this one also to read it, watching these letters also emerge beneath his hand, wondering quietly how they could have clung there, not have been blistered to ashes at the instant of contact with the harsh and unforgiving threat: *Judith Coldfield Sutpen. Daughter of Ellen Coldfield. Born October 3, 1841. Suffered the Indignities and Travails of this World for 42 Years, 4 Months, 9 Days, and went to Rest at Last February 12, 1884. Pause, Mortal; Remember Vanity and Folly and Beware.*

"Yes," Quentin thinks, "I didn't need to ask who invented that." Given the scorching words, the telling omission of Thomas Sutpen's name, and the subtle ways in which what is written and not written fit Judith's life, however, we must ask, and so must Quentin. His choice – "Miss Rosa ordered that one" – is plausible. But Clytie is another possibility, and Judith is surely a third. Strangely, however, the indefiniteness of the author of these words redoubles their force in a book in which authorship is so heavily gendered and yet so widely shared, and in which language, tricky and unreliable though it is, becomes the scene of the only happy, productive marriage we observe.

In some moments, *Absalom, Absalom!* seems to be ruled by principles of isolation and incommensurability so severe that bits and pieces, resistant to meaningful patterns, are all we have. In others, it seems ruled by a principle of repetition so severe that we need not even listen, since everything we encounter comes to us as something already known, to strike once again the "resonant strings of remembering." But flawed model though it is, Quentin's conflicted mind, torn between hope and affirmation, despair and denial, reminds us of three things. First, that, although we are free to fail, we are not free to desist; second, that, to know ourselves in our world, we must study the history that has engendered us; and, third, that that history extends beyond the regional, national, and temporal boundaries that we habitually set.

In multiplying possibilities, Faulkner both gives and takes. He draws us into the search for answers, but he also erodes our confidence in the possibility of finding final answers. He even threatens us with the possibility that he has authorially exhausted the range of possible interpretive moves, leaving us to admire his dexterity. Finally, however, only the first of these threats holds; and despite the losses it entails, it proves to be liberating. For Faulkner's form-ulations have this in common with Miss Rosa's and Quentin's and Judith's: they require as well as invite revisions. It is in this connection, furthermore, that his flawed and limited characters become in one crucial respect model citizens. "What you have as a heritage, now take as a task," Goethe said. "For thus you shall make it your own." "It is not required of you that you complete the work," said Rabbi Tarphon in *Pirke Aboth*, "but neither are you free to desist from it." Where Faulkner's characters pick up such admoni-tions as these is not, finally, hard to say. They permeate the room that Miss Rosa still calls an office because her inadequate father had called it that; they rise from the "rotting shell" of Sutpen's dilapidated mansion and failed mar-riages; and they are encoded in the faint lettering and graved messages found in the Sutpen family cemetery. Quentin's life is tortured in part because he lives a personal lie, particularly where his feelings for Caddy are concerned. But it is also tortured because he knows that his own life figures in larger cultural lies. His personal crisis, like Miss Rosa's and Judith's, cannot be sepa-rated from the larger moral crisis of the rank ambition and ruthlessness of his possessive, sexist, and racist society, which, like Sutpen, is intensely but not peculiarly Southern. Sutpen's origins, his Scots English family, were American before they became Southern, and they were British before they became American. Even in their migrations he and his family are intensely mod-ern. Quentin's personal crisis provides him a way into Sutpen's culturally resonant story and its destruction of Miss Rosa and Judith precisely because his personal crisis, brought on by living a lie, prefigures the moral crisis of his society. Far from celebrating "community" and "tradition" as achievements of the South, as the Agrarians had tried to do, Faulkner presents them as ideas that weigh more heavily precisely because, given the nation's fascination with the new and the individual as well as its divisive greed, they exist only as ideas.

Quentin's conflicts are so fundamental as to *be* the only life he has. Though isolating, furthermore, they turn out to be shared in one way or another by characters as different as Thomas Sutpen, Eulalia Bon, Ellen Coldfield, Miss Rosa, Mr. Compson, Henry Sutpen, Judith Sutpen, Charles Bon, Clytie, and Wash Jones. Quentin discovers scenes one piece at a time, and he passes them on in the same way, with this bit added or that altered. And he hears, word by word, stories that are filled with echoes, resonances, remarkable vacancies, and deletions, like the father's missing name on Judith's tombstone. Time and again he feels what Charles Bon seems likely to have felt at least once – namely, that the whole of his life is about to fall "into pattern." Frustrated, he grasps for something, some "integer," that will solve the "jigsaw puzzle picture," only to meet with new bafflement. To the end, despite a series of remarkable breakthroughs, he must make do with stories that are tentative, provisional, imperfect, on the assumption that they are "probably true enough."

The mood of Faulkner's great fiction remains deeply provisional because, in language as well as action, it is so deeply circumstanced by time and history, as we see in this passage from *Go Down, Moses*:

> The boy would just wait and then listen and Sam would begin, talking about the old days and the People whom he had not had time even to know and so could not remember (he did not remember ever having seen his father's face) . . . .
> And as he talked about those old times and those dead and vanished men of another race from either that the boy knew, gradually to the boy those old times would cease to be old times and would become a part of the boy's present, not only *as if* they had happened yesterday but *as if* they were still happening, the men who walked through them actually walking in breath and air and casting an actual shadow on the earth they had not quitted. And more: *as if* some of them had not happened yet but would occur tomorrow, *until at last it would seem* to the boy that he himself had not come into existence yet.

This passage comes to us as both a celebration and a critique of both language and storytelling. Behind it lie the loss of the old days and the old people, and terrible conflicts: between parents and children as well as two genders and three races of people; and between lives lived and words uttered or written in a certain order. The power Faulkner attributes to words is at one with the power his words display: "And as he talked *about* those old times and those dead and vanished men of another race . . . [they] would cease to be old times and would become." As Faulkner renders Sam's resonating voice, he celebrates it. Yet even as he celebrates it, rendering its power in the plenitude it adds, he insists on an anterior plenitude, prior to division and loss, whose default is the occasion of Sam's song; and he also insists as well on reminding us that Sam's song is a fiction by forcing us to view it under the aspect of the phrase he thrice repeats: *as if*. What Sam finds is not the thing itself, but some more or less adequate substitute for it: it was *"as if . . . until at last it would seem."* Insofar as Sam's voice fills a void, it is *as if* it fills a void.

Faulkner's own effort to live for his world unfolded as an effort to work through the South's tangled story – its lost dream, its lingering guilt, its terrible lies, and its exploitation of people as well as land – by finding words for it. In the process, he not only helped to make the South visible to others; he also helped to make the possibilities of the modern novel and the significances of the Great Depression visible. His techniques include means of expansion, especially through analogical ties and associations; means of extension, especially through the proliferation of voices and tales and versions of voices and tales; and means of establishing relations, including rhetorical relations, with his readers. They also include techniques that work counter to expansion, extension, and connection: techniques of concentration and localization that tie his fiction, as Albert Camus once put it, to the dust and the heat of the South; techniques of regression and escape, as we see in voices such as Quentin's in *The Sound and the Fury*, which moves, not out toward other voices, but in toward his own interior; and techniques of aggression, ranging from terse, laconic understatement to ironic and parodic motions to strange convoluted flights. Through all of this, but especially through the proliferation of narrators, Faulkner's fiction displays an underlying sympathy for those who attempt to create narrative in the pursuit of meaning. That sympathy encodes a secret sympathy for those who have attempted, even with limited success, to fashion a coherent self or create a coherent culture. Informing the interplay among these sympathies is the predicament of an artist who knows that all human beings are circumscribed creatures whose needs include self-transcendence as well as self-definition, a sense of being rooted in the order of being as well as a sense of being responsible to and for something larger than one's own personal status and prosperity.

Like Whitman, Faulkner celebrated the magic of the commonplace. And like Whitman's, his disaffection with life in the United States coexisted with inexhaustible fascination. The disaffection and alienation that mark this country's fiction run deep in Faulkner's work because he felt acutely the failure of his culture to meet needs of mind and spirit that material possessions can never satisfy. Like T. S. Eliot, he was suspicious of the dream of creating a social system so perfect that people would no longer need to be good; and like Herman Melville, he felt more solidarity with the poor, the forgotten, and the defeated than with the rich and the victorious, though it was the latter he wanted to join. More courageously than most, he lived by writing the incongruities, conflicts, anxieties, and even the lies that shaped his own life as well as those of his region and nation. One thing bequeathed by the nineteenth century, besides a suspect faith in the sufficiency of material progress, was the promise of more freedom: a willingness to blur or even dissolve all lines, restrictions, and taboos, in life as well as in art. Faulkner sought the rewards of material progress and enjoyed breaking long-honored rules, including several having to do with narrative fiction. But he remained convinced that freedom suffices only when people are spiritually sure enough of themselves to know what they truly need or, put another way, only when what they want corresponds to their deepest needs and so matches their need for affiliation as well as attention and their capacities for awe and wonder as well as their desires for clarity, comfort, and pleasure.

Like other writers in the United States during the early twentieth century, Faulkner was an heir less of the dominant culture of the nineteenth century than of its great rebels. Much of the daring, even the headiness, of the assaults that Darwin, Marx, Nietzsche, and Freud – to name only four – mounted against accepted beliefs continued to find expression in the brashness of writers like Faulkner, as they set out to invent literature anew. Faulkner's almost fierce determination to deal with the past on his own terms marked him as a rebel and also shaped his art. Like much modern fiction, his is often pessimistic and violent, even brutal and despairing. He is a poet of deprivation and loss. Affluence and plenty mark his work primarily in style and imagination. Yet we find other things there: remnants of the good hope of the Lyric Years, which was political as well as aesthetic; the persistence of the exuberance of the twenties, which was experimental as well as escapist; and the difficult hope against hope that sprang to life during the Great Depression, of creating anew an imperfect community, knit together by imperfectly possessed and painfully held memories and by imperfectly shared and practiced values. These things he infused with the same boldness of spirit and moral courage that we see in the striking formal experiments that give his fiction its special place in a great and varied outpouring of innovative, conflicted, and often self-critical expression.

FICTIONS OF THE HARLEM RENAISSANCE

Rafia Zafar

I

❦

A NEW NEGRO?

WHAT DO WE KNOW today about the literary phenomenon called by some the Harlem Renaissance, by others the New Negro movement? Was it a quixotic though noble failure? Was it the triumph of a black modernism paradoxically ignited by a Victorian brown bourgeoisie? Were its authors who plumbed the color line seeking to remake the very notion of race? How salient a category was gender to its creators? Was its literary nationalism part of larger global movements? A long scholarly debate surrounds the Harlem Renaissance – a debate about its meanings, parameters, and, indeed, its very existence. My title, "Fictions of the Harlem Renaissance," is meant both to invoke the swirling stereotypes and shibboleths of the era, and to indicate the vitality of the literature in our time.

In the early twenty-first century, the scholarly consensus on the Harlem Renaissance runs as follows: the African American intellectual response to historical and social forces in the period immediately following World War I was a cultural construct, a belles-lettristic sleight of hand in which black intellectuals and writers elegantly tossed together a coherent movement that never actually took place. Said another way, the Harlem Renaissance did not really exist – if by a literary movement's existence we mean to indicate an unselfconscious, spontaneous upwelling of artistic endeavor, one untainted by political ideology or commercial encouragement. This belief in aesthetic purity is a lovely sentiment, but few literary movements are innocent of social and economic factors. Almost universally, critics now acknowledge that the Harlem Renaissance was based on artifice and politically motivated social engineering. So understood, this "New Negro" movement spread far beyond the borders of Black Harlem, as the poet Sterling Brown even then insisted. We can see it as a movement that originated decades before World War I, in the period termed "the Nadir" – the late nineteenth and early twentieth centuries – when race relations in the United States were at an all-time low, and organized white violence against blacks was approaching a high-water mark. In the closing years of the nineteenth century, young African American thinkers, from the Fisk- and Harvard-educated W. E. B. Du Bois, newly possessed of his doctorate in history, to the black woman's club movement activist Victoria Earle Matthews, announcing the coming of a "race" literature, called for a "New" Negro.

This turn-of-the-century cohort of African Americans committed to an upward trajectory within white supremacist America predated, and paved the way for, Harlem Renaissance thinkers often seen (if not entirely correctly) as revolutionaries. Here, then, is the trajectory of the Harlem Renaissance: decades of African American political agitation and social thought flower into the now famous outburst of writing, painting, music, and the related expressive arts. What we today *know* as the Harlem Renaissance, as proposed and propagandized by individual thinkers, attests to the self-consciousness of this interwar expressive arts movement. Yet we know, too, the Renaissance came with antecedents and from somewhere specific. So while I invoke the years of artistic and intellectual ferment preceding the post-World War I era, I must at the same time point to a surge in publications and self-imagination that characterized the years between 1919 and 1935. Therefore, and in accordance with oft-cited parameters of the age, I hold the period as running from about 1919 to the mid-1930s.

The intellectuals identified as the leadership cadre of the Renaissance were politically aware, if not outright activists. Several of the best-known contributors to the Harlem Renaissance years – W. E. B. Du Bois; Alain Locke, the first black American Rhodes scholar and long-time Howard University professor; scholar, diplomat, activist, historian, novelist, poet, and musician James Weldon Johnson, the Renaissance's Renaissance Man; *Crisis* editor Jessie Redmon Fauset; "problem novelist" Walter White; Fisk sociologist and president Charles S. Johnson – were officers or members of the major civil rights organizations. Alain Locke wrote in 1925 that it was a past generation that felt "art must fight social battles and compensate social wrongs," but his unflagging promotion of Negro intellectual achievement, beginning with his editorship of the March 1925 *Survey Graphic* special issue on "The New Negro," which appeared in expanded book form shortly thereafter, demonstrated the import of the conjunction of social activism and literary art. That the house organs of the National Association for the Advancement of Colored People (NAACP) – *The Crisis* – and Urban League – *Opportunity* – each ran "talent contests" for young and new writers underscores the alliance between civil rights and arts.

This was not art for art's sake. The use of the Civil Rights organization journals as showcases for artistic and intellectual achievement confirmed the wedding of art and racial advancement. Albert Murray might later decry the reading of black literature as "social science fiction," but his protest, made

decades after Locke's cultural activism, points to the success of that conjunction. There were other, more overtly political, venues, such as activism within
Garvey's Universal Negro Improvement Association (UNIA) and the Communist Party; they, too, made their mark on black creative artists. Still, the
Harlem Renaissance remains in the minds of many of its practitioners a literary movement dedicated to toppling racism and bigotry. A literal space of
resistance to a dominant and dominating white America, Harlem figured as
well as a psychological and political fortress.

More than a state of political consciousness, the Renaissance presents itself
as a metonym for the most significant internal migration within the history
of the United States. Geography loomed large in the New Negro movement,
whether as particular place – Harlem – or philosophical space – the African
diaspora. The historical forces impacting upon its literary productions could
be said to have first appeared in the changing spaces of "Negro" Manhattan, a
point first made in *Black Manhattan* (1931), by James Weldon Johnson. That
survey of black New York from 1626, when Manhattan was still a Dutch
colony with not even a dozen black inhabitants, to the end of the 1920s, when
more than 200,000 blacks lived in Harlem alone, set down the physical,
cultural, and historical significance of their city within a city, even then
asserting Harlem's spatial importance to black and white worlds alike. Lying
within, not physically marginal to, the surrounding city, the black city figured
then, as now, as an actual place in which to fashion an ideal identity. Yet
however much the desires of the migrating African Americans served to shape
Harlem, the physical space that became the ground zero of black America
could not have existed without the collapse of the real-estate speculation in
the Manhattan precincts above 110th street. White landlords who worried
about empty apartments decided to rent to blacks. Many African Americans
got their first chance at decent, ample housing (of course, as Harlem continued
to absorb black renters, this racially inflected housing market would lead to
overcrowding, rent-gouging, and increasingly unattractive quarters). If nationalism can be said to demand a fictive or actual homeland, Harlem's acreage
offered a physical locale to the newly self-conscious African American migrant.

Major social and historical changes had led to this dynamic surge northward.
Harlem grew because of push and pull vectors alike: the Niagara movement,
which led to the formation of the NAACP; Marcus Garvey's electrifying call
to build once more a black kingdom in Africa, and the common people's
embrace of his UNIA movement; the return of African American veterans
who demanded freedom at home now that they'd fought for it abroad; flocks
of rural folk fleeing agricultural serfdom, the boll weevil, and drought; the
horrors of lynch mobs and Klan activity; the encoding of separate but equal in

the Supreme Court's *Plessy v. Ferguson* decision; the attractions of "the North" itself, believed to be less racist than the South, and with greater educational and job opportunities, whatever their limitations. In the years leading up to the Renaissance, the average African American changed from a rural, Southern inhabitant to a dweller in the cities. Along with its American-born citizens Harlem included those from the rest of the African diaspora.

The many and long travels of Africa's descendants were inscribed within that city within a city. Movers and shakers like Garvey, Claude McKay, Eric Walrond, and Arthur Schomburg were all foreign-born. Others, now anonymous, added cultural, religious, class, and national diversity to what outsiders saw as an undifferentiated population of brown-skinned individuals. A uniquely American and urban creation for and of African Americans, Harlem maintained an internationalist presence. With its wealth of young and mature intellectuals and its dynamic mix of diasporic Africans, Harlem offered a space for an anticipatory postcolonial consciousness. Demands for the recognition of national identities were acknowledged and accepted in 1919 at the Treaty of Versailles, but the day of African nations free from colonial intervention would not really occur until after World War II. Whatever arguments other African diasporans could make for their own cities, Harlem, situated in one of the world's urban capitals, became the center for the new black world.

Harlem in this period could not by itself stand in for the entire surge in African American cultural production. From this unarguable fact springs the desire to discuss the literary and arts movement as a New Negro Renaissance, rather than to secure that particular set of cultural expressions to a fixed and literal space. Washington, DC, permanent home to poets Georgia Douglas Johnson and Sterling Brown, served as a way-station for other writers of the era, including Jean Toomer, who spent his boyhood there, and a young Langston Hughes. Those affiliated with Howard – men like Alain Locke and James Porter – of course called Washington their primary home, even if they frequently found themselves elsewhere as arbiters and creators of the New Negro aesthetic. Chicago also laid a claim to the Negro Renaissance, for it too boasted a fast-growing black community with attendant cultural institutions; the University of Chicago's famed sociology department acted as a magnet, drawing the young Richard Wright. Nevertheless, Harlem remains the richest symbol of black creative expression in the period, if for no other reason than that New York City was the cultural nexus of the United States. With New York a world city, Harlem was bound to become a mecca for African Americans.

2

❦

BLACK MANHATTAN

ARLEM and the Renaissance exist as twin *lieux de mémoire*, places
where individual and collective memories transform actual places
and events into metahistorical, communal symbols. 1920s Harlem,
held to be synonymous with the "New Negro" movement, figures as one such
place. Black Harlem, with its shifts in social alignment, its geographic and
transatlantic movements, its breaking-down and interrogation of boundaries
between peoples and art forms, deserves pride of place for its imagined-yet-
actual home for African Americans. If modernism denotes the yoking together
of disparate forms and themes, and the creative efforts of those convinced that
the world was not to return to its prewar "innocence," then the authors of the
Renaissance represent an integral part of that international movement. And if
alienation – from one's land, from one's nation, from one's place in the world –
has been called a salient characteristic of the modernist frame of mind, who
better could represent that anomic status than Americans of African descent?
They too well personified the citizen without rights, the wanderer in new and
strange lands.

For black American intellectuals then and now, the Harlem Renaissance
contains symbolic cruxes. The New Negro movement demanded an end to the
"subservient" Negro, and the beginning of the dismantling of repression. The
Renaissance spoke to the inner self and longings of black Americans in a way
that white mainstream writers could not and would not. When in "The Negro
Speaks of Rivers" (1922) Langston Hughes wrote "I have known rivers" in
both the Congo and the Americas, he spoke to the idea of the African diaspora,
long before the concept became a familiar term in the academy. When Claude
McKay yoked activism to classically scripted verse in "If We Must Die" (1919),
announcing the new, young African American's willingness to die – echoing
Du Bois's pronouncement, "We return. We return fighting" – he wrote as a
modern, conjoining the form of a sonnet with political militancy.

By 1920 a United States Government increasingly hostile to labor organizers and communists persecuted labor and left political organizers alike.

This repressive atmosphere was heightened by the mob lynchings of African American veterans still in uniform. In such a violent climate, many blacks came to believe that cultural achievement, manifested by race-proud publications, could serve as an alternate route to social and political progress. Journalist-activists like A. Philip Randolph and Chandler Owen, founders of the black left journal, *The Messenger*, believed in socialism, a world-wide unity of workers, self-determination, and black pride (in fact, initially the *Messenger* aligned itself with the UNIA, although it would later come to a parting of the ways with Garvey). Although the journal would in time lose much of its radical nature, its early articles bridged politics and thoughtful reflection.

Several years before the appearance of Alain Locke's renowned and influential anthology, *The New Negro: An Interpretation*, the editors of the *Messenger* claimed:

The New Negro arrived upon the scene at the same time of all other forward, progressive groups and movements – after the great world war. He is the product of the same world-wide forces that have brought into being the great liberal and radical movements . . . . His presence is inevitable in these times of economic chaos, political upheaval and social distress. Yes, there is a New Negro. And it is he who will pilot the Negro through this terrible hour of storm and stress.

Everyone, it seemed, believed in the New Negro in some formulation or another. All constructed this new person differently, but all partook of the postwar belief that the old order was irrevocably altered, and that new activism would be necessary and unstoppable. For the editors of the *Messenger*, New Negroes had to understand their position as black men and women within working-class America. In an editorial titled "The New Negro – What is he?" the *Messenger* defined the New Negro as someone who could not be fooled by "political spoils and patronage. A job is not the price of his vote . . . so long as the Negro votes for the Republican or Democratic party, he will have only the right and privilege to elect but not to select his representatives." The New Negro was thereby defined as a worker who demanded adequate compensation, buying power, and social equality; this worker must also be educated and committed to self-defense. For his part, A. Philip Randolph attacked mainstream civil rights activists as being accommodationist and "subsidized by the white [old guard]." His New Crowd–old crowd juxtaposition is meant to conjure up the image of the "old boy system", for his locution "New Crowd" necessarily invokes, and satirizes, the staid "New Negro."

Beyond native-born activists like Randolph, political insurgency also came from the diasporic leaders in the Harlem community. Eric Walrond and W. A. Domingo were but two of a number of diasporan intellectuals drawn to

New York City. Short-story writer Walrond, born in Guyana, regularly partook in Renaissance happenings. First noticed by many through his presence at the Civic Club dinner in 1924 (a fête hosted by Charles S. Johnson to celebrate Jessie Fauset's first novel, *There is Confusion*), young Walrond seemed on the verge of a brilliant career. *Tropic Death* (1926), an intriguing hothouse of Caribbean modernism, collected fewer than a dozen stories, but tales like "The Palm Porch" stand out among the Renaissance's short works for their oddly beautiful evocation of imperial decay and human catastrophe. It is a loss to the literature of the Americas that, despite favorable notices and a second book contract, Walrond never published another volume.

The Jamaican-born Domingo, a contributor to Locke's *The New Negro*, edited and wrote for various periodicals, including the *Messenger* and the *Negro World*. As a Marxist, Domingo's writings concerned the amelioration of the working classes and people of color – and he, like other thinkers of African descent, found himself drawn to the preeminent black metropolis.

Far and away the most prominent of Harlem's diasporic leaders was Marcus Garvey, a charismatic speaker who had once worked for the United Fruit company and claimed to have a doctorate in civil law from a university in England. Garvey promised that he would lead his people – 400 million folks of African descent – out of white imperial bondage and into their own, African, empire; his New World black man would effect a rapprochement and reunion with the African continent. On moving to the U.S. from Jamaica, Garvey discovered that the mainstream black American civil rights movement did not welcome his "Africa for Africans" rhetoric, nor the swelling allegiance he commanded. Garvey's pan-Africanist proclamations – that ordinary folks were descendants of an African aristocracy, that the degradation of life in the United States would be supplanted by a black African empire, that every race should have its own habitat and nation – garnered millions of supporters worldwide. Many middle-class blacks viewed Garvey with distrust, however, even though initially his adherents came from that sector as well. Garveyites' paramilitary costumes and pageantry were disliked, and the Garvey-owned Black Star Line Steamship Corporation was viewed as a charade aimed at bilking money from the poor desperate for hope (it seems clear now that Garvey was cheated by some untrustworthy associates). Garvey's combination of naiveté and confidence confirmed the influential W. E. B. Du Bois in his contempt, and Garvey furthermore stirred enmity by his color-baiting (the dark-skinned Garvey believed in a "pure" black race and attended a Ku Klux Klan rally to affirm his hatred for race amalgamation). Garvey's inspirational message – "black men you were once great; you will be great again. Lose not courage, lose not faith, go forward" – offered an optimistic prospect to the average black. However we weigh his successes and failures, he, like other architects of a New Negro, knew to choose Harlem as his capital.

Activism operated on planes other than the political, as another adoptive Harlemite, Arthur Schomburg, the Afro-Puerto Rican whose library served as the nucleus for the New York Public Library's eponymous Schomburg Collection, realized. Without the collecting of this single-minded bibliophile, the predecessors of the Renaissance – and the works of that era themselves – might no longer be extant. The 135th Street location of the New York Public Library, now known as the Countee Cullen branch, functioned as a literary and intellectual focus-point for the Renaissance and gave Schomburg further impetus for his visionary work. He urged the study of the people and the works of the African diaspora, amassing a collection that would support such research. Schomburg identified one Harlem branch exhibition of black literary productions as capable of "rewriting . . . many important paragraphs of our common American history." He knew that black peoples would continue to be denigrated, if not obliterated, without the preservation of books and ephemera from the centuries of New World African creativity. Harlem could provide the site for the crucial rewriting of black history.

No single date or timespan could demarcate the fading of the "Old" Negro and the arrival of the "New," although some literary historians have pegged the Harlem Renaissance's recognizable "beginning" with the publication in 1925 of Alain Locke's *The New Negro*. Other anthologies compiling African American writers before World War II include Countee Cullen's *Caroling Dusk* (1927), Charles S. Johnson's *Ebony and Topaz* (1927), Nancy Cunard's *Negro* (1935), and Sterling Brown's *Negro Caravan* (1941), among others. Many sought to identify, if not canonize, the literary achievements of a growing group of African Americans, beginning with eighteenth-century foremothers like Phillis Wheatley and continuing with the bright stars of the future, like Langston Hughes.

Perhaps foremost among these early anthologies is James Weldon Johnson's *The Book of American Negro Poetry*, not only for its primacy of chronology and heralding of a body of African American literature but for Johnson's prescient, acute preface. First published in 1922, with a second edition following in 1931, the diplomat, author, musician, and now editor Johnson created an anthology that aimed to be both popular and influential. Remarkable for its astute positioning of Negro poetry, Johnson's introduction functions as a political and didactic take on black expressive art. He boldly asserts that "the final measure of the greatness of all peoples is the amount and standard of the literature and art they produced," an aesthetics of utility echoed by other

Renaissance elders. Although Johnson's adherence to European American ideas of art and universality led him to believe that African Americans could raise their status by creating a certain kind of art, he also advanced the particularity of the black experience. Strikingly, in this preface Johnson enumerates four unique gifts of Negroes to United States civilization, offerings that bring new vigor and beauty to the New World: spirituals, African-inspired folklore, ragtime (which in today's locution we would call jazz) and the cakewalk (that is, African-accented dance). His celebration of these forms anticipates contemporary estimations of the impact of black culture on the American mainstream. Disappointingly, Johnson avers that despite their influence, dance and ragtime are "low art forms" most valuable for pointing the way to a "high art" still to develop. Dialect, too, he views as problematic because of the limitations of accurately pitching vernacular speech: such language offers "but two full stops, humor and pathos," rather than a nuanced range of emotion. Attesting that Negro art must speak to the range of black life in America yet not limit itself to racial themes, Johnson set the terms for the 1926 manifestos of Langston Hughes and George Schuyler.

Ephemeral publications can have great impact – especially when they're planned as the basis for a book. One dramatic example can be seen in the origins of *The New Negro* (1925). By the mid-1920s Paul Kellogg, editor of the popular magazine *Survey Graphic*, was following the goings-on in literary Harlem. Cognizant of the influence of Howard professor and cultural arbiter Alain Locke, Kellogg asked Locke if he would edit a special issue of the magazine devoted to the creative arts of black New York. By the time the special issue of *Survey Graphic* came out early in 1925, Locke was putting together the volume that would become the core of *The New Negro*, which appeared in the same calendar year. That the volume *The New Negro* remains in print attests to Locke's canny inclusion of such authors as Rudolph Fisher, Langston Hughes, Zora Neale Hurston, Countee Cullen, Jean Toomer, Claude McKay, Jessie Fauset, and James Weldon Johnson – authors now well known. Yet the changes in the collection, from its magazine version to the final book form, highlight some of the struggles over how, and what of, African American life should be portrayed: should white artist Winold Reiss be chosen to depict the talented tenth, that slice of educated and middle-class Afro-America said to lead the masses? How deeply behind the scenes of everyday and working-class life should writers peek? The short-lived *Fire!!* (1926), edited by a very young Wallace Thurman, addressed to "younger Negro artists," was aimed in part to shake up the serious world shown in *The New Negro*; although some authors appeared in both compilations (Hughes and Hurston, to name just two), *Fire!!* meant to tread on bourgeois sensibilities. Debates over what, and who, should constitute the portrait of black folk offered to white America reveal the competing ideologies behind the aesthetic scenario.

Alain Locke's several essays in the final volume show the powerful mind behind the watershed project: Philadelphia-born and Harvard-educated, Locke was in 1907 the first, and until 1963, the only black American Rhodes scholar; graduate studies at the universities of Oxford and Berlin completed his education. Locke's eponymous essay "The New Negro" asserts the modern black as a politically aware person whose mission takes place in the cultural realm. Revealing a classist, or "talented tenth" bias – given away by his images of the "unthinking" and "vague urges" of the folk – Locke believes the Negro can seize a "moral advantage" by returning hate and violence with intelligence and dignity. Pan-Africanism, he wrote, can be a healthy outlet for New Negroes in the United States; Harlem should therefore be the home of the Negro's "Zionism" for it represents the "advance guard of African peoples in the 20th century." Locke understood there must be a common space for a common New Negro consciousness, even if that commonality occurs only on a symbolic plane. Harlem, Locke concedes, isn't "typical" but it is "prophetic." The cultural and physical magnitude of Harlem offered an unmatchable arena.

3

❦

AVATARS AND MANIFESTOS

A S A CULTURAL CENTER, Harlem arose after the early careers of two whose lives and work would become inextricably linked with their adopted home town. For many, W. E. B. Du Bois and James Weldon Johnson personified Harlem's intellectual wealth. Born three years apart, and within a decade of the Civil War's end, each man was in his fifties during the 1920s, the era's high-water mark. Du Bois's active career, in fact, would continue decades beyond the relatively brief period of the Renaissance. Yet their creative contributions set the stage for the literary efflorescence of the 1920s and 1930s.

W. E. B. Du Bois was born in Massachusetts in 1868, making him the most senior of those connected with the Renaissance. He lived for nearly a century, his publications appearing over a span of years longer than most American lifetimes. Educated at Fisk, Harvard, and Friedrich Wilhelm University in Berlin, Du Bois pushed his talents in many directions. *The Souls of Black Folk*, which he published in 1903, displays this protean thinker's ability to mix uplift and social insight with lyricism and emotion. Drawn from Du Bois's own experiences in the South as both student and teacher, *Souls* is rightly considered an African American – indeed, an American – classic. *The Souls of Black Folk* encompasses many genres: the essay, sociological study, musicology, fiction, autobiography, and philosophy. In this sense, Du Bois's most widely read work is paradigmatically modernist in form; the hybridity of form of *Souls* may in fact account for its longevity and success in our contemporary estimations. In Du Bois's search to apprehend those like himself – and those unlike himself – who "dwell beyond the veil," his book supports a reading of the African American as the quintessential modern alienated from self and home. It is a foundational text of African American letters. Yet *Souls* does not situate itself as a Renaissance work, if only because the sign for African American modernity had not yet begun to constitute itself: Harlem, as an acknowledged space of resistance, empowerment, and fantasy, was not yet in its planning stages. For the magnitude of its influence, the haunting collection of linked visions in

The Souls of Black Folk outshines any single volume published by an African American between 1918 and 1935. Published just after the turn of the century, *Souls* predates the acknowledged classics of the Harlem Renaissance by years, and has long occupied a primary position in the canon of African American studies. Du Bois's epigrammatic and prophetic encapsulation of the racial situation in the United States – "the problem of the twentieth century is the problem of the color line" – echoes to this day as a kind of holy writ. For African Americans following in the wake of the paradigm shift that *Souls* represented, Du Bois's metaphor of the veil, that actual yet invisible barrier of custom and law erected between blacks and whites, shaped their very ambitions, if not their actual words. The Du Boisian notion of "double consciousness," wherein "one ever feels his two-ness, – an American, a Negro; two souls, two thoughts, two unreconciled strivings, two warring ideals in one dark body," similarly became a controlling idea in black thought from this point on. Du Bois's prominence as a public intellectual and philosopher came not from formal literary achievements but from the scope and nature of his philosophical insights.

Du Bois's novels do not match the remarkable bricolage that characterizes *Souls*. For all of their creator's evident gifts for language, Du Bois's efforts in full-length fiction fall short of the aesthetic pinnacle scaled by *Souls*. His first novel, *The Quest of the Silver Fleece* (1911), has been not unjustly described as a "romantic melodrama" that, in true Progressive-era style, exposed the exploitation inherent in the cotton industry. As could be expected from one intent on eradicating racial servitude and unjust practices, Du Bois poured his politics into his fiction – an effort that did not serve his novels best. *Silver Fleece* follows the fortune of two children of the Deep South, Alwyn Blessed and Zora. Bles, as folks call him, reared in rural Alabama and educated at a struggling Negro school, has a natural dignity and intelligence; he has no material or social advantages. His soulmate, the wild child Zora, born and raised in the swamps near Miss Susan Smith's school for colored children, is equally bright although far more leery of whatever touches the white world. As teenagers they raise a nearly silken crop of cotton in a field cleared by themselves, but are swindled of their riches by the local plantation owner. Years pass, and the two are parted by Bles's naiveté and the machinations – benign and otherwise – of nearby white folk. At the novel's end the two young adults, now possessed of experience gained by separate sojourns in Washington, DC, return to their former life, and a new vocation, among the poor, the landless, and the uneducated. Their devotion to their people rekindles the loving flame each had thought extinguished in the other.

This debut novel showcases many of Du Bois's themes and strains: perorations on the beautiful yet tragic South; noble, educated African Americans who will lead their less fortunate peers to a brighter future; the championing of black womanhood and its corollary, respect for black manhood; an attack on lynching; the recognition of the ways that race, for black folk, has been made to stand in for a permanent low-class status; and the affirmation that poor whites are not, at least materially, any better off than their similarly deprived black neighbors. Du Bois's writing, sometimes almost floral in its phrasing, conveys twentieth-century concerns in language reminiscent of Charles Chesnutt and other nineteenth-century authors: "The black boy, too, went his way in silent, burning rage. Why should he be elbowed into the roadside by an insolent bully? Why had he not stood his ground? Pshaw! All this fine frenzy was useless, and he knew it." At a pivotal reunion, Bles drops to his knees to plead for Zora's hand in marriage. The scene escapes sentimental melodrama because the specter of Zora's childhood rape – and Bles's ignorant, first rejection of her as "impure" – forms the backdrop of his proposal. Bles's abjection affirms the modern black man's triumph over Victorian sexual taboo, and his dedication to the cause of civil, economic, and social rights. In *Silver Fleece* Du Bois weds political issues to a familiar narrative form and plot.

His next novel appeared during the Harlem Renaissance. *Dark Princess* was published the same year – 1928 – as McKay's *Home to Harlem*, Larsen's *Quicksand*, and Fisher's *The Walls of Jericho*. Like *Quest of the Silver Fleece*, it seems a novel from another century. The work is a *Bildungsroman* concerning one Matthew Towns, from his first engagement with educated racism – when a New York medical school dean refuses to allow him to pursue a rotation in obstetrics – to his seeming acquiescence to corrupt ward politics in Chicago, and beyond. Towns's eventual awakening – a sine curve of desire, disappointment, resignation, and reward – refracts a larger story of intercontinental cooperation, of the "colored races" coming together across class lines to throw off their European and white colonizers and oppressors. Star-crossed as Matthew and Kautilya may be, their lives were meant to awake Du Bois's audience to a global politics of people of color. Their love-letters refer to such intimate matters as: "American Negroes are a tremendous social force, an economic entity of high importance." Du Bois's intentions make for laudable goals, but not compelling fiction. Yet even here the philosopher-historian's incisiveness of thought served as spur, incentive, and benchmark for the authors who willingly followed in his footsteps. In much the same way his landmark study, *Black Reconstruction* (1935), contributes to the larger discourse in African America (its appearance in the same year as the Harlem Riots underscored the link between the past and the present day). If his novels do not achieve the loftiest goals of fiction, the entire corpus of Du Bois, crowned by *Souls*, earns him a paramount place in African American letters. His commitment to racial justice, and his efforts

as editor of the NAACP's *Crisis* magazine, helped to stage the literary efflorescence he believed indispensable to the black struggle for personal dignity
and social equality.

James Weldon Johnson was, with Du Bois, one of two key avatars of black
New York's cultural scene. Born in Florida in 1871, Johnson was one of the
many Southern migrants to the city; he represented the acme of the new,
urbanized, American Negro. Cultured and bilingual, a member of the U.S.
diplomatic service to Venezuela and Nicaragua, Johnson was known not only
for his literary talents, but also for musical composition: with his brother
Rosamond, he composed what has long been called the Negro national anthem, "Lift Every Voice and Sing." Perhaps more than any other author of the
period, Johnson was a Renaissance Man. In addition to excelling in the fields
of diplomacy, music, and literature, Johnson could claim the professions of
lawyer, journalist, and academic. (The Renaissance abounded with such individuals: two others are Zora Neale Hurston, novelist, anthropologist, and
performer, and Rudolph Fisher, radiologist, essayist, and novelist.) A polymath
and social activist, Johnson sought through his range of talents to consolidate
and improve the position of black Americans.

James Weldon Johnson's *The Autobiography of an Ex-Colored Man*, a good
deal of which is set in Harlem, was first published anonymously in 1912 and
reprinted under the author's name in 1927. It should not be considered a work
of the Harlem Renaissance, if we adhere strictly to the chronological frame that
posits the New Negro literary movement as beginning after World War I, and
continuing until the mid-1930s. We can view the novel as proleptic, announcing the awakening of the New Negro (the term dates from the 1890s) but, in
its timing, ahead of the curve. Did the young author suspect that his frank and
apparently non-judgmental treatment of passing might ruffle white and black
feathers alike? Johnson's remark in his autobiography, *Along This Way*, "I have
never been able to settle definitely for myself whether I was sagacious or not
[for publishing the novel anonymously]" does not reveal his inmost thoughts.
How many authors try to hide their creations, especially young writers
who have already won some acclaim? By the publication of *Ex-Colored Man*,
Johnson had written and published poetry and musical compositions, most
notably "Lift Every Voice and Sing," with his brother, Rosamond. Insisting
that he took some pleasure in the anonymity, Johnson writes as well that he
was amused by those who claimed the work as their own. In the 1927 edition,
with introduction by Carl Van Vechten, however, Johnson publicly settled the
matter of whether the work was fiction or memoir.

The Autobiography of an Ex-Colored Man strikes unusual notes in the literature
of social protest. Its hero, a never-named narrator, begins life innocent enough

of race. Fair-skinned, wavy-haired, the Georgia-born protagonist grows up in a New England town. Until a teacher asks him to sit with the other, "colored," students, the boy lives in a prelapsarian paradise; after the event, he sees himself, and his very light-brown-skinned mother, as never before, as the "niggers" his taunting white schoolmates see. He meets his Southern white father but once as a child, then years later as an adult. Thus, when his mother dies shortly before his graduation from high school, the boy – now a supremely accomplished pianist – must make his way to college, and through the world, on his own. Unsurprisingly, the young man who was once so naive about his own origins proves to be as unskilled about matters of life as he was of bigotry; when he is robbed of his tuition money for Atlanta University, he free-falls into a picaresque journey that takes him first further into the South, to Florida, then north, to New York City and all the attractions, good and ill, of that alluring metropolis. Johnson's ethnographic descriptions of cigar factories and urban clubs, of Europe's capitals and concert halls, decidedly deepens the texture of his narrative, which grows into a virtual dissection of race and modern consciousness.

The Autobiography of An Ex-Colored Man possesses a psychological intimacy and fictional power unprecedented in African American literature before the twentieth century. In the course of his life, the light-skinned narrator must grapple with a doubled double-consciousness; as a white-appearing black man, Johnson's protagonist feels a veil drawn between him and whites ignorant of his racial identity, but he also feels distanced from African America. Prior to 1900 there had been novels about the constrained lives of the mixed-race descendants of illicit and forced Southern concubinage: for example, Frances E. W. Harper's *Iola Leroy* (1892), has its eponymous white-skinned heroine belatedly, and altruistically, casting her lot with the race of her mother; Charles W. Chesnutt's *The House Behind the Cedars* (1899) portrays a white-skinned, doomed heroine and her cowardly white lover. All the way back to the mid-nineteenth-century origins of the African American novel, near-white black characters had suffered and, usually, died. (That Johnson places a man at the center is worth noting, for more often than not the mulatto in literature had been figured as a woman.) The protagonist's success in love and business, rather than an end culminating in loneliness or death, depends on his remaining in the white, urban fold. The ex-colored man's victory thus presents black readers with a curious test of allegiance: do they condemn the narrator, or applaud him? The ex-colored man's ambivalent and ambiguous conclusions point to the hard reality of the socially constructed "color line."

By 1925 twentieth-century black literature had experienced a number of high points: the publication of *The Autobiography of an Ex-Colored Man*, the two appearances of *The New Negro*, the publication of Jean Toomer's *Cane* (1923) and Jessie Fauset's *There is Confusion* (1924), and the establishment of literary prizes backed by civil rights organizations. Amid such ferment, two figures, one quite young and the other a veteran of World War I, squared off over the meaning of "Negro" literature. George Schuyler's "The Negro Art Hokum" and Langston Hughes's "The Negro Artist and the Racial Mountain" draw aesthetic lines in the sand, seemingly irreconcilable. Appearing in sequential issues of the *Nation*, their debate took up the heart of the matter for black intellectuals and creative artists in the early twentieth century: what is the role of "race" in the work of art? The two essays work together as neatly as opposite sides of a debate team: if Hughes stands for the black-identified artist, then Schuyler calls for a "raceless" American art. Hughes's argument is wonderfully introduced by his recalling a young writer (almost certainly Countee Cullen, although Hughes did not publicly identify him) saying, "I want to be a poet – not a Negro poet." What readers make of that remark will place them either on the side of Hughes's black-identified-black or the un-named poet, Schuyler's raceless artist. There can be no argument for "universal" truths, Hughes maintains, for the subtext in 1920s America can only be the reading, "I would like to be white." In words that fairly vibrate on the page with the intensity of a vigorously and proudly identified racial identity, Hughes asserts that "This is the mountain standing in the way of any true Negro art in America – this urge within the race toward whiteness, the desire to pour racial individuality into the mold of American standardization, and to be as little Negro and as much American as possible." Quite specifically Hughes locates the desire to be raceless as class-based, for the working classes, he observes, are not desirous of such a color-blind society, nor are they "afraid of spirituals."

Hughes has been said to romanticize the working classes, in the way of many left-leaning intellectuals. The author, however, once recalled an invitation to him and his mother from sponsors of a Washington, DC, reading society's annual dinner. At the time, he was working in a laundry, and could not afford the formal dress the evening's organizers expected; his mother was coldly uninvited when it appeared her wardrobe would not measure up to that of other, society, women. Hughes's class-consciousness, then, was not book-learned. He understood that those with any possibility of "rising" economically in the American mainstream worried about blending in; those with no chance of making it in the mainstream could ignore middle-class society's insistence on certain standards of decorum or dress. The serious black artist, Hughes wrote, must search for materials from the folk, from his own people, drawing on their specific heritage of blues, humor, and dialect: "Most of my own poems are racial in theme and treatment, derived from the life I know."

Significantly, Hughes does not say that the white world is bad, indifferent, or anything else; he is more concerned that African Americans not substitute an alien culture for their own. An indefatigable traveler, Hughes loved meeting people of different backgrounds; he journeyed to Mexico, Europe, the Soviet Union, and the west coast of Africa in order to satisfy his desire to know the world. Doing so enabled him proudly to place African American culture within a global context: "I am ashamed for the black poet who [says] his own racial world [is] not as interesting as any other world." And while Hughes was profoundly indebted to his own black American culture, he also drew on that of the European American poets he'd read and admired, among them Whitman and Carl Sandburg. Such canonical and popular poets' highly aural works encouraged, if indirectly, Hughes's own experimentations with blues lyrics and meter.

In contrast to Hughes's wanderings, the life of George Schuyler, armed-services veteran and long-time newspaperman, was a model of stability. Schuyler wrote for the *Messenger*, later became editor of the African American newspaper *Pittsburgh Courier*, and was throughout his life a sharp-tongued critic of American mores. His acid wit was akin to that of the white Baltimorean H. L. Mencken: neither man suffered fools gladly, and each was more than willing to expose the follies of the "mob." Schuyler's iconoclasm led him to launch a broadside against the black and white perpetrators of a hoax he called the "Negro Art Hokum." In that essay he concurs there is indeed Negro art – but insists it can be found only in Africa, not America. Indigenous American "Negro" art is, for him, rural and Southern, the creation of a peasant culture. Whatever their ethnic or racial origins, "any group under similar circum-stances" would produce such works. High-culture producers like Du Bois, Meta Warwick Fuller, and Henry O. Tanner are American artists, not "Negro" ones. Schuyler rejects the idea that a white couldn't have produced creative works nearly identical with those of the major African American authors and artists of his day. He argues that the "Aframerican . . . [is] merely a lamp-blacked Anglo Saxon," adhering to Progressive-era beliefs in a national melt-ing pot that would, after several generations, disgorge Americans all alike, whether of Italian, African, or any other ancestral origin. Enumerating artists of African descent from a number of countries, such as France's Alexandre Dumas and Russia's Alexander Pushkin, Schuyler notes that they participate in national generic traditions, not "Negro" ones. Schuyler anticipates late twentieth-century claims for a level playing-field, insisting that should edu-cation and environment be about the same for blacks and whites there would be no observable difference between them. The very notion of dissimilarity was a virtue "palmed off by Negrophobists," not one self-confident African

Americans should espouse. Ineluctable difference "must be rejected with a loud guffaw." By asserting the sameness, the Americanness, of whites and blacks alike, Schuyler affirms the then widely accepted premise that, in being brought from Africa, and supposedly deprived of both native language and kin networks, Africans were turned into "tabulae rasae" devoid of African culture and identity.

Both Hughes and Schuyler fasten on the notion of cultural difference as problematic in some way, although each sees that difference differently. Schuyler denounces it as indicative of inferiority, Hughes endorses it with pride. The younger man sees an African American's desire to be a poet without racial classification, in a society that determines one's status on the basis of race, as quixotic at best and self-destructive at worst; he advocates a celebration of self-knowledge and black culture. Schuyler's invocation of President Harding's notion of difference as "immutable" inferiority, even as a means of debunking culturally specific art, leaves him vulnerable to charges of having an inferiority complex himself. In Hughes's and Schuyler's perfect worlds, nothing intrinsically good or bad would inhere in difference, despite the fact that millennia of human existence have demonstrated the staying power of xenophobia. When construed as different by the majority, literary works and people alike are consigned to a lower order. Race may be a fictional construct, but it had, and has, actual consequences.

That sobering fact of racial life would be something that white writers and fellow travelers might invoke but could not wholly understand. European Americans flocked to Harlem, the aesthetes to rub shoulders with the latest celebrated talent, the voyeurs to drink prohibited liquor and attend cabaret shows increasingly aimed at well-heeled whites. Many of these tourists would have been surprised to find that their eagerness to mix with blacks was found suspect, patronizing, or worse. Two prominent whites, Carl Van Vechten and Nancy Cunard, considered Harlem part of their world. Cunard, brash and opinionated, commanded the privilege that went with being a member of an internationally known family. Some contemporaries proclaimed that her interest in Harlem followed her affairs with black men, and that her espousal of things Negro had as much to do with personal matters as social justice. Whatever the impetus for *Negro: An Anthology* – Cunard had previously displayed no interest in publishing – the 1935 volume provided a much-needed opportunity for Depression-era black writers (white authors, too, were included). Many black contributors, among them Hughes and McKay and, somewhat later, Ralph Ellison and Richard Wright, were to become sympathetic to the communism lying beneath Cunard's efforts, but more became disillusioned with the somewhat abrasive Englishwoman. Radicals like Cunard often alienated black Americans because they approached racism entirely in terms of class struggle, denying the reality of hundreds of years of institutionalized oppression and racism. Yet many ordinary African Americans became supporters of the communists for their intervention on behalf of the "Scottsboro boys," nine young men falsely accused of raping white women. Nonetheless, the white privilege embedded in bourgeois European America was evident to many black folks, and obvious in the attitudes of many so-called radicals. Cunard's blindness to her own biases can be almost amusing: "I was impressed by . . . the magnificent strength and lustiness of the Negro children." Cunard was the kind of white person intellectuals like Jessie Fauset worried about; Fauset had few whites to her home, Langston Hughes remembered, because she "did not feel like opening her home to mere sightseers, or faddists momentarily in love with Negro life." The success of Cunard's *Negro* reminds us that there was indeed a "vogue" for black culture, and that black Americans would not be the only ones to stake a claim to African American culture.

There was one white fellow traveler with whom the Negro never went out of vogue. The career of Carl Van Vechten (1880–1964) presents us with a much more complex set of issues and problems than other "friends" of the New Negro, for unlike Cunard Van Vechten's deep embrace of things African American lasted his entire adult life. Known during the earlier part of the 1920s as a bon vivant and author of mannered, amusing contemporary novels, the blond, blue-eyed Midwestern Van Vechten's publication of *Nigger Heaven* (1926) might seem to identify him as a racial opportunist. That charge would be unjust. Numerous literary historians have noted that Van Vechten's interest in African Americans preceded the writing of that "scandalous" novel. While a student at the University of Chicago, the young Van Vechten was befriended by some African Americans; later, as a *New York Times* reporter, he called for authentic portrayals of black language. His insistence on hosting heterogeneous social occasions, and his inclusion of black and white among his circle of friends, undermines the claims of those who would paint him as a racist trading on his knowledge of Harlem and its inhabitants. His years-long photographic portraiture of black notables, and his founding of the James Weldon Johnson papers at Yale University, should dispel simplistic accusations of voyeurism. Nevertheless, and despite his evident good intentions, Van Vechten can be said to have overstepped the line of ironic observation in his best-selling *Nigger Heaven*.

The novel's prologue features the serpentine presence of one Anatole Longfellow, a.k.a. the Scarlet Creeper, wending his away among the throngs of Seventh Avenue and its environs. The Creeper takes a haughty attitude with the women who flock to him, although he doesn't hesitate to take their money. Van Vechten's story moves from the exploits of the Creeper to the champagne-soaked precincts of wealthy Harlem and its calm middle-class regions. Mary Love, a librarian befriended by one of the divas of Harlem society, sets aside an offer of marriage from a rich but uneducated numbers banker (a racketeer who manages an illegal betting operation). Instead, Byron Kasson, a feckless aspiring writer, wins her adoration. For his part, Byron is happy with Mary's attentions, and comfortable, at least at first, with her urging him on to middle-class status. But the roiling social mobility of Harlem, with its tendency to mix strivers, show-offs, gangsters, working folk, and deadbeats at the same popular clubs and parties, leads to various upsets. Embittered by his lack of success, and sensitive to Mary's proddings, Byron falls prey to the lures of the city.

In some ways Van Vechten's portrait of slang-slinging, bootleg-gin-swilling, black New Yorkers resembles the kind of Renaissance-era writing that the older black intelligentsia deemed salacious. It differed in one crucial way: the author was a white man. However genuinely and affectionately Van Vechten himself might see the events portrayed in the novel, however much he might insist that his fictional characters, regardless of background, are portrayed as people, rather than racial stereotypes, the fact remains that Van Vechten could not speak as an insider. And as a white outsider, his depictions of gun-toting gamblers and men-discarding vamps struck many African Americans as a betrayal. His depiction of the foibles of college-educated black men and women could be viewed by the less charitable as outright sabotage. A number of his fellow writers defended Van Vechten's artistic freedom, especially in his choice of title. Ironically, the title, locating black New York as both heaven and hell, strikes us still. Yet that same phrase, when taken with the novel's hyperbolic depiction of urban black life, leaves the reader unsettled and unsure of Van Vechten's ultimate intent.

Nigger Heaven stands as a peculiarity of the era, one inextricable from the overall history of the New Negro movement. Although written by a white, the novel became a success against which Van Vechten's African American contemporaries would have to measure their own productions. For that reason, *Nigger Heaven* can almost be seen as a modernist *Uncle Tom's Cabin*. Both authors possessed attitudes about black Americans unusual for their white coevals, but they remained oblivious to, or unwilling to admit, the overwhelming advantages of their racial position. It remains troubling that Van Vechten decided to go ahead with his title, despite the concerns of both his father and black friends like James Weldon Johnson that its irony would be lost on most readers. However mocking Van Vechten intended the word "nigger" to be, his insistence on using it points to a blind spot about his own limitations (if not, less charitably, his own arrogance). In this regard he may resemble white visitors to Harlem such as Nancy Cunard more than he would have liked to admit. Van Vechten's main gift to posterity lies in his patronage and support of black culture. Carl Van Vechten befriended, helped, and preserved the writers of the Renaissance, but he could not himself become a New Negro, no matter how artificial he believed the boundaries of the color line to be.

4

❦

HARLEM AS A STATE OF MIND: HUGHES, McKAY, TOOMER

L ANGSTON HUGHES, life-long friend and fan of Carl Van Vechten, captured the inner black world to which his well-off friend desired entry.
Born in 1902 into rural poverty, the internationally renowned Hughes
counted in his large *œuvre* short stories, novels, plays, operas, two memoirs,
and children's books, as well as edited and translated volumes. Hughes may be
the one New Negro author who honestly could list his occupation as "writer."
He began his ascent to fame when Jessie Fauset published the nineteen-year-
old poet's "The Negro Speaks of Rivers" in the June 1921 *Crisis*. Before the
decade ended, Hughes brought out two much-reviewed collections of poetry,
The Weary Blues (1926) and *Fine Clothes to the Jew* (1927). Rich in vernacular
speech, humor, and musical influence, Hughes's poems reveal his empathy with
the average man and woman and his love for, and pride in, African American
culture. Lines like "Night coming tenderly / Black like me" have fairly earned
Hughes his reputation as the bard of black America. The swinging meter evident in much of his verse – "Droning a drowsy syncopated tune, / Rocking
back and forth to a mellow croon, / I heard a Negro play . . . " – trumpets his
fusion of black literature and music, drawing on both the rhythms and the
images of blues and jazz to create a singularly American poetry. Innovative in
form in ways that much other work of the period could not approach, Hughes's
poetic amalgam of black music and vernacular earns him a high place in the
pantheon of American poets.

Hughes's fiction is no footnote to his poetic abilities. "Luani of the Jungles"
(1928), his first published prose, tells the story of a white traveler and his
African bride's return to her country; the tale invokes themes first treated in
Hughes's poetry, such as the meaning of the African diaspora, the hard life
of the rural dweller, and African American music. Several of his early stories
draw on Hughes's contact with the "mother" continent, which the author
first saw as a seaman in 1923. Yet as in his verse, Hughes's fiction frequently
describes what the author himself might have experienced – America's tortured
race relations, miscegenated family tragedies, brilliant musical forms, and

enduring, wise, and ironic black folk. Hughes's well-received autobiographical novel, *Not Without Laughter* (1930), strikes elegiac, personal, quietly emotional notes, qualities not often found in Harlem Renaissance fiction.

Hughes's early life, in segregated, dusty towns in Missouri and Kansas, was not exactly the stuff of dreams; he was raised by his maternal grandmother, who would cover him as he slept with the bullet-riddled shawl of her first husband, killed during John Brown's raid on Harper's Ferry. Although his fictional alter ego in *Not Without Laughter* has no such firm connection to race royalty, the boy's upbringing gives him sense enough of who he is, where he might find a place in the world. Bright, poor, black, Sandy Rodgers is the son of Annjee Williams and Jimboy, an itinerant musician-laborer whose wanderings cast a pall on his lonely wife. Annjee, more attuned to her husband than her child, leaves the boy to her mother's raising and he grows up in a near-silent, hardscrabble home. One of his mother's sisters, Harriett, is determined to be free of the stunted boundaries of black life in Kansas and runs off to see if she can find a better life. Sandy's other aunt, Tempy, a tight-fisted social climber, self-incarcerates in a brown-faced caricature of white do-good womanhood. Sandy spends much of his childhood in a kind of suspended animation, waiting for his life to begin in earnest. The novel moves into another gear after the death of the boy's laundress grandmother, and subsequent months spent in the cold bourgeois world of his aunt Tempy. A long-awaited summons to his mother and Chicago brings Sandy into precincts of wonder and strife. Almost lost in the throng of rural black emigrants, what little he had – the chance at an education – nearly slips away. The windy city, Hughes shows us, holds all the promise and menace of Harlem and the smaller black cities.

Hughes's Midwest lacks the sensual romanticism of Toomer's South. His work is remarkable for its aversion to sensational imagery, its avoidance of gruesome scenes of racism – although Sandy encounters instances enough of bigotry and ill-will – and its quiet, thorough exploration of the unrelenting little sadnesses of a poor, black child's life. When, on a Christmas morning, Sandy's long-awaited sled turns out to be a rough, homemade thing too big for a boy to carry easily, his emotional state is perfectly conveyed when, somewhat later, he throws into the stove ashes the gold-edged book of stories given to him by his well-off aunt: expensive, didactic gifts from the heartless are not what he craves. With understatement, Hughes reveals Kansas's acquisition of Southern cruelties in the heartless spurning of Sandy and his friends from their town's first amusement park. Recalling the newspaper's avowed "Free Children's Day Party," Sandy sadly admits to his friends, "I suppose they didn't mean colored kids." Much of the power of Hughes's novel stems from his insightful recreation of a boy's point of view, one alternately happy, resigned, indignant, or reflective. Although it is not set in Harlem, *Not Without Laughter* grapples with the dislocation of the Southern migrant to the city. Seen through the not quite comprehending eyes of a boy, the urban mecca remains strange, becoming familiar only when songs from a storefront church remind Sandy and his mother of back home.

Less personal and more overtly political, Hughes's collection of short stories, *The Ways of White Folks*, appeared four years later. This volume of short fiction incorporates protest and a rejection of bourgeois ideals with Hughes's signature humor. Stories like "Cora Unashamed," "Mother and Child," and "Red Headed Baby" take up the unmentionable subject of illegitimate birth, condemning not the children or the mothers, but the society that casts a pall over such life events. Some, like "The Blues I'm Playing," wherein a young pianist chooses love *and* music, to the despair of her white patroness, cast a mordant look on white patrons (Hughes's own supporter, the Park Avenue widow Mrs. Charlotte Osgood Mason, would abruptly drop him after years of support). "Father and Son" returns to the subject of Hughes's 1925 poem "Cross":

> My old man died in a fine big house.
> My ma died in a shack.
> I wonder where I'm gonna die,
> Being neither white nor black.

Bert Norwood, the spurned son of a white plantation owner and his black mistress, kills his father in a rage. The disappointed mob must turn to Bert's brother to have a "real" human sacrifice. (Hughes also wrote a play, "Mulatto," on the same theme.) Moving as it does from irony to affection to harsh criticism, *The Ways of White Folks* may in some ways lack the profound and personal emotion of *Not Without Laughter*, but it more than compensates for this by its frequent comic takes on America's racial stupidities.

Both [whites and blacks] would have told Jean Toomer not to write *Cane*. The colored people did not praise it. The white people did not buy it. Most of the colored people who did read *Cane* hate it. They are afraid of it. Although the critics gave it good reviews the public remained indifferent. Yet (excepting the work of Du Bois) *Cane* contains the finest prose written by a Negro in America. And like the singing of Robeson, it is truly racial.   Langston Hughes

Jean Toomer would have himself rejected Hughes's commendation for being "truly racial." Within a few years of the publication of his sole book, *Cane*, in 1923, Toomer expressed surprise that he had ever been identified as black: "as I was not a Negro, I could not feature myself as one." Toomer's refusal to allow his work to be included in any anthology of African American writing challenges our conceptions of an authentic black voice. Often called his people's

artistic genius, Toomer has also been described as a confused visionary, pathetically race-ashamed. These contradictory estimations of *Cane* and its author
reflect in part the unusual form of the work and its creator's enigmatic intentions. *Cane*'s New Negroes, grappling with roles inherited from an agrarian,
racist past, and haunted by the responsibilities of uplift, mirrored not only the
author's but his generation's uneasy assessment of the place African Americans
would have in a still segregated United States.

Toomer was a product of the "blue vein" aristocracy, that self-anointed
late nineteenth-century association of light-skinned, middle-class African
Americans. His maternal grandparents were P. B. S. Pinchback, the light-
skinned Reconstruction-era politician rumored to have passed for Negro to
win office, and his white wife. Nathan Toomer, a Southerner whose legal classification was black, was only briefly married to Toomer's mother Nina, and
so the boy knew little of his father. After his mother's death, the teenaged
Toomer returned to Washington, DC, the city of his early childhood. Those
years, and a two-month sojourn as a substitute teacher in a black school in rural
Georgia, laid the foundations of his sole published book. A move to New York
City made his career seem predestined, for Toomer there befriended and
was under the influence of avowed modernists such as Sherwood Anderson,
Kenneth Burke, and Hart Crane. *Cane*, published in 1923, won immediate
acclaim, with Waldo Frank announcing: "This book *is* the South...A poet
has arisen in that land." But Toomer's idiosyncratic work baffled most readers,
black and white.

What was *Cane*? A novel, or a collection of short stories and poems? The
form of Toomer's lyric engagement with the South continue to pique the
imagination. Poetry, prose, drama; interior monologue, fragmented syntax,
indirect discourse: a multiplicity of modernisms informs *Cane*. The book resists
categorization. The tripartite structure of *Cane* iterates the Great Migration,
that massive, voluntary emigration north of rural, Southern blacks. Its first
two parts, comprised of short fiction and poems, with verse and spirituals
interwoven into the narrative sections, depict the Deep South's small-town
roots and the almost frenzied move to the cities; the final section, "Kabnis,"
imagines the Southern sojourn of a citified educator. However conflicted its
author's relation to that movement, *Cane*'s significance for the cultural work
known as the Harlem Renaissance, along with its simultaneous engagement
with European modernism, propelled the book into near-mythic status.

Toomer's language reflects and makes concrete the interpersonal, intersexual
communication in American society, and the hidden conversation of race. What
happens, Toomer asks, when the barriers between the races begin to erode under
a changing social order? In "Bona and Paul," a college boy of indeterminate

race looks out his window. Toomer invokes I Corinthians 13:12: "For now we see through a glass, darkly; but then face to face: now I know in part; but then shall I know even as also I am known." Paul's view, bifurcated by a passing L train – "with his own glow he looks through a dark pane" – points to the train as an African American symbol of personal freedom. The reference to the words of the Apostle Paul – "now we see through a glass, darkly . . . then shall I know even as also I am known" – seems to indicate the alternating opacity and clarity of American racial boundaries. Toomer epitomizes Paul's unknowable self through the physiological marker of blood. Imagistically rendered around this sanguinary imagery, the erotic nature of physical play conflates with white notions of black sexuality.

"Blood Burning Moon," the tragedy of a black – white – black triangle, returns to blood imagery as it foreshadows the inevitability of racial and sexual violence. Expressionistic, nonlinear movements are underscored by a sinister, blood-red moon. To highlight the story's debt to classical tragedy, Toomer stages the story in dramatic form. ("Portrait in Georgia," a poem that immediately precedes this story, strikingly condenses horror and beauty, reflecting Toomer's knowledge of both the imagist movement and the metaphysical poets; the densely packed verses and juxtaposition of apparently unrelated elements pack into a few lines most of the themes in *Cane*.) Trapped within the mindset of a feudal patriarchy, the white Stone vaguely acknowledges his enslavement to stereotype – Louisa is "lovely – in her way. Nigger way. What way was that?" Rejecting the idea that he might be attracted to Louisa simply because she is beautiful, he runs headlong into Burwell, a black man more than capable of besting a white man. As elsewhere in *Cane*, the black woman comes across as elemental, magnetic, inarticulate, a characterization often disputed as a romantic stereotype. Although acute in many ways, Toomer's portrait of a near-mythic black folk here slides toward the two-dimensional.

"Kabnis," partially parsed in play form, draws on profound cultural elements – the spiritual, the folktale – to plumb the life of Ralph Kabnis, a teacher at a small black college. His urban upbringing and advanced education block his ability to interpret or appreciate the rural South. Mystified by the Georgia countryside, Kabnis responds with attraction and aversion. One night he is terrified by the nocturnal rustlings around his tumbledown dwelling, for his rational mind is no match for the plangent sounds of the wind. Plaintive music from a nearby black church chills, rather than inspires. His abstract ideals of justice are snapped by a land where lynchings impose "order" on the black population; his downward spiral brings him face to face with the still living relics of slavery. Elliptically critiquing the vocational mission of historically black institutions, the notion of a holistic African American community, and the blindness of intellectuals, Toomer refuses to confirm or deny Kabnis's – or the South's – eventual redemption.

By contrast Toomer's city scenes – as in "Box Seat" or "Seventh Street" – mourn a lost, if admittedly crippling, pastoral. Urban men seem unable to act upon their heterosexual desires, women present a remote aspect. The unnamed narrator in "Avey" at last connects with his childhood idol, only to have her fall asleep in the park as he talks about his innermost feelings; John, in "Theater," loses the bright interest of a dancer through his failure to act. A vivid racial quality nevertheless infuses the sections of the cities where these people live: "black skinned, they dance and shout above the tick and trill of white-washed buildings." The city offers spaces of resistance, places around which to construct a new black identity. But to the near-mystic who in the end rejects all racial categories, the city also fails to support a fundamental humanity.

The critical success that *Cane* achieved proved an ambiguous triumph for Jean Toomer. An insistence on being "nonracial" and adherence to Gurdjieffian doctrine led Toomer away from the African American wellsprings of his earliest, best-known work and into rhetoric more congenial to a metaphysical enthusiast. For decades after the publication of *Cane* Toomer continued to write. Little was published, for his ties with New York writers and editors had been severed, at least in part because of his spiritual questing. A long poem proclaiming an ideal America, "The Blue Meridian," was published in 1936, but that would be the last literary work to appear during his lifetime. Toomer's unwillingness to stay within the parameters of a single genre, his refusal to celebrate uplift or condemn sensationalism, and his insistence on following his own individual path speak not only to his own life situation, but to the quandary of the New World black artist as well.

Claude McKay was born in 1890 in a rural Jamaican village, one of eleven children in a farming family. He benefited from having a schoolteacher as an older brother, and despite, or perhaps because of, his family's piety, McKay considered himself a religious freethinker for most of his adult life (although not long before his death in 1948, he converted to Catholicism). As a young adult, McKay worked as a constable. In enforcing colonial law the young man realized that rural, dark-skinned folk – those most like himself – were often on the lowest rung of the social and economic ladder. McKay's psychological bifurcation anticipates fellow West Indian Derek Walcott's late twentieth-century query: "I who am poisoned with the blood of both, / Where shall I turn, divided to the vein? . . . how choose / Between this Africa and the English tongue I love?" A black colonial British subject, McKay, if not literally "multiracial" like Toomer, occupied a liminal position. His wanderings and migrations, like those of Toomer, Hughes, and other New Negro writers, identify him as a diasporic New Negro.

McKay's earliest publications, classically formed poetry, exhibited the speaker's desire to create a black pastoral and to return to a rural Jamaica. His preference for traditional poetic form, the sonnet and the short lyric, could be complemented by leftist politics; an example of this aesthetic–activist enjambment can be found in the poem "The White House." Following the success of his first two volumes of poetry, McKay tried a return to farming. He left home for the United States and the Tuskegee Institute, and would never again live in Jamaica. Horrified by the harsh racism of Alabama, and eventually equipped with money from an English patron, McKay went to New York, started a restaurant, and married a childhood sweetheart. Both endeavors failed. McKay stayed on in the city, becoming a socialist at the end of World War I. Class-conscious in a way many black writers of his generation were not, few of his peers were more overtly leftist. In fact, his allegiance to radical politics and white bohemians may have kept him from becoming more solidly affiliated with self-identified race men. In truth, many politically active and self-consciously black modernists had extensive relations and friendships within the white intellectual world. McKay, like Toomer and others, published in "white" journals because of those venues' receptiveness to experimentation. Notwithstanding McKay's common causes with white modernists, his poetry and fiction affirmed his solidarity with the common folk of black America, a commonality that was often warmly reciprocated (as seen by the popularity of the poem "If We Must Die").

A first novel, "Color Scheme," completed in 1925, did not find a publisher. It was too frank for the time in terms of sexuality. McKay warned his friend Arthur Schomburg, "I make my Negro characters yarn and backbite and fuck like people the world over." Even before the publication of the novel that would make him famous, McKay voiced his fears, predicting the response of the black bourgeoisie in a letter to Alain Locke: "I must write what I feel what I know what I think what I have seen what is true and your Afro-American intelligentsia won't like it. I know that." *Home to Harlem*, which McKay took care to tone down somewhat, still outraged many. Du Bois, in an often-quoted review in the *Crisis*, said that he felt "unclean" and "in need of a bath" after reading it; the reviewer in the black *Chicago Defender* scoffed that "white people think we are buffoons, thugs and rotters anyway. Why should [McKay] waste so much time trying to prove it?" The black middle class were confirmed in their fears when white reviewers raved about the verisimilitude of *Home to Harlem*. The reviewer in the *New York Times* applauded this "*real thing* . . . the *lowdown*," undoubtedly sending shivers down the collective spine of black America's upper classes. But Langston Hughes, ever the defender of black artistic freedom, called it a great novel.

Home to Harlem was indeed a shock to many, and still provokes arguments among readers, black and white, male and female. Focusing on the virile and dark-skinned veteran Jake, *Home to Harlem* can be described as a picaresque novel: in the narrative we follow the many adventures of a good-hearted rascal. Realistic in manner and episodic in structure, the novel showcases a character who, for all his travels, remains fundamentally good and must make his way through a contradictory world. Curiously, the story line moves in a spiral fashion: to Harlem, away from Harlem, back to Harlem, and away from Harlem once more. In this manner McKay's title and plot ironically comment on the black mecca. The shocking behavior of its principals, and its looping movement, partly obscure an age-old plot: boy meets girl, boy loses girl, boy gets girl. For all the Jazz Age lack of inhibitions, McKay casts his wanderer as a man in search of a domestic berth. As with his sonnets, McKay's novel provides an opportunity for him to demonstrate his talent for combining relatively standard forms (in this case, a realistic novel with a familiar plot) with modern content: vile language, amoral characters, and an insider's view of working-class black American life.

McKay's Jake is a Southern home-boy come north: he's a man's man, and a woman's man, too. Good-looking, Jake is good-hearted as well. The action opens with Jake on board a freighter steaming westward, musing over the exploitation of black servicemen: "he had enlisted to fight . . . [but] toting planks and getting into rows with his white comrades at the bal musette were not adventure." Illustrating McKay's belief that political and class consciousness were at the core of black workers, Jake muses: "why did I want to mix mahself up in a white folks' war?" Jake's brief against scabbing to his underemployed friend Zeddy similarly challenges assumptions about the black lower class. Jake is no ordinary roustabout.

McKay's misogynistic portrayal of women brings the life of this rough but positive fellow to an earthbound thump. Jake's ideal woman turns out to be the hackneyed image of the prostitute with a heart of gold. Meeting the newly returned Jake in a bar, Felice's business is unmistakable – "How much is it going to be daddy?" – yet she reveals her true nature when she returns Jake's money. McKay's sensational Harlem is gender-specific. After that first night with Felice, Jake exults "Harlem is mine!" The other women in the novel – "Gin head" Susy, the dark-skinned Brooklyn cook who prefers light-skinned men; Miss Curdy, described as a "hideous" mulatto; and Congo Rose, the cabaret singer who wants Jake to slap her around – serve as negative contrasts to Felice. (The only middle-class black woman portrayed is unceremoniously dumped by her boyfriend.) The sexualized portrayal of women underscores McKay's bifurcated personification of the black capital as both attainable and rejecting. Black women might find it hard to recognize themselves in McKay's portrait.

Despite McKay's apparent conflation of "home" and "Harlem," he leads Jake to stay away from the city for some time once he finds employment on the railroad. Jake's multiple encounters on the rails enable McKay to address class issues within black society. In more than a passing nod to "proletarian" literature, McKay acutely draws the hierarchy of those who work the passenger trains, whether porters or cooks, unlearned or college-educated. With the introduction of Ray, a Caribbean-born man with some college education, McKay provides us with his alter ego. While Jake at first exhibits some xenophobia, Ray's command of literature and history wins the roughneck's admiration. Jake returns Ray's friendship by showing the young intellectual around the high – or low – spots in black life, even saving him from an accidental drug overdose. Unwilling to participate in the activities at a black bordello, Ray represents, as does Ralph Kabnis, the inability of the lettered African American to connect with "authentic" black life.

McKay's portrayal of the underside of African American life reveals the author's ambivalence about heterosexual relationships. Despite his frankness about heterosexual practices, McKay does not overtly comment on homosexual behavior. References to one character, Billy Biasse, who "boasted frankly that he had no time for women," hint at a gay Harlem subculture. When we later see Billy he is seated with "a straw colored boy . . . made up with high-brown powder . . . lips streaked with the dark rouge so popular in Harlem." Readers can infer from this and other scenes that Biasse is a homosexual, but Jake himself never comments on this sexual difference. Furthermore, Jake and Ray each, on different occasions, express revulsion with heterosexual love, equating it with violence or confinement. McKay's images of a female Harlem playing to a male traveler combine attraction and repulsion. A satire-critique of a supposed urban utopia, *Home to Harlem* forecasts the difficulties of the modern black experience.

McKay's subsequent two novels affirm his diasporan traveler mentality. Although his own ancestors had long been dispossessed from Africa, McKay crosses and recrosses the Atlantic. *Banjo*, McKay's second published novel, appeared in 1929. If *Home to Harlem* begins with the return of African American soldiers, *Banjo* takes New World blacks back to Europe, specifically the polyglot seaport of Marseilles. Tracing the raucous living of an amiable Southern black seaman-stevedore, the eponymously named novel again pairs a likeable rough with a gripped-with-doubt intellectual. Ray of *Home to Harlem*, last seen departing the Negro Mecca, turns up in Marseilles. His best friend is again a working-class man who personifies hard-living masculinity. *Banjo*, more episodic than its predecessor, reworks many of the previous work's themes and scenarios: the often-violent relations between working-class men and women; barroom culture; the underlying causes of strife among workers, black and white; the black thinker crippled by reflection; heterosexual ambivalence. The writing alternates between low-life vernacular ("he was a money cracker as sure as gold ain't no darky's color") and stilted existential musings: "He felt that there was something fundamentally cruel about sex which, being alien to his nature, was somehow incomprehensible." *Banjo* did not have the success of *Home to Harlem*, but McKay realized some income from it and kept on writing.

In 1933 McKay's third and last published novel appeared. Set in early twentieth-century Jamaica, *Banana Bottom* draws on the author's early life and his relationship with the folklorist Walter Jekyll, a transplanted Englishman living in the West Indies. Rather than a devil-may-care working-class hero or a hesitant intellectual, McKay sets at the novel's center a "cultivated Negro girl from the country," one Bita Plant. Sent to England for an education by white missionaries, Bita returns home to find herself between two vastly separated worlds, that of the native brought up to lead her people and that of an educated country woman who must find a meaningful connection between her girlhood and her adult life. Bita's secular mentor, Squire Gensir, embodies the qualities McKay found in his patron Jekyll: Gensir respects the local religion, loves all music, vernacular and European, and genuinely befriends those young Jamaicans interested in the world outside their villages. When Bita announces she will wed an educated young preacher, her English friend offers no discouraging word. With Gensir's support, however, Bita eventually pulls back from the narrow and proper path chosen for her, and strikes out upon her own.

With its rural Jamaican setting, *Banana Bottom* does not fit obviously within a model of Harlem Renaissance writing, if by that we mean works written by those of African descent living in Harlem, or about that city itself. Its female protagonist projects a different sensibility from those of McKay's male characters. Bita Plant believes sexuality to be an integral part of life, but unlike her male predecessors she believes in marriage, if not quite in the bourgeois manner of her white sponsors. *Banana Bottom* continues the tradition of New Negro modernism, especially in its theme of the reconciliation of the educated black with a rural community. Less sensational than McKay's urban novels, this homage to the author's homeland resounds with the shock of the new: "free" sexuality is portrayed without condemnation; an analysis of class

5

❦

A NEW NEGRO, A NEW WOMAN: LARSEN,
FAUSET, BONNER

1928 SAW THE PUBLICATION not only of *Home To Harlem* but also of several
other important Renaissance novels. Nella Larsen's *Quicksand* was one of these
signal appearances. Born in Chicago in 1891, Larsen tried several careers,
beginning and ending her working life as a nurse, but also serving as a librarian
in the New York Public Library system. At some point Larsen decided upon
a writer's life and set out consciously to achieve that goal. Her marriage to
a physicist of impeccable family solidified her position in black New York
society, and recommendations from such notables as Walter White and Carl
Van Vechten helped her become the first black woman to win a Guggenheim.
In addition to two novellas, Larsen published several short stories, one of which,
"Sanctuary" (1930), brought her infamy because of plagiarism charges leveled
against her, accusations of which she was eventually cleared. (The editors of
Forum, who published the work, reviewed Larsen's drafts of her story and
one titled "Mrs. Adis" by Sheila Kaye-Smith; they supported Larsen's claim
of literary coincidence.) In addition to her professional woes Larsen fought a
bitter and public divorce, for her professor-husband had an affair with a white
colleague. Did the strains of her life exhaust her creative energies? Whatever
the reasons, Larsen would publish nothing after 1930, despite announced
plans for a third novel, "Fall Fever." Slender though they may be, Larsen's
two novels remain a valuable legacy of the Renaissance. Their psychologically
astute portraits of women walking the tightrope of color, class, and sexual
respectability continue to win admiring critics.

Much of the action in *Quicksand* centers in black New York City. Chicago,
a hoped-for final destination in *Home To Harlem*, is seen by protagonist Helga
Crane as a less than satisfactory counterpart of Harlem. Helga's experiences
mirror the author's own life, for both came of age in Chicago of white European
and African American parents. Departures and arrivals figure largely in *Quicksand* as they do in other Renaissance fiction, underscoring the travel aspect
prevalent in the modern black novel. As McKay's characters find themselves
moving to and away from Harlem, Helga Crane also finds herself lured to,

away from, back to, and away again from the Negro capital. And it is here that Larsen's mixed-race individual becomes a synecdoche for interracial and intraracial conflict. If black Americans possess a double consciousness, would mulattos be trebly conscious? On an individual level the mulatto's fortunes seem to reflect the larger society: as blacks can't belong to mainstream America, so mulattos struggle to fit in with black America. Often seen as a doomed wanderer of the racial borderlands, the mixed-race character had been popular since the nineteenth century. Few of these stories had optimistic endings. White writers generally saw the mulatto figure simplistically, as the tragedy of a white person trapped in a black body. African Americans knew the shallowness of such a reading, and often used the double whammy of black race and female gender to get at the nature of such liminal figures. To be mixed race was not simply not to be white. Such individuals struggled to belong anywhere. To be thus and female in a patriarchal society heightened the dilemma. Larsen's fascination with African Americans born on the color line was echoed by other Harlem Renaissance authors from Jean Toomer to Langston Hughes. Hughes's "Cross" served as Larsen's epigraph:

> My old man's a white old man
> And my old mother's black.
> If ever I cursed my white old man
> I take my curses back.

Larsen portrays Helga vividly as a damaged person unable to call anywhere, or any nation, home. Her initial appearance, in a dimly lit room at Naxos College, presents her as an isolato defined by her beauty and skin color. Her clothes proclaim her difference: "the colors were *queer . . .* positively *indecent.*" In Harlem, she distinguishes herself from her aptly named roommate Anne Gray by her sartorial choices – a "*fluttering thing* of green chiffon" or a "*cobwebby black net* touched with orange." Much of the action, as it were, takes place within the protagonist's mind, giving Helga's portrait psychological heft. Yet as the young woman's experiences have not equipped her to be objective, readers understand that she is something of an unreliable narrator. Thoughts of her own unworthiness suffuse Helga's consciousness, and her lack of self-love propels her to foolhardy choices in her career, in her residence, in a mate.

If many in the Renaissance sought to celebrate the vibrancy and gifts of the lower classes, Larsen, like Jessie Fauset, the other major black woman novelist of the 1920s, limns the middle and upper classes. The mixed-race Helga's inability to feel membership within black society offers the reader a class analysis situated entirely within African America. Time and again Larsen shows us Helga rejecting others before they can spurn her, whether at Naxos, with the college's own Dr. Anderson, at a bourgeois black Chicago church, or with Harlem's smart set. Despair over her white family's rejection leads to her conviction that she will be forever homeless and unloved. What money Helga obtains she spends on everything but what she needs, an obvious and futile substitution for emotional connection.

Sometimes Larsen appears ambiguous in her delineation of prevailing attitudes on racial uplift and respectability. Occasionally she seems to reject Victorian-era ideals; at other times, she accedes to these bourgeois notions. Still, her treatment of black female sexuality and class in *Quicksand* and *Passing*, her second novel, opens a subject generally aired at the time by female blues singers, not college-educated race women. Larsen's views of club life and intraracial class conflict differ notably from those of black male authors, even if she also describes the clearly sexual allure of the nightclubs. Even more interestingly, the display of sexuality merges with interracial mixing and identity, suggesting a link between unfettered sexuality, homosexual and otherwise, and racial indeterminacy. Helga, in an oft-cited nightclub scene, rejects the spinning, swaying dancers, averring that she is no "jungle creature"; the sight of the alabaster-skinned Audrey Denney, a black woman who can pass for white, socializing with whom she pleases, sends Helga into a frenzy. The protagonist's admiration for the other woman, her desire to *be* her, mixes in with a rising sexuality which she forces back by fleeing, "cold, unhappy, misunderstood, and forlorn."

The forthright expression of female desire presented a taboo for the African American middle class. The "politics of respectability" took precedence over sensual liberation. Sex, a danger zone for black Americans, must be publicly repulsed or displaced. For her physical desire Helga must substitute clothing, jewelry, and color schemes, a material solution that fails to address her psychic turmoil. Fleeing the United States for Denmark doesn't relieve Helga's distress, either. Her white Danish relatives exoticize her, and Helga finds the attention both exciting and repugnant. A Scandinavian suitor, Axel Olson, erotically sees a racial stereotype rather than an actual woman. Helga's inability to resolve the contradiction between repulsion and desire leads her back to America, and a downward trajectory. Her female gender and racial identity place her in a figurative sinkhole, one from which even her creator seems unable to save her.

Passing appeared a year after the well-received *Quicksand*. As in her first novel, Larsen centers the story around the experiences of a middle-class African American woman. *Passing*, however, takes on the myths swirling around those who live on the color line – black folk who can cross over and become "white" – and complicates them to a degree not seen before. Protagonist Irene Redfield is not portrayed as a damaged soul tossed on life's rough currents. Instead, readers meet a calculating woman driving her physician-husband to ever-higher heights of bourgeois comfort. Bent on security and social position, Irene would shudder at the thought of being considered an ordinary Negro. An early scene shows her on a visit to Chicago and cooling off at the Drayton hotel's rooftop café. As it turns out Clare Kendry, a childhood friend also in town, is seated nearby. Both women are patrons because they can pass. "Ah! Surely! They were Negro eyes! mysterious and concealing . . . in that ivory face under that bright hair." This chance encounter, one Irene will forget about for weeks, will result in a storm of envy, desire, and rage.

Irene's friend Clare does not only pass for convenience. Her entire adult life is based on her ability to be read as white, for she had years before said goodbye to African America. Clare's racist husband greets his wife with the endearment "Nig," and comments that his wife seems to be getting darker every year. Irene is enraged, but then recalls with pity the other woman's poverty-stricken youth. When Clare ardently pursues a rekindling of their friendship, insinuating herself into Irene's bourgeois black New York circle, the Harlemite becomes frightened, angry, and jealous. Intriguingly, Irene's negative feelings are mixed with desire: she finds Clare's voice "so very se-ductive," and thinks few women "weep as attractively as Clare." Is it Clare's caressing, magnetic manner Irene desires, or the woman herself? *Passing* ex-plores multiple desires, and the reader must decide which of them propels the novel to its cataclysmic finale.

In *Passing*, Harlem's inhabitants feel the draw of the Negro mecca, of black life itself, no matter what the white world holds. Larsen's indeterminate charac-ters here and elsewhere underscore the contingent nature of belonging, as well as the narrow space in which the black middle class orbits. Her white-black women illustrate the problematic of intraracial class stratification, for a white skin may obtain wealth but not inclusion. Unwanted in the tightly knit world of the brown bourgeoisie, Larsen's light-skinned poor pass over to the white side, hungering for the racial enclave left behind. The return of the racially and class repressed in *Quicksand* and *Passing* makes for an uncomfortable reading of the New Negro.

Jessie Fauset, 1882–1961, the most prolific novelist of the New Negro in-telligentsia, may be the least esteemed. As editor and mentor her work in the cause of African American literature has long been celebrated, although some have called her fiction her weakest contribution to the era. Fauset's prominence as a Harlem Renaissance "midwife," rather than as a novelist, has been rea-sonably attributed to gender: her assistance is lauded, the product is someone else's. This quasi-invisibility was promoted by her profession as literary editor of the *Crisis*, although she frequently contributed poetry and short fiction to that journal. Few other black writers were as educated as Fauset: born in 1882, she nevertheless was awarded two Ivy League degrees – a bachelor's degree, Phi Beta Kappa, in classical languages from Cornell, and a master's in French from the University of Pennsylvania. Despite her achievements, the new graduate worked as a teacher in Washington, DC's segregated Dunbar High School. (Dunbar was hardly the last resort: known for the quality of its education, its graduates included many notable African Americans, Jean Toomer among them.) Finding herself insufficiently challenged, Fauset pulled up roots and moved to New York City, landing her position at the *Crisis*. Known for her supportive readings, Fauset also sponsored literary soirées in her home. Her skills as an editor-mentor rivaled those of Scribner's Maxwell Perkins. Many admired her; some, like Langston Hughes, idolized her.

In spite of her days spent advancing the cause of race literature, Fauset published four novels: *There is Confusion* (1924), *Plum Bun* (1929), *The Chinaberry Tree* (1931), and *Comedy: American Style* (1933). Her initial foray into novel-writing was spurred by the publication and success of *Birthright*, a novel on the "race question" by white novelist T. S. Stribling that appeared in 1921. That debut, *There is Confusion*, follows the career of Joanna Marshall, a young, gifted, and black performer in early twentieth-century New York City. Daughter of a prosperous caterer, and sister to a rising Du Boisian race leader, Joanna's ambition is not matched by a consciousness of race or class strife; in fact, she tells her brother to drop his poor girlfriend. (Her own suitor plans to be a doctor.) Much of the novel concerns itself with the doings of this gifted, yet minuscule, group of middle-class African Americans. The gender status quo, seemingly upended by Fauset's espousal of career women, is in the end undercut by the heroine's submersion of her career in her husband's. As first novels go, *There is Confusion* is well enough plotted and notable for Fauset's depiction of a community unknown to millions of white Americans, the tiny albeit very real world of the brown bourgeoisie. Fauset's placement of a brown-skinned woman at the center of the narrative – "no hair straighteners for her" – strikes at the light-skinned heroines of early black fiction. Fauset's subsequent heroines would lighten in complexion, leaving her open to charges that she was concerned only with the experiences of a negligible and unrepresentative group of blacks.

With her second novel, *Plum Bun*, Fauset began a three-volume exploration of the myth of the "tragic" light-skinned heroine. The narrative is, like *Quicksand*, a black female *Bildungsroman*. Opening on working-class Opal Street in Philadelphia, the novel gives us the white-skinned protagonist Angela Murray, who sees her home as "the dingiest, drabbest chrysalis that had ever fettered the wings of a brilliant butterfly." With an accident of genetics leaving one sister brown-skinned and the other fair, the surrounding racist atmosphere leads to a tragedy in the making: the decision of one Murray to pass, spurning her sibling, with the expected and attendant complications. Written much like a love story or fairy tale, the story depicts poverty and troubles as ineffectual against the romance of the sisters' parents. When mother and father die, the stabilizing force of their tidy home evaporates, leaving Angela with memories of her mother passing for white in order to gain the little indulgences she craves. What's most striking about this novel written over sixty years ago are Fauset's explorations of skin privilege, social mobility, and female liberation.

Born in the intersection of three status handicaps, Angela Murray is "colored," without family and with small economic resources, and female. Having decided to live as a white woman, she moves to Greenwich Village – not Harlem. Fauset sets the terms for her character's freedom from a degraded social status as reliance on self and a rewarding career. When Angela finally learns to acknowledge her race, she does so in the context of learning about herself as an artist: without asserting her racial identity, she cannot succeed at her craft. Life as a white isolato has enabled Angela to see black Americans for who they are, rather than as victims of oppression or unattractive stereotypes. Fauset shows Angela's progress toward a race-conscious morality through the young painter's changing views of the dark-skinned Rachel Powell, a fellow student. Early on in her life as a white woman, Angela cannot decide whether Rachel's "features were good but blurred and blunted by the soft night of her skin or really ugly . . . "; later, when she has repented her walk on the Caucasian side, Angela muses, "To anyone whose ideals of beauty were not already set . . . [Rachel] must have made a breathtaking appeal." When she at last reclaims her African American identity, and chooses a life independent of men, Angela becomes successful – in her painting, in her love-life. Success does not mean unilateral triumph. At the end, Angela's lover proves to be as racially ambiguous as she is. How race-proud can the painter be if she weds another white Negro?

Fauset's third and fourth novels, *The Chinaberry Tree* and *Comedy: American Style*, again portray light-skinned heroines. Although all of her novels include dark-skinned characters, the later novels focus on the lives of the fair. *The Chinaberry Tree* takes on issues of miscegenation and incest akin to those of William Faulkner. Dressmaker Laurentine Strange lives a quiet life as a semi-outcast in her Northern black community, for her mother ignored the community's taboo on white male–black female relationships. The resulting ostracism jeopardizes the seamstress's future, for a new and growing black middle class avoids mixing with the illegitimately born. A visiting cousin, a brown-skinned city girl, thinks that her own romantic failures stem from her association with the marginal Stranges; "still and all," she says, "it is nice to be decent." A modern-thinking doctor and an old-timer join forces to unravel the secrets that threaten the two young women's happiness, and things seem to end happily. But an authorial aside, tendered just before the novel's end, undercuts the rosy picture. For the final scenes, Fauset writes, are but a "brief span of peace in the tragic disorder of their lives." As with much of Fauset's fiction, a smooth surface hides the uncertainty of black lives in early twentieth-century America, whether those lives be middle class or otherwise.

The relative optimism of Fauset's first three novels is undercut by the un-relenting scenes of psychic destruction in *Comedy: American Style*. This last novel, published not long before Fauset's marriage and self-imposed exile to New Jersey, portrays the Stygian depths to which intraracial prejudice can sink a family. As a child Olivia Blanchard was furious with her parents: "how *could* they have made me colored?" As an adult, her desires lead to the perverted belief that her entire family can become white, as opposed to merely appearing so. This delusion leads her to marry a Caucasian-appearing man and to dote on her two oldest children, whose features and complexions suggest pure European ancestry. But her third, last, and most intelligent child takes after his grandfather – beautiful, perfect, and an ineffaceable brown. Tragedy ensues, for father and older siblings prove too weak to protect the youngest Blanchard from a rabidly color-struck mother. Although various elements of *Comedy* have surfaced before in Fauset's novels (the white-appearing child whose mother chases away brown-skinned lovers; the doctors who represent the acme of black achievement; the nobility of those who can pass but instead dedicate themselves to uplift and race progress), in this work her themes combine into an especially bleak vision. The wit of Fauset's earlier works, especially her sly undercutting of middle-class mores, have here been sacrificed to heavy-handed condemnation.

Unfairly characterized as rearguard in her thinking, Fauset was no prude. In *Plum Bun*, Angela Murray has a premarital sexual liaison, but she is not pun-ished for it with illness, poverty, or death. In *The Chinaberry Tree*, illegitimate birth is no bar to a happy marriage. Fauset's first and last novels criticize the color and caste snobbery of the black middle class. In her explorations of that small world – be it through the modes and expression of female desire, the conflict between the individual and her community, or the place of the city in making that class – Jessie Fauset shaped a quiet, genteel critique of a black America in the process of becoming modern.

Few black women published novels during the Harlem Renaissance, although more than a handful published short stories. Of these authors Marita Bonner [Occomy] was the most prolific, creating short fiction, essays, and plays. Born in 1899 in Boston, Bonner grew up there and graduated from Radcliffe College. As a young adult Bonner taught school in Washington, DC, where she met and was befriended by the poet Georgia Douglas Johnson, becoming a member of the older writer's "S" street salon. During the 1930s she moved with her husband to Chicago, where she would spend the rest of her life (Occomy died as the result of a house fire in 1971). She would publish seventeen of her short stories in the New York City-based *Crisis* and *Opportunity* magazines, ten of these before 1935. Drawing as it does on a wealth of influences, whether modernist aesthetics, Greek mythology, psychoanalysis, or African American culture, Bonner's work would be better known had the author published a novel or other volume during her lifetime.

"On Being Young, a Woman, and Colored," Bonner's now classic essay, appeared in a 1925 issue of the *Crisis*. In this and other writings she frequently used both first-person narration and second-person address, making for an intimate and immediate effect. "On Being Young . . ." meditates on the joys, trials, and responsibilities of being who she is, a highly educated African American woman in a society that has not yet accepted the possibility of such a person's existence. After its whimsical beginning – "You start out after you have gone from kindergarten to sheepskin covered with sundry Latin phrases" – Bonner describes the American woman who recently got the vote, who was beginning to smoke in public, who was asserting her rights. In particular she affirms the "colored woman's" status as modern, even though the perks of the elevated, white female identity remained beyond the reach of most African American women. When Bonner writes that when whites see a black woman, they see "an empty imitation of an empty invitation. A mime; a sham; a copy-cat," she points to the specific nature of black women's oppression. Willingly and emphatically shouldering the burden of the race woman, Bonner asserts, "If you have never lived among your own, [when you go south to help] you feel prodigal."

Her fiction struck more pessimistic notes. Published under a male pseudonym, "A Boy's Own Story" is an unsettling first-person narrative incorporating classical Greek myth. A boy of eleven strangely begins, "I'm glad they got me shut up in here. Gee I'm glad! I used to be afraid to walk in the dark and to stay by myself." His memories invoke myths of cursed families – Oedipus, the Oresteia, and Philomela and Procne. By weaving these ancient stories with the boy's present-day horror, Bonner curses the American legacy of slavery and miscegenation. Other short fiction, much of it set on Chicago's working-class Frye Street, pitted black folks against a world that always wins: the one time a poor black mother hits her child, he strikes his head and dies; a working-class couple finally finds love, but the woman has contracted tuberculosis.

Bonner's universe, increasingly full of unnecessary death and corrupted innocents, anticipates the powerful urban realism to come of Richard Wright and Ann Petry.

Like Bonner, most women writing during the Renaissance did not publish novels. Although short stories by African American women regularly appeared in the *Crisis* and *Opportunity*, not until recently were such works gathered up and reprinted. Many of these women published only a handful of stories. Some who are known best as poets also wrote skillful fiction: two such examples are Angelina Weld Grimke's "The Closing Door" (1919), which limns the racially marked outcome of one woman's post-partum depression, and Gwendolyn Bennett's "Wedding Day" (1926), which demonstrates that even a holy sacrament can be blighted by racial prejudice. That many less prolific authors were female speaks to the multiple limitations placed upon the black woman, who had to struggle with both caste and gender perceptions in order to get into print. To read beyond the better-known novels of the day is to discover the full spectrum of Harlem Renaissance writing.

6

🍒

"DARK-SKINNED SELVES WITHOUT FEAR OR SHAME": THURMAN AND NUGENT

ALTHOUGH THE 1920s have been celebrated as the "free love" period, the Renaissance authors were the children of parents born during the Victorian era. Langston Hughes, an outspoken advocate of free expression, was born in 1902 and raised in good part by his grandmother. Claude McKay, like authors Nella Larsen and Zora Neale Hurston, was born in the closing years of the nineteenth century. A significant project of black writers, artists, and activists was the normalization of black sexuality, if not its liberation. For the bulk of African Americans, the post-emancipation period meant a variety of freedoms, including personal ones. "Free love" literature appalled many blacks because African Americans still fought an array of negative stereotypes, chief among them the myths of the sexually rampant male and lascivious female. Yet sexual abandon and illegal stores of alcohol were precisely why many other people came to Harlem, whether white or black. Most of the black middle class eschewed any behavior deemed salacious, or even inappropriate. Working-class folk were less interested in the mainstream's approbation, as they had less to lose than the bourgeoisie. The tension between these levels of black society were played out in fictional settings ranging from the bars of McKay's novels to the stylish living rooms of Jessie Fauset. Gin joints and buffet flats (apartments where musical entertainment, illegal liquor and sexual partners could be obtained) were places where the less inhibited could enjoy themselves away from the disapproving gaze of their social betters. Sexuality within the black community remained contested for decades in black discourse. Because of ascribed and assumed gender roles, black women writers would not always think in concert with their male peers; neither would self-defined gay or bisexual writers choose to tell a reassuring, middle-class story.

For the reasons noted above, the sexual independence of Bessie Smith and other classic urban blues singers has long been celebrated by those wishing to depict the range of black intimacy. As both a lifestyle and a musical form, the blues greatly influenced the writers of the New Negro movement. Although most obvious in the blues poetry of Langston Hughes, whose poem "The Weary

Blues" takes its title from a song composed by the African American pianist W. C. Handy, blues and its close cousin, jazz, served as accent and commentary on many a Renaissance story. Nightclub scenes in *Quicksand* or *Home to Harlem* put music to the task of interpreting the characters' sensual desires and new urban environment. Wallace Thurman, in *The Blacker the Berry* (1929), and Rudolph Fisher, in *The Walls of Jericho* (1928), breathe verisimilitude into their Harlem jazz clubs and vaudeville acts. African Americans are indeed "blues people," as LeRoi Jones has famously asserted. The feelings and emotions of their new, urban life were voiced by blues artists, who laid out for their audiences the facts of working-class black life in an exchange demonstrating the blues were something singer and audience had in common. Volumes of fiction and poetry, especially in their attempt to delineate smaller, less-known black worlds, convey less of a group experience than did black vaudeville acts and "race records" (recordings made during the period that were aimed at African American consumers). When Langston Hughes remarked that the Harlem Renaissance didn't mean much to the average working man and woman, he was pointing to the separation, if not the irrelevance, of the aesthetically refined from the everyday expressive world of the average black American.

The difference between manifestations of so-called high art, such as the novel, and so-called vernacular art, such as the classic blues, is writ large in the treatment of gay Harlem. A subtext in much of Harlem Renaissance fiction, homosexuality and other taboo subjects were straightforwardly tackled by many of the classic blues singers. Ma Rainey and Bessie Smith were said to have been lovers, not just musical mentor and student; references to homosexuality occur in their lyrics. Other performers, too, shared an attraction for either life-long or occasional homosexual behavior. The sexually open buffet flats were memorialized by both blues singers and fiction writers alike. (Langston Hughes roguishly included replicas of buffet flat advertisement cards within his autobiography.) Harlem's unofficial nightclubs attracted many, from black newcomers to venturesome whites from downtown.

Wallace Thurman may be the best known of artists chronicling the Renaissance demimonde. Born in Utah in 1902, like many neo-Harlemites Thurman had emigrated to New York (his undergraduate studies were completed at the University of Southern California). Thurman quickly became immersed in the city's cultural scene, first becoming an editor at the *Messenger* and then at Macauley's, a white-owned book publisher. In 1926 Thurman edited *Fire!!*, a little magazine that ran for one issue alone, but brimmed with the fresh new work of Gwendolyn Bennett, Langston Hughes, Helene Johnson, Zora Neale Hurston, Countee Cullen and the painter Aaron Douglas; its subtitle indicated its aim at "Younger Negro Artists." (In addition to providing a venue for newer black talent, *Fire!!* included a higher percentage of women writers than Locke's *New Negro* anthology: the table of contents lists Hurston's play "Color Struck" and a story, "Sweat," as well as Johnson's poem "Southern Road" and Bennett's story "Wedding Day.") Visible as he was, Thurman didn't try to conceal his lifestyle, although he sometimes expressed ambivalence about his sexual orientation; a brief marriage to Louise Thompson ended with bitter feelings on both sides. Thurman's misery stemmed not so much from his sexual preference, but from his inability to write to the standards he himself set. When Thurman once swore dramatically, "I should commit suicide," he was referring to what he believed were the unfulfilled promises of his own creative career.

Thurman's first novel, *The Blacker the Berry*, attacks head-on the failure of the African American community to accept all of its members. (The title refers to the folk saying, "the blacker the berry, the sweeter the juice.") When Emma Lou, a young Idahoan, goes to the University of Southern California, she hopes to find a life far away from her stultifying and bigoted home town. Her mother, a member of Boise's "blue vein society," never stopped ruing the dark-brown complexion of her daughter, and Emma Lou grows up despising her own skin. Away at college, Emma Lou looks forward to joining a small band of African American collegiates, but to her dismay she finds herself and another student edged out of the sororities and parties by intrarace color prejudice. After two years in school and one unsuccessful love affair, she escapes to Harlem. Surely, she thinks, she will find the acceptance she craves in the black metropolis.

As Thurman knew, Harlem's magic went only so far. Emma Lou soon hits a series of snags. Although her first few weeks fly by – she finds a lover with little difficulty – her efforts to make use of her training fall flat when she is turned away from a stenographer's position at a Harlem real-estate firm. Time and again, Emma Lou finds that color prejudice lives in this biggest of big cities, whether through remarks from sidewalk Lotharios – "I don't haul no coal" – or silences that speak volumes. The self-despising young woman sinks deeper into a mire of self-hate, bleaching her skin and chewing arsenic wafers in a useless effort to lighten her skin. When an opportunistic, but fair-skinned, alcoholic latches on to her, Emma Lou falls hard. Despite her encounters with the best that the city has to offer – an evening with Harlem's brightest young lights, dancing in the hippest clubs, taking in the sights and sounds of vaudeville at the famed Lafayette Theater – Emma Lou can't enjoy herself. With the greatest of efforts she extricates herself from her lover's poisonous attractions, and only then after she finds him embracing another man. Thurman's inconclusive ending leaves us wondering whether Emma Lou has finally ended her career of self-loathing. Harlem, the Holy Grail to many black migrants, cannot solve all problems. Emma Lou finds her demons pursue her even in the city of possibilities.

More widely read than *The Blacker the Berry*, *Infants of the Spring* (1932) is a tart and sarcastic insider's look at some of the "younger Negro artists." A *roman à clef* that still delights readers with its acid estimation of the Renaissance, *Infants* follows the fortunes of writer Raymond Taylor, whose desire to win fame and influence runs up against the usual as well as unexpected obstacles. Set in "Niggerati Manor," an apartment house modeled on the real-life "Dark Tower" where Thurman entertained many of his friends, the novel gleefully portrays young Harlem denizens destined to make history: Langston Hughes appears disguised as the enigmatic Tony Crews, while Alain Locke appears as the progress-spouting aesthete Dr. Parkes. Zora Neale Hurston breezes in garbed as the gifted opportunist Sweetie Mae Carr, and a very young Helene Johnson and Dorothy West have walk-ons as New England visitors Doris Westmore and Hazel Jamison. A thinly veiled Rudolph Fisher and Aaron Douglas have cameos as well, as do other notables of the Harlem 1920s scene. For time-traveling voyeurism, few works match *Infants of the Spring* in outrageousness and vigor. "Ninety-nine and ninety-nine hundredths per cent of the Negro race," Thurman remarks in a characteristically provocative tone, "is patiently [sic] possessed and motivated by an inferiority complex. Being a slave race actuated by slave morality, what else could you expect?"

Just as Thurman broke the taboo against revealing intraracial color prejudice, so too he mocked bourgeois norms with his openly homosexual characters. Thurman's determination to examine 1920s-era sexuality in all of its forms raised concerns in the older generation, who didn't want the younger set washing any dirty linen in public. Thurman celebrated his friend Richard Bruce Nugent's then shocking revolt against his proper upbringing in the portrayal of the polymorphously perverse Paul Arbian, the Oscar Wilde-loving, underwear-averse free spirit who insists he has no sexual preference: "I enjoyed one experience as much as the other." That fluidity of attachments was abetted by the continuous ebb and flow of men and women seeking newer, freer lives in Harlem and the surrounding Manhattan precincts.

Thurman's publication in *Fire!!* of younger writers like Richard Bruce Nugent and Gwendolyn Bennett earned him lasting fame. Yet Thurman could also be ungenerous, even cruel: "Nella Larsen can write, but oh my god she knows so little how to invest her characters with any life like possibilities. . . . Jessie Fauset should be taken to Philadelphia and creamated [sic]." He wasn't any easier on himself, for despite publishing several novels and writing *Harlem* (1929), the first play written in part or wholly by an African American to be staged on Broadway, Thurman felt inadequate. He died at thirty-two years of age, never having met his own impossibly high expectations.

Thurman's good friend Richard Bruce Nugent is one of those literary figures about whom we know so much because they corresponded with so many people. His longevity – Nugent was born in 1906 and lived until 1987 – aids our memories of him as well. Nugent's literary corpus is neither large nor widely read, but his writings helped define the age. His unabashed social iconoclasm made him something of a celebrity while still in his twenties, for his writing treated without condemnation marijuana use and homosexuality. Nugent published some of his stories under abbreviated versions of his name, as a quasi-pseudonymity designed to protect his parents ("Smoke, Lilies, and Jade" appeared with the name "Richard Bruce" and "Sahdji" came out with the byline of "Bruce Nugent.") Chastised by Du Bois, who asked him if he could write about racial matters rather than pansexual explorers, Nugent retorted, "I'm a Negro, aren't I?" Progressivism, Nugent knew, took forms other than racial rights activism.

Nugent's short story "Smoke, Lilies, and Jade" is meant to shake up the black establishment. Shocking to many readers, "Smoke" served as one response to Langston Hughes's 1926 manifesto demanding that African American authors write without regard for the sensibilities of the black middle class. A contribution to the sole issue of *Fire!!*, the story has been called the first overtly homosexual-themed work published by an African American. Although later in life Nugent referred to "Smoke" as "precious folderol," the story's treatment of a nocturnal, same-sex pick-up was bold for its time. "Smoke" is an avant-garde piece that heralds not only a freedom of form, but also a liberation of social-sexual behavior. Alex, the narrator, thinks about a casual encounter – begun over the request for a cigarette light – and compares it to his ongoing heterosexual relationship. In the end, Alex proclaims that one *can* love two ways. Repeated references to smoke most likely refer to marijuana, a common stimulant of the alcohol-deprived Prohibition era, as the interior ramblings of the narrator bring to mind a pot-head's disconnected wanderings: "of course he was an artist . . . his mother didn't understand him . . . [he was] The Tragic Genius . . . it was more or less true." An earlier story, "Sahdji," a fantasy of tribal life, displays Nugent's characteristic style mannerisms (chiefly an over-reliance on ellipses to represent pauses in an interior monologue or narrative). Nugent's fictional forays test the limits of the socially acceptable and fixed racial, and formal, boundaries.

Nugent was not the only author whose sexual preferences underpinned much of his creative output. Countee Cullen's relationship with another young Harlem dweller, Harold Jackman, endured well beyond the poet's brief marriage to Yolande Du Bois, the activist-philosopher's daughter. Cullen was not so flamboyant as Nugent or Thurman, yet his gender nonconformity was commented upon even during the 1920s. Claude McKay's expressions of misogyny may have been an attempt to deflect curious inquiries about his sexual preferences (like Cullen, McKay married briefly, leaving his wife not long afterward and never laying eyes on their daughter). Langston Hughes guarded his personal life fiercely, so that to this day biographers and critics are still unsure as to the nature and duration of what intimate relationships, if any, the writer actually experienced. Less mysteriously, Alain Locke professed his attraction for a number of men, including Hughes, whom he pursued for some months (finally giving up over the young writer's nearly inaccessible persona). That the Harlem writers expressed themselves sexually in ways the mainstream found unacceptable was hardly unique: white modernist authors were equally well known for their free-loving escapades, as their published work, diaries and letters richly detail.

7

❦

GENRE IN THE RENAISSANCE: FISHER, SCHUYLER, CULLEN, WHITE, BONTEMPS

RUDOLPH FISHER surpassed the boundaries of the black middle class. Born in 1897 in Washington, DC, but raised in Providence, Rhode Island, Fisher graduated Phi Beta Kappa from Brown University in biology and English. Subsequently first in his Howard Medical School class of 1924, Fisher took up a postdoctoral fellowship at Columbia University upon graduation. He went on to place articles in medical journals, start up his own radiology practice, work on a musical revue with Langston Hughes, and publish over a dozen short stories, magazine essays, and novels. Fisher's innovative appropriation of the detective genre and humorous insight into the foibles of urban ways deconstruct life in the "City of Refuge," the affectionately ironic name Fisher gave to his beloved Harlem.

Fisher's satiric essay, "The Caucasian Storms Harlem," portrays the black Mecca as in danger of becoming a tourist trap. Spots once limited to blacks out on the town became, by the middle of the 1920s, nightclubs catering to white folks. If James Weldon Johnson was eager to advertise black Harlem as a culturally rich space teeming with talented and brilliant inhabitants, Fisher had reservations about sharing that space, even as he comically addressed such concerns. Returning to Harlem after a long absence, Fisher relates how he went from club to club seeking a Negro ambience. Instead, he finds himself, again and again, the only black person present: "The best of Harlem's black cabarets have changed their names and turned white." Recalling life before the "invasion," Fisher drops the names of such notables as Paul Robeson, football hero, law student, and international theater star; Bert Williams, vaudeville celebrity; and a young and self-possessed *chanteuse* named Ethel Waters. Musing that this Prohibition-fueled, voyeurism-spurred integration may have a positive effect, Fisher ends, "Maybe these Nordics have at last tuned in on our wavelength. Maybe they are at last learning to speak our language."

In Fisher's short lifetime (he died at the age of thirty-seven in December 1934, four days after Wallace Thurman's death), the physician-author participated in popular culture and high art. As a resident observer of the Harlem scene also concerned with his neighbors' physical well-being, Fisher was captivated by everyday folk. Middle-class concerns about his predilection for showing the wrong element of the race were doubtless confirmed by the puckish glossary Fisher appended to his first novel: "jigaboo," "hiney," and "boogy" were decidedly un-talented tenth terminology. His short stories fully demonstrate his affection for the average dweller of Harlem, U.S.A.

Rudolph Fisher began publishing fiction in the mid-1920s, and the celebrated story, "The City of Refuge" (1925), has the satirical edge for which Fisher became famous. A clear-eyed yet affectionate view of the burgeoning city within a city, "Refuge" spins a humorous and cautionary tale of a young black Southerner on the lam; its bumpkin-hero, trapped in an urban scam, nevertheless remains in awe of a place run by black people. Other stories, like "Ringtail" or "Blades of Steel," portray the fortunes and failures of those drawn to the promise of Harlem. Concise and well plotted, Fisher's Harlem stories display African Americans in love, in trouble, and in over their heads. Fisher desires to illustrate all levels of Harlem life, from blue-veined café society to dark-skinned piano-movers. Where Claude McKay would set his Harlem scenes in working-class hangouts, and Nella Larsen set her heroines in colleges and lovely homes, Fisher depicted the high and the low thrown together in one surging tide. Harlem, as desired space, drew them all.

Fisher's first novel, *The Walls of Jericho* (1928) introduces themes and types already familiar to readers of his short stories – the workings of Harlem from its topmost ranks to its lowest levels. Shifting back and forth between various locales, from the shady precincts of a West Indian's pool hall to the parlor of a near-white lawyer, the novel's main focus is the ups and downs of Shine, a hard-working moving man, and Linda, his ambivalent girlfriend. Interwoven with and impeding the progress of their romance are the machinations of two other Harlem denizens – the owners of the aforementioned pool hall and parlor, whose antagonistic maneuverings provide a suspenseful counterpoint. Adding a note of Lafayette Theater-type vaudeville are Jinx and Bubber, the fat-and-lean male pair whose verbal sparring hides their fast friendship. Fisher skewers white flight from Harlem, intraracial stratification, and black and white uplifters alike. Humor and Harlem vernacular heighten rather than obscure the double-edged nature of black America's city of refuge. As in his earlier and later works, Fisher depicts Harlem as both an alluring physical place and a compelling psychic space, a sanctuary with very real liabilities. For those who can negotiate its alternately welcoming and forbidding locales, Harlem mitigates the continual setbacks of its uneducated working class and the limited opportunities for black high society.

Fisher's second novel, *The Conjure Man Dies* (1932), portrays one of the earliest fictional African American detectives. Here Fisher is not interested in plumbing psychological depths; nor is he concerned with promoting working-class internationalism; neither, finally, does he seek to attack in-group ills like color prejudice or sexism. The doctor-novelist wants instead to entertain first and enlighten second, both by his use of the detective genre, and by his incorporation of a tradition well known to all Americans – the ribald, stereotypical, and physical comedy of vaudeville and minstrel shows. (The inspiration for Fisher's detective fiction could in fact have come from a knowledge of black vaudeville stars Bert Williams and George Walker's show "Dahomey," which followed the exploits of a black detective; coincidentally, *The Conjure Man Dies* was produced as a play by the Federal Theater Project in 1936, opening at Harlem's Lafayette Theater.) Jinx and Bubber, minor characters in *Jericho*, move to center stage here, invoking a tradition of comic opposites that brings minstrelsy to mind but antedates that mimicry. Fisher's stock figures illustrate a long-running problem for the black artist: how to create comic black images when the dominant culture has long promoted an image of blacks as buffoonish, stupid, and lascivious? Fisher must have hoped that the style of the *black* vaudeville shows – especially the pair of mismatched comics – would be recognizable to his readers as more than minstrelsy's racist imagery.

Balancing minstrel-like stereotypes with the erudite and learned physician John Archer – tall, light-skinned, possessed of considerable sang-froid – and the police officer Perry Dart, the detective who is Archer's opposite number, Fisher debunks traditional figures of black men as semiliterate buffoons. With the entry of his third protagonist, the Harvard-educated N'Gana Frimbo, Fisher milks the stereotypes for all their worth. The novel's subtitle, "a mystery tale of dark Harlem," winks at Fisher's subterfuge, intriguing whites shopping for exotic locales as well as entertaining Harlemites in the know.

Fisher plays with the notion of black men as oversexed, voracious creatures by having the mysterious N'Gana Frimbo collect "black male sex organs" in laboratory jars. By placing a Harvard-educated African at the center of the novel, the author further signifies on the diasporic past when he figures Frimbo as corpse, possible murderer, and symbol of the supposed "dark continent." Fisher's insertion of a "conjure man" in a genre novel marks a humorous engagement with the modern-day meaning of Africa and Africans. Along with its genre-bound comedy *The Conjure Man Dies* presents a serious riff on Countee Cullen's famous query, "What is Africa to me?" Fisher puns on the darkness of the murderous deed, the opacity of Frimbo's machinations, and, of course, the multiple darknesses of Harlem. Cloaked in the disfiguring stereotypes of Western Europe, black Americans had to sift through and discard a mountain of falsehoods. Buwongo, the mythical African kingdom of Frimbo's birth, is described by the conjure man in a way that reminds us of the autobiography of Olaudah Equiano, the eighteenth-century Anglo-African. Frimbo's mysticism operates as an inquiry into the metaphysical nature of Africa, and the weight of that past when set against the Westernized, Eurocentric world.

If, as Du Bois once said, Negroes are forced to see themselves through other eyes, to feel themselves "ever two," what is a displaced African to make of the paradox of the black intellectual in the United States? Frimbo's railing against racism convinces Dart that the African is walking on the line between reason and insanity – Fisher's underhanded comment on the foolishness of believing that intelligence and reason can eradicate bigotry. When Frimbo bitterly remarks, "the rest of the world would do better to concern itself with why Frimbo was black [than why he's the target of a murderer]," Fisher alludes to more than a particular crime. *The Conjure Man* represents Fisher's ultimately pessimistic meditation on Africa in America. His inability to believe that Africa can offer solutions to the New World black seems to suggest that the lost homeland offers inspiration, romance, and mystery rather than answers. The clues, Fisher seems to say, may come from our Harlem know-it-alls.

Veteran newspaperman George Schuyler's impulse toward a more caustic brand of humor than Fisher's doubtless dictated his choice of satire as favored creative form. *Black No More* (1932) is Schuyler's most notable achievement. Readers do not find in it the unbounded affection Fisher displays for his Harlemites, despite the older satirist's evident pleasure in his tricksters and buffoons. In his youth Schuyler could have been described as a socialist, but by the 1940s he had become perhaps the first, and best-known, of the "black conservatives." Schuyler's mindset, however, cannot simply be evaluated as either "right" or "left" in orientation. At various times he held opinions that could alienate colleagues at one end or the other of the political spectrum, and could hold seemingly diametrically opposed views simultaneously. Apparently contradictory points of view are in keeping with Schuyler's deepest convictions: his mission was to satirize the foibles of his compatriots, whatever their ancestral background, and he spared no one's feelings. H. L. Mencken, perhaps the foremost American satirist, admired Schuyler's skewerings of the body politic, and the similarities between the two men, each dedicated to lampooning peculiar national follies, are obvious. Despite – or because of – his firm stance on the essential similarities of white and black America, Schuyler portrayed American race relations as the most pernicious national folly of all.

Schuyler was tireless in asserting that what most took for authentic black culture was, in reality, Southern culture. Nonetheless he harbored a genuine affection for African America. In *Black No More* he deflates the American way of bigotry through the wisecracks and confidence-man tactics of one Matthew Fisher (né Max Disher). His hero is introduced to his audience as a brown-skinned would-be Romeo spurned on New Year's Eve by a racist white thrill-seeker. When he learns that a Dr. Crookman has invented a process for turning blacks into whites, Max heads the line of would-be clients. Almost immediately after his transformation, Matthew – the former Max – finds white clubs are "pretty dull. There was something lacking in these ofay places of amusement." Heading south to his native Georgia to find the beautiful bigot, Matthew discovers she is the daughter of a former Klansman fronting a new white supremacist group. Chaotic events pile up as millions of African Americans "get white": shortages of cheap black labor panic capitalists; race-proud whites can't determine who's really Caucasian; the specter of mulatto babies from "white" mothers threatens to rend the American fabric. Women, alas, are seen as little more than reproducers of "white" or "black" folk, with two exceptions. While questioning the American racial status quo, Schuyler does not analogously interrogate the sexual politics of a people's wholesale passing: his women remain imprisoned by physiological, if not phenotypical, differences. A carnivalesque series of events leads to a bizarre and violent presidential election. In the end, Matthew and his creator fail to connect racial and sexual stereotyping. But the truly evil do get what they so richly deserve.

Schuyler's Harlem, like that of Rudolph Fisher, Claude McKay, Wallace Thurman, and other black writers, was a place of hucksters and hustlers, an urban heaven-cum-hell that promised excitement and happiness but, in segregated America, could hardly hope to deliver. Although in crucial ways the black mecca drives the circumstances of the plot, Harlem is not the center. *Black No More* fantasizes a process that would not only "erase" race problems, but would obviate racial space as well. Other of Schuyler's works, like the anonymously authored serial fiction of the mid-1930s collected in *Ethiopian Stories* (1994), move well beyond the actual yet metaphoric space celebrated in much Harlem Renaissance writing. There, the European refusal to come out against Italy's invasion of Ethiopia – made even more heinous by the Italian deployment of banned chemical weapons – brought Schuyler to his most race-conscious stance. Schuyler made African Americans global, but he shrank from making them racial.

In his belief that art would transcend race, poet Countee Cullen found common cause with Schuyler, although both writers could never escape the color line. *One Way to Heaven* (1932), Cullen's only novel, can best be described as an entry in the Harlem local color category. Like the protagonist of Fisher's "City of Refuge," Sam Lucas, Cullen's Southern-migrant hero, has a less than savory past. A card-sharping, knife-wielding womanizer, the one-armed Sam attracts attention for his disfigurement and his ethical lapses. Kept from various legitimate careers by disposition, a rudimentary education, and his physical handicap, Sam turns to a con as inventive as it is remunerative. Traveling from church to church, he "gets saved," melodramatically casting down his razor and cards before awe-struck congregations. Admiring worshipers help him out with meals, cash, and – for Sam is handsome – female companionship. In the opening chapters he makes his largest haul ever at a Harlem church's New Year, or "watch night," service. Along with his usual loot, he walks off that evening with a beautiful young woman whose conversion was spurred by his searing tale of Godlessness. Such tales of sin and false redemption Cullen knew well: as the son of a renowned Harlem minister, he saw the world of black religion from a behind-the-scenes perspective.

Although apparently mocking uninformed belief, *One Way to Heaven* shows an unmistakable fondness for its Harlemites. Sam actually weds his latest conquest, Mattie Johnson, for he is finally moved by her fervent religiosity. Eventually, her steadfastness begin to irritate a husband unfamiliar with the straight and narrow. Mattie's chic employer, the black socialite Constancia Brandon, also tries the young woman's patience; the maid finds the doings of wealthy African Americans "exceedingly strange and curiously mannered." The novel shuttles back and forth between two levels of Harlem life until Cullen finally shoves the café-au-lait society subplot into the shadows. Harlem night-spots, churches, and movie theaters serve as a crucial backdrop to the action; as in so much other Renaissance fiction, the city itself becomes a character whose alluring traits are bound up with less appealing ones. Cullen's characters find the black metropolis a promised land struggling to make good on its promises. And although his protagonists never attain textual richness, Cullen brings some verve to the narrative through the depiction of Sam's ambivalences. Ultimately and unfortunately, *One Way to Heaven* does not deliver the wit and energy of other Harlem chronicles.

Literary fashion has moved some distance since the carefully wrought sonnets of Countee Cullen. Walter White, once as lionized in his way as that poet was in his, has nearly passed out of memory. A long time NAACP official, White believed that arts and letters should serve the race. In 1924 White published his first novel, *The Fire in the Flint* (like Fauset, he had been moved to write by the positive reception accorded to white treatments of racial issues). Generally assigned to the category of propaganda or problem novel, the narrative does offer rewards to the attentive reader. Intent on his ascension to a surgeon's life, the Southern-born but Northern-educated Dr. Kenneth Harper soon finds out that his homeland's old ways have hardly passed. Kenneth finds the status quo allows for few challenges, and with the backing of his militant younger brother and a race-conscious young woman he plans for the legal redress of exploited farmers. The doctor's activism is met with a predictable but all too real surge of vigilante violence. Clunky expository passages – "Of such material has the coloured woman been made by adversity" – weaken the story's narrative pull. Much more interesting than White's race relations report is the author's reworking of Charles Chesnutt's *The Marrow of Tradition* (1901). Like that book, *Fire in the Flint* presents a fictionalized account of a Southern race riot. A young black physician of even temper and good faith believes that reason, and the help of good white people, will stave off vigilante violence; as had Chesnutt, White calls his young physician-hero to the house of a white bigot in order to save a life. Revising Chesnutt's original plot in this and other ways underscores the national dishonor of seemingly ineradicable lynch mobs, a horror researched by an undercover Caucasian-appearing White. *Fire in the Flint*'s signifying on an earlier African American novel confirms that Renaissance authors were well aware of their literary ancestors.

White's second novel, *Flight* (1926), dealt with passing. Here the author's foray into a character's psychological depths does not come off so well as had his efforts at fictionalized history. Protagonist Mimi Daquin, a white-skinned New Orleans Catholic, feels out of place among Atlanta's brown Protestant bourgeoisie. Drawn to an aimless acquaintance, Mimi gets pregnant, refuses to marry, and places her infant in an orphanage. Successful in a dress-designing career, then married to a white businessman, Mimi entertains uneasy memories of her lost race and absent son. Without the suspense and narrative drive of White's first novel, yet hampered by weak dialogue and flat exposition, *Flight* becomes a problem novel manqué. Lacking an overt passion for racial justice, White's second and last published novel received a lukewarm response. In his next book, *Rope and Faggot* (1928), White turned to nonfiction to advance the civil rights struggle that so energized his first novel.

Arna Bontemps, like Walter White, was inspired by pivotal events in African American history. Bontemps's early career as an author was supported by the Illinois Writers Project and participation in Richard Wright's Chicago writing group. Born in Louisiana in 1902, the same year as Langston Hughes, the California-raised Bontemps became that poet's life-long friend and a living memory of the New Negro movement, for he lived and worked in Harlem for about ten years. For decades at Fisk University, as both teacher and college librarian, Bontemps talked and wrote about the Harlem Renaissance. Although his first creative appearances came in the 1920s with poetry published in *Opportunity* and the *Crisis*, Bontemps went on to write two novels by the mid-1930s (a third, *Drums at Dusk*, was published in 1939). Neither novel was set in New York, which may reflect the waning strength of the premier black metropolis, or simply indicate Bontemps's greater interest in describing the historical context of the African American. Bontemps's subsequent career as archivist, educator, and editor would support the latter interpretation.

God Sends Sunday (1931), a somewhat sensationalistic novel, tells the story of "Little Augie," a character based on one of Bontemps's own relatives. Born on a plantation with a "lucky caul" over his face, the undersized Augie finds horse-racing a fast route out of poverty for a black boy without education or middle-class connections. Local color and vernacular are used in ways unlikely to dispel set notions about the black poor: when Augie searches black St. Louis to find his sister, he sees "women with thick hips, monstrous breasts, and glossy black skin" and hears "loud-mouthed nigger laughter, and songs in the miserable stone houses". Despite the many life events that should counter any optimism, the jockey unshakably believes in his good luck, a conviction that leads him to one difficult situation after another. Augie lives long, but not easily. Bontemps may have regretted his decision to depict the seamier sides of black life, for his next novel portrayed an epic of pre-Emancipation history.

Black Thunder (1936), a fictionalized narrative of Gabriel Prosser and his doomed revolution, demonstrates Bontemps's increasing sense of the power of history. That his second novel also shows a greater narrative pull may well lie in Bontemps's creative reimagining of preexisting accounts. Rewriting black history in a fictional counterpart to Du Bois's *Black Reconstruction*, Bontemps provides a series of economically sketched characters and a plot that takes off quickly. Gabriel, tall and physically powerful, possesses a questioning mind that rises up against unfairness and cruelty. Prosser, Gabriel's owner, a vile and violent slave-owner and Creuzot, a freethinking French printer, present the opposing poles of white thought. Ben, an old house-slave, will blow the whistle on Gabriel's planned uprising. Other slaves and whites, women and men, are similarly sketched in and put to the service of the plot. Although clichés lurk within the pages of *Black Thunder* – Bontemps repeatedly describes Gabriel's lover Juba as a "tempestuous brown wench" – the author successfully depicts what happens when good people are "strained to the breaking point." The novel sometimes displays predictable language, yet its revisionist militancy reflects the waning of the expressly aesthetic strand of the New Negro movement. *Black Thunder* and *Drums at Dusk* (1939), a novel of the Haitian revolution, mark the rising significance of historical events in the shaping of African American literature. Bontemps's aesthetic and political decision to write historical fiction laid out one path for black writing in the post-World War II age. *Black Thunder* may differ signally in style, tone, and outlook from the historical fiction of Charles S. Johnson and Toni Morrison, but it stands as their worthy predecessor.

8

❦

SOUTHERN DAUGHTER, NATIVE SON: HURSTON AND WRIGHT

ZORA NEALE HURSTON appeared to be the coeval of Anna Bontemps, another ambitious black college student who migrated to Harlem. As it turns out, the anthropologist-author, known for her fondness for trickster stories (and trickster behavior), was not born in the new century, as she led people to believe, but in 1891. She became well known for her shenanigans: Langston Hughes's story of how she took a nickel from a blind man's cup for the subway fare is Renaissance lore. Hurston trained in anthropology and folklore at Barnard College and Columbia University after initiating her studies at Morgan State. As she wrote in the very first sentence of *Mules and Men* (1933), "I was glad when somebody told me, 'You may go and collect Negro folklore.'" To perform such work would validate her own origins as an African American. In addition, her training as a scholar enabled her to look more dispassionately on her upbringing, and see it more clearly than the one who never steps outside of her culture. Part of her love for her own people and place lay in her recognition of the richness of black American oral literature. Born and raised in the Deep South, Hurston lived a childhood that fellow Renaissance scribes Fauset, Larsen, Toomer, and Fisher could only imagine. Hurston declared herself a real Southerner, proudly proclaiming she had "the map of Florida on her tongue."

Hurston's acute ear for figurative and expressive language is now well known. Her passion for the metaphoric richness of everyday speech identifies her style, and stands as one of her chief legacies. Importantly, she marks as beautiful and evocative the language of average, even poor, black people. Folk epistemology is revealed to the reader through parable and tall tale, and illustrated through the community's moral judgments and counsel. For a long time Hurston's literary language was demeaned because of its verisimilitude; its closeness to the way actual people speak led some critics to dismiss the sophistication behind her "simple" stories.

While still a newcomer in Harlem, Hurston became known as an author of folk-based short stories. Her first published story, "John Redding Goes to Sea," appeared in 1921 in a Howard University journal, but it was reprinted in *Opportunity* five years later; by that time, *Opportunity* had published three other of Hurston's stories. Still other stories, such as "Sweat," depicting the dramatic struggle between a hard-working washerwoman and her evil husband, and "The Eatonville Anthology," a harbinger of *Mules and Men*, were brought out in *Fire!!* and the *Messenger* respectively. In all, Hurston published about a dozen short pieces during the period leading to 1934, the year her first novel came out. Hurston's signature mixing of genres – the folding-in of autobiographical elements, anthropological fieldwork, fictional imaginings, and folklore – is evident in these earliest works. (Some material appears in more than one book, such as a set of whimsical directions for fish-eating.) Her empathic characterizations of rural inhabitants, from the thoughtful young man who longs to see the world, to the impish child whose behavior horrifies her grandmother but delights white tourists, represent more than rehearsals for book-length works. The best of Hurston's stories show an artist at her most accomplished – but even her novice efforts display a "whole souled" affection for ordinary folk and an insight into gender relations within the black community.

Hurston's critical essay, "Characteristics of Negro Expression" (1935), describes and celebrates everyday expression, whether verbal, physical, or artistic. Hurston enumerates some eleven such characteristics with which American Negroes dramatize their existence. An interest in performance had already led her to compose several theatrical pieces, from "Color Struck," which appeared in *Fire!!*, to "The Great Day" (1932), which received enthusiastic reviews but for which no text survives, and *Mule Bone*, co-authored with Langston Hughes and completed in 1931, but, because of a conflict over copyright (an argument that ended their friendship), not produced until 1991. Long before performance studies entered the academy, Hurston analyzed and practiced what she called the drama of everyday. Along with her prescience about the performative aspect of daily life, she points to "double-descriptives" and "verbal nouns" as evidence of a "Negro," dramatic penchant for elaborately satisfying language.

Hurston's most significant works can be said to be clustered toward the end of the Renaissance: her first novel, *Jonah's Gourd Vine*, appeared in 1934; *Mules and Men*, a work of folklore, came out the following year; and the novel widely acclaimed as her masterpiece, *Their Eyes Were Watching God*, two years after that. By the 1930s, then, Hurston was fashioning into literature the black expression, folk culture, and lore constitutive of all her works, whether fiction, folklore collection, or autobiography. As had Langston Hughes, Hurston depicted ordinary people in her writings in ways that went beyond the romanticized, socialist views of Claude McKay, or the romanticized, metaphysical views of Jean Toomer. Hurston's upbringing in the black church of rural Florida imbues her work with an insider's knowledge and love. Although her training as a folklorist-anthropologist augmented her immersion in African American language, ritual, and belief systems, scholarship alone could not penetrate the rich fabric of black American life in the way that Hurston's writings do. Her use of biblical and African American folklore mirrors black adaptations of multiple cultural influences. Hurston's familiarity with African American typology is illustrated by her novel *Moses, Man of the Mountain* (1939), the story of Moses told from a black point of view: in Hurston's rendering, Moses becomes one of the greatest conjure men who ever walked the earth.

Jonah's Gourd Vine, the story of a striving country preacher and the woman he woos, marries, and finally disappoints, is based on the marriage of Hurston's own parents. John Buddy Pearson and Lucy Potts take the stage as fully formed individuals whose frailties make them that much more real to the reader. Lucy's sharp self-confidence and John's in-spite-of-himself infidelities collide again and again – but their mature battles are shown in the context of a loving, rural courtship and intraracial color and class hierarchies. Tender exchanges between the two are revealed through the depiction of a coherent black folk community: the courtship scene, in which John asks Lucy if she's a "flying lark" or a "settin' dove," exemplifies Hurston's talent for showing an individual through cultural specifics. A sharp ear for everyday dialogue constitutes one of Hurston's greatest strengths.

A story of love, disillusionment, retribution, and, perhaps, salvation, *Jonah's Gourd Vine* attacks central communal issues subtly and indirectly, in ways that can seem almost insignificant. Her use throughout of animal metaphors, love-knots, and riddles illustrates the intricacies of social ritual and the moral world-view of rural black Americans. Without bias, she depicts two belief systems coexisting alongside one another, with overlap and spillage from one into the other. The alternation of Christianity with practices derived from traditional African societies is shown, for example, when churchgoers attempt to use a "two-headed doctor," or conjure man, to win back a straying spouse. False notes occur when interpolated ethnographic or historical asides within the narratives impede the flow of the story or the recreation of a milieu, as when Hurston describes the activities on the plantation where John was born.

Their Eyes Were Watching God (1937) is generally acknowledged as the pinnacle of Hurston's novelistic achievement. The story "embalmed" – that is Hurston's word – an intense love affair gone defunct. Like most of Hurston's writing, *Their Eyes* portrays Southern blacks in all their specificity of lovings and longings, their richly descriptive speech, their particular American and African syncretic culture. Protagonist Janie Killicks Starks's quest for romance, intimacy, and self-actualization aired themes hitherto only elliptically broached in African American literature. Richard Wright grumbled that the novel "wasn't about anything," caviling that Hurston's characters unrealistically manage to avoid racism and poverty, but his critique ignores crucial elements of Hurston's novel. In contrast to Wright's avowedly politicized writings of the 1930s, Hurston's works detail a world simultaneously more personal and more communal. *Their Eyes Were Watching God* is far more than a fairy tale of Southern black life (as Wright charged), more than a fantasy world without lynchings, substance abuse, or back-breaking endless labor. Hurston's experience is no phantasm. Her work posits an ordinary reality, one without the sensationalism of a *Home to Harlem* or the behind-the-scenes strivings of Larsen's brown bourgeoisie. Protagonist Janie Starks does not attend Harlem parties in expensive shifts; neither is she the mysterious, nearly wordless eternal feminine of Toomer's rural South. Instead, Hurston presents an everyday heroine, a sensual woman who longs to be taken seriously. Janie Starks ushers in the kind of black female character that would become central to the work of Alice Walker and Toni Morrison.

As a girl, Janie experiences a sensual awakening under the blossoming pear tree in her back yard. She yearns for more than the arranged marriage her slave-born grandmother sets into motion. Her grandmother sees security in Mr. Killicks; the girl sees an old man. Not many months after her reluctant acceptance, and without a backward look, Janie runs off with Jody Starks, a can-do big talker whose outsized ambition provides the spark lacking in her life: "The shirt with the silk sleeveholders was dazzling enough for the world." Starks, the prototype of the American who can get the job done, provides Hurston with a canvas on which to paint different kinds of black success stories. Jody, like Janie, offers a model of black self-hood beyond archetypes of nineteenth-century perseverance over adversity.

Once the newly-weds find the all-black town Jody longs to command, he begins his reign as mayor and general store owner. Folks complain, but Jody's ceaseless drive and hectoring get most in line. Janie, for her part, finds life on a pedestal unsatisfying: "Ah felt like de world wuz cryin' extry and Ah ain't read de common news yet." As counterpart to an intimate portrait of individuals, Hurston's interwoven "lying sessions" – tall-tale sessions held in front of Starks's store – offer up an affectionate portrait of Southern black life largely absent from the canon of Renaissance fiction. One long-running town joke, about a man's skinny mule, nicely encapsulates that world: "Yeah,

Matt, dat mule so skinny till de women is usin' his rib bones fuh uh rub-board, and hangin' things out on his hock-bones tuh dry." Everyday black life, on both an individual and group level, propels the action.

In telling the story of one woman's search for love and self-expression, Hurston critiqued unexamined social mobility, a steady questioning that runs throughout *Their Eyes*. The story of Janie's escape from her first, arranged marriage could expect to find sympathizers. Hurston's deconstruction of her character's second marriage to a self-made race man would raise a few eyebrows, for fulfillment still eludes Janie. Widowhood, and a subsequent encounter with a charming, sexy-eyed younger man, finally change the dynamics of Janie's existence. In the eyes of her beau, "Tea Cake" Woods, Janie can do no wrong: she is beautiful, she likes to fish, and she doesn't nag about his gambling. Nevertheless, the outcome of that third and last relationship points to the costs and caveats Hurston herself could not escape.

The triumph of *Their Eyes* lies in its ability to weave a web of black whole-ness, however rare such a life may have appeared. A skillful use of vernacular and folklore, and lively characterization, combine to create a womanist fable that serves still as an anthem. To tell the story of a rural Southern black woman who yearns for something more than a partnership, marriage, and acreage, who seeks sensual satisfaction with a man younger than herself and against the nascent middle-class mores of her community, put in place a fic-tional agenda that goes beyond uplift, beyond aesthetic manifestos. Janie's geographical movements within the South reflect the larger pattern, if not the actual direction, of the Great Migration. James Reese Europe, a black band-leader of the World War I era, sang "How you gonna keep 'em down on the farm / After they've seen Paree?" Janie's escape from the farm does not take her across the Atlantic, nor to the streets of Harlem, but the oceanic horizons she daydreams of suggest liberation and her own, New Negro, status.

Hurston's imagination could not always reach the benchmark she herself set. The author's own personal disappointments, and the limitations and bound-aries firmly set around the black woman in the early twentieth century, would impact upon her achievements. Her autobiography, *Dust Tracks on a Road* (1942), engaged (albeit somewhat evasively) with the challenges of being an African American female; it won her an award from the *Saturday Review* for furthering dialogue between the races and laudatory reviews. In her last two published novels, *Moses, Man of the Mountain* (1939) and *Seraph on the Suwanee* (1948), Hurston tried to break out of the straitjacket of "race" novels; in one she casts Moses as the original conjure man, in the other she used a white female Southerner to address the troubling issues around marriage and commitment. Neither was a success, critically or commercially. Hurston's move away from her bedrock material – the Southern black culture she studied and lived – may have doomed these later works. Their creator, however, may just have been tired, tapped out from trying to make a living as a black female independent scholar and novelist. The questions posed implicitly in Hurston's works of the Renaissance era remain unanswered: how can African American women reconcile independence with the desire to be married or mated? What will be the nature of gender roles in the modern black community? If Du Bois saw the problem of the new century as one mainly of race, Hurston, along with predecessors like Nella Larsen and successors like Ann Petry, knew that long-prescribed race and gender roles would, like the color line, be nearly impossible to escape.

Richard Wright (1908–1960) most clearly marks the divide between the Harlem Renaissance and African American literature in the World War II era and beyond. Wright, who began to publish in the mid-1930s, was born into extreme poverty. His family's desolate existence in Mississippi was somewhat alleviated by a move to Chicago while he was in his teens. For Wright, enraged at the racism he and other blacks had to endure, only the communists seemed to offer a rational way out of what was the irrational nightmare of the poorest blacks, a nightmare he vividly recreated in *Native Son* (1940). Wright's early and key essay, "Blueprint for Negro Writing" (1937), returns to some of the same propagandistic notions of literature that many of the Renaissance-era intellectuals had held, albeit with significant differences. Wright asserted there was no common ground shared by his and others' intent to write Negro works for the Negro masses and earlier, elite, writing; any perceived similarities between the two were tainted by the influence of bourgeois and white patrons. A realistic attention to class will enliven and strengthen black writing, for "every first rate novel, poem, or play lifts the level of consciousness higher." "Blueprint for Negro Writing" serves as a countermanifesto to Hughes's "The Negro Artist and the Racial Mountain," with its simultaneous upholding of a genuine black art and the necessity of artistic freedom. The Chicago-dwelling Wright insisted on the explicit melding of social justice and literature in a way the poet Hughes, himself a sympathizer with socialism, would not.

Lawd Today, Wright's first novel (unpublished until after the author's death, and then in an edited version), does not toe a polemical line. Initially drafted around 1934 and revised regularly during the mid-1930s, the work originally entitled "Cesspool" shows Wright's intellectual range rather than Party loyalty. The action of the novel takes place over a little more than a day (in a likely nod to James Joyce's *Ulysses*), and Wright ironically follows protagonist Jake Jackson around on Lincoln's birthday. The detritus of popular American culture, such as radio broadcasts and bridge-player charts, overlay and highlight black working-class life, be it a dozens competition (a kind of verbal jousting) between two characters or the humble Negro demeanor Jake must feign to keep his post office job. Supposedly a free man, Jake is nevertheless ensnared in a web of drudgery and institutional racism. In that sense he can be seen as an earlier, more anodyne type of Bigger Thomas, the antihero of Wright's fictional high-water mark, *Native Son*.

The literal rude awakening that precipitates the action in *Lawd Today* and *Native Son* illustrates the trajectory that connects the two: in *Native Son* a shrilling alarm clock brings Bigger rudely back into a harsh urban world; in *Lawd Today* a blaring radio shocks Jake into similar consciousness. Iterating a day-long stream of hagiographic broadcasts on the nation's sixteenth president, the repeated invocations of the Great Emancipator's life and legacy in *Lawd Today* produce a mordant commentary on the life of a black postal worker in Depression-era Chicago. Feeling ensnared by his ailing wife, Jake takes Lil's illness personally: "she goes and gets herself a Gawd damn tumor!" Self-absorbed, Jake eats and drinks to excess, patronizes juke joints with his buddies, and wastes what money he gets. When a desperate Lil reports Jake's abuse to his supervisors he almost loses his job – then plunges on into more self-destructive behavior. Kaleidoscopically portraying alienated modern black life, Wright employs fictional strategies as diverse as epigraphs from Van Wyck Brooks, to scatological exchanges, to the replication of an evangelical Christian's handbill. In fact, this unpublished early novel of Wright's offers more modernist elements than his first two published works, themselves seen as classics of mid-century social realism. By turns a discontinuous simulacrum of the working man's tedium and a bleak rendering of black self-hate, *Lawd Today* must have appeared too negative, too nasty a view of America. Not until 1991 would the novel appear in the form the author himself shaped.

Uncle Tom's Children (1938), published two years earlier than *Native Son* (and appearing about the time of Wright's last revisions of *Lawd Today*), was Wright's first book. Foremost in this collection of short fiction are the social concerns of the Depression-era black man; the never-ending oppression, etched in violent terms, echoes the brutality of real-life vigilante mobs. Modernist aesthetics take a smaller role: one hears the young writer's stern admonition that fiction must advance a social, if not even socialist, agenda. While the characters are sympathetically sketched – one has only to remember the terror of Big Boy, shuddering in a muddy hole while outside a childhood friend is lynched – the historical vectors that push and pull African Americans are more emphatically portrayed than psychological interiority. When "In Long Black Song" Sarah, the weary wife of a cotton farmer trying to get ahead, submits to the advances of a clock salesman, her actions do not entirely make narrative sense; her behavior toward a sweating, unattractive white man seems more pointed toward revealing the lurid draw of American capitalism than as showing evidence of her cupidity or adulterous intent. With the appearance of *Native Son* and the ineradicable placement of Bigger Thomas on the literary map, Wright's engagement with social and political fiction hit a zenith (even if his disappointing treatment of black female characters continued). The more playful, if equally serious, experiments of *Lawd Today* seem far away. So too do the fictions of the Harlem Renaissance's meridian.

9

❦

BLACK MODERNISM

THE GREATEST OBSTACLE Harlem Renaissance writers faced was not the withdrawal of the public eye. The Great Depression, beginning in 1929 and continuing until the build-up to World War II, presented the worst barrier to their continued success. As the maid of Fisk sociologist E. Franklin Frazier snorted, she didn't know why people were talking about a Depression; she'd known hard times all her life. The necessity of art was replaced with economic reality and aesthetic theory supplanted by politics. By the mid-1930s the tone and subjects of many writers had shifted from a celebration of Negro culture and the attractions of the black metropolis to the hard facts of breadlines, apartment evictions, and skyrocketing unemployment (at one point during the 1930s about 50 percent of Harlem residents able to work were unemployed). The Republican Party, once the party of choice for African Americans, gave way to the Democratic Party's promises of a safety net for all. Despite his party's gains with African Americans, President Franklin Delano Roosevelt was no radical on race issues. Although he retained black educator Mary McLeod Bethune as an adviser, Roosevelt feared a liberal image would weaken his position with white Southerners, and endanger his larger slate of reforms; no antilynching bill would be supported by him. (Not until 1948, under the leadership of President Harry Truman, would the United States officially begin the process of desegregation.) Federal organizations set up to alleviate the disasters of the Depression ended up replicating the status quo. Blacks would continue to receive lower wages than whites, if indeed they received work and federal assistance at all.

Some progressive movement took place. A number of blacks participated in the Federal Writers' Projects – Wright, Hurston, Richard Bruce Nugent, and Dorothy West, to name a few – but the help they received was negligible when set against the overall picture of destitution. Many writers turned to Marxism as a means of finding a solution to social ills, although few black Americans actually joined the Communist Party. Louise Patterson, the ex-wife of Wallace Thurman, was one of a number of blacks to accept an invitation to travel and work in the Soviet Union; Hughes, whose Marxist-influenced poems would lead to attacks from some quarters, was another member of this group. Authors published increasingly politicized work in the 1930s, demonstrating the sea change in black intellectual thought. The aesthetic battle for the soul of America, the ambassadorships of good will sponsored by writing and art, the legal litigation sponsored by the NAACP and the Urban League began to seem antiquated and inadequate. Life as African Americans had long known it returned in force by the mid-1930s.

In 1935 the suffering of Harlem broke onto the national consciousness when beleaguered and angry citizens took to the streets. The causes of the widespread unrest were numerous, although the precipitating incident was the roughing up of a young Puerto Rican boy, allegedly a shoplifter, by white storekeepers. Passed on from person to person, the story at last reported the boy murdered. Looting by enraged and desperate inhabitants followed. With Harlem wracked by violence, what had been flourishing appeared to lie dead and buried. As Claude McKay wrote, "Docile Harlem went on a rampage, smashing stores and looting them and piling up destruction." Poverty, segregation, and discrimination, emblematized in the pattern of employing only whites in stores with a majority black clientele, had as much to do with the upheaval as the vicious beating of a boy. McKay's essay memorialized "a defeated, abandoned, and hungry army . . . [whose] rioting was the despair of a bewildered, baffled, and disillusioned people."

1935 saw Du Bois espousing Marxian analysis. His commanding study, *Black Reconstruction*, published that year, drew on a radical economic interpretation of U.S. history, all the while placing the racial struggle front and center. Where Du Bois diverged from many other black thinkers was his apparent espousal of separatist principles, as in his essay "A Negro Nation Within the Nation" (1935). His move away from a liberal center on race and politics led to his forced departure from the NAACP, where former colleagues like Walter White were suspicious of communism and anything remotely resembling Garveyism. But the aging Du Bois had reason to feel disillusioned. Despite the NAACP, a coalition of progressive white and black activists, Negro participation in World War I, a solid decade of literary and artistic propaganda, and careful legal tactics, vast black unemployment and racial violence remained the order of the day. The dignified way left, said Du Bois, would be for "Negroes [to] develop in the United States an economic nation within a nation . . . It must happen in our case, or there is no hope."

Most African Americans in the 1920s and 30s found the economy, or rather their place in it, dictating their way of life. Fiction writers of the era may have been somewhat shielded from the financial Depression, but they could not long stay immune. The few who had shortly before basked in admiration at Park Avenue parties discovered themselves little better off than the rest of black America. The prosperity of the 1920s, with its attendant access to white patronage and mainstream publishing houses, had intimated that they were on their way to seizing the American dream. With the Depression's arrival, such dreams appeared to be dashed.

That wasn't really the case. The appearance of the anthology *Negro* in 1935, to use just one example, showed that the Harlem Renaissance writers remained active. Hurston would go on to publish four novels, a major work of folklore, an autobiography, and various essays, with at least two additional novels left unpublished at the time of her death in 1960. Langston Hughes lived in Harlem until his death in 1967, successfully supporting himself as a writer; some of his greatest work lay ahead, including the Simple stories and the jazz–poetry collaborations.

Certainly, silences and tragedies shadowed Hughes's and Hurston's compeers. Jessie Fauset's fourth novel, *Comedy: American Style*, was her last. Marita Bonner, whose pungent stories promised a lustrous career, focused on teaching and family. After winning the loyalties of black and white critics alike, Jean Toomer turned more intensely to spirituality, and found no takers for his metaphysically oriented manuscripts. Nella Larsen dropped from sight after years of personal and professional turmoil; despite a Guggenheim award, an announced third novel was never completed. Rudolph Fisher, Wallace Thurman, Claude McKay and Countee Cullen all died prematurely. These deaths and disappearances, awful as they were, could not obscure the successes of the Harlem Renaissance. The work was out there, if for a time largely inaccessible. It lived on to inspire the generations to follow.

The ultimate success of black Harlem's writers can be seen in the achievements of their successors. During the Depression that followed the boom years of the Renaissance, the U.S. Government's Works Progress Administration provided limited financial aid for some of those authors who would immediately follow. These younger writers also drew sustenance from the examples, if not the mentorship, of those who lived and wrote in those halcyon days before the WPA supplanted the book publishers Boni & Liveright and Knopf as a source of authorial income. Wright's denunciation of the "curtseying Negroes" in the decades before him should not entirely surprise us; neither should James Baldwin's 1950s attack on Wright, whom the younger man accused of being captive to the mode of protest fiction. Ann Petry may have been influenced by Richard Wright, but her investigations into economics, race, and gender owe a debt to Fauset, Hurston, and Larsen, too. Each generation clears its own path to authorial independence as it simultaneously engages with its literary ancestors.

Harlem Renaissance writers provided successive generations with a mode of exploration. They eagerly critiqued the boundaries of race and gender, as decades before Du Bois's "The Conservation of Races" had complicated reigning ideas about the distinctiveness of cultural groupings. During the Renaissance, characters operating on the fault-lines of segregation regularly appeared; these racially indeterminate figures went beyond the tragic mulattos of the nineteenth century. The mulatto in 1920s and 1930s fiction proffers an ironic commentary on a racially bifurcated world. Analogously, heterosexual norms were challenged in fiction and personal memoirs. In Harlem, as elsewhere in the modern world, roles once believed to be fixed were repeatedly interrogated. Even liberal fealties to integration and capitalism could be questioned, as the recurring notes of black nationalism and pan-Africanism demonstrate.

The Harlem Renaissance is one of the triumphs of American modernism. The fabled black city within a city may not have existed as much more than a cluster of stops on the New York City subway and some hundreds of acres of real estate, lovely and not, in upper Manhattan. But black women and men went there for far more than decent living quarters. They moved there to be part of a social upheaval that promised a new home, a new world of the mind, body, and spirit. Their migration was chronicled by the Renaissance novelists, who had themselves made their way to the mecca, sometimes for the briefest of visits, sometimes to live there. Harlem, foremost of black cities, performed a great service to writers, from Missouri or Chicago, Florida or Jamaica. Building on the swell of migrants from the South, and the irresistible pull of Manhattan, Harlem offered to inhabitants and visitors alike the glimmer, if not the reality, of a black utopia. The symbolic space that was and still is Harlem radiates with the presence of those who would, as Langston Hughes predicted, "build our temples for tomorrow, strong as we know how." If as a physical place Harlem perhaps never held the supremacy long assigned to it, as a black city within the nation's cultural capital it stands as the primary metaphysical site around which we organize African American fiction between the two World Wars.

For a moment, Harlem *was* black America. The fictive space that was Harlem in the novels of the Renaissance coexisted with a historic, geographically specific entity. Harlem, as the saying has long had it, was not just a place but a state of mind. Harlemites, then, would exemplify the New Negro. The enormous geographical dis- and re-locations were writ over in individual moves from rural to urban, from Southern to Northern, from farm to the

Lafayette Theater. Harlem's prominence inhered in its metonymic quality. By transforming Harlem into a figurative place for birth and rebirth, for individual and cultural self-fashioning, the writers of the Renaissance contributed to a cultural realignment.

If Harlem's physical and metaphoric space shaped the fiction that appeared within the boundaries of our period, the African diaspora shaped Harlem. West Indians and Africans, however fleeting their romance with New York might prove, reflected the impact of international movements circulating well beyond the borders of the United States. Those black nationals in search of nation also went to make up Harlem. People of African descent remained largely citizens without rights, and moved within and without America's borders embodying the post-imperial, alienated, stateless person. Harlem Renaissance fiction thus draws particular strength and shape from the experience of global circulation. The black migrant's experience – from the South, from Jamaica – was discontinuous, a break from a previous life. Images of individuals on the move, disconnected from community, populate the pages of black writing. Migration sets the tone for much of twentieth-century New York life. Small wonder that Harlem, a prime nexus of black migration, figures so largely in the fiction of the 1920s.

A sense of place, a sense of movement, and a sense of self- and group-consciousness undergirded the fictions of the Renaissance. Feeling a part of something – something black – suffused it all. At some time, in some way, each of the novelists in this study identified her or himself with a literary movement irrevocably linked to social justice. This imagined community of writers forged a poetics of politics, an aesthetics of uplift. Sojourners in and out of Harlem, they found a Renaissance in modernism and blackness alike.

ETHNIC MODERNISM

Werner Sollors

INTRODUCTION

THE PERIOD from 1910 to 1950 was the age of modernism in literature, art, and music. James Joyce's *Ulysses*, T. S. Eliot's *Waste Land* (both published in 1922), and the experiments by Pablo Picasso, Duke Ellington, and Arnold Schönberg defined the aesthetic of the first half of the twentieth century in defiance of artistic developments from the Renaissance to nineteenth-century realism. The modernist emphasis was on "abstract" form rather than on theme and on a new nonlinearity rather than on traditional artistic development and execution. Artists and writers increasingly wished to represent the sense of speed and motion that trains, trolleys, automobiles, and other means of modern transportation made widely available. Modernists were also interested in adapting techniques of nonwestern art and of the new formal language of film. These trends supported the "experimental," detached, and often difficult quality of modernism that took different shape in the various movements (the many "isms") that emerged in the course of the century. Amazingly, what started as the fringe enterprise of a few radical artists at the beginning of the century who set out to "defamiliarize," to "alienate" their small audiences, and what appeared as if it would be replaced by a second wave of realism in the 1930s (when Gertrude Stein bought work by such painters as Christian Bérard, Pavel Tcheletchew, or Francis Rose), became the dominant expression of Western art by the 1950s.

Looking back at modernism, the Harvard University critic Harry Levin marveled at the fact that "The Picasso" could have become the name of an apartment building in New York, and his Columbia University colleague Lionel Trilling wondered what had changed to make modernism teachable in so many colleges and schools around the United States. In the 1920s, Eda Lou Walton, an avant-garde professor of modern literature at New York University, had to smuggle a copy of *Ulysses* through U.S. Customs in order to read and discuss it in her private boudoir, in unorthodox fashion, with adventurous young undergraduate boys. By the 1950s, Joyce could readily be assigned to coed students who had not yet reached the legal drinking age in many states.

Gertrude Stein's famous sentence, "A rose is a rose is a rose," was enough of an irritant so that characters in Richard Wright's *Lawd Today* (finished in manuscript in 1937) would wonder about the "old white woman over in Paris" who had written it and then wouldn't tell what it meant; even Cab Calloway "ain't never said nothing that crazy." In the second half of the century, Stein's line was milked for American Volkswagen commercials ("it runs and runs and runs").

At the beginning of the period, modernism may have still seemed foreign to many Americans. The public reactions were strong against the modernist paintings that were in the minority in the famous 1913 Armory Show, such as Marcel Duchamp's *Nude Descending a Staircase, No. 2* (1912), which was frequently ridiculed by cartoonists. Some saw in it the explosion of a tile factory. The New York *Evening Sun* parodied it, under the general heading "Seeing New York with a Cubist," as *The Rude Descending a Staircase (Rush hour at the Subway)*. Though William Carlos Williams said, "it was not until I clapped my eyes on Marcel Duchamp's Nude Descending A Staircase that I burst out laughing from the relief it brought me," Theodore Roosevelt published "A Layman's View of an Art Exhibition" in *Outlook* (March 22, 1913), in which he wrote:

Take the picture which for some reason is called *A naked man going down stairs*. There is in my bath-room a really good Navajo rug which, on any proper interpretation of the Cubist theory, is a far more satisfactory and decorative picture. Now if, for some inscrutable reason, it suited somebody to call this rug a picture of, say, *A well-dressed man going up a ladder*, the name would fit the facts just about as well as in the case of the Cubist picture of the *Naked man going down stairs*. From the standpoint of terminology each name would have whatever merit inheres in a rather cheap straining after effect; and from the standpoint of decorative value, of sincerity, and of artistic merit, the Navajo rug is infinitely ahead of the picture.

The opposition clearly had the upper hand, and the overwhelming majority of American works of art that were exhibited before World War II at the Venice Biennale, for example, were at first salon art, and later urban realist, regionalist, or social realist – or throughout the decades, recognizably detailed female nudes by hence forgotten painters – but they were not modernist. The single exception was the 1934 Biennale, for which Juliana Force of the brand-new Whitney Museum made the selections, and at which much American modernist work was shown, including Edward Hopper's *Early Sunday Morning*, Georgia O'Keeffe's *Mountains, New Mexico*, Max Weber's *Chinese Restaurant*, Reginald Marsh's *Why Not Use the "L"*, and Walt Kuhn's *Blue Clown*. The exhibit was marred, however, by the central presence of a life-sized and life-like effigy of William Randolph Hearst's mistress, the actress Marion Davies (painted by the once-famous celebrity portraitist Tadé Styka, the son of a

Polish panorama artist) that Hearst's men had managed to sneak into the American pavilion without Force's knowledge; and Force was unable to have it legally removed before the Biennale season ended. This much-commented-on installation (that still appeared in the centenary Biennale catalogue of 1995 as if it had been an official 1934 submission) seemed symbolic of the dominance of nonmodernist art in the period, especially since Hearst's papers had given ample room to caricature modern paintings, comparing them to grandma's quilts or wondering whether the museums were hanging their modern artworks upside down. The conflict between Hearst and Force seemed ominously representative of the intensifying struggle between "fascist realism" and "democratic modernism," since Hearst had also published positive press reports on Mussolini, was on his way to meet Hitler, and knew Count Volpi di Misurata, the fascist director of the Biennale, whereas Force was a democratic spirit and daring amateur who described modern American art in the 1934 Biennale catalogue in cosmopolitan terms as coming out of "the fusion of different races and nationalities which has given the US a rare sensibility of being open to influences from around the world."

When, in 1936, the not yet seven-year-old Museum of Modern Art in New York ran an all-European exhibition on *Cubism and Modern Art* (its curator was Alfred H. Barr, Jr., who had pioneered in teaching modern art at Wellesley College from 1926 to 1929), the U.S. Customs Service determined that many of the sculptures (among them, those by Boccioni, Miró, and Giacometti) were not "art" and subjected them to duties as imported materials (stone, wood, etc.). Under the headline "Furiously They Ask Once More: But Is It Art?" the *New York Times* gave lavish coverage to the show but also voiced the complaint that "these cliqued isms represent the flight from reality. Facing life as it is, they paint life as it isn't."

The exhibitions in Alfred Stieglitz's gallery 291 (1908–17) reached only a relatively small group of intellectuals, who were exposed to shows on African sculpture, Cézanne, Picasso, Braque, Matisse, and children's drawings (newly discovered as an art form). Stieglitz and his *Camera Work* (1903–17) also appealed to a small circle of modernists who were eager to develop photography as art and to distinguish its aesthetic from that of painting. By 1938, this effort had not yet taken root, and photography received no mention in Harold Stearns's stocktaking collection, *America Now* (1938), an updating of Stearns's earlier symposium, *Civilization in the United States* (1922).

Antonín Dvořák had set the tone early for incorporating black American musical elements into modern music when he took the themes of black and Indian songs and made them part of his 1893 *Ninth Symphony* ("From the New World"). Yet ragtime and jazz were still regularly attacked in American newspapers in the 1920s, the so-called "jazz age." Even a calm academic, Walter Damrosch, found it necessary to address the Music Supervisors' national conference in 1928 with a worried and thoroughly derogatory comment on jazz, describing it as "a monotony of rhythm ... without music and without soul" that "stifles the true musical instinct, turning away many of our talented young people from the persistent, continued study and execution of good music." A short time before Duke Ellington launched his intricate musical experiment "Daybreak Express" (1930), the *New York Times* still reported as a matter of fact the belief that "Jazz is quite unsatisfactory to any intelligent person" (April 17, 1928: 26). It is telling that music critic and CBS consultant Deems Taylor's contribution on "Music" to Harold Stearns's *America Now* (1938) makes no reference to jazz, but that Hearst paper columnist Louis Reid's entry on "Amusement: Radio and Movies" mentions that broadcasters were "primly-squeamish about recognizing jazz as such," yet they had unwittingly "accomplished the astounding service of making the whole world jazz-conscious."

William Faulkner, ultimately the most significant American prose writer of the century, wrote his most important works from 1929 to 1942 to mixed reviews and a small audience. It is symptomatic that literary critic John Chamberlain's contribution to Stearns's *America Now*, which discusses many major and minor writers of the 1930s, mentions Faulkner only once: "Erskine Caldwell and William Faulkner have their points, but they have not developed into major artists." This sentence suggests the niche of sensationalist Southern gore within which Faulkner was still buried as a minor regionalist. The immigrant novelist and critic Ludwig Lewisohn held Faulkner in higher esteem as early as 1932, when he characterized him, in *Expression in America*, as the "most gifted" of contemporary "neo-naturalist writers" who, however, in "needlessly intricate and essentially confused books" "has preserved one active emotion, a very fruitful emotion for the naturalist: a fierce hatred for all that has given him pain." (Was Quentin Compson's pained exclamation at the end of *Absalom, Absalom!* (1936), "*I dont hate it! I dont hate it!*," also a response to Lewisohn?)

Even scholar and critic Alfred Kazin's influential interpretation of modern American prose literature, *On Native Grounds* (1942), which devotes more than ten pages to Faulkner, still concludes with the assessment that "Faulkner's corn-fed, tobacco-drooling phantoms are not the constituents of a representative American epic" and that "no writer ever made so much of his failure." Reviewing *Go Down, Moses* in the *Nation* in the same year, Lionel Trilling took a more positive stance toward the book's Southern and racial themes, yet viewed Faulkner's "literary mannerisms" as "faults," found Faulkner's "reliance on the method of memory" "tiresome," his prose "irritating," and complained generally:

> while I am sure that prose fiction may make great demands on our attention, it ought not to make these demands arbitrarily, and there is no reason why Mr. Faulkner cannot settle to whom the pronoun "he" refers. Mr. Faulkner's new book is worth effort but not, I think, the kind of effort which I found necessary: I had to read it twice to get clear not only the finer shades of meaning but the simple primary intentions, and I had to construct an elaborate genealogical table to understand the family connections.

By 1944, virtually all of Faulkner's seventeen books had slipped out of print.

At the beginning of the period, then, modern art seemed like a strange European invention, modern music and jazz had subcultural or popular, not national or artistic, significance, and the best modernist literature had not found many sympathetic readers. American intellectuals could believe that modern art was not art, that modern music was not music or merely entertainment, and that even the best modernist literature was simply an elaborately disguised failure. And on the level of "middlebrow readers" – a newly popular term located between the "highbrow" and "lowbrow" of critic Van Wyck Brooks's *America's Coming of Age* (1915) – the *Saturday Evening Post* expressed its hostility to modern art as alien to America in countless articles, often with the reassuringly homey realism of Norman Rockwell's cover art. It was also the *Saturday Evening Post* which serialized Mussolini's autobiography, a text ghostwritten by the anti-immigration and pro-deportation writer Richard Washburn Child, who had been US ambassador to Italy during the fascist march on Rome in 1922.

By the mid-century, agencies of the U.S. Government proudly adopted abstract art, modern jazz, and the 1950 Nobel Prize winner William Faulkner (his works now partly available in Malcolm Cowley's thematically organized *Portable Faulkner* edition – with genealogies and a map) as true expressions of the American spirit that could be officially endorsed for export around the globe. The fact that the remaining American opposition was shrilly xenophobic and right-wing only enhanced the development. Representative is a 1949 diatribe by Republican Congressman George A. Dondero from Michigan, who worried about the "intolerable situation" that "public schools, colleges, and universities . . . , invaded by a horde of foreign art manglers, are selling to our young men and women a subversive doctrine of "isms." Dondero proclaimed in a thirty-minute address to Congress on August 16, 1949:

> All these isms are of foreign origin, and truly should have no place in American art. While not all are media of social or political protest, all are instruments and weapons of destruction . . . .
> Cubism aims to destroy by designed disorder.

Futurism aims to destroy by the machine myth . . . .
Dadaism aims to destroy by ridicule.
Expressionism aims to destroy by aping the primitive and insane . . . .
Abstractionism aims to destroy by the creation of brainstorms.
Surrealism aims to destroy by the denial of reason . . . .
The artists of the "isms" change their designation as often and as readily as the Communist front organizations. Picasso, who is also a Dadaist, an abstractionist, or a surrealist, as unstable fancy dictates, is the hero of all the crackpots in so-called modern art. . . . But no matter what others call Picasso, he said of himself: "I am a Communist, and my painting is Communist painting."

One of Dondero's deepest worries was that Kurt Seligmann, a Swiss surrealist, had been named as artistic judge by the Hallmark Christmas Card Company of Kansas City to determine the winner in their $30,000 contest. What danger this represented to Christmas in America was obvious to Dondero, for surrealism "holds that our cultural heritage of religion is an obstacle to be overcome." Even Dondero had to concede, however, that "quite a few" sincere individuals now believed that "so-called modern or contemporary art cannot be Communist because art in Russia today is realistic."

Unfortunately for Dondero, President Dwight D. Eisenhower turned out to be one of those individuals, for on the occasion of the twenty-fifth anniversary of the Museum of Modern Art on February 19, 1954, he sent his "warm greetings" – tape-recorded – to all the museum's associates and friends. In this presidential message, which was played to the 2,500 assembled guests, Eisenhower called the MoMA a "great museum," stressed what he called the "important principle" that "freedom of the arts is a basic freedom, one of the pillars of liberty in our land," and said: "For our Republic to stay free, those among us with the rare gift of artistry must be able freely to use their talent." Equally important was that "our people must have unimpaired opportunity to see, to understand, to profit from our artists' work." He continued that "as long as artists are at liberty to feel with high personal intensity, as long as our artists are able to create with sincerity and conviction, there will be healthy controversy and progress in art. Only thus can there be opportunity for a genius to conceive and to produce a masterpiece for all mankind." Though General Eisenhower's own aesthetic sensibility was probably closer to Roosevelt's than their different assessments of modernism might suggest, Ike endorsed modern art as part of a Cold War logic, for such praise helped the anticommunist objective of chastising the way in which modern art was either attacked by state propaganda or banned outright under totalitarian tyranny, the artists imprisoned or persecuted. "When artists are made the slaves and the tools of the state," he argued, "when artists become chief propagandists of a cause, progress is arrested and creation and genius are destroyed." The president ended his greetings with a momentous resolution: "Let us resolve that this precious freedom of the arts, these precious freedoms of America, will, day by day, year by year, become ever stronger, ever brighter in our land."

The *New York Times* described the event, at which such other speakers as New York's mayor and the secretary general of the United Nations also made addresses, under the headline "Eisenhower Links Art and Freedom." Dondero, however, simply could not understand Eisenhower's statements, and saw threatened his life-long goal to "protect and preserve legitimate art as we have always known it in the United States."

Dondero notwithstanding, in the war and postwar years the tide was clearly turning toward an official acceptance of modernism. The American pavilion at the Biennale became more and more modernist each time, starting in 1948; and it began to include photographic art by Ben Shahn, Charles Sheeler, and Diane Arbus in its exhibits. On January 23, 1943, Duke Ellington's ambitious *Black, Brown, and Beige: A Tone Parallel to the History of the American Negro* opened at Carnegie Hall (presented as a benefit for Russian War Relief); and in 1956, the State Department (not being able to afford Louis Armstrong) sent Dizzy Gillespie on a tour of the Near and Middle East. Gillespie was only one of several jazz musicians who went on official government-sponsored tours to many countries, including ultimately the Soviet Union. (It would be hard to imagine Jelly Roll Morton on a Woodrow Wilson-sponsored tour abroad.) The officially financed Congress for Cultural Freedom promoted modern literature, art, and music in opposition to totalitarianism; at its Paris meeting in 1951 music by Arnold Schönberg was performed, and Jean Cocteau designed the stage set for a production of *Oedipus Rex* that was conducted by Igor Stravinsky.

College generation after generation was now being raised on modernism in literature and the arts (Dondero was right at least in this respect). In 1962, Warner Brothers released the animated musical feature film *Gay Purr-ee* in which "Mewsette," a cat with Judy Garland's voice, encounters all versions of modernist art in Paris, from Van Gogh to Buffet, remarkably designed by Victor Haboush; among the film's memorable song lines is "The chestnut, the willow, the colors of Utrillo." In the same year, even Norman Rockwell painted a modernist canvas for a *Saturday Evening Post* cover (January 13) entitled *The Connoisseur*. The large Jackson Pollock-inspired painting in which abstract colors explode dramatically fills two thirds of the image, but it is presented to the viewer behind (and partly obscured by) a realistically rendered, balding, conservatively dressed and professorial-seeming gentleman, whose creased gray trousers, white hat, black umbrella and shoes form a bland antithesis to the painting; he appears more skeptical observer than connoisseur. He also seems like an allegory of the professoriate's relationship to modernist art.

The United States was an intricate part of the development in the course of which modernism emerged as the dominant art form of the twentieth century. In fact, the U.S. became virtually identified with the culture of modernism by mid-century so that modernism now appeared as American as apple pie, the culture of modernism as an American "homemade world," and modern art as "the great American thing." The newly claimed and rapidly disseminated modernist American spirit received a literary genealogy that included proto-modernists like Herman Melville (rediscovered after 1919), among whose early advocates was the modern photographer and jazz supporter Carl Van Vechten. Edmund Wilson stressed, in *Axel's Castle* (1931), Edgar Allan Poe's significance as a "prophet of [French] symbolism." The important nineteenth-century poets were Walt Whitman and Emily Dickinson (in the newly restored unregularized edition published from 1951 to 1955) while Whittier, Longfellow, and Lowell moved into the distant background. The wish to view American culture as the prototypical modern one was pervasive by the 1950s. Thus the art critic Harold Rosenberg surprisingly cast the French pointillists in a tradition of American popular lithographs when he wrote: "I have seen enlarged details of [Currier and Ives's] New York scenes that are a match for Seurat." However forced it seems in retrospect, the connection may have appeared natural enough at the moment.

The change in canonization and the new emphasis on American modernism coincided with the growing international reception of U.S. authors. In 1910, American literature was still of marginal significance outside of the borders of the United States. More American publishers were engaged in disseminating British authors than European houses were in reprinting the Americans. American literary culture lived from importing, not exporting, works. After World War II, however, this changed remarkably – so much so that later in the twentieth century U.S. cultural products were second only to the weapons industry in achieving an export surplus, as the American entertainment industry had become a supplier of the whole world. From 1910 to 1950, the United States shifted from a country of consumers of European culture – "gondola guzzlers," as David Quixano, the hero of Israel Zangwill's play *The Melting-Pot* (1908), put it disparagingly – to a near-universal global "content provider" for all media, old and new.

This development went hand in hand with the dramatic changes brought about by new technological inventions like modern print techniques, records, sound movies, radio, and at the end of the period, television, all of which sim-plified dissemination and export. These inventions, and the continuing proc-esses of urbanization, industrialization, secularization, and migration, are often viewed as aspects of "modernism." In order to differentiate the sociological and technological developments from aesthetic movements, it may be helpful, however, to refer to the former as "modernity" and only the latter as modernism.

The changes from 1910 to 1950 coincided with a growing commercialization of literary production and publishing as part of a larger "entertainment industry," and with an unheard-of expansion of consumer culture. It was a development that changed the publication of literary texts dramatically by new features: there were tie-ins with film releases (e.g. the publishing of Anzia Yezierska's *Salome of the Tenements* on Thanksgiving Day 1922, when the moving picture based on her novel *Hungry Hearts* was also released), blanketing advertising campaigns for creating best-sellers (e.g. Claude McKay's *Home to Harlem* in 1928), and the presentation of authors as "celebrities" among the rich and famous. F. Scott Fitzgerald contributed an essay on the pressing question of "How to Live on $36,000 a year" to the *Saturday Evening Post* in 1924; and Hemingway's mythical biographical persona became the embodiment of an American author of world-wide fame.

At the beginning of the century, ads began to interrupt serialized fiction in publications like Edward Bok's *Ladies' Home Journal*. After the middle of the century, the culture critic Paul Goodman suggested that television programming should properly be viewed as the interruption of commercials. George Horace Lorimer, the editor of the *Saturday Evening Post*, early on presented positively conceived images of the "businessman" and fought hard for expanding advertisements. Later he managed to choose appropriate content to accompany and reinforce advertising messages. By the mid-1920s, the *Post* contained more advertising than editorial matter (the back page alone selling for 15,000 dollars) and reached 10 million readers and consumers. The development from a literary editor who sought business as a theme to a commercial entrepreneur who paid for content to accompany a journal's advertisements was well under way. In 1939 the then-Trotskyite *Partisan Review* sent out a questionnaire to writers – among them James Agee, who incorporated it into *Let Us Now Praise Famous Men* – that included a question concerning the "corruption of the literary supplements by advertising" making difficult fair reviews of books.

The very existence of competitive advertising signaled the presence of large, otherwise untapped, readerships that could be reached, at least temporarily, through the organs that proliferated in the period. In 1920, John Dewey sensed that there was an enormous populace that was "constantly in transit," hence neither nationally American nor locally anchored and ideally suited as the readership for organs like the *Saturday Evening Post*:

They are just what they are – passengers. Hence the S---- E---- P---- and other journals expressly designed for this intermediate state of existence. . . . What becomes of all these periodicals? The man who answered this question would be the final authority on literature in America. Pending investigation, my hypothesis is that the brakeman, the Pullman porter, and those who clean out the street-cars inherit them.

The radical leftist Mike Gold called the *Saturday Evening Post* more vividly a "filthy lackey rag," and in 1924 he found in the journal's pages "hired romanticists; hired liars about life; high salaried thimble-riggers, flim-flam men and circus fakers; Rolls Royce captains of fictional industry; sob sisters," – an industrially produced and ever-expanding mass culture that was aesthetically and politically below contempt.

The dramatic changes in the first half of the century were greatly enhanced by the two big wars in both of which the United States played a decisive role; the country asserted its military strength in World War I and its technological leadership by the first use of two nuclear bombs in World War II. The 1945 nuclear bombings of Hiroshima and Nagasaki were to remain the only two military uses of this quintessentially twentieth-century weapon, its only application in the "nuclear age" of the last century. The two World Wars made the period from 1910 to 1950 one of the most violent times in human history, claiming a total of at least 65 million human lives. Amidst all this violence, no battle or military action took place in the continental United States. However, partly as a consequence of the two World Wars, the U.S. moved from the periphery to the center of the world stage. Starting out as a minor player and debtor nation, it became one of the great world powers and creditor countries in the course of the first half of the century.

❦

African Americans, European immigrants, and members of other minority groups were, *as* immigrants and ethnics, part of modernity, as they lived through experiences of migration, ethnic identification, and often, alienation. In many ways, they also participated in, and significantly advanced, the course of modernism in the United States; Afro-American artists, including Fletcher Henderson, Louis Armstrong, Duke Ellington, and Charlie Parker, were central to the development of the new American music; modern composers Arnold Schönberg and Kurt Weill escaped to America from fascist Europe; immigrant and émigré artists like Joseph Stella, Max Weber, Ben Shahn, Man Ray, and Marcel Duchamp helped to establish modernist art; European exiles like Josef Albers were prominently active in such institutions as Black Mountain College while Hans Hoffmann taught the principles of modernist art and "abstract expressionism" in New York. Important modern art collectors and curators like Leo Stein, Etta Cone, Juliana Force, or Peggy Guggenheim were the children or grandchildren of immigrants.

Works of American "ethnic" prose literature, written by, about, or for persons who perceived themselves, or were perceived by others, as members of ethnic groups, are the central subject of these pages. Ethnic autobiographies, novels, short stories, and nonfiction works participated in the development of an American literary modernism that would carry the day only after World War II. The reception of some of these works resembled that of modernist art and literature in general. Jean Toomer's experimental book *Cane* (1923), a landmark of modernism, sold but a few hundred copies in the 1920s and then disappeared from view, only to reemerge as a Harper "perennial classic" in the 1960s and a mass-market Norton paperback since the 1970s; Henry Roth's novel *Call It Sleep* (1934) reached a couple of thousand readers in the 1930s, vanished, and reappeared as an Avon mass-market paperback in the 1960s, followed by a Farrar, Straus, and Giroux reprint. Both Toomer and Roth received positive *New York Times Book Review* coverage when they were reprinted, a rare occasion in an influential organ in which reprints are infrequently reviewed.

While ethnic writers may have felt at home in modernism, they were not always equally at home in America – only in the utopian notion of what the country might become. In an age of racial definitions of U.S. citizenship, racist immigration restrictions, and eugenicist thought, ethnic writers often invoked America as an ideal, while the real United States was not yet claiming diversity in the spirit of multicultural pride that was to prevail only later. For the United States had yet to be reimagined as the "nation of nations" (that Walt Whitman had first proclaimed) rather than as England's stepchild.

The cultural work of recasting the United States as a multiethnic country was undertaken by American ethnic writers in the period, who like Abraham Cahan or Jessie Fauset were often fluent in other languages and well versed in international debates about cosmopolitanism and art. American ethnic writers were increasingly drawn to ethnic pluralism or at least to a broader definition of the American "host culture" to which immigrants and minorities were to be "assimilated." Like the Russian-born Mary Antin or the Slovenian-American Louis Adamic, they may not have been in the forefront of aesthetic modernism, but they fought for a redefinition of America in the first half of the century though their vision took firmer public hold only in the second. Waldo Frank's manifesto *Our America* (1919) attempted to articulate the literary consequences of the new view of America when he demanded that American writers "study the cultures of the German, the Latin, the Celt, the Slav, the Anglo-Saxon and the African on the American continent: plot their reactions one upon the other, and their disappearance as integral worlds." For Frank, Whitman doubled as the prophet of aesthetic modernism and of a multicultural view of America. Whitman's view of the United States as "nation of nations" was admired and echoed by many twentieth-century authors, as was his observation: "Thus far, impress'd by New England writers and schoolmasters, we tacitly abandon ourselves to the notion that our United States have been fashion'd from the British Islands only – which is a very great mistake." Ethnic writers tended to share Whitman's worry that Americans had not yet learned that their own antecedents were "ampler than has been supposed" and included many points of origin. (These intellectuals were less easily prepared to endorse Whitman's sentiment that English was "the dialect of common sense . . . , the chosen tongue to express growth faith self-esteem freedom justice equality friendliness amplitude prudence decision and courage." And they were probably unaware of Whitman's opposition to racial amalgamation – "Nature has set an impassable seal against it" – in an 1858 *Brooklyn Daily Times* editorial, followed by Whitman's rhetorical question, "Besides, is not America for the Whites? And is it not better so?")

The period from 1910 to 1950 provided the United States with a new vocabulary that was needed for the multiethnic reimagining of the country – as well as for naming the fearful opposite of that vision. The radical New York critic Randolph Bourne was the first to advocate a "Trans-National America" in a 1916 landmark essay. Walter Lippmann gave currency to the term "stereotype" in 1922, a word that assumed a more sinister meaning in the 1930s and 1940s. In 1924 the phrasing "cultural pluralism" was coined by the immigrant philosopher and William James's student Horace M. Kallen, in opposition to the dominant ideology of ethnic assimilation; the significance of Kallen's coinage became palpable only decades later when it was more widely adopted. The word "ethnicity," which had been obsolete since the eighteenth century, was self-consciously revitalized by the anthropologist W. Lloyd Warner in 1941, at a time at which "race" had assumed too many charged connotations by its fascist use; and this usage also "took" only after the 1960s. The word "multicultural" was launched by Edward F. Haskell's little-known *Lance: A Novel about Multicultural Men* (1941). This American novel by an author who was the son of missionaries introduced the adjective "multicultural" to describe the pioneering quality of a few exceptional men who, in the modern age of transportation and communication, transcend the confines of individual nation states, of one language, or of a single religion. The term "identity," omnipresent later in connection with the words "ethnic" and "national," goes back only to the immigrant psychologist Erik Erikson's attempt in *Childhood and Society* (1950) at offering a shortened English formula for Sigmund Freud's notion of "the secret familiarity of identical psychological construction," a notion Freud used to describe his sense of Jewishness that was not based on religious faith, national pride, or race.

It was this vocabulary which helped multiculturalism flourish by the end of the century. The terms began to circulate more widely as they provided an alternative to "racism," "totalitarianism," and "genocide." At first a positive term launched by fascists to describe the importance they assigned to race, the word "racism" came into general use only in the 1930s, and it acquired its pejorative sense when it became the central term to express intellectual critiques of fascism. Magnus Hirschfeld's still remarkable antifascist book, *Racism* (1938), marked the turning point. The same is true for "totalitarianism" which was launched in English in Luigi Sturzo's *Italy and Fascismo* (1926) and assumed its negative meaning only slowly, with Hannah Arendt's *Origins of Totalitarianism* (1951) marking the final point. "Genocide" was another English neologism introduced in a book by Polish scholar and attorney Raphaël Lemkin, entitled *Axis Rule in Occupied Europe* (1944). Lemkin coined the word by combining Greek *genos* (race, tribe) and Latin *cide* (killing), in analogy to tyrannicide or homicide, and suggested *ethnocide* as a synonym. Lemkin studied the new, eliminationist Nazi occupation policies (most especially, toward Jews, but also toward many other national groups in occupied countries) and found that these measures were genocidal because they intended to destroy "the essential foundations of the life of national groups, with the aim of annihilating the groups themselves." Lemkin's coinage was disseminated more widely when the United Nations adopted the term in a 1945 indictment of Nazi leaders for having "conducted deliberate and systematic genocide – namely, the extermination of racial and national groups."

This newly coined twentieth-century vocabulary reflected, and helped to shape, a new emphasis on ethnic identity and on cultural pluralism in modern democratic societies, which were, after World War II and the Holocaust, more unambiguously defined against the fascist trajectory from racist stereotype to genocide.

The ascent of aesthetic modernism, the expansion and dominance of commercialism and mass culture, the growing international importance of the United States in a very violent period of world history, and the changing ethnic and developing multicultural definition of "America" mark a dramatic transformation, and American literature participated in these developments.

The remaining question is what made such enormous changes possible. The attempt to address it, at least in its cultural components, will take us to the cultural policies of the great ideological challenges to bourgeois democracy that were active in the twentieth century – communism and fascism. It will take us to the complicated negotiations of ethnic and national identities at the peak of the assertion of the power of nation states to assimilate, to ignore, to mistreat, or to exclude, its minorities. And it will take us to a variety of works of American literature – a small number of them read very closely – in which the tensions of ethnicity, modernity, and modernism are present, and are often central.

GERTRUDE STEIN AND
"NEGRO SUNSHINE"

THERE MAY BE no better beginning for the story of ethnic modernism
in American prose literature than the ending of Gertrude Stein's
"Melanctha: Each One as She May." This story, which forms the central
part of *Three Lives*, an important book that was first published in 1909, ends:

But Melanctha Herbert never really killed herself because she was so blue, though
often she thought this would be really the best way for her to do. Melanctha never
killed herself, she only got a bad fever and went into the hospital where they took
good care of her and cured her.
    When Melanctha was very well again, she took a place and began to work and to
live regular. Then Melanctha got very sick again, she began to cough and sweat and
be so weak she could not stand to do her work.
    Melanctha went back to the hospital, and there the Doctor told her that she had
consumption, and before long she would surely die. They sent her where she would
be taken care of, a home for poor consumptives, and there Melanctha stayed until she
died.

FINIS

Readers who are used to nineteenth-century aesthetic conventions – one only
has to think of Little Eva in *Uncle Tom's Cabin* or of Mimi in *La Bohème* – will
be startled by the coldness of this "detached" death scene of Stein's heroine.
No effort is made to draw on the reader's sympathy or to develop the narrative
in a way that would sustain emotional engagement and identification. There
is no protracted agony and suffering, there are no tears of near and dear ones,
and no last words are spoken. Instead, Stein "comforts" the reader with the
information that Melanctha did not commit suicide but "only" got ill; then she
immediately reports that Melanctha got well, refusing to build momentum
toward a death scene. Abruptly, the heroine's one-sentence recuperation gives
way to a relapse that leads to her quick death within two further sentences,
before the reader fully realizes what has happened. The doctor's emphatically
noneuphemistic statement "that she had consumption, and before long she
would surely die" seems inappropriately colloquial; and the simple language

and repetitions in this passage do not create a feeling of familiarity but rather instill a sense of distance from Melanctha in readers. The "FINIS" is not the climactic conclusion to the protracted death struggle of a consumptive heroine, but a sudden interruption of the reading process. In many ways, the understated ending of "Melanctha" marks an end of established narrative conventions and readers' expectations.

This effect is reinforced because the other two stories included in *Three Lives* end similarly. "The Good Anna" leaves the reader with the sentences: "Then they did the operation, and then the good Anna with her strong, strained, worn-out body died." "The Gentle Lena" concludes: "When it was all over Lena had died, too, and nobody knew just how it had happened to her." Stein's *Three Lives* is thus a book about the deaths of three working-class women; and no web of feeling or meaning surrounds the abruptness and finality of death.

Stein's death scenes are not without precedent – but they go well beyond Flaubert's "Un Cœur Simple," a tale Stein translated while she was writing *Three Lives*. Stein's scenes are part of a whole arsenal of modern strategies that she employs and that make her stand out among her contemporaries Willa Cather, Theodore Dreiser, and Jack London. Such strategies also separated *Three Lives* from the format of the ethnic life story and from Stein's earlier autobiographically inspired materials (nobody dies in the popular ethnic life stories of the period or in Stein's earlier *Q.E.D.; or, Things as They Are*), making way for a new, unforgettable, and also cold and rather reader-unfriendly style. The themes of searching for love, of triangles, and of jealousy are rendered no more engagingly than are the death scenes. This is a typical passage about Dr. Jeff Campbell who finds out that Melanctha is unfaithful:

Now Jeff began to have always a strong feeling that Melanctha could no longer stand it, with all her bad suffering, to let him fight out with himself what was right for him to be doing. Now he felt he must not, when she was there with him, keep on, with this kind of fighting that was always going on inside him. Jeff Campbell never knew yet, what he thought was the right way, for himself and for all the colored people to be living. Jeff was coming always each time closer to be really understanding, but now Melanctha was so bad in her suffering with him, that he knew she could not any longer have him with her while he was always showing that he never really yet was sure what it was, the right way, for them to be really loving.

The features of Stein's literary style include a strange predilection for the unexpected and the enigmatic use of the word "always," which is also among the most popular words, appearing a total of 745 times in "Melanctha" alone, and, in general relentless repetitions of a relatively simple vocabulary, the pervasive -ing form and the dependent adverbial clause, a meandering narration, and no attempt at differentiating distinct voices so that narrator, characters, and even the letters they write all sound alike, assuming a stylized or stilted, self-conscious, pseudo-colloquial voice. When the narrator asks, "What was it that now really happened to them?" this is not the pleasant intervention of an omniscient narrator who addresses the reader in the way in which Harriet Beecher Stowe would have asked rhetorical questions such as "Who is to blame?" For Stowe, the obvious answer ("You, sir!") could be given by any reader. Stein's interventions raise real questions, and simple though they may seem, they tend to be unanswerable.

There are some minimalist sentences; descriptive "literary" adjectives are usually avoided in favor of flat, "childlike," nonspecific yet strangely evaluative ones (like "good" or "fine"); and there are also long and sprawling sentences generated by repetitions and variations in which the reader desperately tries to recognize a pattern. But the sentences are the essential element of Stein's prose, as she herself put it in *The Autobiography of Alice B. Toklas* (1933): "Sentences not only words but sentences and always sentences have been Gertrude Stein's life long passion." The text of *Three Lives* interrupts, it disturbs, it thwarts expectations; Stein's writing is formal and calls attention to itself. The deadpan, detached narrator avoids grand emotions and all feelings – except maybe those generated by the composition itself.

Form was becoming the central theme of a work of prose fiction. And it would remain the central theme of work after work Stein produced, culminating early in her massive "novel" *The Making of Americans* (finished by 1911 and published in 1925), in which the meandering narration that was present in *Three Lives* takes on a new proportion because of the epic possibilities of variation and repetition. When, in *The Making of Americans*, Stein makes observations about repetition, she articulates even these observations repetitively: "Repeating is the whole of living and by repeating comes understanding, and understanding is to some the most important part of living. Repeating is the whole of living, and it makes of living a thing always more familiar to each one and so we have old men's and women's wisdom, and repeating, simple repeating is the whole of them." And so forth. Carl Van Doren assessed *The Making of Americans* in 1940: "Often praised, this huge novel has seldom been read, nor will it ever be except by enthusiasts who tolerate its tedious, mannered repetitions because of the pleasure they take in the delicate and intricate variety of its sentences." Edmund Wilson voiced a similar sentiment in a famous quip on *The Making of Americans*: "I confess that I have not read this book all through, and I do not know whether it is possible to do so."

It is doubtful that any reader has imagined that being stranded on an island with only a set of Stein's complete works would be an unambiguously exciting and pleasant experience. It is hardly surprising that Stein never became a popular author – excepting only her somewhat more conciliatory *Autobiography of Alice B. Toklas* in which Stein states disarmingly that the newspapers "always say ... that my writing is appalling but they always quote it and what is more, they quote it correctly, and those they say they admire they do not quote." No wonder that Stein "did not believe that anyone could read anything she wrote and be interested." Yet with her strange sense of humor, she continued to contribute to the creation of herself as the enigmatic mother of all American modernists. When Harold Loeb, the editor of the little magazine *Broom*, asked her for something that was as fine as "Melanctha," she sent him a piece entitled "As Fine as Melanctha" (1923).

How did Stein arrive at her experimental mode, in which losing the general reader was part of the program? Perhaps it was merely a matter of Stein's temper, character, and of her willful idiosyncrasies. Yet her appeal to other writers suggests that it was also the result of other historical and cultural factors that were related to the rise of modernism.

Central was the field of modern psychology and its interest in unconscious processes. As a student at the Harvard Annex, later Radcliffe College, Stein participated in Hugo Münsterberg's experiments in automatism, and her very first publication was an essay on the topic of automatic writing. Undertaken jointly with Leon M. Solomons, this study of "Normal Motor Automatism" for the *Harvard Psychological Laboratory* of 1896 describes various experiments in producing automatic writing. To stimulate it, Stein and Solomons note, "dialect stories do not go well at all." Among the observations they made were the following: "Miss Stein found it sufficient distraction often to simply read what her arm wrote, but following three or four words behind her pencil." And: "The stuff written was grammatical, and the words and phrases fitted together right, but there was not much connected thought." The specimen sentences Stein and Solomons cite include "When he could not be the longest and thus to be, and thus to be, the strongest" and "This long time when he did this best time, and he could thus have been bound, and in this long time, when he could be this to first use of this long time ...." "It is very interesting to read," Stein writes of this early essay in retrospect, "because the method of writing to be afterwards developed in Three Lives and Making of Americans already shows itself." She ascribed her interest in representing unconscious processes to her psychological training and to her work with William James who had coined the term "stream of thought" in his *Principles of Psychology* (1890), who called for an examination of the "hidden self," and who claimed that a "*comparative study of trances and sub-conscious states* is ... of the most urgent importance for the comprehension of our nature." In the section entitled "The Stream of Consciousness" that forms part of James's *Talk to Teachers on Psychology: and to Students on Some of Life's Ideals* (1905), he further called attention to the "succession of states, or waves, or fields . . . of knowledge, of feeling, of desire, of deliberation, etc., that constantly pass and repass, and that constitute our inner life" and found the process by which one state "dissolves into another" often very gradual.

Stein represented the unconscious in the nonlinear and repetitious forms in which it seemed to articulate itself. In this sense Stein's modernism can also be seen as an extension of psychological realism. "Henry James in his later writing had had a dim feeling that this was what he knew he should do," as Stein put it. From the point of view of modern psychology, realism was somewhat incomplete. Realism did not represent the characters' meandering thought processes accurately; and modern prose writers wished to correct that (as did the dramatists around the Provincetown Playhouse).

American realism often understated the importance – or at least ignored some physical details – of sexuality in literary representation, and some modernists set out to correct that emphatically. Frankness in sexual matters was, of course, one reason why modern novels from *Ulysses* (1922) and D. H. Lawrence's *Lady Chatterley's Lover* (1928) to William Burroughs's *Naked Lunch* (1959) had difficulties with censors and government agencies, which suspected such books of being pornographic. However, if Stein was one of these modern authors, her unique style probably did little to stimulate, even among suspicious censors, pornographic readings of such sentences as "Feeling or for it, as feeling or for it, came in or come in, or come out of there or feeling as feeling or feeling as for it," written in her "erotic" work *As a Wife Has a Cow: A Love Story* (1926).

Stein did not produce automatic writing in the Harvard psychology experiments or in her later literary output, as she stressed in *Everybody's Autobiography* (1937). Stein stylized very consciously, whether she was writing about thought processes or attempting dialogue in fiction, whether the genre was poetry, drama, opera, or public lecturing. In her prose writings she avoided the conventional distinction of narrator and character and the differentiation between characters, not just in the name of a higher realism but in the name of a new and unmistakable style. It was this intimidating and forbidding "Steinian" style that put off even friends and supporters who had a well-established interest in unconscious processes. Thus William James apologized to his former student Gertrude Stein for never having finished reading *Three Lives*. He wrote her that it was the kind of book about which one says to oneself, "I will go at it carefully when just the right mood comes." He added, "But apparently the right mood never came."

If modern psychology was one element in Stein's literary experimentation, then the development of modernist painting at the beginning of the century formed another important inspiration. As the children of a well-to-do businessman who had invested in the booming streetcar business in Oakland, Gertrude Stein and her brother Leo became art collectors, connected with Bernard Berenson and Daniel-Henry Kahnweiler. In Paris Stein was part of the circle of most illustrious modern artists. She sat for famous Picasso and Francis Picabia portraits and for Jacques Lipchitz and Jo Davidson sculptures, she knew Matisse and Cézanne well, and Juan Gris illustrated her *As a Wife Has a Cow*. She introduced Matisse and Picasso to American audiences in articles for Alfred Stieglitz's *Camera Work* (in 1912, one year before the Armory Show). The guest list of visitors to the apartment she shared with Alice B. Toklas at 27, rue de Fleurus in Paris resembles a dictionary of modern art. Although she included the ironic disclaimer in *The Autobiography of Alice B. Toklas* that she "was not at any time interested in african sculpture," she witnessed, and participated in, the interest in African masks and the beginnings of cubism. The art collector Etta Cone typed a manuscript of *Three Lives*. The list goes on. It is thus helpful to regard Stein as a writer among visual artists, and to see her style in connection with movements from cubism to fauvism. Mabel Dodge, who ran a radical salon off Eighth Street in Greenwich Village attended by Emma Goldman, Mike Gold, and Jean Toomer at various times, commented in 1913 that "in a large studio in Paris, hung with paintings by Renoir, Matisse and Picasso, Gertrude Stein is doing with words what Picasso is doing with paint. She is impelling language to induce new states of consciousness, and in doing so language becomes with her a creative art rather than a mirror of history." And a review of *Three Lives* for the *Philadelphia Public Ledger*, entitled "A Futurist Novel," found that "the blur which this futurist in writing at first creates cannot be cleared until we are willing to bring the thought and intelligence to its interpretation which we needed when examining *The Nude Descending the Stairs*." The analogy to visual modernism is all the more justified since modern artists may have played down the continuities that linked their work to a long tradition of ornamental and decorative art which was generally nonrepresentational, tended to suggest flatness rather than depth, and practiced repetition to the point of serial appearance – qualities that were present in modern paintings as they were in Stein's writing.

Stein also took a strong interest in modern photography, and she kept in touch with Stieglitz and Man Ray. In *Lectures in America* (1935), she also compared her method of repetition with variation to the language of film. "In a cinema picture no two pictures are exactly alike each one is just that much different from the one before." This analogy, phrased in a sentence that provides a formal equivalent for its statement, is all the more interesting since Stein's one-time mentor Hugo Münsterberg also became one of the pioneers of film theory with his book, *The Photoplay* (1915).

Similarly, though not as deeply, Stein was connected with modern music. She commented on the aesthetic effect of Richard Strauss's *Electra*; and she collaborated with Virgil Thomson on the opera *Four Saints in Three Acts*, produced by an organization called "The Friends and Enemies of Modern Music" in 1934, with an all-black cast, tan-faced and in cellophane costumes. "There is a Difference Between Steinse and Nonsteinse," the *New York Times* subtitled its review of the Hartford opening, adding, "What Difference." And the article points out that Stein "apparently uses words for sound instead of meaning." The *sounds* of Stein's words do matter, and the principles of repetition and variation resemble fugues or the musical leitmotif technique, even in texts that are not librettos. Stein also described jazz bands, in *Lectures in America*, as engaged in the difference between the thing seen and the thing felt that causes nervousness in the theatre: "Jazz bands made of this thing an end in itself. They made of this different tempo a something that was nothing but a difference in tempo between anybody and everybody including all those doing it and all those hearing and seeing it."

Stein was attracted to the developments of modern psychology, art, photography, film, and music because she liked to adopt a simple and direct literary voice that was "objective" rather than confessional. This aspect of her work becomes clearer when one compares *Three Lives* with its more straightforwardly autobiographical precursor book *Q.E.D.*, an early and still somewhat confessional work (written in 1903 and published posthumously) which centers on a love triangle among women. Stein's own projection figure is Adele who loves the unfaithful Helen. Interestingly, some of the exact wording was adopted by Stein for "Melanctha," only that the theme of same-sex love relations among white women became predominantly heterosexual and black, with Stein's voice turning into Jeff Campbell's, and Helen's into Melanctha's. But in the process of sexual and ethnic transformation, confession gives way to principles of composition, as the style changes and becomes more experimental and Steinian. Stein's modernist language may thus also have been a mask, a protection against emotional vulnerability, or at the very least an objectification and stylization of the memory of a painful experience. The ethnic mask seemed particularly suited to deflect from the confessional.

❦

No matter how idiosyncratic and difficult it was, Stein's writing – together with Joyce's, Eliot's, Ezra Pound's, and Virginia Woolf's – set a standard to which many twentieth-century English-language writers aspired and against which they measured themselves and each other. Stein's particular emphasis on the sentence as the most important unit of even long works of prose inspired many authors. Once the modernist style existed as a new code of literary representation, it constituted a challenge to modern writers. Especially after World War I, which signaled the violent end of an era, more and more writers tried to live up to that challenge. It is poetically just that it was Stein who coined the phrase "Lost Generation," brought into wide circulation as the famous epigraph to Ernest Hemingway's novel, *The Sun Also Rises* (1926): "'You are all a lost generation.' – GERTRUDE STEIN *in conversation*." Two and a half decades later, Delmore Schwartz wrote in "The Grapes of Crisis" (1951) that victory in World War II was supposed to bring about the end of all totalitarian regimes: "'We are all the last generation,' Adolf Hitler might have remarked to Gertrude Stein or Pablo Picasso in Paris in May, 1940." And a decade and a half after Stein's death, the City Lights Books editors of the *Beatitude Anthology* (1960) ascribed to Stein, tongue-in-cheek, the statement: "'You are all a Beat Generation.' – Gertrude Stein in conversation with Jack Kerouac." Stein's influence on writers like Sherwood Anderson is well known. And William Faulkner could have won a Stein-sound-alike competition with sentences like the following from *Absalom, Absalom!* (1936):

All of a sudden he discovered, not what he wanted to do but what he just had to do, had to do whether he wanted to or not, because if he did not do it he knew that he could never live with himself for the rest of his life, never live with what all the men and women that had died to make him had left inside of him for him to pass on, with all the dead ones waiting and watching to see if he was going to do it right, fix things right so that he would be able to look in the face not only of the old dead ones but all the living ones that would come after him when he would be one of the dead.

(That novel also contains what is probably the longest single sentence in a twentieth-century American novel.)

Of course, modern writers took many paths toward modernism. In Claude McKay's *Home to Harlem* (1928), for example, Ray, the Haitian-born protagonist and counterpart to African American Jake, explains how "the great mass carnage in Europe and the great mass revolution in Russia" had given him the sense of having lived through "the end of an era" and how he felt that this experience required new "dreams of patterns of words achieving form." He mentions Joyce, Sherwood Anderson, D. H. Lawrence, and Henri Barbusse, and he observes that "only the Russians of the late era seemed to stand up like giants in the new. Gogol, Dostoievski, Tolstoy, Chekhov, Turgeniev." But he does not refer to Gertrude Stein in his quest for literary models that would offer a formal equivalent to the experience of World War I. Stein was, after all, only one model of the pervasive trend toward modernism.

The literary modernism of Stein's *Three Lives* developed a specific focus on ethnicity. The book's heroines are not only working-class, but also ethnically marked. Lena and Anna are German American, and Melanctha is mixed-race African American. Stein's family had German American household help, and she stressed in *The Autobiography of Alice B. Toklas* that her interest in blacks originated when she was at Johns Hopkins Medical School. "It was then that she had to take her turn in the delivering of babies and it was at that time that she noticed the negroes and the places that she afterwards used in the second of the Three Lives stories, Melanctha Herbert, the story that was the beginning of her revolutionary work."

Stein's merging of modernist style and ethnic subject matter was what made her writing particularly relevant to American ethnic authors who had specific reasons to go beyond realism and who felt that Stein's dismantling of the "old" was a freeing experience. The realistic mode of narration had included conventions (such as local color dialect writing) and tags that were often negatively charged ethnic stereotypes – and compared to that legacy, Stein's writing seemed perhaps not "realistic" in the sense of the dominant nineteenth-century aesthetic but "convincing" and "truthful," worthy to be upheld as a model and to be adopted, imitated, and varied upon. Strangely enough then, "Melanctha" – which was, as we have seen, the partial result of a transracial projection – came to be perceived as a white American author's particularly humane representation of a black character.

Hutchins Hapgood, whose book *The Spirit of the Ghetto: Studies of the Jewish Quarter of New York* (1902) had established him as an ethnic specialist, read *Three Lives* in manuscript and wrote Stein a genuinely enthusiastic letter, praising the stories for their "reality, truth, unconventionality," and singling out "Melanctha" as "the very best thing on the subject of the Negro that I have ever read." Carl Van Vechten, Stein's close friend, life-long correspondent, and literary executor, who also promoted Harlem Renaissance literature, photographed the most famous black intellectuals of the period, and authored the novel *Nigger Heaven* (1926), claimed that "Melanctha" was "perhaps the first American story in which the negro is regarded . . . not as an object for condescending compassion or derision." This interpretation was indirectly shared even by Wyndham Lewis, the English modernist painter and writer living in Paris, who vehemently opposed populist tendencies in literature. Lewis deplored the "monstrous, desperate soggy *lengths* of primitive mass life" that he sensed in Stein's work, "undoubtedly intended as an epic contribution to the present mass-democracy." "In adopting the simplicity, the illiterateness, of the mass-average of the Melancthas and Annas, Miss Stein gives proof of all the false 'revolutionary' propagandist *plainmanism* of her time." What Van Vechten found admirable in Stein, Lewis considered deplorable; and he diagnosed her prose as cold, "composed of dead and inanimate material."

Stein also had detractors on the left. In *Change the World!* (1936), Mike Gold, the second-generation immigrant author of the book *Jews Without Money* (1930) and advocate of proletarian fiction (who had Americanized his original name Itzok Granich), wrote that Stein's work was "an example of the most extreme subjectivism of the contemporary bourgeois artist, and a reflection of the ideological anarchy into which the whole of bourgeois literature has fallen . . . When one reads her work it appears to resemble the monotonous gibberings of paranoiacs in the private wards of asylums. It appears to be a deliberate irrationality, a deliberate infantilism." Gold claimed that "Stein did not care to communicate because essentially there was nothing to communicate," and he concluded with the strong proclamation that Marxists "see in the work of Gertrude Stein extreme symptoms of the decay of capitalist culture. They view her work as the completed attempt to annihilate all relations between the artist and the society in which he lives . . . The literary idiocy of Gertrude Stein only reflects the madness of the whole system of capitalist values. It is part of the signs of doom that are written largely everywhere on the walls of bourgeois society."

Was Stein an ethnic populist and "plainmanist" who shouted the people's howl and was particularly sensitive to black and immigrant character portrayal, or was she an example of bourgeois decadence and idiocy whose works unwittingly were the writing on the wall that spelled doom for capitalist power relations? Precisely because of the style that so annoyed Mike Gold, many black and white ethnic writers took the former position, and praised Stein for the "populist"-seeming side of her modernism that Wyndham Lewis so detested.

When, after World War II, the African American radical Richard Wright reviewed Stein's *Wars I Have Seen* (1945), he famously defended Stein against Gold's attack. Wright claimed that in order to "gauge the degree to which Miss Stein's prose was tainted with the spirit of counter-revolution" he read "Melanctha" aloud in a Black Belt basement to "a group of semi-literate black stock-yard workers – 'basic proletarians with an instinct for revolution'" (as Wright echoes Gold ironically). And what was the result, according to Wright? "They understood every word. Enthralled, they slapped their thighs, howled, laughed, stomped, and interrupted me constantly to comment upon the

characters. My fondness for Steinian prose never distressed me after that."
Wright thus conferred upon Stein's prose both proletarian and racial credentials. He also held up Stein's "Melanctha" as the best modern prose piece in
the collection *I Wish I Had Written That* (1946) and argued, echoing Van
Vechten, that it was "the first long serious literary treatment of Negro life in
the United States." Wright's love for Stein's "good story, even though slightly
screwy," was based on Stein's language in which he believed he heard his
own grandmother's "deep, pure Negro dialect." "While turning the pages of
'Melanctha,' I suddenly began to *hear* the English *language* for the first time in
my life! . . . English as Negroes spoke it: simple, melodious, tolling, rolling,
rough, infectious, subjective, laughing, cutting." Wright also admired Stein's
What Are Masterpieces (1940); he wrote a blurb for, and reviewed, *Brewsie and
Willie* (1946); and in *American Hunger* (set in galleys in 1945 but published
only posthumously in 1977) Wright described how, under the influence of
Stein's *Three Lives*, he composed such "disconnected sentences for the sheer
love of words" as the following: "The soft melting hunk of butter trickled
in gold down the stringy grooves of the split yam." Or: "The child's clumsy
fingers fumbled in sleep, feeling vainly for the wish of its dream." And: "The
old man huddled in the dark doorway, his bony face lit by the burning yellow
in the window of distant skyscrapers." Stein's and Wright's temperamental
difference is apparent even in the few examples Wright summons to suggest
similarity. Nonetheless, Stein returned Wright's compliments when she said
about his autobiography *Black Boy* (1945): "I do not think there has been
anything like it since I wrote *Three Lives*."

Sounding somewhat like Wright's version of Stein, James T. Farrell's Irish
American trilogy *Studs Lonigan* (completed in 1935) includes sentences like
"He sucked a malted milk through a straw, and watched the soda jerkers
hustle orders amid the noise and clatter of the buzz of the electric malted-
milk shakers." And when Italian American Jerre Mangione returned many
years later to his ethnic neighborhood in Rochester that he had evoked in
Mount Allegro (1942) and found only a 22-acre Coca-Cola bottling plant, he
commented with Stein's proverbial phrasing about Oakland: "When you get
there, there's no there there." In Zora Neale Hurston's *Dust Tracks on a Road:
An Autobiography* (1942), which also contains sentences that resemble Wright's
Stein imitations, the case against racial generalizations is formulated in the
familiar way: "There is no *The Negro* here." Faulkner was not alone in the
occasional wish to sound like Stein; and, for beginning ethnic writers, being
in awe of Stein was so pervasive as to be recognized as a danger. The young
Armenian American writer William Saroyan wrote Stein a virtual fan-letter
on the occasion of Stein's visit to the United States in 1934 in which he stated,

in a Steinian fashion:

Some critics say I have to be careful and not notice the writing of Gertrude Stein but I think they are fooling themselves when they pretend any American writing that is American and is writing is not partly the consequence of the writing of Gertrude Stein and as the saying is they don't seem to know the war is over.

On the strength of the letter, Stein met with Saroyan in San Francisco. Jack Dunphy's little-remembered but very stylishly written Philadelphia Irish American novel *John Fury* (1946) places much emphasis on sentences ("Katie looked down Market Street at the trolley swaying as it came along from side to side like a great happy caterpillar with one round yellow eye"), and each chapter is divided into blocks of prose-poem-like paragraphs in which repetitions and variations are common. When asked about how he came to write the novel, Dunphy said: "Started reading Gertrude Stein's *Making of Americans* but gave it up to write a novel of my own. Gave that up too . . . Finally started (and finished) *John Fury*."

The admiration and support for Gertrude Stein among twentieth-century African American writers was particularly strong. It seems that among the most important figures only Claude McKay was explicitly critical of Stein, accusing her pointedly, in his autobiography *A Long Way from Home* (1937), of being able to see only "black as black and white as white, without any shades." He did not like the cult around Stein and reported that when he examined "Melanctha," he "could not see wherein intrinsically it was what it was cracked up to be."

Most African American writers' views differed from McKay's. In his column "What to Read" for the *Crisis* (December 1910), W. E. B. Du Bois included Stein's *Three Lives* in a short list of the most noteworthy books. James Weldon Johnson believed that with "Melanctha" Stein had established herself as the first "white writer to write a story of love between a Negro man and woman and deal with them as normal members of the human family." Jean Toomer's *Cane* (1923), which includes Steinian sentences throughout the book, opens with a "Melanctha"-inspired section entitled "Karintha." Nella Larsen's novels *Quicksand* (1928) and *Passing* (1929) employed some loosely Steinian modernisms; and at Van Vechten's suggestion, Larsen sent an advance copy of *Quicksand* to Stein, together with a note in which she praised Stein's "Melanctha" as a "truly great story" she had read "many times": "I never cease to wonder how you came to write it," Larsen wrote to Stein, "and just why you and not one of us should so accurately have caught the spirit of this race of mine." In 1937, the poet and critic Sterling Brown judged that "Stein broke the white American literary tradition of portraying black characters as subhuman or as fools." And though the experimental novelist Clarence Major "did not 'hear' the same tonal qualities Wright heard," he still concluded in 1979: "When the speech of Jeff and Melanctha is compared to the speech of Negro characters created by Paul Laurence Dunbar, Joel Chandler Harris, Mark Twain, and even Melville, and Stein's contemporary, Sherwood Anderson, the characters Jeff and Melanctha do seem exceedingly convincing in the way they talk."

It is difficult to see how this could be the case with dialogues like the following: "I certainly do understand Dr. Campbell that you mean you don't believe it's right to love anybody." "Why sure no, yes I do Miss Melanctha. I certainly do believe strong in loving, and in being good to everybody, and trying to understand what they all need, to help them." What in Stein's language had the freeing effect that American writers, and especially immigrant and black authors, reported?

It was certainly not Stein's delicate avoidance of racial stereotypes. On the contrary, she seemed to cherish ethnic tags, and she used them consciously and with great gusto. The word "german" (lower case, as Stein often likes to render her ethnic adjectives) is repeated endlessly in "The Gentle Lena," and in *The Autobiography of Alice B. Toklas* we find such passages as the following: "She did not like the stranger's looks. Who is that, said she to Alfy. I didn't bring him, said Alfy. He looks like a Jew, said Gertrude Stein, he is worse than that, says Alfy." And "french," "german" and "spanish" qualities are abundantly claimed. In *Three Lives*, in "As Fine as Melanctha," and in letters to Van Vechten, Stein uses the word "nigger." Rose Johnson may have been inspired by the minstrel song "Coal Black Rose." In *The Autobiography of Alice B. Toklas*, one can read how Stein reacted to the "quantities of negroes" that Carl Van Vechten sent: "Gertrude Stein concluded that negroes were not suffering from persecution, they were suffering from nothingness." For her, "the african is not primitive, he has a very ancient but a very narrow culture and there it remains. Consequently nothing does or can happen." McKay quipped that not long after Stein published this, "something was happening: Negro Americans were rendering her opera *Four Saints in Three Acts*." Stein's term "nothingness" has been considered a precursor to Ralph Ellison's concept of "invisibility" (and in praising John Kouwenhoven's *The Beer Can by the Highway* Ellison wrote, "A can is a can is a can"). Yet "nothingness" was also enough of a provocation for the black modernist poet Melvin Tolson to ask ironically in *Harlem Gallery* (1965): "Listen, Black Boy. / Did the High Priestess at 27 rue de Fleurus / assert, 'The Negro suffers from nothingness'?" The "Black Boy" addressed here may be a reference to Richard Wright. Stein also advised Paul Robeson ("as soon as another person came into the room he became definitely a negro") not to claim spirituals: "Gertrude Stein did not like hearing him sing spirituals. They do not belong to you any more than anything else, so why claim them, she said. He did not answer." In letters to Carl Van Vechten, Stein praised the addressee for his good taste in friends, called Robeson "a dear," and reported the beginning of her conversation with him as follows: "why you like niggers so much Robeson." McKay faulted Stein for taking Robeson as "*the* representative of Negro culture," but reported that Robeson told him after his encounter with Stein "that she was all right" and that McKay should also seek her out; and Van Vechten wrote Stein that Robeson "adores you."

Perhaps it was Stein's very directness that made the difference. In her fiction, her explicit and programmatic use of stereotypic adjectives and ethnic tags, coupled with her love of repetition, at times seems to deplete racist language of its traditional weight. This is the case with the repetition of the phrase "negro sunshine" throughout "Melanctha." Sterling Brown noticed that "Gertrude Stein speaks of 'the wide abandoned laughter that gives the broad glow to negro sunshine,' but her major characters do not have it." It is true that in the tale, Rose Johnson "had not the wide, abandoned laughter that makes the warm broad glow to negro sunshine" and James Herbert "had never had the wide abandoned laughter that gives the broad glow to negro sunshine." However, Dr. Jefferson Campbell does: "He sang when he was happy, and he laughed, and his was the free abandoned laughter that gives the warm broad glow to negro sunshine." By this point in the story, however, the stereotypical quality of "negro sunshine" that so few characters seem to possess, has already eroded. The next time, Jeff has "a warm broad glow, like southern sunshine." And after that substitution by a regional adjective, the ethnic metaphor turns into a literal weather report: "It was summer now, and they had warm sunshine to wander." A tag became a word again, one might say; and it appeared to have shed much of its hurtful baggage in the process. It is also significant that in *Q.E.D.* Adele was associated with "a land of laziness and sunshine" – well before the racial transformation of the story into "Melanctha" was to take place.

Stein's dismantling of a sinister linguistic feature by repetition speaks to another reward Stein's prose held for writers who came to regard her as a model. Many ethnic stories were painful stories; so how could they be told without making the storytellers vulnerable? In "Melanctha," Stein had taken a tale of personal suffering and turned it into a prose experiment in which the biographical sources were both revealed and hidden. Would this not make a good method for other authors who wanted to give expression to pain? What Ludwig Lewisohn described as a reason for Sherwood Anderson's "instinctive submission to the influence of Gertrude Stein" may thus be particularly applicable to minority and immigrant writers: "In her," Lewisohn writes about

Anderson, "he found a writer driven to utter her secret yet constantly inhibited from doing so and feigning, as a defensive rationalization, that one could no more utter oneself through human speech until that speech was shattered into meaninglessness and the communication at once needed but neurotically inhibited could no longer take place." What made this model all the more attractive was that writers did not have to go to Stein's extremes or, as Lewisohn put it, "follow Miss Stein the whole way to sheer babbling."

What furthermore may have attracted some writers to Stein was the fact that she did not differentiate between a standard-English narrator and dialect-speaking characters. She thus avoided a procedure that, some writers felt, only dramatized racial hierarchies. This lack of differentiation helped to universalize by putting characters and narrator on an equal footing; of course, it also generalized as it took away the specific sound patterns that could be associated with ethnic location. It deserves to be remembered that Claude McKay found that Stein only "reproduced a number of the common phrases relating to Negroes," among them "abandoned laughter" and "Negro sunshine," "all prettily framed in a tricked-out style." In the "telling of the story," he found "nothing striking or informative about Negro life" and noted that "Melanctha, the mulattress, might have been a Jewess."

Whatever the ultimate reasons, there clearly were aspects of Stein's writing that made her work surprisingly congenial for ethnics who tended to be skeptical of American local color and race-differentiated dialect writing and who – like Sterling Brown – were otherwise quick to denounce ethnic stereotyping in literature, for authors who wanted to reveal pain without doubling the pain in the telling, and for writers who realized the benefit of going part of the way into Stein's direction.

Richard Wright's claims about the stockyard workers' reactions notwithstanding, Stein's writing defamiliarized and alienated its readers, whereas so much ethnic writing rested on making ethnic outsiders seem familiar to "general American" readers – in part by stereotyping minority characters, whether for progressive or reactionary motives. *Three Lives* may thus be viewed both as an aesthetic departure from the genre of the ethnic life story and as an example of it.

What was noticeably absent in the appreciation was the attempt to read Stein as an "ethnic" writer. Stein was a second-generation German Jewish immigrant child and an American expatriate who returned to the United States only once between 1903 and the time of her death in 1946; she was an outsider to prevailing American sexual norms, as Hemingway made sure to remind readers even after his death, and long after hers, in his authorized posthumous publication of *A Moveable Feast* (1964). There Hemingway spoke of Stein's "strong German-Jewish face" and reported to a mass audience that "Miss Stein and her friend" had forgiven Hemingway and his wife "for being in love and being married." Hemingway insisted on revealing that Stein had told him that male homosexuals commit "ugly and repugnant" acts, then are "disgusted with themselves" and drink, take drugs, and always change partners, but that the situation of female homosexuals was the opposite: "They do nothing that they are disgusted by and nothing that is repulsive and afterwards they are happy and they can lead happy lives together." This sounds suspiciously like Jake Barnes's definition of immorality in *The Sun Also Rises* as "things that make you disgusted afterward." In a July 1956 letter to Harvey Breit, Hemingway wrote bluntly: "Stein was a nice woman until she had change of life and opted for fags and fags alone."

In *Three Lives* Gertrude Stein had set up a model for literature that would be both "ethnic" and "modernist." Yet *Three Lives* was not read for the author's ethnicity in a manner that differentiated Stein as a supposed "insider" writing about German American women Lena and Anna and as a white "outsider" depicting mixed-race Melanctha and Jeff Campbell. It was not Stein's ethno-biographical persona (was she "ethnic"?), her gender (did she write "women's literature"?), her sexual orientation (did she write "as a lesbian"?), or her possible ethnic bias (how did she really feel about black, mixed-race, Jewish or German Americans?) but her style that mattered most to minority writers who were her contemporaries. Her innovations in writing seemed too important to be read in light of social categories that otherwise may have defined her existence. If the need for biographical material arose, it was filled not with ethnic genealogies but with intellectual party scenes of Stein and Toklas among the painters and artworks at the mythical rue de Fleurus in Paris.

2

❦

ETHNIC LIVES AND "LIFELETS"

W HEN Gertrude Stein's "Gentle Lena" realizes that her marriage plans have failed, she goes home alone in a streetcar crying, and the conductor and the other passengers empathize with her: "And everybody in the car was sorry for poor Lena." The conductor kindly promises her, "You'll get a real man yet, one that will be better for you," and Lena feels slightly better. Stein may have thwarted the reader's expectation to express empathy in the brief death scenes of *Three Lives*, but she did represent the kindness of strangers in the streetcar setting of her modern city of "Bridgepoint."

Streetcars are a prototypical modern symbol that the reader often encounters in literature of the first half of the twentieth century. Henry James, returning to America in 1904–5 after a very long absence, found in the electric cars that had arrived in New York in 1887 the concentrated presence of new immigrants: "The carful, again and again, is a foreign carful; a row of faces, up and down, testifying, without exception, to alienism unmistakable, alienism undisguised and unashamed," he writes in *The American Scene* (1907). Streetcar settings – as well as scenes on subways, trains, buses, and other means of public transportation – may provide local background, may bring friendly, hostile, or indifferent strangers together, may inspire a hero to seek a revelation on the tracks, or may serve as a formal inspiration to convey the sense of movement, speed, or electric power. One only has to think of Ezra Pound's "In a Station of the Metro" ("The apparition of these faces in the crowd; / Petals on a wet, black bough."). "'Trams and dusty trees'" (the line that opens the song of one of the Wagnerian Thames daughters) in Eliot's *Waste Land* also suggests the intimate connection between this theme and literary modernism. Eliot's line is not only a version of contrasting machine and garden but also juxtaposes the tramway of modernity with trees, the ultimate image of rootedness, though the trees are dusty in this cityscape. There are also numerous representations of trolleys in modern art. Examples include Mary Stevenson Cassatt's *In the Omnibus (The Tramway)* (1891), the Italian Carlo Carrà's futurist painting *What the Street-Car Told Me* (1910–11), the Russian Kazimir Malevich, who did an oil canvas

384

entitled *Lady in a Tram* (1913) just before he moved toward the pure abstraction of suprematism, the German Nikolaus Braun's primitivist *Berliner Strassenszene* (1921), and the Canadian Miller Gore Brittain's Hopper-like *Two Waitresses on a Streetcar Crossing the Reversing Falls* (1940). Numerous modern works of art represent subways and trains, including Max Weber, *Grand Central Terminal* (1915), Edward Hopper, *Night on the 'El' Train* (1920), Reginald Marsh, *Why Not Use the 'L'* (1930), and George Tooker's *The Subway* (1950). In 1920, John Dewey thought that train and streetcar passengers were the ideal readers of periodicals that seemed "designed" for the mobile passengers' "intermediate state of existence." Streetcar scenes are especially interesting in retrospect since electric streetcars, once a prime symbol of modernity, have now assumed an aura of nostalgic quaintness after their literal disappearance from most American cities in the course of the twentieth century.

At about the same time that Stein was working on her *Three Lives*, the New York *Independent*, the *Outlook*, and several other American newspapers and periodicals ran brief life stories which aimed, as the editor of the *Independent* put it, to "typify the life of the average worker in some particular vocation, and to make each story the genuine experience of a real person." One of the autobiographical contributions to the *Independent* was entitled "The Race Problem – an Autobiography by a Southern Colored Woman" (March 17, 1904). Its anonymous author relates a visit to "a Southern city where" (she did not know) "the 'Jim Crow' law is enforced." On boarding an electric car, she takes the most convenient seat.

The conductor yelled, "What do you mean? Niggers don't sit with white folks down here. You must have come from 'way up yonder. I'm not Roosevelt. We don't sit with niggers, much less eat with them."

I was astonished and said, "I am a stranger and did not know of your law." His answer was: "Well, no back talk now; that's what I'm here for – to tell niggers their places when they don't know them."

Every white man, woman and child was in a titter of laughter by this time at what they considered the conductor's wit.

The Southern colored woman is refused full participation in those means of transportation that seem to embody modernity: shortly afterward she is denied entrance to an elevator in a skyscraper and is sent instead to the freight lift. The modern settings serve as a contrast to the inhuman treatment the autobiographer receives; and, unlike in "The Gentle Lena," empathy is a stranger to the story of the Southern colored woman.

Who were the "white people" on the colored woman's streetcar? Did they include immigrants from Europe who were here benefiting from "whiteness"? It is telling that the conductor justifies segregation by alluding to Theodore

Roosevelt's famous lunch with Booker T. Washington in the White House on October 18, 1901 that caused a public stir against interracial meals, with some white voices professing "horror that a white gentleman can entertain a colored one at his table." The day after the meal, the *Baltimore Sun* published the somewhat misleading front-page headline, "The Black Man to be Put on Top of the White Man," editorializing that this association on the basis of "social equality" was unacceptable to the South because the "inevitable result of this association is the intermarriage between black men and white women and white men and black women." The interracial Roosevelt lunch was a central public event in the age of the color line. It was enough of a theme to form the basis of a paranoid novel, Robert Lee Durham's *The Call of the South* (1908), a book actually premised on the assumption that the daughter of a president who had invited black leaders for lunch would herself fall in love with and tragically marry a man who had an African great-grandfather – with the most disastrous consequences for the president and his daughter. Readers of the *Independent* were obviously expected to catch the Roosevelt allusion.

Touchiness about interracial dining was only one symptom of the tense and explosive volatility of race relations. American ethnic heterogeneity at the beginning of the twentieth century was intensely debated and conflict-ridden. The color line between black and white marked the deepest divide; but there were many other ethnic fault lines. The United States had grown from a small, rural, provincial, and British-dominated country into a large, modern, polyethnic, and increasingly urban nation. In 1910 there were 92 million Americans (a fourfold growth from only 23 million before the Civil War); among them nearly 10 million blacks (up from 3.5 million in 1850) and only 280,000 Native American Indians. Immigration had reached impressive proportions: more than 13 million of those counted in 1910 were foreign-born, mostly in Europe; and the number increases to over 32 million if one includes the second-generation children of foreign-born Americans that the Census then counted under the category "total foreign white stock." Two and a half million had come from Germany, more than 1.5 million from Russia, and more than 1 million each from Ireland, Italy, Austria, Scandinavia, and Great Britain. The majority of the newcomers were arriving during the "new immigration," the wave that peaked between the 1880s and the 1920s. There were 23,000 Japanese, 85,000 Chinese immigrants (their number declined once Chinese exclusion took effect), and many people of Spanish and some of French descent who had been incorporated into the United States by annexation and territorial expansion. Large-scale internal migration from the South to the North and from the countryside to cities added to the changing composition of American cities starting with World War I. For example, while in 1910 approximately a quarter of all African Americans lived in cities, by 1950 more than half of a new total of about 15 million did.

The chance to establish a sense of multiethnic American nationhood that would include cross-cultural and interracial empathy seemed slim in this period when the ideal of the homogeneous nation state was at its peak. Ethnic and linguistic heterogeneity were successfully portrayed as political dynamite and as the serious cultural danger of "balkanizing" the United States and transforming it into a "house divided" or a new "Babel." Proponents of continued immigration often viewed assimilation into Anglo-America as the best method of integrating newcomers, while opponents (who doubted that assimilation was ever possible for heterogeneous "racial stocks") opted for restriction and exclusion. The Americanization movement of World War I was accompanied by language bans and the Anglicization of foreign words and names. Walter Lippmann observed in 1929 that the "Americanization movement, in some of its public manifestations, has as much resemblance to patriotism as the rape of the Sabine women had to the love of Dante for Beatrice." And after 1920 immigration was legislated to decline dramatically from the nearly 10 million who came between 1910 and 1930 to a mere 1.5 million who arrived between 1930 and 1950 – exactly when millions would have needed asylum. (By comparison, in the year 1907 alone, more than 1.25 million immigrants had come to the United States.) In 1910, more than one in seven Americans was foreign-born; by 1950 the percentage had dropped by more than half, for then only one fifteenth of a total of 150 million Americans was foreign-born. Immigration restrictions, often fueled by racial prejudice, were part of many social expressions of a growing white American conservatism that was particularly hostile to the made-up social category of "non-whites."

The further curtailment of African American rights and advancement of racial segregation, the terror of lynching and white mob violence euphemistically referred to as "race riots" (in East St. Louis and Tulsa), the expansion of bans on racial intermarriage, and the passing of eugenicist-inspired and explicitly racist laws like the Virginia Act to Preserve Racial Purity (1924), a dramatic change in American Indian policy from coercive assimilation, to the Indian Reorganization Act (1934) which enforced tribal organization, the severe discriminative framework surrounding Asian immigrants, and a more pervasive dissemination of an aggressive white "race consciousness" all found support among American citizens and intellectuals at least until World War II. In short, it was not a very comfortable time for ethnic minorities in the United

States, for the pressures of the fiercely asserted hegemony of "whiteness" and of Anglo-American assimilation were enormous.

The published output of ethnic prose writing in the decades from 1910 to 1950, however, was truly impressive; and literature of American ethnic minorities moved from the margins toward the center of American literature in those years. Black America saw the flourishing of the Harlem Renaissance, and strong literary production of fiction continued through the 1930s and 1940s, paving the way for the full entrance into American mainstream literature marked by the Book of the Month Club selection of Richard Wright's *Native Son* (1940) and the winning of the National Book Award by Ralph Ellison's *Invisible Man* (1952). American Jewish prose writers offered strong works from the still-marginalized beginnings with Abraham Cahan, Anzia Yezierska, Samuel Ornitz, and Daniel Fuchs to the high point of Saul Bellow's National Book Award-winning *Adventures of Augie March* (1953), and on to the fullest possible public recognition signaled by the conferral of the Nobel Prize for literature on Saul Bellow in 1976 and on Isaac Bashevis Singer in 1978. Immigrant and ethnic autobiography and fiction represented the lives of many different groups, ranging from Syrian (Samuel Rizk) to Jamaican (Claude McKay), from Irish (Mary Doyle Curran) to Italian (John Fante), and from Slovak (Thomas Bell) to Slovene (Louis Adamic). Ethnic writers benefited – as did many American authors – from new institutions: Rosenwald and Guggenheim fellowships permitted uninterrupted writing time, writers' centers like Yaddo or Taos provided congenial settings, and many journals supported modern-fiction writers. Whit Burnett and Martha Foley's *Story Magazine* (1931–53) published and awarded such "new" writers as Nelson Algren, William Saroyan, Zora Neale Hurston, James T. Farrell, and Richard Wright; and the annually published volumes *Best Short Stories* (1915–32) and *Best American Short Stories* (1942–77) helped many short-fiction writers – among them Konrad Bercovici, Nelson Algren, Saul Bellow, Leo Surmelian, and Carlos Bulosan as well as Vladimir Nabokov and Lionel Trilling – to reach a wider national audience. Louis Adamic's journal *Common Ground* (published from 1940 to 1949 by the Common Council for American Unity) and Edwin Seaver's *Cross Section* anthologies (1944–48) specifically aimed for a polyethnic representation among contemporary American authors. Most importantly, the Works Progress Administration (WPA) gave support to many artists and authors who would later become famous. From 1935 to 1943 the Federal Writers' Project (FWP) helped to employ writers of diverse backgrounds, created a wide forum for exchanges of opinions (such as theaters, journals, and conventions), and involved authors in a large-scale, government-sponsored enterprise of taking stock of America, which included interesting historical or social science research projects such as the background work for, and writing of, the Writers' Guide Series, interviews with many ex-slaves, and the collecting of rural and urban folklore. The fact that on June 14, 1939, during his work on the Federal Writers' Project in Harlem, Ralph Ellison heard and recorded the black tale of Sweet-the-monkey who "could make hisself invisible" is suggestive of the importance of the FWP in the development of American literature. As time went on, writers would also be more and more likely to teach "creative writing" in colleges throughout the United States.

While the hostility to languages other than English that was fomented in the World War I years, in a powerful mix of Anglo-American ethnocentrism and political reasoning, had a dampening effect on American ethnic literature in languages apart from English, the publication of non-English-language prose writing in the United States continued. The surveillance of all foreign-language papers from 1917 into the 1920s by the vast translation supervision enterprise of the Postmaster General affected two thousand American periodicals written in Ruthenian, Syrian, Bohemian, "Spanish-Jewish" (Ladino), Tagalog-Visayan, Romanian, and many other languages, as well as bi- and tri-lingual journals in Polish Latin, Danish Norwegian Swedish, or German Hungarian. Yet just a few years later, *I de dage* (In Those Days, 1924) and *Riket grundlægges* (Founding the Kingdom, 1925), the first two volumes of Ole E. Rölvaag's Norwegian-language immigrant saga, a high point of non-English literature of the United States, were received with great enthusiasm in Lincoln Colcord's English translation under the title *Giants in the Earth: A Saga of the Prairie* (1927).

The foundations for modern multicultural literature were being laid in those decades. Not only did Oliver LaFarge's widely read *Laughing Boy* (1929) include a prayer ("House made of dawn light, House made of evening light") to which N. Scott Momaday's novels *House Made of Dawn* (1968) would later allude, but the first important modern novels by Native Americans John Joseph Mathews, *Sundown* (1934) and D'Arcy McNickle, *The Surrounded* (1936), were also published then. Asian American fiction and autobiography began to take off with Sui Sin Far's sophisticated story collection, *Mrs. Spring Fragrance* (1912), as well as with Younghill Kang's *East Goes West: The Making of an Oriental Yankee* (1937), Pardee Lowe's *Father and Glorious Descendant* (1942), Carlos Bulosan's *America is in the Heart: A Personal History* (1946), Toshio Mori's *Yokohama, California* and Hisaye Yamamoto's "Seventeen Syllables" (both published in 1949). The first use of the word "Chicano" (derived from "mexicano") appeared in Mario Suárez's short story "Señor Garza" (1947) which anticipated features of the later Chicano literary movement that would begin, after 1950, with John Rechy's sketches, such as "El Paso del Norte" (1958), and with José Antonio Villareal's novel *Pocho* (1959).

The difficulties ethnic writers faced affected their literary production. Legislative changes were accompanied by an intense debate about the future of the country and the nature of various ethnic groups. In such contexts, ethno-autobiographical literature was an eminently political genre, as it seemed to provide information for the general reading public about the "desirability," potential "assimilability," or "compatibility" of whole groups of people. While American authors who were not ethnically marked often extolled free-standing individualism, ethnic writers operated under a system that has been called "compulsive representation," for they were often read as informants about the collectivities they were believed to embody. It is hardly surprising, then, that English-language American ethnic autobiography has, with some important exceptions, tended to present a positively conceived collective self and curbed too candidly self-critical individual representation that might be held against the authors *and* their groups, turning literary revelation into a "debit to the race." A negatively shaped self-portrait, as in Richard Wright's autobiography *Black Boy* (1945), was a strategic ploy, intended to show the terrible effects of racial segregation on human consciousness – though, despite this anti-segregationist political purpose, Wright was often taken to task for not offering a more positive representation of African American life in *Black Boy*.

As debate raged about who should and should not be included in the category "American," the ethnic writers' answer often was, "We *are* Americans." In the very titles of their books they pronounced their compatibility with the culture and the political system of the United States where their presence had become so questionable. Jacob Riis set the tone with his autobiography *The Making of an American* (1901), a title Mary Antin later wished had still been available to her when she was writing her autobiography; she ultimately chose the title *The Promised Land* (1912) for what became a truly representative work of the genre. Other writers who adopted "American" titles were Edward Steiner, *From Alien to Citizen* (1914), Marcus Ravage, *An American in the Making* (1917), Horace Bridges, *On Becoming an American* (1919), *The Americanization of Edward Bok* (1920), Louis Adamic, *My America* (1938), and Salom Rizk, *Syrian Yankee* (1943). The title of Gertrude Stein's *The Making of Americans* was thus also a response to a flourishing genre.

Whereas immigration restrictionists and liberal reformers alike discussed ethnic heterogeneity in terms of the problems posed by crime, health, housing conditions, and poverty, the representative ethnic texts of the period were typically written by American immigrants and their descendants and by members of minorities who not only claimed America but also stressed that they had "made it." Following such famous titles as Booker T. Washington's autobiography *Up From Slavery* (1901, partly ghostwritten by Max Bennett Thresher), the Irish immigrant Alexander Irvine gave his auto- biography the telling title *From the Bottom Up* (1910), anticipating the slogan of American social historians in the 1960s. Other titles in this vein included Michael Pupin, *From Immigrant to Inventor* (1923) and Richard Bartholdt, *From Steerage to Congress* (1930). In the manner of the American uplift saga "from log cabin to White House," ethnic autobiographers attempted to include immi- grants and minorities in tales of educational and economic upward mobility, transforming their marginality into a version of the typical American story. The illustrations that accompanied some of the autobiographies often sup- ported this message, as the reader who just leafs through these volumes is taken from images of modest beginnings like S. S. McClure's birthplace in Ireland to encounters with famous Anglo-American or English people (for Jacob Riis and Edward Bok, Theodore Roosevelt; for Mary Antin, Edward Everett Hale; for S. S. McClure, Robert Louis Stevenson), and to an arrival in an enviable American residence such as shown in the full-page photographs of "'Happy Hollow,' Mr. Irvine's Present Home Near Peekskill, New York" or of "Edward Bok's Present Home 'Swastika' (named by Rudyard Kipling), at Merion, Pennsylvania."

Part of the ethnic writer's perceived task was to go against commonly held ethnic stereotypes: Mike Gold's *Jews Without Money* (1930) announces this strategy in its title, and the narrator is indignant when he reports that his teacher called him a "little kike." (A nice counterpoint would be to read Myra Kelly's chapter "H. R. H. The Prince of Hester Street" in *Little Citizens: The Humour of School Life* (1904) which tells stories about Lower East Side schools from the Irish American teacher Constance Bailey's point of view, including an episode in which Isidore Belchatosky "with growing fluency . . . cursed and swore and blasphemed; using words of whose existence Teacher had never heard or known and at whose meaning she could but faintly guess.") The Jamaican immigrant Claude McKay includes much stereotype-questioning in his autobiography *A Long Way from Home* (1937): for example, when a Russian poet's wife asks McKay to "dance a jazz" with her, he obliges, but ironically adds that he probably did not "live up to the standard of Aframerican choreography." Thomas Bell's Slovak American steel-mill-workers' novel *Out of this Furnace* (1941) was viewed by the author as an "answer to all those unthinking people who looked down on the Slovaks," stereotyping them as "Hunkies." Jerre Mangione's autobiographically inspired *Mount Allegro* (1942) describes the young protagonist Gerlando Amoroso's attempts to convince his teachers that, though Italian, he was neither talented as a singer nor as a painter; and, on a more serious note, he was taught that as a male of Sicilian parentage, he ought never to be seen publicly holding a knife – not even at dinner. It could be difficult to become in the eyes of others the cliché of the knife-wielding Sicilian. Ironically, this stereotype-confronting tendency has led to the strange fact that a reader who searches for ethnic stereotypes against a given group is most likely to encounter them in literature by members of that group – who often tried to name, attack, and refute these clichéd notions. As the narrator of John Fante's short story "The Odyssey of a Wop" (1940) puts it: "As I grow older, I find out that Italians use Wop and Dago much more than Americans." Yet he also reports an incident when, working as a waiter, he is taunted so much by the chef that he actually becomes the knife-wielding stereotype for moment: "I am not thinking of throwing it, but since he says I won't, I do. It goes over his head and strikes the wall and drops with a clatter to the floor."

American ethnic autobiographers sensed that the stakes were high, for a "general reader" might judge the merit of a writer's ethnic group on the basis of reading a single book. Thus ethnic authors tended to flash their accomplishments, identifying their achievement and upward mobility with the respective ethnic group as a whole and with America, instead of revealing their individual perversions, nightmares, fears, or human failings. They often made a particular case for their own ethnic group by arguing for a special connection, an early historical link, a blood sacrifice, or a shared destiny with America. This claim of a special affinity has been called "homemaking myth," and many ethnic groups have made themselves at home in America by emphasizing an early arrival in the New World, a linguistic connection, a shared war experience, a "gift" or an ideological relationship, or any other element suited to establish the putative unity of the respective group culture and the dominant culture of the United States. Ethnic heroes – among them the autobiographers themselves – were sometimes the living symbols of such homemaking myths.

Immigrants and members of minority groups also made their case by testifying against other ethnic groups. The representation of Italian boys in Gold's *Jews Without Money*, of the Irish neighbors in Ole Rölvaag's *Giants in the Earth* (1927), and of Polish farmers in Edna Ferber's *American Beauty* (1931) are just a few examples of this common strategy. In Anzia Yezierska's *Salome of the Tenements* (1922), the Jewish heroine Sonya Vrunsky finds in her Anglo-American beloved John Manning "the Anglo-Saxon coldness, its centuries of solid ice that all the suns of the sky can't melt." Yet Yezierska's narrator balances this cliché with quite unironic and rather antisemitic sounding descriptions of her heroine: "The eternal urge of her race to rise – to rise – to transmute

failure, heartbreak and despair into a driving will to conquer – swept her up
to the heights of hope again." As if in direct opposition to Jerre Mangione, a
butcher's wife in Henry Roth's *Call It Sleep* (1934) warns her husband: "Do you
oppose an Italian? Don't you know they carry knives – all of them?" In short,
the lives narrated by outsiders, marginals, immigrants, and ethnics could easily play a problematic role in affirming ethnic stereotypes. Even when ethnic
writers included social criticism and an attack on specific laws and customs,
on bigotry, racism, or on narrow notions of Americanness, they could also be
more upbeat than, and just as biased as, certain authors from then-dominant
groups.

An offbeat contribution to the immigration debate was made by *The Sieve;
or, Revelations of the Man Mill* (1921), an unusual narrative by the immigrant
Felix Feri Weiss, who arrived in the United States in 1892 (apparently from
Hungary) and became an immigration inspector. He writes almost nothing
about his own life and past, focusing instead on his difficult work of sorting out
bad aliens from desirable ones. Latvian anarchists, stowaways from many lands,
a trachoma-infected Armenian girl (whose case as "the girl without a country"
goes all the way to the Supreme Court), young European girls lured away
from their parents by Mormon missionaries and headed for a fate of polygamy
in Utah, Italian picture brides, smuggled-in Chinese, and legal immigrants
from many countries who come with near-unintelligible information about
their destination in the United States – these are some of the problem cases
that cause "leaks in the sieve" that Weiss tries to mend with the conviction
of a believer in "the Religion of Eugenics." His book makes a telling counterpoint to the many immigrant narratives with arrival scenes. Yet despite his
cautiously restrictionist outlook, Weiss saw his job as a contribution to the
rededication of Plymouth Rock and proudly ended his book with his participation at an immigrant education conference in Plymouth, on the occasion of
the tercentenary of the Pilgrims' journey.

As a balancing element to strategies of ethno-American compatibility, ethnic literature also tended to include positive references to country-of-origin
communities and their character traits that were *not* "American." In such references often lay a point of subtle resistance to, or overt critique of, America.
This was the case even in the most pro-American and apparently assimilation-
ist works. *The Americanization of Edward Bok: The Autobiography of a Dutch Boy
Fifty Years After* (1920), written in the third person, was a model of the cheery
quality of the genre of the success story, and it celebrated the joys of progress
and acquisition. Yet near the end of his autobiography even Bok, the famed
editor of the *Ladies' Home Journal*, included a section entitled "Where America
Fell Short With Me." There Bok remembers how wasteful America appeared to

him upon his arrival: "it was an easy calculation that what was thrown away in a week's time from Brooklyn homes would feed the poor of the Netherlands." He attacks such "infernal Americanisms" as the phrase "That will do," for preventing Americans from aspiring to thoroughness and excellence. (A quarter of a century earlier Abraham Cahan had seen the adoption of the phrase as a symptom of shallow Americanization when the narrator of *Yekl: A Tale of the Ghetto* (1896) says: "America for a country and '*dod'll do*' for a language.") Bok also criticizes the popular movement to Americanize immigrants, claiming boldly that the Americanizers themselves needed Americanization. And he wonders "whether, after all, the foreign-born does not make in some sense a better American – whether he is not able to get a truer perspective; whether his is not the deeper desire to see America greater; whether he is not less content to let its faulty institutions be as they are; whether in seeing faults he does not make a more decided effort to have America reach those ideals or those fundamentals of his own land which he feels are in his nature, and the best of which he is anxious to graft into the character of his adopted land?" The reason Bok gives for his decision to retire from the editorship of the *Ladies' Home Journal* at age fifty-six comes as no surprise: "After all, he was still Dutch; he held on to the lesson which his people had learned years ago . . . that the Great Adventure of Life was something more than material work, and that the time to go is while the going is good!" Ironically then, Bok argued that it was being and remaining Dutch that made him a better American. Amazingly, he said so at the peak of the Americanization movement, and with Roosevelt's explicit endorsement.

   The possibilities and constraints of American ethnic autobiography and prose fiction are apparent in the short life stories that were published in the *Independent*, and of which the Southern colored woman's was an example. More than seventy such life stories appeared in the *Independent* before World War I, and the labor-and-reform-oriented Progressive editor Hamilton Holt perceived the potential of these "lifelets" (as they were called) to form a collective image of the new polyethnic America. Holt's idea of collecting such life stories for the *Independent* was carried out with the help of several professional writers, including Sydney Reid, the already-mentioned Irish American Alexander Irvine, and the Princeton-trained writer Ernest Poole who had also helped Upton Sinclair to find sources for *The Jungle* and was the author of the novel *The Voice of the Street* (1906), a book about New York's Lower East Side, to be followed by *The Harbor* (1915), and *Millions* (1922). In 1925 Holt became the President of Rollins College in Winter Park, Florida, where he instituted educational reforms and attracted an illustrious faculty some of whose members, after a serious crisis in 1933, left Rollins only to found the even more experimental (and more famous) Black Mountain College – one of the seedbeds of American aesthetic modernism.

Holt collected sixteen lives in a book entitled *The Life Stories of Undistinguished Americans as Told by Themselves* (1906). The programmatic title suggested that everyone in the world could be American and that being "undistinguished" could be a mark of distinction. The collection opens with the story of Antanas Kaztauskis, a Lithuanian refugee from Russian oppression who works in the brutal Chicago stockyard and joins a union (there are similarities with Upton Sinclair's *The Jungle*, published in the same year). The machinery of death becomes chillingly real in this practical account of a world of profit:

My job was in the cattle killing room. I pushed the blood along the gutter. Some people think these jobs make men bad. I do not think so. The men who do the killing are not as bad as the ladies with fine clothes who come every day to look at it . . . . The cattle do not suffer. They are knocked senseless with a big hammer and are dead before they wake up. This is done not to spare them pain, but because if they got hot and sweating with fear and pain the meat would not be so good. I soon saw that every job in the room was done like this – so as to save everything and make money. One Lithuanian who worked with me, said: "They get all the blood out of those cattle and all the work out of us men."

The volume ends with a Chinese merchant's wish to return from New York's Chinatown to his native village in China: Lee Chew even draws a floor plan of his father's house. In the book, the American Indian Ah-nen-la-de-ni is prevented at his Pennsylvania school from expressing himself in the only language he knows, and the African American experiences the hell of a Georgia peon camp. A farmer's wife in Illinois has to struggle against an overwhelming workload and her own husband, in order to follow her calling as a writer, and an itinerant Southern Methodist minister pursues his career against the physical handicap of his defective eyesight. The Italian bootblack Rocco Corresca and the Swedish farmer Axel Jarlson build their lives in New York and Minnesota. A Japanese servant describes how California employers have humiliated him. Nothing is more telling than the Polish sweatshop worker Sadie Frowne's understated and almost casual remark: "Where the needle goes through the nail it makes a sore finger, or where it splinters a bone it does much harm." This destructive side of industrial labor gives a serious dimension to her naively comic premodern account of always arriving very early at work because she does not believe in the existence of alarm clocks: "I have heard that there is a sort of clock that calls you at the very time you want to get up, but I can't believe that because I don't see how the clock would know." A Greek peddler misses the flavor of Greek fruit in America and mentions a 10 percent return migration rate to

Greece; and the French dressmaker Amelia des Moulins knows that there is only one Paris and is looking forward to the voyage that will take her back to France. The German nurse girl Agnes describes the ups and downs of her work and looks forward to getting married to a grocery store assistant. The pro-Turkish Syrian church sentences the Syrian journalist L. J. A. to death for having published critical articles on the Armenian massacres in New York's Arab-language press.

Some of the immigrant stories include arrival scenes at the Statue of Liberty. Sadie Frowne noted that upon arriving in New York she "saw the beautiful bay and the big woman with the spikes on her head and the lamp that is lighted at night in her hand (Goddess of Liberty)"; and the Syrian journalist mentions that he "passed close by the grand Statue of Liberty" and saw in the distance the "beautiful white bridge away up in the blue sky and the big buildings towering up like our own mountain peaks." Such descriptions belong to the long series of texts starting with Emma Lazarus's poem "The New Colossus" (1883) which reinterpreted the Statue of Liberty, officially designated as embodying Franco-American friendship, as a symbol of welcome to immigrants. Some lifelets contain interesting misreadings of the symbol. Thus Mike Trudics, the Hungarian peon, describes the statue's torch as a broom: "A well-dressed man who spoke our language told us that the big iron woman in the harbor was a goddess that gave out liberty freely and without cost to everybody. He said the thing in her hand that looked like a broom was light – that it was to give us light and liberty too . . . he told us a man could stand inside the broom."

The stories portray fun and leisure, and we hear of fortune-tellers, cafés, the theater, picnics, or concerts, and, again and again, of Coney Island – where, however, the Igorrote chief Fomoaley Ponci is on display, brought to America from the recently conquered Philippines. He serves as a reminder of the stark inequality that is pervasive in the New World, and present even in the world of entertainment. Interestingly, the *Independent* published Russian writer Maxim Gorky's contemporary critique of Coney Island as a "paying business, as a means to extract their earnings from the pockets of the people" who experience "boredom" (the title of the essay) as a result of their monotonous jobs. Coney Island is not the only site of social tension among the various Americans who speak in *The Life Stories*: they belong to different classes, so much so that just a part of the Greek peddler's income could have completely saved the African American from his fate of peonage. The volume as a whole suggests the broadening of the term "American" that its editor intended. Yet it also revealed the problems and conflicts of a multiethnic society in which great riches and dramatic poverty coexist.

Ethnic tensions are as widespread as is class inequality. Because of their differences in culture, religion, and language the undistinguished Americans measure each other by incompatible yardsticks and at times look at each other with skeptical and biased eyes – as "foreigners" or "devils," "red-haired savages" or "infidels." When the Irish cook learns that her American employers are Jewish, she packs her bags and says, "I beg your pardon, ma'am, but I cannot eat the bread of them as crucified the Saviour." (The lady's answer that Christ also was a Jew only confirms the maid in her decision to quit.) The Chinese businessman maintains that "No one would hire an Irishman, German, Englishman or Italian when he could get a Chinese, because our countrymen are so much more honest, industrious, steady, sober and painstaking." Each life story develops a sympathetic and individualized view of the group it represents, while many propagate "stereotypes" of other groups. Thus the Italian bootblack can say: "He was Irish, but a good man . . . ." The Swedish farmer notes that his French Canadian friend "was part Indian, and yet was laughing all the time" whereas he found that the steerage passengers "were Swedes and very pleasant and friendly." The feature of viewing one's own group in positive terms and members of other groups as types was pervasive in American ethnic literature. One novel of the period, Jessie Fauset's *Plum Bun* (1929), explicitly lets its heroine become self-conscious of this general trait. In *Plum Bun*, the mixed-race artist Angela Murray recognizes that her award-winning project of creating a great painting of "Fourteenth Street types" at New York's Union Square is flawed because Angela herself would also be nothing but a social "type" to others. As her wisdom and her sympathy with the down-and-outs grow, she comes to understand "how fiercely she would have rebelled had anyone from a superior social plane taken her for copy."

What were the common denominators of an increasingly polyethnic country? One person's utopia could be another person's hell. This makes a widely shared expression of nostalgia for one particular sacred past difficult. Religion, for example, could mean unpredictably diverse things for different Americans: the Lithuanian does not often go to church in the New World because he finds religious services too "slow" in America. The Italian bootblack notes that there are "here plenty of Protestants who are heretics, but they have a religion, too" and that their churches "have no saints and no altars, which seems strange." The Jewish garment worker comments that in America, unlike in Poland, only men go to synagogue; and compared to China, Lee Chew writes, America is a country where people pay no regard to the precepts of Kong-foo-tsze (Confucius) and the Sages.

For the people who speak in this collection there is no agreed-upon "sacred" realm that is being secularized. In this respect they are representative of

Americans. To whose religious past can a polyethnic society dream of returning? Christianity? (Catholicism? Protestantism? Greek or Maronite Orthodoxy?) Islam? Judaism? Hinduism? Confucianism? or nature worship? The inhabitants of this book have left many different sacred and secular pasts behind – yet they continue to view the modern through the lenses provided by these various pasts. Is "secularization" merely a convenient metaphor in such a state of affairs, leaving open the issue of which specific form of sacredness is to be left behind and focusing instead on the shared process of becoming "modern" and secularized? Might not a rhetoric of "making it new" create the hope for a unity to emerge in the future – so that Americans, in Lee Chew's grandfather's critical words, are "constantly showing disrespect for their ancestors by getting new things to take the place of the old." Would not specific forms of religious fundamentalism, of precisely defined "faith-based values," or of a single dogmatically designated meaning of the civil-religion formula "In God We Trust" simply have to be exclusionary and divisive in a society of many past and present creeds?

The problem of heterogeneity also affects expectations for the future. While the majority of the life-story subjects imagine a better future in America, there are those who will go back to a country of origin, those who only dream of return emigration, those who have no country to which they can return, and those who have little hope for a future anywhere. (In representing the theme of return migration, *The Life Stories* reflected the fact that more than thirty of each hundred immigrants returned to their country of origin between 1910 and 1930.) When the French dressmaker announces that she is going back to Paris, she is embracing a past to which no other undistinguished American could hope to return. This highlights a problem with many "back to . . ." movements in the modern United States – unless what followed was a mere abstraction, a vague generalization that could then be fleshed out in the most heterogeneous fashion. It was a problem that stood out in an era when nation states cherished myths of homogeneity, shared origins, and a common destiny.

Even the constitution of individual ethnic identity could be the result of complex interethnic interaction and negotiation. The Indian describes his first encounter with the generalization "Mohawk" to which he supposedly belonged but also a name in which he senses an insult (he was right since the name means "cannibals" or "cowards" in Algonquin); the Greek peddler alternates between a description of Greeks as "they" and as "we," as does the Syrian when he speaks about "his" people. Axel Jarlson may say "with us" and mean "in Sweden" but he also uses the phrase "this country" to refer to the United States; whereas the term "Americans" or even "Swedes who live in America" does not command the narrator's use of the pronoun "we" which most often refers to personally known groupings of family and friends of any nationality.

These ethnic issues and interethnic differences are not only recognizable in hindsight. Some undistinguished Americans directly responded to the lifelets of others. The Southern colored woman wrote the *Independent* in response to other first-person stories that had appeared in it before hers. She explicitly addresses two of the other autobiographers.

I would be contented and happy if I, an American citizen, could say as Axel Jarlson (the Swedish emigrant, whose story appeared in THE INDEPENDENT of January 8th, 1903) says, "There are no aristocrats to push him down and say that he is not worthy because his father was poor." There are "aristocrats" to push me and mine down and say we are not worthy because we are colored. The Chinaman, Lee Chew, ends his article in THE INDEPENDENT of February 19th, 1903, by saying, "Under the circumstances how can I call this my home, and how can any one blame me if I take my money and go back to my village in China?"

Happy Chinaman! Fortunate Lee Chew! You can go back to your village and enjoy your money. This is my village, my home, yet I am an outcast!

The various lifelets add up to a polyethnic panorama, a "complete picture of America in all its strata," and for the book Holt selected those stories that would best typify what he thought of as "the five great races" and a series of representative professions. More than that, these life stories suggest the global interconnectedness of working-class Americans at the beginning of the century. They also make vivid the difficulty of associating a single "type" with the word "American," and of taking for granted a historical sense of a widely shared past among a heterogeneous populace.

What could the Founding Fathers, or the American nineteenth century, or almost any aspect of American history mean to so many ethnic Americans? The slim output by English-writing ethnic authors of the otherwise so popular genre of historical fiction is symptomatic of this problem. An example of minor contributions to the genre is provided by Frances Winwar. Born "Vinciguerra" in Taormina, Sicily, she adopted her Anglicized pen-name, an exact translation of her Italian name, when she published *The Ardent Flame* (1927), a thirteenth-century romance based on the tale of Francesca di Rimini; and she also wrote an American historical novel about the hysteria of the Salem witchcraft trials, *Gallows Hill* (1937). Yet only one single African American historical novel was published between 1910 and 1950, Arna Bontemps's *Black Thunder* (1936); and Henry Roth's attempt at completing a second novel in the 1930s failed precisely because he could not imagine what the historical memory of the Civil War could have meant to a twentieth-century native-born American radical.

In many ways, the short autobiographical sketches, presented from the point of view of a liberal reformer, represent the more general tensions in ethnic autobiography in the first half of the century, though *The Life Stories of Undistinguished Americans* do not reveal much of the subjects' psychology. The social questionnaire that the storytellers answered or anticipated and addressed implicitly did not provide much of an opening for such revelations. "Where do you come from? Why, when, and how did you come to America? Are you better off now? Where do you work? How much money do you make? Where do you live? How do you spend your day? What is the role of the family in your group?" The authors or informants were busy answering the cluster of direct or implied questions that surrounded the debates about immigration and race. Their lives seemed to be interesting to the extent that they were socially representative of the groups they "typified," a fact the titles or subtitles of many life stories made clear. (One only has to think of "The Race Problem – an Autobiography by a Southern Colored Woman.") The narrators conveyed social meaning and found little time for introspection. After all, such short "lifelets" may not be the appropriate place for laying bare one's inner soul. They were a popular genre with American readers, and Ernest Poole followed Holt's lead, authoring such first-person stories as "Up from the Ghetto: From a Dweller to a Speculator in Slums" and "Getting That Home: Told by Jan, the Big Polish Laborer," even for the anti-immigration *Saturday Evening Post* (1906).

Numerous "authentic" and "inauthentic" ethnic autobiographies followed, and the borderline between "real" and "fake" is more difficult to draw than one might think, as the genre of ethnic autobiographies written by impersonators suggests. Now, if one sees a nonrepresentational, modernist painting and learns that the artist was Jewish, that fact alone does not necessarily add anything to the understanding or enjoyment of the work. Only fascists, nativists, or racists believed that Jews were determined to paint *as* Jews; hence the revelation that a painter was Jewish could have enormous consequences in a fascist world. Outside of racist paranoia, there might only be a mild recognition of kinship, group pride, or of very subtle difference that would not necessarily have a bearing on the appreciation of the work itself. Similarly, if we were then told that the first ascription had been false and that the artist actually was not Jewish but Anglo-American, that information would just result in an unemotional correction process in our brains.

These rules do not apply to American ethnic autobiography (or to much ethnic literature in general). For better or worse, ethnic literature has often been read as social evidence; and the "ethnic authenticity" of the work in question (which largely depended on the ethnic background of the author) was therefore a crucial element for ethnic advocates and detractors alike. This issue can be traced back at least to the early abolitionists who, like Richard Hildreth's immensely popular *The Slave; or, Memoirs of Archy Moore* (1836), had created the fake slave narrative and were challenged for it by Southerners. Reading texts for an author's ethnicity was also not uncommon in discussions of American literature that tried to excise some parts of that literature as too foreign. The University of Illinois literary historian Stuart P. Sherman, for example, attacked Theodore Dreiser in the *Nation* in 1915 for his "barbaric naturalism" that was representative of "a new note in American literature, coming from the 'ethnic' element of our mixed population." Dreiser's ethnic background, Sherman implied, seemed to make him less of an "American," less of a "main stream" writer.

Yet even a casual survey of American ethnic autobiography shows a great variety of forms that complicate a reading process which aims for clear ethnic boundaries on which inclusion or exclusion, appreciation or dismissal could be based. As in the case of *The Life Stories*, the borderline between "authentic," "as-told-to," ghostwritten, and fabricated texts is fluid.

Some autobiographies were published by an ethnic author who was identified by name, and they were narrated in the first-person singular. Mary Antin's *The Promised Land* (1912) is representative, but it begins with the warning, "I am absolutely other than the person whose story I have to tell." Antin proposed to her publisher the use of two different names for her past and present self throughout the book. Other ethnic autobiographies were published under the author's name and were narrated in the third person. *The Americanization of Edward Bok* (1920) is a good example, yet the use of the third person here is universal only for the Edward of the past, whereas the Bok of the present uses the first person to describe his current views and opinions. Thus, one chapter is entitled "A Bewildered Bok," another one, "What I Owe to America." The confusion of pronouns in *The Life Stories* was merely an example of a more widespread phenomenon. Gertrude Stein was to be the master at confusing pronouns in *The Autobiography of Alice B. Toklas*; it was an "autobiography" ostensibly written in Toklas's voice which logically referred to Gertrude Stein in the third person (and always by her full name). Yet at the very end of the book this fiction is surprisingly given up: "About six weeks ago Gertrude Stein said, it does not look to me as if you were ever going to write that autobiography. You know what I am going to do. I am going to write it for you. I am going to write it as simply as Defoe did the autobiography of Robinson Crusoe. And she has and this is it."

Some writers adopted pen-names that would make the reader expect "ethnic" works. In the nineteenth century, Henry Harland had published Jewish romances under the name "Sidney Luska"; and after the end of our period

Daniel James published a Chicano book under the ethnically more appropriate pseudonym "Danny Santiago." The story of the Eaton sisters Winifred and
Edith Maude constitutes an interesting example of the complicated boundaries between literary fiction and ethnic authenticity. The daughters of an
interracial Anglo-Chinese couple, Edith chose the Chinese American identity of "Sui Sin Far" and published "Leaves from the Mental Portfolio of an
Eurasian," an autobiographical lifelet for Holt's *Independent* (1909), whereas
the younger Winifred concealed her partly Chinese origins and opted for the
Japanese pen-name "Onoto Watanna" and wrote Geisha romances such as
Miss Nume of Japan: A Japanese–American Romance (1899), some of which made
it to Hollywood. At first glance, one sister would seem to be "authentic"
and the other "fake," yet both had to work at imagining and sustaining the
divergent Asian images they wished to project. And books by both sisters were
lavishly designed in an "oriental" manner.

Anonymous publication also permitted full fictionalization of the genre
expectation, as in the case of the first-person-singular *Autobiography of an
Ex-Colored Man* (1912), taken to be a confession by a man of partly black
ancestry who had passed for white and was now revealing the secrets of race
relations by drawing aside the "veil," but the book was really a novel written
by James Weldon Johnson. The immigrant intellectual Abraham Cahan's first-
person novel, *The Rise of David Levinsky* (1917), praised by Carl Van Doren as
"the most notable of the immigrant novels before 1920," was first published
in partial serialization in *McClure's Magazine*, illustrated, and under the title,
"The Autobiography of an American Jew" (1913). Originally, Samuel Ornitz's
novel, *Haunch, Paunch and Jowl* (1923), was published anonymously, advertised by its publisher Boni and Liveright with a big question mark instead of
an author's photograph, and classified by the philosopher Horace Kallen as a
"pseudo-autobiography." Sylvester C. Long's *Long Lance* (1928) was published
as an American Indian autobiography, and though the author lived as a Native
American, his claim of Indian ancestry is now often considered invalid. When
the editors of *Esquire* wanted to accept the story "Christ in Concrete" (1937) by
the Italian American bricklayer Pietro di Donato, they were worried that they
might have fallen for a "Union Square or Greenwich Village gag" and they sent
Jewish American writer Meyer Levin to "look up, and over, Mr. di Donato and
confirm or deny our cynical suspicion." Fortunately, Levin found di Donato
to be the real article; Levin reported that the young Italian American writer
was "indeed a bricklayer, and apparently a very good one," who furthermore
looked "like young Dante." Elizabeth Stern's works *My Mother and I* (1917,
introduced by Theodore Roosevelt) and *I Am a Woman – And a Jew* (1926),
long read as authentic autobiographical expressions by an American Jewish

woman, were later dismantled by Stern's own son who claimed that Stern had made up her Jewish birth. The dispute around these dramatically conflicting claims has not yet been resolved.

Other autobiographies were published under an ethnic author's name, but were commissioned and ghostwritten, or resulted from different degrees of collaboration. Thus *My Autobiography* (1914), the Irish immigrant memoir "by S. S. McClure," was in reality ghostwritten by Willa Cather. McClure, a powerful editor who had invented syndicated writing, had control over his text, but the ethnic subjects whose life stories were published in "as told to" format (among them, several of Holt's *Life Stories* and many of the first-person lifelets published in American magazines) had no such power. The growing phenomenon of ghostwriting affected both "celebrities" (a concept that has been on the ascent since the 1920s) and the truly poor (who often had little or no control over the shaping or the thrust of their published autobiographies). Various euphemisms were used to describe the relationship of subject and writer, such as "in collaboration with," "given by," "reported by," "with," and even "directed by" (in a 1928 *Saturday Evening Post* life story about the actor Harold Lloyd). Past and present self, first and third person, and authorized and spoken-for subjects have populated the books with alternating genre ascription, yet all were often read for the "ethnic character" – however problematically it may have been constituted.

There was considerable confusion about the literary genres of ethnic writing. Louis Adamic began writing *Laughing in the Jungle: The Autobiography of an Immigrant in America* (1931) as a novel, but then augmented it by previously published essays as well as new first-person materials about the author's Slovenian childhood in the province of Carniola and emigration to America in 1914, so that the subtitle of the book characterizes only a part of what is really a mixed-genre work.

Some autobiographies were published alternately as "novel" or as "memoir." Jerre Mangione's *Mount Allegro* (1942) is representative. Although *Mount Allegro* is narrated in the first-person singular, the first publisher persuaded the author late in the writing stage to change the narrator's name to "Gerlando Amoroso" and identified the book as "fiction." The first edition, however, made the best-seller lists both in fiction and in nonfiction. The last authorized reprint in Mangione's lifetime received the subtitle, "A Memoir of Italian American Life." Mike Gold's *Jews Without Money* (1930) is written in the first-person singular, reads like a memoir, and was billed as an autobiography when Liveright first published it in 1930, but was labeled a novel when it was reissued by Sun Dial Press in 1946; and it is now often viewed and discussed as autobiographical fiction.

In ethnic prose literature of the first half of the twentieth century, ethnic personae and novelistic inventions were close to each other, since even the most "authentic" autobiographies published in English had to imply certain American audience expectations and since even the most inauthentic ones could contain much intuitively truthful or well-researched social information. Whether true or made up, ethnic autobiographies often implied the questionnaire that was behind Holt's *Life Stories* and constituted answers to what Henry James called "the ethnic question" that loomed large in the period from 1910 to 1950.

3

☙

ETHNIC THEMES, MODERN THEMES

THNIC LITERATURE of the first half of the twentieth century developed a repertoire of ethnic themes. In addition to class mobility and assimilation, generational tensions appear often (at times in ethnic trilogies), as does the conflict between arranged marriage and romantic love. Rifts between children and parents are prominent, and the often complex mother–son and father–daughter relations receive particular emphasis. Encounters with ethnic hatred or hypocrisy are frequently represented, as are friendly and amorous relations across ethnic boundaries. The attenuation of older religious beliefs and ethical standards finds manifold expression in these works. Since a central persona is often correlated to the figure of the aspiring author, difficult negotiations between the world of work and the realm of artistic creation are common. Education tends to be central, both as a school setting and as a possible symbolic area of resolution of the various tensions. Protagonists tend to be relatively young so that the general process of socialization can be described in the context of cultural conflicts and the pressures of American assimilation. Getting lost in a foreign-language cityscape or feeling lost in the vast-seeming countryside are common experiences. The tensions of poor ethnic families in working-class polyethnic neighborhoods in an often mythic-seeming America are omnipresent and at times decisive for the plot. Shame and pride may alternate in characters' responses to their ethnicity. There are scenes in which the contrast between the ethnic group and America is dramatized and others in which it is bridged. Ethnic foodways are mentioned favorably, at times with the appropriate non-English name, and sometimes the details that are given amount to a recipe. The Americanness of a given moment may be underlined by the presence of flag, a song, or another national symbol, like the Statue of Liberty; and ethnic protagonists may recognize their own Americanness when they travel abroad, and especially, to a place of symbolic significance for their ethnic identity, in the case of immigrants, when they return for a visit to their country of origin. A sense of double consciousness pervades the literature and often finds its expression in the simultaneous presence of general

American and ethnic symbols, of two intertwined flags, for example, or in the descriptions of two settings in terms of each other. In short, ethnic literature offers many details, large and small, that have been of interest to sociologists, anthropologists, and ethnic historians.

When it is not read for its ethnic themes, however, ethnic literature of the first half of the twentieth century shows a remarkable concern for the American world of modernity. In part, this tendency reveals itself in fleeting instances when the ethnic group in question is associated with an older, premodern, or "medieval" ethos. Mary Antin described immigration as if it were time-traveling and focused on the paradox that her life metaphorically spanned centuries: "My age alone, my true age, would be reason enough for my writing. I began life in the Middle Ages, as I shall prove, and here I am still, your contemporary in the twentieth century, thrilling with your latest thought." African American intellectuals, too, used the distinction between the middle ages and the modern period to describe the history of the race. Alain Locke wrote in the introduction to his landmark anthology *The New Negro* (1925) that each wave of migration is "in the Negro's case a deliberate flight not only from countryside to city, but from medieval America to modern." Since America is the proverbial "country without middle ages," such rhetorical (and heavily ideological) strategies put urban America into sharp relief as the embodiment of modern society against the presumably community-and-tradition-oriented ethnic group, especially prior to migration. And the term "middle ages" serves as a convenient unifier of the heterogeneous premodern pasts that are assimilated to a single notion of progress. Moreover, this imaginative belief in a single, Anglo-American notion of progress as the embodiment of the "modern" had the effect of giving an appearance of unity to dramatically divergent experiences of modernization: those forms of modernization that came from within American culture and transformed it tended to replace rather than transform existing cultural features in minority and ethnic groups. Yet the pervasive concern with modernity goes far beyond this form of metaphorical postmedievalism, as the reader finds in American ethnic literature images of the details of modernity, from skyscrapers to automobiles and airplanes, and from the machinery of the workplace to fast food and the many features of modern leisure culture.

Mary Antin has a keen eye for such New World features as the speaking-tube, the soda fountain, cold lemonade, hot peanuts, and pink popcorn as well as chewing candy. Leo Kobrin stages an encounter of strangers at the automat in New York City. Jean Toomer notes cardboard advertisements for Chesterfield cigarettes and Chero-Cola. Zora Neale Hurston (in her "Story in Harlem Slang," 1942) incorporates the soft-drink bottle into urban banter:

"But baby! . . . Dat shape you got on you! I bet the Coca Cola Company is paying you good money for the patent!" Henry Roth includes such details as the "sword with the big middle on Mecca cigarettes." Anzia Yezierska mentions ketchup stains and "ready-made" clothing (in *Salome of the Tenements*). In *Home to Harlem*, Claude McKay comments on the novelty of hip pockets in his character Jake's suit, and James T. Farrell calls attention to electric malted-milk shakers. Richard Wright's Bigger Thomas sees airplanes flying over Chicago. Popular songs are in the background of Carl Van Vechten's *Nigger Heaven* (1926), and the "Indian Love Call" can be heard on a phonograph in Pietro di Donato's *Christ in Concrete* (1939). In Daniel Fuchs's *Homage to Blenholt* (1936), the character Ruth dozes off at a manicurist's – an event which is stylistically marked by a one-page catalogue of popular and commercial culture items ranging from Bing Crosby and Myrna Loy to Hindu brown stockings and an "E.Z. Hair Removing Glove." In Willard Motley's *Knock on Any Door* (1947) the Italian American Nick Romano looks at a sign in a plate-glass window that reads, in mirrored reverse, "CHILI 10¢" as he leans against a gum machine. And everybody goes to the movies, listens to the radio (some protagonists build crystal radio sets), notices newspaper headlines, leafs through magazines, and takes electric streetcars and subways.

In these aspects ethnic literature participates in general American features. Henry James and Henry Adams may have been the first to introduce brand names to American literature when they wrote of a "Remington" (James's typewriter) or a "Kodak" (Adams's camera); and Hemingway expanded the horizons of American Prohibition-era readers when he gave brand names from Pernod and Cinzano to Veuve Cliquot champagne a firm presence in *The Sun Also Rises* (1926). Salesmen who peddle modern gadgets are ubiquitous in American prose from Mark Twain's *A Connecticut Yankee in King Arthur's Court* (1889) to Eudora Welty's "Death of a Traveling Salesman" (1936). Mark Twain, Gertrude Stein, John Dos Passos, and Richard Wright were fascinated by newspaper headlines and incorporated them into their writing. Gertrude Atherton mentions nail polish as a device to camouflage supposed "tell-tale" signs of mixed-race origins on the fingernails of "suspicious brunettes." Other writers offered whole inventories of modernity: F. Scott Fitzgerald's *The Great Gatsby* (1925) included the *Saturday Evening Post*, the car repair shop, and the gigantic billboard; John Dos Passos's *U.S.A.* (1938) imitated the forms of camera eye, newspaper clipping, and newsreel.

There are some subtle differences: ethnic literature, because of its more pervasive working-class affinities and urban locales, was more likely to show encounters with public transportation than with the beauty of the most fanciful automobiles, with technology in the world of labor, typified by concrete mixing in di Donato's book, rather than in the realm of conspicuous consumption. At times, ethnic authors also were inclined to dramatize the features of modernity against the background of a premodern community that still seemed within reach. It is indubitable that the themes of modernity are pervasive in American ethnic literature from 1910 to 1950; and it is quite possible that ethnic literature was even more extensively engaged with features of modernity than were many mainstream writers. In some cases, the ethnic writers who were connected with modern means of publication reached such a wide or intense dissemination as to elicit envy from more traditionally positioned authors. Thus Theodore Roosevelt yearned for Edward Bok's ability to reach millions of Americans who would read the *Ladies' Home Journal* leisurely in their private sphere. Roosevelt wrote Bok: "My messages are printed in the newspapers and read hurriedly, mostly by men in trolleys or rail-road cars."

Being thematically modern could, but did not necessarily, mean being formally modernist. In a social setting in which incongruity resulting from the incompatibility of various pasts may have been the most widely shared cultural feature, there was perhaps no alternative to modernity. Migration and accelerated culture contacts helped to produce "marginal men," a term the Chicago sociologist Robert E. Park derived from Georg Simmel's concept of the "stranger" who is simultaneously inside and outside a community; and the artists among them may have wished to translate the experience of modernity into the aesthetic experiments of modernism. In other words, their marginal location in a world of modernity may have pushed some writers who were immigrants and migrants toward modernism. The "translated" quality of some of their expressions makes them resemble avant-garde prose, as in the story of the Japanese man-servant in Holt's *Life Stories*: "The way to open the door, salute the guest, language to be used according to the rank of the guests and how to handle the name card. Characteristic simplicity of democracy could not be seen in this household." Or one may think of Genya Schearl's expression "it grows late" in Henry Roth's *Call It Sleep*, or of the magical word *girarihir* that, Jerre Mangione writes in *Mount Allegro*, Italian immigrants learned even before they landed in America, and that turns out to mean, "Get out of here." Such cases of a defamiliarization of the English language seem to straddle a borderline between naturalistic verisimilitude and modernist prose.

Yet the language of modernity only occasionally overlaps with that of modernism; and no matter how much some modernists may have invoked modernity, there was no inescapable linkage of modernity and modernism. The ways in which individual writers reacted to the modern world of cities and technology varied significantly. It is useful to remember the distinction between modernity (embodied by the processes of secularization on the one hand, and of urbanization and industrialization on the other) and modernism (the formally experimental ways in which many writers, composers, and artists chose to express themselves in the twentieth century). After all, a given writer's views of modernity could be at variance with his or her attitudes toward modernism. Thus four basic literary types emerged:

(a) Some writers were critical of modernity and used traditional, premodern (nonmodernist, or antimodernist) literary forms in order to voice their criticism. This was the case for some genteel or nostalgic writing, at times articulated in the name of a mythic homogeneous rural or small-town past. Some *Saturday Evening Post* writing and the Norman Rockwell covers illustrate this orientation; but it was a mode that was relatively rare in ethnic literature.

(b) Other authors expressed the themes of modernity yet refrained from employing modernist forms. This was a common mode in ethnic literature (Bok, Yezierska), that described migration, immigration, ethnicity, and modernity in premodernist prose and plotlines.

(c) Writers could also be deeply critical of modernity, and prefer, for example, traditional religious beliefs, but express themselves in a modernist fashion. Much literature commonly discussed under the modernist label falls into this category of experimentally expressed critiques of (or laments about) technological modernity. T. S. Eliot is a prime example.

(d) Finally, some writing was both promodern and modernist. This was the case for many ethnic and minority writers, especially those from groups who look back to pasts that offer too little invitation for sustained nostalgia (e.g. slavery, persecution, or severe class oppression).

Of course, many writers voiced ambivalence about the mixed blessings of modernity and some were open to at least occasional moments of nostalgia, including nostalgia for pasts that never existed. Furthermore, one cannot always distinguish easily between a writer's fascination with, and contempt for, modernity. Some writers believed, for example, that the movement toward modernity was inevitable, preferable to any alternative, yet ultimately tragic.

What this obviously simplified fourfold distinction helps to visualize, however, is that modernity may have been more popular than nostalgia in ethnic writing. Though some outstanding ethnic works did emerge in the period that were part of the modernist movement, the general trend of American ethnic literature may have been toward modernity without modernism. What is often associated with "high modernism" may have been a particular Anglo-American blend of opposition to modernity expressed in aesthetically modernist forms, whereas African American, immigrant, and other ethnic writers may have been less frequently inclined to endorse the modernist strategy of opposing modernity. From a vantage point of classic high modernism, this form of modernism, especially its populist side (the tradition that is audible in modernity-oriented modernist writers) seems lacking in "detachment," hence appears to be "not really" modernist.

4

❧

MARY ANTIN: PROGRESSIVE OPTIMISM AGAINST THE ODDS

IN A SHORT SKETCH called "First Aid to the Alien" and published in *Outlook* in 1912, Mary Antin describes a trolley-car encounter between an American botanist and the little Italian immigrant boy Tomaso Verticelli. Upset by the mess that Italian children have made in the car, and by the helplessness of the conductor who cannot get through to the immigrants because they do not understand a word he is saying, the botanist sternly lectures the little boy, "*No – rubbish – on – the – floor*," adding, "That's not *American*." The Italian boy and his sister seem to understand, and, "like a pair of brown monkeys," they clean the car thoroughly. Later, the boy's teacher discovers that "Thomas" Verticelli strangely believes that the Star-Spangled Banner stands for "America! *No rubbish on the floor!*"

This streetcar encounter resembles that of Stein's "Gentle Lena" more than that of the Southern colored woman in the *Independent*, for it seems to show an act of kindness, of "first aid," among strangers on an electric car. Yet Antin's light and vaguely humorous vignette also represents the issue of "Americanization" as a problem of cleanliness, implies that it was foreign-tongued immigrants who made America dirty, and suggests that the problem could be resolved by education, and especially by teaching the English language and American patriotism. The story literally shows "dirty foreigners" (as xenophobic propaganda would vilify immigrants) but then proceeds to persuade the reader that a good-hearted, scholarly Yankee father figure can get the right message across, even to "monkey"-like little aliens. In other words, Antin engaged the negative stereotype, and even accepted some validity in it, in order to transform it. The strategy of going into the stereotype in order to overcome it was characteristic of much of Antin's writing, including her autobiography *The Promised Land* (1912), probably the most outstanding American immigrant autobiography of the twentieth century.

Antin, the daughter of Israel and Esther Weltman Antin, was born at Polotzk in czarist Russia (now Belarus) on June 13, 1881. Her father emigrated to the United States in 1891, and three years later the mother followed with the four children, arriving in Boston on the *Polynesia* on May 8, 1894. The Antin family lived in generally poor circumstances in the Boston area, where Mary and the younger siblings began public school in Chelsea, whereas her sister "Fetchke/Frieda," only a year older than Mary, had to work as a seamstress. Though Antin's native language was Yiddish, and she came to Boston at age thirteen without knowing a word of English, she became an excellent writer in the English language. As she put it memorably, "I learned at least to think in English without an accent."

Antin was keenly interested in modernity and developed an elaborate contrast between the "medieval" Old World and modern America. Yet her writing clearly was not modernist. She directly attempted to address the "ethnic question" that hung in the air in the period. And she gave much room not only to her social self, but also to some of her inner motives and feelings.

There is no doubt that Antin was deeply aware of the growing hostility to immigration in the United States, for she campaigned in lectures and in much of her published writing against the immigration restrictions that were legislated in 1917, 1921, and 1924. Yet she was among ethnic writers who published autobiographical writing that not only answered the ethnic questionnaire (so familiar from Hamilton Holt's *Life Stories*) but also offered glimpses of a subtle self-revelation that had much power independent of the social context of the immigration debate.

Antin's autobiographical writing followed a trajectory that made her wonderfully representative of the times. Her writing career started with a personal letter in Yiddish about her emigration experience that she sent to an uncle in 1894. She later translated this account into English (with some dramatic changes) and published it, in a circle of philanthropists and Jewish intellectuals, under the title *From Plotzk to Boston* (1899, the printer misspelling the name of her home town). The little book carried a glowing introduction by Israel Zangwill, whose celebrated immigrant melodrama, *The Melting-Pot* (1908), helped to popularize the term that would soon be commonly used to describe American ethnic assimilation. The essayist Josephine Lazarus – the sister of Statue of Liberty poet Emma Lazarus – reviewed the volume, and Antin became known as a child prodigy, all the more so since it was generally believed that she was two years younger than her actual age. Antin also benefited from the South End Settlement House of Edward Everett Hale – who was famous for such literary works as "The Man Without a Country" (1863) – and she described her own experiences with allusions to Hale's novella, as when she states that in Russia Jews had been "a people without a country." She alludes to the Bible, to Augustine's *Confessions*, *Robinson Crusoe* (which she read in translation while she was still in Russia), Coleridge's "Ancient Mariner,"

Emerson's essays, Sewell's *Black Beauty*, Sue's *Wandering Jew*, and the Aladdin of *The Arabian Nights*, Robert Louis Stevenson, George Eliot, Mark Twain, Tennyson, Longfellow, and Whittier. She also mentions popular works ranging from Russian and Yiddish periodical romances to Jacob Abbott's *Rollo* series (which started in 1839) and George Madden Martin's *Emmy Lou: Her Book and Heart* (1902). In short, her literary canon was extensive, and it was also exclusively premodernist. For a Russian immigrant, it was also a remarkably Western list; and one notices the absence of those great Russian writers whom Claude McKay saw as embodiments of the modern spirit: Gogol, Dostoyevsky, Tolstoy, Chekhov, and Turgenyev.

At age thirty she carried out the project of a full-length literary autobiography, some chapters of which appeared first in Ellery Sedgwick's prestigious *Atlantic Monthly*. In April, 1912, the leading publishing house in Boston, Houghton Mifflin Company, printed the nicely designed book, illustrated with eighteen photographs, and with a golden Statue of Liberty in outline engraved on the front cover, its torch on the spine. The dust-jacket, also decorated with a Statue of Liberty, carried the subtitle "The Autobiography of a Russian Immigrant," which appeared nowhere else in the book.

In its twenty chapters, *The Promised Land* gives a vivid account of the author's life in Russia and America, of her childhood, her emigration to Boston, and her Americanization in the public schools. She comes across as a precocious, intellectually probing Jewish child and a happy and observant American adolescent and adult. She had to face much adversity: as a girl in Polotzk, she was excluded from the world of Jewish learning; and because of her father's occupational failings, she lived under truly poor circumstances in and around Boston. However, as a teacher's pet, she thrived in the American school, and the autobiography sounds a note of promise. She pioneers in articulating what became known as "the American dream" ("America became my dream," she writes), embraces America as "my country" (thus rewriting Hale), and ultimately comes to consider herself the "heir of the ages," a biblical phrasing that had been used by Tennyson, John Fiske, and Henry James.

America is the youngest of the nations, and inherits all that went before in history. And I am the youngest of America's children, and into my hands is given all her priceless heritage, to the last white star espied through the telescope, to the last great thought of the philosopher. Mine is the whole majestic past, and mine is the shining future.

This is the upbeat end of the narrative, followed in the manuscript by a bold "FINIS." Antin's book was published three years after Gertrude Stein had so heartlessly undermined the literary convention of endings. *The Promised Land* reaches such an emphatic crescendo that the end was brought out on a

78 r.p.m. record, read by an agitated male voice. This climactic ending was not only explicitly premodern (in the sense that it adhered to the very conventions Stein sought to undermine), but it also appealed to the general reader and was used as social evidence in books like William P. Shriver's *Immigrant Forces: Factors in the New Democracy* (1913).

In her approach to the frail magic of memory, Antin is representative of the importance of the act of remembering in immigrant literature. *The Promised Land* is the self-conscious, and self-consciously literary, attempt to give aesthetic shape, in remarkably subtle language, to what remain recognizable as fragile memories, wrested from the threatening gray blank of oblivion and cold facts. Memories may fail to return when she invokes them, as the excellent American cherries she eats in a concentrated effort to bring back the taste of Russia cannot evoke in her the fragrant sweet remembrance of things past. She recognizes that this is not just a matter of the contrast between the two countries of her life: "And if I should return to Polotzk, and buy me a measure of cherries at a market stall, and pay for it with a Russian groschen, would the market woman be generous enough to throw in that haunting flavor? I fear I should find that the old species of cherry is extinct in Polotzk." On the other hand, memories may suddenly erupt, as when eating "ripe, red, American strawberries" she is shocked to experience, in breathless amazement, the "very flavor and aroma of some strawberries" she ate twenty years earlier.

Antin started her autobiography as she looked back to half a life spent in the Old World and half in the New. "I was born, I have lived, and I have been made over. Is it not time to write my life's story?" she asks at the opening, and it is at this point that she considers herself "absolutely other than the person whose story I have to tell." From the manuscript stage on, her autobiography was always more or less evenly divided between a Russian and an American half.

As a good stylist, Antin supplements her description of the immigration experience by sounding out the vocabulary commonly used to explain it. She writes that she was "transplanted to the new soil" at a most impressionable age. "All the processes of uprooting, transportation, replanting, acclimatization, and development took place in my own soul." And she applied the language of the biblical Exodus to the secular migration from Russia to America, with such chapter headings as "The Tree of Knowledge," "Manna," and "The Burning Bush."

Antin made many fresh and some startling observations. She captures the sense of endlessness that the Russian railroad tracks in Polotzk conveyed to her as a child – a technologically modern feature present in her "medieval" childhood. Later, the view of the "dim tangle of the railroad tracks below"

South Boston Bridge gives Antin a sense of the difficulty of finding her own "proper track." She is also fascinated by Boston streetcars, the "constant clang and whirr of electric cars," and she plays the dangerous children's game of cutting "across the tracks in front of an oncoming car." "[I]t was great fun to see the motorman's angry face turn scared, when he thought I was going to be shaved this time sure." She uses images of modernity to account for her own situation, and that of immigrants in general. "We are the strands of the cable that binds the Old World to the New," she writes. She comments hauntingly on the fears of death the emigrants experienced when they underwent compulsory disinfection in Germany, on their way from Russia to America:

[O]ur things were taken away, our friends separated from us; a man came to inspect us, as if to ascertain our full value; strange-looking people driving us about like dumb animals, helpless and unresisting; children we could not see crying in a way that suggested terrible things; ourselves driven into a little room where a great kettle was boiling on a little stove; our clothes taken off, our bodies rubbed with a slippery substance that might be any bad thing; a shower of warm water let down on us without warning; again driven to another little room where we sit, wrapped in woollen blankets till large, coarse bags are brought in, their contents turned out, and we see only a cloud of steam, and hear the women's orders to dress ourselves, – "Quick! Quick!" – or else we'll miss – something we cannot hear. We are forced to pick out our clothes from among all the others, with the steam blinding us; we choke, cough, entreat the women to give us time; they persist, "Quick! Quick! – or you'll miss the train!" Oh, so we really won't be murdered! They are only making us ready for the continuing of our journey, cleaning us of all suspicion of dangerous sickness. Thank God!

(This passage was adapted from the Yiddish letter she wrote to her uncle at age thirteen and that was freely translated and first published in *From Plotzk to Boston* in 1899, where Antin continued that they were "assured by the word 'train.'" This sample attests to her early gift as a writer.)

In *The Promised Land* Antin distinguishes the horrifying crowd description of the Russian pogrom – "They attacked them with knives and clubs and scythes and axes, killed them or tortured them, and burned their houses" – from the elating and freeing crowd experience among the milling pedestrians in Chelsea: "A million threads of life and love and sorrow was the common street; and whether we would or not, we entangled ourselves in a common maze."

Again and again, Antin is drawn to explain the vocabulary of her Old World past and of Jewishness, and a linguistic glossary is appended to *The Promised Land*. This is an exceptionally detailed instance of a widespread strategy in ethnic writing. Such a glossary cannot be a systematic instrument; and an unexplained rest always tends to remain. Yet the glossary establishes Antin as the mediator who gives to the English-speaking non-Jewish reader (for whom it was prepared and who was imagined by Antin to be ignorant of and perhaps even somewhat hostile to Jews) a minimal ethnic vocabulary. That this is not done value-free is apparent when one reads, for example, under "*Hasid*, pl. *Hasidim*": "A numerous sect of Jews distinguished for their enthusiasm in religious observance, a fanatical worship of their rabbis and many superstitious practices."

One purpose of *The Promised Land* was to offset a growing sense of American nativist hostility to immigration by presenting a young woman's consciousness that successfully underwent the transformation from foreign immigrant to American citizen. Antin at times addresses the imagined gentile reader as "my American friend" and tries to convince him or her of her point: "What if the ragpicker's daughters are hastening over the ocean to teach your children in the public schools?" (These direct addresses to the reader are in the old vein of Harriet Beecher Stowe, not in the Steinian fashion.)

Antin's American patriotism gives poor Jewish immigrants a special place and an entitlement. In America, a Senator and an obscure child from the slums may "seal a democratic friendship based on the love of a common flag." Shouts like "Three cheers for the Red, White, and Blue!" are justified in a country in which a Jewish immigrant schoolgirl can recite poems addressed to Washington, as Antin famously did. Interestingly, while this poem establishes Antin's Americanization, she also states that "a special note" ran through her patriotic Washington poem that "only Israel Rubinstein and Beckie Aronovitch," her Jewish classmates, "could have fully understood." Her homemaking myth is that Jewish immigrants have a special understanding; paradoxically, that is what makes them ideal Americans.

Antin cheers the Red, White, and Blue at another, more troubling, occasion when she praises the American system of justice for punishing a "great, hulky colored boy, who was the torment of the neighborhood" and had treated her "roughly." The court hearing seemed completely fair to her. "The evil-doer was actually punished, and not the victim, as might very easily happen in a similar case in Russia. 'Liberty and justice for all.' Three cheers for the Red, White, and Blue!" It is remarkable that Antin is not able here to imagine any analogies between the roles of Jews in the Pale and of blacks in turn-of-the-century America.

What interests Antin foremost is the psychological consequence of the social experience of immigration on her as a child and as an adult. She embarks upon the course of becoming an American, but she does not suppress how difficult the shift in immigrant orientation can be. Like many other immigrants, Antin movingly evokes the specific tastes of her homeland: she recognizes that it takes history to make a Polotzk cheesecake, and concedes that the fragrance of childhood cherries may be lost even in the Russia of the author's later years. Thus it is all the more remarkable that even though her faith in America is expressed in such metaphors as "manna," America hardly seems appetizing. In Boston, the family may eat "without any cooking, from little tin cans that had printing all over them." By far the most detailed American eating scene Antin describes is also a haunting ethnic-loyalty test. When her Chelsea schoolteacher Miss Mary S. Dillingham invites her to tea, Antin realizes that the strange meat served to her was "ham – forbidden food." She is afraid, then angry at her weakness:

> I to be afraid of a pink piece of pig's flesh, who had defied at least two religions in defence of free thought! And I began to reduce my ham to indivisible atoms, determined to eat more of it than anybody else at the table.
> Alas! I learned that to eat in defence of principles was not so easy as to talk. I ate, but only a newly abnegated Jew can understand with what squirming, what protesting of the inner man, what exquisite abhorrence of myself.

Taking "possession" (as she repeatedly puts it) of the New World was also like swallowing down undesirable food, in defense of principles but over the protests of her "inner man," her conscience that accuses her of ethnic treason. What is all the more disturbing about this scene is that this was Antin's "first entrance into a genuine American household" and that her host was the well-intentioned teacher who brought about Antin's first publication of a school composition and who encouraged her to translate her emigration letter into English. Is the stilling of her "hunger" for reading and writing, of which she repeatedly speaks, in any way connected with this painful, traumatic scene of kin betrayal and self-destruction? And does her experience not dramatize the anxiety of many ethnic intellectuals that, in giving up religiously based maxims of their childhood, they might not be joining, on an equal footing, an international group of modern, cosmopolitan freethinkers but only ingratiating themselves to the host society's sets of superstitions based on another, alien, religion that merely passes itself off as more "modern"?

Antin is extremely self-conscious of the autobiographical project and articulates, in a first-person narrative, the lure of other identity (and pronoun) options in order to examine her pervasive sense of doubleness: "I could speak in the third person and not feel that I was masquerading. I can analyze my subject; I can reveal everything; for *she*, and not *I*, is my real heroine." The word "heroine" suggests the conscious use of novelistic strategies. Of all the American immigrant narratives in which pronoun confusion abounds, Antin's may be the most self-conscious. Antin even proposed to her editor, Ellery Sedgwick, that she would use her own (maiden) name only on the

title page, but a "different name – Esther Altmann, as I have it – in the text."
("Esther Altmann" would have been the symmetrical opposite of Henry James's
"Christopher Newman," for Esther was not only Antin's mother's first name,
but also an allusion to the biblical figure of the queen who saved the Jews
in Persia, and the surname literally means "old man" and is evocative of Old
World origins, but also close to Antin's mother's maiden name Weltman.)

Antin's interactions with the Boston editor are telling, for Sedgwick published such genteel little pieces as Estelle M. Hart's "Trolley-Car Ornithology,"
Atlantic Monthly (1908), which encouraged tramway-riders to watch birds on
ordinary routes since "more of their habits can be noted from a rushing trolley-
car than one would at first thought deem possible." But he also ran Randolph
Bourne's essay "Trans-National America" (1916), with the central tenet of
which he strongly disagreed; in a letter Sedgwick criticized Bourne for sounding "as though the last immigrant should have as great an effect upon the determination of our history as the first band of Englishmen." Tellingly, Sedgwick
seriously questioned the wisdom of Randolph Bourne's vision of a transnational
America, and simply turned down Gertrude Stein's submissions, but he was
very hospitable to Mary Antin – who in their correspondence teasingly asked
the Boston Brahmin editor to verify the spelling of some Yiddish words for her.

The book's stylistic range is impressive, from lyrical-mystical to historical-
descriptive, from analytical to evocative, from understated to emphatic passages, and from somber notes to the humor of sudden punch-lines; it is not
surprising that it became a big success. Reviews were often enthusiastic, and
the book's welcoming reception in public libraries and educational institutions
was especially remarkable: Sedgwick had already noticed the interest of librar-
ians who are "in contact with a large number of foreign-born" when the section
"My Country" was published in the *Atlantic Monthly*, but in the summer of
1912 the *New York Sun* reported "the name of the books most called-for at the
various libraries; and Mary Antin's name 'led all the rest.'" *The Promised Land*
was also published in special educational editions with teacher's manuals and
student questions, and it was used as a public school civics-class text as late
as 1949. It has been taken, with Abraham Cahan's fiction, as the beginning of
Jewish literature in America. The editors of the *Outlook* hardly overstated the
case when they observed: "Few recent American books have made as strong an
impression on the reading public as 'The Promised Land'"; and the publisher
also ran blurbs by Louis D. Brandeis and Rabbi Stephen S. Wise. Antin's success undoubtedly inspired the writing of autobiographies by other immigrants
to the United States.

It goes without saying that there were also negative voices. The same Mike
Gold who accused Gertrude Stein of "literary idiocy" attacked Antin, with

similar restraint, for explaining "away all the horror and injustice man has established." Gold calls Antin a "bright slum parvenu who wrote that exuberant book of gratitude." As if she had not written about slums and tenements, Gold addresses and admonishes her directly: "See, Mary, how the . . . roaches and bedbugs venture from our moldy walls." He concludes: "America's slums could never dim the faith of Mary Antin in the spirit of '76, for she and her type have climbed up into a place in the bourgeois sun, and they are grateful – so grateful for their deliverance! Ah, the good God; ah, the Promised Land!" Published in the radical, low-circulation *Liberator*, and six years after the publication of *The Promised Land*, Gold's comment did little to stem the book's success.

Newspapers and periodicals praised Antin's patriotism and compared her with Benjamin Franklin, Jacob Riis, Carl Schurz, Booker T. Washington, W. E. B. Du Bois, and James Weldon Johnson. Reviewers accentuated both the individual and the ethnic aspects of the autobiography, viewing Antin as an "extreme individualist" and the book as "a treatise on sociology, of which education is the dominant feature." With the success of her autobiography, Antin's career seemed made. Yet success was not to be her ultimate destiny.

Under the management of the Boston agency "The Players," she embarked upon a lucrative career as a public lecturer speaking on behalf of Progressive causes and in favor of immigrants. She also showed a rather moderate feminist side (more moderate at least than Roosevelt thought), claiming her right as "woman" and as "immigrant" to speak as a "citizen." She said before the election of 1912: "I am not a suffragist, but I wish I had a vote just this once." Her wish for America to be "the leading nation of this age in respect to justice and humanity" made her want to "send a Progressive President to the White House." This would also be good for immigrants. "I call the attention of all naturalized citizens to the fact that the Progressive party is the only one that has any idea of what is due to the immigrant," she concluded, thus making a special appeal to the immigrant vote.

She traveled extensively and lectured on such topics as "The Responsibility of American Citizenship," "The Civic Education of the Immigrant," "The Public School as a Test of American Faith," "Jewish Life in the Pale: A Lesson for Americans," or "The Zionist Movement." She contributed a series of essays to the *American Magazine* that then became her last book, *They Who Knock at Our Gates: A Complete Gospel of Immigration*, published in 1914, again by Houghton Mifflin Company, Mary Antin's Progressive plea for the immigrant and her impassioned brief against immigration restriction.

The book was illustrated by Joseph Stella, the Italian immigrant whose work had already taken a modernist turn toward his famous Brooklyn Bridge images and become popular in the wake of the Armory Show; yet the portraits used here by Antin were of his earlier, realistic stage, and some had previously accompanied such write-ups of immigrants as "A Mixing Bowl for Nations" by Ernest Poole (one of the ghostwriters for *The Life Stories*) in *Everybody's Magazine* (1910). Joseph Stella had also illustrated Poole's novel *The Voice of the Street* (1906) and produced the perfect visual equivalent to Holt's *Life Stories* when he published in the *Outlook* of 1905 a collection of images called *Americans in the Rough: Character Studies at Ellis Island*. Stella's images enhanced the "typical" reading of specimens of various ethnic groups in the United States, and their titles – such as "A Russian Jew" or "Pittsburgh Types," they could vary from one use of an image to another – asked the viewer to think of the specific person who was represented in terms of larger, often ethnic, collective abstractions. For Stella, an aesthetic turning point came in 1913 during a bus ride to Coney Island when he was struck by the amusement park's "dazzling array of light" and decided to abandon his earlier realist style for a "new kind of art" in order to be able to capture the "brilliance and the dynamic energy of modern life so evident in America." And he focused on subjects like the New York skyscrapers, Brooklyn Bridge, and on such trite settings of modernity as gas tanks (that would also be threateningly present in *Call It Sleep* when David accompanies his father on the milk delivery route). At this time, then, Stella was widely identified with the modern movement, yet Antin chose his earlier, realistic charcoals of immigrant types as illustrations for *They Who Knock*.

What Antin had done on an individual level in *The Promised Land*, she now extended to a full social view of America as a country in which Jewish immigrants can rightly invoke Pilgrims and Revolutionary heroes as "our Fathers." "The notion of the dignity of man, which is the foundation of the gospel of democracy, is derived from Hebrew sources, as the Psalm-singing founders of New England would be the first to acknowledge," she writes. And: "many of the Russian refugees of to-day are a little ahead of the Mayflower troop, because they have in their own lifetime sustained the double ordeal of fight and flight, with all their attendant risks and shocks."

Like her autobiography, *They Who Knock* featured the Statue of Liberty on the cover. For Antin was a pioneer in supporting Emma Lazarus's reading of the Statue as a symbol of welcome to immigrants. Antin also offered a mild correction to the ambiguous phrase "wretched refuse" from Lazarus's poem "The New Colossus" that was affixed to the Statue in 1903 but became increasingly identified with the Statue only after immigration was stopped in 1924. Antin found "convincing proof that what we get in the steerage is not the refuse but the sinew and bone of all the nations," a statement that was particularly emphasized by Joseph Stella's heroic-realist immigrant portrait that served as the book's frontispiece: "THE SINEW AND BONE OF ALL THE NATIONS." What Antin did for the Statue of Liberty, she boldly extended to core symbols of the American nation: "The ghost of the Mayflower pilots every immigrant ship, and Ellis Island is another name for Plymouth Rock," she wrote, imagining the United States as a cosmopolitan model nation in which no background should convey any particular privilege. Though Mike Gold had criticized Mary Antin rather sharply, his book *Jews Without Money* (1930) not only contained a juvenile Washington poem resembling Antin's but also elaborated the analogy Antin made between modern mass immigration and the Pilgrims' arrival. In a chapter that starts with the young narrator's discovery that some new immigrant family is sleeping in his bed, "in their foreign baggy underwear" and smelling "of Ellis Island disinfectant, a stink that sickened me like castor oil," Gold goes on with the pronouncement that "every tenement home was a Plymouth Rock like ours." Louis Adamic, who in 1917 arrived in the United States from Austrian Slovenia at age seventeen, was to develop the rhetorical fusion of Plymouth Rock and Ellis Island further in the 1930s and 1940s; but at the time Antin was writing this was still a very radical proposition. Nobody could have foreseen that it would one day become the rationale for the Ellis Island Museum. After all, in 1956 the Eisenhower administration was ready, two years after the immigration center had closed, to put up Ellis Island for sale and private development.

Antin used the title *They Who Knock at Our Gates* and started a representative sentence with the phrasing, "If we took our mission seriously, – as seriously, say, as the Jews take theirs . . . "; Antin's "we" obviously refers to non-Jewish Americans. As has already become apparent, this confusion of pronouns was common in ethnic autobiography and literature: the Jewish immigrant Edward Steiner wrote similarly in *From Alien to Citizen* (1914), "whether or not we threw the immigrant to the dogs did not matter, so long as he was eaten up and his bones gnawed free of anything foreign." In Antin's case the pronoun-switching had the effect that she was not pleading "we, who knock at your gates," but, having become an American, was assuming "the American point of view." Yet at the same time she stylized immigrants as more protypically "American" than "native born citizens" who were bent on restricting immigration and had lost the sense of Pilgrim and Revolutionary beginnings. Antin thus offered more than merely a personal or Jewish American homemaking myth: hers was a homemaking myth writ large that included all immigrants to the United States.

5

❧

WHO IS "AMERICAN"?

WHAT ANTIN argued in her autobiography and her lectures consti-
tuted in the eyes of some critics an erosion of the word "American."
As that word was increasingly claimed, or "usurped," by "aliens,"
alternative terms were launched such as "100 percent Americans," "native
Americans," "only Americans," "real Americans," or "American-Americans."
Edward Bok asked in his second autobiography, *Twice Thirty: Some Short and
Simple Annals of the Road* (1925): "How many of us, born here or elsewhere,
could qualify as a 'hundred per cent American'? Scarcely one, because, in
truth, there is no such American." Yet both Brander Matthews and Nicholas
Roosevelt resorted to the term "American-Americans" when they critically
reviewed Horace Kallen's 1924 book of essays *Culture and Democracy in the
United States*, the book in which Kallen introduced to print the term "cultural
pluralism," Matthews under the worried headline, "Making America a Racial
Crazy-Quilt." The negatively charged image of the quilt which also appeared
in satirical cartoons of the cubists at the Armory Show had yet to be reimagined
as a positive symbol of America's happily diverse folk heritage.

Antin's own story of Americanization served as a litmus test for the meaning of the word "American." The New Englander Barrett Wendell, who was
among the first professors of English to teach American literature at Harvard
University, wrote in a letter of 1917 that Antin "has developed an irritating habit of describing herself and her people as Americans, in distinction
from such folks as [Wendell's wife] Edith and me, who have been here for
three hundred years." For Wendell – whose conceit of epic longevity was more
sedentary and New World-based than Antin's metaphorical medievalism –
being "American" specifically meant *not* being "Hebrew" or "Ethiopian." Yet
Wendell, like Mary Antin, also identified the original Puritan settlers and
Old Testament Jews. Perhaps he believed even in an actual kinship; yet he
found it impossible to include twentieth-century Jewish immigrants in the
"American" category.

Wendell articulated his opinion of Antin in a personal letter to an English friend. Yet the provocation embodied by Antin's stance also led to a more public debate about the nature of "America" and the question of just *who* was entitled to call it "our country" or to view Pilgrims and Revolutionaries as ancestors. Whereas some native-born liberals praised Antin for her "admiration" of America, and some immigrant readers found her "gratitude" toward her new country disloyal to her origins, the conservative journalist Agnes Repplier was among those Americans who were troubled by Antin's presumptuousness in calling the Pilgrim Fathers "our forefathers" as well as by her critical attitude. "[W]hy should the recipient of so much attention be the one to scold us harshly, to rail at conditions she imperfectly understands, to reproach us for . . . our slackness in duty, our failure to observe the precepts and fulfill the intentions of those pioneers whom she kindly, but confusedly, calls '*our* forefathers.'" Repplier, who failed to see any parallels between Plymouth Rock and Ellis Island, expressed her wartime fear that, for example, German Americans would now fight the battle of Germany in the American ballot by supporting neutralist peace candidates, and argued pointedly that no other nation cherishes the melting-pot illusion, for "An Englishman knows that a Russian Jew cannot in five years, or in twenty-five years, become English."

It must have been particularly troubling for Antin to find Repplier's sentiment on the pages of "her" *Atlantic Monthly*, edited by "her" editor Ellery Sedgwick, a man with whom she corresponded as late as 1937. Repplier seemed to resent Antin, and she even invoked the Jewish immigrant philosopher Horace Kallen in order to support her dislike of "Mrs. Amadeus Grabau," alluding publicly to the fact that Antin had married an "American" (with a foreign-sounding surname). Kallen, who had been one of Wendell's and James's students at Harvard, was described by William James as "a Russian Jew by birth, very intense in character, very able and with high potentialities of all round cultivation, an enthusiastic and aggressive 'pragmatist', an active political worker, a *decidedly* original mind, neurotic disposition." In his critical essay, "Democracy versus The Melting-Pot," published in the *Nation* in 1916, Kallen, who was also one of Antin's correspondents and friends, partly adopted Antin's argument and compared Polish immigrants with the Pilgrims when he wrote: "the urge that carries [the Poles] in such numbers to America is not so unlike that which carried the pilgrim fathers"; yet he also criticized Antin for being "intermarried, 'assimilated' even in religion, and more excessively, self-consciously flatteringly American than the Americans." Still, it was assimilation, full American identity, even if claimed unilaterally by declaration of will rather than by American birth or by easy acceptance from old-stock

Americans, that entitled Antin to criticize her adopted "promised land" – or to praise it for qualities the United States would still have to acquire by fully including people like her. It was as if Antin was saying, Yes! in thunder.

The radical Columbia intellectual and culture critic Randolph Bourne was acutely aware of the political implications of the Brahmins' critical reactions to Mary Antin's claims. Bourne was depicted vividly in "Newsreel 22" of John Dos Passos's *1919* (1932); and the ever-critical Mike Gold praised Bourne for examining "all the political and economic facts . . . when he discussed literature." The term Brahmin had been coined in Oliver Wendell Holmes's novel *Elsie Venner* (1859) where it referred to a collegiate "race of scholars" different from the common country boy. Among American intellectuals who embraced the term were not only old-stock descendants but also upwardly mobile young men, some of whom had married into old families. Such intellectuals also adopted and increasingly stressed the symbols of the *Mayflower* and Plymouth Rock as mythic points of origin. Bourne understood that this invented Brahmin identity served as a tool for excluding immigrants. "We have had to watch," Bourne wrote in his famous programmatic essay of 1916, "Trans-National America," "hard-hearted old Brahmins virtuously indignant at the spectacle of the immigrant refusing to be melted, while they jeer at patriots like Mary Antin who write about 'our forefathers.'" Against that position Bourne argued memorably: "We are all foreign-born or the descendants of foreign-born, and if distinctions are to be made between us they should rightly be on some other grounds than indigenousness." For Ellery Sedgwick who criticized Bourne in letters, the United States "was created by English instinct and dedicated to the Anglo-Saxon ideal," and Bourne's essay was thus simply a "radical and unpatriotic paper" – though he did publish it in the *Atlantic Monthly*.

In the course of Bourne's essay he entered a dialogue with Antin, who had let an American teacher tell the immigrant protagonist David Rudinsky in her story "The Lie" (published in the *Atlantic Monthly* in 1913): "Every ship that brings your people from Russia and other countries where they are ill-treated is a *Mayflower*." Bourne set a different accent:

Mary Antin is right when she looks upon our foreign-born as the people who missed the Mayflower and came over on the first boat they could find. But she forgets that when they did come it was not upon other Mayflowers, but upon a "Maiblume," a "Fleur du mai," a "Fior di Maggio," a "Majblomst."

While implying in this example that various ethnic histories could be understood simply as "translations" of an original *Mayflower* voyage, Bourne did perceive the tremendous cultural opportunity of creating a cosmopolitan civilization that thrives upon the linguistic and cultural richness that ethnic variety brings to a country in which each citizen could also remain connected with another language and another culture. Bourne opposed the English orientation in American culture that Antin had come to love and the requirement that all non-English newcomers shed their cultural, religious, or linguistic pasts, yet he did not think that immigrants would or could remain fixed to their pasts. Instead Bourne advocated the new ideal of "dual citizenship," both for immigrants who came to the United States and for the increasing number of internationally oriented individuals who, like American expatriates in France, were born in one country but went on to live in another. In Bourne's hands the contemplation of Americanness in the face of ethnic diversity led to a reconsideration of the nationalist premises of citizenship.

Yet Bourne's pluralism also alienated radical young intellectuals like him from working people – except insofar as they belonged to distinct ethnic groups. Nowhere is Bourne's blind spot more apparent than in his disdain for assimilation. He writes: "It is not the Jew who sticks proudly to the faith of his fathers and boasts of that venerable culture of his who is dangerous to America, but the Jew who has lost the Jewish fire and become a mere elementary, grasping animal."

It must have been hard for Antin to find that a friend could be so insensitive toward the position she had presented. She had written in *The Promised Land*, with a nod (noted above) to Edward Everett Hale, that in Russia Jews had been "a people without a country," making the great love of "a little Jewish girl from Polotzk" for "her new country" all the more understandable and genuine. It is telling that Bourne echoed Antin's adaptation of Hale's phrase when he deplored the assimilated "men and women without a spiritual country, cultural outlaws without taste, without standards but those of the mob" – all of this in the context of a passage that reserves animal imagery for the assimilated and employs the nativist term "hordes" to describe them. Bourne's transnationalism preferred stable ethnic identities based on fixed national origins, a dilemma of many pluralist models of American culture from the 1920s to the age of multiculturalism. Antin's advocacy of assimilation was thus controversial to the hostile Repplier on the restrictionist right as well as to the friendly Bourne on the pluralist left. Neither political camp provided much room for an assimilated immigrant who claimed an American identity and the full rights of a citizen.

What would it mean to an immigrant child to sing "Land where my fathers died," or "our fodders" in *Call It Sleep*, was a question both Antin and Henry Roth asked. Can the "founding fathers" be the symbolic "fathers" of children whose real fathers are visible reminders of their own foreignness, who retain

exotic accents, fail to conform to American codes, live in the worst neighborhoods, and may ardently believe in America as something to which they can
never belong though their children or children's children might? This question, that nativism as well as cultural pluralism of the 1920s came to resolve
more and more negatively, was boldly and unequivocally answered with a "yes"
by Mary Antin, whose autobiography constituted not only a success story but
also a provocation. The patriotism of much of her writing was connected with
an egalitarian hope, especially for an integrative, open-door policy toward new
immigrants. Yet it was a hope that was to be dashed. The big public and
private crisis for Antin came with World War I. It was, in fact the context of
the war in which Repplier, Kallen, and Bourne had argued with Antin.

The Promised Land implies that Antin graduated from Boston Latin School
and went on to Radcliffe College. The facts of life were somewhat grimmer: she
never finished high school or became a regular college student anywhere. And
her life took a sharp downturn that was marked by the caesura of World War I.
At the time when she wrote *The Promised Land*, Antin was living in New York
and was married, against her father's wishes, to Amadeus William Grabau, a
(non-Jewish) German American science professor at Columbia, who is never
mentioned in *The Promised Land*, yet who is implicitly addressed throughout.
Some of Antin's cosmically mystical language also appears to echo or foreshadow such Grabau works as "Paleontology and Ontogeny" (1910) or *The
Rhythm of the Ages: Earth History in the Light of the Pulsation and Polar Control
Theories* (1940). The language of the study of nature permeates the book
from the way in which Antin traces her genealogical origins on a paleontolog-
ical time frame to the inspiration she gets in the "stupendous panorama which
is painted in the literature of Darwinism" and in the "book of cosmogony" to
learn about what she calls the "promised land of evolution."

In New York City and Scarsdale, Antin and Grabau led a rich social life
during the few golden years in her literary and public life that had started
with the publication in the *Atlantic Monthly* of the magnificent short story
"Malinke's Atonement" (1911), worthy of comparison with Sholem Aleichem's
tales. Antin corresponded with Theodore Roosevelt, Horace Kallen, and the
literary critic Van Wyck Brooks, entertained such diverse figures as Randolph
Bourne, Rabbi Abraham Cronbach, also a correspondent who later published
a warm memoir of Antin, and, her profession unknown to Antin, the prostitute Maimie Pinzer, who wrote a mean-spirited account of her visit to
Antin's house in a letter to Fanny Howe. The Grabaus' circle included writers,
artists, scientists, rabbis, and ministers, Christians and Zionists. Though both
Antin and Grabau were very busy professionally, their relationship, a gentile
Christian intermarriage of a native-born American Lutheran of German

ancestry and a naturalized American freethinker of East European Jewish origins, seems to have been very harmonious. Antin referred to her husband, who was eleven years her senior, as her "counselor and guardian."

The war ended that. Antin remembered a decade later that World War I turned her husband "into a dreadful hostile stranger who terrorized the household and scandalized the community (no, I am not exaggerating; these are matters of history)" and that as a consequence she suffered a nervous breakdown. The native-born Grabau, who also experienced serious setbacks in health, argued for an American neutralist position in the war (which was considered pro-German and simply untenable for a German American in the propagandistically heated war climate of 1917 America), lost his position at Columbia, accepted the invitation to become director of research for the China Geological Survey, moved to Peking, and ended up spending the rest of his life as an active and prolific scientist in China. The foreign-born American patriot Antin firmly supported the Allied cause. Their daughter later remembered that the war was fought right in their home. Antin felt that an *Atlantic Monthly* article on "Wives of German-Americans" portrayed the general situation so accurately that it might well have been written with her case specifically in mind. The marriage broke up. At the same time, her father died, the Scarsdale house was sold at a great loss, and she was left destitute after being released from psychiatric care. She spent many years at Gould Farm in the Berkshires and was connected at some points with Zionism but also became deeply interested in Christian universalism, the Indian mystic Meher Baba, and Rudolf Steiner's anthroposophy. She had become estranged from her political positions and felt, after the victory of the immigration restrictionists, that *They Who Knock* had become so dated that she wanted Houghton Mifflin to stop selling the book she now contemptuously called "The Knockers."

Antin's disillusionment was stark. In 1895 her dream of seeing patriotic poetry she wrote on Washington's birthday published in the Boston *Herald* was fulfilled. In *The Promised Land* Antin wrote up this experience with enthusiasm and mentioned that she dreamed of finding her name "Antin, Mary" in an encyclopedic dictionary, not far from "Alcott, Louisa M." In 1926, however, when she was asked by the publicity department of Houghton Mifflin to contribute something for a portrait gallery of contemporary New Englanders for the Boston *Herald*, she sarcastically commented that it would "soon be time for them to reheat the patriotic hash from *The Promised Land* which they have served up at shortish intervals, about Washington's Birthday, ever since Houghton Mifflin have been paying me royalties." She called her bitter self-assessment a "nice obituary," and she published only two more pieces – one of them, an account of a mystical vision – in the remaining twenty-three years of her life.

6

❧

AMERICAN LANGUAGES

H. L. MENCKEN was always a provocative essayist, ready to surprise his readers with unpredictable attacks or new directions of cultural inquiry. Ethnic works from Louis Adamic's *Laughing in the Jungle* (1931) to Richard Wright's *Black Boy* (1945) and authors from Claude McKay to John Fante attested to the freeing influence of Mencken's essays. Among the many topics he pursued, Mencken's deepest interest was in language as it was actually spoken in the United States. He observed the linguistic enrichment that came with features of modernity such as the streetcar: "Trolley crews, in the days of their glory, had their jargon, too," he wrote in 1948, "*e.g.*, *boat* for a trolley-car, *horse* for a motorman, *poor-box* for a fare-box, *stick* for a trolley-pole and *Sunday* for any day of light traffic." Drawing on the "Lexicon of Trade Jargon," a Federal Writers' Project manuscript, he also noted that the trolley-car "gave us the expression *to slip one's trolley*."

Mencken was fascinated by the linguistic consequences of America's multi-ethnic makeup, and undertook a still unparalleled effort to examine the many ethnic and non-English tributaries to the "American Language." It is telling that Zora Neale Hurston's "Story in Harlem Slang," published in Mencken's *American Mercury*, was accompanied by a glossary of the slang she employed, including "Big Apple" for New York, apparently still in need of annotation in 1942. Mencken was interested in all semantic and grammatical features that made American different from British English, and he called attention to many aspects of multilingualism that were present in America. One of Mencken's specific interests was in mixed languages that combined English and non-English elements. In *The American Language* (1919) he recorded features of what he referred to as "Finglish," "American-Greek," "Negro-French," and twenty-five other "non-English dialects in American."

Consciously or unconsciously, many ethnic writers used features of the mixed languages known as Spanglish, FrAnglais, Germerican, or Portinglês and supplied Mencken with materials. At Mencken's suggestion, Louis Adamic contributed an essay on "The Yugoslav Speech on America" to the *American Mercury*

(1927), in which he described an imaginary American Yugoslav housewife who "orders the wailing *bebi* to *šerap* (shut up), and tells two of her other children to cease their *fajtanje* (fighting) and *garjep* hurry up) to the *rejrod jards* (railroad yards) with the biggest *bosket* in the house and see if they can't pick up some *kol* (coal)." Jerre Mangione also explicitly responded to Mencken's work on ethnic languages. In his *Mount Allegro* (1943) – the very title of which combines an English and an Italian word – he pointed out that if his relatives believed that, after many years in America, they were "still speaking the same dialect they brought with them from Sicily, they were mistaken," for, influenced by "hearing American, Yiddish, Polish, and Italian dialects other than their own, their language gathered words which no one in Sicily could possibly understand." Citing such examples as *storo* for store, *ponte* for pound, *barra* for bar, or *giobba* for job, he agrees that "Mr. Mencken's collection of Italian American words is a good indication of what happened" to his relatives' vocabulary. And he adds *baccauso*, the word for toilet that Mangione used in Sicily to the bafflement of his Sicilian relatives, until the reader realizes that it must be an adaptation of "back house" and mean "toilet." Both *Mount Allegro* and *Jews Without Money* mention the immigrant use of the pat phrase, "get out of here," rendered as *girarahir* (in Mangione, already cited) or *gerarahere* (by Mike Gold). Such terms were part of an American *lingua franca*. Among Konrad Bercovici's many accounts of what was yet to be called multicultural America is the following in *Manhattan Side-Show* (1931): "Bearded Jews, tailors from Russia, Italians, Syrians in their red fezes, Turkish women just out of harems, Greeks and Levantines, worked side by side, day and night, to make our coats and pants. They created their own language: Mercer Street English."

Code-switching and mixed languages are prevalent in American ethnic literature, whether such literature was originally written or published in English or in one of the many other languages that have been used in the United States. For American literature was also written in Yiddish (as was the letter that became Antin's *From Plotzk to Boston*), Polish, Swedish, Welsh, Norwegian, Portuguese, Spanish, Chinese, or German – the list goes on and on – and this little-known non-English literature of the United States offers fascinating insights into American ethnic diversity in some formally accomplished and many thematically provocative works. The propaganda against foreign languages in the course of World War I marked only an interruption in a long tradition of non-English-language literary production in what is now the United States that started with recorded works in Native American and all colonial languages and continued with literature in scores of immigrant tongues. The propaganda may have been at least effective in removing this literature from scholarly attention in the second half of the twentieth century. The present section on prose literature of the first half of the twentieth century is not the place to review the long multilingual history in all genres of American literature. Yet one only has to recall that the first African American short story ("Le Mulâtre" by Victor Séjour, 1837) and anthology (*Les Cenelles*, 1845) were both published in French; that an Arabic slave narrative from North Carolina, written by Omar Ibn Said in 1831, predates Frederick Douglass's by fourteen years; that the first American novel depicting a lesbian love scene was published in German (*Die Geheimnisse von New Orleans*, 1854–55), or that Eusebio Chacón published Spanish-language novellas in New Mexico in 1892, in order to have a first understanding of what is omitted when "American literature" is defined as literature in English only. There was even a "Streetcar Song, Gay '90's," written by Kurt M. Stein in the humorously mixed idiom of Germerican, which appeared in 1927 in Stein's collection *Die schönste Lengevitch*; the title poem confronts a German American with a newcomer whose question "Pardong, Sir, holds ze tramway here?" the old settler needs to have translated before answering it in the same mixed fashion of "die schönste lengevitch."

Despite the linguistic xenophobia (glottophobia?) generated by World War I (when not only German *sauerkraut* officially turned into "liberty cabbage" but when also Spanish, Yiddish, Scandinavian languages and almost any foreign tongue were under siege), literary publication continued, and even increased in some languages. Some examplars of this literature received a new national recognition from the 1920s to the mid-century. One only has to think of Ole Rölvaag (writing in Norwegian), Vladimir Nabokov (writing in Russian and English), Sholem Asch (writing in Yiddish and English), or Isaac Bashevis Singer (writing in Yiddish) in order to see the centrality of non-English-language works to American fiction from 1910 to 1950. *The Multilingual Anthology of American Literature* (2000) has made some texts available bilingually. For each known author, however, there are dozens of unknown ones, and many works have not yet been identified, let alone been translated into English. There are, for example, the Japanese-language works by Kyuin Okina ("Boss," 1915) and Saburo Kato ("Mr. Yama and the China Incident," 1938), still unrecognized in the United States and little known in Japan. German-language writing was perhaps the hardest-hit by World War I. Yet even though no new high point comparable to Reinhold Solger's remarkable social novel *Anton in Amerika* (1862) has been identified in the modern period, German-language writing did continue after World War I. The rise of fascism also brought a lively German-language exile literature and culture to the United States in the 1930s and 1940s; it included writers Bertolt Brecht, Lion Feuchtwanger, and Thomas Mann, modernist artists like George Grosz, and composers like Arnold Schönberg. It is telling that in 1942 the philosopher

Theodor W. Adorno published his American dreams (literally, transcripts of his dream life in New York and California) in the German-language New York newspaper *Aufbau*.

Even American authors known for their English-language writings may hold surprises when their non-English *œuvre* is examined: thus the Chinese American Lin Yutang, whose best-selling English-language China book *My Country and My People* (1935) established his fame that increased with his novel *Chinatown Family* (1948) continued to write in Chinese, and there he sounded a more radical note than he did in English. While bibliographies and historical scholarship for the earlier periods are often available, at the end of the twentieth century no one knew just how many short stories, novels, and autobiographies were published in the United States in the twentieth century in languages apart from English, though it is safe to assert that there must be thousands of them, for which the following handful can merely serve as an unrepresentative sampling.

As part of a wave of Welsh-language publishing in Utica, New York, Dafydd Rhys Williams wrote the story collection *Llyfr y Dyn Pren ac Eraill* (The Book of the Wooden Man and Others, 1909). The book, which draws on such traditions as the Welsh folktale and the ancient heroic narrative, includes stories against drinking, smoking, and assimilation. Among the prolific authors who published prose in Yiddish in the United States was Leo Kobrin whose collected American short stories (published in Yiddish in 1910) added up to more than 900 pages. Often told in the first-person singular, his tales and sketches portray immigrants in their new environments, or focus on chance encounters of strangers in New York. In "Di shprakh fun elnt" (The language of misery, translated by Max Rosenfeld under the title "A Common Language"), the greenhorn narrator gets a job as a night watchman and finds out that the burglars he has beaten to a retreat one night turn out to be a middle-aged Italian immigrant and his small daughter. The narrator feels a strong bond of sympathy toward these poor criminals, even though they have no language in common: "We talked in sign language, with our hands, with gestures. But we understood each other." He lets them free and even gives them kindling wood, but loses his job for this act of kindness. Later his "Italian friend" offers him a banana in return. The solidarity that connects the poor and separates them from the world of hypocritical employers bridges national and linguistic boundaries in Leo Kobrin's tale.

Ole Amundsen Buslett's Norwegian-language tale *Veien til Golden Gate* (The Road to the Golden Gate, 1915) depicts the allegorical road, an immigrant's *Pilgrim's Progress* of sorts, from Norway to America's Golden Gate and warns its readers against going too fast on the road of Americanization which may lead to a "Yankee Slough" (Buslett's version of the Slough of Despond) in which all would become alike and ultimately go under and drown. Only those Norwegians who retain their sense of origin and their know-how are able to build safe roads across that slough of Americanization. Yet the tale does not advocate remigration and dismisses the road back to the old country as "the road of nostalgia." The story ends when Rosalita declares her love for Haakon. They will form a couple that has just the right degree of ethnic loyalty, sharing neither Rosalita's father's shallow Americanism nor Haakon's mother's static Old World outlook.

Dorthea Dahl's "Kopper-kjelen" (The Copper Kettle) was published in the Chicago Norwegian-language literary journal *Norden* (1930). Born in Norway, Dorthea Dahl came to South Dakota with her parents at age two, and lived in Moscow, Idaho, for most of her life. Her story focuses on a Norwegian immigrant couple, Trond Jevnaker (the center of consciousness in this third-person narrative) and his wife Gjertrud. Gjertrud is assimilated; she has come to America before her husband, whom she asks to Anglicize her name as "Gørti" – which he refuses indignantly. Dahl's Gjertrud is the typical "language traitor" who rushes into (incomplete) Americanization and is embarrassed by her husband's adherence to old-country ways, symbolized here by an old kettle: it belonged to Trond's grandfather in Norway, but Gjertrud is planning to discard it – when an American lady sees the kettle and expresses her wish to buy it as an antique. Neither Trond nor Gjertrud knows what she means by "*æntik*," but Gjertrud wants to sell the kettle. Surprisingly, Trond takes command at this point and decides to give the kettle to the American lady as a present. This changes Gjertrud's relationship to Trond, and she now defers to him and promises to abandon her plan for an American "skrinportsen" (screen porch). The eyes of the American native had seen the value of the Norwegian heirloom that the too speedily assimilated immigrant woman had regarded only as a source of embarrassment.

The Portuguese-language short story "Gente da Terceira Classe" (Steerage, 1938) is representative of José Rodrigues Miguélis's *œuvre*. Born in Lisbon in 1901, Miguéis died in Manhattan in 1980, having spent the last forty-three years of his life in political exile in New York City. University-trained and a Portuguese translator of F. Scott Fitzgerald, Erskine Caldwell, and Carson McCullers, he wrote numerous short stories in America. "Steerage," cast in the manner of a log, is set on an ocean liner returning from South America to Portugal. Among the third-class passengers of the title are returning emigrants whose hopes have been dashed, as well as new and hopeful emigrants, "Poles, Portuguese, some lower-class Englishmen (Irish surely), an incommunicative German couple, a large Syrian clan returning from the north of Brazil with jaundiced children, and others of the same breed." The misanthropic narrator mulls over the signs of class and ethnic discrimination, *"For Spanish and Portuguese people only,"* and wonders at the end whether the voyage has created a bond of sympathy among these heterogeneous and largely unsympathetically portrayed passengers.

At first glance, there seems to be in such works only the shared condition of not having been written in English. Yet there are certain features they have in common. Thematically, many tales could be classified as allegorical love-and-assimilation stories. Others stress the possibility of empathy across ethnic and linguistic boundaries, while still others express critique of Anglo-America freely in the non-English tongue. Formally, such works inscribe an English linguistic presence in the texts in a way that works in English – in which English has to serve as the medium of communication – cannot adequately replicate. Dahl spices up his Norwegian with "Hadjudusør" (how do you do, sir), "spærrummet" (spare room), "nervøsbreikdaun," and some complete sentences in English in order to suggest the different speed of assimilation that separates Trond and Gjertrud. Miguéis includes many English words, entire sentences in English and French (suggesting also the importance of "third" languages in such mixed-language locations), and such "Portinglês" (or Luso-American) terms as "cracas" (crackers), "dolas" (dollars), "bossa" (boss), or "racatias" (racketeers).

Even the most obscure non-English-language works shed light on the inward dimensions of America's multicultural past and on linguistic aspects of assimilation; they also offer a multidimensional view of American group relations in the first half of the twentieth century. The founder of modern American immigration history, Marcus Lee Hansen, was right when he wrote in the essay "Immigration and American Culture" (1940): "The student of the future who is willing to conceive of American literature in more than a parochial sense must be the master of at least ten or a dozen languages."

7

❦

"ALL THE PAST WE LEAVE BEHIND"?
OLE E. RÖLVAAG AND THE
IMMIGRANT TRILOGY

ONE OF THE GREAT and widely recognized works of modern American ethnic literature in a language apart from English was a trilogy originally written in Norwegian by O. E. Rölvaag. It consists of *Giants in the Earth: A Saga of the Prairie* (originally published as two separate novels *I de dage*, 1924, and *Riket grundlægges*, 1925; Engl. both 1927), *Peder Victorious: A Tale of the Pioneers Twenty Years Later* (orig. *Peder Seier*, 1928, Engl. 1929), and *Their Fathers' God* (orig. *Den signede dag*, 1931, Engl. 1931). Rölvaag's work marked a high point of American literature, but also the beginning of the end of Norwegian-language writing in the United States, a rich body of works that includes not only Buslett and Dahl, but a long line of novelistic precursors. Singularly noteworthy among them is the beautifully melancholy (and social-reformist) novel *En saloonkeepers datter* (1887, Engl. A Saloonkeeper's Daughter) by the Norwegian-born author Drude Krog Janson. The heroine of the novel's title is the memorable character Astrid Holm, the daughter of a stern bourgeois businessman and a melancholy actress, who, after her mother's death and the failure of her father's business, follows him (with her much younger brothers) from Norway to Minnesota – where none of the Old World maxims seem to apply any more and where her new identity is simply that of *A Saloonkeeper's Daughter*. The central part of the novel shows the heroine's attempt to find her own way through different suitors, and, ultimately, as an ordained minister and close friend of a woman doctor. Janson's novel contains some familiar themes of American-immigrant fiction: the differences between the Old World and the New, generational conflict between immigrant parents and children, the difficulties of courtship by "American" suitors. Yet the novel also has a specifically Scandinavian aura in its pervasive allusions to the ogres of Norse mythology and its evocation, in Astrid's love for the stage, of a particularly Norwegian ideal of serious dramatic art, embodied by Henrik Ibsen and Bjørnstjerne Bjørnson. Published both in Copenhagen and in Minneapolis, the novel calls attention to its transnational character in its original title, *En saloonkeepers datter*, which sandwiches an English term between two Norwegian words.

Also worth mentioning is the Norwegian American novelist and journalist Waldemar Ager who publicly criticized the "melting-pot" concept of assimilation as a metaphor of destruction whose function was "to denationalize those who are not of English descent," as he wrote in 1916. In Ager's novel *Paa veien til smeltepotten* (1917, On the Way to the Melting Pot; transl. 1995), the antihero Lars Olson embodies the destructive lure of the American melting pot that brings him outward success but destroys him spiritually.

Johannes B. Wist published an immigrant trilogy consisting of *Nykommerbilleder* (Immigrant Scenes, 1920), *Hjemmet paa prærien* (The Home on the Prairie, 1921), and *Jonasville* (Jonasville, 1922), in which he pokes fun at the shallow Americanization of the Norwegian immigrant Salomonsen who has changed his name to Mr. Salmon and whose examples of code-switching make him another ridiculous language traitor: "Amerika er en demokratisk *kontry, ju 'no!* . . . Jeg har *getta saa jused te'* aa *speak English*, at jeg *forgetter* mig *right 'long*, naar jeg *juser* norsk." (In Orm Øverland's translation: "America is a democratic country, you know! . . . . I have gotten so used to speaking English that I forget myself right along when I use Norwegian.") How could a balance be struck between ethnic and linguistic heritage and the promise of American life?

O. E. Rölvaag answered this question and, like Ager, he polemicized against too rapid a process of Americanization and against the melting pot in essays collected in *Omkring fædrearven* (Concerning Our Heritage, 1922). Rölvaag was born in 1876 in a little Norwegian fishing village near the Arctic Circle, on the island of Dönna, and emigrated to the United States in 1896. After some years of farm labor, he worked his way through college, graduating from St. Olaf's College in Minnesota at age twenty-eight, and then studying for a year at Oslo. Later he started teaching at St. Olaf's College where he became an active professor of Norwegian with a special interest in immigrant history. He published numerous books, among them the novel *Amerika-Breve* (Letters from America, 1912), based on immigrant letters and published under a pseudonym, and the novel *To tullinger* (1920), significantly revised and altered in its English version under the title *Pure Gold* (1930). Until his death in 1931, he published his literary works in Norwegian. As long as he wrote for a Norwegian American audience only, there was little interest in him in Anglo-America. However, when his books started to appear in Oslo and received recognition in Norway, things began to change. And it is in this context that his trilogy (or Norwegian tetralogy) emerged.

Giants in the Earth, the first and most famous of the three novels (in the work's English version), follows the lives of Norwegian farmers who in 1873 establish a lonely settlement in Spring Creek in the Dakota Territory. At the center of a small number of families are the Holms. Per Holm, known as

Per Hansa, is an active pioneer who faces all kinds of obstacles in establishing the settlement, ranging from winter storms to a plague of locusts. His wife Beret suffers from the isolation in the prairie, is given to bouts of melancholy, and almost loses her sanity. They have two sons, Ole and Store-Hans, and a daughter And-Ongen. Beret almost dies giving birth to their third son, Peder Victorious. Peder is born on Christmas Eve, and, like David Copperfield, he is born with a "helmet" – a caul or veil – often taken as a sign of second sight in Norwegian folklore, for example, as well as in Du Bois's *Souls of Black Folk* (1903). Beret turns toward stricter observance of Lutheran religion under the guidance of a visiting minister. When Per goes out one bitter-cold winter day to fetch a minister to visit a seriously ill neighbor, Per dies in a snowstorm; and the novel ends in the spring afterwards when his frozen body is found seated on a haystack, his eyes set toward the West.

The sequel, *Peder Victorious*, is set when Peder goes to an American, then a Norwegian school, but his Americanization and alienation from his mother are unstoppable. After the marriages of the two older sons, who always helped the widowed mother in the farm work, Beret is lonelier and more fanatically religious than ever; and Peder becomes the second-generation rebel against the mother's conservatism. He first associates with the daughters of religious dissenters, then falls in love with the Irish American Catholic Susie Doheny, the sister of an old schoolfriend of his. Surprisingly, Beret consents to the marriage at the end of the book.

The concluding volume, *Their Fathers' God*, continues with Peder and Susie's wedding in 1894. Despite the intergenerational religious, linguistic, and cultural differences, the young couple lives on Beret's farm. Conflicts increase when Susie gives birth to a boy, Petie, and three different ideas of how to raise the child collide. In Susie's absence, Beret arranges a secret Lutheran baptism for Petie; Susie has him christened secretly as a Catholic. Meanwhile freethinking Peder is indifferent to religion and embarks on a political career, during which the bitter political opposition between Irish and Norwegian immigrants becomes apparent. Peder ends an affair with Nikoline Johanson, a young Norwegian immigrant who then returns to Norway, and he goes back to Susie when his mother falls ill. On her deathbed, Beret confesses the child's secret baptism. Susie almost dies from a miscarriage, but survives thanks to Peder's care. Yet during Peder's political election campaign, his character is publicly maligned by his Irish American opponent with details from his private life, including Petie's secret Catholic baptism, that Peder believes must have come from Susie. Angrily he destroys the Catholic symbols in front of her eyes: he stomps on the white porcelain figure of the crucifix, on the vessel with holy water, and on the beads of the rosary that he first takes apart. Susie is horrified and swoons; the next day she leaves Peder, taking little Petie along with her. If the novel progresses from the faith of the immigrant generation to a secularization of their children, then that process is complicated and disrupted by the different and mutually exclusive meanings of the "fathers' god" for the third and doubly baptized generation. The novel ends with the breakup of the interethnic and interreligious marriage and Susie's return to her father.

Rölvaag's trilogy is a remarkable work. It is a contribution to the classic historical novel, for its beginning is set approximately fifty years before the first volume was written. The three novels trace the historical outline from immigrant settlement to second-generation assimilation to the arrival of a third, American, generation, and the books richly represent the themes of language loyalty and loss and of intergenerational tension. Rölvaag is interested in the pressures that migration exerts on language, audible in some inevitable Anglicisms; on religion, either succumbing to sectarian intensification in the case of Beret or to secularization in Peder; on the changing code of values, including ethnic embarrassment or the wish to possess things; and on interethnic relations, especially with Indians and with Irish neighbors. Rölvaag devotes much space to inward feelings and to landscape description – or better, lyrical evocation – so that a sharp portrait emerges of the loneliness of the Norwegian settlers on the prairies of the Dakotas. "A grey waste . . . an empty silence . . . a boundless cold. Snow fell; snow flew; a universe of nothing but dead whiteness. Blizzards from out of the northwest raged, swooped down and stirred up a greyish-white fury, impenetrable to human eyes." In the first volume, Beret's changing states of mind are especially well portrayed. In Beret's mind, the immigrant family chest, marked "Anno 16 – " becomes associated with a coffin; later the Lutheran minister uses it as an altar, thus literally transforming and sacralizing an object that accompanied the modern secular process of emigration. The small pieces of wood that mark the confines of the Hansas' territory and that Per moves, so as to own more land, also give rise to Beret's fear, mythically justified in America, that she lives on stolen land. Subtle details add further life to the story. The sod house is vividly represented. The rhetoric of "Promised Land" is developed fully in the course of the novel. English appears as a *lingua franca* for communication between the Norwegian settlers and the Indians, one of whom Per Hansa daringly treats and cures of an infected wound. And the arrival of the railroad is a sinister symbol of nineteenth-century modernity: "The monster crawled along with a terrible speed; but when it came near, it did not crawl at all; it rushed forward in tortuous windings, with an awful roar, while black, curling smoke streaked out behind it in the air." These and many other details that are often presented rather understatedly come into focus through the different lenses in which they acquire meaning for the settlers. In the sequels to the novel, Rölvaag pursues the question of what can hold diverse Americans together by focusing on a Norwegian–Irish, Lutheran–Catholic intermarriage in the second generation, and how American political campaigns reflect and shape ethnicity. *Peder Victorious* presents different and at times incompatible points of view through the metaphor of living in different rooms. In one of them, Peder "lived everything in English," yet a teacher has to tell his mother that Peder "must by all means get rid of that accent!"

As did many other ethnic works – from Willa Cather's *O Pioneers* (1913) to Maxine Hong Kingston in *Tripmaster Monkey* (1987) – Rölvaag explicitly invokes and adapts Walt Whitman's poetry. At a moment when Peder is on horseback in a state of exultation, the lines from "Pioneers! O Pioneers!" that he copied from the blackboard at school become intertwined with the narrative: "Sitting thus high, he could speed away on the wings of the wind. *'Fresh and strong the world we seize'* – heigh, ho! heigh, ho! . . . He would surely read this poem to Mother! Lashing his horse he raced away to the rhythm of the verse: *Fresh and strong the world we seize.*" The Whitmanian hope of "All the past we leave behind" is a hope that Peder's mother cannot share, of course, and the text she lives in is that of the Bible, interspersed in Gothic typefont in the second novel. It is another sign of Rölvaag's imaginative powers that, as he is becoming more frank in representing sexual matters, he draws on the language of the Song of Songs (not set in Gothic font). In the third volume, Rölvaag gives room to an elaborate polemic against assimilation, when Reverend Kaldahl challenges Peder's claiming of an American identity: "If we're to accomplish anything worth while," he says, "we must do it as Norwegians." He holds up the example of Jews who made their great contributions to civilization "because they stubbornly refused to be dejewed." By contrast, the American melting pot would only produce "a dull, smug complacency."

The trilogy has an unmistakable sound to it. Rölvaag employs a lyrical realism which he sets forth with a unique style. Where there are touches of modernism, they are more in the vein of Whitman, or of Carl Sandburg, who wrote a rave review of *Giants in the Earth*, than of T. S. Eliot or Joyce. Other sources of inspiration come from the historical novel tradition of Scott, Cooper, and Bulwer-Lytton, from Rölvaag's systematic study of the modern Norwegians – Ibsen, Bjørnstjerne Bjørnson, Knut Hamsun – and from a famous nineteenth-century collection of Norwegian folktales.

With effective flow and pacing the sentences move easily from third-person description to direct and indirect discourse; and the pervasive use of ellipses (". . ."), suggestive of elisions in the narrative, intensifies the effect of the writing. For example, Per Hansa

asked Beret and Hans Olsa to help pick the best building place; his words, though few and soberly spoken, had in them an unmistakable ring of determination . . . . This vast stretch of beautiful land was to be his – yes, *his* – and no ghost of a dead Indian would drive him away! . . . His heart began to expand with a mighty exaltation. An emotion he had never felt before filled him and made him walk erect . . . . "Good God!" he panted. "This kingdom is going to be *mine!*"

One is amazed at such qualities in what is, after all, a work "translated from the Norwegian."

In his modest introduction to the first American edition, Rölvaag expressed his gratitude to Lincoln Colcord, without whose "constant encouragement" and "inimitable willingness to help" *Giants in the Earth* never would have "seen the light of day in an English translation." And he noted the difficulty of rendering the characters' untranslatable Norwegian dialect in English. Colcord, a professional writer who during World War I had brought out a volume of poetry entitled *Visions of War* and was best known in the 1920s for volumes of stories of the sea, raised the question of how Rölvaag's novel should be classified, "so European in art and atmosphere, so distinctly American in everything it deals with."

The translation of *Giants in the Earth*, a leading Rölvaag critic tells us, was really a complex process, in the course of which Colcord alone would work through student-and-amateur-produced draft translations before meeting with Rölvaag to decide together on the final version. In those sessions the original text was apparently significantly expanded, in part made more poetic, by the addition of descriptive adjectives, adverbs, and whole phrases. The cited passage about Per Hansa's vision of the kingdom on the prairie, for example, was, in its entirety, added to the English "translation" only; an equivalent passage is not to be found in the earlier Norwegian "original" text of *I de dage*. Apart from such expansions and from the introduction of American colloquialisms, Rölvaag's English version differs in its absence of the subtle effect of having more and more Anglicisms in the characters' Norwegian as the trilogy progresses, an untranslatable feature.

Rölvaag worked with other translators for the second and third volumes, but he adhered to the method of "double action" for the translation that he had worked out with Colcord. One might speak, in this case, of two authorized versions of the same work, not an uncommon phenomenon in those instances of American ethnic literature in which an author tells the same story twice in different languages – as did Luigi Ventura in the French and English versions of *Peppino* (1885, 1886), Abraham Cahan in the English and Yiddish versions of *Yekl* (1896), and Mary Antin in the transformation of the 1894 Yiddish letter to her uncle into *From Plotzk to Boston* (1899).

The aesthetic accomplishment of Ole E. Rölvaag's *Giants in the Earth, Peder Victorious*, and *Their Fathers' God*, as well as of his larger *œuvre*, makes one wonder how many other masterpieces will yet emerge from the now dusty shelves of non-English-language literature of the United States. As Lincoln Colcord wrote in his introduction, "It has not yet been determined, even, what America is, or whether she herself is strictly American." And three quarters of a century later, one can only agree with Colcord's conclusion that some of this literature should be "translated into English, to enrich our literature by a pure stream flowing out of the American environment – a stream which, for the general public, lies frozen in the ice of a foreign tongue."

If Mary Antin set the standard for immigrant autobiography, then Rölvaag – whose *Giants in the Earth* also was a popular success and a 1927 Book of the Month Club selection – provided the most compelling model for the American immigrant saga, fiction that spans generations and that often found expression in the form of a trilogy. Among the other ethnic trilogies published in the period were John Cournos's *The Mask, The Wall*, and *Babel* (the third volume appearing in 1922, about a Russian Jewish immigrant coming of age in America), James T. Farrell's Irish American *Studs Lonigan* trilogy (completed in 1935), Danish-born Sophus Keith Winther's *Take All To Nebraska* (1936), *Mortgage Your Heart* (1937), and *This Passion Never Dies* (1938), and Daniel Fuchs's Jewish *Williamsburg Trilogy* (completed in 1937).

Published after the watershed of World War I and after the deep divide marked by the end of immigration in 1924, Rölvaag's work viewed immigration and assimilation in far more somber terms than did Antin's *Promised Land*. This may be due, in part, to the original use of a medium other than English. However, Rölvaag also represented the historical shift that Horace Kallen had seen coming when he wrote his critique of Mary Antin and Edward Bok: "*The Americanization of Edward Bok* . . . may indeed be regarded as the climax of the wave of gratulatory exhibition which Mary Antin's *Promised Land* began. Now there are signs that the ebb is at hand, and the doctrinal pattern of autobiography for the Americanized is likely to be more analytical, discriminative, and sad." Kallen was thinking of Ludwig Lewisohn and Samuel Ornitz. James T. Farrell who was part of the "new" literature, written after World War I and conscious of the watershed that the war years came to mark, vividly described in similar terms what he perceived as the progress of ethnic literature as it emancipated itself from the local-color formula:

In early years, there was the literature of the American immigrant, of first-generation groups, written in an unreal and patronizing vein. The melting pot was a typical literary theme. The treatment in such works was without vitality, conventional, intended to be humorous. The stories contained little truth and were written from the outside . . . . It was a literature of the Cohens and the Kellys, of Abie's Irish Roses, Uncle Remus, a literature of the upper classes and of good old Star-Spangled Banner patronage.

Writing starting with Abraham Cahan's *Rise of David Levinsky* (1917) and continuing with Rölvaag's trilogy bore out such observations more broadly. The new, "sad," and reflexive attitude was not only present in Rölvaag but also in the later writing by Antin herself for whose career World War I was so traumatic an event. And it characterized the best ethnic literature at the peak of modernism, from Jean Toomer to Henry Roth.

8

❧

MODERNISM, ETHNIC LABELING, AND THE QUEST FOR WHOLENESS: JEAN TOOMER'S NEW AMERICAN RACE

"Seventh Street," set in post-World War I Washington, DC, opens and closes with the same short poem:

> Money burns the pocket, pocket hurts,
> Bootleggers in silken shirts,
> Ballooned, zooming Cadillacs,
> Whizzing, whizzing down the street-car tracks.

The page that is framed by this poem of urban modernity is both lyrical invocation and apostrophe of the black migrants who form a "wedge" of jazz songs and life driven into "the white and whitewashed wood of Washington." "Seventh Street" is part modernist prose poem that expresses the rhythms and noise of the city of Prohibition, and part meditation on the meaning of migration. At its center is the repeated question, "Who set you flowing? Flowing down the smooth asphalt of Seventh Street, in shanties, brick office buildings, theaters, drug stores, restaurants, and cabarets?"

"Seventh Street" opens the second part of Jean Toomer's *Cane* (1923), an experimental book that marks the full arrival and a high point of achievement of American ethnic modernism. Published by the prestigious house of Boni and Liveright in 1923, still before Ernest Hemingway's and William Faulkner's first important books were to appear, *Cane* was a powerful contribution to the specific stream of modernism that included Stein's *Three Lives*, James Joyce's *Dubliners*, and Sherwood Anderson's *Winesburg, Ohio*, though Toomer also was inspired by modern poetry (Hart Crane's poem *The Bridge*), Eugene O'Neill's plays, Waldo Frank's manifesto *Our America*, Georgia O'Keeffe's paintings, and Alfred Stieglitz's photographs. An avid reader, Toomer was drawn to Shaw, Ibsen, Dostoyevsky, Tolstoy, Baudelaire, Flaubert, and Melville. *Cane* is on our side of the transformation toward aesthetic modernism, psychological scrutiny, bohemian self-searching, increasing ethnic expression, and engagement with new ideologies, a transformation that was initiated at the beginning of the century and accelerated by the experience of World War I.

Toomer took up, but never completed, studies in history, anthropology, agriculture, and physical training; he was early attracted to atheism and socialism, and later to the mystical and introspective Gurdjieff movement, to the Quakers, and to an Indian guru. He spent important years in such artists' colonies as Greenwich Village, Mabel Dodge Luhan's Taos, New Mexico, and Carmel, California, and participated in an early experiment in group psychology in Portage, Wisconsin, that neighbors suspected was a free love movement. He published poems, plays, and prose pieces on the pages of such small, experimental, and often radical literary magazines as *Broom*, *Dial*, *Liberator*, and *Modern Review*. Toomer submitted a play to O'Neill's Provincetown Playhouse and wrote a rave notice on O'Neill's "The Emperor Jones," was friends with Sherwood Anderson and Hart Crane, and was intimate with Georgia O'Keeffe; his second wife Marjorie Content had previously been married to Harold Loeb, the editor of *Broom* who had published Stein's "As Fine as Melanctha" and was caricatured as Robert Cohn in Hemingway's *The Sun Also Rises* (1926). Both Toomer and Stein contributed a homage to Stieglitz in a volume published in 1934.

Toomer's outlook had a strong visionary component. One April evening in 1926 Toomer had a mystical conversion experience at a prime site of modernity, the platform of the 66th Street L stop in Manhattan, where he was waiting idly, not hurrying to get home, when he felt "a mysterious working in [his] depths," as if he were "being taken apart," and sensed a soft light unfolding behind him and in his body: "This was no extension of my personal self, no expansion of my ordinary awareness. I awoke to a dimensionally higher consciousness. Another being, a radically different being, became present and manifesting." The apt metaphor he used to describe this experience was "transport": "Precisely *I* was being transported from exile into Being. Transport is the exact term. So is transcendence . . . . Liberation is the exact term. I was freed from my ego-prison." He felt as if he were towering above the platform now and saw the "dark earth . . . far down." And he realized that the earth-beings sitting on the train could only see his body and not his Being – which made him wonder whether their true selves were also hidden to *him*, since he could only see their bodies. It was this experience that confirmed him in his turn toward Gurdjieff's "Harmonious Development of Man" (but also distanced him from his focus on literary efforts).

Toomer was deeply and existentially concerned about American ethnic issues, and his writing, most excellently embodied by *Cane*, represents an attempt to answer his close friend Waldo Frank's demand that American writers "study the cultures of the German, the Latin, the Celt, the Slav, the Anglo-Saxon and the African . . . and their disappearance as integral worlds." Frank and Toomer spent some time together in Spartanburg, South Carolina; inspired by this trip, Frank contributed to the little magazine *Secession* "Hope," an odd short story of a nameless white man who makes love to a nameless black woman, and published an experimental and lurid novel of perverted interracial lust and violence, *Holiday* (1923).

Toomer had previously worked as acting principal in a black school in Sparta, Georgia, for two months – the Washingtonian's first extended stay in the rural South – during which time the idea for *Cane* germinated. He read the town newspaper, the *Sparta Ishmaelite*, and lived in a former slave cabin. *Cane* was published in 1923, a year that marked the sixtieth anniversary of the end of slavery as well as the tenth anniversary of the Armory Show. It is the most important American book to contemplate the legacy of African slavery in a thoroughly modernist idiom.

What struck Toomer about the rural South was that "the trend was toward the small town and then toward the city – and industry and commerce and machines. The folk-spirit was walking in to die on the modern desert. That spirit was so beautiful. Its death was so tragic. Just this seemed the sum of life to me. And this was the feeling I put into *Cane*. *Cane* was a swan-song. It was a song of an end." *Cane* is a meditation on what Toomer felt was the disappearing African culture in the modern desert of the American continent.

It is also an ambivalent book that describes modernity both with exuberance and with melancholy. Against the background of the mass movement from soil to pavement, *Cane* reflects on the country without idyllic nostalgia and on the city without teleological hope. Both are historically changing worlds of failed human understanding and of at times comic and at other times horrifyingly brutal encounters. The reader is drawn into a magical and mysterious world of pine needles and clay, of autumn leaves and dusk, of spiritual striving and human failing, of love and violence, but is also exposed to the exciting movement from country roads to city streets and from natural to industrial sounds.

Toomer achieves his effects by a carefully orchestrated system of verbal repetition and musical progression in a book whose very form resists classification by genre. It is *sui generis*, as it fuses poetry, prose, and drama (in "Bona and Paul" and "Kabnis"), and its form attempts to find a literary equivalent for the dislocations wrought by modernity. Can the lost soul of a fertile peasant past be recuperated in the elusively modernist form of a book that artistically, even artificially, reconstitutes life-asserting wholeness by resisting easy generalizations and *a priori* assumptions? *Cane* attempts to do just that – even though Toomer articulated his keen awareness that there is no possibility for modern Americans to be going back to a shared past.

"Back to nature," even if desirable, was no longer possible, because industry had taken nature unto itself. Even if he wanted to, a city person could not become a soil person by changing his locale and living on a farm in the woods.

So then, whether we wished to or not, we *had to go on*.

Toomer's answer to the problem could not lie in a nostalgic wish for a return to traditional country values, for "those who sought to cure themselves by a return to more primitive conditions were either romantics or escapists." No, going on, and going on to create, searching for aesthetic wholeness and a new vision in a fragmented modern world, those were the only viable answers. The contemplation of modernity impelled Toomer to move forward the project of modernism.

Cane makes its readers self-conscious in order to let them yearn for a fresher and fuller look at the world. This effort is captured in the book's repeated allusions to St. Paul's first letter to the Corinthians: "For now we see through a glass darkly; but then face to face; now I know in part; but then shall I know even as I am known" – a passage that Ralph Waldo Emerson and Nathaniel Hawthorne had also cherished, that Henry Roth and Ralph Ellison were to draw on later, and that Isaac Rosenfeld's *Passage from Home* (1946) used as general motto. Toomer also searched for a more cosmic understanding of the wholeness of a polyvocal America as it was once sung by Walt Whitman and now proclaimed by Waldo Frank. Like many earlier visionaries, Toomer espoused the fragmentary as the necessary part of larger totalities.

The interrelatedness of fragmentation and quest for wholeness structures *Cane*. The book is divided into three parts that are marked by figures that resemble parentheses: (,), and ( ). "Between each of the three sections, a curve. These, to vaguely indicate the design," Toomer wrote to Frank. The two segments realign and aim for a circle without fully achieving its closure in the third part.

Part one is set in Georgia, the rural South. It is mostly focused on women, starting with Karintha, whose very name is reminiscent of Gertrude Stein's "Melanctha." "Karintha" originally appeared in the context of the drama *Natalie Mann* (1922) in which Toomer's mouthpiece Nathan Merilh reads the story as an artist's valid response to modern Marxist and nationalist interrogators. Men bring Karintha money, and her imagistic constitution is that of a woman whose running is a "whir" and whose "skin is like dusk when the sun goes down" – a leitmotif of the story in the repetition of which Toomer visibly blurs the line between poetry and prose: it appears typeset as a prose sentence and as a poem.

Fragments of a passing rural world in which natural images (especially those of sunsets and autumn), and religious sentiments, increasingly give way to such intrusions of modernity as railroad tracks and factory door – and to scenes of violence. Becky, introduced as "the white woman who had two Negro sons," lives on a "ground islandized between the road and railroad track." Fern is presented as if narrator and reader were seeing her from a segregated train thundering by: "I ask you, friend, (it makes no difference if you sit in the Pullman or the Jim Crow as the train crosses her road), what thoughts would come to you . . . had you seen her in a quick flash, keen and intuitively, as she sat there on her porch when your train thundered by?"

Toomer's enigmatic questions to the reader seem located somewhere between Stowe's and Stein's. They too may ultimately be unanswerable, but they suggest a lyrical feeling altogether different from Stein's cold interrogations.

Esther, who has come to sexual maturity, walks like a somnambulist into a jeering crowd, and the story ends as if it were a Franz Kafka tale: "She steps out. There is no air, no street, and the town has completely disappeared." The undercurrent of violence erupts at the end of the first section as the factory town mob lynches Louisa's black lover Tom Burwell whose steel blade had slashed across his white rival Bob Stone's throat.

In part two *Cane* takes us to cities, especially Washington and Chicago in the age of mass migration and urbanization. As in "Seventh Street," this world has a new and fast-paced rhythm, characterized by postwar disillusionment, by a proliferating entertainment industry, and by the syncopation of jazz that Toomer incorporates into his prose in order to render a life that is "jagged, strident, modern." The surrealistic Rhobert who wears his house like a diver's helmet is an urban counterpart to Becky, as the narration again repeats prose sentences as poems. The image of the man who sinks is connected with the World War I experience, which violently reduced God to "a Red Cross man with a dredge and a respiration-pump" and makes the singing of the traditional spiritual "Deep River" seem out of place in a secularizing world. The self-conscious narrator of "Avey" resembles that of "Fern." Again, the wish for a performance of the spiritual "Deep River," this time by the Howard University Glee Club, marks the contrast to rural religion, a contrast that shapes also the vignette of the young woman on the street in "Calling Jesus." "Theater" continues the jazz theme, and Toomer adopts some blues lines here: "Arms of the girls, and their limbs, which . . jazz, jazz . . by lifting up their tight street skirts they set free, jab the air and clog the floor in rhythm to the music. (Lift your skirts, Baby, and talk t papa!)." In "Box Seat," Dan Moore reflects on a man who saw the first Oldsmobile but was born a slave: "He saw Grant and Lincoln. He saw Walt – old man, did, you see Walt Whitman?" The new urban world is not even one lifetime removed from Civil War and slavery; and this recent history also casts its shadow over the failed interracial romance between

Bona and Paul in the story that ends the second part and corresponds most directly to "Blood-Burning Moon": just as Bob Stone wanted Louisa because she was black and "went in as a master should and took her. Direct, honest, bold," so Bona in the new world of a Chicago gymnasium and the nightclub Crimson Gardens is attracted to Paul *because* she suspects he is black: "That's why I love –." Bona's (and Toomer's) lyrical labels "harvest moon" and "autumn leaf" cannot displace the racial slur "nigger" – that is, for Bona, however, a source of attraction. The weight of such historical racial categories (the phrase "a priori" recurs) impinges upon the consciousness of the youths: "Bona is one window. One window, Paul." Rölvaag's *Peder Victorious* shared with *Cane* this association of different identities with divided interiors. This may be an ironic affinity, since Toomer's narrator also contrasts the racially ambiguous Paul ("What is he, a Spaniard, an Indian, an Italian, a Mexican, a Hindu, or a Japanese?") with his friend Art, who is described as "this pale purple facsimile of a red-blooded Norwegian friend of his."

The representation of the nightclub Crimson Gardens gives Toomer an opportunity to find verbal equivalents for the musical experience in strong-sounding sentences with striking images that amount to a prose poem:

Crimson Gardens. Hurrah! The bare-back rider balances agilely on the applause which is the tail of her song. Orchestral instruments warm up for jazz. The flute is a cat that ripples its fur against the deep-purring saxophone. The drum throws sticks. The cat jumps on the piano keyboard. Hi diddle, hi diddle, the cat and the fiddle. Crimson Gardens . . . hurrah! . . jumps over the moon.

The stride piano merges with Joyce's technique of playing with familiar nursery rhymes, and puns and conceits intensify the progression from "rider" to "tail" and from a furry sound to the literal presence of a cat on the piano, to the cat and the fiddle from the nursery rhyme. This modernist blending was inspirational to young Langston Hughes when he wrote the poem "The Cat and the Saxophone (2 A.M.)." Toomer's pervasive interest in jazz was related to his hope for an aesthetic fusion brought about by new forms of artistic expression. This put him at odds with contemporary conservatives who deplored the growth of jazz, as well as with some political radicals who believed, as did Mike Gold in the *New Masses*, that African American strategies of resistance should be modeled not on "saxophone clowning" but on "Beethoven's might."

In part three, "Kabnis," the artist himself is a character *seen* rather than being merely an observing subject. Like Toomer, Kabnis is a secular urban intellectual who goes to rural Georgia to teach. Partly inspired by Joyce's *Portrait of the Artist as a Young Man*, "Kabnis" – written as a play – shows the development of a tortured mind through encounters with nursery rhymes, religion, and the various role models such as a teacher, preacher, cartwright, radical, and visionary. Kabnis must face many issues in society, history, and in himself, but the core of what he must come to terms with is a legacy of violence. The ending of "Kabnis" is like a rebirth, and the book ends as a birthsong with a sunrise.

The three parts of *Cane* confront the divisions of South and North, women and men, and black and white, while the structure of the book tends to bridge such divisions and strive toward unity. The fact that words, phrases, shorter and longer sentences are repeated throughout the book gives the reader a sense of acoustic and visual familiarity, a phenomenon reminiscent of *Three Lives*. For example, *Cane* is a book of repeated "thuds," harsh knocking sounds that syncopate the reading from "Becky" to the end of "Kabnis." In "Blood-Burning Moon" the "thud" is the sound of Bob's lynched body falling and of the mob's yell, giving a menacingly violent undercurrent of meaning to such later thuds as those in the gymnasium of "Bona and Paul." The book is woven of recurring sounds and images in such words as sawmill, pine, cotton, dixie pike, street, smoke, wedge, window, moon, cloud, purple, cradle, sin, and, of course, cane. Toomer shared Gertrude Stein's love for -ing forms, and "Seventh Street" alone offers the examples "zooming," "whizzing," "thrusting," "pouring," "flowing," "eddying," and "swirling." These examples suggest also how sensuous Toomer's sense of language is and how little he shares Stein's thrust toward abstraction. *Cane* is a book full of sunset and dusk imagery that is virtually omnipresent in the poems and the prose, thus calling particular attention to the very emphatic sunrise at the end.

"Fern" opens with a simple sentence in which "face" is the grammatical subject: "Face flowed into her eyes." The image is strong, the precise meaning elusive. Such a phrasing is reminiscent of Ezra Pound's "In a Station of the Metro." Toomer may, in fact, be consciously following F. S. Flint's and Ezra Pound's 1913 imagist maxims which exhorted poets to arrive at an image which presents an intellectual and emotional complex in an instant of time. The "oracular" strangeness in Toomer's images comes out of this poetic tradition.

He writes (about Louisa): "Her skin was the color of oak leaves on young trees in fall." The strongly visual image makes the reader see things freshly, yet it would be difficult to associate one very specific color with the description. Perhaps, for Toomer, an oak was not an oak was not an oak? It is no coincidence that for Toomer lyricism also functions as an avoidance of a label; after all, he chose to publish under the enigmatically androgynous first name "Jean" (rather than his correct baptismal first names "Nathan Eugene"). Toomer shared with the imagists a disdain for labels and abstractions and a desire to let fresh metaphors take their place. It is no coincidence that Toomer does not call

Karintha a "prostitute" (though reviewers like W. E. B. Du Bois did); the narrator only says that men bring her their money. Yet Toomer brings to this program a wish that goes beyond the aesthetic.

Louisa's skin color is particularly an alternative to a racial label, a needling engagement with a reader's desire to know whether a character is black or white. Toomer's response is, "Her skin was the color of oak leaves on young trees in fall." Toomer's aesthetic modernism was thus connected to an attack on false perceptions, prejudices, *a priori* assumptions, and stereotypes. "Damn labels if they enslave human beings – above race and nationality there is mankind," he writes in one of his aphorisms. If America was fragmented, black and white, male and female, Southern and Northern, rural and urban, Toomer saw his own mission, by contrast, in providing a literary ground for spiritual unity. His method of subverting ethnic stereotypes was different from Stein's "Negro sunshine" approach.

Toomer was not alone in the belief that modernist forms helped to complicate facile notions about social life. Georgia O'Keeffe, for example, had painted *Birch and Pine Trees – Pink* (1925), as a modern version of a "surrogate portrait" of her friend Jean Toomer, to whom she wrote, "there is a painting I made from something of you the first time you were here." This was, of course, also a way of deflecting from portraits as realistic representations (including typical ones) to portraits as purely *formal* expression. Toomer told O'Keeffe in a letter that there was an analogy between his "Bona and Paul" and Stieglitz's cloud photographs, the "Equivalents," though most people would probably not be able to see either: "When I say 'white', they see a certain white man, when I say 'black', they see a certain Negro. Just as they miss Stieglitz's intentions, achievements! Because they see 'clouds.'"

Toomer had a modern, analytical understanding of the mechanisms of racial differentiation. In his essay "Race Problems and Modern Society" (1929), he wrote that "the new Negro is much more Negro and much less American than was the old Negro of fifty years ago." The greater similarity of professional types "makes the drawing of distinction supposedly based on skin color or blood composition appear more and more ridiculous." Paradoxically, however, these "lines are being drawn with more force between the colored and white groups." This was certainly the case, as segregationist laws proliferated; for example, the Virginia legislature passed the Act to Preserve Racial Purity in 1924, defining any person "in whom there is ascertainable any Negro blood" as colored.

Against this trend, Toomer kept stressing the unity of what was being separated, and, as Charles W. Chesnutt had done before him in the prophetic essay "The Future American" (1900), Toomer imagined the term "American" in a utopian fashion. In the essay, "The Americans," he viewed America ethnically as the place "where mankind, long dismembered into separate usually repellent groupings, long scattered over the face of the earth, is being re-assembled into one whole and undivided human race." However, to arrive at this goal of an inclusive "America," one had to first break "the suggestion of hypnotic labels and false beliefs." And here he became a prophetic visionary who proclaimed that "these labels and beliefs will die": "And the sight of people will be freed from them, and the people will become less blind and they will use their sight and see." Toomer likened the blending of races and bloods into something new to the formation of water out of hydrogen and oxygen, but then amended his comparison, "for the blood of all the races is *human* blood. There are no differences between the blood of a Caucasian and the blood of a Negro as there are between hydrogen and oxygen. In the mixing and blending of so-called races there are mixtures and blending of the same stuff." Stressing in 1929 – in a very modern way – the sociological (not biological) nature of racial distinctions he concluded:

There is only one pure race – and this is the *human* race. We all belong to it – and this is the most and the least that can be said of any of us with accuracy. For the rest, it is mere talk, mere labeling, merely a manner of speaking, merely a sociological, not a biological, thing.

In his collection of aphorisms, *Essentials* (1931), he drew the consequences from such reflections and wrote about himself: "I am of no particular race. I am of the human race, a man at large in the human world, preparing a new race." Toomer would express similar sentiments in his Whitman-inspired poem "Blue Meridian" (1936) and in autobiographical prose writings in which he tended to see not only his utopian "America" but also the first-person singular "I" as potentially all-inclusive. He polemicized in "On Being an American" against those who "put value upon, their hearsay descents, their groupistic affiliations" and are not "aware of being *Americans*." And he suggested to the editor of *Prairie* magazine: "It is stupid to call me anything other than an American."

Nathan Eugene Pinchback Toomer was born into a family with a long-standing tradition of racial ambiguity on both sides. He described his own ethnic background as consisting of "seven blood mixtures: French, Dutch, Welsh, Negro, German, Jewish, and Indian. Because of these, my position in America has been a curious one. I have lived equally amid the two race groups. Now white, now colored." Though the experience preceding the writing of *Cane* pulled him "deeper and deeper into the Negro group," he concluded on his familiar note: "From my own point of view I am naturally and inevitably an American." "American" as an ideal self-description meant for Toomer an identification for people of all backgrounds who can acknowledge their shared and mixed characteristics – against the more common silent usurpation of the term "American" to stand for "white American."

When in March of 1931 (after the group psychology experiment at Portage, Wisconsin), Toomer married Margery Latimer, the author of the interracial short story "Confession" (1929), and a descendant of Anne Bradstreet, he proclaimed the arrival of "A New Race in America": "It is neither white nor black nor in-between. It is the American race, differing as much from white and black as white and black differ from each other . . . . My marriage to Margery Latimer is the marriage of two Americans." By contrast, the *World Telegram* headline read "NEGRO WHO WED WHITE NOVELIST SEES NEW RACE." Toomer's vision of a world beyond ethnic labeling was not shared by popular journalism at a time when interracial marriage was prohibited in a solid majority of the United States. Toomer would not only deplore such sensationalist and hostile labeling; upon the completion of *Cane* he also came to reject the label "Negro writer." He did not wish to be included in anthologies such as Nancy Cunard's *Negro* and was apprehensive of friendly writers who, like Sherwood Anderson, saw him too exclusively as, and thus limited him to, "Negro." On the other hand, he was critical of attempts to understand America ethnically without including the Negro: "No picture of a southern person is complete without its bit of Negro-determined psychology," he wrote about Frank's own failure to include the Negro more fully in *Our America*.

In one of his later manuscripts (written between 1937 and 1946), Toomer describes another mystical experience of oneness in modern Manhattan that shows his continuing quest for human unity among "beings called bums" and others called "street walkers, and business men, Americans, foreigners, Jews, Christians, blacks, whites. I rode a street car up Broadway. Beings were packed close around me. I could smell their body-odors, hear their bodies breathing." The Whitman-inspired experience of being close to these heterogeneous human bodies in a streetcar gave Toomer a sudden sense of a divine presence. Whether he aimed for this goal through the poetics of *Cane*, through the experiment of some of his later "sound poems" ("Mon sa me el kirimoor, /Ve dice kor, korrand ve deer"), or through his various spiritual undertakings, the quest for a divinely inspired human oneness remained.

Toomer conceived of his art and striving as a spiritual analogy to a much-needed "racial intermingling." He thought that *Cane* was only the beginning of a long road. Though, indeed, many projects and fragments, long manuscripts, a few literary works, and published essays and aphorisms followed, no second Toomer book equal to the brilliance of *Cane* ever appeared.

FREUD, MARX, HARD-BOILED

In the course of the interwar period ethnic literature proliferated, turned to new themes, and developed a new tone. Among many other influences, Freud, Marx, and Hemingway made their presence felt in some of the new writing. Freudian issues were brought to the fore, for example, by the German Jewish immigrant and critic Ludwig Lewisohn whose marriage-as-hell novel *The Case of Mr. Crump* (1926) was termed "an incomparable masterpiece" by no less a person than Freud himself; and in his introduction Thomas Mann places Lewisohn – who also published the autobiographies *Up Stream* (1922) and *The Island Within* (1929) – "in the forefront of modern epic narrative" and praises him for his "manly style," his "dry and desperate humor," and his characterization: "even the woman, Anne Crump, remains human in all her repulsiveness," Mann comments.

Lewisohn's little-known novel *The Vehement Flame: The Story of Stephen Escott* (1930) was a particularly noteworthy attempt to represent the theme of repressed sexuality in the interaction among Jews and gentiles in New York at the turn of the century. The narrator is the lower-middle-class Southern Christian Stephen Escott (who is symbolically positioned between his Jewish immigrant hometown friend David Sampson and the upper-class Oliver Clayton). Stephen and David work as law partners in Manhattan; Oliver is a genteel publisher who is shocked by modernist literature. Their differing attitudes toward sexuality, class-based expectations of life's rewards, and art come to a head in a traumatic murder trial of the Freud-savvy, avant-garde Greenwich Village poet Paul Glover, who publishes in the *Little Review* and *Poetry*, embodies the modern defiance of aesthetic and sexual conventions, yet kills Jasper Harris for having an affair with Paul's wife Janet. Though David defends Paul well enough to secure a mistrial, Paul joins "some army" and gets killed "on an obscure and alien field." David, who still remembers the Jewish village in Poland where he was born and who vividly recalls the emigration experience, "the dreadful herding in freight-cars of immigrant families to Hamburg and the more dreadful steerage," resigns from the law firm and prophesies with a sad smile that "Western mankind has an evil conscience and there are people in all countries who need a scape-goat for their sins. The scape-goat, as always, are the Jews."

Indeed, the public outrage at the outcome of the trial leads to David's disbarring. Yet David is strangely calm about the antisemitically inflected reactions even by his former friend Oliver Clayton; and the novel ends as Stephen Escott takes a Sabbath dinner at the Sampsons' house and Ruth Sampson toasts "to a time when things will not be so unevenly divided, when all people will have love enough and justice enough to make life bearable."

As a student, Stephen represses his erotic reveries and reacts hypocritically to David's admonition that what he needs "is a little honest dissipation." His marriage to Dorothy is the logical consequence of this attitude, for Stephen's wife is extremely repressed, upwardly mobile (she worships Oliver Clayton) and – as it turns out in her sharply negative reaction to the Sampsons – also antisemitic. Dorothy feels threatened by the Sampsons, both sexually and socially, and defensively says that they are "vulgar," adding revealingly: "I suppose it's because they are Jews." Stereotyping, a pervasive issue in ethnic writing, is here examined psychologically.

Stephen is unhappy that he cannot get real affection from Dorothy, and her negative reaction to David Sampson (who has become Stephen's law partner) heightens Stephen's attraction to him. He confesses to the reader that he "might not have clung so assiduously to David's friendship had Dorothy been indifferent to it and to him." Dorothy's opposition makes Stephen aware that he has to hold on to and do what she dislikes in order to preserve his "individuality." Dorothy becomes sickly and ultimately dies.

When Stephen starts a relationship with the sexually free "new woman" Beatrice Loth, a female Don Juan figure and Hemingwayesque libertine, he soon finds out that Beatrice is merely the obverse of Dorothy – what one repressed the other expresses more or less exclusively. Stephen realizes that Beatrice is ever-afraid of boredom, has no real tenderness, and has merely "driven love back within its physiological limits." Beatrice was "as much as Dorothy a victim of Puritanism. Only she was rich and free and belonged to the feminist generation." When Dorothy says that "sentimental intimacy" makes her sick and adds, "You don't expect me to baby talk to you, I hope," Stephen asks her whether there isn't "a happy medium between baby talk and being hard boiled." (Lewisohn here employed the term that was coming in vogue in the 1920s and 1930s and that will concern us later.)

Such a happy medium, the novel suggests, is actually achieved by "quite a number" of Jewish marriages that are as good and sound as the Sampsons', and this is, David explains, due to the fact that Jewish women "have learned humility . . . in the face of life." In the novel, only David and Ruth Sampson have a sexually fulfilled union; and the dissatisfaction and sexual frustration of the others serves as a partial explanation of their antisemitism. The Sampsons are not only free from Clayton's overt bigotry or Stephen's own earlier hypocrisy; David Sampson also has a benignly condescending understanding of Paul Glover's modernism, with its "libertarian theories" and "revolutionary ardors," for he has "heard them years ago expressed in Russian and Yiddish at the old Café Monopole on Second Avenue."

This is made clear by an encounter of Paul with Berl Fligelmann, the ultimate embodiment of the Old World modernist spirit who responds to Paul's wish for the "liberation of people through the world" by spreading out "his hands in his old, strangely birdlike fashion" and proclaiming: "How younk! How younk! Dese t'ings come late to America. Ve hav finished wit dem. Do you know de 'Faust' from Goethe? 'In de beginnink vass de *deet*!'" From the point of the ancient-seeming Fligelmann, Paul's deed is nothing but the absurd reenactment of Faust's attempt to rewrite the beginning of the gospel of St. John. The "vehement flame" of American modernism may destroy Paul, reveal Oliver's hypocrisy, and force Stephen to rethink his life, but it is nothing but an old story for Jewish figures like Fligelmann or Sampson. In view of this assessment of modernism, Lewisohn's choice of a realistic narrative seems programmatic. In Jewish wisdom about human strivings and artistic stirrings – however comically accented its articulation may be – Lewisohn seems to see a safeguard against American Puritanism and its modern inversion. However, the possibility that Jews will get scapegoated for their very wisdom is also very real in a novel that is quite unusual in ethnic fiction, though it has been dismissed as too much of a *roman-à-thèse*.

Whether or not Freud was explicitly invoked, sexual frankness in ethnic writing increased in the 1930s. Richard Wright wrote (but excised for Book of the Month Club considerations) a scene from *Native Son* (1940) in which Bigger Thomas and his friends masturbated in a movie theater. Of all ethnic writers in the period, Henry Miller, third-generation German American, was probably the most sexually explicit author, so much so that much of his work, most famously his trilogy *Tropic of Cancer* (1934), *Black Spring* (1936), and *Tropic of Capricorn* (1939), remained inaccessible in the United States until the early 1960s. In addition to extending misogyny to greater physiological detail than did most of his competitors, Miller, whose Brooklyn birth certificate was in the German language, also wrote an ethno-autobiographical narrative, "The Tailor Shop," and included it in the center of the middle volume of his trilogy. It continued not only Miller's sexual story but also gave ample room to reminiscences about working in his father's shop during World War I and about German American festivities, ascribing to this milieu the first inklings of his artistic development.

In *The Story of American Literature* (1939) Ludwig Lewisohn developed in depth a Freudian view of American literary history, in which immigrant, ethnic, and minority writers are in the modern phalanx in combating Anglo-American repression, neo-Puritanism, and hypocrisy. Lewisohn saw the legacy of Puritanism in the modern American folk-beliefs "that men are either total abstainers or drunkards, either monkish or libertine, either hustlers or idlers, either political and economic conformers or enemies of all social order." World War I brought the Anglo-Americans into sharp confrontation with "the later immigrant strains: the German, the Jewish, the Latin and the Slav." The war years also heightened the "sexual ambivalence toward the Negro" in the whole country. Yet despite powerful neo-Puritan repression, the modern writers – not only the ethnics among them, but also "men and women of undivided American and Puritan descent" – set out to "destroy and transform Puritanism." The result was the "treatment of the sexual life in the books of Farrell and Caldwell" as well as similar themes in "the fictions of John O'Hara and James M. Cain and Bessie Breuer and the overrated John Steinbeck." The new literature's excessive, hardly ironic, and unveiled preoccupation "with the body as love-object and with the immediate sexual act" shows that "contemporary America has set a new standard of frankness – mild word enough! – in the treatment of man's sexual life." Lewisohn deplored this tendency, for it sought "not only ecstasy but anodyne, not so much life as a kind of death." He was no more enthusiastic about the bulk of social protest fiction, though he did think of James T. Farrell's *Studs Lonigan Trilogy* as "one the most massive and impressive literary achievement" of the 1930s.

❦

Marxian themes of class struggle and dismal social conditions in city and country took center stage in the genre of proletarian fiction to which several ethnic writers contributed with growing intensity during the Great Depression. Apart from Farrell, there were Edward Dahlberg, Pietro di Donato, Richard Wright, and, perhaps most notably, Mike Gold, who also propagated proletarian realism in book reviews and theoretical essays and who ended his autobiographically inspired *Jews Without Money* (1930) with a communist soap-box orator who effectively merges the immigrant-ethnic with the proletarian tendency in literature:

A man on an East Side soap-box, one night, proclaimed that out of the despair, melancholy and helpless rage of millions, a world movement had been born to abolish poverty.

I listened to him.

O workers' Revolution, you brought hope to me, a lonely suicidal boy. You are the true Messiah. You will destroy the East Side when you come, and build there a garden for the human spirit.

O revolution, that forced me to think, to struggle and to live.

O great Beginning!

This may have been an abruptly propagandistic ending to a book which presents some classic immigrant themes such as greenhorns and American-ization, inter-ethnic encounters, name changes, the problem of ethnic slurs ("Christ-killer!"), the protective immigrant mother, and the father's remark-able love for the Yiddish theater. Gold engages with common ethnic stereo-types: "Jews are as individualized," he writes very directly, "as are Chinese or Anglo-Saxons. There are no racial types. My father, for instance, was like a certain kind of Irishman more than the stenciled stage Jew." As in the case of Mary Antin's *Promised Land*, the reader is imagined to be non-Jewish and is provided with numerous explanations (though no glossary) of Jewish customs: "The Jewish holidays were fascinating to children. It was like having a dozen Christmases during the year."

Jews Without Money also represents many facets of modernity: Gold interest-ingly writes of the "newsreel of memory" in evoking the past, he describes the death of a playmate who is run over by a horse car, and he gives an account of a Sunday outing to the Bronx Park on an elevated train:

The train was worse than a cattle car. It was crowded with people to the point of nausea. Excited screaming mothers, fathers sagging under enormous lunch baskets, children yelling, puking and running under every one's legs, an old graybeard fighting with the conductor, a gang of tough Irish kids in baseball suits who persisted in swinging from the straps – sweating bodies and exasperated nerves – grinding lurching train, sudden stops when a hundred bodies battered into each other, bedlam of legs and arms, sneezing, spitting, cursing, sighing – a super-tenement on wheels.

Well before the ending of the book, then, the focus on the injuries of class is unmistakable, as Gold writes about the many horrors of urban life among the poor: the lack of privacy in overcrowded, filthy, and infested tenements, badly paying jobs and unemployment, gangsters, crime, and violence, and pimps, prostitution, and syphilis.

Granville Hicks's *The Great Tradition: An Interpretation of American Literature since the Civil War* (1933) ends with "Direction," a forward-looking, hopeful chapter which predicts the broadening of the Marxist tendencies in American literature and mentions such novels as Albert Halper's *The Foundry* (1934, focusing on everyday working-class life), Isidor Schneider's autobiographical *From the Kingdom of Necessity* (1935), and Nathan Asch's experimental *Pay Day*

(1930), a remarkable novel set on a single night that happens to be the date of Sacco and Vanzetti's execution.

Nathan Asch was the son of the Polish immigrant Sholem Asch, a versatile Yiddish writer in many genres who was to achieve his highest American fame for his multiethnic New York novel *East River* (1946). Nathan Asch had caught Hemingway's attention when he submitted a short story to the *transatlantic review* that Hemingway was eager to help revise and usher into print. *Pay Day*, a Joyce-inspired novel, follows the clerk Jim Cowan through such sections as "Subway," "The L," "The Street," and "The Speakeasy." Public transportation provides occasions for melting-pot encounters ("There were two wops talking in Italian, every now and then saying 'All right' in English") and for sexual fantasies ("A desire came over him to reach down and touch those breasts, fondle them; his hand even relaxed its grip on the strap, but quickly he controlled himself, tightened his hold, and still he looked"). The section entitled "The Movie" is a montage experiment of simple prose sentences strongly evocative of images – a long, avant-garde prose poem rather than a novel chapter. In the background of the novel are newspaper headlines about the Sacco and Vanzetti case, and only the last section, "Home Again," intertwines the two stories, as Jim says at dawn, "Oh, my God. They're dead." Asch's Bloomsday was August 23, 1927.

Hicks saw in revolutionary novelists who "come from very different backgrounds," are experts on social conditions and strikes, strive for a new sensibility, and find themselves attracted to communism, the confirmation of Marx and Engels's prophecy that honest and clear-sighted intellectuals from all classes would join the anticapitalist ranks. "And participation in the common struggle against the exploiters brings these very different persons closer and closer together, so that there is a fundamental unity side by side with a rich diversity." Interestingly, Henry Adams, who was seen as a hero in Lewisohn's Freudian view, also is praised by Hicks for his Marxian understanding of social relations.

❦

Perhaps the most remarkable development in the literature after the mid-1920s was a changing tone in prose writing. Gertrude Stein remained the large super-ego figure hovering over modern American prose writers, so that even her detractor Gold used fourteen -ing forms in his brief description of the Third Avenue L (just quoted). Yet many readers could not warm up to Stein as a model, even though they may have been mesmerized and occasionally influenced by her. The truth is that no matter how much they invoked Stein, many writers did not actually like her cold style.

Young writers were therefore also looking for different, established, yet modern-sounding models. One option was F. Scott Fitzgerald, but his obsession with unrequited love for the very rich remained an idiosyncrasy – though his most famous hero's upwardly mobile name-change from Gatz to Gatsby and his made-up past would also have held an obvious appeal to immigrant and ethnic writers concerned with assimilation and racial "passing." Sherwood Anderson's humanity and impressive sharpness of perception were marred by more than occasional flashes of naiveté and pettiness. John Dos Passos was intriguing in his remarkable and unparalleled openness to modernity, yet he also frightened writers by the sprawling endlessness of his enterprise, so that it seemed more interesting to talk about him than to read him page by page, or sentence by sentence – let alone to follow his work as a model.

In retrospect, William Faulkner would appear to be the most likely candidate for a position of central importance to modern immigrant and ethnic writers. Yet, as has already been suggested, Faulkner was still understood as an unnecessarily difficult regionalist writer. Faulkner's career started in the opposite manner from the way in which Henry Roth's came to a halt. If the immigrant Roth could not imagine what the meaning of the Civil War could be for American culture, then the native-born Faulkner knew only too well – though the sources of his knowledge came from the wrong, the defeated, side. Faulkner did valiantly start out, in good Lost Generation fashion, to write *Soldier's Pay* (1926), a novel about a veteran returning from World War I. Faulkner even stylized himself as a World War I war hero and made up tales of his supposed experiences as a fighter pilot who had received a war wound and needed to drink much bourbon because of the pain (tall tales in which Sherwood Anderson seriously believed and which he foolishly wrote up in print). But Faulkner's significant past was symbolized not by World War I but by the Civil War. Faulkner's major works reach back to the memory of the Old South, and it is telling that his chronology informs readers that his protagonist Quentin Compson commits suicide in 1910 – well before World War I.

Like many ethnic writers, Faulkner represented a very specific past, marginalized and "ethnicized" by the dominant Yankee culture, a problematic and often traumatic past that was examined at times against the implied or explicit voice of questions from the outside ("Why do you hate the South?"). In *Light in August* (1932), *Absalom, Absalom!* (1936), and *Go Down, Moses* (1942), Faulkner explored the tragic web of race relations within the Southern family, making him particularly relevant to all writers concerned with issues of ethnicity, race, interracialism, and multigenerational families. Like many modernists, Faulkner tried his hand at imitating T. S. Eliot and, as has already been seen, wrote many a Steinian sentence. Developing his own style, he arrived at experiments in time shifts and different points of view that set a new standard for modernist authors after World War II (Ann Petry's *The Narrows*, James Baldwin's *Go Tell It on the Mountain*, Ross Lockridge's *Raintree County*, and Ralph Ellison's *Invisible Man* come to mind). Faulkner came to be the most revered American writer for the Latin American magical realists like Gabriel García Márquez and for Europeans like Günter Grass. Toni Morrison, whose relation with Faulkner is complex, wrote her 1955 M.A. thesis at Cornell University on "Virginia Woolf's and William Faulkner's Treatment of the Alienated."

Faulkner's haunting themes and his meditations on fragments of the past found their perfect equivalent in experimental sentences, as in the use of fragments rendering Quentin Compson's state of mind in *The Sound and the Fury* (1929):

If that was the three-quarters, not over ten minutes now. One car had just left, and people were already waiting for the next one. I asked, but he didn't know whether another one would leave before noon or not because you'd think that interurbans. So the first one was another trolley. I got on. You can feel noon. I wonder if even miners in the bowels of the earth. That's why whistles; because people that sweat, and if just far enough from sweat you won't hear whistles and in eight minutes you should be that far from sweat in Boston . . . .

I could hear my watch whenever the car stopped, but not often they were already eating *Who would play a* Eating the business of eating inside of you space too space and time confused Stomach saying noon brain saying eat o'clock All right I wonder what time it is what of it. People were getting out. The trolley didn't stop so often now, emptied by eating.

It would be hard to find a modernist match to Faulkner's stream-of-consciousness trolley. Jean-Paul Sartre wrote that "for young writers in France, Faulkner is a god." Yet this was in 1945; and in the United States of the 1930s and early 1940s Faulkner's many accomplishments did not yet give him a position of centrality, for he still seemed intractable and forbidding.

As late as 1956 Ernest Hemingway bluntly expressed what was undoubtedly a more widespread American opinion about Faulkner. "Faulkner gives me the creeps," Hemingway wrote in a letter and continued: "Never trust a man with a Southern accent," He went on to expand on his prejudice against Southerners: "They could talk reasonable English as we talk it if they were not phony." Elsewhere Hemingway also referred to Faulkner simply as "a no good son of a bitch."

Hemingway's reaction might have been colored by the fact that the versatile Faulkner had parodied Hemingway's style in (the idiot) Benjy's section in *The Sound and the Fury*, a book in which Faulkner writes in many different stylistic registers. Benjy has a most radically limited point of view in which only external perception matters, since the center of consciousness lacks the power of synthesis. Benjy describes his first drunken experience:

The ground kept sloping up and the cows ran up the hill . . . . Quentin held my arm and we went toward the barn. Then the barn wasn't there and we had to wait until it came back. I didn't see it come back. It came behind us and Quentin set me down in the trough where the cows ate. I held on to it. It was going away too, and I held to it. The cows ran down the hill again, across the door.

This flat, noninterpretive accounting of sensations in a clear, childlike vocabulary which forces the reader to supply an interpretation sounds very much like a parody of Hemingway's voice. Here is Jake Barnes experiencing drunkenness in *The Sun Also Rises*:

I went out the door and into my own room and lay on the bed. The bed went sailing off and I sat up in bed and looked at the wall to make it stop . . . . I got up and went to the balcony and looked out at the dancing in the square. The world was not wheeling any more.

Faulkner also parodied himself, using the pen-name "Ernest V. Trueblood," and Wyndham Lewis thought that both Faulkner and Hemingway were "men without art." Faulkner was certainly not alone in imitating and perhaps parodying Hemingway. In fact, the writer who did become identified with modern American literature and who was the most imitated and parodied author in the interwar period was Ernest Hemingway.

Hemingway himself had started imitating Sherwood Anderson and, especially, Stein, but he seemed to have written Anderson out of his system with the parody *The Torrents of Spring* (1926), a book in which Hemingway also took on Stein in a section entitled "The Making and Marring of Americans." "A bitch is a bitch is a bitch," Hemingway also penned in capital letters arranged in a circle on the front page of the copy of his *Death in the Afternoon* (1932) that he gave to Stein. Yet no matter how much he distanced himself from her at times, Hemingway continued to use some of Stein's idiosyncrasies (repetitions, simple adjectives, an objective and detached stance) and achieved the widest national and international audience appeal of any serious American author in the first half of the century. He shared Stein's emphasis on the sentence as the most important element of modern prose; and he wrote in *A Moveable Feast*: "I would stand out and look over the roofs of Paris and think, 'Do not worry. You have always written before and you will write now. All you have to do is write one true sentence. Write the truest sentence that you know.'" Hemingway self-consciously thought of single sentences as possibly the truest legacy of a writer and said: "Some writers are only born to help another writer to write one sentence."

What happened to Stein's sentences in Hemingway's hands? Among Hemingway's representative sentences is the following (from *The Sun Also Rises*) in which the detached observer adds an aspect of masculine-coded violence: "He was a good trout, and I banged his head against the timber so that he quivered out straight, and then slipped him into my bag." In an example of a ride on a bus (in *Paris 1922*) the narrator plays the insider to Paris life: "I have stood on the crowded back platform of a seven o'clock Batignolles bus and lurched along the wet lamp lit street while men going home to supper never looked up from their newspapers as we passed Notre Dame grey and dripping in the rain." In *The Sun Also Rises* there is an abundance of such Paris scenes, for example:

In the morning I walked down the Boulevard to the Rue Soufflot for coffee and brioche. It was a fine morning. The horse-chestnut trees in the Luxembourg gardens were in bloom. There was the pleasant early-morning feeling of a hot day. I read the papers with the coffee and then smoked a cigarette . . . . The Boulevard was busy with trams and people going to work. I got on an S bus and rode down to the Madeleine, standing on the back platform.

Lady Brett Ashley articulates an ethos of secularized modernity when she announces that "it makes one feel rather good deciding not to be a bitch," adding: "It's sort of what we have instead of God." A battlefield description in *A Farewell to Arms* (1929) shows Hemingway's readiness to face the loss of meaning in wars: "the sacrifices were like the stockyards at Chicago, if nothing was done with the meat except to bury it."

Carl Van Doren, assessing Hemingway's power in 1940, writes: "If Hemingway had learned about style and cadence from Gertrude Stein, he had none of her obscurity and he used none of her materials . . . . He had a terse, cold magic in his story-telling that made Scott Fitzgerald seem flimsy in comparison, Dos Passos loose-gaited." Hemingway "took" – for his highly stylized yet surprisingly "natural"-seeming prose gave readers a full experience of taking part in modernism while still getting some traditional characterization, story lines, and sentiments (all the more so if these aspects were withheld or suppressed on the page). His was a modernism that was both "easy," never as difficult for the reader as was Stein's, and "tough," as he demonstratively embodied the particularly "masculine" flavor of the term "hard-boiled." Mark Twain had used the word once in the 1883 speech "General Grant's Grammar," when he defended Grant's, perhaps ungrammatical, phrase "I propose to fight it out on this line if it takes all summer" because "it did certainly wake up this nation as a hundred million tons of A No. 1, fourth-proof, hard-boiled, hide-bound grammar from another mouth could not have done." Yet the word "hard-boiled" (in reference to an attitude, or to prose writing rather than to eggs) was coming into wider circulation only in the 1920s. Hemingway's Jake Barnes, for example, employs it to name a pose; feeling "like hell again," he declares at the end of chapter four of *The Sun Also Rises*: "It is awfully easy to be hard-boiled about everything in the daytime, but at night it is another thing." (In the draft manuscript of the novel, the narrator still felt "like crying again," and the chapter ended without any comment on being hard-boiled.) The *Nation* ran Allen Tate's review of *The Sun Also Rises* under the heading "Hard-Boiled." In the same year, 1926, the *Ladies' Home Journal* wrote that "the hard-boiled cynic has a shell" that satire "can never penetrate." Even the arch-conservative literary critic Stuart Sherman used the term "hard-boiled" when he argued in *The Main Stream* (1927) that it was impossible to take Ring Lardner's "hard-boiled Americans" seriously. Sherman's own meandering style serves as a perfect counterpoint to hard-boiled prose when, in support of the term "main stream" to which his book helped give currency, he imagines the ideal literary critic as a man who

conceives of literature perhaps as a river, himself as a scout seeking for the main channel of intellectual and emotional activity in his own tract of time, recurring constantly to the point where the full rush of living waters comes in from the past, and eagerly searching for the point where the flood breaks out of the backwater and through the dams, and streams away into the future.

Lewisohn, as we saw, used "hard boiled" as the opposite excess to "baby talk."

Overtly anti-sentimental, Hemingway's detached, stoic, and wisecracking narrators and characters manage to feed sentimental reader expectations at the same time. Hemingway may have been the most successful compromise modernist, parallel to Edward Hopper in painting or George Gershwin in music. When *Scribner's* published Hemingway's short story "The Killers" in 1927, Hopper wrote the editors that he found it "refreshing" to read such an "honest piece of work in an American magazine, after wading through the vast sea of sugar coated mush that makes up most of our fiction."

Hemingway produced the first full version of American modernism for the millions that made the subculture of artists, existentialists, and bohemians in avant-garde cliques generally available as an object of popular identification. He appealed to artists, to middle-brow readers, and to a wide general audience who became vicarious *aficionados* and insiders *en masse*. Hemingway's penchant for parataxis may have helped in this process, for as the literary critic Joseph Warren Beach observed in 1941, Hemingway worked "to reduce all ideas to a single order of relationship, the conjunctive coordinate relationship, in which no one item is subordinated to any other." Here is an example from "The Snows of Kilimanjaro" (1936): "It was evening now and he had been asleep. The sun was gone behind the hill and there was a shadow all across the plain and the small animals were feeding close to camp." Hemingway's love for parataxis, Beach noted, may have run against the attempts of English teachers to inspire their students to express "their ideas in the proper order of subordination." Hemingway wanted storytelling "to flow and not be lost in eddies of logic" – which is why he relied on what Beach called "the great leveling democracy of the *and*."

Hemingway was also a master of dead-pan dialogues:

> "This is a good place," he said.
> "There's a lot of liquor," I agreed.

The response was the result of revision, for the manuscript still read: "'It's a nice place,' I agreed." Or, most famously:

> "Oh, Jake . . . we could have had such a damned good time together."
> "Yes . . . . Isn't it pretty to think so?"

This quick and memorable repartee was also refined in the revision process from the original manuscript's "It's nice as hell to think so."

These dialogues in simple, vigorous words suggest nothing so much as a fatalistic ethos that comes across more persuasively because it is understated. Hemingway's art follows what he called the "principle of the iceberg," for "there is seven-eighths of it underwater for every part that shows." A feeling of modern hopelessness, symbolized by Jake's war wound, combines with a Quixotic element of chivalry in a bad time, a quest for a "Roncevaux" that may have become more elusive after World War I than it ever was.

The stylized vernacular absorbed everyday language, including advertisements and ubiquitous brand names. While many writers incorporated the names that attached themselves to articles of consumption, Hemingway extracted near-transcendental meaning from them. For example, when the German artist Kandisky describes to the narrator in *Green Hills of Africa* (1935) the pleasure of having a thirteen-year-old daughter, he says that her participation in the family conversations is "the Heinz ketchup on the daily food."

Hemingway's tone struck the right chord for the time. His ethos of finding oneself in a strange world, in which the codes one believes in no longer seem to apply, spoke to immigrant and minority writers and readers. Themes of suddenly erupting violence and of complex initiation were compatible with the experience of ethnoracial hostility and of socialization into, or exclusion from, American codes of conduct. Hemingway's style was equally resonant with lives lived in translation, and his repetition of simple words like "nice," "fine," and "pretty" resembled the immigrants' famous "all right" or the under-stated terms derived from black slang ("cool"). In a passage Delmore Schwartz highlighted from the short story "The Gambler, the Nun and the Radio" (1933; first entitled "Give Us a Prescription, Doctor") an American detective asks a mortally wounded Mexican gambler to tell him who shot him:

"Listen," the detective said, "this isn't Chicago. You're not a gangster. You don't have to act like a moving picture. It's all right to tell who shot you. That's all right to do."

Yet an American writer goes right on to "translate" the detective for the Mexican:

"Listen, amigo . . . The policeman says that we are not in Chicago. You are not a bandit and this has nothing to do with the cinema."
"I believe him," said Cayetano softly. "*Ya lo creo.*"
"One can with honor denounce one's assailant. Everyone does it here, he says."

Hemingway's deceptive simplicity of language was not only attractive to writers who had come from backgrounds in which English did not have a multigenerational presence or was not the writer's family or first language, but Hemingway's style also suggested the presence of translation or created the illusion of being a literal translation from another tongue. Perhaps this is one reason for Hemingway's tremendous international success also. Here is an example from *For Whom the Bell Tolls* (1940): "Thou wert plenty of horse." As Harry Levin noted in 1951, Hemingway may have been simply translat-ing "*Eras mucho caballo.*" Levin marveled that, "having cut down his English vocabulary," Hemingway "should augment it by continual importation from other languages." These imported words are often placed right next to the English equivalent, as in *The Sun Also Rises*, when Jake asks Robert what he would like to drink: "'Sherry,' Cohn said. 'Jerez,' I said to the waiter."

IO

❦

HEMINGWAY SPOKEN HERE

Delmore Schwartz argued in 1951 that Hemingway's style was neither primitive nor proletarian:

Its devices include eloquent reticence, intensely emotional understatement, and above all the simplified speech which an American uses to a European ignorant of English . . . .

Hemingway's style is a poetic heightening of various forms of modern colloquial speech — among them, the idiom of the hardboiled reporter, the foreign correspondent, and the sportswriter. It is masculine speech. Its reticence, understatement, and toughness derive from the American masculine ideal, which has a long history going back to the pioneer on the frontier and including the strong silent man of the Hollywood Western. The intense sensitivity to the way in which a European speaks broken English, echoing his own language's idioms, may also derive from the speech of the immigrants as well, perhaps, as from the special relationship of America to Europe which the fiction of Henry James first portrayed fully.

Schwartz's linking of Hemingway's "Americanness," employment of the international theme, and possible reliance on immigrant speech was perceptive. "Hemingway spoken here" might well have been the motto of much prose writing of the 1930s, and American ethnic writers gave ample testimony to their indebtedness.

Meyer Levin, a Jewish novelist from Chicago who wrote the trilogy-length novel *The Old Bunch* (1937) and was later instrumental in publishing Anne Frank's *Diary of a Young Girl* (1952) in English translation, started his career with two Hemingwayesque novels. *Reporter* (1929), a city desk book, and *Frankie and Johnnie* (1930), the story of a failed romance with such sentences as: "All the time Johnnie was thinking these things Frankie wasn't riding home on the L at all. All that time, Frankie was riding home on the bus."

In his autobiography *A Long Way From Home* (1937) Claude McKay confessed to "a vast admiration" for Hemingway and reported that left, liberal, as well as some conservative writers he met in France "all mentioned Hemingway with admiration." "Many of them felt that they could never go on writing as before after Hemingway." McKay also thought that it was not Hemingway's fault if in the 1930s he came to be "mainly admired by a hard-boiled and unsophisticated public." Yet at the same time McKay felt that Hemingway had achieved a quality "distinctly and definitely American" (and "altogether un-European") in illuminating "the hard-boiled contempt for and disgust with sissyness expressed among all classes of Americans" – a "conventionalized rough attitude." And further: "Mr. Hemingway has taken this characteristic of American life from the streets, the barrooms, the ringsides and lifted it into the realm of literature. In accomplishing this he did revolutionary work with four-letter Anglo-Saxon words." With all this praise McKay also found it worth mentioning that his own "loose manner and subjective feeling" had little in common with Hemingway's "objective and carefully stylized form" and that his own novel *Home to Harlem* (whose protagonist happens to be a proto-existentialist World War I veteran named Jake) followed the "clearly consistent emotionalist realist thread" that McKay had established before Hemingway started publishing.

James T. Farrell's 1943 essay on Hemingway's *The Sun Also Rises* mentions the imitations it generated, not only among younger authors but also in real life: "Boys and girls on campus after campus began to talk like Hemingway characters." There is thinness in his imagination, Farrell observes: his Europe is a tourist's Europe and most of his characters have only a meager past, do not really think, and feel quite alike in the stoic acceptance of the ills of life. Yet in *The Sun Also Rises*, which "remains one of the very best American novels of the Twenties," "he has saved himself from the crudities of simple behaviorism because of his gift of suggestiveness and his developed skill of understatement."

Ludwig Lewisohn thought that before *A Farewell to Arms* Hemingway had been "merely the most gifted of the new 'hard-boiled' writers, that is to say, of those impelled to depict life in order to express their disgust for it and hence their own spiritual despair." But with a novel of such excellence Hemingway had transcended "the moral nihilism of the school he had himself helped to form." Lewisohn admired one of the novel's culminating moments and singled out a sentence, "with its classically curbed rage and pity" about the interrogation by the battle police: "The questioners had that beautiful detachment and devotion to stern justice of men dealing in death without being in any danger of it."

Alfred Kazin noted in *On Native Grounds* (1942) that Hemingway's example "as a stylist and craftsman"

was magnetic on younger men who came after him; as the progenitor of the new and distinctively American cult of violence, he stands out as the greatest single influence on the hard-boiled novel of the thirties, and certainly affected the social and left-wing fiction of the period more than some of its writers could easily admit . . . . Hemingway is the bronze god of the whole contemporary literary experience in America.

(Sartre had not yet propagated the other "god.")

Kazin's observation was true even for the extremely qualified Hemingway assessment that the ever-critical Mike Gold offered in 1928. Gold complained that Hemingway only satisfied the daydreams of the "American white-collar slave" with his chief three themes of liquor, sex, and sport, and gave the young "liberal" authors who wrote "advertising copy meekly all day" a fantasy world of an "irresponsible Europe, where everyone talks literature, drinks fine liqueurs, swaggers with a cane, sleeps with beautiful and witty British aristocrats, is well informed in the mysteries of bullfighting, has a mysterious income from home." The gratification of these fantasies explained why Hemingway was "suddenly popular." However, "the revolutionary writers of the future will be grateful to him; they will imitate his style. But they will have different things to say."

One such revolutionary writer was Richard Wright, who explained at Columbia University in 1938:

When I was employed on the Federal Writers' Project in Chicago, practically all us young writers were influenced by Ernest Hemingway. We liked the simple, direct way in which he wrote, but a great many of us wanted to write about social problems. The question came up: how could we write about social problems and use a simple style? Hemingway's style is so concentrated on naturalistic detail that there is no room for social comment. One boy said that one way was to dig deeper into the character and try to get something that will live. I decided to try it.

One of the short stories first published in *Uncle Tom's Children* (1938), "Long Black Song," was the result.

Hemingway did not only inspire the ethnic left to imitate his style. When Farrell pointed out that boys and girls had started to speak like Hemingway characters, he was thinking of colleges as one arena in which Hemingway dissemination was taking place. Another such arena was the increasingly proliferating popular culture of the 1930s and 1940s. A ready example is the genre of pulp fiction, represented for example by a writer like Raymond Chandler, whose life shares some features with an immigrant's. Although he was born in Chicago in 1888, his British mother took him to England at age seven when his parents divorced, and he completed a thoroughly English education and began a career in the Admiralty before returning to the United States at age twenty-four. His early writings had a distinctly English style; and when, after a checkered career, he returned to writing in the early 1930s, he did so with reflections on the differences between English and American prose, with sketches, and with a Hemingway parody. In his "Notes (very brief, please) on English and American style," Chandler commented sharply on American English. Among the critical points he made were its overworking of catch-phrases, the phony sound of its slang, "being invented by writers and palmed off on simple hoodlums and ballplayers," its feeble awareness of "the continuing stream of culture," due to the lack of the historical sense and to shoddy education," and its "too great a fondness for the *faux naïf*," that is "the use of a style such as might be spoken by a very limited sort of mind." Here Chandler qualifies his critique: "In the hands of a genius like Hemingway this may be effective, but only by subtly evading the terms of the contract, that is, by an artistic use of the telling detail which the speaker never would have noted. When not used by a genius it is as flat as Rotarian speech."

Chandler clearly aimed for the genius spot; and if as a youth he had imitated Henry James, in 1932 he parodied Hemingway on his way to write his major "hard-boiled" detective novels of the 1930s and 1940s. The exercise was not so subtly called "Beer in the Sergeant Major's Hat (or The Sun Also Sneezes)" and dedicated "with no good reason to the greatest living American novelist – Ernest Hemingway." This is a sample:

Hank drank the alcohol and water. It had a warm sweetish taste. It was warm as hell. It was warmer than whiskey. It was warmer than that Asti Spumante they had that time in Capozzo when Hank was with the Arditi. They had been carp fishing with landing nets. It had been a good day. After the fourth bottle of Asti Spumante Hank fell into the river and came out with his hair full of carp. Old Peguzzi laughed until his boots rattled on the hard gray rock. And afterward Peguzzi got gonorrhea on the Piave. It was a hell of a war.

Only after such writing exercises did Chandler begin to publish in the pulp magazine *Black Mask* (that H. L. Mencken had helped found) and develop his most famous detective novels *The Big Sleep* (1939), *Farewell, My Lovely* (1940), *The High Window* (1942), and *The Lady in the Lake* (1943). Some of the hard-boiled terms Chandler coined gained wide currency later, for example, Marlowe's novel use of the phrase "I'll take him out" (in the approximate sense of neutralizing or killing one of General Sternwood's blackmailers so that "he'll think a bridge fell on him") in *The Big Sleep*.

In an imaginary interview on "The New American Novelists" (1949), André Gide praised Hammett's dialogues," in which every character is trying to deceive all the others and in which the truth slowly becomes visible through the haze of deception," as comparable "only with the best in Hemingway." It was through Chandler, Dashiell Hammett, and James M. Cain, and even more so through the Hollywood movies that were made from their novels, that the hard-boiled style became universalized. What took place, especially in the genre of film noir, might be termed the Hemingwayization of American culture. The effect of the hard-boiled dialogues was further enhanced by the visual aid of film-noir movie sets: a critic noted that in Fritz Lang's *Scarlet Street* (1945) the "unpeopled streets, the elongated shadows, the angular buildings that guard empty space like grim sentinels, recall the eerie night-time cityscapes in the paintings of Edward Hopper." This was true for many films of the genre, including Henry Hathaway's *The Dark Corner* (1946), based on a story by ethnic writer Leo Rosten (of Hyman Kaplan fame), with jazzy interludes and a professional, Hopperesque set designed by Paul S. Fox and Thomas Little.

To be sure, Gertrude Stein's style also inspired occasional moments in Hollywood movies. The film *The Awful Truth* (1937), for example, directed by Leo McCarey, and with a screenplay by Viña Delmar based on a 1922 play by Arthur Richman, lets the nearly divorced Mr. and Mrs. Warriner (played by Cary Grant and Irene Dunne) find their way back into their marital bed literally at the last minute before a divorce decree takes effect. This reconciliation is accompanied by what sounds like a pure Steinian dialogue:

> LUCY: It's funny that everything is the way it is on account of the way you feel.
> JERRY: Huh?
> LUCY: Well, I mean, if you didn't feel the way you do, things wouldn't be the way they are, would they? I mean, things could be the same if things were different.
> JERRY: But – eh – things are the way you made them.
> LUCY: Oh no! No, things are the way you think I made them. I didn't make them that way at all. Things are just the same as they always were. Only you are the same as you were, too, so I guess things will never be the same again.

And a little later:

> LUCY: You are all confused, aren't you?
> JERRY: Uh-uh. Aren't you?
> LUCY: No.
> JERRY: But you should be because you are wrong about things being different because they are not the same. Things are different, except in a different way. You're still the same, only I've been a fool, but I'm not now.
> LUCY: Ah!
> JERRY: So long as I am different, don't you think that, well maybe things, could be the same again, only a little different, huh?
> LUCY: You mean that, Jerry? Are you sure?

This wonderful insertion of a Steinian moment into an otherwise more conventionally scripted screwball comedy of remarriage sent a critic to double-check Plato's *Parmenides* as a possible source. Still, *The Awful Truth* may have been an exception. More pervasive were the prolific contributions to the film-noir cult of the 1930s and 1940s. They created the illusion that a stylistic convention derived from Hemingway was actually a lived idiom that was spoken by America's existentialist detectives and gangsters.

In Billy Wilder's *Double Indemnity* (1944), adapted for the screen by Wilder together with Raymond Chandler from James M. Cain's novella "Three of a Kind" (*Liberty Magazine*, 1936), the insurance agent Walter Neff admits: "Yes, I killed him. I killed him for money and for a woman. I didn't get the money and I didn't get the woman. Pretty, isn't it?" What makes this confession all the more intriguing is that Neff makes it in the form of a dictated office memorandum: even that typically tame genre could take on the irresistible, tough-talking, hard-boiled, and Hemingwayesque tone of film noir. In Howard Hawks's *The Big Sleep* (1946), based on the 1939 Chandler novel and adapted (in part) by William Faulkner, we hear the following dialogue:

> STERNWOOD: How do you like your brandy, sir?
> MARLOWE: In a glass.

As in the case of Hemingway, revision strengthened the wisecracking repartee, for in Chandler's novel Marlowe had still answered "Anyway at all."

In his essay on "The Language of Hollywood" (1944) Farrell disagrees with Horace Kallen's more optimistic view of mass culture and looks at Hollywood as a "counterfeit culture" in which "common speech" may create the illusion of a democratic emphasis but actually only serves "to glorify the status quo." He observes that much "literary talent of America is now diverted to Hollywood and radio writing" and mentions the "penetrating influence of Hollywood on the novel" that can be seen in "the stimulation it has given to a kind of hard-boiled realism that imitates all the manners of serious writing but contains none of the inner meaning, the inner protest against evils, the revelation of the social mechanisms and social structures found in serious realism." He cites as examples *The Postman Always Rings Twice* and *Double Indemnity*.

James Agee examined twice the relationship of the movies to the spirit of hard-boiled prose. Agee commented on the 1946 movie version of Hemingway's *The Killers* that "Hemingway's talk, which on the page used to seem so nearly magical and is still so very good, sounds, on the screen, as cooked-up and formal as an eclogue." Yet writing about the movie version of Chandler's *Farewell, My Lovely* on December 16, 1944, Agee found that this film preserved both the faults and virtues of the book, and he came up with an excellent formula that describes the intellectual limits of the hard-boiled genre, including some of its ethnic contributors: "poetic talent, arrested-adolescent prurience, and the sort of self-pity which, in rejoicing in all that is hardest-boiled, turns the two former faculties toward melodramatic, pretentiously unpretentious examination of big cities and their inhabitants."

The literary beginnings of James T. Farrell, Pietro di Donato, Meyer Levin, Richard Wright, Ralph Ellison, and even some of Mike Gold's works would have been different had it not been for Hemingway's example. This was not always a matter of the nurture these writers received (as did Nathan Asch), for Hemingway was not famous for being generous to all literary newcomers, as the example of the young William Saroyan shows.

Fresno-born, William Saroyan was the only son of the Armenian immigrants Armenak and Takoohi Saroyan who had come to the United States from Bitlis in eastern Anatolia. Saroyan published a story in *Hairenik* (Homeland), an Armenian journal in Boston, and then in Edward J. O'Brien's *Best Short Stories of 1933*. After this first success, other stories followed in Mencken's *American Mercury*, in *Harpers*, in the *Atlantic Monthly*, and in Burnett and Foley's *Story Magazine*; and soon Random House published Saroyan's first book collection, *The Daring Young Man on the Flying Trapeze and Other Stories* (1934). Reviews were mixed, though Saroyan was generally read in the context of modernism. The *Christian Century* opined that Saroyan's book "has qualities in common with the 'Nude Descending a Staircase,' but it is better than 'a rose is a rose is a rose.'" Saroyan had invited such contexts, since he mentioned some modernists by name, for after contemplating the possibility of continuing the Tarzan series if Edgar Rice Burroughs were to die, he pronounced: "if I felt inclined, I could write like John Dos Passos or William Faulkner or James Joyce." As he himself observed, however, he did not actually write like any of them; and only in a few instances – such as the experimental short story, "Quarter, Half, Three-Quarter, and Whole Notes" (in *Three Times Three*, 1936) – did he write like Stein to whom he had written the adulatory letter already cited. Another author whom he occasionally imitated was Hemingway. In the story "Aspirin is a Member of the N.R.A." (first published in *American Mercury*) Saroyan contemplates the certainty of death and the pervasiveness of human pain, visible on the faces of everybody on the subway. "I looked everywhere for one face that was not the mask of a pained life, but I did not find such a face. It was this that made my study of the subway so fascinating." He reaches the decision that "the subway is death, all of us are riding to death." (The theme of the sad lonely faces in crowded urban subways remained with Saroyan, and in his play *Subway Circus* he permitted some of the subway riders, Thornton Wilder-style, to reveal their thoughts to the audience.) From the recognition that aspirin is an evasion of death, he imagines a future advertisement in the *"Saturday Evening Post*, making a slogan on behalf of death. *Do not be deceived ... die and see your dreams come true ... death does not harm the heart ... it is absolutely harmless ... doctors everywhere recommend it ...* and so on." And this is when he nods toward Hemingway: "You hear a lot of sad talk about all the young men who die in the Great War. Well, what about this war? Is it less real because it destroys with less violence, with a ghastlier shock, with a more sustained pain?"

In another story in *The Daring Young Man* Saroyan half-seriously sets up Hemingway as an ideal:

I hope some day to write a great philosophical work on the order of *Death in the Afternoon*, but I am aware that I am not yet ready to undertake such a work. I feel that the cultivation of tennis on a large scale among the peoples of the earth will do much to annihilate racial differences, prejudices, hatred, etc.

Worried that some sophisticated readers might think that he is making fun of Hemingway, Saroyan states: "I am not. *Death in the Afternoon* is a pretty sound piece of prose .... Even when Hemingway is a fool, he is at least an accurate fool. He tells you what actually takes place and he doesn't allow the speed of an occurrence to make his exposition hasty. That is a lot."

This was too much for the master. In January 1935 Hemingway commented on the book for *Esquire*, a men's magazine founded in the fall of 1933 in which Hemingway regularly contributed letters from Tanganyika, Paris, and Cuba, and in which Dreiser, Farrell, James M. Cain, and Meyer Levin were publishing and Dos Passos's realist watercolors of the port of New York and of a Spanish fiesta appeared. Their contributions were interrupted by ads for whiskey, cigarettes, sharp-looking men's clothing (including not only hats and shirts but also such paraphernalia as cuff-links, socks, and even zippers), and enticingly illustrated *Esquire* self-promotion focusing on such forthcoming taboo-breakers as Langston Hughes's story "A Good Job Gone" (a story of interracial romance and intrigue that "no commercial magazine would touch with a ten foot pole"). There were also risqué cartoons, off-color jokes, and somewhat revealing photographs of actresses.

Writing in the context of this man's magazine, Hemingway was not generous when he took to task Saroyan, the ethnic newcomer to the literary scene, whose first *Esquire* story had just been published, who had invoked and attempted to imitate Hemingway in his first book, and in whose writings Edmund Wilson had also noticed some Hemingway traits. Hemingway struck the pose of a drunkard picking a barroom fight with Saroyan "who tells the boys in his stories how he can write like, or better than, other people if he wanted to try." Hemingway lectures the young contender: "Anybody can write like somebody else. But it takes a long time to get to write like yourself and then what they pay off on is having something to say . . . . You've got only one new trick and that is that you're an Armenian." But that was hardly enough, Hemingway said, invoking the example of Michael Arlen, who had disappointed after some early promise. "Now you see us, the people you can write like and better than, have some of us been shot, and some of us been cut, and all of us been married, and we've been around a long time and we've been a lot of places and seen a lot of things that you haven't seen, Mr. Saroyan, and that you won't ever see because the things are over and lots of the places aren't there any more." After more derogatory comments on Saroyan's abilities, Hemingway asks: "Do I make myself clear? Or would you like me to push your puss in. (I'm drunk again now you see. It's a wonderful advantage when you're arguing.)" And on and on the brawling style goes, as Hemingway calls Saroyan to whose name the world may echo "like Roland's horn at Roncevaux," a "poor ignorant bastid." He asks rhetorically whether there is a doctor in the house: "Good. Mr. Saroyan wants him . . . . Mr. Saroyan isn't feeling so good." The champion clearly felt that he had knocked out the lightweight contender and that ethnic credentials were meaningless in the battle for good writing. Saroyan answered this public attack with a restrained personal letter in which he conceded that Hemingway might be "right" that Saroyan was an Armenian but added: "I hope you don't want me to feel bad about being what I am because I don't feel any worse about this than any Englishman (for example) feels about being who he is, although I suppose neither of us feels any too good about it."

One of the ethnic writers Hemingway publicly supported was Nelson Algren. Upon Algren's collection *The Neon Wilderness* (1947) Hemingway conferred lavish and wisecracking praise: "Mr. Algren, boy are you good – one of the two best authors in America," the blurb read (and the reader just knew who the other one had to be). Algren, who had worked on the Illinois Project of the Writers' Guide Series, was one of the first major ethnic writers to take up the theme of heroin addiction on such a large scale in twentieth-century America that the rise of the Mafia during the Prohibition years made possible. A typical sentence from *The Man with the Golden Arm* (1949) reads: "The light was fading in his eyes now, they were sinking to his head and the freshness the drug had brought to his cheeks had turned into a dull putty-gray." Algren, who was also famous for a love relationship with Simone de Beauvoir that affected her (and Sartre's) view of the United States, elicited this comment from Hemingway in a 1956 letter: "if Nelson is as tough a boy inside as he thinks he is how could he have devoted more than one evening to Simone [de Beauvoir]

HENRY ROTH: ETHNICITY, MODERNITY, AND MODERNISM

IN HENRY ROTH'S novel *Call It Sleep* (1934), the strands of ethnicity, modernity, and modernism come together inseparably, and at a very high point of American literary achievement. This autobiographically inflected novel is an outstanding example of their fusion into "ethnic modernism." When the eight-year-old Jewish immigrant protagonist David Schearl attempts, in the experimental twenty-first chapter of book four ("The Rail"), to stick a milk ladle into the electric rail of the Eighth-Street trolley tracks on New York's Lower East Side, a high modernist verbal explosion accompanies this climactic moment in the novel.

On Avenue D, a long burst of flame spurted from underground, growled as if the veil of earth were splitting. People were hurrying now, children scooting past them, screeching. On Avenue C, the lights of the trolley-car waned and wavered. The motorman cursed, feeling the power drain.

Such external descriptions alternate with, and the pervasive -ing forms here seem to echo, the sounds of the streetcars: "Klang! Klang! Klang!" – as an avant-garde anticipation of Hugh Martin and Ralph Blane's cheerier and more popular "Trolley Song" in the film *Meet Me in St. Louis* (1944). A surrealistic melting-pot melange of people's *eyes* observes David's body lying on the tracks.

Eyes, a myriad of eyes, gay or sunken, rheumy, yellow or clear, slant, blood-shot, hard, boozy or bright swerved from their tasks, their play, from faces, newspapers, dishes, cards, seidels, valves, sewing machines, swerved and converged.

There are familiar echoes of St. Paul's letter to the Corinthians and of Isaiah's prophetic image of burning coal.

(*As if on hinges, blank enormous mirrors arose, swung slowly upward face to face. Within the facing glass, vast panels deployed, lifted a steady wink of opaque pages until an endless corridor dwindled into night.*) . . . .
(*Coal! And it was brighter than the pith of lightning and milder than pearl,*) . . (*And made the darkness dark because the dark had culled its radiance for that jewel. Zwank!*)

James Joyce- and T. S. Eliot-inspired, Yiddish-inflected, and multilingually enriched expressions by the bystanders also sustain the fusion of the secular and the sacred in the modern city:

> "Oy! Oy vai! Oy vai! Oy Vai!"
> "Git a cop!"
> "An embillance – go cull-oy!"
> "Don't touch 'im!"
> "Bambino! Madre mia!"
> "Mary. It's just a kid!"

While David is shaken by the electric power on the streetcar tracks, all the strands of thinking about modernity seem to coalesce. He views the electric current as if it were a divine power. It is telling that he disregards a rabbi's admonition that "God's light is not between car-tracks."

❦

Call It Sleep has been justly praised as a twentieth-century masterpiece of American literature. Written by a young communist, it became part of the controversies surrounding proletarian art; yet it includes only a brief moment in which a soap-box orator makes overt social commentary: "Only the laboring poor, only the masses embittered, bewildered, betrayed, in the day when the red cock crows, can free us!" This was not enough for the *New Masses*, where an anonymous reviewer (who sounds very much like Mike Gold) expressed anger at the "sex-phobias" of "this six-year-old Proust" (Gold had also accused Proust of masturbatory modernism). "It is a pity," the reviewer complained, "that so many young writers drawn from the proletariat can make no better use of their working class experience than as material for introspective and febrile novels." This dismissal of *Call It Sleep* provoked Kenneth Burke and Edwin Seaver to come to Roth's defense for his honesty and skill in portraying the "pre-political thinking of childhood."

Call It Sleep was also developed with evident psychoanalytic interest in such concepts as Freud's "family romance," the child's wish to imagine a fantasy ancestry and to regard his real parents as foster parents, a wish intensified here in the immigrant situation. Another famous Freud essay seems to have provided the model for a passage in the novel. In *Beyond the Pleasure Principle* Freud, exploring "repetition" and its connection to the death instinct, gave an account of a lonely child's imaginative method of making himself disappear during absences of his mother, whom he greeted with an enigmatic "Baby o-o-o-o!" upon her return. "He had discovered his reflection in a full-length mirror which did not quite reach the ground, so that by crouching down he could make his mirror-image 'gone.'" In *Call It Sleep*, there is a memorable scene in which David sees his mirror image appear and disappear in shop windows:

Only his own face met him, a pale oval, and dark, fear-struck, staring eyes, that slid low along the windows of the stores, snapped from glass to glass, mingled with the enemas, ointment-jars, green globes of the drug-store – snapped off – mingled with the baby clothes, button-heaps, underwear of the dry-goods store – snapped off – with the cans of paint, steel tools, frying pans, clothes-lines of the hardware store – snapped off. A variegated pallor, but pallor always, a motley fear, but fear. Or he was not.

– On the windows how I go. Can see and ain't. Can see and ain't. And when I ain't, where? In between them if I stopped, where? Ain't nobody. No place. Stand here then. BE nobody. Always. Nobody'd see. Nobody'd know. Always. Always? No. Carry – yes – carry a looking-glass. Teenchy weenchy one, like in pocket-book, Mama's. Yea. Yea. Yea. Stay by house. Be nobody. Can't see. Wait for her. Be nobody and she comes down. Take it! Take looking-glass out, Look! Mama! Mama! Here I am! Mama, I was hiding! Here I am! But if Papa came. Zip, take away! Ain't! Ain't no place! Ow! Crazy! Near! I'm near! Ow!

David's vividly rendered experience of losing his self-image is connected to his obsession with death, with "sleep eternal years," and with coffins. Yet Henry Roth claimed not to have read Freud at the time of the novel's publication.

Call It Sleep was, as the quoted excerpts suggest, part of the modernist movement as it experimented with stream-of-consciousness technique, with a literary equivalent of cinematic montage, with allusions to Stein, Eliot, Joyce, Conrad, Yeats, and other moderns and contemporaries. As a young man, Roth helped the New York University professor Eda Lou Walton edit the volume of modern urban poetry *The City Day* (1929). The novel's many stylistic registers show this exposure, as he incorporates into the book, without apparent effort, such Stein-like phrases as "A bath-tub is a bath-tub," alludes to Eliot's "Jugjugjugjugjugjug," "unreal" city, or "heap" – Roth calls it "swirl" – "of broken images" from *The Waste Land*, invokes Joseph Conrad with the phrasing "heart of darkness," or makes a Joycean pun, as in the dialect rendition of "a whore master" as "a hura mezda" – sounding like the Zoroastrian god of light, Ahuramazda. And the novel's central biblical image from Isaiah of the power of the seraph's coal that can cleanse dirty lips (which feeds David's wish to seek a vision and to find purification on the trolley tracks) may have been inspired by William Butler Yeats's poem "Vacillation" (1932) where it is connected with the theme of modern art. There are also brief and, on the whole, exceptional moments where the style gestures toward Hemingway: "'And this is the Golden Land.' She spoke in Yiddish." Or: "'No, I don't want it.' He answered in Yiddish."

Authored by an immigrant who had come as a young child from Polish Galicia (then belonging to Austria-Hungary), the book that opens with a prologue at Ellis Island and the Statue of Liberty is also part of "immigrant fiction." Significantly, the prologue is set in 1907, a peak year for immigration during which more than 1.28 million people came through Ellis Island. The steamer on which the family that is at the center of the novel arrives is named *Peter Stuyvesant*, after the Dutch governor who attempted (in vain) to prohibit the immigration of the "deceitful race" of Jews to New Amsterdam in 1654; and the novel may be the very best literary representation of the "second generation" of immigrants to the United States, and the most successful experiment in using immigrant dialect and non-English-language elements as an idiom in an English-language novel. In *Call It Sleep*, the Statue of Liberty is described somewhat differently from the tradition marked by Holt's *Life Stories* or of Emma Goldman's autobiography:

And before them, rising on her high pedestal from the scaling swarmy brilliance of sunlit water to the west, Liberty. The spinning disk of the late afternoon sun slanted behind her, and to those on board who gazed, her features were charred with shadow, her depths exhausted, her masses ironed to one single plane. Against the luminous sky the rays of her halo were spikes of darkness roweling the air; shadow flattened the torch she bore to a black cross against flawless light – the blackened hilt of a broken sword. Liberty.

This is a modernist defamiliarization of the silhouetted Statue. Franz Kafka's *Amerika* deforms Lady Liberty in a similar fashion: "a sudden burst of sunshine seemed to illumine the *Statue of Liberty* so that he saw it in a new light, although he had sighted it long ago. The arm with the sword rose up as if newly stretched aloft, and round the figure blew the free winds of heaven." Roth's description contains some of the key terms of the novel: brilliant light, the raised broken hilt of a menacing sword, and the cross. Whereas Mary Antin had helped to redefine the official meaning of Liberty to stand for a welcome to immigrants, Roth casts her as the war god Ares or the angel with the flaming sword ready to drive humans out of paradise. And near the end of the novel the Statue of Liberty returns as Roth incorporates a voice that says that "you can go all the way up inside her for twenty-five cents" – as if Lady Liberty were a cheap prostitute.

❧

The prologue, written after the rest of the novel was completed, introduces the central characters, as David Schearl and his mother Genya arrive at Ellis Island and meet David's father Albert. It prepares the reader for a sociological novel about immigrant life that does not follow this opening, though it significantly establishes a crossing, a migration, as the first action of the book. If Roth had not added the prologue, the novel's first sentence would have come closer to the opening of Joyce's *Ulysses*: "Standing before the kitchen sink and regarding the bright brass faucets that gleamed so far away, each with a bead of water at its nose, slowly swelling, falling, David again became aware that this world had been created without thought of him."

Roth represents the Jewish immigrants' Yiddish as *good* English – for Roth a highly stylized and lyrical language – and their English as broken English. This procedure suggests an inner world of richness and lyrical expression, a full range of feelings and words that might remain hidden to an English-only reader were it not for the narrator's mediation. In the "broken English" sections, however, Yiddish words do enter into the text, at times with the humorous effect of a bilingual pun. One example hinges on the double meaning of the word "kockin" as English "cocaine" and Yiddish "to shit," which explains the apparent paradox that in America "kockin" "will clear the mouth of pain." Sometimes Yiddish meanings are rendered in English, at other times they remain on the level of in-jokes; for Roth does not put the reader in the comfortable position of the standard-English speaker who finds amusement in the fully accessible humorous dialect of the kind that Leo Rosten ("Leonard Q. Ross") created with great public resonance for *New Yorker* readers and in *The Education of H*y*m*a*n K*a*p*l*a*n* (1937).

On many occasions, the reader is invited to hear a Yiddish original *through* a strangely poeticized English text in which it is buried but apparently not completely lost in translation. Albert repeatedly asks, "Where is the prayer?" (referring to David who will presumably say Kaddish upon the father's death) and Genya's sister Bertha wonders, "How fares a Jew?" At times, the technique is subtle: "Do you still ask?", "It grows late", or "Nothing fulfills itself with me! It's all doomed!" In other instances, an unfamiliar English phrasing calls attention to itself, as in: "Will you vomit up past shame?", "Go talk to my buttocks!", "All buttocks have only one eye", or "May your brains boil over!" This form of linguistic transposition, in which even vulgar terms may take on a poetic glow, was also tried out by Roth's contemporaries. Alter Brody's "Lowing in the Night" (1927), for example, includes such lines as "Try to joke with such a blister on your tongue," "Who smears salt on a herring?," and "Just a bed pan for you to empty your lust in." (Brody's comic man–woman dialogue also serves as an antidote to Lewisohn's idealization of Jewish marital rapport in *The Vehement Flame*.)

Roth uses, without translation, Hebrew, Aramaic, Slavic, and Italian words and phrases. Here is the Italian–Yiddish exchange between a butcher and a sweeper: "Verstinkeneh Goy!" . . . "Sonnomo bitzah you! I fix" . . . "You vanna

push me? . . . I'll zebreak you het." "Vai a fanculo te! . . . Come on! Jew bast!"
Roth employs various dialects, and he makes the reader listen to a boy's speech-
impediment: "If I blyibm duh ywully ylyod, den he wonthye hilyt me so
moyuch, myaytlybe." As the narrator puts it, "In trying to divine Benny's
meaning, one could forget all else."

Roth's varied method of representing language difference contributes much
to the poetic quality of *Call It Sleep*. It also permitted Roth to insert many
literary phrasings that, whether they had their origins in Anglo-American
modernist aesthetics, in the world of technological modernity, or in conventional Yiddish speech, seem natural parts of dialogue or narration. It may be
hard to determine what, in a given instance, is sociolinguistic reference to
a foreign-language original ("the prayer"), what is a mistake ("I'm losted"),
and what is specific to an interior monologue in the modern novel ("Tomorrow came"). Is Bertha's (hardly traditional) curse "May a trolley-car crack his
bones" a translation from the Yiddish? Is her expression, "A bath-tub is a
bath-tub," a common immigrant wish or an echo to Gertrude Stein? When
the phrase "suddeh vuddeh" appears, is this merely the dialect deformation of
"soda water" – or is it an allusion to Mrs. Porter and her daughter who wash
their feet in soda water, from *The Waste Land*? Is there a correct English
equivalent of "Boddeh" Street on which David says he lives when he is lost
in Brownsville? Bodder, Potter, Poddeh, Bodder, Body, Pother, Powther,
Bahday, and Barhdee Street are among the suggestions offered in the book; yet
does such a street exist at all? Are there limits to translation, the novel seems
to ask – which is extraordinarily successful in giving the English-language
reader the feeling of living in an uneasily translated world.

At times, translation and explanation to linguistic and religious outsiders
come close to ethnic treason in the novel, when David "explains" things Jewish
to his admired Polish American and Catholic friend Leo Dugovka whom he
considers part of a "rarer, bolder, more carefree world" and who has a "glamour
about him."

When Leo had asked him whether Jews wore amulets on their persons, David had
described the "Tzitzos" that some Jewish boys wore under their shirts, and the "Tfilin",
the little leather boxes, he had seen men strap around their arms and brows in the
synagogue – had described them, hoping that Leo would laugh. He did. And even
when Leo had said of the "Mezuzeh", the little metal-covered scroll that all Jews tacked
on the door-posts above their thresholds – "Oh! Izzat wotchuh call 'em? Miss oozer?
Me ol' lady tore one o' dem off de door w'en we moved in, and I busted it, an' cheez!
It wuz all full o' Chinee on liddle terlit paper – all aroun' an' aroun'." David had not
been hurt. He had felt a slight qualm of guilt, yes, guilt because he was betraying all
the Jews in his house who had Mezuzehs above their doors; but if Leo thought it was
funny, then it was funny and it didn't matter. He had even added lamely that the only

things Jews wore around their necks were camphor balls against measles, merely to hear the intoxicating sound of Leo's derisive laugh.

Interestingly, the narrator provides explanations to a presumed non-Jewish reader even as the danger of explaining religious secrets to outsiders is being invoked. David (and Roth) thus seem to be doing here what Rabbi Judah Leib Lazerow explicitly worried about when he wrote in his sermon *The Staff of Judah*, published in New York in 1921: "I hereby order the translator upon oath not to translate these following statements of mine . . . . I do not want the gentiles to know what is taking place amongst us." One of Lazerow's concerns was the forsaking of the wearing of *tzitzis*, or fringes on four-cornered garments, in America.

Call It Sleep does not only highlight linguistic divides between established adult languages, but also follows the process of a child's language acquisition. David is twenty-one or twenty-two months old in the prologue, and the novel focuses on his life from just before his sixth birthday to a little after his eighth. For example, in contemplating the omnivorous nature of non-Jews, David, at age six, thinks of the following:

Ham . [. . .] And chickens without feathers in boxes, and little bunnies in that store on First Avenue by the elevated. In a wooden cage with lettuce. And rocks, they eat too, on those stands. Rocks all colors. They bust 'em open with a knife and shake out ketchup on the snot inside. Yich! and long, black, skinny snakes. Goyim eat everything.

The context permits us to decode "snot" (a word Joyce had helped to poeticize) in "rocks" as David's personal term for "oyster" (a word withheld by the narrator in order to approximate David's consciousness), just as the "snakes" are recognizable but not identified as "eels."

The oedipally charged child's point of view accounts for the view of the mother "tall as a tower" and representing physical closeness and intimacy by the "faint familiar warmth and odor of her skin and hair." The father is seen in more grotesque or surrealistic but generally menacing close-ups: "The fine veins in his nose stood out like a pink cobweb."

The parents' emigration distances (and alienates) David forever from the world of their origins:

Filled with a warm, nostalgic mournfulness, he shut his eyes. Fragments of forgotten rivers floated under the lids, dusty roads, fathomless curve of trees, a branch in a window under flawless light. A world somewhere, somewhere else.

This passage makes vivid the second (or the first *American*) generation's difficulty with nostalgia. The village Veljish, David's own place of birth, is available to him only through his mother's narration (called "mother's yarn" in the novel's manuscript) and not through concretely remembered sensual experience. The mother's warm and living body, the goal of David's oedipal yearnings, is also the physical space designating his origins, a space all the more important to David since he does not directly know his geographic place of birth. In the world of objects, David's "warm, nostalgic mournfulness" has only fragments to work with, a hill, or a tree. (It is indicative of Roth's stylistic self-consciousness that the sentence starting with the word "fragments" is itself followed by a sentence fragment.) Even when his mother gently chides him, her reference is to a world that has to remain inaccessible to David: "You're like those large bright flies in Austria that can fly backwards and forwards or hover in the air as though pinned there." Yet there are no dragon-flies in David's New York. Much of the past is lost to him, and Roth uses the Joycean technique of incorporating English children's tales ("Goldilocks and the Three Bears") and nursery rhymes to show David's odd cultural situation. The following passage is characteristic of Roth's experimental method of rendering David's chain of associations:

Hickory, dickory dock. Clock. Never had. But – wheel-what? Once . . . Once I . . . Say again and remember. Hickory, dickory, wickory, chickory. In the coffee. In a white box for eight cents with yellow sides. In a box. Box. Yesterday. God it said and holier than Jew-light with the coal.

His "nostalgia" becomes, paradoxically, *forward*-looking, directed away from concrete and local sensual memory impressions and toward transportable abstractions such as the "flawless light" that he ultimately seeks to find through electricity on the trolley tracks.

Genya and Albert incorporate into their New York home cheap and inauthentic items of nostalgia that turn out to be charged with deeper meaning. This is something that David senses. There is a strange parallelism in the aesthetic representations Albert and Genya choose. For the mother, it is a ten-cent reproduction of a generic country scene that she hangs up and that significantly gives a name to one of the four books of the novel. Can "The Picture" "of a small patch of ground full of tall green stalks, at the foot of which, tiny blue flowers grew" evoke the aura of Veljish to Genya and David?

"I bought it on a pushcart," she informed him with one of her curious, unaccountable sighs. "It reminded me of Austria and my home. Do you know what that is you're looking at?"
"Flowers?" he guessed, shaking his head at the same time.
"That's corn. That's how it grows. It grows out of the earth, you know, the sweet corn in the summer – it isn't made by pushcart pedlars."
"What are those blue flowers under it?"

"In July those little flowers come out. They're pretty, aren't they? You've seen them, yes, you have, fields and fields of them, only you've forgotten, you were so young."

The mother–son dialogue marks the distance of the urban boy not only from the place of his mother's youth but from *any* countryside: he has forgotten the country and cannot even identify corn. David finds himself staring at the picture, searching for hidden meanings behind what was "only a picture of long green corn and blue flowers under it."

And she had said that he had seen it too, real ones, long ago in Europe. But she said he couldn't remember. So maybe he was trying to remember the real ones instead of the picture ones. But how? If – No. Funny. Getting mixed and mixed and –

The picture constitutes David's opening to and veil over "real" memories. It also elicits Bertha's ironic question, "Are you starting a museum?" (Sixty years later, Roth described the impression the art in Eda Lou Walton's apartment made on him: "He had never seen sheer white walls like that before. So simple, plain, with just three pictures on them, reproductions, one of crude golden flowers almost leaping out of the frame. And another of a blue farm wagon. Whose were they?" This raises the question whether even such small fictional details as the picture were merged out of childhood and adulthood materials.)

    Albert would have preferred a picture of "something alive," for example, a "herd of cattle drinking such as I've seen in the stores. Or a prize bull with a shine to his flanks and the black fire in his eyes." The father ultimately gets something in this genre, a plaque with bull's horns that has a more threatening effect on David:

Before him on a shield-shaped wooden plaque, two magnificent horns curved out and up, pale yellow to the ebony tips. So wide was the span between them, he could almost have stretched his arms out on either side, before he could touch them. Though they lay there inertly, their bases solidly fastened to the dark wood, there pulsed from them still a suggestion of terrific power, a power that even while they lay motionless made the breast ache as though they were ever imminent, ever charging.

David recognizes what he thinks is a cow – not from life but from pictures and from a movie he saw with Aunt Bertha. Genya responds with a laugh, "A cow, but a he-cow!" She explains that "it reminded him of the time when he took care of cattle," and significantly, her eyes wander "to the picture of the corn flowers on the wall." Both parents thus establish an equivalence between the two purchased items. David is affected by the horns and contemplates them:

Somehow he couldn't quite believe that it was for memory's sake only that his father had bought this trophy. Somehow looking at the horns, guessing the enormous strength of the beast who must have owned them, there seemed to be another reason. He couldn't quite fathom it though.

David's relationship to his parents' city-bought fetishes strengthens his oedipal view of the laughing mother as land, summer, beauty, and fertility, and the scowling father as enormous and unfathomable animal power; yet Roth's fictionalization of David's predicament – the city boy does not recognize corn and cannot tell a cow from a bull – also brings his aesthetic close to Eda Lou Walton's observation that young urban writers are no longer "intimate with the ritual of the seasons" and "have no associations with the names of flowers." Hence they suffer from "rootlessness," a topic Nathan Asch proposed to investigate in a (denied) Guggenheim fellowship application of 1936. They may become interested in "country" as an abstraction, embracing, for example, anthropology as a way of understanding past folkways *in general*, and substitute a lost realm of their own family experience by reading Sir James Frazer's *Golden Bough* (1890) or any of the sources that the footnotes to *The Waste Land* sent them to read, and where they found comprehensive and global accounts of mistletoe, corn-spirit, magical coal, fertility, and "Fire King" lightning myths from Galicia to Cambodia. The mythical method (as advocated by T. S. Eliot) permitted artists to unite past and present, letting modernism function as a curious equivalent for twentieth-century nostalgia.

David's aunt Bertha plays the *buffo* part in this drama, providing comic relief. Bertha is hardly uncritical of the New World, yet she prefers the restlessness and the noise of the city to the boredom of the country.

True I work like a horse and I stink like one with my own sweat. But there's life here, isn't there? There's a stir here always. Listen! The street! The cars! High laughter! Ha, good! Veljish was still as a fart in company. Who could endure it? Trees! Fields! Again trees! Who can talk to trees? Here at least I can find other pastimes than sliding down the gable on a roof!

The trees of Bertha's origins are not only dusty, they are boring; and her vulgar metaphor of the idiocy of country life, "still as a fart in company," provides a dramatic alternative view to Genya's picture of Veljish. Bertha wishes to see America as the fulfillment of everything the immigrant could not be in the country of origin. It is fitting that she is thrilled by shopping in New York and comments on the huge underpants she bought that "when I hold them at a distance upside down this way they look like peaks in Austria." For Bertha, purchasing cheap and large-sized underpants seems to take the emotional place of remembering the sublime view of the Carpathian mountains – and by bargain-hunting in the American marketplace she can symbolically take revenge on the Old World class hierarchies: "Twenty cents, and I can wear what only a baroness in Austria could wear."

Bertha and Genya are not only "worlds apart in temperament," but in their combination they also suggest the ambivalence of immigrants toward embracing new environments and yearning for the past. Bertha lacks depth, yet she is the catalyst who makes Genya speak about her past secret. For Genya, corn is associated with the romantic figure of Ludwig, a Christian organist with whom she was in love but who spurned her before she married Albert. When Ludwig gets married, Genya watches the wedding procession, as she confides to Bertha: "I hid in the corn-field nearby. [...] I felt empty as a bell till I looked at the blue cornflowers at my feet. They cheered me. That was the last I saw of him I think." Genya has substituted an image of beauty for an experience of pain and loss; and she repeats the substitution when she buys the picture. This lends meaning to her unaccountable sighs. David, who overhears the conversation, senses a connection though he does not get the full meaning. Genya's corn story becomes part of David's family romance of imagining the "organist" not only as the mother's first lover but also as his real father. Thus David fancies that he is an illegitimate child, a "benkart."

For Albert the specific meaning of cattle is the story of his guilt for his father's death: although Albert could have saved his father, who was gored by a bull, he did not lift a finger. No wonder David notices a speech hesitation, a hitch, whenever Albert says "my father." Albert's sense of persecution would seem to derive from that trauma of the past, and his guilt for his father's death becomes fear of his own son, fear that another "prayer" will continue the drama and become a "butcher."

This heavily charged family drama is accentuated by David's own guilt feelings connected with sexuality and betrayal of family and ethnic group to his non-Jewish peers. In his childish beginnings with sexuality he experiences a fairy-talelike double-bind in "playing bad" with Annie. These "dirty" sexual games draw on family language and would require David to play the "poppa." David's quest is for the purification of the "dirt" inherent in the family story, for an escape from the darkness of the cellar and the closet to the world of light.

In his friendship with Leo Dugovka, David feels a "bond of kinship." This cross-ethnic kinship looks all the more glamorous to David since it starts with a rooftop encounter that appeals to his visionary side. David instantly worships the blond and blue-eyed boy who is four years older and not afraid. Leo flies kites, is daring, and, David thinks, "There was no end to Leo's blessings – no father, almost no mother, skates." (Skates are associated by the rabbi with non-Jews.) Their bond is based on David's weakness and stems from all the charged areas of his young life including family, sex, and faith. It leads David right back into the darkness of the cellar. He reaps the reward of the rosary only for letting Leo "play bad" with David's cousin Esther and witnessing this momentous event while pretending not to care and exploring the "Big-little-big-little-little-little-big-busted" beads of the rosary against the background of gurgles and whines.

David's forward-looking nostalgia for "flawless light" is thus also a wish for an escape from his traumas and predicaments. The religious schooling in the *cheder* strengthens his wish for a cleansing transformation of the profane into the sacred that would reenact the power of Isaiah's coal. Reading the sacred text about the seraph's coal that can cleanse dirty lips focuses David's energies onto his attempt to seek a vision, to find purification, and to provoke a crisis that will resolve his generational impasse, address his religious needs, and fuse the fragments of the past with modern technology as a secular substitute for transcendence. David has a vision of hypnotizing brilliance at the edge of the river. Afterwards David feels "as though he had seen it in another world, a world that once left could not be recalled. All that he knew about it was that it had been complete and dazzling." The world elsewhere of the parents' past has been transformed into a mysteriously surrealistic and modern vision that can be experienced in the city. It is at this point that the gentile boys Pedey and Weasel – to whom David denies his Jewishness – make him drop a sword-shaped zinc sheet on the live electric wire under the trolley tracks. Fascinated by the terrific light that is unleashed and consumes the mock-Arthurian "sword" with radiance, David now embarks on the project of seeking an illuminating experience on the streetcar tracks. He breaks into the *cheder* in order to reread Isaiah and continues to build up associations between his idea of a sacred vision and the world of technology, the rabbi's laughter notwithstanding.

Later David interrupts the recital of the biblical verse, crying that his mother died "Long ago! Long ago!" He calls his mother his aunt and, when asked about his father, says that his father was an organ-player in a church in "Eu-Europe," a Christian! Asked "in what land" the mother met the organ-player, David, misunderstanding the concrete land for the abstract country, answers: "In where there was – there was c-corn." It is Freud's family romance – but with the difference that the immigrant child was separated early from his father, has no recollection of the meaningful physical world of the parents, and may perhaps develop a more exaggerated drive not toward Freud's exaltation of the actual father, but toward the creation of a homemaking myth, a whole vision that would symbolically fuse David's divided worlds.

Moving toward the climax of the novel, David picks up a milk dipper and breathlessly approaches the trolley tracks with the statement, "*Now I gotta make it come out,"* and the "crack" out of which the rebirth is to take place blends technological site, sexual allusion, and reference to the fissure between worlds that David acutely experiences. David miraculously survives his near-electrocution from a shock of 550 volts. His burnt foot reinforces the Oedipus motif; but preliminary intergenerational recognition and family reconciliation also emerge as the result of the crisis of David's injury.

In the last paragraph of the novel Roth uses three times the phrasing that gives the novel its title, and the passage is a masterpiece at sustaining ambiguity: what is the "it" of *Call It Sleep*? Answers have ranged from rebirth and hope to oblivion and nothingness. Roth stated variously that the title referred to "an artistic accession or an assumption into artistry" or to "the end of that kind of creative life" – a contradiction that is analogous to Coriolanus's proclaiming "a world elsewhere" only in haughty reaction to his banishment, so that "accession" also means "end." (Roth's allusion to Coriolanus's phrase was applied also to Edward Hopper, who was misunderstood as realist because he adhered to the American belief that visionaries need not retreat to "a world elsewhere" but can turn to the experience of their daily lives.

The ending is also the extraordinary realization of "a world elsewhere" that David experiences and that finds its aesthetic equivalent in the world of the arts that Roth hoped to enter with the writing of *Call It Sleep*. David's electric experiment finds its counterpart in Roth's aesthetic experimentation. Roth's method in this chapter is an alternation between external scenes and italicized passages, set as prose poems, that continue David's interior monologue, like cinematic cross-cutting. The bantering vulgarities of the various characters on East 10th Street are juxtaposed ever more rapidly against David, who is about to reach the third rail with his milk dipper.

> *And his eyes*
> "Runnin' hee! hee! hee! Across the lots hee! hee! jerkin' off."
> *lifted*
> "An' I picks up a rivet in de tongs an' I sez – "
> *and there was the last crossing of*
> *Tenth Street, the last cross—*
> "Heazuh a flowuh fer ye, yeller-belly, shove it up yer ass!"
> *ing, and beyond, beyond the elevateds,*
> "How many times'll your red cock crow, Pete, befaw y' gives up? T'ree?"

In the manuscript of the novel the cinematic procedure is evident, as Roth wrote the different sections sequentially and indicated with a system of Greek letters where they should be cut and spliced into each other.

If only for a moment David's electric vision of light, power, and modernity makes possible a sense of "a world elsewhere." The ending brings together the central images of the novel. Cellar, picture, coal, and rail, sword, dipper, electricity, transcendent vision, and polyethnic setting, father and mother, parents and child, Old World and New World, vulgarity and the sacred, sexual imagery, cusswords, and metaphysical yearning, Christianity, Judaism, Zoroastrianism, and secularism, revolutionary action and betrayal, fear and triumph, coexist and fuse in one powerful surge of dangerous brightness that lasts for only a moment but holds in suspension all the tensions under which David suffered – as if he were one of Sir James Frazer's "sacred or tabooed persons" who is, according the *The Golden Bough*, "charged just as a Leyden jar," an early device used for storing and discharging static electricity, "is charged with electricity."

Roth had originally planned to use materials of his own life "from ghetto child to Greenwich Village," yet he ended *Call It Sleep* when David is only eight years old. In later writings, Roth emphasized the importance of Eda Lou Walton with whom he became intimate in the mid-1920s, when he was not yet twenty years old and she was twelve years his senior. Roth recalled Walton's Greenwich Village apartment, where "dust scuffed up from hectic Eighth Street, just above the window." He heard the "clash of crosstown trolley, blast of auto horn, brought into the room along with the normal drone of the city" and remembers "for the nth time, conning T. S. Eliot's 'Waste Land'" while "Eda Lou tittered girlishly in the arms of her young lover," a friend of Roth's. He read *Ulysses* under similar circumstances.

After he became the New York University professor's young love interest, he started writing the manuscript of what became *Call It Sleep* – on NYU blue and pink exam books. In the light of Roth's later writings, the "clash of crosstown trolley" connected not only to Eliot's imagery ("Trams and dusty trees") but also referred literally to the line that connected the two poles of his life, the Lower East Side and Greenwich Village. The world of the Lower East Side, culminating in the electric shock at the Eighth Street trolley, was thus remembered and recreated at the other end of the Eighth Street crosstown line. It must have seemed like magic that, from both points of view, the "world elsewhere" was only a trolley ride away, linked by rails; and there was all the more autobiographical significance to the trolley since Roth's father worked as a motorman on a New York tramway for some time.

It only reinforces the symbolism of the Eighth Street trolley that its tracks led not only from the immigrant ghetto to Greenwich Village, but also went by the Cooper Union (where the radical soap-box orator can be heard), by the first site of the Whitney Museum (where "Eighth Street Rebels" Juliana Force and Gertrude Vanderbilt Whitney exhibited the modernist art that the Metropolitan Museum had refused to accept as a gift), by the Hans Hoffman

School for modernist artists, and close by where Mabel Dodge had held her radical bohemian salon at 23 Fifth Avenue. As art critic Clement Greenberg remembered in 1957, Eighth Street was "the center of New York art life." Eighth Street was also a world off limits to Marjorie Content (married first to Harold Loeb and later to Jean Toomer) when she grew up in midtown Manhattan and was not permitted to ever go further south than Fourteenth Street.

Although Roth's novel ends shortly after his protagonist has turned eight, the whole span of Roth's life "from ghetto child to Greenwich Village" may yet be secretly represented in the book. Crossing worlds, the defining experience of the prologue, may also be the central theme for the "detached artist" Roth.

The fusion of ethnicity and modernism was so successful in *Call It Sleep* because both ethnic childhood and artistic modernism were strongly and simultaneously felt by the writer, each reminding him of the other – and thus doubly moving the reader. The novel may present a deep expression of second-generation art by merging East Side and Village origins so fully that a powerful and haunting bilateral descent myth of Jewish immigrant childhood and American modernist initiation emerges. Two worlds are connected in such a way that there was always "a world somewhere, somewhere else," different from and yet similar to the one inhabited *or* fictionalized. This process was also experienced as a deep crisis, a burnout, and a short-circuit (metaphors close to the language of the novel's ending that Roth also applied to his life), and as an intense experience for which such a price had to be paid that – even though Roth began a novel about a Cincinnati-born proletarian in the 1930s and completed and published several autobiographically inspired books near the end of his life – no new work emerged that was comparable to his 1934 masterpiece.

12

THE CLOCK, THE SALESMAN,
AND THE BREAST

ENRY ROTH'S verbal explosion, and his hero's near-execution at the trolley tracks, marked a violent escalation from such streetcar scenes as Stein's enactment of sympathy or Antin's memories of daring trolley-track games among immigrant children. As a setting of a vision, Roth's choice of the Eighth Street trolley also resembled Toomer's mystical experience at the 66th Street L station. By contrast, Richard Wright returned to the troubling historical legacy that the means of modern transportation were also prime places of racial segregation and tension, an experience that the Southern colored woman's life story had recorded. In the racially bifurcated world that Wright confronted in his life and exposed in his writing, violent explosions were always a possibility. Wright made it his life-long task to attack segregation, calling attention to its social and psychological consequences, as he often focused on the transformation of fear into violence or rage.

In a section tellingly entitled "Squirrel Cage" that forms part of Wright's first novel *Lawd Today* (completed in 1937), a conversation takes place among four young black men who have migrated from the South to the city of Chicago.

"I heard a man say he saw a black guy slash a white streetcar conductor from ear to ear."

"It's bad luck for a black man anywhere."

"There's somebody always after you, making you do things you don't want to do."

"You know, the first time I ever set down beside a white man in a streetcar up North, I was expecting for 'im to get up and shoot me."

"Yeah, I remember the first time I set down beside a white woman in a streetcar up North. I was setting there trembling and she didn't even look around."

"You feel funny as hell when you come North from the South."

In *Lawd Today*, the wish to combine a social message with modernist experimentation comes together, as the novel focuses on a day in the life of Jake Jackson, postal employee in Chicago, a jealous and mean husband who seems happiest with male peers. He roams Chicago, goes to work, is robbed in a nightspot, comes home drunk, and beats up his wife who has a tumor and needs an operation. Unlike Wright's later works, *Lawd Today* presents its characters in rich social detail and in a web of human (or perhaps better, dehumanized) relations.

Wright's employment and mixing of various modernist methods is noteworthy. Following Joyce's *Ulysses*, the apprenticeship novel is set on one single day. Ironically, it is the date of Lincoln's birthday, for Wright's Bloomsday was February 12, 1936. The protagonist is, after Hemingway, another Jake, a monosyllabic tough guy at least in part indebted to the hard-boiled school. The novel does not only invoke Gertrude Stein directly and by name, but also plays around with Steinian techniques. When Jake looks at movie posters for "The Death Hawk," Wright sets the seven posters as blocks of prose, without punctuation or capitalization, and with many -ing forms. For example: "A bluehelmeted aviator in a bloodred monoplane darting shooting speeding zooming careening out of a bank of snowwhite clouds in hot pursuit of two green monoplanes." And in a scene in which Jake's friend Bob laughs so contagiously that not only Jake, but also their opponents Al and Slim, just have to laugh along, Wright begins with a physiological account of laughter ("a sharp expulsion of breath coming from the diaphragm") but then uses the occasion to experiment with repetitions of the simple word "laugh": "And they laughed because they had laughed. They paused for breath, and then they laughed at how they had laughed; and because they had laughed at how they had laughed, they laughed and laughed and laughed." This passage which aims at finding a formal equivalent to the experience and rhythm of contagious laughing, is all the more noteworthy since Wright would refrain from representing mirth, humor, or laughter in most of his later writings. In *Lawd Today*, interior monologues, modernist collages of newspaper headlines ("Hitler Calls on World to Smash Jews"), the incorporation of radio programs, diagrams of card games, and mottos by Van Wyck Brooks, T. S. Eliot, and Waldo Frank round off the experiment. Rejected by several publishers, for one of which James T. Farrell was the reader, *Lawd Today* was published only in 1963, after Wright's death; ironically, Granville Hicks's lukewarm review stressed Farrell's influence on the young Wright.

Compared to *Lawd Today*, Wright's next and most famous novel, *Native Son* (1940), was more mature and accomplished but also seemed less experimental in form. Its dramatic opening signaled the end of an era and the full arrival of a sociologically inspired and realist-inflected left-wing modernism. The "undistinguished American" sweatshop worker Sadie Frowne had been able to live without an alarm clock and maintain the premodern belief that no such clocks could possibly exist because she could not imagine how "the clock would know" how to call you "at the very time you want to get up." Henry Roth's sketch "Impressions of a Plumber" (1925) had started with the sentence, "The alarm clock rings with frightened intensity." Wright's own *Lawd Today* and several manuscript versions of *Native Son* had started with the scene of a protagonist slowly waking up (because "somebody was calling," or "a loud knock at the door made him jerk fully awake"). By contrast, the published version of *Native Son* (1940) opened very dramatically with the word "*Brrrrrriiiiiiiiiiiiiiiiiiiiinng!*" – an onomatopoeic representation of the ringing of an alarm clock. It is a first line that few readers are likely to forget and that has been regarded as the end of the Harlem Renaissance or the beginning of a Chicago Renaissance. The sound is intelligible to readers around the globe – the novel has been translated into most European languages as well as Japanese, Turkish, Hebrew, Chinese, and other tongues – as it embodies the intrusion of the most familiar instrument of modern time into the natural world of sleepers, a small, capsule version of *the* story of modernization.

The topics of modernity reached Wright and other authors through the writings of the Chicago School of Sociology – works by W. I. Thomas and Robert E. Park (both from small-town backgrounds), Ernest W. Burgess, the immigrant Louis Wirth (whose wife was the welfare supervisor for Wright's aunt), and the African American Horace Cayton (whom Wright befriended). Burgess, for example, famously argued in a landmark manifesto of 1924, "The Growth of the City: an Introduction to a Research Project," that the "manifestations of modern life which are peculiarly urban – the skyscraper, the subway, the department store, the daily newspaper, and social work – are characteristically American." Wirth's 1940 essay, "Urban Society and Civilization," viewed "culture" and "civilization" as two poles of human existence, correlated to folk societies on the one hand and to the rise of cities on the other, for "what we call civilization as distinguished from culture has been cradled in the city." Burgess's and Wirth's approaches went back to Park's work on the "ecological organization" of the city, his research emphasis on "transportation and communication, tramways and telephones, newspapers and advertising, steel construction and elevators – all things, in fact, which tend to bring about at once a greater mobility and a greater concentration of the urban populations." And Park's son-in-law Robert Redfield published *Tepoztlán* (1930), an influential study of a Mexican village which theorized about modernity transforming natural into clocked time, traditional, sacred, local, rural, "primitive" life into modern, secular, widely shared, urban and industrial life; "folk" into people and orally transmitted folklore into mechanically reproduced popular arts; *Gemeinschaft* into *Gesellschaft*, in short, culture into civilization. These were concepts that held an obvious appeal to ethnic writers.

The Mississippi-born Richard Wright, like Hemingway, never went to college; and, unlike any other major American modernist, never even finished high school; but as a poor Southern migrant to Chicago he was drawn to, and absorbed, the milieu of the Chicago sociologists. In his preface to St. Clair Drake and Horace Cayton's sociological study *Black Metropolis* (1945), Wright summarized the Chicago sociologists' assessment of modernization: "Holy days became holidays; clocks replaced the sun as a symbolic measurement of time. As the authority of the family waned, the meaning of reality, emotion, experience, action, and God assumed the guise of teasing questions." Wright claimed: "It was not until I stumbled upon science that I discovered some of the meanings of the environment that battered and taunted me. . . . The huge mountains of fact piled up by the Department of Sociology at the University of Chicago gave me my first concrete vision of the forces that molded the urban Negro's body and soul."

Many writers around the world fictionalized modernization. What made Richard Wright's version of the story of the rupture brought about by modern time particularly powerful was the fact that the beginning of *Native Son* eradicates any sense of a "sacred" folk existence prior to the alarming intrusion of clocked time. In the novel, in which the family has no authority and religion has become meaningless, there is literally no *word* before the sound of the alarm clock; and the clock is also the subject of the first sentence after the "*Brrrrrriiiiiiiiiiiiiiiiiiiiinng!*": "An alarm clock clanged in the dark and silent room." After that opening, and for the rest of the book, characters are thrown into, and live and die in, the modern world of the city of Chicago.

Human beings seem to be little but objects of modernization. Their first appearance is consciously reified: they make themselves felt simply as "a woman's voice," "a surly grunt," or "naked feet," as if they were parts rather than a whole. The hero's or antihero's name is Bigger Thomas, his last name probably an allusion to Harriet Beecher Stowe's *Uncle Tom's Cabin*; after all, Wright's first published book was entitled *Uncle Tom's Children* (1938). In the famous scene of Bigger's killing of the rat with a kitchen skillet that follows soon, the animal image seems like an allegory of the protagonist himself: both are killed in metallic environments. Significantly, the three-part novel, divided into the books entitled "Fear," "Flight," and "Fate," ends as Bigger Thomas, sentenced to death, "heard the ring of steel against steel as a far door clanged shut." Bigger's life in *Native Son* is thus framed by two clangs. He is trapped in a world that here seems to extend only from the clock to the cell door on death row.

Eager to show Bigger's fascist potential, Wright makes him a hero who first commits an accidental homicide of his white employer's daughter Mary Dalton and then atrociously rapes and murders his black girlfriend Bessie; yet Bigger never is capable of confronting his own guilt, an inability which Wright insisted was central to the characterization. Instead, Bigger settles on the unforgettable nonconfession, "what I killed for I *am*!" This is not so much in the hard-boiled manner as it conveys a frighteningly existentialist sensation: "What I killed for must've been good!" In the absence of recognition or access to social meaning, Bigger Thomas ultimately had only his murders to define him; and for Wright this was both an existentialist option of experiencing a perverse self-definition in the most negative social image and the frightening possibility that someone like Bigger could become the violent parody of a Christlike redeemer figure: "Had he not taken fully upon himself the crime of being black? Had he not done the thing which they dreaded above all others? Then they ought not to stand here and pity him, cry over him; but look at him and go home, contented, feeling that their shame was washed away."

In describing Bigger's brutal actions Wright employs a tough style that creates an urban-gothic effect and inhibits an easy identification of the reader with Wright's protagonist who is both pitiable victim and horrifying perpetrator: "The head hung limply on the newspapers, the curly black hair dragging about in blood. He whacked harder, but the head would not come off." Or: "He lifted the brick again and again, until in falling it struck a sodden mass that gave softly but stoutly to each landing blow." It is such sentences that have earned Wright the reputation of being a "naturalist," but *Native Son* has many different levels of style, including the following *tour de force* of a single sentence:

It sounded suddenly directly above his head and when he looked it was not there but went on tolling and with each passing moment he felt an urgent need to run and hide as though the bell were sounding a warning and he stood on a street corner in a red glare of light like that which came from the furnace and he had a big package in his arms so wet and slippery and heavy that he could scarcely hold onto it and he wanted to know what was in the package and he stopped near an alley corner and unwrapped it and the paper fell away and he saw – it was his *own* head – his own head lying with black face and half-closed eyes and lips parted with white teeth showing and hair wet with blood and the red glare grew brighter like light shining down from a red moon and red stars on a hot summer night and he was sweating and breathless from running and the bell clanged so loud that he could hear the iron tongue clapping against the metal sides each time it swung to and fro and he was running over a street paved with black coal and his shoes kicked tiny lumps rattling against tin cans and he knew that very soon he had to find some place to hide but there was no place and in front of him white people were coming to ask about the head from which the newspapers had fallen and which was now slippery with blood in his naked hands and he gave up and stood in the middle of the street in the red darkness and cursed the booming bell and the white people and felt that he did not give a damn what happened to him and when the people closed in he hurled the bloody head squarely into their faces *dongdongdong*. . . .

This is a truly Faulknerian sentence, part of a self-consciously modernist prose experiment employed by Wright in representing a dream sequence. The *dongdongdong* is the "trigger," the sensory stimulus that connects the inner world of Bigger's dream with the outer world of the bell ringing, a common stream-of-consciousness device. And this is not the only instance of Wright's modernism, even though modernist techniques were less prevalent in *Native Son* than they had been in *Lawd Today*.

Wright also alluded to T. S. Eliot's *Waste Land* when he called Chicago an "unreal city." In his manifesto "Blueprint for Negro Writing," Wright invoked Joyce's famous phrasing when he encouraged black writers to "forge in the smithy of our souls the uncreated conscience of our race," a Joyce adaptation later echoed by Ralph Ellison. The ending of his short story "Bright and Morning Star" was a response to the conclusion of Joyce's "The Dead." His experimental novella "The Man Who Lived Underground" (1945) used a collage technique. Wright was fascinated by D. H. Lawrence, and, as we saw, admired Stein and Hemingway.

For Wright, the central question was the one he asked in his preface to *Black Metropolis* (1945): "What would life on Chicago's South Side look like when seen through the eyes of a Freud, a Joyce, a Proust, a Pavlov, a Kierkegaard?" The point was not to choose between realism and modernism, but to use any technique that was likely to shake up readers and direct them toward the serious questions of the times, among which class inequality and racial segregation were prominent.

In order to suggest the psychological consequences of racism, Wright invoked William James who wrote in the section "The Self" of *The Principles of Psychology*:

No more fiendish punishment could be devised, were such a thing physically possible, than that one should be turned loose in society and remain absolutely unnoticed by all the members thereof. If no one turned round when we entered, answered when we spoke, or minded what we did, but if every person we met "cut us dead," and acted as if we were non-existent things, a kind of rage and impotent despair would ere long well up in us, from which the cruelest bodily tortures would be a relief; for these would make us feel that, however bad might be our plight, we had not sunk to such a depth as to be unworthy of attention at all.

Wright applied James's observation to African Americans: "The American Negro has come as near being the victim of a complete rejection as our society has been able to work out, for the dehumanized image of the Negro which white Americans carry in their minds, the anti-Negro epithets continuously on their lips, exclude the contemporary Negro as truly as though he were kept in a steel prison, and doom even those Negroes who are as yet unborn."

For Wright, it was the condition of social inequality that helped to sustain the belief in racial difference, and he was anything but an essentialist. He wrote in the nonfictional *Twelve Million Black Voices* (1941): "The differences between black folk and white folk are not blood or color, and the ties that bind us are deeper than those that separate us. The common road of hope which we all have traveled has brought us into a stronger kinship than any words, laws, or legal claims. Look at us and know us and you will know yourselves, for *we* are *you*, looking back at you from the dark mirror of our lives."

Wright took pains to emphasize the human condition in the black experience and wrote in a blurb he prepared for the publicity of his autobiography *Black Boy* (1945): "[To] those whites who recall how, in the early days of this land, their forefathers struggled for freedom, BLACK BOY cannot be a strange story. Neither can it be a strange story to the Jews, the Poles, the Irish, and the Italians who came hopefully to this land from the Old World."

If there was a writer of the 1930s and 1940s who was truly at odds with Wright it was Zora Neale Hurston. The young Wright, who had not yet published a single book, attacked Hurston's most famous novel *Their Eyes Were Watching God* (1937) in the *New Masses* with a then rarely noticed but later frequently invoked diatribe that includes the verdict that "Miss Hurston *voluntarily* continues in her novel the tradition which was forced upon the Negro in the theater, that is, the minstrel technique that makes the 'white folks' laugh," a passage which also helps to explain why Wright grew reluctant to portray humor in his own work. A year later, the Rosenwald and two-time Guggenheim fellowship winner Hurston retaliated when she panned *Uncle Tom's Children* in the widely circulating *Saturday Review*: "Mr. Wright serves notice by his title that he speaks of people in revolt, and his stories are so grim that the Dismal Swamp of race hatred must be where they live. Not one act of understanding and sympathy comes to pass in the entire work.... Since the author himself is a Negro, his dialect is a puzzling thing. One wonders how he arrived at it. Certainly he does not write by ear unless he is tonedeaf." The disagreements were profound; and they were aired publicly.

Yet like Wright, Hurston saw a need to stress universalism and the inequalities that inhibited the growth of a shared culture. Hurston was a professional anthropologist who received her graduate training from a central figure of twentieth-century anthropology, the Columbia professor Franz Boas, and who worked for Melville Herskovits, wrote for Ruth Benedict, and knew Margaret Mead. Like Wright, she seems to have found her story through an academic discipline: "I needed my Barnard education to help me see my people as they really are." And elaborating upon anthropology as a vehicle for her perception, Hurston wrote that the folklore she was familiar with since childhood was too close to her, so she "had to have the spy-glass of Anthropology to look through at that." What Hurston saw through that spy-glass was the resilience and adaptability of common folk. She was more interested in folk culture than in urban civilization and focused on the internal cohesion of black culture rather than on the social interaction of blacks and whites.

As a universalist, Hurston was one of many African American writers who commented upon the "forced grouping" that takes place in many social as well as intellectual encounters. Using an example set in a means of modern transportation she observed that when a black student couple (Barnard–Yale) goes on a New York uptown subway after a concert and, at 72nd Street Station, two scabby-looking Negroes enter the same car, all other identities of the couple (college students on a date, theatergoers, etc.) get eclipsed by the category "Negro." The white passengers identify the students with the two low-lifes who "woof, bookoo, broadcast, and otherwise [discriminate] from one end of the coach to the other," and are perceived to be "typical." Hurston spelled out the silent comments in the white glances: "Only difference is some Negroes are better dressed" or "You are all colored aren't you?" The students are left with paradoxical thoughts of the kind, "My skinfolks but not my kinfolks." Hurston's point was to expose the strange cultural logic of "forced grouping" that corresponds to a denial of individuality to members of visible minorities. As a writer Hurston therefore tried to resist compulsive representation. "I know," she wrote in a chapter intended for her autobiography *Dust Tracks on a Road* (published in 1942, one year after Wright's programmatically entitled *Twelve Million Black Voices*), "that I cannot accept responsibility for thirteen million people. Every tub must sit on its own bottom regardless."

Hurston echoed Boas's environmentalism and universalism when she wrote in her autobiography: "It seemed to me that the human beings I met reacted pretty much the same to the same stimuli. Different idioms, yes. Circumstances and conditions having power to influence, yes. Inherent difference, no." And in "What White Publishers Won't Print" (1950), Hurston emphasized not only the analogies of blacks and Jews in the American imagination but also stressed the significance of *all* minorities for the country: "But for the national welfare, it is urgent to realize that the minorities do think, and think about something other than the race problem. That they are very human and internally, according to natural endowment, are just like everybody else."

Both Wright and Hurston were part of the greater emphasis placed on universalism in the 1940s and 1950s and of which novels that crossed lines of expected racial representation were representative. A perfect genre novel for the universalist postwar moment was the African American Willard Motley's best-selling *Knock on Any Door* (1947), which was also made into a Hollywood movie. Inspired by the hard-boiled crime writers, by James T. Farrell, and by Richard Wright, *Knock on Any Door* focused not on a black man but on the Italian American criminal Nick Romano and ended with a detailed description of his execution on the electric chair. As did Ann Petry in *Country Place* (1947), William Gardner Smith in *Anger at Innocence* (1950), James Baldwin in *Giovanni's Room* (1956), and Frank Yerby in much of his *œuvre*, both Hurston and Wright also published novels without major black characters (books that were once called "raceless novels"), Hurston's *Seraph on the Suwanee* (1948) and Wright's *Savage Holiday* (1954).

Both Hurston and Wright also worked for the Federal Writers' Project, Hurston in New York and on "The Florida Negro," and Wright on *New York Panorama* and in Illinois. Other writers who participated in the FWP or had WPA jobs were Nelson Algren, Saul Bellow, Arna Bontemps, Sterling Brown, Jack Conroy, Pietro di Donato, Ralph Ellison, Claude McKay, Henry Roth, Margaret Walker, and Frank Yerby as did social scientists W. Lloyd Warner, Horace Cayton, Allison Davis, Burleigh B. and Mary Gardner. And Jerre Mangione administered the FWP and later published a history of it.

What Hurston and Wright saw in the theme of modern clocked time also marked their difference. For example, Hurston collected a cheery song poem in which measured time has become part of a courtship story that goes literally "around the clock": "When the clock struck ten I was in the bin, in the bin with Sue,/ in the bin with Sal, in the bin with that pretty Johnson gal/ When the clock struck eleven, I was in heaven, in heaven with Sue,/ in heaven with Sal, in heaven with that pretty Johnson gal." Hurston also included a lively story in her folklore-inspired *Mules and Men* (1935) in which a man takes a turtle on a string as if it were a pocket watch on a chain, and, when asked what time it is, pulls out the turtle and says: "it's quarter past leben and kickin' like hell for twelve." This was an instance of resilient folk survival and even tricksterish folk one-upmanship in response to modernization. In *12 Million Black Voices* Wright imagines another type of dialogue about telling time that grimly connects it to racial domination:

If a white man stopped a black man on a Southern road and asked: "Say, there, boy! It's one o'clock, isn't it?" the black man would answer: "Yessuh."

If the white man asked: "Say, it's not one o'clock, is it, boy?" the black man would answer: "Nowsuh."

For Wright, the power of modernity, compounded by racial domination, was simply crushing. For Wright, segregation was omnipresent, for Hurston it was so marginal that she was the only major black writer to attack the first important Supreme Court decision for integration, *Brown v. Board of Education* in a segregationist white Southern newspaper.

❦

One way in which the confrontation of the premodern world with modernity was represented in literature was through the figure of a seductive stranger, typically a salesman of sorts, who brings modern commercial leisure culture to remote, traditional settings. For some reason, "tradition" could readily be imagined as a good, but temptable, young black woman in a rural or provincial setting who had to brave the salesman's lure. And readers could marvel at the attractiveness of the new that those handsome-seeming modern devils of the trade tried to sell.

Julia Peterkin's tale "The Merry-Go-Round," first published in *Smart Set* (1921), was one such story from the 1920s. The intruder is the white man Carson who brings, as a symbol of leisure culture, a merry-go-round to a black village setting. Soon Jesse Weeks and his girlfriend Meta, Maum Mary's daughter, ride the merry-go-round every night. Maum Mary, who cooks Carson's food, rejects his request to let him sleep in her house, saying firmly, "No white man ain' nebber sleep in no bed o'mine, an' I know I ain't gwine sta't wid you." Meta, too, resists the white man's temptation to take some "free rides" when she brings him her mother's food. When Carson approaches Meta on the merry-go-round while Jesse is buying peanuts, Jesse strikes Carson who takes revenge a day later and shoots Jesse. The whites of the town, mobilized by the village store clerk, and the black policeman escort Carson onto a train; and the black townsfolk set fire to the merry-go-round. Carson becomes involved with a tent mission; Jesse who was crippled by the shot works as a basket-and-fish-trap maker; Maum Mary and Meta make a living by taking in washing and give part of their income to the preacher. The temptation of secular modernity and leisure culture had been resisted, though it leaves wounds.

Both Hurston and Wright wrote stories following this pattern and intensifying it. In Hurston's "The Gilded Six-Bits," first published in 1933 in Martha Foley and Whit Burnett's *Story* magazine, the Florida factory-worker Joe wants to take his wife Missie May to a new ice-cream parlor operated by a stranger, Mister Otis D. Slemmons from Chicago who has the distinction of owning a five-dollar gold piece for a stickpin and a ten-dollar gold coin on his watch chain and whom Joe worships as a black Rockefeller or Ford. Joe is excited after their visit to Slemmons's parlor, though Missie May thinks that the gold would look better on Joe.

One night when Joe comes home early from his shift in the plant, he finds Slemmons in bed with his wife. He beats him, chases him away, and is left with the golden watch chain in his hands, which he now sulkingly uses to remind Missie May of her unfaithfulness. After months of acting sullenly like a "stranger," they finally make love again, but when Missie May afterwards finds the gold piece in their bed she wonders if Joe meant it as "payment" for her lovemaking. She also discovers that the coin is merely a gilded half-dollar. Soon Missie May is pregnant and, before long, gives birth to a baby boy who, according to Joe's mother, looks exactly like Joe. The husband feels reconciled, goes to Orlando, and buys the coin's worth of candy kisses for his wife. The couple's life continues as it had before the Slemmons episode.

Wright's four-part story "Long Black Song," first published in *Uncle Tom's Children* (1938), is told from the point of view of Sarah, whom Wright once described as "a very simple Negro woman living in the northern hills of Mississippi." Sarah is waiting for her husband Silas to return, soothes her baby, Ruth, and thinks of the past, her first love Tom, who was sent, almost a year earlier, to Europe to fight in World War I, and for whom she still yearns. A white salesman arrives in a car. He demonstrates to Sarah a gilt-edged fifty-dollar clock-phonograph, plays a religious recording of a song about judgment day, and makes sexual advances to her. Sarah keeps saying "no" to him, but the salesman succeeds in making love to her. He leaves the clock-phonograph behind and offers it to Sarah, now for the reduced price of forty dollars, promising to return the next morning.

When Silas comes home, his happy mood soon changes when he discovers the graphophone and the white salesman's suspicious traces. Silas explodes, breaks the phonograph, and starts whipping his disloyal wife, who manages to escape with Ruth into the hills. The next morning Sarah observes from the hills the arrival of the salesman's car and the ensuing struggle between Silas, the salesman, and the salesman's associate. Silas shoots one of the two white men as the second one drives off. Silas drags the white man's body into the street and throws Sarah's belongings out of the house. Cursing all white men he bitterly accepts his fate – certain death. From the hills Sarah sees the arrival of a long line of cars full of white men. Silas shoots some of them until they set fire to the house in which Silas dies without a murmur. Sarah runs away from the scene crying "Naw, Gawd!"

Compared with Peterkin's story from 1921, these two tales of the 1930s suggest that "The Merry-Go-Round" seems not to have been taken to the possible climactic moment of the rural woman's actual unfaithfulness; in Peterkin's tale the modern, seductive, and ruthless aspects of the merry-go-round man are ultimately rejected even by the intruder himself. At the end of the story, the vehicle of leisure-culture seduction is burned and religious authority reasserted. Peterkin thus offered a resolution to the drama that no longer seemed plausible to either Wright or Hurston. Peterkin's Meta is also much more passive than Sarah in Wright's story, let alone Missie May in Hurston's tale. And neither Wright nor Hurston were willing to adopt the patronizing voice of Peterkin's narrator who describes the arrival of the merry-go-round with the sentence: "Every evening when work on the plantations was over the gay music sounded clear in the still air, and the darkies flocked down to the village and rode out all the money they had."

Wright's and Hurston's stories, in pushing further the kind of plot Peterkin had told, let the tradition-oriented female characters yield to the temptation from the snake of the salesmen of leisure, and showed that the glitter of leisure-oriented capitalism is not golden but merely gilded. In both stories, the intrusion is represented, not simply as a loss of innocence, but as married women's adultery and unfaithfulness to relatively good though jealous husbands who furthermore also have achieved some, and yearn for more, access to the world of modernity that the seducers perhaps can also pretend to represent. Missie May and Sarah, as well as Peterkin's Meta, can thus be said to be pivots "between men."

There is a particular tension in the stories' imagery between breast as home and nature and breast as an erogenous zone susceptible to the modern seducer. Wright's Sarah first offers to breast-feed her baby, Ruth; then her breasts are touched sexually by the salesman. Hurston describes the still faithful Missie May in a bathtub with a phrasing that may vaguely foreshadow the ice-cream parlor: "Her stiff young breasts thrust forward aggressively like broad-based cones with the tips lacquered in black." At the end Joe buys so many candy kisses because the baby boy can "suck a sugartit."

Yet Wright and Hurston conclude their stories in a virtually antithetical fashion. For Hurston, natural time works as a great healer. For Wright, the story steers toward a violent catastrophe. Hurston's seducer is *black*, which gives the whole story an intraracial focus that is characteristic of much of Hurston's *œuvre*. Wright's modern tempter is white, which intensifies the dramatic interracial collision: "If it were anybody but a white man," Sarah ponders when she considers pleading with Silas, "it would be different." When Hurston panned *Uncle Tom's Children*, she sarcastically commented that

in "Long Black Song," the hero gets the white man most Negro man rail against – the white man who possesses a Negro woman. He gets several of them while he is about the business of choosing to die in a hurricane of bullets and fire because his woman has had a white man. There is lavish killing here, perhaps to satisfy all male black readers.

The killing had been even more lavish in the story's manuscript version. In a fifth section, omitted in publication, Sarah's old lover Tom reappears,

together with her brothers Bill and Leroy, and all three black men, uniformed
veterans who have just come back from World War I, die fighting at Silas's
burning house. The unpublished section is formally distinguished by rapidly
alternating Sarah's direct speech, third-person narration, and Bill, Leroy, and
Tom's words in an italicized, lower-case language stream, creating the effect
as if Sarah heard the words of others only in a swimming blur.

Hands shook her again. *sarah when this happen sarah tell us whut happened* "They killed
'im!" *where they kill im show us where yuh live sarah* She bent over again and moaned. [. . .]
  The car stopped. *Look look that mus be the place its on fire lawd it's a gawddam mob them
sonsofbitches them bastards ef ah killed them germans ah kin kill some of them sarah tha you
place* "They killed im . . ." *drive on down bill naw not wid sarah in this car hell ah wanna
go somebody has t stay here n watch sarah n this baby stay here tom its best we go bill c mon
c mon*

This is a splicing-technique that resembles Roth's experimentations. Wright's
plotline was the one that Frantz Fanon would later consider the typical Third
World story: the black veteran has fought for a country that denies him his right
to live upon his return. Hurston instead incorporates the phrase "bookooing"
which black soldiers had picked up in France, from the word "beaucoup."
  If for Wright the image of the clock was more traumatic than for Hurston
and his salesman brought death rather than knowledge, Wright also took little
comfort in the metaphor of the breast as marking happy maternal origins in a
community. It is telling that Wright's worst nightmare recorded in *Black Boy*
(1945), which occurs after he has been beaten to unconsciousness by his religiously fanatic parents, seems to describe the horrible transformation of what
might have been a nourishing breast into a terrifying vehicle of torture and
destruction: "Whenever I tried to sleep I would see huge wobbly white bags,
like the full udders of cows, suspended from the ceiling above me. Later, as
I grew worse, I could see the bags in the daytime with my eyes open and I was
gripped by the fear that they were going to fall and drench me with some
horrible liquid. Day and night I begged my mother and father to take the
bags away, pointing to them, shaking with terror because no one saw them
but me." If the symbol of the clock spelled doom, that of the breast could
be equally deadly. One thinks of such famous autobiographical statements as
Wright's line from *Black Boy*: "This was the culture from which I sprang. This
was the terror from which I fled." Yet for Wright escape led only to new terror.

❦

There were other ethnic writers in the 1930s and 1940s whose sense of modernity drew on the disciplines of anthropology and sociology. James T. Farrell,

who was at the University of Chicago as an undergraduate and wrote a term paper for Ernest Burgess that the famous sociologist saved in his papers, remained so close to a Chicago School of Sociology perspective that he incorporated it quite directly into *Studs Lonigan*, letting a Chicago street orator recite it in the novel. John Connolly, "the King of the Soap Boxers," summarizes, as he puts it, the "plausible ideas presented by members of the Department of Sociology at the University of Chicago," and explains "that the city of Chicago could be divided into three concentric circles." After a differentiated account of these three circles and the city's growth, Connolly proceeds to show that "social and economic forces" created the pressure for black migration into "the white residential districts of the South Side. Blather couldn't halt the process." This is a very close paraphrase of Ernest Burgess's previously cited essay, "The Growth of the City" (1924) which, written at the time when Farrell was a student at Chicago, argued that the "typical processes of that expansion of the city can best be illustrated, perhaps, by a series of concentric circles, which may be numbered to designate both successive zones of urban expansion and the types of areas differentiated in the process of expansion." Perhaps for the sake of academic balance, Farrell's next speaker by the Cottage Grove side of the Park, "a small, untidy Jew," invokes the anthropologists who had "proven that no one race is superior to any other race" – which Studs's buddy Red translates crudely as the Jew's wish to "prove that a Jew was a white man."

Henry Roth was exposed, through the Alfred Kroeber-trained Eda Lou Walton, whose own doctoral work had focused on Navajo poetry, to the anthropological perspective of Frazer's *Golden Bough*, a book Walton admired, that helped Roth understand past folkways *in general* and substitute them for the specific rural family origins that were lost to the urban immigrant, in his version of the "mythical method." Through Walton, Roth also met the anthropologist Margaret Mead.

Mario Suárez is the Mexican American author who introduced the word "Chicano" to printed literature in 1947 in his modern folk vignettes of life in "El Hoyo" (the ethnic "hole" of Tucson) and his portraits of the section's barber, "Señor Garza." Published in the *Arizona Quarterly*, these sketches strike the familiar anthropological note and fall into the category of ethnic humor, reminiscent of Hurston or Saroyan. Suárez draws a reader, presumed to be an outsider, into an unfamiliar ethnic world. Thus the sketches explain that El Hoyo's "inhabitants are *chicanos* who raise hell on Saturday night, listen to Padre Estanislao on Sunday morning, and then raise more hell on Sunday night. While the term *chicano* is the short way of saying *Mexicano*, it is the long way of referring to everybody." Here Suárez departs from any notion of presenting ethnic homogeneity: "Pablo Gutierrez married the Chinese grocer's daughter and acquired a store; his sons are *chicanos*." Suárez included accounts of parties and suggested a rich folklife, described mixed loyalties and explained folk expressions, but he also stressed that El Hoyo was not a closed, only internally defined universe, for Felipe, for example, came back "from the wars after having killed a score of Germans with his body resembling a patchwork quilt."

In *Out of this Furnace* (1941), Thomas Bell's novel about Slovak American miners in Braddock, Pennsylvania, there are examples of Wright-like modernist-industrial-urban-gothic prose that was increasingly present in sociologically inspired immigrant writing. Bell attempted to sound both an ominously mystical and a socially conscious note in representing industrial modernity, and he was drawn to the use of -ing forms. The following passage is typical of Bell's narrative voice:

A Talbot Avenue streetcar, waiting to begin its long trip through the sleeping towns, the lonely streets, to Pittsburgh, made a yellow glow for the young people to sing by. The voice of the mill was harsher than theirs. It came over the wall like a breathing of a giant at work, like a throb of an engine buried deep in the earth. In it were the piping of whistles and the clash of metal on metal; the chuffing of yard locomotives, the rattle of electric cranes and skip hoists, the bump-bump-bump of a train of cars getting into motion; the wide-mouthed blow of the Bessemers, the thud of five-ton ingots dropping six inches as they were stripped of their moulds, the clean, tenpin crack of billets dropping from a magnet, the solid, unhurried grind of the ore dumper, lifting a whole railroad gondola of iron ore and emptying it, delicately; the high whine of the powerhouse dynamos, the brute growl of the limestone and dolomite crushers, the jolting blows of the steam hammers in the blacksmith shop, the distant, earth-shaking thunder of the blooming mill's giant rolls. A hundred discords merged into harmony, the harsh triumphant song of iron and flame.

Bell, whose father's baptismal surname was Belejcak, was a second-generation immigrant who found his modernist voice not only in the tough tragic-heroic struggle of the men in the brutal industrial world, but also in brief experiments with stream-of-consciousness writing in order to render the feelings of the mother, Mary, who has to raise the children alone after her husband's death.

The differences between two Italian American prose works, Pietro di Donato's *Christ in Concrete* (1939) and Jerre Mangione's *Mount Allegro* (1942), most specifically resemble those between Wright's and Hurston's *œuvres*. Di Donato portrayed immigration as death and a modern industrial cruci-fixion, Mangione created an immigrant community centered on the culture of the banquet and the tale. Di Donato represented clocks, both setting the rhythm of industrial labor and providing the theme of such Abruzzese songs as "The heart tick-tock alike the clock." He also included an episode in which a phonograph plays twice, and, quite incongruously, the American popular song

"Indian Love Call," composed, incidentally, by the Czech immigrant Rudolf Friml who had married his Chinese secretary in California. There are also advertisements, radios playing the Billy Rose song, "Barney Google," and there are other reminders of modern commercial culture. Mangione, on the other hand, leaned toward the representation of Sicilians as a "natural" people, part of "culture" rather than of "civilization," a notion which is, however, informed not only by the emotions evoked in going back to one's roots, but also expressly by Mangione's reading of D. H. Lawrence. Lawrence had claimed that Sicilians "never leave off being amorously friendly with almost everybody, emitting a relentless physical familiarity that is quite bewildering." Mangione raises the issue of punctuality in discussions of Mussolini: some relatives tell the narrator not to find fault with fascism, for did not the American newspapers admit that "Mussolini was a great man who made the trains run on time"? However, when the narrator leaves Realmonte, the Sicilian birthplace of Mangione's mother, he notices and emphasizes with an obvious political intention that in fascist Italy the train arrived half an hour late.

Di Donato's short-story version of "Christ in Concrete" first appeared in 1937 in *Esquire*, where it was hyperbolically touted as among the best of forty short stories that *Esquire* had accepted for publication from among 18,000 submissions. Told from the point of view of the construction-site foreman Geremio di Alba, an Italian who emigrated from the Abruzzi to the U.S. in order not to have to fight for "God and Country" in the Italian war against Turkey that ended with the Italian annexation of Libya in 1912, "Christ in Concrete" opens with a description of various immigrant laborers, among them cheery-faced Tomas, the scaffoldman, Old Nick "the Lean" (a war veteran), Snoutnose, Giacomo Sangini, Sandino, Joe Chiappa, and Mike "the Barrelmouth." They all work on a New York construction site which is operated in violation of safety regulations by the Anglo-American Boss, "Mister Murdin."

Dorothy Canfield Fisher called attention to the "extraordinary language" in which di Donato's *Christ in Concrete* was written, "the sonorous gift for colorful use of an English which is ringing with memories of Italian." Indeed, there are such literally translated phrases as "I sense badly," for "mi sento male." The workers are largely assumed to be speaking Italian with each other, and when they do speak English it is, as in Roth's *Call It Sleep*, a stereotypically broken idiom. Mike's phrase, "somebodys whose gotta bigga buncha keeds and he alla times talka from somebodys else," is representative. There are also Italian words and phrases interspersed into the English text that enhance the translated feeling, though they are not always idiomatic and seem to imply an English rather than an Italian reader, as in "Ah, *bella casa mio*."

The construction workers are seen as objects of forces beyond their control, forces that are like gods and that di Donato capitalizes, "Job" or "Boss" or

"Tenement." Here is an example for the young author's attempt to sound a tough modernist staccato tone – with frequent ellipses marked by " . . . " – a tone that drives home the violence of labor and the reification of the workers:

Trowel rang through brick and slashed mortar rivets were machine-gunned fast with angry grind Patsy number one check Patsy number two check the Lean three check Vincenzo four steel bellowed back at hammer donkey engines coughed purple Ashes-ass Pietro fifteen chisel point intoned stone thin steel whirred and wailed through wood liquid stone flowed with dull rasp through iron veins and hoist screamed through space Carmine the Fat twenty-four and Giacomo Sangini check. . . . The multitudinous voices of a civilization rose from the surroundings and melded with the efforts of the Job.

That the workers live under the rule of secular, not sacred, time is made explicit since the gruesome story is set on a cold and snowy Good Friday in March. At a dreamy moment during lunch break (the Catholic Geremio does not eat meat on Fridays) when everything seems unreal to him, Geremio tells Vincenz that he has been thinking "funny! A – yes, what is the time – " and Vincenz tells the time, apparently from a clock on an advertisement: "My American can of tomatoes says ten minutes from two o'clock." Five minutes later, Snoutnose checks the time again, and Geremio "automatically" takes out his watch, rewinds, and sets it. However, "automatic" processes suggest not aesthetic inspiration, as they did for Stein, but reification and dehumanization; and for di Donato as for Wright, clocked time spells doom, not the impending end of the work-day, as Geremio hopes.

Indeed, Murdin has economized too much on the underpinning and ignores Geremio's warning with a simple "Lissenyawopbastard! If you don't like it, you know what you can do!" As a result of the workplace violations, "Job tore down upon them madly." The whole structure collapses, and the men are thrown about in -ing-rich sentences: "Walls, floors, beams became whirling, solid, splintering waves crashing with detonations that ground man and material in bonds of death." Several of the workmen die, and some are injured in this immigrant catastrophe caused by an Anglo-American's greed.

The second half of the story is a protracted representation of Geremio's slow and gruesome death, as he is buried alive in construction-site concrete under girders, "the gray concrete gushing from the hopper mouth, and sealing up the mute figure." His inside point of view, following Geremio's "train of thought," presented at times in a stream-of-consciousness technique, alternates with third-person narration: "'Ahhh-h, I am not dead yet. I knew it – you have not done with me. Torture away! I cannot believe you, God and Country, no longer!' His body was fast breaking under the concrete's closing wrack. Blood vessels burst like mashed flower stems." Di Donato's interest in the way in which a violent death may turn human beings into things resembles Toomer's description of Tom Burwell's death in "Blood-Burning Moon." "The stricken blood surged through a weltering maze of useless pipes and exploded forth from his squelched eyes and formless nose, ears and mouth, seeking life in the indifferent stone." In Geremio's last conscious moment of suffering he moans "the simple songs of barefoot childhood" as if he were returning to culture from the horrors of civilization. His long, very self-consciously Christlike agony includes prayers, thoughts of his wife Annunziata and their children, memories, curses, and attacks on national and labor exploitation: "they have cheated me with flags, signs and fear." Di Donato also builds upon a contrast to Geremio's vitality and virility: "The strongly shaped body that slept with Annunziata nights and was perfect in all the limitless physical qualities, thudded as a worthless sack among the giant debris that crushed fragile flesh and bone with centrifugal intensity." Before the accident, the men who obviously did not share David Schearl's view of shellfish as "snot" in "rocks," had spoken about going to Mulberry Street for oysters "for the much needed steam they put into the – " but now Geremio's "genitals convulsed. The cold steel rod upon which they were impaled, froze his spine." Di Donato makes Hemingway's Jake Barnes's war wound seem like a mere scratch.

When di Donato made the *Esquire* story the opening chapter of the novel of the same title, he revised and trimmed the death scene; the chapter now ends with the point of view of Geremio's son Paul, who hears a tarantella on his crystal radio at the moment of the father's dying prayer; and the bulk of the novel carries on with the story of the family after the father's death.

Against this grim novel by di Donato stands Jerre Mangione's memoir-novel *Mount Allegro* (1942), a book that evokes the author's experience of growing up in an Italian American (or more precisely, Sicilian American) family in a mixed neighborhood of Rochester, New York, and that starts with this passage:

"WHEN I GROW UP I WANT TO BE AN AMERICAN," Giustina said. We looked at our sister; it was something none of us had ever said.

"Me too," Maria echoed.

"Aw, you don't even know what an American is," Joe scoffed.

"I do so," Giustina said.

It was more than the rest of us knew.

"We're Americans right now," I said. "Miss Zimmerman says if you're born here you're an American."

"Aw, she's nuts," Joe said. He had no use for most teachers. "We're Italians. If y' don't believe me ask Pop."

But my father wasn't very helpful. "Your children will be *Americani*. But you, my son, are half-and-half. Now stop asking me questions. You should know those things from going to school. What do you learn in school, anyway?"

When Jerre Mangione's *Mount Allegro* was reprinted in 1952 (without a subtitle or genre identification), it carried an introduction by the novelist Dorothy Canfield Fisher who had also introduced the first edition of Wright's *Native Son* and commented on di Donato's language. Fisher praised *Mount Allegro* for its "light-hearted gaiety in the life portrayed," with "none of the sombre tensity which for so long has been a literary fashion" as the book "fortifies the hope in all our hearts that life is not necessarily a martyrdom, but is often a variegated delight." *Mount Allegro* gives the reader a warmly ironic sense of vividly drawn characters who are not victims of circumstances but who spin their tales of Old World memories and New World mishaps, who celebrate their meals, and who give their American-born descendants a magical sense of a world elsewhere. Like Hurston, Mangione includes fairly precise recipes of particular dishes, jokes, and just stories after stories. Aunt Giovanna, rejected by immigration officials for the suspicion of trachoma, spent eight days at Ellis Island "looking through iron bars at the Statue of Liberty and the New York skyline, and weeping," before being sent back to Palermo. Uncle Luigi whose anti-Catholicism made him become a Baptist and also go to as many as "three or four services in as many churches of different denominations," would eat two courses of meat on Fridays and attend "a synagogue with some of his Jewish friends." Yet Uncle Luigi notwithstanding, the relatives' Catholicism was a firm part of their lives, and was also "enveloped in a heavy blanket of fatalism" that helped to explain any misfortune as an act of (capitalized) "Destiny."

Both *Mount Allegro* and *Christ in Concrete* include a scene of a séance in which communication with dead relatives is established or at least attempted. Mangione tells the story of a salesman, an Armenian immigrant who was formerly a rug vendor and who now offers to provide the spiritualist contact on a Saturday midnight in the Catholic cemetery. They go there by streetcar, the Armenian ridiculously wearing "plaid golf knickers and a bright yellow sport cap" and displaying "the offensive eagerness of an aggressive salesman." For Mangione, this is an occasion to comment ironically on superstitions, as the narrator's father, unlike two of his Italian American fellow workers in a candy factory, never believes in the charade. This becomes quite apparent when the "spirits" speak broken Italian in what is recognizably the Armenian's voice. The fraudulent salesman of premodernism escapes, but at least the father is happy not to have paid in advance. For di Donato, the séance provides an opportunity to create a scene of deep human communication among the poor and oppressed. After the séance, the crippled woman who serves as the medium and Paul's mother Annunziata talk with each other, the medium telling Annunziata "of her two sons killed in the War" and of the bribes she has to pay the police to run her business. Annunziata "felt for her, and in return passionately unburdened to her of Geremio, her Paul, and her children." They drink tea together, the medium charges little, and the night after the séance, both Paul and his mother feel that Geremio's "love surmounted the distance of death."

One motif in which the contrast between di Donato and Mangione becomes apparent is, again, that of the breast. In *Christ in Concrete*, Geremio imagines floating off "to blessed slumber with [his] feet on the chair and the head on the wife's soft full breast," and breasts appear more frequently in their overtly sexual dimensions. Both Mangione and di Donato place at the center a young American-born boy on his way to manhood. In the masculine world of *Christ in Concrete*, following the path toward manhood means giving up being a "titty-drinker" (as the pre-adolescent Paul is called when he starts working as a bricklayer in his father's place) and feeling, instead, "intoxicating consternation" and "hot blood" sheeting one's face (as the injured Luigi does in his sickbed when Cola swarms her breasts over his face). Cola, Tomas's widow, virtually has the epic epithet "big-titted" accompanying her name throughout the novel; and her comment on Luigi is that she "hugged her breast with one hand and sighed . . . : 'Even big strong men are like children.'" In an urban melting-pot scene on the New York subway, Paul is pushed against a female subway passenger: "When the train bent around a curve she fell heavily upon him and remained there after the train righted itself. Her body brought him an immediate disturbing message. He shut his eyes. Spongy breasts pulsed against his chest." It is a situation not unlike the one Jim Cowan fantasized about in Nathan Asch's *Pay Day* (1930).

In *Mount Allegro*, a whole cultural distinction between Sicilian immigrants and Anglo-Americans is derived from attitudes toward breasts:

[M]y Sicilian relatives had little regard for privacy. They brought all their infants with them on their picnics and the women had no inhibitions about baring their breasts to feed them, no matter where they were or how many Americans might be about to watch them.

Never having seen the exposed breasts of an American mother, I imagined they were never as large and as sprawling as Sicilian breasts, but rather neat and delicate, like the food they packed for picnics. In my prudishness, I was also confident that the breasts of American mothers were purely ornamental and never used for the messy business of hungry brats.

Mangione may here be alluding to, and playing with, the expectation that breast-feeding mothers were a "sight" in immigrant communities, an ambivalent symbol of the immigrants' strange foreign ways as well as of their supposedly natural and admirably premodern qualities. Reports about ethnic communities have included this feature at least since 1898 when E. S. Martin's well-intentioned reportage, "East Side Considerations," for *Harper's Monthly Magazine* dwelled on the fact that "you may walk up and down Fifth Avenue for ten years and never see a Fifth Avenue mother nursing her latest born on the doorstep, but in Mott or Mulberry or Cherry Street that is a common sight and always interesting to the respectful observer." At the same time, these examples may be indications of the cultural change from the flat-and-"ornamental"-chested American female ideal of the 1920s toward the busty pin-up idols that proliferated after Betty Grable's success and dominated the 1950s, making what used to be an "ethnic" marker a globally exported feature of "American" culture. The women who represented this new ideal were variously referred to in the 1940s as "anatomic bomb" or "sex bomb."

The contrasts that have been drawn out between the different sets of writers resemble each other enough to justify the question addressed to writers of a sociological bent like Wright and di Donato, how come, if the world was as oppressive and destructive as they describe it, that anybody ever survived? And to the anthropological camp of Hurston and Mangione: why on earth, if the ethnic world was so wonderful, did their autobiographical projection figures and protagonists choose to leave the community rather than stay in it forever?

Each perspective seems to rest on an assertion as well as a denial; and occasionally the other side comes through: for example, Hurston loved the all-black Florida town of Eatonville enough to claim it as her 1907 birthplace (though she was actually born on January 15, 1891 in Notasulga, Alabama), yet in *Dust Tracks* she once calls Eatonville a "dull village," very much in the way in which Aunt Bertha from *Call It Sleep* looked at her native Veljish, and Jerre Mangione tellingly describes the end of a family party with the adults sitting around "reminiscing about Sicily" while "the youngsters danced and listened to jazz." Mangione also speaks of his determination to "make the break" and leave Mount Allegro – which is a strange description of a departure from paradise. The fact that Hurston invokes a "calling," while Mangione gives as a reason that he was going to college, hardly seems sufficient.

❦

Illustrations of the period reinforced the divergent tendencies in the prose. The *New Masses* (May 1930) self-consciously offered a cartoon that juxtaposed the alternatives of representing black life in the period, William Siegel's two-part illustration, "The white bourgeois version of the Negro" and " – as the white worker knows him." The former image represents singing, comedy, jazz, gamblers, bare-breasted dancers, and so forth, the latter shows somber scenes of labor and oppression as well as a lynching. It was symptomatic that one of Wright's stories, "Almos' a Man," was fittingly illustrated in the serious

WPA style of Thomas Hart Benton, with emaciated and elongated figures and a haggard mule, whereas Hurston had *Mules and Men* cheerily illustrated by the slicker Miguel Covarrubias who had earned his fame as a *Vanity Fair* artist. *Esquire's* art director Eric Lundgren accompanied "Christ in Concrete" by line drawings depicting sullen workers walking toward the viewer with pick-axes and Geremio praying desperately at the collapsed construction site; the dust-jacket for the 1939 hardback featured a pick-axe and a shovel surrounded by a crown of thorns and a glowing halo; and the 1962 mass-market popular library edition also chose an image of workers with shovels and pick-axes against the New York skyline for the front and back covers. Jerre Mangione's *Mount Allegro* was illustrated by Peggy Bacon who focused more on the children than the adult characters as subjects of her drawings. In the cases of Mangione–Bacon and Hurston–Covarrubias, the art accompanying ethnic accounts of an all-black home town and of second-generation immigrant childhood resembled illustrations of children's books or light and comic cartoons. This is also true of William Saroyan's *My Name is Aram* which had colored artwork by Don Freeman, whereas Mike Gold's *Jews Without Money* carried stark woodcuts by Howard Simon.

What all of this artwork had in common on either side of the divide, and was shared also by much cover art of the period, was that it was far more realist and less experimental than modernist art had been since the Armory Show or than were the African-mask-inspired art-deco patterns that were such prevalent book designs in the 1920s. Judging by the images accompanying ethnic literature of the 1930s and early 1940s it would seem that realism (modified only by touches of modernism) had returned in full force.

13

❦

WAS MODERNISM ANTITOTALITARIAN?

OR THE IMMIGRANT and ethnic narratives from *The Life Stories*, *The Promised Land*, and *Giants in the Earth* to *Call It Sleep*, *Laughing in the Jungle*, and *Mount Allegro* the decisive international connections were those that linked "Americans in the making" with various countries, or villages, of origin. For Antin, it was Polotzk, for Rölvaag, the island of Dönna, for Saroyan, Bitlis in eastern Anatolia, and for Roth's David, the village Veljish. In the last two chapters in *Mount Allegro*, Mangione returned to his mother's birthplace Realmonte (or "Munderialli," as the natives called it), his father's original home in Porto Empedocle, and other places in the vicinity of the Sicilian city Agrigento.

The Native's Return: An American Immigrant Visits Yugoslavia and Discovers His Old Country (1934) took Louis Adamic, on a Guggenheim fellowship he received with the help of Sinclair Lewis and H. L. Mencken, back to his birthplace in the Slovenian village of Blato. His first home seemed much smaller than the emigrant had remembered it, for now he had the "consciousness of the Empire State Building and the interior of the Grand Central in New York City." Adamic was impressed, however, by the "bright green of the meadows" with "big splashes of buttercups and purple clover ahum with bees" as well as "forgetmenots in abundance" and "more lilies-of-the-valley in one spot" than he had seen in "nineteen years in America." America seemed to stand for the impressive scale of its man-built environment, while Blato had nostalgic value as pure nature, and Adamic clearly cherished both.

For Stein, Hemingway, Roth, and countless modernist artists, expatriate writers, and musicians, Paris played an important role as the "capital of the arts," a Prohibition-free city that appreciated jazz and was the location of publishers who would dare to bring out works like *Ulysses*. For Toomer, the Château de Prieuré near Fontainebleau may have held more meaning as the international headquarters for Gurdjieff's "Institute for the Harmonious Development of Man."

Starting in the 1920s, accelerating in the 1930s, and intensifying to its highest pitch in the years of World War II and the beginning of the Cold War, a new international context emerged that was of some significance not only for individual writers and books but for the whole trajectory of modernism, ethnic writing, and jazz in the twentieth century. It was the global battle of the ideologies of fascism (originating in Italy and Germany) and communism (located in Russia and then expanding to Eastern Europe, China, and Korea) that pulled American writers into these new international constellations. These constituted real lures for some intellectuals in the period, and threats for others. The authoritarian systems of government, in which only one political party ruled and which controlled all other institutions and demanded absolute obedience of the individual, were called "totalitarian," a term that assumed a generally pejorative meaning only after World War II, notably in Hannah Arendt's widely read work.

Take *My Autobiography* by Benito Mussolini as an example, not exactly a work of "American literature," one might think. Still, published in 1928 by Hemingway's and Fitzgerald's publisher, Charles Scribner's Sons, it was illustrated with the typical photographs that had accompanied American immigrant autobiographies like S. S. McClure's, ranging from an image of the poor-looking house where the author was born, a stone cottage in Varano di Costa, to one showing him associating with a famous personage – in his case, the Italian king Victor Emmanuel III. The book described the decisive role of World War I, for as a soldier Mussolini was wounded by a bursting grenade, experienced "indescribable suffering," and underwent "twenty-seven operations in one month; all except two...without anaesthetics." In his disgust for the routine of postwar politicians who "forgot our 600,000 dead and our 1,000,000 wounded," he sounded like a member of another lost generation. But he did something about what he called "the beast of decadence," and the book emphasizes the protagonist's young age at the time of his March on Rome in October of 1922, with which he took power. Mussolini also expressed his admiration for the United States, "now in its golden age," for its discipline, praised the American people for their "sense of organization," and concluded:

As the reserves of wealth are gone now from the continents to North America, it is right that a large part of the attention of the world should be focused upon the activity of this nation that has men of great value, economists of real wisdom and scholars that are outlining the basis for a new science and a new culture.

In Mussolini's autobiography, "America, the land harboring so many of our immigrants," still called "to the spirit of the new youth." But unlike immigrants, who would at times imagine the American ideal as a fulfillment in the New World of childhood dreams from elsewhere, Mussolini suggested that this ideal was also being fulfilled in fascist Italy, for though he looked to American "youth for her destinies and the preservation of her growing ideals" so did he look "to the youth of Italy for the progress of the Fascist state. It is not easy to remember always the importance of youth. It is not easy to retain the spirit of youth." Was fascism simply one way of realizing the American ideal, as Mussolini's autobiography seemed to suggest?

That appears to have been the opinion of Richard Washburn Child, the U.S. ambassador to Italy at the time of the March on Rome, who not only introduced the book but also, as was mentioned earlier, actually ghostwrote it and helped to serialize it in the *Saturday Evening Post*. It was a book that was pitched to an American reading public and was, in fact, not available in Italian for the entire duration of fascist rule. Incidentally, S. S. McClure was also trying to sell Mussolini in the U.S. at the time, but Child had better connections. Child idolized the leader ideal that Mussolini represented and put such sentences in Mussolini's mouth as "I am strict with my most faithful followers," apparently expecting the reader's approbation and applause. Child exemplified an American intellectual so enamored by fascism that he simply ignored the political terror and repression that had taken command in Italy, and proclaimed from the Olympian distance and safety of the U.S.: "It is absurd to say that Italy groans under discipline. Italy chortles with it! It is victory!"

Bigger lights would follow, among them, for example, the arch-modernist Ezra Pound, who in 1937 wrote in *Germany and You*, a Nazi progaganda publication, about "Totalitarian Scholarship and the New Paideuma" – an early and notably positive American use of the word "totalitarian." Pound's rambling essay argued that "with the march on Rome, which was led not by secluded artists but by men in action, a new phase was initiate[d]." He also criticized those who did not understand the "spirit of the rising Germany," mistaking "the end of demo-liberal us[u]rer's Europe for the end of race vigours in Europe." Pound had a long-standing obsession with "Jewish usury" and made English-language propaganda radio broadcasts in fascist Italy during the war years, in which he warned English and American listeners that they were being subjected to Jewish propaganda, or, as he put it in a 1941 broadcast, "clever Kikes runnin' ALL our communication system." In broadcasts of 1942 he argued against pogroms, the "old-style killing of small Jews," for "that system is no good whatsoever." Yet he added: "Of course, if some man had a stroke of genius and could start a pogrom UP AT THE TOP, there might be something to say for it." In 1944, Pound advised Mussolini, now reduced to the Hitler-protected Republic of Saló, that his government should support translations of such a strange array of works as e. e. cummings's *Eimi* (1933), Joyce's *Ulysses*, and Stalin's *Leninism* (1928), and near the very end of the war he wrote the orthodox fascist cantos 72 and 73 (published in 1987). Throughout these years Pound seems to have believed in the fascist ethos as a version of his American maxim of "making it new." Like Child, he explicitly saw Mussolini as the political leader who would fulfill the American promise – for Pound, most especially Jefferson's project – and he said so in print in his *Jefferson and/or Mussolini*, a book which Pound offered to the British Union of Fascists for publication, which T. S. Eliot (who called it "Jeff & Mutt" in his correspondence with Pound) tried to place, and which in 1936 also appeared in the U.S. with Horace Liveright, Mike Gold's and Jean Toomer's publisher. In *Jefferson and/or Mussolini*, Pound found that "the fundamental likenesses between these two men are probably greater than their differences" and that the "heritage of Jefferson, Quincy Adams, old John Adams, Jackson, Van Buren, is HERE, NOW *in the Italian peninsula* at the beginning of the second fascist decennio, not in Massachusetts or Delaware."

Among other American authors of the period, Thomas Wolfe cherished sympathies for Nazi Germany and attended the 1936 Berlin Olympics. Zora Neale Hurston's pre-Pearl Harbor manuscript of *Dust Tracks on a Road* included some chapters which were omitted, at the publisher's suggestion, in the 1942 book publication, among them the concluding "Seeing the World as It Is," which expressed some surprising views on Japan and Hitler. "We Westerners," Hurston commented on the brutal Japanese invasion of China, "wrote the song about keeping a whole hemisphere under your wing. Now the Nipponese are singing our song all over Asia." And with equal sarcasm, she commented on the Nazi military campaigns at the beginning of World War II:

All around me, bitter tears are being shed over the fate of Holland, Belgium, France, and England. I must confess to being a little dry around the eyes. I hear people shaking with shudders at the thought of Germany collecting taxes in Holland. I have not heard a word against Holland collecting one twelfth of poor people's wages in Asia. Hitler's crime is that he is actually doing a thing like that to his own kind.

Written in 1941, this does not seem to be a very perceptive comment by a writer who was interested in ethnic issues and whose novel *Their Eyes Were Watching God* had been translated into Italian in 1938 by the antifascist Turin intellectual Ada Prospero, the widow of Piero Gobetti, who had died after being arrested and tortured by the fascist authorities. Ironically, the back cover of Hurston's published autobiography showed a patriotic Hurston advertising U.S. war bonds.

Gertrude Stein was "encouraged" by her French translator and friend Bernard Faÿ, the Vichy regime director of the Bibliothèque Nationale and Croix de Feux member who also edited antimasonic and antisemitic reviews, to translate Marshal Pétain's speeches. Stein executed the translation in an intriguingly literal fashion, and she introduced the speeches with the description of Marshal Pétain (a man whom Pound also called, affectionately, "ole Pete Pétain") as a historical figure "who like George Washington, and he is very like George Washington because he too is first in war first in peace and first in the hearts of his countrymen, who like George Washington has given them courage in their darkest moment." Stein who spent the war years in occupied France reportedly also recommended Hitler for the Nobel Prize.

By contrast, the clear-sighted W. E. B. Du Bois, who visited Nazi Germany for five months in 1936, stressed in essays published in the *Pittsburgh Courier*, a Negro weekly, that an integral part of Nazi policy "just as prominent now as earlier and perhaps growing in prominence, is world war on Jews. The proof of this is incontrovertible, and must comfort all those in any part of the world who depend on race hate as the salvation of men." He perceptively noticed the power of propaganda, the "greatest single invention" of World War I, which actually made the mass of people believe in what it said:

Every misfortune of the world is in the whole or in part blamed on Jews – the Spanish rebellion, the obstruction to world trade, etc. One finds cases in the papers: Jews jailed for sex relations with German women; a marriage disallowed because a Jewish justice of the peace witnessed it; Masons excluded from office in the National Socialist Party, because Jews are Masons; advertisements excluding Jews; the total disfranchisement of all Jews; deprivation of civil rights and inability to remain or become German citizens; limited rights of education, and narrowly limited right to work in trades, professions and the civil service; the threat of boycott, loss of work and even mob violence, for any German who trades with a Jew; and, above all, the continued circulation of Julius Streicher's [*Stürmer*], the most shameless, lying advocate of race hate in the world, not excluding Florida. It could not sell a copy without Hitler's consent.

Du Bois thus highlighted the antisemitic racism of the National Socialists while also reminding readers of the antiblack racism at home. He stressed that he, a colored man, had been "treated with uniform courtesy and consideration" in Nazi Germany and added: "It would have been impossible for me to have spent a similarly long time in any part of the United States, without some, if not frequent, cases of personal insult or discrimination. I cannot record a single instance here."

Far more widespread among American intellectuals, and better-studied by scholars, was the lure of communism, a lure to which Du Bois also succumbed late in his life. For the enticement of communism grew out of the Marxian interests that were understandably widespread among ethnic intellectuals and among many others who were indignant about the inequalities under capitalism, especially during the years of the Great Depression in the United States. Communism also seemed to present a stronger alternative to fascism than did the capitalist democracies – at least until the 1939 Stalin–Hitler agreement. The attraction was not only strong in the early revolutionary years symbolized by Trotsky, when the new Soviet Union seemed to be the political home for all sorts of modernist artists and when suprematism and objectivism constituted something like a state art, but it continued well into, and for some all the way through, the Stalinist years of brutal political repression, the kulak liquidation, and the infamous show trials to which many intellectuals and artists fell victim. In Myra Page's novel *Moscow Yankee* (1935), for example, Andy, an incredibly naive cardboard working-class American, goes to Russia and becomes an equally unbelievable "new Soviet man," while the novel is blissfully blind to the human costs of collectivization and Stalin's Five Year Plan, the praises of which are sung at the end of the book. The death toll in the Soviet Union for the period 1931–33 alone has been estimated at around 7 million. Was communism, was Stalinism, twentieth-century Americanism, as American communist Earl Browder's Popular Front slogan had it?

A good number of American intellectuals thought so. Among writers who have been cited or discussed in these pages, Mike Gold remained loyal to the Communist Party through all its ideological shifts and changes, and both Henry Roth and Richard Wright remained enthusiastic about the Soviet Union in very dark times. Tellingly, Roth referred to the Soviet Union as his "cherished homeland," and in the statement "Where My Sympathy Lies" (1937), he publicly condoned the Stalinist show trials, for he felt that all defendants had "confessed their guilt." Roth added: "I do not believe together with the Hearst press that these men were under the influence of mesmerism or mysterious narcotics; therefore, I believe them to be, as they themselves acknowledged, guilty." Even at the time of the Hitler–Stalin pact of August 1939 which divided Poland, gave the Baltic states to Stalin, and made possible the beginning of World War II, Richard Wright wrote a brief, unpublished essay that was entitled, "There are still men left" in which he confessed: "The most meaningful moments of experience I have gotten from this world have been in either making an attempt to change the limits of life under which men live, or in watching with *sympathy* the efforts of others to do the same. For that reason I am a card-carrying Communist.... Communism to me is a way of life, ... an unusual mode of existence." This was not a question of rightness or wrongness of the Party's position, for Wright stated parenthetically and revealingly: "(sometimes I feel myself most deeply attracted to it when most people are repelled – that is, for instance, when the USSR signed the pact with Nazi Germany)." By implication, Wright spoke not only about communists but also about Nazis when he concluded: "They are men who are used to seeking, not comfort, security, *individual* happiness, equality, but *meaning*, meaning in terms of feeling and knowing in its most concrete and literal sense." That such convictions approached the level and intensity of a religious experience became clear when Wright, having left the Party, participated, together with Ignazio Silone and Arthur Koestler, in Richard Crossman's collection of testimonials entitled *The God That Failed* (1949). Even Hemingway, who was left-leaning and antifascist from the very beginning of that movement and who learned anti-Stalinism from the experience of the Spanish Civil War, never commented in any of his writings or his correspondence on the Nazi–Soviet pact.

The point is neither to idealize nor to vilify cultural participants in hindsight but to show the real attractions and challenges that authoritarian movements presented to modern American writers and intellectuals. One should also not forget that the term "totalitarian" tended to blur important differences among various fascist and communist systems and between fascism and communism. Fascism seemed to reestablish and exaggerate – often by very modern means – some traditional forms of authority that modernity had challenged and that seemed to have collapsed in World War I; in its Nazi version, it put "race" at the center of its idea of order. It was a movement that aestheticized power and displayed it as spectacle that was constantly reenacted and amplified with the new means of radio, sound-track-accompanied newsreels, and propaganda films. Fascism appealed to the paradoxical need of some writers for a "forward-looking nostalgia," to a mix of military-style order and ethnic homogeneity, of ritual and "roots." Communism – equally adept at using the modern arts of persuasion – made "class" the central category of human divisions and promised to act on the egalitarian ideal that had been established in the French Revolution, an ideal that was deeply in need of revitalization in the Depression years following the global economic crisis of 1929. However different they were, both the communist and fascist revolutions projected youthful images and would thus appeal to a culture that had always emphasized the importance of youth, novelty, and a fresh start. One only has to remember Lee Chew's grandfather's verdict from *The Life Stories*, that Americans "were constantly showing disrespect for their ancestors by getting new things to take the place of the old."

How could the by now aged and ancestral political system of democracy, which had attracted little deeply felt cultural enthusiasm after Antin's World War I writings, become as magnetic as the young-isms with which it was increasingly confronted? Cool and hard-boiled indifference was hardly synonymous with a commitment to democracy: the Italian American author

John Fante, for example, wrote to his editor on May 26, 1940, "They can tear this over-rated civilization apart, they can have their fascism and nazism and bolshevism and democracy. I shall type with one hand, the fingers of the other pinching my nostrils. It will be slower, less convenient, but it will be great writing anyway." In other letters, Fante struck a hedonistic or self-serving note describing himself as an advocate neither of communism nor of capitalism but of what he actually called "Clitorism." He wrote bluntly: "The only menace I find in poverty is that I can't fuck enough." Fante also thought that "the Italians rushing into this war will cause a lot of Italian-American interest here in this country, and for that reason I give you odds that [Fante's novel] Dago Red will be a success." War could simply be good for the ethnic writer's business and did not compel him to take sides.

Still, perhaps it was the tough Hemingwayesque film-noir style – which Fante often employed, but also explicitly satirized in the piece "We Snatch a Frail" (1936) as the ridiculous prose of the "Caldwell–Hemingway–O'Hara school of scribblers" – that exerted the kind of appeal in America that foreign totalitarian leaders commanded abroad. In the absence of an enthusiastically presented and compelling democratic literature, the film-noir style could take on a democratic meaning and ultimately also become one basis of allied self-understanding and propaganda, all the more so since it was often coupled with plotlines centering on apolitical and tough-talking but basically fair-minded existentialist loners, who were ultimately forced into political action for democracy because of the aspirations toward global domination that their sinister opponents tried to realize. Michael Curtiz's film *Casablanca* (1942) was only the most famous stylization of existentialists for democratic action.

The confrontation with totalitarianism also generated shriller and more extreme articulations of individualism as the true essence of American capitalist democracy. Perhaps the sharpest opponent of Russian communism among immigrant writers was Ayn Rand who, born Alissa Zinovievna Rosenbaum in St. Petersburg in 1905, left the Soviet Union in 1926 and came to the United States. She published an autobiographically inspired novel *We the Living* (1936), in which she first developed her idealization of individualism as the ideology of freedom. Her novel is set in communist Russia, and it represents the experiences of the young individualist, Kira Argounova, enmeshed in a politically charged love triangle in a gloomy world of state terror and collectivism. The novel is interspersed with political headlines and Party slogans. When it was reissued in 1958, Rand stressed that this was "not a story about Soviet Russia in 1925" but about "Dictatorship, any dictatorship, anywhere, at any time, whether it be Soviet Russia, Nazi Germany, or – which this novel might do its share in helping to prevent – a socialist America." Rand also revised

We the Living stylistically, changing "awkward or confusing lapses" that were the sign of "a particular kind of uncertainty in the use of the English language, which reflected the transitional state of a mind thinking no longer in Russian but not yet fully in English."

Rand's most famous novel, *The Fountainhead* (1943), extolled the extreme and antialtruistic individual freedom of the idealist modernist architect, Howard Roark, who defies dominant conventions and mediocre standards, deciding ultimately to destroy the building he had designed rather than to compromise. Roark was apparently inspired by Frank Lloyd Wright. Made into a 1949 movie directed by King Vidor and starring Gary Cooper, this novel helped to propel Rand into national prominence, and her work keeps attracting a following among readers who may not be worried that the extremist endorsement of the strong individual shares features with the fascist ideal of the superman who lives above and beyond the standards of the mass. Though Rand proposes the heroic individual as an answer to totalitarianism, *The Fountainhead* is less an embodiment of the democratic ideal than an expression of contempt for conventions and for people who care about them.

Another possibility for boosting morale and for fleshing out the democratic ideal at a time of threat lay in the notion of the "American dream" that Antin had evoked in *The Promised Land* and the mention of which proliferated in the Depression era. Michael Foster's novel, *American Dream* (1937), helped to popularize the phrase itself; and Shelby Thrall, the novel's protagonist, ultimately embraces and defines what the narrator calls "that queer phrase, '*the American dream.*'" "Shelby saw suddenly that the dream did live, as it had lived forever through bloody centuries ruled and spoiled by the grabbers and the shouters; as it would live forever, and be seen always by a few men, sometimes by a nation, through slaughter and ruin and loud follies. Because it was not merely the American dream – it was the old, old human faith that somehow, somewhere, a time might come when man would stand on the ruins of an old world and an old self, with the starlight on his shoulders. That a time might come when men would live and deal among themselves with justice. And tenderness. And truth."

Michael Foster's was an all-American story; but the "American dream" also flourished particularly in immigrant writing, as immigrants in the interwar period often brought a comparative understanding of political systems to their appreciation of democracy. Louis Adamic was instrumental in reviving the tradition that Antin had established in calling attention to the immigrant's story as perfect for the possible realization of the American dream, thereby helping to expand and make more inclusive the term "American" and to give new and multiethnic meaning to American democracy. Antin had made the argument to stem the nativist tide of the 1910s, whereas Adamic developed it further in the 1930s and 1940s in the context of opposition to fascism; and, somewhat prophetically, he found the core value of American democracy in its ethnic heterogeneity. In the section "Ellis Island and Plymouth Rock" in a book entitled, in the Antin tradition, *My America* (1938), and in lectures to hundreds of audiences, the immigrant Adamic wrote euphorically that Americans must

work toward an intellectual–emotional synthesis of old and new America; of the Mayflower and the steerage; of the New England wilderness and the social–economic jungle of the city slums and the factory system; of the Liberty Bell and the Statue of Liberty. The old American Dream needs to be interlaced with the immigrants' emotions as they saw the Statue of Liberty. The two must be made into one story.

Adamic hoped for the production of a great encyclopedia that would describe the inspiring ethnic diversity of Whitman's "nation of nations," a phrase he adopted for the title of a 1945 book. For Adamic, realizing the American dream meant acknowledging and honoring the country's many diverging origins and its continuing cultural diversity. His journal, *Common Ground*, was emphatically multiethnic, boasted Mary Antin and Zora Neale Hurston among its contributors, and in 1941, for example, carried one piece about Fante as an all-American writer, the punch-line comparing him with Will Rogers, and another by Fante on his Armenian American friend William Saroyan. In his book programmatically entitled *From Many Lands* (1940), Adamic encouraged both native-born and old-stock Americans to think of a greater diversity when speaking of "Americans," and criticized newcomers for not adopting the term "American" quickly enough: "I find that most of the new people, when they say 'we,' don't mean 'we Americans' or 'we the people in this town,' but 'we who live in this section and are of Polish or Armenian, etc., origin or background.' When they say 'Americans,' they don't mean themselves." As has already become clear, immigration created confusing uses of personal pronouns; and Adamic wanted immigrants to be entitled to think "we" when they heard the word "Americans."

In her war-effort-sponsored national character study *And Keep Your Powder Dry* (1942) the anthropologist Margaret Mead addressed the problem from the opposite side and asked all Americans, ordinary and "old-stock," to view themselves *as immigrants*, for "however many generations we may actually boast of in this country," she explained, "we are all third generation." Without quoting him, she thus echoed Bourne's universalist position from World War I days as she urged Americans to think "we" when they heard the term "immigrants."

One immigrant who had no hesitation in adopting the term "American," and who also provided a striking example of the presence of the notion of the "American dream" in an immigrant autobiography of the period, was Salom Rizk. His *Syrian Yankee* (1943) is the story of an Arabic-speaking Lebanese boy who finds out at age twelve that he could (through his mother) actually claim American citizenship. The chapter title "Passport to Heaven" suggests how he feels about this discovery, and from his schoolmaster's account an image of America emerges in Salom's mind: " . . . the land of hope . . . the land of peace . . . the land of contentment . . . the land of liberty . . . the land of brother-hood . . . the land of plenty . . . where God has poured out wealth . . . where the dreams of men come true . . . where everything is bigger and grander and more beautiful that it has ever been anywhere else in the world . . . " And so on and so on.

Rizk's "Land of My Dreams," the title of the next chapter, seems like a fairy tale, even to him, though he adds: "But I wanted to believe all this, I had to believe it, and I did." Rizk finally gets his passport and lives his American dream. The dream is fully confirmed, however, only after he takes a trip back to his impoverished homeland, in the course of which he is almost arrested in fascist Italy and has to travel on a boat together with hundreds of Jewish refugees from Nazi Germany headed for Palestine. Now he knew that "bad as things were" in Depression America, "they were infinitely better than in Europe or, for that matter, anywhere else in the world." Rizk finds that his new feelings for America were not merely patriotic,

for I had an overwhelming wish that the whole world might share in all of it; that the kindly, poverty-stricken people I had so recently visited in Syria, and who had yearned, even begged, so pathetically for passage to America, might have a land like this to live in; that the Jewish exiles returning to the lean and stony ridges of Palestine might have found resources as rich as these, an air to breathe as free of hate and fear as this, and a welcome – yes, a welcome as warm and rousing as the words inscribed to the huddled masses of the Old World on our own Statue of Liberty.

Salom Rizk's wartime articulation of the American dream would not have been complete without his explicit opposition to the totalitarian threat. Since "racial prejudice, poverty, unemployment, discontent, despair of democracy" might also take root in America, he saw it as his task to warn Americans of the evils that could result from the organization of hatred and intolerance:

Mussolini's brags about Fascismo solving poverty had found welcome lodging in certain American ears. Hitler's maltreatment of the Jews appealed to some of my friends as good common sense. There were those, especially disillusioned young people, who applauded Stalin's arbitrary arrests, killings, and starvation as the future liberation of humanity from the evils of arbitrary arrest, killings, and starvation.

The American dream was, for immigrants like Rizk and for many others who came to know fascism and Stalinism, a hopeful and promising alternative.

Less ideologically charged, Mangione's *Mount Allegro* also emphasized an immigrant child's "return," in manhood, to a now fascist homeland, a political change which resolves any ambivalence toward ethnic origins in favor of the democratic location of his parents' adopted country. At the end of the book, the narrator simply wanted to leave Sicily for Rochester, as if he were reenacting the original event of the parents' emigration, with the added justification of getting away from fascism: "I was beginning to get lonely for America and I thought how good it would be to be home again."

In Henry Roth's representation of David Schearl's Lower East Side childhood of 1911 to 1913, the political situation of the early 1930s – the time when the novel was written – made itself felt in some small but telling details. Roth stated explicitly that *Call It Sleep* "violates the truth about what the East Side was" in the 1910s, describing it instead as a "montage of milieus," and specifically suggested the rise of antisemitism epitomized by Hitler as an inspiration for the scene in which David Schearl denies his Jewishness to the antisemitic boys Pedey and Weasel. In his new preface to the 1935 edition of *Jews Without Money*, Gold reports a friend's account who had heard Nazis laugh hysterically when they saw the book, for they simply could not believe that there were any "Jews without money."

Adamic's *The Native's Return* includes discussions of Mussolini's forced Italianization and suppression of the Slovenian language in the part of the country that Italy received at the end of World War I. He found that opportunistic rulers dangerously played one party leader against the other: "Serbs against Croats, Croats against Serbs, Slovenes against both, Moslems against Orthodox Christians, the latter against Catholics." His conclusion for the American reader appears in italics: Balkan policy *"created a spirit under which the various racial and religious groups became more attentive to their differences than their resemblances."* This was an implicit appeal for multiethnic democratic unity, for finding a "common ground." Adamic was so convinced of the democratic commitment of immigrants to the United States that he proposed in *Two-Way Passage* (1941) that American immigrants from Europe should return to their various countries of origin and help to establish democracies there, educating Europeans in democracy. However, Adamic also held high hopes for communism as the answer to problems of the Balkans, and of Eastern Europe in general; before World War II, he was hopeful that a new war, though "millions of people might die in it," would bring along with it some positive change for the region. "I see now that the salvation of the Yugoslav people and other small backward nations in that part of the world lies, clearly and inescapably, in the direction of Russia." After the war, he supported Tito (with whom he had a correspondence and who awarded Adamic the Yugoslav Order of National Unity) against Stalin; and in 1951, Adamic died under suspicious circumstances in his house in New Jersey.

Various forms of cultural opposition to totalitarianism helped to redefine American democracy as totalitarianism's opposite. The American dream might still be incomplete, but the new wisdom seemed to be that the dream was destined to be completed in the multiethnic, nontotalitarian United States and not anywhere else; in Massachusetts and Delaware, and not in Rome, Berlin, or Moscow. American culture was being viewed as vital because it was the culture of democracy, of process, of mobility, and of plenty.

According to John Kouwenhoven, it was characteristic that an American "invented chewing gum (in 1869) and that it is the Americans who have spread it – in all senses of the verb – throughout the world. A nonconsumable confection, its sole appeal is the process of chewing it." Chewing gum could also appear as a secular equivalent to a communion: thus Toomer's early poem "Gum" (c. 1920) juxtaposed a Christian billboard with the advertisement "WRIGLEYS/eat it/after/every meal/It Does You Good." It was also in a culture that cherished process, that was not "a closed system," in which jazz emerged expressing love for improvisation, or the skyscraper with its arbitrary height, or the serial assembly of parts into a whole, or the aesthetic formula of the soap opera. The changes that took place during the 1930s and 1940s were changes that deeply affected American self-understanding as well as the image of America that it would from now on project abroad.

Yet there were some fairly obvious contradictions. Immigrants turned into typical Americans in Margaret Mead's hands, and Mead also wanted to kindle "the enthusiasm and devotion of every young adult" so as to resist the lure of the "fascist organizer," yet legislation restricting immigration that was enacted in the 1920s remained in full force during much of the period and barred desperate refugees from entering the United States. As the post-Pearl Harbor wartime logic supported Louis Adamic's project of imagining the United States as the nation of immigrants, of giving dominance to Emma Lazarus's view of the Statue of Liberty as a welcome to immigrants and Mary Antin's interpretation of Ellis Island as another name for Plymouth Rock, Japanese Americans were called "non-alien Japanese" and put in internment camps, their U.S. citizenship notwithstanding.

The wartime internment of about 120,000 West Coast Japanese Americans was made possible by Roosevelt's Executive Order 9066, as in the panicked atmosphere after the attack on Pearl Harbor it was possible to subject to forced relocation and detention so many people exclusively on the basis of their ethnic background. Racetracks and stadiums served as temporary centers; then concentration camps were built in usually remote areas of the Southwest. Many haunting literary works of the 1940s emerged in the context of this traumatic experience. The War Relocation Authority provided mimeographing machines, and nine camps had newsletters or papers, many of which included literary contributions. Toshio Mori, for example, wrote for the Topaz (Utah) *Times*. One representative piece published on January 1, 1943 was simply entitled "A Sketch." It understatedly presented the conversation of two men about a fence that was being erected around the camp. One asks, "What are the fences for? We won't run away." The other quietly replies: "There are two ways of looking at it. It might limit your travels but it also protects you. Don't you think it is meant for protection too? For example, suppose we start a poultry farm. Coyotes roam nearby and the animals need protection. You can never tell when a fence comes in handy." He continues: "We all have fences – within and without. A fence is a symbol of our limited capabilities. And another thing, friend. We have our own fences within ourselves which hinder understanding and cooperation." The critique of fences is thus articulated in the same breath that voices their justification by the somewhat absurd coyote story. Immediately after the war, Miné Okubo published *Citizen 13660* (1946) which, accompanied by drawings, describes her internment, starting at the Santa Anita Racetrack in Tanforan near San Francisco where she was assigned to horse stable 16, stall 50.

Indirection and understatement characterize Hisaye Yamamoto's writing. California-born, she was taken to Poston, Arizona, when she was turning twenty-one; and she started publishing in the Poston *Chronicle*. Her first contribution was a serialized detective story that was set "aboard the last car of the evacuee train," "Death Rides the Rails to Poston." In the middle of a murder mystery, the reader learns about the feelings of the evacuees from Oceanville's Little Tokyo; and the solving of the initial murder ultimately seems less important than Pat Nori's recognition "that since evacuation had become a reality her life had somehow taken on the quality of a dream." After the war, Yamamoto returned to the theme of the camp setting as a background to tales of quiet passion.

"The Legend of Miss Sasagawara" (*Kenyon Review*, 1950) is an interesting attempt to represent the fate of a modernist artist in the detention camp. The first sentence of the story seems to take for granted the reader's knowledge of the setting: "Even in that unlikely place of wind, sand, and heat, it was easy to imagine Miss Sasagawara a decorative ingredient of some ballet." Slowly, the precise meaning of the place comes into focus: block 33, "this Japanese evacuation camp in Arizona," or, about Miss Sasagawara and her father: "They were occupying one end of the Block's lone empty barracks, which had not been chopped up yet into the customary four apartments." The first-person narrator is a waitress, and the heroine, who refuses to act normal, remains mysterious, refracted only in the reactions of others; and they tend to consider her crazy. Only later does the narrator find a poem by Mari Sasagawara, published in a poetry magazine. "It was a *tour de force*, erratically brilliant and, through the first readings, tantalizingly obscure."

In Yamamoto's story, "Yoneko's Earthquake" (1951), another particularly sensitive female internee reacts to the experience with more terror than the others, the crisis here coming with an earthquake:

The others soon oriented themselves to the catastrophe with philosophy, saying how fortunate they were to live in the country where the peril was less than in the city and going as far as to regard the period as a sort of vacation from work, with their enforced alfresco existence a sort of camping trip. They tried to bring Yoneko to partake of this pleasant outlook, but she, shivering with each new quiver, looked on them as dreamers who refused to see things as they really were.

The situation of Japanese Americans was extreme, calling for later presidential apologies and for the rare case of governmental reparations. Many other ethnic groups were also pitted against each other, making harmonious dreams of a "common ground" somewhat difficult to realize. A 1938 survey, for example, showed that a majority of Americans believed that Jews themselves were at least partly to blame for the treatment they received in Nazi Germany. The African American *Pittsburgh Courier* warned its readers in 1936 of the many Italian Americans who were secretly Mussolini sympathizers and racists. Many Italian Americans and German Americans were also interned during the war. And while Victory records and the American Forces Network began to use swing – black and white – as if it were the national music, racial segregation was still the dominant ethnic model in place in the U.S.: interracial marriage was prohibited in more than half of the states and, three quarters of a century after the end of slavery, black voting rights remained severely restricted. In William Gardner Smith's novel *The Last of the Conquerors* (1948), which focuses on the interracial love story of the black G.I. Dawkins and the German woman Ilse, a German character says that when he was a prisoner of war in Virginia, the black American soldiers who guarded the white Germans were not permitted to eat in the same restaurant where the Germans ate. During World War II, fought in the name of democracy against an axis of racist, fascist dictatorships, blood banks of the American Red Cross carried separate blood for the black soldiers fighting for democracy, a public health policy that eerily literalized the metaphor of "black" and "white" blood which Toomer had questioned so memorably. "Hitler could hardly desire more," Langston Hughes commented, for the Red Cross had "failed thirteen million Negroes on the home front, and its racial policies [were] a blow in the face of American Negro morale." Richard Wright cited the existence of separate blood banks in the war as one reason why he left the United States to settle permanently in France in 1946. Such paradoxes led to the "double victory" campaign (at home and abroad), as ethnic intellectuals (like Du Bois) put their finger on prevailing American hypocrisies and helped to provide the momentum for the sea change in American race relations starting with *Brown v. Board of Education* in 1954 and with the end of racially based immigration restrictions in the 1960s.

Delmore Schwartz's short story "A Bitter Farce" (*Kenyon Review*, 1946) vividly portrays some of the ironies that complicated the issues of race and national unity in the situation of teaching during World War II. The story is set in 1943. A young Jewish instructor teaches English composition both to a group of Navy students, some of whom have been in the Pacific war, and to a class of girls. The boys, many of them Southern, talk with their teacher about current events, the existence of a secret weapon, Hitler, the Detroit race riots and so forth, but the toughest question a student asks the teacher is the sudden, "would you marry a Negro woman?" Mr. Fish is thinking of saying that "he would marry any woman to whom he made love because otherwise his children might be illegitimate," hoping that this might "touch both the sense of honor and the memory of experience in some of them." Yet anticipating the giggles and smirks that might accompany the mentioning of sexual intercourse in class, Fish wonders what to do. Answering in the affirmative would make him lose faith with his students; but saying no would mean that he shared their belief in social inequality. After evading the question with the statement that he has not been introduced to any Negroes, he finally answers, and though he appears calm, "his inner being was suddenly full of fear and trembling": "I would not marry a Negro woman, . . . but there are many white women whom I would not marry for the same reasons that I would not marry a Negro woman. Thus it is not a question of discrimination against the Negro race." Though the answer goes over well, he realizes that his students must think that his reply meant that he "would not marry many white as well as Negro women because he was a Jew."

Teaching in the different ambience of the "passive, polite and docile" girls in which Fish finds conferences with individual students most fruitful, a blonde and blue-eyed student gives him a journal entry in which three girls discuss the question, "If you had to marry one of them, which of these would you choose, a Chinaman, a Jew, or a Negro?" And the deliberation of the question reiterates familiar stereotypes, such as "Jews have managed to wangle themselves into good positions and make money," and leads two of the girls to choose the Chinese, allies in the war. Fish is so amazed that he chooses to talk about form, as he attempted to do when he told the Navy class "we had better return to the difference between the use of the semicolon and the comma. It is possible . . . that the absence of a comma may result in the death of a man – " only to be interrupted. Now, after commending the girl for drawing on her own feelings, he offers her stylistic advice: "You ought not to use such a colloquialism as 'wangled' in a piece of writing." After this formal approach, he states that he need not comment on the content, yet adds that the Chinese also were despised, at least on the Pacific Coast.

Back in the Navy class the topic is Louis Adamic's "Plymouth Rock and Ellis Island" with its hope for the "American dream" of a "universal culture, a pan-human culture, such as had never before existed on the globe." Fish feels it necessary to offer a criticism of Adamic: "What Adamic has to say is true, in part; but we ought also to remember that if America has always been the land of liberty, it has also been the land of persecution and the land where everyone feared that he was a stranger or was conscious of a fear of the stranger." Fish expands Adamic's formula to describe America as "the land of liberty and of persecution," using the Los Angeles zoot-suit riots as an example. This encourages an Irish student who disagrees with Adamic to say that "something is wrong with a lot of Jews." In a long dialogue between teacher and student, Fish raises the question that goes to the heart of preconceptions on the basis of ethnicity, "Can a moral act be inherited?" Race prejudice "is a denial of the freedom of the will and of moral responsibility." At the end of the class, the Irish student wants to reassure the Jewish teacher that he has nothing against him personally, but also complains, "They shouldn't have put such essays in the textbook. They're troublemakers."

Schwartz's amusing story illuminates how explosive the topic of inter-marriage was and what obstacles Adamic's "nation of nations" faced, even in the middle of the wartime effort of unifying the country.

The confrontation with totalitarianism affected not only American political self-understanding and the new, more positive stress on ethnic pluralism but also the fate of modernism and jazz, which were increasingly presented as proto-typically democratic and quintessentially American art forms in the period of the greatest political opposition of the United States to totalitarianism, the years of World War II and of the Cold War.

Juliana Force's 1934 confrontation at the Venice Biennale and Alfred Barr's 1936 MoMA exhibition on *Cubism and Modern Art* were character-ized by the ideological conflicts of the moment. As we saw, Force's Whitney Museum-based and exceptionally modernist display at the American pavilion ran into difficulties with Hearst's scheming and the Italian fascist authorities; and Barr fell foul of New York's customs officials who did not want to accept cubist works as art but merely as matter. Force developed a multiethnic and cosmopolitan rationale for modern American art as the result of "the fusion of different races and nationalities" that made American art the truly international one and also marked an implicit contrast with the fascist ideal of "racial purity." Barr emphasized the term "abstract art," a phrase that had been used occasionally around the time of the Armory Show, but that came into common use only in the 1930s and 1940s. Barr's exhibition catalogue defined the term "abstract" as a welcome modernist break with a long artistic tradition characterized by "nature" and "imitation," and praised the "more adventurous and original artists" for being "driven to abandon the imitation of natural appearance."

Yet Barr also included a section on abstract art and politics which mentioned that Lenin dismissed experimental art and literature as "the infantile disorder of Leftism" and that the National Socialists considered the art of the Weimar Republic *Kunstbolschewismus*; in short, abstract art was, as Barr put it understatedly, "discouraged" by both totalitarian regimes. Hence he concluded that the 1936 cubist "exhibition might well be dedicated to those painters of squares and circles... who have suffered at the hands of philistines with political power." Modernism was at odds with totalitarianism.

But was American modernism antitotalitarian? The belief that it was helped the growing official sanctioning of modernism in the United States, but it was a belief difficult to reconcile with the example of such prominent modernists as Ezra Pound. What may have given rise to this notion was nothing inherent in Force's fusion-of-races America or in Barr's squares-and-circles modernism, but the political developments in the two totalitarian countries to which Barr alluded. What ultimately may have proved decisive was not any particular action undertaken by modernist writers and artists, but the aesthetic choices that were made official doctrines by totalitarian governments; and these choices can be described quite simply: in the 1930s, totalitarianism turned antimodernist.

In the 1920s and 1930s, the course of the official aesthetic of the Soviet Union changed to the new antimodernist order signaled by Lenin's dismissal of modernism and cemented by Stalin's official propagation of the exclusive aesthetic of socialist realism and, simultaneously, the banning of jazz, first in the Soviet Union and later in all communist countries. The writer Maxim Gorky was central to both those developments. His essay "On the Music of the Gross," or "the Degenerate," as the English translator put it, was published in 1928 in no less an organ than *Pravda* and soon became the backbone of

Stalinist repression of jazz music as exploitative, vulgar, sexualized, animalistic, threatening, and degenerate. Gorky heard the music, "a fox-trot executed by a negro-orchestra," as follows:

One, two, three, ten, twenty strokes, and after them, like a mud ball splashing into clear water, a wild whistle screeches; and then there are rumblings, wails and howls like the snorting of a metal pig, the shriek of a donkey, or the amorous croaking of a monstrous frog. This insulting chaos of insanity pulses to a throbbing rhythm. Listening for a few minutes to these wails, one involuntarily imagines an orchestra of sexually driven madmen conducted by a man-stallion brandishing a huge genital member.

The instruments seemed equally monstrous to Gorky who complained, for example, that "the saxophone emits its quacking nasal sound." Among the effects the music, disseminated by radio, was having on the white middle class were, Gorky actually seemed to believe, obesity and homosexuality of epidemic proportions, as the master class was turning toward the barbarism of jazz that America's oppressed Negroes had been leaving behind. Jazz was "bourgeois," a sign of deep "decadence" from the pinnacle of musical developments such as Mozart or Beethoven. It was an opiate and a tool of capitalist control. It seems hard to believe that such a biased and paranoid little vignette should have formed the theoretical backbone for the official Soviet policy toward jazz; but soon after the publication of this article, its tenets were reiterated by the Commissar for Public Enlightenment Anatoly Lunacharsky, and the prohibition of jazz and much black popular music in communist countries was the ultimate result.

Similarly, the term "socialist realism," which first appeared in the Soviet Union in 1932, became official doctrine in 1934 after Gorky delivered a programmatic speech to the First All-Union Congress of Soviet Writers, in which he envisioned "a new direction essential to us – socialist realism, which can be created only from the data of socialist experience." Realism was the appropriate method of exposing capitalism, affirming, in an optimistic spirit, the advances of socialism, and of educating the proletariat to realize its revolutionary potential. "Socialist realism affirms being as action, as creation, whose aim is the uninterrupted development of each person's most valuable qualities so as to attain victory over the forces of nature, man's health and long life, and the great happiness of living on earth," Gorky proclaimed somewhat mystically. Gorky, the famous author of works like the autobiographical trilogy beginning with *My Childhood* (1913), who had early on polemicized against capitalist leisure culture at Coney Island, thus appears to have been the single intellectual who formulated both the attack on jazz and the advocacy of realism as central features of Soviet art policy, features that remained in place until the Gorbachev era.

This did not make Gorky any less popular among writers and intellectuals in the United States. One would expect this from Mike Gold, who liked to be seen as "the American Gorky," but not from the most eminent jazz poet of the period, Langston Hughes. Yet Hughes reported cheerily how, during his train travels through Kazakhstan, he participated in a 1932 celebration honoring the fortieth anniversary of Gorky's literary career, sending "a telegram to Comrade Gorky from the passengers of the train, and another from [Hughes's] Negro group." Hughes may simply not have known Gorky's position on jazz, though Gorky's diatribe was published – without rebuttals – in Marie Budberg's English translation, in the December 1928 issue of the avant-garde *Dial*, a few pages after a contribution by Jean Toomer. In Kunitz's *Twentieth-Century Authors* (1942), Hurston listed Maxim Gorky among her favorite authors: did she – an eager student of black music, who in 1941 wrote that while she was not a joiner she saw "many good points" in the Communist Party, but who also was to launch violent attacks on African American communists in the *American Legion Magazine* of the Cold War years of 1950 and 1951 – know that Gorky was one of the Stalinist architects of socialist realism and the intellectual who had laid the cornerstone for the Soviet ban on jazz?

Though it was "racially" sanctioned rather than motivated by political theory, the defining act of the official Nazi aesthetic in the 1930s was surprisingly similar to that which had just emerged in the Soviet Union: a ban on jazz and on modernist art and literature accompanied by an official endorsement of realism. The covers to notorious exhibition guides from the 1930s illustrate this point.

The guidebook for the "Degenerate Music" show in Düsseldorf 1938 had a specially designed cover page on which a stereotyped saxophone-playing black appears wearing a Star of David. "Niggerjazz" – this was the official term – was not permitted to be broadcast on the radio in Nazi Germany, and it was officially dismissed as music stemming from a "sick mental disposition" which could only be "found interesting by snobs who are aloof from the people"; characterized by the "prominence of the saxophone which alone carries the tune while all other instruments grotesquely emphasize the rhythm." The saxophone, the signature instrument of a U.S. president half a century later, thus seems to have enjoyed communist as well as fascist censure.

Although Goebbels, the Nazi minister of propaganda, had published the novel *Michael* (1931) in which great and effusive admiration was voiced for Van Gogh's experimental art, the Nazi dismissal of modernist art was comprehensive, unambiguous, and articulated by the highest authority, for it was Hitler who proclaimed at a Nuremberg Party rally in 1935 that decades of a "Jewish regime" of modernism would now come to an end:

> What reveals itself to us as the so-called "cult of the primitive" is not the expression of a naïve, uncorrupted soul but of a thoroughly corrupt and sick degeneracy. He who wishes to exculpate the paintings and sculptures – to take only a particularly crass example – of our Dadaists, Cubists, and Futurists or imaginary Impressionists has obviously no comprehension of the task of art, which is not to remind man of the symptoms of his degeneracy but rather to oppose symptoms of degeneracy by showing what is eternally healthy and beautiful.

In Hitler's view, the German people had long outgrown the primitiveness of such artistic barbarians and in the present time did not only "reject this nonsense but consider[ed] its manufacturers to be either charlatans or madmen." And he added authoritatively and menacingly: "we do not intend to let them loose on the people any longer." The ostracizing and banning of "racially inferior, sick, and Jewish-bolshevist art" was the consequence.

The "Degenerate Art" show in Munich 1937 used as the cover of the exhibition guide a reproduction of the African-inspired primitivist sculpture *The New Man* by Otto Freundlich. The consequences of this prominent exposure were terrible: Freundlich, one of the pioneering practitioners of abstract art and founders of an international "abstraction-création" group, was killed in the concentration camp Majdanek in 1943. At the opening of the "Degenerate Art" show, Hitler explicitly condemned "Cubism, Dadaism, Futurism, Impressionism, Expressionism" as "completely worthless for the German people." Photographs of the exhibition show men in uniforms inspecting paintings such as Emil Nolde's *Mulattin* (The Mulatto, 1913) under a banner that reads: "The niggerizing of music and theater as well as the niggerizing of the visual arts was intended to uproot the racial instinct of the people and to tear down blood barriers." All Jews were considered *inherently* the producers of "degenerate art," and politically antifascist artists like George Grosz were predictably banned; but too modernist a style or too racially charged a theme could also make apolitical "Aryan" artists "degenerate" in Nazi eyes – including the painter Emil Nolde who had joined the Nazi Party as early as 1920 and wanted desperately to be accepted by the Party, but who was exhibited as degenerate nonetheless. He simply did not understand why he was expelled from the Prussian Academy of Arts in 1933. Nolde's "Mulatto" painting was undesirable to the Nazis because of its modernist style as well as its theme; for the very title seemed to endorse (or at least represent) the racial mingling that, inspired by eugenicists in the United States, the National Socialists so vehemently opposed in the name of "racial purity."

While jazz and modernist art were considered "degenerate" in Nazi Germany and "bourgeois decadent" in the Stalinist Soviet Union, ideologues in both countries espoused realism as the more appropriate art form. In Russia the term "socialist realism" became the catchword for "progressive" art in official terminology as well as in government- (and terror-) sanctioned policy, whereas in Germany realist art was praised as being "healthy" and "close to the beauty ideal of the people" – with equally brutal consequences for those who dared to deviate.

It was the fact that realist doctrine prevailed so virulently and violently in two totalitarian countries that gave an altogether new life and significance to modernism in the United States. In the 1930s one could still observe a turning away from modernism toward realism. Force and Barr were hardly in central positions of cultural authority in the United States; they were merely making arguments that seemed widely compelling only later. The change came around 1939, as the possibility of a second world war grew.

Ironically, it was one of the employees of the U.S. Customs Service that had so annoyed Barr, who developed what was to become perhaps the most widely adopted rationale for modernism in America – though it was only one of many similar interventions. The young intellectual's name was Clement Greenberg, and his 1939 essay "Avant-Garde and Kitsch" was only his second publication. He knew Harold Rosenberg, who was then the art director for the WPA's *American Guide* series and who introduced him to the artists' circle at the Hans Hofmann School. Dwight Macdonald invited Greenberg to write for the initially communist and recently Trotskyist-reborn *Partisan Review*, and Greenberg submitted the essay in 1939, just before he left for a two-month trip to Europe. The piece was at first rejected by Dwight Macdonald who was dissatisfied "because of its unsupported & large generalizations," an assessment that made Greenberg "furious." When it was published after revisions, "Avant-Garde and Kitsch" became a landmark essay that was included in the *Partisan Reader*, reprinted in Britain and the United States, and discussed very widely as a prophetic argument in favor of abstract expressionism. It also established Greenberg as an authority on modern art.

Greenberg's essay began with the serious pronouncement that popular and high art had bifurcated in modern America: "One and the same civilization produces simultaneously two such different things as a poem by T. S. Eliot and a Tin Pan Alley song, or a painting by Braque and a *Saturday Evening Post* cover." Similarly, who could put a poem by Eliot and a poem by once-famous radio poet Eddie Guest "in an enlightening relation to each other?" The poles which Greenberg establishes as opposites ultimately settle around the terms *avant-garde* ("the only form of living culture we now have" though it is endangered) and the "ersatz culture" of *Kitsch* ("popular, commercial art and literature with their chromotypes, magazine covers, illustrations, ads, slick and pulp fiction, comic, Tin Pan Alley music, tap dancing, Hollywood movies, etc. etc."). Predictably, the *Saturday Evening Post* is pure kitsch. But there are also stages in-between; for example, "a magazine like the *New Yorker*, which is fundamentally high-class kitsch for the luxury trade, converts and waters down a great deal of avant-garde material for its own uses." And there are borderline authors like Steinbeck. But the situation has reached global proportions so that "the Chinaman, no less than the South American Indian, the Hindu, no less than the Polynesian, have come to prefer to their native art magazine covers, rotogravure sections and calendar girls." As the popular support of kitsch has grown, the opposition to modern art has taken on a decidedly political aspect, too.

If kitsch is the official tendency of culture in Germany, Italy and Russia, it is not because their respective governments are controlled by philistines, but because kitsch is the culture of the masses in these countries, as it is everywhere else. The encouragement of kitsch is merely another of the inexpensive ways in which totalitarian regimes seek to ingratiate themselves with their subjects . . . the main trouble with avant-garde art and literature, from the point of view of Fascists and Stalinists, is not that they are too critical, but that they are too "innocent," that it is too difficult to inject effective propaganda into them, that kitsch is more pliable to this end. Kitsch keeps a dictator in closer contact with the "soul" of the people.

Hence it was a matter of expediency and not of an inevitable, inner ideological affinity of realism and totalitarianism that made the fit appropriate at the moment, Greenberg argues: "Nevertheless, if the masses were conceivably to ask for avant-garde art and literature, Hitler, Mussolini and Stalin would not hesitate long in attempting to satisfy such a demand."

What Greenberg's essay did was not only to develop a sense of populist–totalitarian conformism associated with mass art of kitsch, but also to suggest the danger that kitsch posed to capitalist America. The strong implication was that given the political context of the period, only the avant-garde art of Eliot, Picasso, and even of the modernist poet and one-time Nazi sympathizer Gottfried Benn, presented hope for resistance. From the point of view of anti-Stalinist socialists as embodied by *Partisan Review*, modernism alone seemed ready to resist the incorporating logic of both totalitarian state art and of capitalist consumer culture.

There were connections between the antipopulists of the *Partisan Review* group and of the Frankfurt School, now in exile as the "Institute for Social Research in New York City." Symptomatic was the Institute's 1941 collective research project entitled "Cultural Aspects of National Socialism" which proposed to determine "the factors that prepared public opinion for authoritarianism prior to the advent of political power," including the "non-political section of the daily press, the illustrated magazines, and the popular biographies," all of which "may play a considerable role in transforming independent men into beings ready to surrender their individual rights." Though focused on Germany, the project rationale emphasized that "American democracy may not be entirely beyond this danger." A part of Theodor W. Adorno's contribution was to undertake psychological as well as sociological analysis of the violent reactions voiced by large sections of the German middle classes against features of what they termed "modernism," such as the putative distortion of the human face by radical painters, dissonance in music, the flat roof, and even jazz.

The attempts by Frankfurt School and New York intellectuals to cast modernism in this way – and in addition as an ally in the struggle against racial segregation – were surprisingly successful. Gold had once claimed that "Stein did not care to communicate because essentially there was nothing to communicate," – and in the context of proletarian writing, this had been a devastating critique. Now, in the hands of Greenberg or Adorno, the refusal to communicate could become the central achievement of an artist, and a sign of his or her resistance to the ideologies of the market – and of the ultimate fascist and Stalinist panderers. This was a position that seemed all the more plausible because it mirrored, and was mirrored by, the shriller tone of totalitarian aesthetics.

In 1947, for example, Vladimir Kemenov officially condemned artists like Georgia O'Keeffe as reactionaries, combining an exegesis of Marx with indignation at comparatively mild sexual aspects. Kemenov also excoriated Picasso and Jacques Lipchitz, two artists who had portrayed Stein. "The basic features of decadent bourgeois art are its falseness, its belligerent anti-realism, its hostility to objective knowledge and to the truthful portrayal of life in art." He contrasted "contemporary mystical and pathological art which reflects the spiritual slough of the contemporary reactionary bourgeoisie" with the "new form of realistic art which is completely popular" that Soviet artists had created. Kemenov also stressed that the focus on "abstract art" was very new, citing a 1943 study of American painting that still concluded that the mass of American artists had been "unaffected by modernism." But by 1947, *Life* and the United States Information Service publication *America* were propagating modernism, a sign that it was advancing to a status of capitalist state art.

The debate had become part of the Cold War, and attacks like Kemenov's only had the effect of strengthening the American resolve to recast modernism as the art of democracy. In that process, the opinions of a small group of intellectuals came to affect government policy and decision-making processes on many levels of the cultural apparatus. The Committee for Cultural Freedom sponsored concerts by modern composers whose work had been banned by Hitler or Stalin, and in some cases, like Alban Berg's, prohibited by both.

In 1951, the State Department paid for a production of Gertrude Stein and Virgil Thomson's opera *Four Saints in Three Acts*, the work that had mystified reviewers in 1934. The fact that Stein chose an all-Negro cast in 1934 seemed questionable then, but by 1951 the organizers' official correspondence stressed that "for psychological reasons the entire cast of *Four Saints* should be American Negro: to counter the 'suppressed race' propaganda and forestall all criticisms to the effect that we had to use foreign negroes because we wouldn't let our own 'out.'" The production starred Leontyne Price.

The official press release that accompanies the 1951 modern art exhibition curated by former MoMA director James Johnson Sweeney announced the show (with works by Matisse, Derain, Cézanne, Seurat, Chagall, Kandinsky from American collections) as a self-evident argument for freedom of the arts: "On display will be works that could not have been created nor whose exhibition would be allowed by such totalitarian regimes as Nazi Germany or present-day Soviet Russia and her satellites, as has been evidenced in those governments' labeling as 'degenerate' or 'bourgeois' of many of the paintings and sculptures included." This was quite compatible with the way in which Eisenhower would see things at the 25th anniversary of MoMA in 1954. Congressman Dondero with his long diatribe against modernism (cited here in the introduction) had no political effect, for he sounded as if he were echoing Hitler or sharing Stalin's artistic taste. In this context, supporting modernism came to seem mere common sense.

Even Hollywood cartoons reflected the change toward modernism and jazz. In 1939, the typical cartoonist working for the Schlesinger studio was described in *Exposure Sheet* as a high-school-educated person who "thinks Norman Rockwell" is "tops" and who has "no use for Picasso, Van Gogh, Renoir, or any of those 'futuristic guys.'" Yet in 1951, the painter Eyvind Earle joined Disney and received credit for extraordinarily experimental background painting in the ambitious Goofy short *For Whom the Bulls Toll*. Bob Clampett's *Coal Black and the Sebben Dwarfs* (Warner Brothers, 1943), with a black cast, was famously set to the music of Duke Ellington's *Jump for Joy*, but was marred by the employment of controversial black-face stereotypes and drew protests from the NAACP.

Modernism seeped into popular culture (supposedly its kitschy opposite) on many fronts. On August 8, 1949, *Life* famously carried an illustrated story on Jackson Pollock. In *Vogue* of March 5, 1951, one could admire fashion models in front of Pollock backdrops. In March 1954 *House and Garden* carried ads for African masks at five dollars each, postage paid, by a mail-order company in Ohio.

Modern American authors, including Faulkner and James T. Farrell, were promoted abroad by U.S. Government agencies; and their works were exported and translated. The Cold War constellation gave artists and intellectuals a central role in the ideological confrontation. In Richard Wright's novel *The Outsider* (1953), the protagonist Cross Damon

marveled at the astuteness of both Communist and Fascist politicians who had banned the demonic contagions of jazz. And now, too, he could understand why the Communists, instead of shooting the capitalists and bankers as they had so ardently sworn that they would do when they came to power, made instead with blood in their eyes straight for the school teachers, priests, writers, artists, poets, musicians, and the deposed bourgeois governmental rulers as the men who held for them the deadliest of threats to their keeping and extending their power.

Avant-garde artists and educators, intellectuals mattered in this world. The very fact that works had been banned (or were still banned) meant that they were important; and American intellectuals and artists played a state-supported role which they have not regained in later years.

❦

What the story of antitotalitarian modernism omitted was the fact that many artists and much writing developed from modernist emergence toward a new realism: Joseph Stella's "Coney Island: Battle Of Lights" (1913) and his many Brooklyn Bridge paintings were followed by Catholic neorealist (or magical-realist) art representing the Virgin or the Nativity; and Max Weber's famous stage (around 1915) in which he produced the Duchamp-inspired "Rush Hour, New York" and "Grand Central Terminal" as well as his signature cubist work, the collage-like "Chinese Restaurant," gave way to a new representational phase in which Weber emphasized Jewish, and especially Hasidic, religious themes in works like "Patriarchs." In the 1930s and 1940s, Stein collected now forgotten realist painters, and in 1933, she published her least modernist book, *The Autobiography of Alice B. Toklas*. Richard Wright toned down his modernist strategies in rewriting "Long Black Song," or in moving on from *Lawd Today* to *Native Son*. The tale of modernist emergence notwithstanding, there was a general strengthening of realism in the 1930s and 1940s. What the tale also omitted was the fact that this new American realism of the 1930s had a strong social focus as an art of political opposition – a feature that was confronted indirectly in associating engaged literature with Stalinism or totalitarianism and stylizing modernism as the true art of resistance.

And it is in this aspect that a conflation was successful: it was the mythical fusion of all stories of modernist emergence, according to which Van Gogh's movement from *The Potato Eaters* to *Starry Night*, or Jackson Pollock's from the Federal Arts Project to abstract expressionism, could be seen as one single story of progress, understood both in aesthetic terms and as the political advance of American democracy. Superimposing the older and newer stories of modernism and making them into one single and somewhat timeless modern story carried the advantage that this story helped to cast any realism not only as old-fashioned and obsolete but also as inherently linked to totalitarianism. Imagining realism at best as the mold out of which modernism must always emerge, and at worst as the handmaiden of terror, helped to make modernism appear as the truly expressive art of antifascist and anti-Stalinist resistance, as the signature expression of American democracy.

The modernist orthodoxy that arose among New York intellectuals and the Frankfurt School in the 1940s avoided a head-on confrontation with some unpleasant facts. Most prominent among the obstacles to the sacralization of modernism was the fact that Italian fascists, German national socialists, and Soviet communists all had modernist phases, and that (as Adorno himself noted) many high modernists were "reactionaries," some of whom had voiced antisemitic sentiments and were hardly the stalwarts of democracy. And it removed from view the possibility that modernism was also a failure of nerve. For instead of naming nameable political ills, the modernist aesthetic forced readers to contemplate the disappearance of meaning and to accept that we live in a world of futility and the absurd in which aesthetic form is the only theme that matters.

14

❦

FACING THE EXTREME

THE FILM DIRECTOR Joseph Losey once commented on the disillusioning quality of the 1940s and early 1950s: "After Hiroshima, after the death of Roosevelt, after the investigation, only then did one begin to understand the complete unreality of the American dream." How did American writers fictionalize some of the extreme experiences of the 1940s – among them, the Holocaust of the European Jews and the nuclear destruction of the cities of Hiroshima and Nagasaki? How did ethnic writers react at a time when countless people were arrested, tortured, or killed, not for what they had done but for who they were, and when civilians were killed simply for where they were? Were modernist strategies helpful in representing the world of modernity that World War II had so brutally redefined?

World War II seemed to have made true and even surpassed the most nightmarish fears of modernity. The Lithuanian of *The Life Stories* described tourism of fine ladies to Chicago's industrial slaughterhouses. Antin gave an account of a disinfection at the German border. Mike Gold experienced a subway trip as a cattle-car ride. Saroyan imagined death as the subject of advertising slogans. Roth had a vision that drew on one of the highest sources of energy he could imagine. Now, means of transportation like planes and trains had become means of killing. "Streetcars," in soldier slang going back to World War I, meant "heavy long-range shells."

In her last printed essay, "House of the One Father," published in Louis Adamic's journal *Common Ground* (1941), Mary Antin reflected on group af-filiation in a new time of crisis, for the piece appeared just before the full on-slaught of the Holocaust. The SS *Einsatzgruppen* massacred seven thousand Jews in Antin's native Polotzk alone in December 1941. Contemplating Hitler's "object lesson on the fruits of intolerance" Antin reviewed her own attitudes and practices and questioned her own "divorcement" from Jewish life: "Today I find myself pulled by the old forgotten ties, through the violent projection of an immensely magnified Jewish problem. It is one thing to go your separate way, leaving your friends and comrades behind in peace and prosperity; it is

another thing to fail to remember them when the world is casting them out."
Yet this sense of solidarity did not mean for Antin that it was easy or even
possible to return to "her people" or her past.

> I can no more return to the Jewish fold than I can return to my mother's womb;
> neither can I in decency continue to enjoy my accidental personal immunity from the
> penalties of being a Jew in a time of virulent anti-Semitism. The least I can do, in my
> need to share the sufferings of my people, is declare that I am as one of them.
>
> Here, in my own case, is a hint of the historic tragedy of the individual Jew whose
> nature is to lose himself in universal relationships, but who is driven back into some
> Ghetto without walls by the action of anti-Semitism. God helping, I shall not let
> myself be stampeded.

In fact it was on freedom of thought and of association that she now based a
broader sense of group loyalty:

> Humbly, respectful of those who feel called to that bitter labor, I shall no more spend
> myself in defense of the Jew on sectarian or folk lines, except incidentally, as my
> knowledge of things Jewish may illumine a given situation. Not to dissociate myself
> from the Jewish lot, but to establish the more unassailable bond, I here declare that
> the point where I come to life as a member of modern society, where my fullest sense
> of responsibility is kindled, is deep below the ache and horror of the Jewish dilemma,
> at the juncture of social forces where I see the persecution or belittlement of a group –
> *any* group, whether of race, creed, or color – as an attack on democracy.

Antin's wish for responsible, democratic group membership included the
individual's right to express solidarity with the persecuted of any group while
maintaining a freethinking person's entitlement to refuse to be stampeded into
some "Ghetto without walls." Antin's assertion of bonds was based on past
experience with "things Jewish" and a modern sense of democratic humanism
and universalism, not on what she termed "sectarian or folk lines." Antin died
in 1949, and this was her last published word.

Also in 1949, Jean Toomer, who had by then become a Quaker, delivered the William Penn lecture in Philadelphia, entitled "The Flavor of Man."
In his published address Toomer reflected upon some serious issues of the
times. Starting in a light vein, he related a seed catalogue listing for a mysterious "crystal apple," described as an "amazingly attractive cucumber, perfectly
round, crystal-white at all stages, with a sweetness and lack of cucumber flavor
that is remarkable." Toomer considered this "typical of twentieth-century
man," ingeniously producing a cucumber that isn't a cucumber. And similarly
bread had lost the flavor of bread. That modern America was relatively flavor-
less had been observed by many immigrant and ethnic writers before, starting
with the Greek peddler from *The Life Stories* who complained about American
tomatoes. Toomer also struck an environmentalist note when he found that

water no longer tasted like water, for American streams had deteriorated. "The air of our cities is becoming smog," and "our literature" is "without the flavor of literature." Commenting on the Cold War and World War II, he continued: "Outstanding at this time is the fact that we have peace without the flavor of peace. But the wars we wage have the full horrible flavor of war. The bombs we make are not Crystal Apples." A little later he took a billboard as the point of departure for another commentary: "As I ride into Philadelphia the train stops at a station near which is a building bearing in large letters this sign: Wrecks Our Specialty. It refers to motor-cars. I am thinking of human beings." Now Toomer asked his listeners to remember the human wrecks "by the millions" of "so-called peace-time society," in slums, hospitals, and poorhouses, as well as the wrecks of wartime society which abound all over the world as do the "mutilated bodies of countless thousands" that are "buried out of sight." Focusing on the wrecks in a Pennsylvania institution for the insane, Toomer quoted an investigator who compared the patients' grim situation with "the pictures of the Nazi concentration camps at Belsen and Buchenwald." Toomer extended and universalized this strong parallel: "So many of our kinsmen are in asylums so-called, in ghettos, in concentration camps and colonies, and in some high places, critically reduced below the par of man. Does it matter that some have white bodies, some black, that some are Jews, some Gentiles, some Republicans, some Democrats? It matters that they are human." And contemplating the fact that "the rulers of the two most powerful nations of the world are contemplating and preparing for – or, as they would say, preparing against – a war that may indeed end war by ending man," Toomer dramatically described the "desperate race between education and catastrophe." "The alternatives, I am convinced, are starkly these: Transcendence or extinction."

Antin and Toomer were part of the turn toward universalism that seemed to be the first lesson of World War II drawn by those who did reflect on it. Stressing ethnicity had been part of the problem, and the time had come to emphasize our common humanity.

Another strategy was indirection, either by a passing reference or by willful omission. Martha Foley's collection, *The Best American Short Stories of 1944*, for example, includes contributions by Saul Bellow, Shirley Jackson, Carson McCullers, Leon Zurmelian, Lionel Trilling, and others. In a few stories, there are hints of the extremities of World War II. Brooklyn-born Irwin Shaw's "The Veterans Reflect" includes a long interior monologue of a man who is approaching the Swiss border: "Today his name was known in every home on the face of the earth, in every jungle . . . Thirty million people had died earlier than they expected because of him and hundreds of cities were leveled to the ground because of him." What is revealed only later is that "he" is Hitler.

The narrator of Russian émigré Vladimir Nabokov's story "That in Aleppo Once..." reports in a single sentence that he heard that those among the Russian refugees in France

who chanced to have Jewish blood talk of their doomed kinsmen crammed into hell-bound trains; and my own plight, by contrast, acquired a commonplace air of irreality while I sat in some crowded café with the milkly blue sea in front of me and a shell-hollow murmur behind telling and retelling the tale of massacre and misery, and the gray paradise beyond the ocean, and the ways and whims of harsh consuls.

Dorothy Canfield (Fisher)'s "The Knot Hole" is set among prisoners traveling in a crowded box-car to France only to be returned to Germany. After a frame narrative the account starts in a Kafkaesque manner: "I thought it was probably by accident that I was among those in the box-car. I never knew why I was. Perhaps there had been room – if you can call it room – for one more."

A good example for a framing of a novel so as to exclude direct representation is Isaac Bashevis Singer's *The Family Moskat*, which appeared in English in 1950 after being serialized in Yiddish in the *Jewish Daily Forward* for two years. It offers a three-generation family story that ends just as World War II has started and the German bombs hit Warsaw. While Singer thus made the choice to stop short just before the Warsaw ghetto years and the Holocaust, the knowledge of what is about to happen after the novel ends informs the whole book, from the topography of the streets that are not yet disrupted by the ghetto wall to the novel's last words, uttered by Hertz Yanovar in clarification of his prophecy, in Polish, that "the Messiah will come soon." "Death is the Messiah. That's the real truth." And here the novel ends.

Singer also draws an analogy between the experience of residential bombing and modernism:

On Zlota Street they came across a bombed house. From it issued an odor of whitewash, coal, gas, and smoking cinders. The front of the house had collapsed; a ceiling lay sloping above a pile of bricks, plaster, and glass. They made out the interior of rooms, with their beds, tables, and pictures. Asa Heshel was reminded of modernist theater settings.

Had the grim realities of World War II surpassed the wildest modernist nightmares?

The novel starts with the arrival of Reb Meshulam in Warsaw: "From time to time a red-painted tramcar rumbled by, the electric wires overhead giving off crackling blue sparks." The Warsaw streets that the characters traverse in Singer's novel had already become lines of imprisonment; the ghetto streetcar with the Jewish star and the horsedrawn omnibuses in the walled-in ghetto had become associated with the genocide of Warsaw's Jewry. The train station that is the setting for the arrival in the city had become the transfer to the killing center at Treblinka. Yet in 1950 Singer, who had grown up in Warsaw and left it only in the 1930s when he emigrated to New York, chose to be silent about, to imply rather than to represent, what was to follow after the end of his novel.

In this respect Singer's *Family Moskat* is radically different from John Hersey's novel of the same year, *The Wall* (1950), which offers a full-fledged representation of life in Jewish Warsaw from the forced establishment of the Jewish Council by the Nazi occupation authorities to the closing of the ghetto and the mass deportations to Treblinka. Told in the form of a found document, Noach Levinson's archive, the novel is written as if it were an English translation from a Yiddish original, with editorial annotations. A day-by-day, dated and annotated account of experiences and reflections in the Warsaw ghetto, *The Wall* is perhaps the first American novel to confront the Holocaust fully and centrally. It is not anachronistic to use the word "Holocaust," for Hersey employs it to describe the genocide of European Jews, perhaps as the first novelist to do so: when a couple discusses whether or not a baby prematurely born in a hidden basement in 1943 should be circumcised, the father thinks "that circumcision would be folly in the time of an anti-Jewish holocaust," while the mother disagrees and Noach Levinson adds that "at one point Spinoza considered circumcision alone sufficient to keep the Jewish nation alive."

Levinson registers external events and emotions, small details and momentous occurrences in his archive, and the book focuses closely on a small group of individuals who respond variously to the terror of the Warsaw ghetto. Levinson is close to the socialist Hashomer group, but the political divisions as well as the character differences are described in detail. The communists, for example, have a very hard time making sense of Stalin's policy in 1939–40. Some figures rise to small and large acts of heroism, but Hersey also depicts a young man who asks his own parents to agree to be deported so that he can save his own life. Before "Jews are barred from trolleys and buses," Rachel Apt takes "long, idle walks and streetcar rides outside the Jewish section – along the Vistula, to Saxon Garden, to Pototzki Palace, past the Bristol and the Europejski Hotels, even to the suburbs, Praga and Zoliborz and Brudno. It was as if she were trying to memorize the Polish parts of her city, the Polish parts of her life." As the wall is being built, Levinson describes it in such precise detail that the official explanation of it being an "epidemicwall" becomes absurd: "This wall is actually intended to keep human beings from passing." Yet his inner reaction puzzles him also: "We will be together, without the constant, sandy rub of life among the Poles and Germans. . . . I *am* glad."

The cumulative effect of different measures is not easily recognizable as part
of a plan. When the "resettlements" begin, a pattern emerges: whatever the
people around Levinson find out is worse than they could possibly have feared.
One chilling turning point is when Slonim goes on a mission to determine
where the cattle trains are going. He discovers the truth about Treblinka, and
the underground socialist broadside *Storm* reports his findings in a way that
actually assumes that the reader already knows – but is reluctant to believe.
Hersey does not simply reproduce the report, but creates a staccato, a modernist
effect by showing fragments of the report as Rachel Apt reads them, for the
words "seemed to jump and jerk before her eyes; she could scarcely credit the
snatches as she saw them."

> ... *three blank-walled rooms, about two meters high, area 25 square meters, with a narrow
> corridor fronting all three... pipes with valves... outside, curious scoops reminding one of ship
> ventilators... power room at one end... hermetic seals around the doors and at the scoops and
> valves... floors with terra-cotta inlay which moisture renders very slippery....*
>
>   *... was especially struck by the irony of the classification sign in the first enclosure – Tailors,
> Hatmakers, Carpenters, Road-builders, and so on – tending to make the Jews believe they were
> to be sorted for labor farther east... kindly speech by a gentle-looking* S.S. *officer:...* After the
> bath and disinfection, this property will be returned to you in accordance with your
> receipts... *along the path naked, carrying a small piece of soap and his documents... about 15
> minutes... are carried by the Jewish auxiliary, led by* Kapos *whose identification is a yellow
> patch at the knee, to the cemetery... and this duty, according to the escaped* Kapo *interviewed by
> our courier in a hut a few kilometers south of Malkinia, is trying in the extreme... covered over
> by bulldozers, the exhausts of whose Diesel motors provide the constant music of Treblinka....*

When Levinson hears the the debates as to whether the Slonim account is
"true," "accurate," "exaggerated," "a calculated attempt by the Socialists to
create panic," and even ... "totally imaginary – a sick fantasy!", he worries,
"if there is apathy and incredulity right here, what must there be, what will
there not be forever and ever, at the untouched ends of the earth, in Melbourne,
in Rio de Janeiro, in Shanghai, in Chicago?" Now he decides to fight to
preserve his archive as testimony. As the ghetto is reduced in size, workers like
Mordecai have to tear down what they had been forced to build, and Mordecai
feels as if he were in a trick German slow-motion film played backwards.
One of Levinson's entries describes the accelerated living on the brink of
death in staccato, Hemingway-like sentences: "We want to cram as much
as possible into our remaing hours. Appetites are exaggerated. Flirtation is
hurried. Courtship is telescoped. In conversation, even, we come quickly to
the point. We live as if by telegraphy." When people's names at the Jewish
Council are read off, they would say, "*Deported*, or, *Alive*, as the case might be."
The German commander enforces ever higher "resettlement" rates and asks

the Jewish Council for "a tax of one million zlotys *to pay*, he said, *for damage done to railroad stock by Jews while being resettled.*"

As did Singer, Hersey represented the surrealism of the ruins, in *The Wall*, of the burned-out ghetto in May 1943: "This was some other planet. Nothing was left of the part of the ghetto where we were, it seemed, but fires and trash. Dunes of fallen brick were silhouetted against weird little separate sunsets of flame-touched smoke. The streets were only valleys in the general rubbish-desert. Where parts of walls or frames or chimneys still stood, they were ragged, tapered, and naturalistic; of a stalagmitic architecture. The scene was eerie and unsettling." Miraculously, Levinson is among the few survivors, though he dies of lobar pneumonia within a year after the destruction of the ghetto, due to the physical attrition. His archive is saved.

Hersey, having mapped out the novel as a third-person narrative, switched to the first-person singular of Levinson in the process of drafting the book, for the story "could not be told by an all-knowing, all-seeing John Hersey." Levinson's meticulous, even pedantic style, the format of referencing date of event and entry and source at the beginning of each episode, strangely draw in rather than distance the reader. The translated quality of some of the writing creates a similar effect. David Daiches characterized *The Wall* as a "miracle of compassion" when he reviewed it in 1950.

John Hersey, a non-Jewish American author born in China and trained at Groton and Yale, may appear to be a surprising choice in a survey of major American ethnic modernists. He was a realist, though did occasionally employ modernist devices, and one does not think of him as "ethnic," though, because he spent his formative years in China as the child of American missionaries, his life story had certain similarities with that of an immigrant. Henry Luce, Pearl S. Buck, and Edward F. Haskell had also grown up outside the United States as the children of missionaries. Hersey was an author who made several important contributions to ethnically themed literature. After having worked as secretary for Sinclair Lewis, Hersey served as World War II correspondent for Luce's *Time* and *Life* covering the Pacific theater, the advancing Red Army, and the Italian campaign.

In his Pulitzer Prize-winning novel *A Bell for Adano* (1944), he portrayed the familiar ethnic theme of the return of an immigrant to his ancestral homeland. Hersey's novel takes this familiar plotline into the war and presents the arrival of the U.S. Major Joppolo, whose parents had emigrated from Florence, in the fictitious town of Adano in Sicily where he helps restore life to normal after fascism and war. He is an ordinary American hero who has to deal with an insensitive army bureaucracy and the conflicting needs of a poor village. Just when his scheme to procure a new bell for the town has succeeded, he is relieved of his duties due to the meddling of an inane general, modeled on George S. Patton: the ethnic hero is not just an "American" but the better American. Joppolo was inspired by a real man, Frank E. Toscani, who had, indeed, been in Italy during the Allied invasion and provided a bell for the town Licata. Hersey's popular and rather cheery novel of 1944 was awarded the Pulitzer Prize on VE Day, turned into a Broadway hit starring Fredric March and a Hollywood movie with John Hodiak, had a New York restaurant named after it, and was panned by Diana Trilling as a journalist's novel "for the war effort."

Readers of *A Bell for Adano* were probably glad when they received the *New Yorker* of August 31, 1946, with a happy cover of summer leisure activities, for apart from the "Goings on about Town" section, the entire issue consisted of a single, long contribution by John Hersey, interrupted only by advertisements. Yet what the reader found was "Hiroshima," a hard-hitting report about the experience of ordinary people who were in Hiroshima when the nuclear bomb was dropped by the American B 29 bomber plane named "Enola Gay" after the pilot's mother. Hersey's writing was considered nonmodernist, even "flat" by some reviewers, as he attempted to create empathy with the people who had faced the extreme and the unimaginably horrifying, and had miraculously survived, for the time being, these new forms of mass annihilation, if not their eerie after-effects.

The wound may have been the symbol of a cool, exceptional Hemingway protagonist or of the inevitable fate that meets di Donato's hero who is sacrificed as a new Christ, in concrete. In Hiroshima there was nothing exceptional or heroic about the wounds that had become very widespread, and in fact seemed universal. What had happened to empathy, one of the targets of modernist attacks on realism? Was empathy "kitsch," and should one simply shut up about the sufferings of the victims of the twentieth century, in the way in which Gertrude Stein seemed to suggest in what seems a clear trajectory from the deaths of the three women in *Three Lives* to Stein's "Reflections on the Atom Bomb" in 1946:

They asked me what I thought of the atomic bomb. I said I had not been able to take any interest in it. . . . What is the use, if they are really as destructive as all that there is nothing left and if there is nothing there nobody to be interested and nothing to be interested about. If they are not as destructive as all that then they are just a little more or less destructive than other things and that means that in spite of all destruction there are always lots left on this earth to be interested or to be willing and the thing that destroys is just one of the things that concerns the people inventing it or the people starting it off, but really nobody else can do anything about it so you have to just live along like always, so you see the atomic [bomb] is not at all interesting, not any more interesting than any other machine, and machines are only interesting in being invented or in what they do, so why be interested. I never could take any interest in the atomic bomb.

One would have to be a hard-boiled modernist, indeed, to appreciate Stein even in this articulation, for Stein displayed about as much empathy here as her narrator of *Three Lives* had toward death-bound Melanctha. "A bomb is a bomb is a bomb," as one critic put it.

The atomic destruction of Hiroshima caused an estimated 100,000 immediate human casualties, and many more died later from the burns and the effects of radiation. How could this unimaginable mass death be presented to readers so that they would care, empathize, and identify with the victims – and at a time when newspapers had offered a full coverage of the technical details of the bombing? Hersey begins with the tried old device of creating scenes with which readers anywhere in the modern world could identify – waking up, doing the chores of everyday life, or going somewhere by streetcar – when the extraordinary happens, and his characters have to face the extreme, the full extent of which they begin to realize only slowly. The "noiseless flash" some of them see is far, far worse than Richard Wright's *Brrrrrriiiiiiiiiiiiiiii-iiiinng!* The moment Hersey chooses, is "exactly fifteen minutes past eight in the morning, on August 6, 1945," and his focus is on six survivors who are spared the fate of an instant death at that moment:

Each of them counts many small items of chance or volition – a step taken in time, a decision to go indoors, catching one streetcar instead of the next – that spared him. And now each knows that in the act of survival he lived a dozen lives and saw more death than he ever thought he would see.

The witnesses he interviewed were a German Jesuit, Father Wilhelm Kleinsorge; the Methodist Reverend Mr. Kiyoshi Tanimoto; Dr. Terufumi Sasaki, a Red Cross Hospital surgeon; Miss Toshiko Sasaki, a clerk not related to Dr. Sasaki; another physician, Dr. Masakazu Fujii; and a tailor's widow with three small children, Mrs. Hatsuyo Nakamura.

It is Dr. Sasaki who "caught a streetcar at once" on his way to work. "He later calculated," Hersey adds, that "if he had had to wait a few minutes for the streetcar, as often happened, he would have been close to the center at the time of the explosion and would surely have perished." The trams also served as part of one of the post-explosion myths that offered to explain the extraordinary to people who could not possibly comprehend what had happened: "The bomb was not a bomb at all; it was a kind of fine magnesium powder sprayed over the whole city by a single plane, and it exploded when it came into contact with the live wires of the city power system," something that was only possible to do to "big cities and only in the daytime, when the tram lines and so forth are in operation." Hiroshima certainly fit the bill for that story, for it boasted a fleet of 123 tramcars – out of which only three were in working condition after the attack. Some cars remained only as shadows that the gigantic light of the explosion left on streets and some stone walls.

The creation of these permanent shadows helped experts figure out where the hypocenter of the explosion, named "ground zero" in an Americanism of 1945, must have been by triangulating various shadows of buildings. The shadows themselves seemed like another violent parody of surrealist art.

A few vague human silhouettes were found, and these gave rise to stories that eventually included fancy and precise details. One story told how a painter on a ladder was monumentalized in a kind of bas-relief on the stone façade of a bank building on which he was at work, in the act of dipping his brush into the paint can; another, how a man and his cart on the bridge near the Museum of Science and Industry, almost under the center of the explosion, were cast down in an embossed shadow which made it clear that the man was about to whip his horse.

Modern forms of destruction seemed to make a mockery of modern art. The shadows were not the only strange pseudomodernist creations brought about by the sudden change "from a busy city of two hundred and forty-five thousand that morning to a mere pattern of residue in the afternoon." The strangeness of so much destruction caused, without warning, by only one single plane flying in a clear sky remains unmitigated even after the scientists' explanations. Nature was changed. Father Kleinsorge sees a pumpkin "roasted on the vine" and "potatoes that were nicely baked under the ground. Miss Sasaki notices that "wild flowers were in bloom among the city's bones. The bomb had not only left the underground organs of plants intact; it had stimulated them." Ground zero was so quickly covered by sickle senna that it seemed "as if a load of sickle-senna seed had been dropped along with the bomb."

Hersey is strong in describing the horrors of human destruction and deformation; he writes about a group of Japanese soldiers: "Their faces were wholly burned, their eyesockets were hollow, the fluid from their melted eyes had run down their cheeks. (They must have had their faces upturned when the bomb went off; perhaps they were anti-aircraft personnel.) Their mouths were mere swollen, pus-covered wounds, which they could not bear to stretch enough to admit the spout of the teapot."

Hersey is careful to universalize reactions of stoicism: the phrase used was "'Shikata ga nai,' a Japanese expression as common as, and corresponding to, the Russian word 'nichevo': 'It can't be helped. Oh well. Too bad.'" While staying closely to the points of view of the people he interviewed, he lets moral points emerge only in an understated manner, for example by Dr. Sasaki: 'I see . . . that they are holding a trial for war criminals in Tokyo just now. I think they ought to try the men who decided to use the bomb and they should hang them all." The atomic bomb was part of war action – but was mass killing and was maiming of so many civilians justifiable, as the Vatican asked?

The interruptions of the *New Yorker* ads were eerie at times and a reminder of the impassiveness of the world of the market and commerce to even the most extreme human atrocities. Opposite the page on which Hersey describes the change "from a busy city of two hundred and forty-five thousand that morning to a mere pattern of residue in the afternoon," RCA Victor promoted its commercial products by highlighting the company's engineering skill in developing "Sniperscope," an infrared telescope that, mounted on a carbine, enabled a soldier in total darkness to hit a target the size of a man at 75 yards, an invention that was, the ad announced proudly, responsible for "thirty percent of the Japanese casualties during the first three weeks of the Okinawa campaign." A little later, when Hersey describes the analysis by Japanese scientists of the bombing, an ad for a "federal union" warns readers that "now – in this atomic age . . . a bomb could destroy the statue . . . and Liberty, too. We can no longer afford to leave it to a statue to carry that torch." Another ad for "Hair Pieces FOR PARTLY OR ALL BALD SCALPS" seemed pasted, as if intentionally by a perverse editor at the *New Yorker*, precisely next to the passage in which Hersey gives a harrowing account of the many ailments of the survivor-victims who had been exposed to radiation; and at the level between the words "Hair" and "Pieces" in the ad, Hersey's text reads: "the main symptom was falling hair." Next to Hersey's information that the city of Hiroshima "authorized and built four hundred one-family 'barracks'" a Honeywell ad informed readers under the slogan "Modern Art, eh, Gertie?" that a Honeywell "M-H Personalized Heating Control" was a little object more important than a collection of Dali originals." The fact that modernism was on its way toward becoming a safe part of the commercial culture and a commodity was also visible in an ad for a lower-case and all-in-one-word "modernage" shop on 34th Street. And a Pullman ad that represented all-white customers on a platform of a suburban station looking for their own names, as investors and co-owners of the company that were written on a car out of which a happily smiling black porter was looking on, suggested the extent to which the double victory campaign and the sense of an "American dilemma" had reached the country.

Hersey's reportage was immensely successful, as readers seemed to look at what had happened as if for the first time. The cumulative effect of the stories of individual survivors was more powerful than many other, more "objective" accounts which had been published before. The *New Yorker* was quickly sold out, the book publication that followed has never since gone out of print, and the government felt obliged to develop a more full-fledged rationale for the employment of the weapon than it had offered before Hersey's *Hiroshima*.

New York intellectuals may have looked at Hersey's work as what Greenberg called "kitsch." Dwight Macdonald complained that in *Hiroshima*, Hersey's "suave, toned-down, underplayed kind of naturalism" was "no longer adequate, either esthetically or morally, to cope with the modern horrors." According to Macdonald, Hersey had "no eye for the one detail that imaginatively creates a whole." And worse: "the 'little people' of Hiroshima whose sufferings Hersey records in antiseptic *New Yorker* prose might just as well be white mice, for all the pity, horror, or indignation the reader – or at least this reader – is made to feel for them." Mary McCarthy thought that the "human interest" method of *Hiroshima* constituted an "insipid falsification of the truth of atomic warfare." She added an impossible demand: "To have done the atom bomb justice, Mr. Hersey would have had to interview the dead."

Lacking the quality of being "difficult" for readers, of being very self-consciously concerned with formal experimentation, Hersey certainly would not qualify as a full-blown modernist, even though Harry Levin, in his introduction to the 1947 *Portable James Joyce* (a companion to Cowley's *Portable Faulkner*) asked: "How many of those who read John Hersey's *Hiroshima* recognize its literary obligation to *Ulysses*?" This may have been hyperbole, for Hersey appears to have received more formal inspiration from the search for transcendence in the coincidence of a handful of characters who share an accidental death in Thornton Wilder's novel *The Bridge of San Luis Rey* (1927) than from any of Joyce's stylistic devices. The point is not to claim Hersey as an ethnic modernist, but to suggest by the discussion of some of his works in the 1940s what American modernists and ethnic writers stayed away from in the same period: a full-fledged confrontation with the horrors of World War II.

James Agee left only a strange novel fragment, entitled "Dedication Day," in which a nuclear scientist commits suicide to atone for his participation in the building of the bomb. In his Simple tale "Here to Yonder: Simple and the Atom Bomb" (August 18, 1945) Langston Hughes seems to start seriously but then make light of the subject. Simple is worried that the bomb may end all human relations: "The way it kills people for miles around, all my relations and – me, too – is liable to be wiped out in no time." The narrator assures him:

"Nobody is dropping that bomb on you . . . We are dropping it way over in Asia."
"And what is to keep Asia from dropping it back on us?" asked Simple.
"The Japanese probably do not have any atomic bomb to drop," I said.

From there, the conversation drifts to why the bomb was not used in Germany, to the cost of the bomb and better ways to spend the money and to the Mississippi election. This little sketch still makes Hughes exceptionally engaged, for Hurston and Wright, for example, barely mentioned the Holocaust or Hiroshima in their writing, published or unpublished.

John Hersey's report *Hiroshima* and his novel *The Wall* both address the very issue of genocide that came to matter so much to the many writers who would *later* invoke the legacy of Hiroshima and the *univers concentrationnaire* of Auschwitz. The very fact that a young writer, an outsider trained as a journalist, wrote and published such works at a time of much silence about these themes points to the remarkable absence of those issues in American modernist and ethnic fiction right after World War II. Perhaps the time has come to think of modernism not as an inherently redemptive, progressive, or resistant category but merely as a set of stylistic conventions – not unlike realism or neoclassicism – that helped artists achieve some extraordinary aesthetic accomplishments but that also could, and did, serve many different ideological purposes, some good and some bad.

15

❦

GRAND CENTRAL TERMINAL

A SHORT STORY by the Hungarian émigré Leo Szilard, entitled "Report on 'Grand Central Terminal,'" written in 1948 and first published in the *University of Chicago Magazine* in 1952, engages the reader as an interpreter of the meaning of artifacts – against an unusual background. A research team of extraterrestrial scientists investigates Manhattan after a neutron-bomb war has destroyed all human, animal, and plant life on earth (hence all subjects of empathy), but has left buildings intact. The story develops a tension between the conservative narrator and the radical scientist Xram. Their conflicting views come to the fore as they investigate Grand Central Terminal, the New York train station that had been the subject of a 1915 Max Weber oil canvas and of several Berenice Abbott photographs, and that made Louis Adamic's Slovenian birthplace seem so small. Szilard's narrator explains: "What its name 'Grand Central Terminal' meant we do not know, but there is little doubt as to the general purpose which this building served. It was part of a primitive transportation system based on clumsy engines which ran on rails and dragged cars mounted on wheels behind them." The narrator concludes that there must have been two kinds of people in the city of Grand Central Terminal, those with a "smoky" and those with a "nonsmoky" complexion; and he theorizes that in this primitive transportation system they were probably segregated as "smokers" and "nonsmokers." A third strain of earth-dwellers, endowed with wings, appears to have died out earlier, since none of the numerous skeletons belonged to this winged strain and since their images "are much more frequently found among the older paintings than among the more recent paintings."

The scientists are puzzled by the public toilets at the station, "small cubicles which served as temporary shelter for earth-dwellers while they were depositing their excrements." Here is the investigators' problem:

[T]he door of each and every cubicle in the depository was locked by a rather complicated gadget. Upon investigation of these gadgets it was found that they contained a

number of round metal disks. By now we know that these ingenious gadgets barred entrance to the cubicle until an additional disk was introduced into them through a slot; at that very moment the door became unlocked, permitting access to the cubicle.

These disks bear different images and also different inscriptions which, however, all have in common the word "Liberty." What is the significance of these gadgets, the disks in the gadgets and the word "Liberty" on the disks?

A scholarly consensus emerges that these disks suggest "a ceremonial act accompanying the act of deposition" and that "the word 'Liberty' must designate some virtue which was held in high esteem by the earth-dwellers or their ancestors." But why the gadgets at the locks? The scientists assume that "earth-dwellers were perhaps driven by a certain sense of urgency, that in the absence of the gadgets they might have occasionally forgotten to make the disk sacrifice and would have consequently suffered pangs of remorse afterward." Xram disagrees, however, and we hear his opinion filtered through the narrator:

[Xram] believes that these disks were given out to earth-dwellers as rewards for services. He says that the earth-dwellers were not rational beings and that they would not have collaborated in co-operative enterprises without some special incentive.

He says that, by barring earth-dwellers from depositing their excrements unless they sacrificed a disk on each occasion, they were made eager to acquire such disks. . . . He thinks that the disks found in the depositories represent only a special case of a more general principle and that the earth-dwellers probably had to deliver such disks not only prior to being given access to the depository but also prior to being given access to food, etc.

Xram is now in a state of excitement as he develops a larger theory, with which the condescending narrator clearly does not sympathize:

He had made some elaborate calculations which show that a system of exchanging disks cannot be stable, but is necessarily subject to great fluctuations vaguely reminiscent of the manic-depressive cycle in the insane. He goes so far as to say that in such a depressive phase war becomes psychologically possible even within the same species.

The narrator has no difficulty disproving Xram's obviously "nonsensical ideas," for "a spot check of ten different lodging houses of the city, selected at random" reveals "a number of depositories but not a single one that was equipped with a gadget containing disks." This leaves only the assumption that disks in the "Grand Central Terminal" depositories "had been placed there as a ceremonial act. Apparently such ceremonial acts were connected with the act of deposition in *public* places, and in public places only."

The thoroughly ironic Jewish author of the story was the same Budapest-born Leo Szilard who, after emigrating to the United States in 1938, was among the "Manhattan Project" pioneers in the development of nuclear chain reactions that made possible the building and use of the first atomic bombs. He once reported that, having read H. G. Wells's "The World Set Free," a visionary science fiction story about atomic energy, he had a sudden burst of inspiration (while he was waiting for a traffic light to change at the corner of Southampton Row in London) that a neutron chain reaction could release energy from fissioning atoms. Szilard was an adventurer in the world of modernity who filed a patent for an electron microscope and, with Albert Einstein, for a refrigerator pump; and who devised his own advertising copy for the book which included "Report on 'Grand Central Terminal'": "In Philadelphia almost everybody reads *The Voice of the Dolphins*.... On sale in the Harvard Coop. If you do not buy it to-day you will forget it."

Szilard also had a strong sense of political responsibility. In 1932 he tried to organize a boycott of Japan in protest against the brutal war Japan was waging against China. And in 1945, Szilard vehemently opposed the use of the atomic bomb in Hiroshima and Nagasaki on moral grounds. After trying unsuccessfully to appeal directly to Roosevelt and then Truman, Szilard circulated a "Petition to the President" among Manhattan Project scientists (dated July 17, 1945) which argued that while the use of an atomic bomb would have been justified had the United States been attacked with such a weapon by Germany, "such attacks on Japan could not be justified, at least not unless the terms which will be imposed after the war on Japan were made public in detail and Japan were given an opportunity to surrender." Worrying about the moral responsibilities involved in such a step, the scientists warned that "a nation which sets the precedent of using these newly liberated forces of nature for purposes of destruction may have to bear the responsibility of opening the door to an era of devastation on an unimaginable scale." Anticipating the arms race of "rival powers," the petition to the U.S. Commander-in-Chief argued that the lead in the field of atomic power gave the United States "the obligation of restraint and if we were to violate this obligation our moral position would be weakened in the eyes of the world and in our own eyes." Szilard's appeal, although it was signed by sixty-nine other atomic scientists, had no effect on Truman's decision-making. Szilard made his efforts the point of departure of another sarcastic tale, "My Trial as a War Criminal" (1947), in which Russians, having taken control of the United States after a biological weapons attack on New Jersey, were rounding up those Americans who were involved in the development and employment of the atomic bomb, in order to try them for Nuremberg-trial-defined crimes such as "violation of the customs of war" and "planning a war in violation of international agreements."

In "Report on 'Grand Central Terminal'" Szilard presented a model case for a minority view held by Xram (an inversion of the name of a famous theorist) that is infuriatingly dismissed by the narrator of the story. Could the "Liberty" disks have something to do with peace and war? Szilard's question is all the more haunting since he defamiliarizes such fixtures of modern life as pay toilets in a postwar, and also chillingly post-human, setting. An extraordinary example of immigrant writing in the post-Hiroshima mode, this subtle tale suggests that modernity, the wish to acquire disks in "manic-depressive" market cycles, and moral irresponsibility had taken mankind to the last stop of a "Grand Central Terminal," indeed.

❧

The period from 1910 to 1950 had a certain four-decade-long unity. But it was also marked by deep ruptures. The teens were both prewar and war-years, and the war marked a deep caesura: the international republic of letters generally gave way to nationalized intellectuals who supported or opposed war efforts – though there was a good amount of neutralism, pacifism, and new internationalism also. World War I developed political propaganda to a new high pitch, and, after the war, its target could be redirected from "Huns" (the term inadvertently launched by Kaiser Wilhelm himself in a pep talk to German soldiers departing for China in 1900) to "Reds" or Jews or "Japs" or social equality or to any other enemy construction throughout the period up into the Cold War. On the home front, the Americanization movement and assimilation drives set out to Anglicize immigrants: the hyphen was a minus sign and English the language of the Declaration. World War I had a deep effect on the marginalization and demonization of languages other than English – a process of which Spanish was ultimately to become the main target. The color line was being drawn more and more sharply, and eugenicist research offered the most comprehensive rationale for racism in the war years and the subsequent two decades.

The years from the end of World War I to 1929 were boom years, with isolationism growing, and they were deeply conservative. At the same time ethnic autobiography and literature became more modernist, self-reflexive, and somber. The Stock Exchange crash of 1929, another event marking a deep rupture in the period, may or may not have affected literary production, but some social themes moved to the foreground in literature during the Great Depression of the 1930s. Perhaps more importantly, there was a return of the realist aesthetic on many political fronts; and the victory of Hemingway's compromise modernism might also be understood in this context.

The next big caesura was World War II. The war years, with their multi-ethnic platoon stories and Roosevelt's articulation of the four liberties, popularly illustrated by Norman Rockwell, ushered in a double victory campaign over fascism abroad and racism at home, and an intensified effort toward intercultural education as a safeguard against the genocidal danger stemming from group hostilities and stereotyping. Yet American modernist and ethnic writers – with very few exceptions – did not confront the "concentration camp universe" until the Beat Generation came along. Nineteen forty-five to 1950 marked the transformation from war alliance to new anticommunism and Cold War; 1940 to 1950 also brought the ultimate acceptance of modernism as the art of democracy. As the period ended, the civil rights movement was about to get going, and it accelerated from the 1954 *Brown v. Board of Education* decision to the Civil Rights legislation of the 1960s. In 1967, the Supreme Court in the *Loving v. Virginia* case also declared unconstitutional one of the oldest and most widespread racist sets of laws, prohibiting interracial marriage.

In the period from 1930 to 1950 economic mobility prevailed in the United States: whereas the richest 1 percent of American households controlled more than 40 percent of the nation's wealth in 1930, the figure had declined to under 30 percent by 1949 (only to rise again to nearly 40 percent by 1990). This means that the economic developments from 1930 to 1950 gave mobility narratives a certain plausibility whereas by the end of the twentieth century economic mobility rates in the United States were actually lower than those in other democratic countries.

The acceptance of modernism as the art of democracy and of resistance could become more widespread because the totalitarian opposition made such an acceptance plausible – despite the continued populist resistance to art that wasn't about anything. Yet this populism (embodied by Dondero's Congressional appearance) could not find effective political expression during the Cold War years.

As modernism became more what one could call normal practice in the 1950s, it stabilized the story line of its own emergence as its central myth. Retold in the shape of so many biographically informed narratives (from Cézanne, Van Gogh, Ensor, Monet, and Picasso to American immigrant artists Joseph Stella, Emmanuel Radnitsky – who became better known as Man Ray – and Max Weber), the story always moved from a premodern, Victorian, realist code to the formal explosion of style and color that marked the achievement of each modern artist. Stein's story could be told in similar terms as a development from *Q.E.D.* to *Three Lives* and *The Making of Americans* and toward the world of Picasso, Cézanne, and Matisse. It was a very powerful story of emergence and it may still dominate much of the landscape of modernism. Yet it was also a selective story that was based on omissions and conflation. It was a story that may now have run its course.

CHRONOLOGY 1910–1950

Jonathan Fortescue

	American Literary Texts	American Events, Texts, and Arts	Other Events, Texts, and Arts
1910	**Addams, Jane** (1860–1935), *Twenty Years at Hull House* (personal narrative)	Mann-Elkins Act gives Interstate Commerce Commission control of telephone, telegraph, cable, and wireless companies.	Mexican Revolution begins against the autocratic rule of Porfirio Diaz.
		Victor Berger is first socialist to be elected to the U.S. Congress.	China abolishes slavery.
	Churchill, Winston (1871–1947), *A Modern Chronicle* (novel)	U.S. population is 92,228,496.	Portugal becomes a republic.
	Huneker, James (1857–1921), *Promenades of an Impressionist* (personal narrative)		
	James, Henry (1843–1916), *The Finer Grain* (fiction)	President Taft dismisses Gifford Pinchot, U.S. Forest Service chief, when he alleges that the administration is undermining conservation efforts.	Japan annexes Korea.
			Halley's Comet passes near the Earth.
	Johnson, Owen (1878–1952), *The Varmint* (novel)	William Boyce charters the Boy Scouts of America.	
	Kobrin, Leo (1872–1946), *Di shprakh fun ehnt* [The Language of Misery] (fiction)	**W. E. B. Du Bois** begins to publish *Crisis* under auspices of newly founded NAACP.	**Henri Matisse** finishes *Music* (painting).
	London, Jack (1876–1916), *Lost Face* (fiction)	**Myers, Gustavus** (1872–1942), *History of the Great American Fortunes* (economic history)	**Igor Stravinsky** composes *The Firebird* (ballet).
	Roosevelt, Theodore (1858–1919), *African Game Trails* (personal narrative)	**Child Hassam** finishes *Against the Light* (painting).	King Edward VII dies. George V succeeds him.
		George Herriman publishes first "Krazy Kat" (cartoon).	Leo Tolstoy dies.

1911		
Bierce, Ambrose (1842–1914?), *The Devil's Dictionary* (satire)	U.S. Supreme Court orders break-up of the Trusts – Standard Oil, American Tobacco, DuPont Co.	U.S., Great Britain, and Japan sign treaty to abolish seal hunting in the north Pacific for 15 years.
Dreiser, Theodore (1871–1945), *Jennie Gerhardt* (novel)	Triangle Shirtwaist fire kills 146 workers, mostly women, who were locked inside the factory by the management.	Roald Amundsen becomes the first person to reach the South Pole.
Du Bois, W. E. B. (1868–1963), *The Quest of the Silver Fleece* (novel)	Charles Kettering perfects the electric starter for the automobile.	Ernest Rutherford formulates theory of the structure of the atom.
Harrison, Henry (1880–1930), *Queed* (novel)	Procter & Gamble debut Crisco.	**Conrad, Joseph** (1857–1924), *Under Western Eyes* (novel)
Johnson, Owen (1878–1952), *The Tennessee Shad* (novel)	**Boas, Franz** (1858–1942), *The Mind of Primitive Man* (anthropology)	Georges Braque finishes *Man With a Guitar* (painting).
Muir, John (1838–1914), *My First Summer in the Sierra* (personal narrative)	**Taylor, Frederick** (1856–1915), *Principles of Scientific Management* (economics)	Paul Klee finishes *Self-Portrait* (painting).
Sedgwick, Anne (1873–1935), *Tante* (novel)	*The New Masses* publishes its first issue.	Richard Strauss composes *Rosenkavalier* (opera).
Wharton, Edith (1862–1937), *Ethan Frome* (novel)		
Wright, Harold (1872–1944), *The Winning of Barbara Worth* (novel)		
1912		
Antin, Mary (1881–1946), *The Promised Land* (nonfiction)	"Memphis Blues" (popular song)	The *Titanic* sinks on her maiden voyage across the Atlantic. 1,513 people drown.
Dreiser, Theodore (1871–1945), *The Financier* (novel)	Woodrow Wilson defeats Theodore Roosevelt and William Taft in the election for president of the United States.	U.S. Marines invade Nicaragua.
	New Mexico and Arizona admitted to the Union as 47th and 48th states.	

American Literary Texts	American Events, Texts, and Arts	Other Events, Texts, and Arts
Grey, Zane (1875–1939), *Riders of the Purple Sage* (novel)	U.S. Supreme Court dissolves the merger of Union Pacific and Southern Pacific railroads.	Jung, C. G. (1875–1961), *The Theory of Psychoanalysis* (psychology)
Johnson, James Weldon (1871–1938), *The Autobiography of an Ex-Colored Man* (novel)	Jerome Kern writes *The Red Petticoat* (musical).	Pablo Picasso finishes *The Violin* (painting).
London, Jack (1876–1916), *Smoke Bellew* (novel)	Jim Thorpe wins the decathlon and pentathlon at the 5th World Olympics.	Claude Debussy composes *Images* (orchestral music).
Sui Sin Far [Edith Maud Eaton] (1865–1914), *Mrs. Spring Fragrance* (fiction)	The presence of electrons and protons is detected in a cloud-chamber photograph.	
Bourne, Randolph (1886–1918), *Youth and Life* (essays)	16th Amendment to the U.S. Constitution authorizes the federal income tax.	Niels Bohr formulates his theory of the structure of the atom.
Cather, Willa (1876–1947), *O Pioneers* (novel)	17th Amendment to the U.S. Constitution permits the direct election of senators to the U.S. Congress.	London Peace Treaty divides European Turkey among the victors of the first Balkan War.
Glasgow, Ellen (1874–1945), *Virginia* (novel)	Garment workers strike over the length of the workday.	Lawrence, D. H. (1885–1930), *Sons and Lovers* (novel)
Glaspell, Susan (1882–1948), *Lifted Masks* (fiction)	Ford Motor Co. installs the first assembly-line in its factories.	Mann, Thomas (1875–1955), *Death in Venice* (novella)
Herrick, Robert (1868–1938), *One Woman's Life* (novel)	Gideon Sundback invents the zipper.	Proust, Marcel (1871–1922), *Swann's Way* (novel, vol. 1 of *In Search of Lost Time*)
James, Henry (1843–1916), *A Small Boy and Others* (autobiography)	Keokuk Dam across the Mississippi River is completed.	Claude Debussy composes *Preludes* (piano music).

1913

1914

La Follette, Robert (1855–1925), *Autobiography* (autobiography)
London, Jack (1876–1916), *The Valley of the Moon* (novel)
Wharton, Edith (1862–1937), *The Custom of the Country* (novel)
Burroughs, Edgar (1875–1950), *Tarzan of the Apes* (novel)
Dreiser, Theodore (1871–1945), *The Titan* (novel)
Herrick, Robert (1868–1938), *Clark's Field* (novel)
James, Henry (1843–1916), *Notes of a Son and Brother* (autobiography)
Lewis, Sinclair (1885–1951), *Our Mr. Wrenn* (novel)
McClure, Samuel Sidney (1857–1949), *My Autobiography* [ghostwritten by Willa Cather] (autobiography)
Stein, Gertrude (1874–1946), *Tender Buttons* (fiction)
Steiner, Edward (1866–1956), *From Alien to Citizen* (autobiography)
Tarkington, Booth (1869–1946), *Penrod* (novel)

Federal Reserve Act passes.

Armory Show of modern art in New York City

"Danny Boy" (popular song)

The Great Migration of blacks from rural South into Northern industrial cities accelerates.

Merrill, Lynch brokerage house opens for business.

Federal Trade Commission Act passes.

The New Republic and *The Little Review* publish their first issues.

Brandeis, Louis (1856–1941) *Other People's Money* (essay)

Davis, Richard Harding (1864–1916), *With the Allies* (nonfiction)

John Sloan finishes *Backyards, Greenwich Village* (painting).

W. C. Handy composes "St. Louis Blues" (popular song).

Igor Stravinsky composes *The Rite of Spring* (ballet).

World War I begins after the assassination of Archduke Ferdinand.

Mexican Revolution unsettles Latin America.

Mahatma Gandhi returns to India to support national sovereignty movement.

Panama Canal opens to shipping.

Oscar Barnack develops the 35mm still camera in Germany.

Joyce, James (1882–1941), *Dubliners* (fiction)

Adolf de Meyer takes *Sur le Prélude à L'Après-midi d'un faune* (photographs)

	American Literary Texts	American Events, Texts, and Arts	Other Events, Texts, and Arts
1915	Buslett, Ole (1855–1924), *Veien til Golden Gate* [The Road to the Golden Gate] (allegory)	J. P. Morgan & Co. agree to loan $500 million to Britain and France to help finance war.	*Lusitania* torpedoed by German submarine. 1,198 people drown.
	Cather, Willa (1876–1947), *The Song of the Lark* (novel)	First transcontinental phone call made from New York to San Francisco.	Tetanus epidemic breaks out across World War I battlefields.
	Dreiser, Theodore (1871–1945), *The "Genius"* (novel)	Taxicabs arise as new form of local transit in the major cities.	Latin American nations convene with the U.S. to seek end to Mexican Revolution.
	Glaspell, Susan (1882–1948), *Fidelity* (novel)	State of Georgia grants the Ku Klux Klan a new charter.	Albert Einstein proposes the general theory of relativity.
	Grey, Zane (1875–1939), *The Lone Star Ranger* (novel)	*Birth of a Nation* (film) dir. D. W. Griffith	Kafka, Franz (1883–1924), *The Metamorphosis* (novella)
	Muir, John (1838–1914), *Travels in Alaska* (travel narrative)	Max Weber finishes *Chinese Restaurant* (painting).	Lawrence, D. H. (1885–1930), *The Rainbow* (novel)
	Poole, Ernest (1880–1950), *The Harbor* (novel)	Provincetown Players, a dramatic group, is formed.	Woolf, Virginia (1882–1941), *The Voyage Out* (novel)
	Wister, Owen (1860–1938), *The Pentecost of Calamity* (nonfiction)		Claude Debussy composes *Etudes* (piano music).
1916	Anderson, Sherwood (1876–1941), *Windy McPherson's Son* (novel)	U.S. Senate orders the build-up of the armed forces.	Theory of shell shock emerges from treatment of WWI veterans.
	Clemens, Samuel (1835–1910), *The Mysterious Stranger* (novel)	Federal Farm Loan Act makes money available for farmers in need.	Dadaists converge on Zurich.
	Glasgow, Ellen (1874–1945), *Life and Gabriella* (novel)	Congress averts a railroad workers' strike by passing 8-hour workday legislation.	British troops suppress the Easter Rising in Ireland.
	Howells, William Dean (1837–1920), *The Leatherwood God* (novel)	Federal Child Labor Law passes.	Pancho Villa invades U.S. at New Mexico border. U.S. sends troops to Mexico.

La Motte, Ellen (1873–1961), *The Backwash of War* (personal narrative)

Lardner, Ring (1885–1933), *You Know Me Al* (fiction)

Tobenkin, Elias (1882–1963), *Witte Arrives* (novel)

1917   Ager, Waldemar (1869–1941), *Paa veien til smeltepotten* [On the Way to the Melting Pot] (nonfiction)

Anderson, Sherwood (1876–1941), *Marching Men* (novel)

Austin, Mary (1868–1934), *The Ford* (novel)

Bourne, Randolph (1886–1918), *Education and Living* (essays)

Cahan, Abraham (1860–1951), *The Rise of David Levinsky* (novel)

Garland, Hamlin (1860–1940), *A Son of the Middle Border* (autobiography)

James, Henry (1843–1916), *The Middle Years* (autobiography)

Phillips, David (1867–1911), *Susan Lenox: Her Fall and Rise* (novel)

Poole, Ernest (1880–1950), *His Family* (novel)

Sinclair, Upton (1878–1968), *King Coal* (novel)

Woodrow Wilson appoints first Jew, Louis Brandeis, to the U.S. Supreme Court.

Dewey, John (1859–1952), *Democracy and Education* (philosophy)

U.S. enters World War I. 2 million land in France. 49,000 killed. 230,000 wounded.

Woodrow Wilson delivers Ten Points speech in favor of a World Federation.

The Jones Act makes Puerto Rico a territory of the U.S.

Congress overrides Wilson's veto of literary test for immigrants and exclusion of Asians.

Cabell, James (1879–1958), *The Cream of the Jest* (historical romance)

Empey, Arthur (1883–1963), *Over the Top* (war narrative)

The Original Dixieland Jazz Band debuts in New York City.

A. Philip Randolph and Chandler Owen launch *The Messenger*.

Joyce, James (1882–1941), *A Portrait of the Artist as a Young Man* (novel)

Ballet Russe tours the United States.

Germans begin unrestricted submarine warfare.

British secret service intercepts the "Zimmerman note" proposing alliance between Mexico and Germany against the U.S.

The Red Army deposes the czar as the communists rise to power in Russia.

The Third Battle of Ypres is fought.

Maurice Ravel composes *Le Tombeau de Couperin* (piano music).

Erik Satie composes *Parade* (ballet).

	American Literary Texts	American Events, Texts, and Arts	Other Events, Texts, and Arts
1918	**Adams, Henry** (1838–1918), *The Education of Henry Adams* [first public printing] (autobiography) **Beebe, William** (1877–1962), *Jungle Peace* (naturalist narrative) **Cather, Willa** (1876–1947), *My Ántonia* (novel) **Gale, Zona** (1874–1938), *Birth* (novel) **Tarkington, Booth** (1869–1946), *The Magnificent Ambersons* (novel)	Woodrow Wilson presents his Fourteen Points for fighting the war to Congress. Sedition Act passes. Eugene Debs sentenced to 10 years in prison for "wartime sedition." **Streeter, Edward** (1891–1976), *Dere Mable: Love Letters of a Rookie* (humor) Debut of Giacomo Puccini trio of one-act operas: *Il tabarro, Suor Angelica, Gianni Schicchi.*	U.S. and Allies score big victories in Aisne-Marne and Meuse-Argonne. World War I ends on 11 November. Virulent strain of influenza sweeps the world and over 20 million die. **Strachey, Lytton** (1880–1932), *Eminent Victorians* (biographical history)
1919	**Anderson, Sherwood** (1876–1941), *Winesburg, Ohio* (fiction) **Bercovici, Konrad** (1882–1961), *Dust of New York* (fiction) **Bridges, Horace** (1880–??), *On Becoming an American* (autobiography) **Cournos, John** (1881–1956), *The Mask* (novel) **Frank, Waldo** (1889–1967), *Our America* (essay)	The 18th Amendment to the U.S. Constitution prohibits the making, selling, or transportation of alcohol in the United States. Woodrow Wilson presents League of Nations covenant to Peace Conference. U.S. Senate rejects Treaty of Versailles. Postwar recession leads to labor unrest that paralyzes many major cities. Woodrow Wilson suffers devastating stroke.	Versailles Peace Conference begins. Red Army scores major victory in the Russian Revolution. Indians massacred by troops of the British Empire at Amritsar. **Walter Gropius** founds the Bauhaus in Weimar.

Glasgow, Ellen (1874–1945), *The Builders* (novel)

Hergesheimer, Joseph (1880–1954), *Linda Condon* (novel)

Mencken, H. L. (1880–1956), *Prejudices* (essays, vol. 1 of 6)

O'Brien, Frederick (1869–1932), *White Shadows in the South Seas* (personal narrative)

Reed, John (1887–1920), *Ten Days That Shook the World* (nonfiction)

Sinclair, Upton (1878–1968), *The Brass Check* (novel)

1920 Anderson, Sherwood (1876–1941), *Poor White* (novel)

Bok, Edward (1863–1930), *The Americanization of Edward Bok* (autobiography)

Day, Clarence (1874–1935), *The Simian World* (essays)

Dell, Floyd (1887–1969), *Mooncalf* (novel)

Racial strife around the country peaks in Chicago where a weeklong riot kills 15 whites, 23 blacks, and leaves 1,000 people homeless.

Communist Labor Party of America is founded, adopts platform of the 3rd International.

Cabell, James (1879–1958), *Jurgen* (historical romance)

Mencken, H. L. (1880–1956), *The American Language* (nonfiction, 1st edition)

Jack Dempsey becomes the Heavyweight Champion of the World.

New York Daily News, the first tabloid newspaper, publishes its first issue.

U.S. population is 105,710,620. First time in history that more than 50% live in urban areas.

Warren Harding wins the election for president of the U.S. over James Cox and Eugene Debs.

The 19th Amendment to the U.S. Constitution gives women the right to vote.

U.S. attorney general Palmer persecutes supposed Bolsheviks in the "Red Scare."

Proust, Marcel (1871–1922), *Within a Budding Grove* (novel, vol. 2 of *In Search of Lost Time*)

Kafka, Franz (1883–1924), *In the Penal Colony* and *A Country Doctor* (fiction)

The Cabinet of Dr. Caligari (film) directed by **Robert Wiene**

Nosferatu (film) directed by **F. W. Murnau**

Treaty of Sèvres dissolves the Ottoman Empire.

Freud, Sigmund (1856–1939), *Beyond the Pleasure Principle* (psychology)

American Literary Texts	American Events, Texts, and Arts	Other Events, Texts, and Arts
Dos Passos, John (1896–1970), *One Man's Initiation* (novel)	New York public schools authorize the firing of teachers who belong to Communist Party.	Lawrence, D. H. (1885–1930), *Women in Love* (novel)
Fitzgerald, F. Scott (1896–1940), *This Side of Paradise* (novel)	Woodrow Wilson wins Nobel Peace Prize.	
Gale, Zona (1874–1938), *Miss Lulu Bett* (novel)	Radio Station KDKA in Pittsburgh, PA begins first regular broadcasting.	
Huneker, James (1857–1921), *Painted Veils* (novel)	Only 5,000 radio sets, mostly experimental, exist in the U.S.	
Lewis, Sinclair (1885–1951), *Main Street* (novel)	Illiteracy in the U.S. declines to a new low of 6%.	
Mencken, H. L. (1880–1956), *Prejudices* (essays, vol. 2 of 6)	Life expectancy in the U.S. rises to 54.09 years.	Proust, Marcel (1871–1922), *The Guermantes Way* (novel, vol. 3 of *In Search of Lost Time*)
Tarkington, Booth (1869–1946), *Alice Adams* (novel)	Eight members of the Chicago White Sox are indicted for "throwing" the 1919 World Series.	Man Ray creates *Rayographs* (photograph).
Wharton, Edith (1862–1937), *The Age of Innocence* (novel)	Dewey, John (1859–1952), *Reconstruction in Philosophy* (philosophy)	
Wist, Johannes (1864–1923), *Nykommerbilleder* [Immigrant Scenes] (novel)	Holmes, Oliver Wendell (1841–1935), *Collected Legal Papers* (nonfiction)	
Yezierska, Anzia (1880–1970), *Hungry Hearts* (novel)		

1921

Anderson, Sherwood (1876–1941), *The Triumph of the Egg* (fiction and poetry)

Cournos, John (1881–1956), *The Wall* (novel)

Dell, Floyd (1887–1969), *The Briary Bush* (novel)

Dos Passos, John (1896–1970), *Three Soldiers* (novel)

Garland, Hamlin (1860–1940), *A Daughter of the Middle Border* (autobiography)

Hecht, Ben (1894–1964), *Erik Dorn* (novel)

Lewisohn, Ludwig (1882–1955), *Up Stream* (autobiography)

Panunzio, Constantine (1884–1964), *The Soul of an Immigrant*

Stribling, T. S. (1881–1965), *Birthright* (novel)

Congress sets limit of 357,000 new immigrants per year.

U.S. Supreme Court rules that labor unions can be prosecuted for restraining interstate trade.

President Harding commutes the sentence for espionage of Eugene Debs.

Ku Klux Klan rampages in the South and attracts widespread media attention.

Industries around the U.S. make broad wage cuts.

Radio station WJZ broadcasts first live coverage of a World Series game.

Albert Einstein arrives in New York and lectures on relativity; introduces the concept of time as the fourth dimension.

Cable Act makes it legal for an American woman to marry a foreigner.

The U.S., Britain, France, Italy, and Japan sign the Naval Limitation Treaty.

The BBC (British Broadcasting Company) is founded.

Rapid inflation in Germany destabilizes its economy.

Faisal I becomes king of Iraq.

Reza Kahn leads coup d'état in Iran.

Galsworthy, John (1867–1933) returns to work on *The Forsyte Saga* (novel, 4 vols.).

Proust, Marcel (1871–1922), *Sodom and Gomorrah I* (novel, vol. 4 of *In Search of Lost Time*)

Wittgenstein, Ludwig (1889–1951), *Tractatus Logico-Philosophicus* (philosophy)

American Literary Texts	American Events, Texts, and Arts	Other Events, Texts, and Arts
Tarkington, Booth (1869–1946), *Alice Adams* (novel)	Knee-length skirts dominate women's fashion.	
Wist, Johannes (1864–1923), *Hjemmet paa praerien* [The Home on the Prairie] (novel)		
Cather, Willa (1876–1947), *One of Ours* (novel)		
Cournos, John (1881–1956), *Babel* (novel)	The U.S. Supreme Court upholds the constitutionality of the 19th Amendment (women's suffrage).	The Soviet Union forms under the rule of Lenin.
Cummings, E. E. (1894–1962), *The Enormous Room* (novel)	WEAF, New York, broadcasts first program with a commercial sponsor.	Mussolini rises to power in charge of a fascist state.
Fitzgerald, F. Scott (1896–1940), *Tales of the Jazz Age* (fiction) & *The Beautiful and the Damned* (novel)	Bell Telephone installs in New York City the first mechanical switchboard: the "Pennsylvania" exchange.	Britain recognizes the sovereignty of the kingdom of Egypt.
Frank, Waldo (1889–1967), *Rahab* (novel)	Dr. Alexis Carrel discovers the existence and purpose of white blood cells in the human body.	Insulin proves to be an effective treatment for diabetic patients.
Lewis, Sinclair (1885–1951), *Babbitt* (novel)		Hesse, Herman (1877–1962), *Siddhartha* (novel)
Mencken, H. L. (1880–1956), *Prejudices* (essays, vol. 3 of 6)	Louis Armstrong moves from New Orleans to Chicago to join King Oliver's Creole Jazz Band.	Joyce, James (1882–1941), *Ulysses* (novel)
	Eliot, T. S. (1888–1965), *The Waste Land* (poetry)	

1922

1923

Wilson, Harry Leon (1867–1939), *Merton of the Movies* (novel)

Wist, Johannes (1864–1923), *Jonasville* (novel)

Yezierska, Anzia (1880–1870), *Salome of the Tenements* (novel)

Anderson, Sherwood (1876–1941), *Many Marriages* (novel)

Atherton, Gertrude (1857–1949), *Black Oxen* (novel)

Boyd, Thomas (1898–1935), *Through the Wheat* (novel)

Cather, Willa (1876–1947), *A Lost Lady* (novel)

Dell, Floyd (1887–1969), *Janet March* (novel)

Pupin, Michael (1858–1935), *From Immigrant to Inventor* (autobiography)

Sinclair, Upton (1878–1968), *The Goose-Step* (novel)

Toomer, Jean (1894–1967), *Cane* (novel)

Post, Emily (1873–1960), *Etiquette* (manual)

Nanook of the North (film) directed by Robert Flaherty

President Harding dies in office. Vice-president Calvin Coolidge becomes president.

Senate begins to investigate oil leases in Wyoming leading to the Teapot Dome Scandal.

Governor J. C. Walton places Oklahoma under martial law to quell Ku Klux Klan violence.

Colonel Jacob Shick patents the first electric razor.

DuPont and Co. purchases the patent to Cellophane.

Crowds gather to hear Emile Coué whose autosuggestive mental therapy includes the saying, "Every day in every way I am getting better and better."

Bessie Smith records "Down-Hearted Blues." 1 million copies sell within year of release.

"Barney Google" (popular song)

Time magazine publishes its first issue.

Proust, Marcel (1871–1922), *Sodom and Gomorrah II* (novel, vol. 4 of *In Search of Lost Time*)

Woolf, Virginia (1882–1941), *Jacob's Room* (novel)

The Beer Hall Putsch in Germany fails to bring Hitler to power.

French armed forces occupy the Ruhr valley in Germany to exact war reparations.

Edwin Hubble calculates the astronomical distance to the Star Nebula.

Freud, Sigmund (1856–1939), *The Ego and the Id* (psychology)

Hamsun, Knut (1859–1952), *The Last Chapter* (novel)

Lawrence, D. H. (1885–1930), *Studies in Classic American Literature* (criticism)

Proust, Marcel (1871–1922), *The Captive* (novel, vol. 5 of *In Search of Lost Time*)

	American Literary Texts	American Events, Texts, and Arts	Other Events, Texts, and Arts
1924	Bercovici, Konrad (1882–1960), *Around the World in New York* (nonfiction)	Calvin Coolidge wins election for president of the U.S.	Greece becomes a national republic.
	Bromfield, Louis (1896–1956), *The Green Bay Tree* (novel)	Number of radios in the U.S. tops 2.5 million.	The socialist Giacomo Matteotti is killed in Italy.
	Chacón, Felipe Maximiliano, *Obras* (fiction)	Ford Motor Co. makes its 10 millionth car.	The German dirigible Z-R-3 crosses the Atlantic ocean.
	D'Angelo, Pascal (1894–1932), *Son of Italy* (novel)	National Origins Act passes.	Insecticides are sprayed for the first time.
	Fauset, Jessie (1882–1961), *There is Confusion* (novel)	Radio Corporation of America transmits first photograph to London via wireless telegraph.	Breton, André (1896–1966), *Manifesto of Surrealism* (art theory)
	Hemingway, Ernest (1899–1961), *In Our Time* (fiction)	General Assembly of the Presbyterian church rules the theory of evolution is wrong.	Hitler, Adolf (1889–1945), *Mein Kampf* (autobiography)
	Lardner, Ring (1885–1933), *How to Write Short Stories* (fiction)	Nathan Leopold and Richard Loeb are found guilty of the thrill-killing of a child.	Kafka, Franz (1883–1924), *A Hunger Artist* (fiction)
	Melville, Herman (1819–1891), *Billy Budd* (novel, first date of publication)	Proposed amendment to the Constitution against child labor does not pass.	Mann, Thomas (1875–1955), *The Magic Mountain* (novel)
	Mencken, H. L. (1880–1956), *Prejudices* (essays, vol. 4 of 6)	H. L. Mencken and George Nathan found *The American Mercury*.	Dmitri Shostakovich composes *First Symphony* (orchestral music).
	Suckow, Ruth (1892–1960), *Country People* (novel)	George Gershwin, *Rhapsody in Blue* (orchestral music)	*The Last Laugh* (film) directed by F. W. Murnau
	White, Walter (1893–1955), *The Fire in the Flint* (novel)	*Sweet Georgia Brown* (popular song)	

1925		
Anderson, Sherwood (1876–1941), *Dark Laughter* (novel)	At Scopes Trial, Clarence Darrow humiliates William Jennings Bryan when questioning him about his disbelief in the theory of evolution.	Physicist Wolfgang Pauli proposes exclusion theory. Theory of quantum mechanics develops.
Bercovici, Konrad (1882–1960), *On New Shores* (fiction)	Army court-martials Col. Billy Mitchell because he insists that air power is key to war strategy.	Hindenberg becomes the president of Germany.
Bodenheim, Maxwell (1893–1954), *Replenishing Jessica* (novel)	Mrs. William Ross, Wyoming, becomes first woman governor in U.S. history.	Abd el-Krim revolt in Morocco against Spanish rule.
Bojer, Johan (1872–1959), *The Emigrants* (novel)	Dillon, Read & Co. buy Dodge Bros. automobile co. for then record $146 million.	Border disputes in Western Europe settled in Locarno Conference.
Bonner, Marita (1899–1971), "On Being Young, a Woman, and Colored" (essay)	15 companies are making cars in the U.S.: Apperson, Buick, Cadillac, Ford, Franklin, Haynes, Locomobile, Maxwell, Olds, Overland, Packard, Peerless, Pierce-Arrow, Stearns, and Studebaker.	Kafka, Franz (1883–1924), *The Trial* (novel)
Cather, Willa (1876–1947), *The Professor's House* (novel)		
Cautela, Giuseppe (1883–?), *Moon Harvest* (novel)		
Dell, Floyd (1887–1969), *Runaway* (novel)	Florida land boom peaks.	
Dos Passos, John (1896–1970), *Manhattan Transfer* (novel)	DuPont introduces production of isopropyl alcohol.	Proust, Marcel (1871–1922), *The Fugitive* (novel, vol. 6 of *In Search of Lost Time*)

	American Literary Texts	American Events, Texts, and Arts	Other Events, Texts, and Arts
	Dreiser, Theodore (1871–1945), *An American Tragedy* (novel)	Drs. George Frederick and Gladys Dick formulate antitoxin for scarlet fever.	**Woolf, Virginia** (1882–1941), *Mrs. Dalloway* (novel)
	Fisher, Rudolf (1897–1934), "The City of Refuge" (fiction)	William Green replaces Samuel Gompers as president of American Federation of Labor.	*Battleship Potemkin* (film) directed by **Sergei Eisenstein**
	Fitzgerald, F. Scott (1896–1940), *The Great Gatsby* (novel)	**Frank Lloyd Wright** builds Taliesin in Spring Green, Wisconsin.	
	Glasgow, Ellen (1874–1945), *Barren Ground* (novel)	*New Yorker* magazine founded	
	Lewis, Sinclair (1885–1951), *Arrowsmith* (novel)	The "Charleston" becomes a popular dance step.	
	Locke, Alain (1886–1954), *The New Negro* (anthology)	**Aaron Copland**, *Symphony for Organ and Orchestra* (orchestral music)	
	Loos, Anita (1893–1981), *Gentlemen Prefer Blondes* (novel)	*The Gold Rush* (film) dir. **Charlie Chaplin**	
	Ostenso, Martha (1900–1963), *Wild Geese* (novel)	**Barton, Bruce** (1886–1967), *The Man Nobody Knows* (advice manual)	
	Stein, Gertrude (1874–1946), *The Making of Americans* (fiction)		
	Yezierska, Anzia (1880–1970), *Bread Givers* (novel)		
1926	**Bennett, Gwendolyn** (1902–1981), "Wedding Day" (fiction)	The U.S. fails to join World Court when the two sides cannot agree on U.S. demands.	Germany is admitted to the League of Nations.
	DeKruif, Paul (1890–1971), *Microbe Hunters* (nonfiction)	Congress passes the Air Commerce Act.	Hirohito succeeds as emperor of Japan.

Faulkner, **William** (1897–1962), *Soldier's Pay* (novel)

Hemingway, Ernest (1899–1961), *The Sun Also Rises* (novel)

Lardner, Ring (1885–1933), *The Love Nest and Other Stories* (fiction)

Mencken, H. L. (1880–1956), *Prejudices* (essays, vol. 5 of 6)

Nugent, Richard (1906–1987), "Smoke, Lilies, and Jade" (fiction)

Stribling, T. S. (1881–1965), *Teeftallow* (novel)

Van Vechten, Carl (1880–1964), *Nigger Heaven* (novel)

Walrond, Eric (1898–1966), *Tropic Death* (fiction)

White, Walter (1893–1955), *Flight* (novel)

Wilder, Thornton (1897–1975), *The Cabala* (novel)

President Coolidge signs the Revenue Act in his continued effort to repeal taxes.

Henry Ford shocks industrial leaders when he orders 8-hour day, 5-day work week.

Act of Congress creates the Army Air Corps.

Richard Byrd and Floyd Bennett make first airplane flight over the North Pole.

Drs. George Minoz and William Murphy devise a cure for pernicious anemia.

"Jelly Roll" Morton and his Red Hot Peppers make a series of seminal jazz recordings: i.e. "Black Bottom Stomp," "Jelly Roll Blues."

Fire!!, ed. **Wallace Thurman**, publishes its only issue.

The General (film) directed by **Buster Keaton**

Ibn Saud becomes king of Saudi Arabia.

Aragon, Louis (1897–1982), *The Paris Peasant* (novel)

Gide, André (1869–1951), *The Counterfeiters* (novel)

Kawabata Yasunari (1899–1972), *The Izu Dancer* (novel)

Lawrence, T. E. (1888–1935), *Seven Pillars of Wisdom* (memoir)

Max Ernst finishes *Mary Spanking the Christ Child* (painting)

Metropolis (film) directed by **Fritz Lang**

	American Literary Texts	American Events, Texts, and Arts	Other Events, Texts, and Arts
1927	Aiken, Conrad (1889–1973), *Blue Voyage* (novel)	Nicola Sacco and Bartolomeo Vanzetti are executed.	Chiang Kai-shek oppresses communists in China.
	Cather, Willa (1876–1947), *Death Comes for the Archbishop* (novel)	U.S. Supreme Court declares unconstitutional a Texas law forbidding black vote in primaries.	German economy collapses.
	Hemingway, Ernest (1899–1961), *Men Without Women* (fiction)	Charles Lindbergh makes first solo nonstop transatlantic flight.	Heidegger, Martin (1889–1976), *Being and Time* (philosophy)
	Lewis, Sinclair (1885–1951), *Elmer Gantry* (novel)	Commercial transatlantic telephone service begins.	Werner Heisenberg (1901–1976) writes 14-page letter to Wolfgang Pauli in which he outlines the uncertainty principle.
	Mencken, H. L. (1880–1956), *Prejudices* (essays, vol. 6 of 6)	Radio Act allows for public ownership of the airwaves.	Hesse, Herman (1877–1962), *Der Steppenwolf* (novel)
	Mourning Dove (1888–1936), *Cogewea, the Half-Blood* (novel)	First experimental television broadcast from New York to Washington DC.	Mauriac, François (1885–1970), *Thérèse Desqueyroux* (novel)
	Rölvaag, Ole (1876–1931) *Giants in the Earth* (novel) trans. Lincoln Colcord	Drs. Phillip Drinker and Louis A. Shaw devise the first "iron lung" respirator.	Proust, Marcel (1871–1922), *Time Regained* (novel, vol. 7 of *In Search of Lost Time*)
	Sinclair, Upton (1878–1968), *Oil!* (novel)	*The Jazz Singer* (film) with Al Jolson is first major film with sound.	Woolf, Virginia (1882–1941), *To the Lighthouse* (novel)
	Wilder, Thornton (1897–1975), *The Bridge of San Luis Rey* (novel)	Aaron Copland, *Concerto for Piano and Orchestra* (orchestral music)	

1928		
Bradford, Roark (1896–1948), *Ol' Man Adam an' His Children* (fiction) Fisher, Rudolf (1897–1934), *The Walls of Jericho* (novel) Larsen, Nella (1891–1964), *Quicksand* (novel) Lewisohn, Ludwig (1882–1955), *The Island Within* (autobiography) McKay, Claude (1890–1948), *Home to Harlem* (novel) Rosenfeld, Paul (1890–1946), *A Boy in the Sun* (novel) Sinclair, Upton (1878–1968), *Boston* (novel)	Congress passes Alien Property Act to compensate Germans for property seized in the U.S. during World War I. Herbert Hoover defeats Al Smith in the election for president of the United States. George Eastman shows first color motion pictures in his lab in Rochester, NY. Boas, Franz (1858–1942), *Anthropology and Modern Life* (anthropology) Mead, Margaret (1901–1971), *Coming of Age in Samoa* (anthropology) White, Walter (1893–1955), *Rope and Faggot* (nonfiction) *Plane Crazy* (cartoon) by Walt Disney marks first appearance of Mickey Mouse.	Alexander Fleming cultures penicillium, the first antibiotic. First Five Year Plan begins in the Soviet Union. Lawrence, D. H. (1885–1930), *Lady Chatterley's Lover* (novel) Mussolini, Benito (1883–1945), *My Autobiography* (autobiography) trans. Richard Washburn Child Waugh, Evelyn (1902–1966), *Decline and Fall* (novel) Maurice Ravel composes *Bolero* (ballet).
1929		
Dreiser, Theodore (1871–1945), *A Gallery of Women* 2 vols. (fiction) Fauset, Jessie (1882–1961), *Plum Bun* (novel) Faulkner, William (1897–1962), *The Sound and the Fury* (novel) Glasgow, Ellen (1874–1945), *They Stooped to Folly* (novel)	The U.S. Senate agrees to the Brand–Kellogg Pact banning war as an instrument of national policy. Agricultural Marketing Act fails to hold prices when farmers refuse to reduce acreage under cultivation.	The Great Depression hits the world economy. Astronomer Edwin Hubble proves that the Universe is expanding. Leads to development of the Big Bang theory.

American Literary Texts	American Events, Texts, and Arts	Other Events, Texts, and Arts
Hammett, Dashiell (1894–1961), *Red Harvest* (novel)	Stock market crashes furthering an already deepening economic downturn.	Minority Labour government forms in Great Britain.
Hemingway, Ernest (1899–1961), *A Farewell to Arms* (novel)	The Great Depression begins.	The Lateran Treaty establishes Vatican City as an independent region in Italy.
LaFarge, Oliver (1882–1961), *Laughing Boy* (novel)	Gangland slaying in Chicago: the St. Valentine's Day Massacre.	Jews and Arabs clash at the Wailing Wall.
Larsen, Nella (1891–1964), *Passing* (novel)	**Lynd, Robert** (1892–1970) and **Helen Merrell** (1894–1982), *Middletown, U.S.A.* (social commentary)	**Remarque, Erich Maria** (1898–1970), *All Quiet on the Western Front* (novel)
Lewis, Sinclair (1885–1951), *Dodsworth* (novel)	**Lippman, Walter** (1889–1974), *A Preface to Morals* (social philosophy)	**Woolf, Virginia** (1882–1941), *A Room of One's Own* (feminist criticism)
McKay, Claude (1890–1948), *Banjo* (novel)	**Georgia O'Keeffe** finishes *Black Flower and Blue Larkspur* (painting).	*The Blue Angel* (film) directed by **Josef Von Sternberg**
Rölvaag, Ole (1876–1931), *Peder Victorious* (novel)	**Cole Porter** has first hit show with *Fifty Million Frenchmen*.	
Thurber, James (1894–1961) & **White, E. B.** (1899–1985), *Is Sex Necessary?* (satire)		
Thurman, Wallace (1902–1934), *The Blacker the Berry* (novel)		
Wolfe, Thomas (1900–1938), *Look Homeward, Angel* (novel)		

| 1930 | Dahl, Dorthea (1881–1958), "Kopper-kjelen" (fiction)

Dahlberg, Edward (1900–1977), Bottom Dogs (novel)
Dos Passos, John (1896–1970), The 42nd Parallel (novel)

Faulkner, William (1897–1962), As I Lay Dying (novel)
Fisher, Dorothy (1879–1958), The Deepening Stream (novel)
Gold, Mike (1894–1967), Jews Without Money (novel)

Hammett, Dashiell (1894–1961), The Maltese Falcon (novel)
Hughes, Langston (1902–1967), Not Without Laughter (novel)

Lewisohn, Ludwig (1882–1955), The Vehement Flame (novel)
Porter, Katherine Anne (1890–1980), Flowering Judas (fiction)
Roberts, Kenneth (1885–1957), Arundel (novel)
Whitfield, Raoul (1898–1945), Death in a Bowl (novel) | President Hoover signs the Smoot–Hawley Tariff Act to boost farm economy. It fails to do so.

Hoover asks Congress for $100 million for public works projects designed to stimulate the economy.
The population in the U.S. is 122,775,046.
1 of every 5 Americans owns an automobile.
The Democrats regain control of the House of Representatives in mid-term elections.
Clyde Tombaugh discovers Pluto, the 9th planet in the solar system.
Parrington, Vernon (1871–1929), Main Currents in American Thought (criticism, 3 vols.)
Edward Hopper finishes Early Sunday Morning (painting).
Grant Wood finishes American Gothic (painting).

Fortune magazine publishes its first issue. | France starts construction of the Maginot line.

Haile Selassie becomes emperor of Ethiopia.

The Turks rename Constantinople as Istanbul.
Yellow fever vaccine is developed.

Gas turbine is invented.

Musil, Robert (1880–1942) The Man Without Qualities (novel) |
|---|---|---|

	American Literary Texts	American Events, Texts, and Arts	Other Events, Texts, and Arts
1931	Adamic, Louis (1899–1951), *Laughing in the Jungle: the Autobiography of an Immigrant in America* (autobiography)	Congress sets aside funds to run Muscle Shoals power plant on Tennessee River. Forerunner of the Tennessee Valley Authority.	Japan invades Manchuria.
	Buck, Pearl (1892–1973), *The Good Earth* (novel)	Congress overrides Hoover veto of Veterans Compensation Act.	Alfonso XIII is overthrown in Spain. Spanish Republic is formed.
	Cantwell, Robert (1908–1978), *Laugh and Lie Down* (novel)	More than 3,800 banks fail as debtors default on loans and financial panic spreads across nation.	The planned capital of India, New Delhi, opens.
		Commission reports on bootlegging and declares Prohibition unenforceable.	
	Faulkner, William (1897–1962), *Sanctuary* (novel)	Chicago mob boss, Al Capone, is sentenced to 11 years in prison for tax evasion.	Gödel, Kurt (1906–1978), incompleteness theorem (mathematics)
	Fauset, Jessie (1882–1961), *The Chinaberry Tree* (novel)		
	Goldman, Emma (1869–1940), *Living My Life* (autobiography)	Empire State Building and George Washington Bridge are completed in New York City.	
	Rölvaag, Ole (1876–1931), *Their Fathers' God* (novel)	Dreiser, Theodore (1871–1945), *Tragic America* (social commentary)	
	Steffens, Lincoln (1866–1936), *Autobiography* (autobiography)	Santayana, George (1863–1952), *The Genteel Tradition at Bay* (social commentary)	Woolf, Virginia (1882–1941), *The Waves* (novel)
	Stribling, T. S. (1881–1965), *The Forge* (novel)	Wilson, Edmund (1895–1972), *Axel's Castle* (criticism)	
	West, Nathanael (1903–1940), *The Dream Life of Balso Snell* (novel)	*City Lights* (film) directed by Charlie Chaplin	*M* (film) directed by Fritz Lang

1932

Caldwell, Erskine (1903–1987), *Tobacco Road* (novel)

Cullen, Countee (1903–1946), *One Way to Heaven* (novel)

Dos Passos, John (1896–1970), *1919* (novel)

Farrell, James T. (1904–1979), *Young Lonigan* (novel)

Faulkner, William (1897–1962), *Light in August* (novel)

Fisher, Rudolf (1897–1934), *The Conjure Man Dies* (novel)

Glasgow, Ellen (1874–1945), *The Sheltered Life* (novel)

Hammett, Dashiell (1894–1961), *The Thin Man* (novel)

Hemingway, Ernest (1899–1961), *Death in the Afternoon* (nonfiction)

Schuyler, George (1895–1977), *Black No More* (satire)

President Hoover calls for friends, charities, and local governments to help those in need.

Hoover recommends creating the Reconstruction Finance Corporation to provide loans to large businesses.

The Glass–Steagall Act separates brokerage and banking businesses.

Norris–LaGuardia Act forbids employers from discriminating against workers in unions.

Farmers begin to refuse to accede to bank foreclosures.

Unemployment in some cities reaches 40%.

Douglas MacArthur uses force to remove protesting servicemen from Washington.

Franklin Roosevelt defeats Herbert Hoover in election for president of the United States.

Crosby, Harry (1899–1929), *The War Letters* (correspondence)

World-wide economic depression leaves many millions unemployed.

James Chadwick discovers the neutron.

English physicists split the atom for the first time.

German industrialists back Hitler.

British government declares Congress of India illegal. Arrests Gandhi.

Japan attacks Shanghai.

Huxley, Aldous (1894–1963), *Brave New World* (novel)

Mauriac, François (1885–1970), *The Viper's Tangle* (novel)

American Literary Texts	American Events, Texts, and Arts	Other Events, Texts, and Arts
Stong, Phil (1899–1957), *State Fair* (novel)	**Wilson, Edmund** (1895–1972), *American Jitters: A Year of the Slump* (social documentary)	Hitler becomes chancellor of Germany.
Stribling, T. S. (1881–1965), *The Store* (novel)	**Charles Burchfield** finishes *November Evening* (painting).	Severe famine in the Soviet Union.
Thurman, Wallace (1902–1934), *Infants of the Spring* (novel)	"Brother Can You Spare a Dime" (popular song)	Japan withdraws from the League of Nations.
Aiken, Conrad (1889–1973), *Great Circle* (novel)	President Roosevelt announces new federal banking policy in first radio "fireside chat."	**Mann, Thomas** (1875–1955), *Joseph and his Brothers* (multivolume novel)
Caldwell, Erskine (1903–1987), *God's Little Acre* (novel)	Harry Hopkins heads the new Federal Emergency Relief Administration.	**Orwell, George** (1903–1950), *Down and Out in Paris and London* (memoir)
Campbell, William (1893–1954), *Company K* (novel)	Federal Securities Act mandates public information to accompany new stock issues.	**Brassaï** produces *Paris du Nuit* (photography).
Conroy, Jack (1899–1980), *The Disinherited* (novel)	Congress passes National Industrial Recovery Act, including Public Works Administration.	
Fauset, Jessie (1882–1961), *Comedy: American Style* (novel)	Prohibition is repealed.	
Hemingway, Ernest (1899–1961), *Winner Take Nothing* (fiction)	Confidence in banking system in the U.S. gradually returns.	
Herbst, Josephine (1897–1969), *Pity Is Not Enough* (novel)	Judge John M. Woolsey lifts the ban on James Joyce's *Ulysses*.	
McKay, Claude (1890–1948), *Banana Bottom* (novel)		
Roberts, Kenneth (1885–1957), *Rabble in Arms* (novel)		

1933

Stein, Gertrude (1874–1946), *The Autobiography of Alice B. Toklas* (autobiography)

West, Nathanael (1903–1940), *Miss Lonelyhearts* (novel)

1934

Cain, James (1892–1977), *The Postman Always Rings Twice* (novel)

Cantwell, Robert (1908–1978), *Land of Plenty* (novel)

Cowley, Malcolm (1898–1989), *Exile's Return* (autobiography)

Farrell, James T. (1904–1979), *The Young Manhood of Studs Lonigan* (novel)

Fitzgerald, F. Scott (1896–1940), *Tender is the Night* (novel)

Fuchs, Daniel (1909–1993), *Summer in Williamsburg* (novel)

Herbst, Josephine (1897–1969), *The Executioner Waits* (novel)

Hughes, Langston (1902–1967), *The Ways of White Folks* (fiction)

Hurston, Zora Neale (1891–1960), *Jonah's Gourd Vine* (novel)

Mathews, John Joseph (Osage, 1894–1979), *Sundown* (novel)

Aaron Copland composes *Short Symphony.*

Nye Committee implies that military-industrial leaders caused World War I in order to profit from it.

Massive drought plagues the Great Plains. The dust bowl.

Congress creates the Federal Communications Commission to regulate radio and telegraph.

Federal Housing Administration created to insure home mortgages.

Du Pont patents the formula for nylon.

Police kill John Dillinger, and Bonnie and Clyde, in shoot-outs.

Juliana Force organizes the American pavilion at the Venice Biennale.

Cole Porter composes *Anything Goes* (musical).

Reginald Marsh finishes *Negroes on Rockaway Beach* (painting).

Hitler orders the assassination of his rivals in Germany.

The Soviet Union is admitted to the League of Nations.

Mao's army begins the "Long March" to northern China.

Kirov is assassinated in the Soviet Union.

Aragon, Louis (1897–1982), *The Bells of Basel* (novel)

Beckett, Samuel (1906–1989), *More Pricks Than Kicks* (fiction)

Waugh, Evelyn (1902–1966), *A Handful of Dust* (novel)

Wodehouse, P. G. (1881–1975), *Thank You, Jeeves* (novel)

Henri Cartier-Bresson takes *Enfants jouant dans les ruines* (photograph).

	American Literary Texts	American Events, Texts, and Arts	Other Events, Texts, and Arts
	Miller, Henry (1891–1980), *Tropic of Cancer* (novel)	The Hays Code (1930) for moral decency in films goes into strict effect.	Italy invades Abyssinia.
	O'Hara John (1905–1970), *Appointment in Samarra* (novel)	*It Happened One Night* (film) directed by **Frank Capra**	Germany incorporates the Saarland.
	Roth, Henry (1906–1995), *Call It Sleep* (novel)	*It's a Gift* (film) starring **W. C. Fields**	The Nuremberg Laws against Jews come into effect in Germany.
	Slesinger, Tess (1905–1945), *The Unpossessed* (novel)		
	Stribling, T. S. (1881–1965), *Unfinished Cathedral* (novel)		
	West, Nathanael (1903–1940), *A Cool Million* (novel)		
	Wharton, Edith (1862–1937), *A Backward Glance* (autobiography)		
1935	**Algren, Nelson** (1909–1981), *Somebody in Boots* (novel)	Roosevelt creates Works Progress Administration.	
	Anderson, Sherwood (1876–1941), *Puzzled America* (social commentary)	Harry Hopkins, WPA head, employs artists, writers, actors, to document state of nation.	
	Du Bois, W. E. B. (1868–1963), *Black Reconstruction* (nonfiction)	Rural Electrification Commission provides service to remote areas of the United States.	
	Farrell, James T. (1904–1979), *Judgment Day* (novel, vol. 3 of Lonigan trilogy)	Congress passes the Social Security Act.	

	Authors	Events	World Events
	Glasgow, Ellen (1874–1945), *Vein of Iron* (novel)	Revenue Act of 1935 sharply increases the taxation of the rich in the U.S.	Persia changes its name to Iran.
	Hemingway, Ernest (1899–1961), *Green Hills of Africa* (personal narrative)	Congress of Industrial Organizations (CIO) forms as a labor union.	British Parliament separates Burma and Aden from India.
	Hurston, Zora Neale (1891–1960), *Mules and Men* (folklore)	Riots in Harlem mark the start of decreasing opportunity for blacks in New York.	Xiao Hong (1911–1942), *The Field of Life and Death* (novel)
	Lewis, Sinclair (1885–1951), *It Can't Happen Here* (novel)	Huey Long is assassinated in Louisiana.	
	McKay, Claude (1890–1948), *Banana Bottom* (novel)	George Gershwin composes *Porgy and Bess* (opera).	
	McCoy, Horace (1897–1955), *They Shoot Horses, Don't They?* (novel)	*Top Hat* (film) starring Fred Astaire and Ginger Rogers	
	O'Hara, John (1905–1970), *Butterfield 8* (novel)	*The Informer* (film) directed by John Ford	
	Steinbeck, John (1902–1968), *Tortilla Flat* (novel)		
	Wolfe, Thomas (1900–1938), *Of Time and the River* (novel)	*David Copperfield* (film) directed by Mack Sennett	Spanish Civil War begins between fascist forces and Republican government.
1936	Barnes, Djuna (1892–1982), *Nightwood* (novel)	Congress passes Soil Conservation Act to boost efforts to end erosion of Great Plains.	Germany, Italy, and Japan form Axis Alliance.
	Bontemps, Arna (1902–1973) *Black Thunder* (novel)	Robinson–Putnam Act forbids national chains from underselling businesses in small towns.	Japanese invade China and capture Beijing.
	Cain, James (1892–1977), *Double Indemnity* (novel)	Hoover Dam is completed near Las Vegas, Nevada.	

American Literary Texts	American Events, Texts, and Arts	Other Events, Texts, and Arts
		The British Broadcasting Corporation begins television broadcasts.
	Sitdown strikes and industrial unrest sweep the nation.	Jesse Owens wins four gold medals at the Berlin Olympics, upsetting Hitler's theories of Aryan racial superiority.
Dos Passos, John (1896–1970), *The Big Money* (novel)	Radar system developed by the U.S. Signal Corps.	Oil is found in Saudi Arabia.
Faulkner, William (1897–1962), *Absalom, Absalom!* (novel)		Arabs revolt in Palestine.
Fuchs, Daniel (1909–1993), *Homage to Blenholt* (novel)	Brooks, Van Wyck (1886–1963), *The Flowering of New England* (criticism)	General labor strike in France.
Gunther, John (1910–1970), *Inside Europe* (nonfiction)	Freeman, Joseph (1897–1965), *An American Testament* (autobiography)	Keynes, John Maynard (1883–1946), *A General Theory of Employment, Interest, and Money* (economics)
McNickle, D'Arcy (Cree, 1904–1997), *The Surrounded* (novel)	Luhan, Mabel Dodge (1879–1962), *Movers and Shakers* (autobiography)	Sergei Rachmaninov composes *Symphony No. 3* (orchestral music)
Miller, Henry (1891–1980), *Black Spring* (novel)	Frank Lloyd Wright designs Fallingwater in Bear Run, Pennsylvania.	
Mitchell, Margaret (1900–1949), *Gone with the Wind* (novel)	Samuel Barber's *First Symphony* premieres in Rome, Italy.	
	The Plow that Broke the Plains (documentary film) directed by **Pare Larentz**	
Steinbeck, John (1902–1968), *In Dubious Battle* (novel)	*Life* magazine publishes its first issue.	
Winther, Sophus Keith (1893–1983), *Take All To Nebraska* (novel)		

1937		
Fante, John (1909–1983), *Wait Until Spring, Bandidni* (novel)	U.S. Steel recognizes the United Mine Workers as a legitimate labor union.	Leon Trotsky exiled from the Soviet Union.
Fuchs, Daniel (1909–1993), *Low Company* (novel)	President Roosevelt signs the Neutrality Act.	Neville Chamberlain becomes prime minister in Britain.
Hemingway, Ernest (1899–1961), *To Have and Have Not* (novel)	Roosevelt appoints Hugo Black to the U.S. Supreme Court thereby solidifying a pro New Deal court.	Spanish forces under Francisco Franco bomb Guernica.
Hurston, Zora Neale (1891–1960), *Their Eyes Were Watching God* (novel)	Golden Gate Bridge is completed.	Sino-Japanese war resumes near Beijing.
Kang, Younghill (1903–1972), *East Goes West: The Making of an Oriental Yankee* (novel)	The news account of the Hindenburg explosion is first nation-wide radio broadcast.	**Masuji Ibuse** (1898–1993), *John Manjiro, the Cast-Away* (novel)
Levin, Meyer (1905–1981), *The Old Bunch* (novel)	**Asch, Nathan** (1902–1964), *The Road: In Search of America* (personal narrative)	**Sartre, Jean-Paul** (1905–1980), *Nausea* (novel)
Marquand, John (1893–1960), *The Late George Apley* (novel)	National Cancer Institute founded	**Dinesen, Isak** (1885–1962), *Out of Africa* (travel narrative)
McKay, Claude (1890–1948), *A Long Way from Home* (autobiography)	**Caldwell, Erskine** (1903–1987) and **Bourke-White, Margaret** (1904–1971), *You Have Seen Their Faces* (social commentary)	Pablo Picasso finishes *Guernica* (painting)
Roberts, Kenneth (1885–1957), *Northwest Passage* (novel)	**Lin Yutang** (1895–1976), *My Country and My People* (nonfiction)	**Carl Orff** composes *Carmina Burana* (orchestral music)
Steinbeck, John (1902–1968), *Of Mice and Men* (novel)	**Lippmann, Walter** (1889–1974), *The Good Society* (social commentary)	*La Grande Illusion* (film) directed by **Jean Renoir**
Thurber, James (1894–1961), *Let Your Mind Alone!* (humor)		
Winther, Sophus Keith (1893–1983), *Mortgage Your Heart* (novel)		
Wright, Richard (1908–1960), *Lawd Today* (novel, ms. finished)		

	American Literary Texts	American Events, Texts, and Arts	Other Events, Texts, and Arts
1938	Adamic, Louis (1899–1951), *My America* (social commentary) Dos Passos, John (1896–1970), *U.S.A.* (trilogy collected) Miguéis, José Rodrigues (1901–1980), "Gente de Terceira Classe" [Steerage] (fiction) O'Hara, John (1905–1970), *Hope of Heaven* (novel) Peattie, Donald (1898–1964), *A Prairie Grove* (naturalist narrative) Steinbeck, John (1902–1968), *The Long Valley* (fiction) Winther, Sophus Keith (1893–1983), *This Passion Never Dies* (novel) Wright, Richard (1908–1960), *Uncle Tom's Children* (fiction)	President Roosevelt asks Congress for funds to begin military build-up. Civil Aeronautics Act ushers in era of passenger airplanes. MacLeish, Archibald (1892–1982), *Land of the Free* (social documentary) Stearns, Harold E. (1891–1943), *America Now: An Inquiry into Civilization in the United States* (symposium) Walker Evans produces *American Photographs* (photography). *The War of the Worlds* (radio play) by Orson Welles scares public who take it literally.	Neville Chamberlain signs Munich Accord with Adolf Hitler. Stalin purges the Communist Party of USSR after several show trials. Anti-Jewish pogrom, Kristallnacht, in Germany. Otto Hahn experiments successfully with nuclear fission. Beckett, Samuel (1906–1938), *Murphy* (novel) Greene, Graham (1904–1991), *Brighton Rock* (novel)
1939	Chandler, Raymond (1888–1959), *The Big Sleep* (novel)	*Snow White and the Seven Dwarves* (feature cartoon) by Walt Disney. Roosevelt consolidates the Public Building Administration, Public Roads Administration, Public Works Administration, Works Progress Administration, and the U.S. Housing Authority within the Federal Works Agency.	Germany invades Czechoslovakia and Poland.

di **Donato, Pietro** (1911–1992), *Christ in Concrete* (novel)

Herbst, Josephine (1897–1969), *Rope of Gold* (novel)

Hurston, Zora Neale (1891–1960), *Moses, Man of the Mountain* (novel)

Lovecraft, H. P. (1890–1937), *The Shadow out of Time* (science fiction)

Miller, Henry (1891–1980), *Tropic of Capricorn* (novel)

Parker, Dorothy (1893–1967), *Here Lies* (fiction)

Porter, Katherine Anne (1890–1980), *Pale Horse, Pale Rider* (fiction)

Steinbeck, John (1902–1968), *The Grapes of Wrath* (novel)

Warren, Robert Penn (1905–1989), *Night Rider* (novel)

West, Nathanael (1903–1940), *The Day of the Locust* (novel)

Drs. Philip Levine and Rufus Stetson discover the presence of Rh factors in human blood.

Sears, Roebuck catalogue carries fashion dresses for the first time.

Nylon stockings appear for sale.

Lange, Dorothea (1895–1965) and **Taylor, Paul** (1917–), *An American Exodus: A Record of Human Erosion in the Thirties* (documentary)

McKenney, Ruth (1911–1972), *Industrial Valley* (social documentary)

Frank Lloyd Wright builds Taliesin West and the Johnson Wax Co. building.

First performance of the *Second Piano Sonata* by Charles Ives

Stagecoach (film) directed by John Ford

Germany and Soviet Union sign nonaggression pact. Russia invades Finland.

Italy invades Albania.

Swiss scientist, Paul Müller, synthesizes dichlorodiphenyltrichloroethane (DDT).

Britain employs radar to protect its coast.

Joyce, James (1882–1941), *Finnegans Wake* (novel)

The Rules of the Game (film) directed by **Jean Renoir**

	American Literary Texts	American Events, Texts, and Arts	Other Events, Texts, and Arts
1940	Anderson, Sherwood (1876–1941), *Home Town* (social commentary)	President Franklin Roosevelt reelected for third term.	
	Chandler, Raymond (1888–1959), *Farewell, My Lovely* (novel)	Congress passes law requiring alien residents to register with the U.S. Government.	Germany invades Norway, Denmark, Belgium, and Paris.
	Chávez, Fray Angélico (1910–1996), *New Mexico Triptych* (fiction)		
	De Capite, Michael (??), *Maria* (novel)	29.5 million households in the U.S. own a radio. U.S. population is 131,669,275.	Leon Trotsky is assassinated in Mexico.
	Fante, John (1909–1983), *Dago Red* (fiction)	Life expectancy in the U.S. reaches 64, 15 years higher than at the turn of the century.	Germany, Italy, and Japan sign an alliance for mutual protection.
	Faulkner, William (1897–1962), *The Hamlet* (novel)	First compulsory peacetime draft in the U.S. begins.	Japan invades Indochina.
	Flanner, Janet (1892–1978), *An American in Paris* (personal narrative)	Woody Guthrie writes "This Land is My Land" (folk song)	Winston Churchill becomes prime minister of Britain.
	Hemingway, Ernest (1899–1961), *For Whom the Bell Tolls* (novel)	*The Philadelphia Story* (film) directed by **George Cukor**	Greene, Graham (1904–1991), *The Power and the Glory* (novel)
	Hughes, Langston (1902–1967), *The Big Sea* (autobiography)	*The Great Dictator* (film) directed by **Charlie Chaplin**	
	Maltz, Albert (1908–1988), *The Underground Stream* (novel)	Adamic, Louis (1899–1951), *From Many Lands* (social commentary)	
	McCullers, Carson (1917–1967), *The Heart is a Lonely Hunter* (novel)	Brooks, Van Wyck (1886–1963), *New England: Indian Summer* (criticism)	
	Saroyan, William (1908–1981), *My Name is Aram* (fiction)	Wilson, Edmund (1895–1972), *To the Finland Station* (social commentary)	
	Wolfe, Thomas (1900–1938), *You Can't Go Home Again* (novel)		
	Wright, Richard (1908–1960), *Native Son* (novel)	"Blueberry Hill" (popular song)	

1941	Agee, James (1909–1955), *Let Us Now Praise Famous Men* (documentary narrative) Bell, Thomas (1903–1961), *Out of This Furnace* (novel) Fast, Howard (1914–), *The Last Frontier* (novel) Fitzgerald, F. Scott (1896–1940), *The Last Tycoon* (novel) McCullers, Carson (1917–1967), *Reflections in a Golden Eye* (novel) Nabokov, Vladimir (1899–1977), *The Real Life of Sebastian Knight* (novel)	Lend-Lease Act signed with Britain Advent of common use of penicillin Coal and steel workers lead protracted strikes. Japan bombs Pearl Harbor. U.S. declares war on Axis powers. Shirer, William (1904–1993), *Berlin Diary* (nonfiction) Snow, Edgar (1905–1972), *The Battle for Asia* (nonfiction)	Germany and Italy combine to invade the Balkans. Germany bombs London and invades Russia. Soviet Union and Japan sign nonaggression treaty. Edwin McMillan and Glenn Seaborg discover plutonium. Borges, Jorge Luis (1899–1986), *The Garden of Forking Paths* (fiction) Dmitry Shostakovich composes *Symphony No. 7* in Leningrad siege.
	Welty, Eudora (1909–2001), *A Green of Curtain* (novel)	Wright, Richard (1908–1960), *Twelve Million Black Voices* (social documentary) Edward Hopper finishes *Nighthawks* (painting). *Citizen Kane* (film) directed by Orson Welles	
1942	Algren, Nelson (1909–1981), *Never Come Morning* (novel) Faulkner, William (1897–1962), *Go Down, Moses* (novel) Glaspell, Susan (1884–1948), *Norma Ashe* (novel)	Executive Order 9066 sends Japanese Americans to internment camps. U.S. Supreme Court finds Georgia labor laws violate the 13th Amendment. First nuclear chain reaction produced in the labs of Enrico Fermi at the University of Chicago.	Battle of the Coral Sea: first naval fight conducted only by airplane Battle of Midway: first major defeat of Japanese navy Battle of El Alamein forces German retreat out of North Africa.

American Literary Texts	American Events, Texts, and Arts	Other Events, Texts, and Arts
	First electronic computer developed.	Germans begin to use gas chambers to murder Jews in mass numbers.
Hersey, John (1914–1993), Men on Bataan (nonfiction)		
Hurston, Zora Neale (1891–1960) Dust Tracks on a Road (autobiography)		
Mangione, Jerre (1909–1998), Mount Allegro (memoir-novel)	Cousins, Norman (1912–1990), The Democratic Chance (nonfiction)	Magnetic recording tape is invented.
McCarthy, Mary (1912–1989), The Company She Keeps (fiction)	White, W. L. (1900–1973), They Were Expendable (nonfiction)	Camus, Albert (1913–1960), The Stranger (novel); The Myth of Sisyphus (essay)
Thurber, James (1894–1961), My World and Welcome to It (essays)		
Welty, Eudora (1909–2001), The Robber Bridegroom (novel)	Irving Berlin writes "White Christmas" (popular song)	
White, E. B. (1899–1985), One Man's Meat (personal narratives)		
		Russians push back German invasion at Battle of Stalingrad.
Lovecraft, H. P. (1890–1937), Beyond the Wall of Sleep (science fiction)	U.S. Government forbids racial discrimination by war contractors.	American and British forces invade Sicily.
	U.S. Government begins to collect paycheck withholding tax.	Mussolini deposed
	Widespread rationing of food and clothes in the United States	
Mitchell, Joseph (1908–1998), McSorley's Wonderful Saloon (essay)	Jackson Pollock (1912–1956), Mural Painting (painting)	Hesse, Herman (1877–1962), The Glass Bead Game (novel)
Rand, Ayn (1905–1982), The Fountainhead (novel)	Rodgers and Hammerstein's Oklahoma premieres on Broadway.	Sartre, Jean-Paul (1905–1980), Being and Nothingness (philosophy)
Smith, Betty (1904–1972), A Tree Grows in Brooklyn (novel)		

1943

	Stegner, Wallace (1909–1993), *The Big Rock Candy Mountain* (novel)	*Casablanca* (film) directed by **Michael Curtiz**	D-Day: Allied forces invade Normandy on June 6.
	Mori, Toshio (1910–1980), "A Sketch" (fiction)		Allied forces march toward Berlin and score several victories in the Pacific.
	Wolfert, Ira (1907–1997), *Tucker's People* (novel)		Germans launch V-1 and V-2 rockets toward London.
1944	Bellow, Saul (1915–), *Dangling Man* (novel)	Franklin Roosevelt reelected to a fourth term as president.	**Borges, Jorge Luis** (1899–1986), *Fictions* (fiction).
	Brown, Harry (1917–1986), *A Walk in the Sun* (novel)	Congress passes the GI Bill of Rights.	**Sartre, Jean-Paul** (1905–1980), *No Exit* (drama).
	Hersey, John (1914–1993), *A Bell for Adano* (novel)	Communist Party of the U.S. reconfigures itself into Communist Political Association.	**Francis Bacon** finishes *Three Studies for Figures at the Base of a Crucifixion* (painting).
	Porter, Katherine Anne (1890–1980), *The Leaning Tower* (fiction)	Government freezes prices on rationed domestic goods to prevent inflation.	
	Pyle, Ernie (1900–1945), *Brave Men* (battle narrative)	**Lemkin, Raphaël** (1900–1959), *Axis Rule in Occupied Europe* (nonfiction)	
	Smith, Lillian (1897–1966), *Strange Fruit* (novel)	**Mumford, Lewis** (1895–1990), *The Condition of Man* (nonfiction)	
	Stafford, Jean (1915–1979), *Boston Adventure* (novel)	**Myrdal, Gunnar** (1898–1987), *An American Dilemma* (nonfiction)	Victory in Europe: May 8, V-E Day.
1945	Glaspell, Susan (1882–1948), *Judd Rankin's Daughter* (novel)	U.S. Senate ratifies United Nations charter.	U.S. drops atomic bombs on Hiroshima and Nagasaki.
	Himes, Chester (1909–1984), *If He Hollers Let Him Go* (novel)	Franklin Roosevelt dies. Harry Truman becomes president.	Winston Churchill, Josef Stalin, and Franklin Roosevelt meet in Yalta.
	Miller, Arthur (1915–), *Focus* (novel)	President Truman announces the "Fair Deal" social policy.	

American Literary Texts	American Events, Texts, and Arts	Other Events, Texts, and Arts
Niggli, Josephina (1910–1983), *Mexican Village* (novel)	Tupperware invented	The United Nations is established.
Stein, Gertrude (1874–1946), *Wars I Have Seen* (nonfiction)		
Vidal, Gore (1925–), *Williwaw* (novel)	*The Lost Weekend* (film) directed by **Billy Wilder**	Orwell, George (1903–1950), *Animal Farm* (novel)
Wong, Jade Snow (1922–), *Fifth Chinese Daughter* (personal narrative)	Dizzie Gillespie (1917–1993) and Charlie Parker (1920–1955) record *Groovin' High, Ko Ko* (jazz).	Waugh, Evelyn (1902–1966), *Brideshead Revisited* (novel)
Wright, Richard (1908–1960), *Black Boy* (autobiography)		*Ivan the Terrible* (film) directed by **Sergei Eisenstein**
Bulosan, Carlos (1913–1956), *America is in the Heart* (personal narrative)	Atomic Energy Commission created	Joseph Stalin warns of anticommunist threat to Russia.
Hersey, John (1914–1993), *Hiroshima* (nonfiction)	In a speech in Fulton, Missouri, Winston Churchill declares that an "Iron Curtain" divides Eastern and Western Europe.	Communists in Indochina resist the reassertion of French rule.
McCullers, Carson (1917–1967), *The Member of the Wedding* (novel)	Hobbs bill passed, preventing unions from interfering with interstate commerce.	British and French forces pull out of Lebanon.
Petry, Ann (1911–1997), *The Street* (novel)	U.S. Marines put down an inmate riot at Alcatraz prison.	First majority Labour government nationalizes health care in Britain.
Rosenfeld, Isaac (1918–1956), *Passage from Home* (novel)	First houses are built in Levittown, New York, as suburban housing tracts rise on periphery of U.S. cities.	Nuremberg tribunal convicts 13 Nazis for crimes against humanity.
Schwartz, Delmore (1913–1966), "A Bitter Farce" (fiction)	*The Big Sleep* (film) directed by **Howard Hawks**	Juan Peron elected president of Argentina.

1946

Stein, Gertrude (1874–1946), *Yes is for a Very Young Man* (nonfiction)
Warren, Robert Penn (1905–1989), *All the King's Men* (novel)
Welty, Eudora (1909–2001), *Delta Wedding* (novel)

1947

Bellow, Saul (1915–), *The Victim* (novel)

Burns, John Horne (1916–1953), *The Gallery* (novel)

Dreiser, Theodore (1871–1945), *The Stoic* (novel)
Himes, Chester (1909–1984), *Lonely Crusade* (novel)
Hobson, Laura (1896–1986), *Gentlemen's Agreement* (novel)

Michener, James (1907–1997), *Tales of the South Pacific* (novel)
Motley, Willard (1912–1965), *Knock on Any Door* (novel)
Nabokov, Vladimir (1899–1977), *Bend Sinister* (novel)
Stafford, Jean (1915–1979), *The Mountain Lion* (novel)

The Best Years of Our Lives (film) directed by **William Wyler**

George Marshall proposes a plan to rebuild the war-ravaged nations of the world.

Congress passes Taft–Hartley Labor Act in an effort to limit power of organized labor.

An Act of Congress founds the Central Intelligence Agency.

President Truman consolidates armed forces into the Department of Defense and announces commitment to fight communism in foreign nations (Truman Doctrine).

The long-playing, or LP, record is invented.

The transistor is invented.

Chuck Yeager breaks the sound barrier in a rocket plane.

Beauty and the Beast (film) directed by **Jean Cocteau**
Open City (film) directed by **Roberto Rossellini**

India and Pakistan gain independence from United Kingdom.

Civil war in Greece and Soviet actions against Turkey cause U.S. to send aid.

The U.S. becomes trustee of Pacific islands once claimed by Japan.

Thor Heyerdahl and colleagues sail reed boat across Pacific: Kon-Tiki voyage.

The Dead Sea Scrolls are discovered.

Calvino, Italo (1923–1985), *The Path to the Nest of Spiders* (novel)
Camus, Albert (1913–1960), *The Plague* (novel)
Frank, Anne (1929–1945), *Diary of a Young Girl* (autobiography)
Kawabata, Yasunari (1899–1972), *Snow Country* (novel)

	American Literary Texts	American Events, Texts, and Arts	Other Events, Texts, and Arts
1948	Suárez, Mario (1925–1998), *Arizona Quarterly* stories (fiction)	Spiller, Robert (1896–1988), *Literary History of the United States* (nonfiction)	Levi, Primo (1919–1987), *If This is a Man* (memoir)
	Trilling, Lionel (1905–1975), *The Middle of the Journey* (novel)	Charlie Parker (1920–1955) records *Quasimado* (jazz).	Mann, Thomas (1875–1955), *Doktor Faustus* (novel)
	Capote, Truman (1924–1984), *Other Voices, Other Rooms* (novel)	Harry Truman reelected president	Mahatma Gandhi assassinated in India
	Cozzens, James Gould (1903–1978), *Guard of Honor* (novel)	Television becomes a national phenomenon (number of stations grows from 11 to 65).	State of Israel created
	Faulkner, William (1897–1962), *Intruder in the Dust* (novel)	Alger Hiss is indicted for espionage.	World Health Organization founded
	Lewis, Sinclair (1885–1951), *Knightsblood Royal* (novel)	Mine workers strike but return to work after the federal government levies heavy fines.	Communists seize power in Czechoslovakia.
	Lin Yutang (1895–1976), *Chinatown Family* (novel)	President Truman desegregates the armed forces.	Soviets blockade West Berlin. Americans airlift supplies to the city. Holograph invented in Britain
	Mailer, Norman (1923–), *The Naked and the Dead* (novel)	U.S. Supreme Court declares religious instruction in public schools unconstitutional.	
	Shaw, Irwin (1913–1984), *The Young Lions* (novel)	Kinsey, Alfred (1894–1956), *Sexual Behavior in the Human Male* (sociology)	Kobo, Abé (1924–1993), *The Road Sign at the End of the Street* (novel)
	Szilard, Leo (1898–1964), "Report on 'Grand Central Terminal'" (fiction)	Willem de Kooning (1904–1997), *Asheville*	Greene, Graham (1904–1991), *The Heart of the Matter* (novel)

1949

Taylor, Peter (1917–), *The Long Fourth and Other Stories* (fiction)

Vidal, Gore (1925–), *The City and the Pillar* (novel)

Algren, Nelson (1909–1981), *The Man with the Golden Arm* (novel)

Bowles, Paul (1910–1999), *The Sheltering Sky* (novel)

Capote, Truman (1924–1984), *The Tree of Life* (fiction)

Curran, Mary Doyle (1917–1981), *The Parish and the Hill* (novel)

Hawkes, John (1925–1998), *The Cannibal* (novel)

Mori, Toshio (1910–1980), *Yokohama, California* (fiction)

O'Hara, John (1905–1970), *A Rage to Live* (novel)

Welty, Eudora (1909–2001), *The Golden Apples* (fiction)

Yamamoto, Hisaye (1921–), "Seventeen Syllables" (fiction, collected in 1988)

Key Largo (film) directed by John Huston

Housing Act supports low-income housing development.

U.S. courts convict 11 members of the U.S. Communist Party for plot to overthrow the government.

U.S. Justice Department files antitrust suit against American Telegraph and Telephone.

Cortisone is discovered.

Samuel Barber (1910–1981), *Knoxville: Summer of 1915* (orchestral music)

Philip Johnson (1906–), Glass House (architecture)

Schlesinger, Arthur, Jr. (1917–), *The Vital Center* (nonfiction)

Miles Davis and Gil Evans release *The Rebirth of Cool* (cool jazz).

The Third Man (film) directed by Carol Reed

Paton, Alan (1903–1988), *Cry, the Beloved Country* (novel)

Bicycle Thieves (film) dir. **Vittorio de Sica**

NATO founded

Mao Tse-tung establishes communist rule in China.

Soviets explode their first atomic bomb.

Apartheid established in South Africa

J. F. J. Cade introduces lithium for treatment of manic depression.

de Beauvoir, Simone (1908–1986), *The Second Sex* (feminist theory)

Böll, Heinrich (1917–1985), *The Train Was on Time* (novel)

Borges, Jorge Luis (1899–1986), *The Aleph* (fiction)

Mishima Yukio (1925–1970), *Confessions of a Mask* (novel)

Orwell, George (1903–1950), *Nineteen Eighty-four* (novel)

	American Literary Texts	American Events, Texts, and Arts	Other Events, Texts, and Arts
1950	Asimov, Isaac (1920–1992), *I, Robot* (science fiction)	U.S. Army takes over railroads to prevent a labor strike.	North Korea invades South Korea. Korean War begins.
	Bradbury, Ray (1920–), *The Martian Chronicles* (science fiction)	Senator Joseph McCarthy incites fear of communism as head of Permanent Subcommittee on Investigations.	Klaus Fuchs arrested for espionage.
	Hemingway, Ernest (1899–1961), *Across the River and into the Trees* (novel)	House Committee on Un-American Activities accuses broad spectrum of citizens of subversive activity.	American military advisers arrive in South Vietnam.
	Hersey, John (1914–1993), *The Wall* (nonfiction)	45 million households own a radio.	China invades Tibet.
	Kerouac, Jack (1922–1969), *The Town and the City* (novel)	Sales of televisions reach 1 million.	Albert Einstein proposes the general field theory.
	Salinger, J. D. (1919–), "For Esmé – with Love and Squalor" (short story)	Riesman, David (1909–2002), *The Lonely Crowd* (sociology)	Duras, Marguerite (1914–1996), *The Sea Wall* (novel)
	Singer, Isaac Bashevis (1904–1991), *The Family Moskat* (novel)	Trilling, Lionel (1905–1975), *The Liberal Imagination* (criticism)	Lessing, Doris (1919–), *The Grass Is Singing* (novel)
	Stegner, Wallace (1909–1993), *The Women on the Wall* (fiction)	*All About Eve* (film) directed by Joseph K. Mankiewicz	*Rashomon* (film) directed by Akira Kurosawa
	Warren, Robert Penn (1905–1989), *Wild Enough and Time* (novel)	*The Men* (film) directed by Fred Zinneman	
	Yamamoto, Hisaye (1921–), "The Legend of Miss Sasagawara," "Wilshire Bus" (fiction)	"Your Show of Shows" debuts on television.	
		Charlie Brown (cartoon) by Charles Schulz first appears in syndication.	

BIBLIOGRAPHY

This selected bibliography is drawn from lists provided by the contributors to this volume. It represents works that they have found to be especially influential or significant. The bibliography does not include dissertations, articles, or studies of individual authors. We have also excluded primary sources, with the exception of certain collections that present materials that have been generally unknown or inaccessible to students and scholars.

Aaron, Daniel. *Men of Good Hope: A Story of American Progressives.* New York: Oxford University Press, 1961.

Abrahams, Edward. *The Lyrical Left: Randolph Bourne, Alfred Stieglitz, and the Origins of Cultural Radicalism in America.* Charlottesville: University of Virginia Press, 1986.

Ahlstrom, Sydney. *A Religious History of the American People.* New Haven, CT: Yale University Press, 1972.

Anderson, Benedict. *Imagined Communities: Reflections on the Origin and Spread of Nationalism.* London: Verso, 1983.

Anderson, Quentin. *The Imperial Self.* New York: Knopf, 1971.

Bakhtin, M. M. *The Dialogic Imagination: Four Essays.* Ed. Michael Holquist; trans. Caryl Emerson and Michael Holquist. Austin: University of Texas Press, 1981.

Baker, Houston A., Jr. *Modernism and the Harlem Renaissance.* University of Chicago Press, 1987.

Banta, Martha. *Imaging American Women: Ideas and Ideals in Cultural History.* New York: Columbia University Press, 1987.

Barr, Alfred H., Jr. *Cubism and Abstract Art* (1936). Repr., with an introd. by Robert Rosenblum, Cambridge, MA: Harvard University Press, 1986.

Barrier, Michael. *Hollywood Cartoons: American Animation in Its Golden Age.* New York and Oxford: Oxford University Press, 1999.

Beach, Joseph Warren. *American Fiction, 1920–1940.* 1941. Repr. New York: Russell & Russell, 1960.

Bell, Bernard W. *The Afro-American Novel and Its Traditions.* Amherst: University of Massachusetts Press, 1987.

Benjamin, Walter. *Illuminations*. Ed. Hannah Arendt; trans. Harry Zohn. New York: Brace & World, 1968.

Benstock, Shari. *Women of the Left Bank: Paris, 1900–1940*. Austin: University of Texas Press, 1986.

Berman, Avis. *Rebels on Eighth Street: Juliana Force and the Whitney Museum of American Art*. New York: Atheneum, 1990.

Berman, Patricia Gray and Martin Brody, curators. *Cold War Modern: The Domestic Avantgarde*. Chandler Gallery, Wellesley College, September 15, 2000–June 17, 2001.

Berthoff, Warner. *The Ferment of Realism: American Literature, 1884–1919*. New York: Free Press, 1965.

Biennale di Venezia, La. *La Biennale di Venezia: Le Esposizioni Internationali d'Arte 1895–1995*. Venice: Electa, 1996.

XIX^A Esposizione Biennale Internazionale d'Arte 1934: Catalogo. Prima edizione. Venice: Carlo Ferrari, 1934.

Boelhower, William. *Immigrant Autobiography in the United States (Four Versions of the Italian Self)*. Venice: Essedue, 1982.

Bone, Robert A. *The Negro Novel in America*. New Haven, CT: Yale University Press, 1958; rev. ed., 1965.

Bradbury, Malcolm. *The Modern American Novel*. New ed., New York: Viking, 1992.

Brinnin, John Malcolm. *The Third Rose: Gertrude Stein and Her World*. New York: Grove Press, 1959.

Browder, Laura. *Slippery Characters: Ethnic Impersonators and American Identities*. Chapel Hill and London: University of North Carolina Press, 2000.

Brown, Dee. *The Gentle Tamers: Women and the Old Wild West*. Lincoln, NE: Putnam, 1958.

Brüderlin, Markus. *Ornament und Abstraktion. Kunst der Kulturen, Moderne und Gegenwart im Dialog*. (Catalogue of an exhibition at Fondation Beyeler, Riehen, Switzerland). Cologne: DuMont, 2001.

Burke, Kenneth. *The Philosophy of Aesthetic Form: Studies in Symbolic Action*. Baton Rouge: Louisiana State University Press, 1941.

Cappetti, Carla. *Writing Chicago: Modernism, Ethnography, and the Novel*. New York: Columbia University Press, 1993.

Carby, Hazel. *Reconstructing Womanhood: The Emergence of the Afro-American Woman Novelist*. New York: Oxford University Press, 1987.

Cash, W. J. *The Mind of the South* [1941]. New York: Vintage Books, 1960.

Chametzky, Jules. *Our Decentralized Literature: Cultural Mediations in Selected Jewish and Southern Writers*. Amherst: University of Massachusetts Press, 1986.

Chipp, Herschel B., ed. *Theories of Modern Art: A Source Book by Artists and Critics*. Berkeley, Los Angeles, and London: University of California Press, 1968.

Christian, Barbara. *Black Women Novelists: The Development of a Tradition, 1892–1976*. Westport, CT: Greenwood Press, 1980.

Cohn, Jan. *Creating America: George Horace Latimer and the Saturday Evening Post.* University of Pittsburgh Press, 1989.

Conn, Peter. *The Divided Mind: Ideology and Imagination in America, 1898–1917.* Cambridge University Press, 1983.

Corn, Wanda M. *The Great American Thing: Modern Art and National Identity, 1915–1935.* Berkeley, Los Angeles, and London: University of California Press, 1999.

Cowley, Malcolm. *Exile's Return: A Literary Odyssey of the 1920s* [1934]. New York: Viking Press, 1951.

Cunard, Nancy. ed. *Negro Anthology, Made by Nancy Cunard, 1931–1933.* London: Wishart & Co., 1934.

Das Cabinet des Dr. Caligari: Drehbuch von Carl Mayer und Hans Janowitz zu Robert Wiene's Film von 1919/20. Introd. Siegbert S. Prawer. Munich: Edition Text + Kritik, 1995.

Davis, Angela Y. *Blues Legacies and Black Feminism: Gertrude "Ma" Rainey, Bessie Smith and Billie Holiday.* New York: Pantheon Books, 1998.

Dearborn, Mary V. *Pocahontas's Daughters: Gender and Ethnicity in American Culture.* New York: Oxford University Press, 1986.

Degler, Carl. *Out of Our Past: The Forces That Shaped Modern America.* New York: Harper, 1959.

Denning, Michael. *The Cultural Front: The Laboring of American Culture in the Twentieth Century.* London and New York: Verso, 1996.

Djupedal, Knut *et al.*, eds. *Novwegian-American Essays.* Oslo: The Novwegian Emigrant Museum, 1993. (See especially solveig zempel, "Rølvaag as Translator: Translations of Rølvaag," pp. 40–50).

Dolan, Marc. *Modern Lives: A Cultural Re-reading of "The Lost Generation."* West Lafayette: Purdue University Press, 1996.

Douglas, Ann. *Terrible Honesty: Mongrel Manhattan in the 1920s.* New York: Farrar, Straus & Giroux, 1995.

duCille, Ann. *The Coupling Convention: Sex, Text, and Tradition in Black Women's Fiction.* New York: Oxford University Press, 1993.

Farrell, James T. *The League of Frightened Philistines and Other Papers.* New York: Vanguard Press, n.d. [ca. 1945?].

Favor, J. Martin. *Authentic Blackness: The Folk in the New Negro Renaissance.* Durham, NC: Duke University Press, 1999.

Ferraro, Thomas J. *Ethnic Passages: Literary Immigrants in Twentieth-Century America.* Chicago and London: University of Chicago Press, 1993.

Fine, David M. *The City, the Immigrant and American Fiction, 1880–1920.* Metuchen, NJ, and London: Scarecrow Press, 1977.

Fussell, Paul. *The Great War and Modern Memory.* New York: Oxford University Press, 1975.

Gates, Henry Louis. *Figures in Black: Words, Signs, and and the Radical Self.* New York: Oxford University Press, 1987.

Geertz, Clifford. *The Interpretation of Culture: Selected Essays.* New York: Basic Books, 1973.

Gelfant, Blanche H., ed. *The Columbia Companion to the Twentieth-Century American Short Story*. New York: Columbia University Press, 2000.

Gilbert, Felix. *The End of the European Era, 1890 to the Present*. New York: W. W. Norton, 1970.

Gilmore, Michael T. *Differences in the Dark: American Movies and English Theater*. New York: Columbia University Press, 1998.

Greenberg, Clement. *The Harold Letters. 1928–1943*. Ed. Janice van Horne. Washington, DC: Counterpoint, 2000.

Griffin, Farah Jasmine. *"Who Set You Flowin": The African-American Migration Narrative*. New York: Oxford University Press, 1995.

Handlin, Oscar. *The Uprooted: The Epic Story of the Great Migrations That Made the American People*. New York: Grosset & Dunlop, 1951.

Harrison, Daphne Duval. *Black Pearls: Blues Queens of the 1920s*. New Brunswick, NJ: Rutgers University Press, 1998.

Hathaway, Heather. *Caribbean Waves: Relocating Claude McKay and Paule Marshall*. Bloomington and Indianapolis: University of Indiana Press, 1999.

Heilbut, Anthony. *Exile in Paradise: German Refugee Artists and Intellectuals in America from the 1930s to the Present*. 2nd ed. Berkeley, Los Angeles, and London: University of California Press, 1997.

Higham, John. *Send These to Me: Immigrants in Urban America* [1975]. Baltimore: Johns Hopkins University Press, 1984.

Hofstadter, Richard. *The Age of Reform: From Bryan to FDR*. New York: Knopf, 1955.

Howe, Irving. *World of Our Fathers: The Journey of the East European Jews to America and the Life They Found and Made*. New York: Harcourt, Brace, Jovanovich, 1976.

Huggins, Nathan Irvin. *Harlem Renaissance: The Afro American Ordeal in Slavery*. New York: Pantheon Books, 1977.

Hull, Gloria T. *Color, Sex, and Poetry: Three Women Writers of the Harlem Renaissance*. Bloomington: Indiana University Press, 1987.

Hulten, Pontus. *Futurismo and Futurismi*. Milan: Bompiano, 1986.

Hutchinson, George. *The Harlem Renaissance in Black and White*. Cambridge, MA: Harvard University Press, 1995.

Ickringill, Steve, ed. *Looking Inward, Looking Outward: From the 1930s through the 1940s*. (European Contributions to American Studies.) Amsterdam: VU Press, 1990.

Ickstadt, Heinz, ed. *The Thirties: Politics and Culture in a Time of Broken Dreams*. (European Contributions to American Studies.) Amsterdam: VU Press, 1987.

Inglehart, Babette F. and Anthony R. Mangione. *The Image of Pluralism in American Literature: The American Experience of European Ethnic Groups*. New York: The Institute on Pluralism and Group Identity of the American Jewish Committee, 1974.

Joachimides, Christos M. and Norman Rosenthal, eds. *American Art in the 20th Century*. Munich: Prestel, 1993. Royal Academy of Arts and ZEITGEIST-Gesellschaft.

Johnson, Charles Spurgeon. *Ebony and Ivory: A Collectanea, 1931.* Reprint: Freeport, NY: Books for Libraries, 1971.

Juliana Force and American Art: A Memorial Exhibition September 24–October 30, 1949. New York: Whitney Museum of American Art, n.d. [1949]

Kalaidjian, Walter. *American Culture Between the Wars: Revisionary Modernism and Postmodern Critique.* New York: Columbia University Press, 1993.

Kazin, Alfred. *On Native Grounds: An Interpretation of Modern American Prose Literature.* New York: Reynal & Hitchcock, 1942.

King, Richard. *A Southern Renaissance: The Cultural Awakening of the American South, 1930–1955.* New York: Oxford University Press, 1980.

Klein, Marcus. *Foreigners: The Making of American Literature 1900–1940.* Chicago and London: University of Chicago Press, 1981.

Knopf, Marcy. *The Sleeper Wakes: Harlem Renaissance Stories by Women.* New Brunswick, NJ: Rutgers University Press, 1993.

Kolodny, Annette. *The Lay of the Land: Metaphor as Experience and History in American Life and Letters.* Chapel Hill: University of North Carolina Press, 1975.

Kucklick, Bruce. *The Rise of American Philosophy: Cambridge, Massachusetts, 1860–1930.* New Haven, CT: Yale University Press, 1977.

Lears, Jackson. *No Place of Grace: Antimodernism and the Transformation of American Culture, 1880–1920.* New York: Pantheon, 1981.

Leuchtenberg, William E. *The Perils of Prosperity, 1914–1932.* Chicago University Press, 1958.

Levine, Lawrence. *Black Culture and Black Consciousness: Afro-American Folk Thought from Slavery to Freedom.* Oxford University Press, 1977.

Lewis, David Levering. *When Harlem Was in Vogue.* New York: Oxford University Press, 1979.

Lott, Eric. *Love and Theft: Blackface Minstrelsy and the American Working Class.* New York and Oxford: Oxford University Press, 1993.

Ludington, Townsend, ed. *A Modern Mosaic: Art and Modernism in the United States.* Chapel Hill and London: University of North Carolina Press, 2000.

Lukács, Georg. *The Theory of the Novel: A Historico-Philosophical Essay on the Forms of Great Epic Literature.* Trans. Anna Bostock. Cambridge, MA: Harvard University Press, 1971.

Lynn, Kenneth S. *The Dream of Success: A Study of Modern American Imagination.* Boston: Little, Brown, 1955.

MacShane, Frank, ed. *The Notebooks of Raymond Chandler and English Summer: A Gothic Romance.* New York: Ecco Press, 1976.

Mangione, Jerre and Ben Morreale. *La Storia: Five Centuries of the Italian American Experience.* New York: HarperCollins, 1992.

May, Henry F. *The End of American Innocence: A Study of the First Years of Our Time, 1912–1917.* New York: Oxford University Press, 1979.

Melnick, Jeff. *A Right to Sing the Blues: African Americans, Jews, and American Popular Song.* Cambridge, MA: Harvard University Press, 1999.

Mencken, H. L. *The American Language*. New York: A. A. Knopf, 1919 (and supplements).

Middleton, William D. *The Time of the Trolley*. Milwaukee: Kalmbach Publishing, 1967.

Mishkin, Tracy. *The Harlem and Irish Renaissances: Language, Identity, and Representation*. Gainesville: University Press of Florida, 1998.

Morrison, Toni. *Playing in the Dark: Whiteness and the Literary Imagination*. Cambridge, MA and London: Harvard University Press, 1992.

Mumford, Kevin. *Interzones: Black/White Sex Districts in Chicago and New York in the Early Twentieth Century*. New York: Columbia University Press, 1997.

Noble, David. *America by Design: Science, Technology, and the Rise of Corporate Capitalism*. New York: Knopf, 1977.

North, Michael. *The Dialect of Modernism: Race, Language, and Twentieth-Century Literature*. New York: Oxford University Press, 1994.

Nyman, Jopi. *Men Alone: Masculinity, Individualism, and Hard-Boiled Fiction*. Amsterdam: Rodopi, 1997.

O'Meally, Robert and Genevieve Fabre, eds. *History and Memory in African American Culture*. New York: Oxford University Press, 1994.

Øverland, Orm. *Immigrant Minds, American Identities: Making the United States Home, 1870–1930*. Urbana and Chicago: University of Illinois Press, 2000.

Owens, Louis. *Other Destinies: Understanding the American Indian Novel*. Norman and London: University of Oklahoma Press, 1992.

Pattee, Fred Lewis. *The New American Literature, 1890–1930*. New York and London: The Century Co., 1930.

Peretti, Burton W. *The Creation of Jazz: Music, Race, and Culture in Urban America*. Urbana and Chicago: University of Illinois Press, 1992.

Poirier, Richard. *A World Elsewhere: The Place of Style in American Literature*. New York: Oxford University Press, 1966.

Radway, Janice A. *A Reading of the Romance: Women, Patriarchy, and Popular Literature*. Chapel Hill: University of North Carolina Press, 1984.

Rideout, Walter. *The Radical Novel in the United States, 1900–1954*. Cambridge, MA: Harvard University Press, 1956.

Rosenberg, Harold. *The Tradition of the New*. [1959] New York and Toronto: McGraw-Hill, 1965.

Ryland, Philip and Enzo Di Martino. *Flying the Flag for Art: The United States and the Venice Biennale, 1895–1991*. Richmond, VA: Wyldbore and Wolferstan, 1993.

Saunders, Frances Stonor. *The Cultural Cold War: The CIA and the World of Arts and Letters*. New York: New Press, 1999.

Silva, Umberto. *Ideologia e arte del fascismo*. Milan: Mazzotta, 1977.

Slotkin, Richard. *The Fatal Environment: The Myth of the Frontier in the Age of Industrialization*. Middletown, CT: Wesleyan University Press, 1985.

Smith, Henry Nash. *Virgin Land: The American West as Symbol and Myth*. Cambridge, MA: Harvard University Press, 1950.

Sollors, Werner. *Beyond Ethnicity: Consent and Descent in American Culture*. New York: Oxford University Press, 1986.

Starr, S. Frederick. *Red and Hot: The Fate of Jazz in the Soviet Union, 1917–1980*. New York and Oxford: Oxford University Press, 1983.

Steinberg, Salme Harju. *Reformer in the Marketplace: Edward W. Bok and The Ladies' Home Journal*. Baton Rouge and London: Louisiana State University Press, 1979.

Stepto, Robert B. *From Behind the Veil: A Study of Afro-American Narrative*. Urbana: University of Illinois Press, 1979.

Taylor, William R. *In Pursuit of Gotham: Culture and Commerce in New York*. New York: Oxford University Press, 1992.

Tedeschini Lalli, Biancamaria and Maurizio Vaudagna, eds. *Brave New Worlds: Strategies of Language and Communication in the United States of the 1930s*. Amsterdam: VU University Press, 1999.

Terkel, Studs. *Hard Times: An Oral History of the Great Depression*. New York: Pantheon, 1970.

Todorov, Tzvetan. *The Conquest of America: The Question of the Other*. Trans. Richard Howard. New York: Harper & Row, 1984.

Trachtenberg, Alan. *The Incorporation of America: Culture and Society*. New York: Hill & Wang, 1982.

Trilling, Lionel. *The Liberal Imagination: Essays on Literature and Society*. New York: Viking Press, 1950.

Turner, Victor. *Dramas, Fields, and Metaphors: Symbolic Action in Human Society*. Ithaca, NY: Cornell University Press, 1974.

Ueda, Reed. *Postwar Immigrant America: A Social History*. Boston and New York: Bedford Books of St. Martin's Press, 1994.

Van Doren, Carl. *The American Novel 1789–1939*. New York: Macmillan, 1940.

Wald, Priscilla. *Constituting Americans: Cultural Anxiety and Narrative Form*. Durham, NC and London: Duke University Press, 1995.

Wall, Cheryl. *Women of the Harlem Renaissance*. Bloomington: Indiana University Press, 1995.

Wecter, Dixon. *The Age of the Great Depression: 1929–1941*. New York: Macmillan, 1948.

Weiss, M. Lynn. *Gertrude Stein and Richard Wright: The Poetics and Politics of Modernism*. Jackson: University of Mississippi Press, 1998.

Weston, Richard. *Modernism*. London: Phaidon Press, 1996.

White, Newman I. *American Negro Folk-Songs*. Cambridge, MA: Harvard University Press, 1928.

Williams, Raymond. *Culture and Society*. London: Chatto & Windus, 1958.

Wintz, Cary D. *Black Culture and the Harlem Renaissance*. Houston: Rice University Press, 1988.

Wirth-Nesher, Hana. *City Codes: Reading the Modern Urban Novel*. New York and Cambridge: Cambridge University Press, 1996.

Wolff, Edward N. *Top Heavy: A Study of the Increasing Inequality of Wealth in America*. New York: Twentieth Century Fund, 1995.

Woodcock, George. *20th Century Fiction*. Basingstoke and London: Macmillan, 1983.

Wyatt-Brown, Bertram. *Southern Honor: Ethics and Behavior in the Old South*. New York: Oxford University Press, 1982.

Yin, Xiao-huang. *Chinese American Literature since the 1850s*. Urbana: University of Illinois Press, 2000.

Zwerin, Mike. *La Tristesse de Saint Louis: Swing under the Nazis*. London: Quartet Books, 1985.

INDEX

NOTE: the index is arranged in alphabetical order word by word, covering pages xiii to 596. Titles of works appear only under the author's name. Page references in **bold** refer to main sections of the topic.

Aaron, Daniel *Men of Good Hope*, 233; *Writers on the Left*, 233
academic authority, xiv–xv
Act to Preserve Racial Purity (Virginia 1924), 449
Adamic, Louis, 388, 421, 429, 520–21, 523–24; *Common Ground*, 521; *From Many Lands*, 521; *Laughing in the Jungle*, 403, 428, 578; *My America*, 190, 241, 251, 390, 521, 585; *The Native's Return*, 512, 523; *Two-Way Passage*, 523
Adams, Henry, 34, 39, 44, 48–56, 84, 457; *Democracy*, 106; *Education of Henry Adams*, 48–56, 102–07, 564; *Mont-Saint-Michel and Chartres*, 103, 104
Addams, Jane, 95, 126, 558
Adorno, Theodor W., 53, 431
advertising, 119, 135–36, 164–65; and reading public, 363–64; and Wall Street Crash, 184
aesthetic modernism, xvii
aestheticism in Thirties, 210
African Americans, 301–02; life, 152; literature, xviii–xix, 497; *see also* Harlem Renaissance
Agee, James, 7, 190, 199, 255; on atomic bomb, 550; on Hemingway and film, 470–71; *Let Us Now Praise Famous Men*, 7, 190, 198, 246–49, 363, 589
Ager, Waldemar, *On the Way to the Melting Pot*, 435, 563
agriculture, xviii, 24–25, 44–45; collapse of market (1920), 251; serfdom in South, 287; *see also* rural life in novels
Aiken, Conrad, 242, 574; *Great Circle*, 580
Alcott, Louisa May, 16
Alger, Horatio, 200, 201, 203, 237
Algren, Nelson, 227, 233; *The Man with the Golden Arm*, 473, 595; *Never Come Morning*, 589; *The New Wilderness*, 473; *Somebody in Boots*, 190, 582
Allen, Frederick Lewis, 187
Allen, Hervey, *Anthony Adverse*, 186

"American," meaning of term, 422–27, 449–51, 521–22
American Caravan (publishers), 193
American Civil Liberties Union (ACLU), 126
American dream/way of life, 191, 237, 252, 520, 522–23; and the South, 256
American Literature, definition, xv, 390
American Magazine, 164
American Mercury, 428
"American Risorgimento," 68–69
American Writers' Congress, 232–33
Anderson, Margaret, 133; *My Thirty Years' War*, 108
Anderson, Maxwell, 127
Anderson, Sherwood, 13, 130–33, 134, 170, 458; Ludwig Lewisohn on, 381–82; and middle class values, 208; *Dark Laughter*, 571; *Home Town*, 190, 243, 588; *Many Marriages*, 569; *Marching Men*, 131, 563; *Poor White*, 565; *Puzzled America*, 190, 225, 250, 582; *Sherwood Anderson's Memoirs*, 130; *A Story-Teller's Story*, 130; *Tar: A Midwest Childhood*, 130; *The Triumph of the Egg*, 567; *Windy McPherson's Son*, 131, 562; *Winesburg, Ohio*, 131–33, 199, 564
"Angry Decade," 189
anthropology, 5
Antin, Mary, xix, 406, 440; background and career, 411–21; on immigration, 416–17; modernity, 415; patriotism and meaning of "American", 422–27; as public lecturer, 419; sense of doubleness in writing, 417–18; "First Aid to the Alien" 411; *From Plotzk to Boston*, 412, 415, 429; "House of the One Father," 539–40; "The Lie," 424; "Malinke's Atonement," 426; *The Promised Land*, 390, 401, 411–16, 418–19, 425–26, 427, 440, 559; *They Who Knock at Our Gates*, 419–20, 421
antinomianism, xiv
antisemitism, 202, 233, 514–15, 516, 526, 539–45

Anvil magazine, 210

Arendt, Hannah, 6, 233; *On Revolution*, 6; *Origins of Totalitarianism*, 367

Armory Show (New York), 71–73, 356

Arnold, Matthew, 3, 191

Arnow, Harriette, 27

art, collectors, 364; cultural role, 12–13; and freedom, 360–61; of James Agee, 248–49; kitsch, 534; and Nazis, 531–32; New Art, 71–73; rendered ornamental, 243–44; *see also* Armory Show; Cubism and Modern Art; "Degenerate Art Show"; modernism; music; painting

artwork *see* illustrators of prose; photography

Asch, Nathan *East River*, 456–57; *Pay-Day*, 456–57, 509; *The Road: In Search of America*, 190, 225, 241

Asimov, Isaac, *I, Robot*, 596

Atherton, Gertrude, *Black Oxen*, 569

Atlantic Monthly, 413, 418, 423, 424

atomic bomb, 546–51, 554

Austin, Mary, 41, 66; *The Ford*, 563

authority of writers, 14

authors, xvi–xvii

autobiography in ethnic literature, 390–404

automatism in writing, 371

Ayres, C. F., 104

Babbitt, Irving, 119

Bacon, Francis, 17

Bacon, Peggy, 511

Baedeker, Karl, 38

Bagehot, Walter, 162

Baker, Roy Stannard, 40

Bakhtin, Mikhail, 7

Baldwin, James, 350, 459, 498

Ballard, John, 255

Baltimore Sun, 386

bankruptcy, 194

Barnes, Djuna, 155, 199, 255; *Nightwood*, 198, 204–05, 583

Barney, Natalie, 155

Barr, Alfred, 528–29, 533

Bart, Lily, 3

Bartholdt, Richard, 391

Barton, Bruce, 164; *The Man Nobody Knows*, 164–65

Beach, Sylvia, 155; *Shakespeare and Company*, 108

Beard, Charles, 104; *Economic interpretation of the Constitution*, 104

Beat Generation, 556

Beebe, William, 564

Bell, Thomas, 388; *Out of this Furnace*, 190, 231, 245, 391, 504, 589

Bellow, Saul, 233, 242; *Adventures of Augie March*, 388; *Dangling Man*, 591; *The Victim*, 593

Benchley, Robert, 210

Benét, Stephen Vincent, 220

Benjamin, Walter, 163

Bennett, Gwendolyn, 325; *Wedding Day*, 572

Bercovici, Konrad, 429; *Around the World in New York*, 570; *Dust of New York*, 564; *On New Shores*, 571

Berkman, Alexander, 90

Best American Short Stories, 388

Best Short Stories, 388

Bierce, Ambrose, 559

biographies, 191

Bishop, Elizabeth, 8

Bishop, John Peale, 109, 193

Black Mask magazine, 219, 468

Black Sox scandal (1919), 125

Blackmur, R. P., 258

Boas, Franz, 496, 497; *The Mind of Primitive Man*, 104, 559

Bodenheim, Maxwell, *Replenishing Jessica*, 571

Bogan, Louise, 155

Bohr, Niels, 52

Bojer, Johan, *The Emigrants*, 571

Bok, Edward, *The Americanization of Edward Bok*, 153, 390, 393–94, 401, 408, 422, 440, 565

Bonner, Marita (Occomy), 323–25, 350, 571

Bonnie and Clyde, 211

Bontemps, Arna, 242; *Black Thunder*, 339, 399, 583; *Drums at Dusk*, 338, 339; *God Sends Sunday*, 339

The Bookman, 92, 152

Borges, Jorge Luis, 158

Boston, 25, 129, 161

Bourke-White, Margaret, 245; *You Should Have Seen Their Faces*, 190, 241, 243

Bourne, Randolph, 66, 69, 89, 171, 173, 208; on Americanization, 424–25; essays, 89, 366; *Education and Living*, 89, 563; *Youth and Life*, 89, 560

Bower, B. M. (B. M. Sinclair), 213–14

Bowers, Claude, *The Tragic Era*, 172

Bowles, Paul, *The Sheltering Sky*, 595

Boyd, Thomas, *Through the Wheat*, 173

Boynton, H. W., 92

Bradbury, Ray, *The Martian Chronicles*, 596

Bradford, Roark, *Ol' Man Adam an' His Children*, 575

"Brahmin" term, 424

brand names in literature, 407

Brandeis, Louis, 561

breast imagery, 501–02, 509–10

Bridges, Horace, *On Becoming an American*, 390, 564

Bromfield, Louis, 135; *The Green Bay Tree*, 570

Brooklyn Daily Times, 366

Brooks, Cleanth, 257

Brooks, Van Wyck, 67, 69, 75, 89;
  disenchantment, 134; and regional
  marginality, 161; *America's Coming of Age*, 69,
  251, 359; *The Flowering of New England*, 192,
  251; *The Life of Emerson*, 251; *New England:
  Indian Summer*, 192, 251; *The Ordeal of Mark
  Twain*, 171; *The Wine of the Puritans*, 251
Broom magazine, 371, 443
Brown, Harry, *A Walk in the Sun*, 591
Brown, John, 232
Brown, Sterling, 285, 288, 379–80; *Negro
  Caravan*, 292
Brown, Theodore, *Lysistrata*, 242
Buck, Pearl, *The Good Earth*, 578
Bulosan, Carlos, 389, 592
Buntline, Ned (Edward Z. C. Judson), 35
Burgess, Ernest, 492, 503
Burgess, John W., 125
Burke, Kenneth, 7, 8, 122, 189, 193; in *Southern
  Review*, 258; *Attitudes Toward History*, 7
Burns, John Horne, *The Gallery*, 593
Burroughs, Edgar, *Tarzan of the Apes*, 561
Burroughs, William, *The Naked Lunch*, 372
Buslett, Ole Amundsen, *The Road to the Golden
  Gate*, 431–32, 562
Bynner, Witter, 127

Cabell, James, 563; *Jurgen*, 113, 154–55, 201, 565
Cage, John, 167
Cahan, Abraham, 388, 439–40; *The Rise of David
  Levinsky*, 64, 402, 441, 563; *Yekl: A Tale of the
  Ghetto*, 64, 394
Cain, James M., 220–22, 468; *The Butterfly*, 221;
  Double Indemnity, 221, 583; *The Postman Always
  Rings Twice*, 220, 581; *Serenade*, 220, 224
Cain, Paul, 237
Caldwell, Erskine, 242, 246, 255; *God's Little Acre*,
  256, 258–59, 580; *Tobacco Road*, 258–59, 579;
  You Have Seen Their Faces, 190, 241
Calkins, Ernest Elmo, 136
camera *see* photography
Campbell, William, *Company K*, 580
Camus, Albert, 3, 183; *The Rebel*, 3
Cantwell, Robert, *Land of Plenty*, 190, 227, 233,
  581; *Laugh and Lie Down*, 578
capitalism, xviii; and bureaucracy, 119
Capote, Truman, *Other Voices, Other Rooms*, 594;
  The Tree of Life, 595
Carnegie, Andrew, 12
Cash, W.J., 255
Cassatt, Mary, *Modern Woman*, 41
caste, 198
Cather, Willa, 10, 13, 21, 49; middle-class values,
  208; natural landscape, 171; World War I, 93;
  Death Comes for the Archbishop, 45, 99, 124,
  574; *A Lost Lady*, 45, 99, 569; *My Antonia*, 23,
  26, 27–30, 564; *O Pioneers*, 438, 560; *One of

Ours*, 93–94, 97, 568; *The Professor's House*, 45,
  571; *Song of the Lark*, 82, 562
Cautela, Giuseppe, *Moon Harvest*, 571
Cayton, Horace, 492, 493, 495
Chacón, Eusebio, 430
Chacón, Felipe Maximiliano, 570
Chamberlain, John, 104, 358
Chandler, Raymond, 213, 218–19, 467–68;
  The Big Sleep, 218, 468, 470, 586; *Farewell My
  Lovely*, 587
Chang Tsu, 19, 55
Chávez, Fray Angélico, *New Mexico Triptych*, 588
Chesnutt, Charles W., *The House Behind the Cedars*,
  299; *The Marrow of Tradition*, 338
Chicago, "Dream City", 37–42, 54; expansion,
  xviii, 25, 26, 30–31; and modernization, 493;
  Negro Renaissance, 288; *Official Manual* of
  city, 40; Prohibition and crime, 129; *see also*
  Frederick Jackson Turner
Chicago Defender, 312
Chicago Renaissance, 492–93
Chicago School of Sociology, 492
Chicano literature, 389–90, 503–04
Child, Richard Washburn, 359, 514
Chinese-language writing, 431
Chopin, Kate, 40; *The Awakening*, 40, 81–82, 83
Christmas, Joe, 3
Chronology (1910–1950), xviii, 557–96
Churchill, Winston S., 4, 558
cinema *see* film industry
cities, in literature, 166–67; and migration, 23,
  25; and productive processes, 164
Civil Rights movement, 290, 556
Civil War, 13, 24–25, 34, 91
Civilian Conservation Corps, 195
class, 169, 455–57; and wealth, 142–50, 160;
  writers on, 198
class problems, 198
Clemens, Samuel *see* Twain, Mark
clocks and time theme, 491–92, 493, 498
code-switching, 429
Cody, William F. ('Buffalo Bill'), 34, 35–36, 37, 46
Colcord, Lincoln, 439–40
Cold War, xix, 535, 537, 555–56
Columbus, Christopher, 24, 37
commitment *see* political commitment
Common Ground, 388, 539; Adamic, Louis, 521
Communism, 187, 194–95, 197, 516–18; and
  black creative artists, 287; defections from
  Party, 233; in Depression, 227, 232, 348–49,
  517; *see also* Marxism
community and literature, xv, xviii
Coney Island in stories, 396
confidence and uncertainty, 15–22
Conrad, Joseph, 51
Conroy, Jack, 210, 245; *The Disinherited*, 190,
  225–26, 230, 231, 580

Cooke, Alastair, 164
Coolidge, Calvin, 117–19, 184–85
Cooper, Anna Julia, *A Voice from the South*, 41
Cott, Carrie Chapman, 95
Coughlin, Father Charles, 187
Cournos, John, 440; *Babel*, 568; *The Mask*, 564; *The Wall*, 567
Covarrubias, Miguel, 511
Cowley, Malcolm, 104, 151, 160; disenchantment, 134, 187; *An Exile's Return*, 108, 130, 581; *A Second Flowering*, 108
Cozzens, James Gould, 233, 594
Crane, Hart, 24, 100, 108, 210–11; *The Bridge*, 166, 442
Crane, Stephen, 40; *George's Mother*, 64; *Maggie: A Girl of the Streets*, 40, 64
Crash *see* Wall Street Crash (1929)
creative reading/writing, 4
Crisis, 286, 298, 306, 321, 324
Croly, Herbert, 68
Cromwell, Dorothea, 108
Cromwell, Gladys, 108
Crosby, Caresse, 155
Crosby, Harry, 108; *War Letters*, 100
Cross Section, 388
Crossman, Richard, *The God That Failed*, 518
cubism, xix
Cubism and Modern Art (MoMA exhibition), 528–29
Cullen, Countee, 151, 152, 330–31; *Caroling Dusk*, 292; *One Way to Heaven*, 336–37, 579
culture, xviii; African American, 301–02; feminization, 152–53; literature, xix, 362; multiethnicity of USA, 365–67; nature, 48; political commitment, 188–89, 190–99, 248–49; popular, 136–37; *see also* art; modernism; music; painting
Culture and Crisis pamphlet, 194
Cummings, E. E., 66, 69, 106; *Eimi*, 515; *The Enormous Room*, 110–11, 163, 173, 568
Cunard, Nancy, *Negro, An Anthology*, 292, 302–03
Curran, Mary Doyle, 388; *The Pariah and the Hill*, 595

Dahl, Dorthea, *The Copper Kettle*, 432, 433, 577
Dahlberg, Edward, 455; *Because I Was Flesh*, 230; *Bottom Dogs*, 190, 229, 231, 577
Daiches, David, 104
D'Angelo, Pascal, *Son of Italy*, 570
Darwinism, 49, 105
Davidson, Donald, 255, 257
Davies, Arthur, 71
Davis, Richard Harding, 92, 561
Day, Clarence, 565

De Capite, Michael, *Maria*, 588
"Degenerate Art Show" (Munich 1937), 532–33
DeKruif, Paul, *Microbe Hunters*, 572
Dell, Floyd, 64, 66, 68, 69, 208; *The Briary Bush*, 567; *Janet March*, 569; *Mooncalf*, 565; *Runaway*, 571
Depression, xviii, xix, 118, 192, 194–95, 198, 203; and black writers, 348–52; and escapist writing, 212; flood and drought, 252; Hollywood, 220; Marxist themes, 455–57; obstacle to Harlem Renaissance, 348; photographic record, 244–45; social writing, 229–32; *see also* Faulkner, William; Miller, Henry; Wall Street Crash
detective stories, 198, 212, 216–19
Deutsch, Babette, 127
Dewey, John, 170–71, 385; *Reconstruction in Philosophy*, 566; *Studies in Logical Theory*, 104
di Donato, Pietro, xix, 231, 402, 407, 455; *Christ in Concrete*, 504–07, 508–09, 511, 587
Dial, 193
Dickinson, Emily, 174, 362
Dillinger, John, 211
disenchantment, 134–39, 181
dissensus and consensus, 6
documentary literature, 190–91, 198, 250; and disarming of dissent, 241–49
"domestic" novels, 213–14
Domingo, W. A., 290, 291
Dondero, George A., 359–61
Dos Passos, John, 10, 90, 93, 127, 133, 255; background, 165–66; on cities, 166–67; openness to modernity, 458; *The 42nd Parallel*, 128,168, 577; *1919*, 173, 579; *The Big Money*, 66, 128, 168, 213, 251, 584; *The Ground We Stand On*, 192, 251; *The Living Thoughts of Thomas Paine*, 251; *Manhattan Transfer*, 166, 167–68, 201, 571; *One Man's Initiation*, 111,166, 566; *Three Soldiers*, 129, 166, 172–73, 567; *U.S.A*, 10, 110,111, 132,166, 169, 188, 198, 204, 205–07, 585
Dougherty, Henry, 117
Drake, St Clair, 495
Dreiser, Theodore, 8, 10, 13, 49, 83–85, 559; "barbaric naturalism" attacked, 401; childhood deprivation, 142; *An American Tragedy*, 10, 84, 87, 142–43, 572; *The Financier*, 86, 142, 559; *A Gallery of Women*, 113, 575; *The "Genius"*, 562; *Jennie Gerhardt*, 559; *Looking Backward*, 86; *Sister Carrie*, 5, 8, 23, 26–27, 28, 29–33, 84–85; *The Stoic*, 142, 593; *The Titan*, 86, 142, 561; *Tragic America*, 190, 250
Du Bois, W. E. B., xix, 14, 151, 286; and fascism, 516; and Harlem Renaissance, 295–98; on marginality, 160; *Black Reconstruction*, 297, 339, 349, 582; *Dark Princess*, 297; *Haiti*, 242;

"A Negro Nation Within the Nation," 349; *The Quest of the Silver Fleece*, 296–97, 559; *The Souls of Black Folk*, 295–96, 436

Dunbar, Paul Laurence, *The Sport of the Gods*, 64; *The Uncalled*, 64

Duncan, Isadora, 67

Dunphy, Jack, *John Fury*, 379

Durham, Robert Lee, *The Call of the South*, 386

Durkheim, Emile, 4

Eastman, Max, 68

economy, and African Americans, 349–50; economic corruption, xviii; economic mobility, 556; growth and expansion, 121–22; protest at worsening situation, 187; *see also* Depression; New Deal; Wall Street Crash

Eden, Martin, 3

Eisenhower, Dwight D., 360–61

Eisenstein, Sergei, 166

Eliot, Charles William, 153

Eliot, T. S., 87, 103, 208; as outsider, 160, 161; and the South, 253; *The Waste Land*, 112, 166, 384, 495, 568

elitism and writers, 198, 208

Ellison, Ralph, 242, 266, 380; *Invisible Man*, 388, 389, 459

Emerson, Ralph Waldo, 4, 169, 189, 234

Empey, Arthur, 93, 563

Equiano, Olaudah, 335

Erikson, Erik, *Childhood and Society*, 366

Espionage Act (1917), 90

Esquire, 402, 472

ethnic literature, xix, 44, 364–67, 382–83; 1910–1950, 388–90; against other ethnic groups, 392–93, 397; American Jewish, 388, 475 (*see also* anti-Semitism); autobiography, 390–404, 418; authentic/inauthentic, 400–01; brand names, 407; country-of-origin references, 393–94; ghostwriting, 403; immigration and assimilation, 440–41; language features, 428–33; Roth and Yiddish, 479–81; New World features noted, 406–07; pen-names, 401–02; sexual frankness increasing, 454–55; and Statue of Liberty, 396, 420–21; themes, 405–06; USA as multiethnic country, 365–67; writers' places of origin, 512; *see also individual authors*; modernism; modernity

Evans, Walker, 190, 246, 247

exclusion and writing *see* marginality and authority of writers

exploration literature, 24

Fall, Albert, 117

Fante, John, 388, 392, 519; *Dago Red*, 588; *Wait Until Spring, Bandini*, 585

Farrell, James T., 255, 407, 466; *Father and Son*, 227; *Judgment Day*, 226, 582; "The Language of Hollywood," 470; *My Days of Anger*, 227; *No Star is Lost*, 227; *Studs Lonigan Trilogy*, 226–27, 378, 440, 455, 503, 579, 581; *A World I Never Made*, 227

fascism, xix, 430, 513–17, 555–56

Fast, Howard, *The Last Frontier*, 589

Falkner, W. C., (great-grandfather of William Faulkner), 267

Faulkner, William, 3, 6–7, 8, 13, 22; American dream and the South, 256; importance to immigrant and ethnic writers, 458–59, 460; maturity in Thirties, 210; novels and history, **266–81**; and Pierrot symbol, 174; *Portable Faulkner* edition of works, 359; techniques, 280; *Absalom, Absalom*, 107, 110, 198, 254, 268, **273–79**, 375, 458, 584; *As I Lay Dying*, 110, 198, 268, 270, 577; *Go Down, Moses*, 132, 198, 267, 268, 279–80, 358–59, 458, 589; *The Hamlet*, 258, 268, 588; *Intruder in the Dust*, 594; *Light in August*, 198, 268, **270–73**, 458, 579; *The Mansion*, 258; *Mosquitoes*, 267; *Sanctuary*, 578; *Sartoris (Flags in the Dust)* 255, 274; *Soldiers' Pay*, 172, 267, 458, 573; *The Sound and the Fury*, 110, 198, 255, 267, 269–70, 274, 459–60, 575; *The Town*, 258

Fauset, Jessie Redmon, 152, 161, 286, 303, **320–23**, 329; *The Chinaberry Tree*, 321, 322–23, 578; *Comedy: American Style*, 321, 323, 350, 580; *Plum Bun*, 321–22, 323, 397, 575; *There is Confusion*, 291, 300, 321, 570

Federal Writers' Project (FWP), 242–43, 348–49, 388–89, 498

Ferber, Edna, *American Beauty*, 392

Fiedler, Leslie, 232–33

Fields, W. C., 210

film, 137, 166, 186, 361, 362, 519; Gertrude Stein, 373–74; and pulp fiction, 469–70

Fire!!, 293, 327–28, 341

Fisher, Dorothy Canfield, 133, 505, 542; *The Deepening Stream*, 97, 172, 577; *The Home-Maker*, 154; *The Walls of Jericho*, 297

Fisher, Rudolph, 293, 332–35; "The Caucasian Storms Harlem," 332; "The City of Refuge," 333, 572; *The Conjure Man Dies*, 334–35, 579; *The Walls of Jericho*, 327, 333, 575

Fitzgerald, F. Scott, xviii, 8, 13, 21, 23, 54, 130, 458; background and marginality, 160, 161, 171; commitment in Thirties, 188; disillusionment, 140–41; and the Jazz Age, 108–09; professionalism, 134, 143; and Wall Street Crash period, 184; *All the Sad Young Men*, 113; *The Beautiful and the Damned*, 568; "Echoes of the Jazz Age," 187; *Flappers and Philosophers*, 113; *The Great Gatsby*, 5, 55, 106,

110, 129, 138, **143–50**, 163–64, 572; *The Last Tycoon*, 237, 589; "The Scandal Detectives," 138–40; *Tales of the Jazz Age*, 109, 113, 145, 568; *Taps at Reveille*, 113; *Tender is the Night*, 141, 188, 199, 581; *This Side of Paradise*, 109, 140–41, 566

Fitzgerald, Zelda, 100

Flanner, Janet, 133, 155, 182; *An American in Paris*, 108, 588; *Paris Was Yesterday*, 182

Flinn, John, 43

Floyd, Charles "Pretty Boy," 211

Foley, Martha, 541–42

folklore, black American *see* Hurston, Zora Neale

Forbes, Charles R., 117

Force, Juliana, 528–29, 533

Ford, Ford Madox, 67, 155, 258

Ford, Henry, 130

foreign influence, 152

formula stories, 212

Fortune magazine, 233, 247

Forum, 317

Foster, Michael, 520

fragmentation, xvii

Frank, Anne, 465

Frank, Waldo, 194, 443–44; *Our America*, 365, 564; *Rahab*, 568; *The Re-Discovery of America*, 115

Frankfurter, Felix, 126, 127

Franklin, Benjamin, 155; *Autobiography*, 145, 149

freedom, personal, 3

Freeman, Don, 511

Freeman, Joseph, 67, 68, 70, 85, 137, 173–74; *An American Testament*, 108

Freud, Sigmund, 49, 366, 452; *Beyond the Pleasure Principle*, 476–77; *The Interpretation of Dreams*, 104; in Roth's *Call It Sleep*, 476–77

Friedman, I. K., *By Bread Alone*, 225; *The Radical*, 225

frontier literature, 34–36, 43–44, 55

Frost, Robert, 170

Fuchs, Daniel, 388, 440; *Homage to Blenholt*, 227, 407, 584; *Low Company*, 227, 585; *Summer in Williamsburg*, 190, 227, 581

Fugitive magazine, 255

Fuller, Henry, 30–31

Fuller, Meta Warwick, 301

FWP *see* Federal Writers' Project

Gale, Zona, 133, 171; *Birth*, 564; *Miss Lulu Bett*, 566; *Preface to a Life*, 130

Garland, Hamlin, 23; *A Daughter of the Middle Border*, 567; *A Son of the Middle Border*, 26, 563

Garvey, Marcus, xix, 287, 291–92

Gellhorn, Martha, 231

gender, 160; writers on, 198, 351; *see also* feminization fear; masculinity of writers threatened; women

genocide, 367

Genteel Tradition, 64–65, 69, 91

geography, New Negro movement, 287; origins of Twenties writers, 133; *see also* Midwest; South

German Americans and internment, 526

German-language writing, 430–31

ghostwriting, 403

Gilpin, William, 24

Giovannitti, Arturo, 70

Glasgow, Ellen, *Barren Ground*, 82, 256, 260–61, 572; *The Builders*, 92, 565; *Life and Gabriella*, 562; *The Sheltered Life*, 261, 579; *They Stooped to Folly*, 255, 261, 575; *Vein of Iron*, 583; *Virginia*, 560

Glaspell, Susan, *Fidelity*, 562; *Judd Rankin's Daughter*, 591; *Lifted Masks*, 560; *Norma Ashe*, 589

Globe, 71

Goebbels, Josef, 531–32

Gold, Mike (Itshak Isaac Granich), 36, 93, 127–28, 455; and Communism, 517; on Gertrude Stein, 377, 535; on *Grapes of Wrath*, 234; on Hemingway, 467; on Mary Antin, 418–19; and realism, 208, 209; on *Saturday Evening Post*, 364; *Change the World*, 377; *Go Left, Young Writers*, 230; *Jews Without Money*, 190, 229–30, 391, 392, 403, 421, 455–56, 523, 577; *see also New Masses*

Goldman, Emma, 67, 90; *Living My Life*, 578; *Mother Earth*, 126

Gorky, Maxim, 529–31

government sponsorship of writers, 242

Grabau, Amadeus William (husband of Mary Antin), 426–27

Grant, Madison, *The Passing of the Great Race*, 125

Great Crash *see* Wall Street Crash (1929)

Great War *see* World War I

Green, Paul, *Hymn to the Rising Sun*, 242

Greenberg, Clement, 533–34

Gregg, Frederick James, 71

Grey, Zane, 171, 213; *Code of the West*, 214, 215; *The Lone Star Ranger*, 562; *Nevada*, 214, 215–16; *Riders of the Purple Sage*, 214, 215, 560; *West of the Pecos*, 214, 215

Griffith, D.W., 166

Grimke, Angela Weld, 325

guilt feelings of writer, 248–49

Gunther, John, *Inside Europe*, 584

Gurdjieff movement, 443

H. D. (Hilda Doolittle), 155

Hadden, Briton, 162

Haeckel, Ernst, *The Riddle of the Universe*, 58

Hagglund, Ben, 227

Hakluyt, Richard, 24

Hale, Edward Everett, 412, 425

Hale, Marie Louise Gibson *see* Rutledge, Marice

Halper, Albert, 456
Hammett, Dashiell, 213, 468; *The Dain Curse*, 219; *The Glass Key*, 218, 219; *The Maltese Falcon*, 218, 219, 577; *Red Harvest*, 218, 219, 576; *The Thin Man*, 579
Hansen, Marcus Lee, 433
Hapgood, Hutchins, *The Spirit of the Ghetto*, 68, 376
Hapgood, Norman, 71
Hapgood, Powers, 127
"hard-boiled" writing, 461–62, 468–71
Harding, President, 117
Harlem Renaissance, xviii–xix, 285–86, 388, 492; avatars and manifestos, 295–305; Black Manhattan, 289–94; Black Modernism, 348–52; blues and jazz, 326–27; free-love period, 326–31 (*see also* Nugent, Richard Bruce; Thurman, Wallace); genre, 332–39 (*see also* Bontemps, Arna; Cullen, Countee; Fisher, Rudolph; Schuyler, George; White, Walter); growth of Harlem area, 287–88; Harlem rioting (1935), 349; Harlem as state of mind, 306–16, 351–52 (*see also* Hughes, Langston; McKay, Claude; Toomer, Jean); New Negro movement, 285–88, 289–90, 292–94; New Negro, new woman, 317–25; Southern daughter, native son, 340–47; *see also* Hurston, Zora Neale; Wright, Richard; Chicago Renaissance
Harlem writers, 151, 152
Harper, Frances E. W., *Iola Leroy*, 299
Harrison, Henry, 559
Hartz, Louis, *The Liberal Tradition in America*, 233
Haskell, Edward F., 366
Hawkes, John, *The Cannibal*, 595
Hawthorne, Nathaniel, 213
Haywood, Bill, 67, 126
Heap, Jane, 155
Hearst, William Randolph, xix
Hecht, Ben, *Erik Dorn*, 567
Heisenberg, Werner, 19, 28, 50–51, 54–55, 120
Held, John (Jr.), 112
Hemingway, Ernest, 13, 21, 51, 93, 133; background, 176–78, 474; breakdown in Thirties, 199; and Communism, 518; his egotism, 174–75; on Faulkner, 459; and Gertrude Stein, 174, 175, 382–83, 460; hunting and fishing, 176; influence on ethnic literature, 452, 465–74; influence on pulp fiction, 467–68; popular modernism, 462–64; short stories, 176, 180, 183, 199, 463–64; style of writing, 180–81, 465–74; war as metaphor, 172, 174–83; violence, 175, 176, 177–78; war service, 175–76, 178–79; and William Saroyan, 472–73; *Across the River and into the Trees*, 596; *A Clean, Well-Lighted Place*,

50; *Death in the Afternoon*, 179–80, 460, 579; *A Farewell to Arms*, 100–01, 173, 181, 255, 461, 576; *For Whom the Bell Tolls*, 182–83, 220, 464, 588; *Green Hills of Africa*, 112, 463, 583; *In Our Time*, 132, 178, 180, 219,570; *Men Without Women*, 574; *A Moveable Feast*, 108, 159, 174–75, 177–78, 460; *The Old Man and the Sea*, 183; *The Sun Also Rises*, 55, 109, 181, 183, 219, 383, 460, 461, 466, 573; *To Have and Have Not*, 219, 220, 585; *The Torrents of Spring*, 460; *Winner Take Nothing*, 580
Herbst, Josephine, 133, 187, 188–89, 230–31; *The Executioner Waits*, 581; *Pity Is Not Enough*, 267, 580; *Rope of Gold*, 587
Hergesheimer, Joseph, 134, 153; *Linda Condon*, 565
hermeneutics of suspicion, 9
Herrick, Robert, 92, 153–54; *Clark's Field*, 561; *One Woman's Life*, 560
Hersey, John, *A Bell for Adano*, 545–46, 591; *Hiroshima* report, 546–51, 592; *Men on Bataan*, 590; *The Wall*, 543–45, 596
Hickerson, Harold, 127
Hicks, Granville, 190, 456, 457
high-society novel, 5
Hildreth, Richard, 401
Hillis, Marjorie, 222
Himes, Chester, 591, 593
Hiroshima *see* atomic bomb
Hirschfeld, Magnus, *Racism*, 367
historicity of text, xv
history, and ethnic Americans, 399; historical novels, 250–51; lines of expansion, 23; and literature, xvi, 3, 49–50; local, 253; and the novel, 11–12, 15–16, 18, 209, 211; moral function, 267; William Faulkner, **266–81**; and photography, 241; reinvention of US literary history, 171; textuality of history, xv
Hitler, Adolf, 233, 532, 542
Hobson, Laura, 593
Hofstadter, Richard, *Age of Reform*, 233
Hollywood, 220, 237–39
Holmes, Oliver Wendell, 424, 566
Holmes, Oliver Wendell (Jr.), 91–92
Holocaust, 543; *see also* World War II
Holt, Hamilton, 394–95; *The Life Stories of Undistinguished Americans*, 395–400, 404, 408
Home Owners Loan Act, 196
Homestead Act (1862), 24–25, 34, 44–45
Hoover, Herbert, 185
Howells, William Dean, 10, 12, 23, 38, 40, 90; *The Leatherwood God*, 562; *Literary Friends and Acquaintances*, 161; on regional marginality, 161
Hubbell, Jay B., *American Literature*, 193
Huebsch, B. F., 126

Hughes, Langston, xix, 133, 151, 152, 288, 331, 350; on atomic bomb, 550–51; and Black Modernism, 349, 350; on Gorky, 531; in Harlem Renaissance, 300–01, 302; on wartime blood banks, 527; *The Big Sea*, 588; *Fine Clothes to the Jew*, 306; "Luani of the Jungles," 306; "Negro Artist and Racial Mountain," 300; "The Negro Speaks of Rivers," 289; *Not Without Laughter*, 307–08, 577; *The Ways of White Folks*, 308, 581; *The Weary Blues*, 306, 326–27

Huizinga, Johan, 243

Huneker, James, 558; *Painted Veils*, 566

hunger, 187, 194

Hurston, Zora Neale, xix, 151, 161, 255, **340–45**, 350, 496–97; breast imagery, 501–02; compared with Richard Wright, 496–02; on Gorky, 531; short stories, 340–41, 406–07; theatrical pieces, 341; *Dust Tracks on a Road*, 344, 378, 497, 515, 590; "The Gilded Six-Bits" 499–500; *Jonah's Gourd Vine*, 341, 342, 581; *Moses, Man of the Mountain*, 342, 344, 587; *Mules and Men*, 340, 341, 498, 511, 583; *Seraph on the Suwanee*, 344, 498; *Their Eyes Were Watching God*, 198, 341, 342–44, 496, 585

Huxley, Aldous, 258

Ibn Said, Omar, 430

I'll Take My Stand manifesto of Southern Agrarians, 256–57, 258

illustrators of prose, 510–11; *see also* photography

imagism, 448

immigration and migration, xvii, xviii, 23, 25, 44, 65, 229; African diaspora and Harlem, 352; and city transport, 384–86; debated by immigrants, 392–94; Jewish refugees, 233; New Negro movement, 287; population, 386–87; return to homeland, 545–46; in Roth's *Call It Sleep*, 478; seen as threat, 152, 393; South to North, 251–52; and unemployment rise, 186; *see also* ethnic literature

Independent (New York), 385, 394

indirection in writing, 531–32

individualism, residual, 208–09, 212–13; *see also* detective novels; Westerns

internment in World War II, 524–26

ironic reflection 10–14

Irvine, Alexander, 391, 394

Irwin, John T., 211

Isherwood, Christopher, 172

isolation and loneliness, 133; *see also* marginality

isolationism, 555

Italian American literature, 504–10; *see also* di Donato, Pietro; Mangione, Jerre

Italian Americans and internment, 526

Ives, Charles, 17

Jackman, Harold, 330

James, Henry, xviii, 4, 10, 34, 60–61, 168, 558; on ironic reflection, 12–13, 49; on streetcar settings, 384; *The American*, 10; *The American Scene*, 12, 13, 384; *The Bostonians,* 16; *The Golden Bowl*, 15, 16; *The Lesson of the Master*, 20; *The Middle Years*, 563; *Notes of a Son and Brother*, 561; "The Passionate Pilgrim," 24; *The Portrait of a Lady*, 8, 15–22, 23, 31,61; *The Princess Casamassima,* 5; *A Small Boy and Others*, 560; *Watch and Ward*, 16

James, William, 371–72, 423, 495

Janson, Drude Krog, 434

Japanese Americans and internment, 524–26

jazz, xix, 112–13, 327, 528, 530–31

Jazz Age, xviii, 108–09, 112–13

Jefferson, Thomas, 25

Jewett, Sarah Orne, 161, 170

Jewish Daily Forward, 542

Jews see antisemitism

Johnson, Charles S., 286; *Ebony and Topaz*, 292

Johnson, Georgia Douglas, 288

Johnson, James Weldon, 151, 152, 286, 298; *Along This Way*, 298; *The Autobiography of an Ex-Colored Man*, 64, 298–300, 402, 560; *Black Manhattan*, 287; *The Book of American Negro Poetry*, 292–93

Johnson, Owen, 558, 559; *Stover at Yale*, 139; *The Tennessee Shad*, 559

Josephson, Matthew, *Life Among the Surrealists*, 108, 114; *Portrait of the Artist as American*, 114

Joyce, James, 68, 447, 495; *Finnegans Wake*, 18; *Dubliners*, 131; *Ulysses*, xix, 355, 372, 515, 550

Judaism see anti-Semitism

Judson, Edward Zane Carroll (Ned Buntline), 35

Kafka, Franz, 478

Kallen, Horace M., 366, 422, 423

Kang, Younghill, 389; *East goes West*, 585

Kansas City Star, 179

Kato, Saburo, 430

Katzmann, Frederick G., 127

Kazin, Alfred, 197–98, 199, 466–67; *On Native Grounds*, 358; *Starting Out in the Thirties*, 197–98

Keller, Helen, 126

Kellogg, Paul, 293

Kelly, Myra, 391

Kerouac, Jack, *The Town and the City*, 596

Kesey, Ken, *One Flew over the Cuckoo's Nest*, 55

Kingston, Maxine Hong, 438

Kobrin, Leo, 406, 431, 558

Kouwenhoven, John, 524

Kronenberger, Louis, 104
Krutch, Joseph Wood, *The Modern Temper*, 255
Ku Klux Klan, 125, 126, 151, 287, 291

La Follette, Robert, 561
La Motte, Ellen, 97; *The Backwash of War*, 563
labeling, ethnic, 448–50
Ladies' Home Journal, 135, 153, 363, 393–94, 408, 462
LaFarge, Oliver, 389; *Laughing Boy*, 575
Lange, Dorothea, "Migrant Mother" photograph, 245; *An American Exodus* 241, 243
language, of Hollywood versions, 469–70; linguistic xenophobia, 430; of modernity, 408–09; other than English, 389, 415–16, 429–33, 439–40; of race, 152, 153; renewal and the "Lost Generation," 110; *see also* ethnic literature, language features; modernism, writing; neologisms of twentieth century
Lardner, Ring, 462; *How to Write Short Stories*, 570; *The Love Nest and Other Stories*, 573; *You Know Me, Al*, 563
Larsen, Nella, xix, 152, 161, 329, 350; *Passing*, 319–20, 379, 576; *Quicksand*, 297, 317–19, 379, 575
Latimer, Margery, 451
Laurent, Henri, 135–36
Lawrence, D. H., 245, 253; *Lady Chatterley's Lover*, 372; *Studies in Classic American Literature*, 66, 171
Lazarus, Josephine, 412
Le Sueur, Meridel, 231
League of American Writers, 233
Lefebvre, Henri, 136
Leighton, George, *Five Cities*, 245
Lemkin, Raphaël, *Axis Rule in Occupied Europe*, 367
Lenin, Nikolai, *The State and the Revolution*, 104
Lerner, Max, 104
Leslie, Shane, *The Celt and the War*, 126
Levin, Harry, 355
Levin, Meyer, 465; *Frankie and Johnnie*, 465; *The Old Bunch*, 465, 585; *Reporter*, 465
Lewis, Sinclair, 114, 133, 170; as amateur sociologist, 198–99; *Arrowsmith*, 572; *Babbitt*, 114–17, 120–21, 130, 164–65, 568; *Dodsworth*, 255, 576; *Elmer Gantry*, 574; *It Can't Happen Here*, 583; *Kingsblood Royal*, 594; *Main Street*, 114, 170, 566; *Middletown*, 114, 118, 194; *Our Mr Wrenn*, 561
Lewis, Wyndham, 168, 376–77, 460
Lewisohn, Ludwig, 358, 381–82, 455, 466; *The Case of Mr Crump*, 452; *The Island Within*, 452, 575; *The Story of American Literature*, 455; *Upstream*, 64–65, 452, 567; *The Vehement Flame*, 452–54, 577

Liberator, 419
liberty, civil, 3
Life magazine, 233
Lin, Yutang, 431; *Chinatown Family*, 594
Lindsay, Vachel, 5, 53, 63, 136
lines of expansion, 23–33
Lippmann, Walter, 64, 67, 68, 85, 130, 366; on Americanization, 387; *The Good Society*, 196; *The New Imperative,* 196
literary history, American, xiii–xiv
Locke, Alain, xix, 286, 293–94, 331; *The New Negro: An Interpretation*, 151–52, 292, 294, 328, 406, 572
Lockridge, Ross, 459
Lodge, Henry Cabot, 125
Loeb, Harold, and Gertrude Stein, 371; *The Way It Was*, 108
London, Jack, 3, 49, 57–62, 77, 79, 208, 558; influencing detective stories, 219; *The Call of the Wild*, 58, 59, 61; *The Iron Heel*, 225; *John Barleycorn*, 79; *Martin Eden*, 40, 60, 65, 77–80; *The People of the Abyss*, 58, 59; *The Sea Wolf*, 58; *Smoke Bellew*, 560; *The Son of the Wolf*, 57; *The Valley of the Moon*, 561; *White Fang*, 59, 61–62
Long, Huey, 187
Long, Sylvester C., 401
Loos, Anita, *Gentlemen Prefer Blondes*, 572
Lorentz, Pare, 242
Losey, Joseph, 539
loss of continuities, 13
"Lost Generation," xviii, 108, 109, 112, 181; and language, 110, 375
Lovecraft, H. P., *The Shadow out of Time*, 587; *Beyond the Wall of Sleep*, 590
Lowe, Pardee, 389
Loy, Mina, 155
Luce, Henry, 162, 197
Luhan, Mabel Dodge, and Armory Show, 71, 73; *Movers and Shakers*, 64–65, 66–67, 108
Lundgren, Eric, 511
Lyric Years (1900–916), xviii, 10–12, 66–70, 75–76, 77; communication changes, 67; compared with the Jazz Age, 112, 113; fading hope of, 168; harking back to, 228; and Wall Street Crash, 185, 200
Lytle, Andrew, 255

McAlmon, Robert, *Being Geniuses Together*, 108
McCarthy, Mary, 231; *The Company She Keeps*, 590
McClure, Samuel Sidney, 513, 514, 561
McClure's Magazine, 402
McCoy, Horace, 220; *I Should Have Stayed at Home*, 222; *Kiss Tomorrow Goodbye*, 222; *No Pockets for a Shroud*, 222; *They Shoot Horses, Don't They?*, 222–24, 237, 583

McCullers, Carson, *The Heart is a Lonely Hunter*, 588; *A Member of the Wedding*, 592; *Reflections in a Golden Eye*, 589
MacDonald, Duncan, 126
Macdonald, Dwight, 533
McKay, Claude, 151, 288, 311–16, 331, 349, 388; on Gertrude Stein, 379; on Hemingway, 465–66; *Banana Bottom*, 315–16, 580, 583; *Banjo*, 314–15, 576; *Color Scheme*, 312; *Home to Harlem*, 297, 312–15, 375, 407, 466, 575; "If We Must Die", 289, 312; *A Long Way from Home*, 391, 465, 585
McKenney, Ruth, 232; *Industrial Valley*, 231, 245; *My Sister Eileen*, 240
MacLeish, Archibald, *Land of the Free*, 190, 241, 243
MacMonnies, Mary Fairchild, *Primitive Woman*, 41
McNickle, D'Arcy, *Cree*, 389, 584
magazines, 135; *see also individual titles*
Mailer, Norman, *The Naked and the Dead*, 594
Major, Clarence, 380
Malamud, Bernard, 233
Mallarmé, Stéphane, 11
Malraux, André, 12
Maltz, Albert, 588; *The Underground Stream*, 190, 245
Mangione, Jerre, xix, 378; *Mount Allegro*, 391–92, 403, 429, 507–08, 509–10, 511, 590; and fascism 523
Mann, Thomas, 233, 452
March, William, *Company K*, 98
marginality and authority of writers, 14, 160–69; in ethnic literature, 408; and regional boundaries, 161–62
Marquand, John, *The Late George Apley*, 585
Marx, Karl, 4, 452
Marxism, 49, 58, 105; Americanization of, 197; in the Depression, 194, 208, 226, 230, 348–49, 455–57; neo-Marxists' utopian theory of art, xv; *see also* Communism
masculinity, 155, 213–15; "hard-boiled" writers, 461–62, 468–71
mass production, 122–23
Masses magazine, 68, 69–70, 73, 75, 90
Masters, Edgar Lee, *Spoon River Anthology*, 131
Mather, Frank, 71
Mathews, John Joseph, 389; *Sundown*, 581
Matthews, Brander, 422
Matthews, Victoria Earle, 286
Matthiessen F. O., 258
Mead, Margaret, 521, 524
mean streets novels, xviii, 5
Mellon, Andrew, 117, 130, 185
Melville, Herman, 58, 362; *Billy Budd*, 570
Mencken, H. L., 65, 68, 99, 113, 114; interest in language, 428–29; and middle-class values, 208; on the Midwest, 170; on the South, 254;

The American Language, 113, 428, 565; *Prejudices*, 565, 566, 568, 570
Messenger, 290, 327, 341, 563
Michener, James, *Tales of the South Pacific*, 593
Midwest and literature, 67, 161, 170, 171, 307
migration *see* immigration and migration
Miguéis, José Rodrigues, *Steerage*, 432–33, 586
Millay, Edna St Vincent, 127
Miller, Arthur, 233, 591
Miller, Henry, 200–04, 255; antiheroes, 199; commitment to self, 201, 202; and the Depression, 203–04; *Black Spring*, 200, 202, 454, 584; *The Rosy Crucifixion* (trilogy), 205; *Tropic of Cancer*, 200, 201, 202, 454, 582; *Tropic of Capricorn*, 198, 200, 201, 454, 587
miners' strikes, 194
Minter, David, xvii, xviii
Mitchell, Joseph, *McSorley's Wonderful Saloon*, 590
Mitchell, Margaret, 255; *Gone with the Wind*, 259–60, 261–62, 584
modernism, xvii, xviii, xix, 21, 49, 51; black, 348–52; cartoons, 536; ethnic labeling, 448–51; four literary types, 409–10; international, 266–67; interracial dining, 386; music, 357–58, 361, 364, 374, 536 (*see also* jazz); period covered, 355; photography, 373–74; post-World War II, 556; and totalitarianism, 528–35; writing, 374–75, *see also* Antin, Mary; art; ethnic literature; Hemingway, Ernest; Pound, Ezra; Rölvaag, Ole E.; Roth, Henry; Stein, Gertrude; Toomer, Jean; Wright, Richard
modernism, ethnic, 355–67; American languages, 428–33; fragmentation and quest for wholeness, 445–46; meaning of "American," 422–27; modern themes, 405–10; segregation, 385–86
modernism, paintings, 356–67, 359–61, 364, 373; city transport depicted, 384–85, 411, 415
modernity, xvii, 13, 362, 406–09, 415, 492–93; modernization in fiction, 493; and salesman figure, 499; and World War II, 539; *see also* Roth, Henry; Wright, Richard
Momaday, N. Scott, 389
money, and Wall Street Crash, 184; and writing, 134, 137–38
Monroe, Harriet, 133
Moore, Marianne, 159
More, Paul Elmer, *Aristocracy and Justice*, 54; *Shelburne Essays*, 167
Mori, Toshio, 389, 591, 595
Morrison, Toni, 473–74
Mother Earth journal, 70
Motherwell, Robert, 252
Motley, Willard, 407; *Knock on Any Door*, 497–98, 593

Mourning Dove, *Cogewea, the Half-Blood*, 574
movies *see* film industry
Muir, John, *My First Summer in the Sierra*, 559;
    Travels in Alaska, 562
multiethnicity in USA, 365–67
Mumford, Lewis, 104; *The Brown Decades*, 171; *The Culture of Cities*, 166; *The Golden Day*, 171
Münsterberg, Hugo, 374
Murger, Henri, 134
Murray, Albert, 286–87
Museum of Modern Art (New York), 357, 360
music, 357–58, 361, 364, 374; and environment, 167; *see also* jazz
Mussolini, Benito, 513–15, 522, 523

NAACP *see* National Association for the Advancement of Colored People
Nabokov, Vladimir, 542; *Bend Sinister*, 593; *The Real Life of Sebastian Knight*, 589
"Nadir" period in race relations, 285–86
Nassau Literary Magazine, 126
Nathan, George Jean, 68, 99, 113
Nation, 71, 423
National Association for the Advancement of Colored People (NAACP), 286, 287, 349
national identity, xv, xvii, 46–7
National Origins Act (1924), 125
National Recovery Act (NRA), 252
Native Americans, 34–5
Nazism and art, 531–32; *see also* anti-Semitism; racism and Nazis
Negro World, 291
Nelson, George "Baby Face," 211
neologisms of twentieth century, 367
New Criticism, xv, 157, 208
New Deal, 196–97, 232, 241–42, 243, 250; and build-up to World War II, 252
New England and literature, 161, 170
New Masses, 127, 194, 228, 229, 476, 510, 559
The New Negro, 292, 300
"New Negro" movement, xix, 285–88, 289–90, 292–94, 449
New Republic, 68, 92, 194
"New" as talisman, 64, 66, 67
New World features and gadgets, 406–07
New York, 25, 52, 132–33, 161–62; black Manhattan, 287, 304; capital of nation's literature, 165; Public Library, 292; Stock Exchange, 185–86
New York Panorama, 498
New York Sun, 418
New York *Times*, 185, 312–13, 358, 361, 365
New Yorker, 210, 546, 550
Nietzsche, Friedrich, 11, 13, 59, 78; works, *Human, All-Too-Human*, 11
Niggli, Josephina, 592
Nin, Anaïs, 155; *Diaries*, 159

Norris, *McTeague*, 87
North American Review, 102
Norton, Richard, 90
Norwegian-language writing, 431–32; *see also* Ager, Waldemar; Buslett, Ole Amundsen; Dahl, Dorthea; Janson, Drude Krog; Rölvaag, Ole E.; Wist, Johannes B.
novel, function and technique, 3–6; *see also* detective stories; "domestic" novels; history and the novel; *individual titles*; Westerns
Nugent, Richard Bruce, 329–30; "Smoke, Lilies, and Jade," 330, 573

O'Brien, Frederick, 565
Occomy, Maria *see* Bonner, Maria
O'Connor, Julia, 126
Odets, Clifford, 238; *Till the Day I Die*, 238; *Waiting for Lefty*, 238
Odum, Howard, 255
Ogan, Sarah, 232
O'Hara, John, 237; *Appointment in Samara*, 582; *Butterfield 8*, 583; *Hope of Heaven*, 586; *A Rage to Live*, 595
O'Keefe, Georgia, 171, 449, 535
Okina, Kyuin, 430
Okubo, Miné, 525
Olsen, Tillie, *Silences*, 231
O'Neill, Eugene, 443
Oppenheimer, James, 68, 75, 89
Opportunity, 286, 324, 341
oppositionalism, xv
Ornitz, Samuel, 388, 402
Orwell, George, 187, 200
Ostenso, Martha, *Wild Geese*, 572
Outlook, 385, 418
"outsiders" of Thirties, 210
Owen, Chandler, 290
Owsley, Frank, 255

Page, Myra, *Moscow Yankee*, 517
Paine, Thomas, 189, 232
painters of protest, 64
painting, 356–57, 359–61, 364, 373, 537; *see also* art; modernism
Palmer, A. Mitchell, 125
Palmer Raids(1919–20), 125–26
Panunzio, Constantine, 567
Paris and modernists, 512
Park, Robert E., 408, 492
Parker, Dorothy, *Here Lies*, 587
Parsons, Elsie Clews, 153
Partington, V. L., *Main Currents in American Thought*, 104
Partisan Review, 231, 363, 533–34
Pater, Walter, 10–11; *Studies in the History of the Renaissance*, 10
Patterson, Louise, 348–49

Pearson, Karl, 48
Peattie, Donald, *A Prairie Grove*, 586
Perry, Ann, 350
Pershing's Crusaders (film), 92
personal writings of Thirties, 229
Peterkin, Julia, *The Merry-Go-Round*, 499,
    500–01
Petry, Ann, 459, 498; *The Street*, 592
Philadelphia Public Ledger, 373
Phillips, David, 563
photography, 190, 241, 243–46, 250, 361; *see also*
    illustrators of prose
Pittsburgh Courier, 301
Plessy v. Ferguson Supreme Court case, 288
pluralism of literature, xiv
Poe, Edgar Allen, 52–53, 362; "A Man of the
    Crowd," 172
political commitment, search for "culture,"
    190–99; in the Thirties, 188–89,
    248–49
Pollock, Jackson, 536
Poole, Ernest, 394, 400, 420; *The Harbor*, 562; *His
    Family*, 563; *The Voice of the Street*, 420
popular discourse, 57–62
population, 63, 186, 386–87; *see also* immigration
    and migration
populism, 208
Porter, Katherine Anne, 199, 255, 264–65;
    Flowering Judas, 577; *The Leaning Tower*, 591;
    Pale Horse, Pale Rider, 587
Portuguese-language writing, 432–33
Potter, David, 255
Pound, Ezra, 5, 21, 68, 73–74, 108; his fascism,
    514–15; *Cantos*, 166; "Hugh Selwyn
    Mauberley," 98; "In a Station of the Metro,"
    384; *Jefferson and/or Mussolini*, 515
poverty, 142, 184–87, 198, 455; in the South,
    251–53, 348
Prager, Robert, 90
Praz, Mario, 258
printing, 362, 363
privatization, 209
professionalism, rise of, 134–35
Prohibition, 128–29
proletarian writing, 190, 198, 211, 227, 229;
    effect of the New Deal, 232–33
protest literature, 63–64, 199; *see also* Harlem
    Renaissance
Proust, Marcel, 198, 199
psychology, 5
publishing and marketing, 212, 363
Pulver, Mary Brecht, 92
Pupin, Michael, 391; *From Immigrant to Inventor*,
    569
Purinton, Edward Earl, 118
Puritanism, 66, 152, 168, 455
Pyle, Ernie, *Brave Men*, 591

Quakerism, 540–41

race, xix, 204, 367, 451; ethnic stereotyping,
    380–81, 391–92; marginality and authority,
    160–62; riots, 349, 387; universalism in
    1940s and 1950s, 497–98; writers on, 198,
    351; *see also* ethnic literature
racism, anti-Semitism, 516, 532; in the
    Depression, 204; ethnic labeling, 448–49; in
    Henry Miller's writing, 202, 204; language,
    152, 153; laws encouraging, 387; "Nadir"
    period, 285–86, 302–03; and Nazism,
    532–33; psychological consequences, 495; in
    World War II, 526–28, 556; *see also*
    multiethnicity of USA
radical novels of Thirties, 190, 202, 211, 225
Radical Reconstruction, 34
Radin, Paul, 104
radio, 195, 197, 362
Raleigh, Sir Walter, 24
Rand, Ayn, *The Fountainhead*, 520, 590; *We the
    Living*, 519–20
Randolph, A. Philip, 290
Rankin, Jeanette, 126
Ransom, John Crowe, 154, 255, 257
Ravage, Marcus, 390
Read, Herbert, 258
realism, 208–09, 372, 530–31
Rechy, John, 390
"Red Decade", 189
Red Scare (1919), 125, 151
Redfield, Robert, 492
Reed, John, 67, 70, 90, 208; *Ten Days that Shook
    the World*, 565
regions and marginality, 161–62, 170
Reid, Sydney, 394
Reiss, Winold, 293
religion, in ethnic lives, 397–98; in the novel,
    213; Southern fundamentalism, 254
Repplier, Agnes, 423
revolutionary tradition, 6
Rice, Elmer, *Prologue to Glory*, 242
Richards, I. A., *The Principles of Literary Criticism*,
    104
Ricketts, Edward F., 234
Ridge, Lola, 127
Riis, Jacob, 390
Rilke, Rainer Maria, 122
Rizk, Samuel/Salom, 388, 390; *Syrian Yankee*,
    522–23
Roberts, Kenneth, 250–51; *Arundel*, 250, 577;
    Northwest Passage, 186, 250, 585; *Oliver
    Wiswell*, 251; *Rabble in Arms*, 250, 580
Robeson, Paul, 332, 380–81
Robinson, Edwin Arlington, 66
Rölvaag, O. E., 23, 438–39; *Amerika-Breve*, 435;
    Concerning Our Heritage, 435; *Giants in the*

Earth, 25–26, 27–29, 389, 392, 435–41, 574; *Peder Victorious*, 576; *Pure Gold*, 435; *Their Fathers' God*, 578; *Totullinger*, 435

Roof, Katherine 152, *The American Sense of Humor*, 152

Roosevelt, Franklin D., 195–97, 348

Roosevelt, Nicholas, 422

Roosevelt, Theodore, 356, 386, 558

Rosenbaum, Alissa Zinovievna *see also* Rand, Ayn

Rosenberg, Harold, 362

Rosenfeld, Isaac, 445; *Passage from Home*, 592

Rosenfeld, Paul, *A Boy in the Sun*, 575

Ross, Leonard Q. *see* Rosten, Leo

Rosskam, Edwin, 190, 241, 243, 246

Rosten, Leo, 469, 479

Roth, Henry, xix, 25, 199, 233, 407, 503; and communism, 517; fascism, 523; Freudian influence, 476–77, 481, 487; language, 479–82; masterpiece of ambiguity, 487; and modernism, 477; nostalgia and memory, 481–83, 486; *Call It Sleep*, 228–29, 365, 425–26, **475–89**, 490, 582

Rourke, Constance, *American Humor: a Study of the National Character*, 194

Russell, Bertrand, 51

Rutledge, Marice, *Children of Fate*, 172

Ryan, Father John, 187

Sacco-Vanzetti trial, 125, 126–28, 151, 168, 457

salesmen in literature, 499–501, 508–09

Salinger, J. D., 596

Sandburg, Carl, 438

Santayana, George, 13–14, 64

Saroyan, William, 378–79, 471–73, 511; *My Name is Aram*, 588

Sartre, Jean-Paul, 207, 459

Saturday Evening Post, 135, 359, 361

scapegoats for materialism, 152

Schneider, Isidor, 456

Schomburg, Arthur, 288, 292

Schuyler, George, 302–03; *Black No More*, 335–36, 579; *Ethiopian Stories*, 336; "The Negro Art Hokum," 300, 301

Schwartz, Delmore, 168, 375, 464, 465, 527–28; "A Bitter Farce," 592

science, 120

Scott, Evelyn, *The Wave*, 255

Scott Fitzgerald, F. *see* Fitzgerald, F. Scott

Scottsboro arrests (Alabama), 211

Scribner's magazine, 462

Sedgwick, Anne, 559

Sedgwick, Ellery, 417–18, 423

Seeger, Alan, 91, 92

Seemuller, Anne Moncure Crane, 16

segregation laws, xix

Séjour, Victor, 430

self-determination, xvii

Service, Robert W., *Rhymes of a Red Cross Man*, 93

Seven Arts magazine, 68, 75, 76, 90

sexuality, 198, 210, 216; and American realism, 372; Djuna Barnes, 204–05; frankness in ethnic writing, 454–55; "free love" literature, 326–31; Henry Miller, 201, 202–03, 454; and Hollywood, 239; Ludwig Lewisohn, 452; Nella Larsen, 319; Wallace Thurman, 329

Shaler, N. S., 125

sharecroppers, 246–47, 254

Shaw, Irwin, *The Young Lions*, 594

Sherman, Stuart, 401, 462

Siegel, William, 510

Simmel, Georg, 408

Simon, Howard, 511

Sinclair, B. M. *see* Bower, B. M.

Sinclair, Upton, *Boston*, 127, 208, 575; *The Brass Clock*, 565; *The Goose-Step*, 569; *The Jungle*, 63, 90, 225, 394, 395; *King Coal*, 563; *Oil!*, 574

Singer, Isaac Bashevis, 388; *The Family Moskat*, 542–43, 596

Sitting Bull (Sioux leader), 34, 35

Sklar, George, *Stevedore*, 242

slavery, 34, 253–54, 258, 444

Slesinger, Tess, 231; *The Unpossessed*, 190, 582

Sloan, John, 64

Smith, Adam, 193

Smith, Bernard, 104

Smith, Bessie, 326, 327

Smith, Betty, *A Tree Grows in Brooklyn*, 590

Smith, June, 200

Smith, Lillian, 255, 591

Smith, Louis, 68

Smith, Jesse, 117

Smith, William Gardner, 498; *The Last of the Conquerors*, 526

social experimentation and literature, 194

social fiction, 230–32

socialist realism, 530–31, 533

Solger, Reinhold, 430

Sollors, Werner, xvii, xviii, xix–xx

Soule, George, 104

South, decade of great writing, 255; economic success and failure, 253–54; government agencies, 252; and literature, 7, 161, 170, 252, 254–55; negative heritage, 257; slavery, 253–54; Southern Agrarians, 256–57; Southern Renaissance, **252–65**; *see also* Faulkner, William

Southern Review, 257–58

Soviet Union and antimodernism, 529–31; *see also* Communism

Spain, 233

Spargo, John, *The Bitter Cry of the Children*, 63

spectatorial attitudes in literature, 172–73

Spencer, Herbert, 58

Spengler, Oswald, *The Decline of the West*, 104

Spiller, Robert, xiii; *Literary History of the United States*, 158–59
Sports Illustrated, 233
sports and popular culture, 137
Stafford, Jean, *Boston Adventure*, 591; *The Mountain Lion*, 593
Stalin, Josef, 233
Statue of Liberty, 396, 420–21, 478
Stearns, Harold (ed.), *Civilisation in the United States*, 152–53
Steffens, Lincoln, 66; *Autobiography*, 227, 578; *The Shame of the Cities*, 63
Stegner, Wallace, *The Big Rock Candy Mountain*, 591; *The Women on the Wall*, 596
Stein, Gertrude, xvii, 13, 21, 57, 68; admiration and support for, 377–79; and Armory Show, 71; on atomic bomb, 546–47; death scenes in prose, 368–69, 384; ethnic modernism, 336, 368, 457; as experimental writer, 155–58; and fascism, 516; and film dialogue, 469–70; grammar/style of writing, 156–58, 369–70, 381–82; Hemingway on, 460–61; influence of modernist painting/photography, 373–74; interest in modernist music, 374; interest in psychology, 371–72; and the "Lost Generation," 109; "negro sunshine" phrase, 381; and racial stereotyping, 380–81; as teacher of writers, 110, 156; *As a Wife Has a Cow: A Love Story*, 372, 373; *The Autobiography of Alice B. Toklas*, 156, 175, 370, 371, 373, 401, 537, 581; *Everybody's Autobiography*, 372; *Four Saints in Three Acts* (opera) 536; *The Genealogical History of America*, 158; *Lectures in America*, 373–74; *The Making of Americans*, 10, 157, 193, 370, 390, 572; "Melanctha: Each One as She May," 368–69, 374, 376, 377–78; *Q.E.D.*, 374, 381; *Tender Buttons*, 157, 561; *Three Lives*, 85–86, 131, 157, 167, 201, 368–69, 373, 383; *Wars I Have Seen*, 157, 158, 592; *What Are Masterpieces*, 157, 378; *Yes is for a Very Young Man*, 593
Steinbeck, John, 233–35; *The Grapes of Wrath*, 233–35, 587; *In Dubious Battle*, 233, 235, 584; *The Long Valley*, 234, 586; *Of Mice and Men*, 235, 585; *Tortilla Flat*, 234, 583
Steiner, Edward, 390; *From Alien to Citizen*, 421, 561
Stella, Joseph, 419–20
stereotyping, ethnic, 380–81, 391–92
Stern, Elizabeth, 402–03
Stieglitz, Alfred, 25, 30–31, 72, 357
Stoddard, Lothrop, *The Rising Tide of Color Against White World-Supremacy*, 126
Stong, Phil, *State Fair*, 580
Story Magazine, 242, 388
streetcar in writing, 384–86, 428, 430, 451, 459, 475–76, 487–88; *see also* transport in literature

Stribling, T. S., *Birthright*, 567; *The Forge*, 258, 578; *The Store*, 258, 580; *Strange Moon*, 255; *Teeftallow*, 573; *Unfinished Cathedral*, 258, 582
Strong, Philip D., 128
Sturzo, Luigi, *Italy and Fascism*, 367
Suárez, Mario, 389–90, 503–04, 594
Suckow, Ruth, 133; *Country People*, 570
Sui Sin Far (Edith Maude), 389; *Mrs. Spring Fragrance*, 560
suicide rate increase, 186
Sumner, William Graham, *Folkways*, 104
surrealism, 209
Survey Graphic, 286, 293
Szilard, Leo, "Report on Grand Central Terminal," 552–55, 594

Taggard, Genevieve, 66, 70, 173, 187
Tanner, Henry O., 301
Tarbell, Ida, *History of the Standard Oil Company*, 64
Tarkington, Booth, 84; *Alice Adams*, 566; *The Magnificent Ambersons*, 564; *Penrod*, 561
Tate, Allen, *The Fathers*, 261; *Jefferson Davis: His Rise and Fall*, 255
Taylor, Frederick, *Principles of Scientific Management*, 66, 559
Taylor, Paul S., 241, 245
Taylor, Peter, 595
technology, 119–20, 362
television, 362, 363
Teller, Charlotte, *The Cage*, 225
Thayer, Webster, 127
Thirties, looking toward the past, 191–92; political commitment, 188–89; search for "culture," 190–91
Thomas, Norman, 126
Thomas, W. I., 492
Thoreau, H. D., *Walden*, 59
Thresher, Max Bennett, 391
Thurber, James, 187; *Let Your Mind Alone!*, 585; *My World and Welcome to It*, 590
Thurber, James and White, E. B. *Is Sex Necessary?*, 576
Thurman, Wallace, 293, 327–30; *The Blacker the Berry*, 327, 328–29, 576; *Harlem*, 329–30; *Infants of the Spring*, 329, 580
Time magazine, 162, 233
Tobenkin, Elias, *Witte Arrives*, 563
Tocqueville, Alexis de, 92, 105
Todorov, Tzvetan, 9
Tolson, Melvin, 380
Toomer, Jean, xix, 151, 152, 288, 309, 350, 406; background, 443, 450–51; on term "American," 449–51; and universalism, 540–41; writing style, 444–45; "The Blue Meridian", 311; *Cane*, 132, 300, 308–10, 365, 379, **442–51**, 569; *Essentials*, 450; *Natalie Mann*, 445

totalitarianism, 367, 518, 524
translation process, 439
transport in literature, 384–85, 407–08, 411, 415, 428, 430, 490, 525
Treaty of Versailles (1919), 288
Trilling, Lionel, 52, 358–59; *The Middle of the Journey*, 594
Troeltsch, Ernst, 4–5
trolley-car *see* streetcar; transport in literature
Tugwell, R. G., 104
Turgenev, Ivan, *A Sportsman's Sketches*, 131
Turner, Frederick Jackson, 24, 43–47, 48; *The Frontier in America*, 104, 170–71
Twain, Mark (Samuel Clemens), 174; *Huckleberry Finn*, 11, 14, 21, 23; *The Mysterious Stranger*, 562
Twenties, 125–33; in retrospect, 187–188; *see also* Jazz Age; Lost Generation
Tyler, Alice Felt, *Freedom's Ferment*, 233
Tzara, Tristan, 69

uncertainty and confidence, 15–22
unemployment, 186, 226
Universal Negro Improvement Association (UNIA), 152, 287
urban decline and fall, 45
Urban League, 286

Valéry, Paul, 258
Van Doren, Carl, 461
Van Vechten, Carl, 66, 302, 362; *Nigger Heaven*, 303–05, 376, 407, 573
Veblen, Thorstein, *Business Enterprise*, 104
Ventura, Luigi, 439
Vidal, Gore, *The City and the Pillar*, 595; *Williwaw*, 592
Villareal, José, 390
violence, in detective stories, 219–24; in documentary works, 211–12; public, 211; mob lynchings, 287, 290, 387; in social writing, 231
Volstead Act (1919), 128
Vorse, Mary Heaton, 70, 194, 231

Walcott, Derek, 311
Walker, F. A., 125
Walker, Margaret, 242
Wall Street Crash (1929), 184–87, 199, 203; and Southern Renaissance, 252–53; and writers' hopes, 209
Wall Street Journal, 185
Walrond, Eric, 288, 290, 291, 573
Walton, Eda Lou, 488, 503
war *see* Civil War; Native Americans; World War I; World War II
war as metaphor, 170; *see also* Hemingway, Ernest
Ward, A. C., 112

Ward, Harry, 126
Warner, W. Lloyd, 366
Warren, Robert Penn, *All the King's Men*, 163, 216, 593; *John Brown: The Making of a Martyr*, 255; *Night Rider*, 587; *Southern Review* (ed.), 257; *Wild Enough and Time*, 596
Washington, Booker T., 386; *Up from Slavery*, 391
waste, economic, 209
Watanna, Onoto (Winifred Maude), 402
Waters, Ethel, 332
Watson, John B., *Behaviorism*, 136
wealth and poverty, 142–50, 160, 185
Weatherman, Clara, *Marching! Marching!*, 190
Weber, Max, 4, 54
Weiss, Felix Feri, *The Sieve*, 393
Wellington, C. G. (Pete), 179
Wells, H. G., *The War That Will End War*, 94
Welsh language writing, 431
Welty, Eudora, 242, 255, 589; *Delta Wedding*, 593; *The Golden Apples*, 595; *The Robber Bridegroom*, 590
Wendell, Barrett, 422–23
West, Nathanael (Nathan Weinstein), 199, 233, 236–40, 255; *A Cool Million*, 237, 582; *The Day of the Locust*, 198, 237–40, 587; *Dream Life of Balso Snell*, 236–37, 578; *Miss Lonelyhearts*, 155, 163, 198, 236–37, 240, 581
Westcott, Glenway, *Goodbye, Wisconsin*, 151
Westerns, 198, 212–16
Wharton, Edith, xviii, 3, 13, 23, 49, 80–81, 83; and World War I, 93; *The Age of Innocence*, 85, 123, 428, 566; *A Backward Glance*, 108, 123, 124, 582; *The Custom of the Country*, 85, 92, 124, 561; *Ethan Frome*, 92, 559; *Fighting France*, 93; *French Ways and Their Meaning*, 123; *The House of Mirth*, 40, 80, 81–83, 84–85, 92; *The Marne*, 91, 93; *A Son at the Front*, 93
Wheatley, Phillis, 292
Whipple, T. K., *Study Out the Land*, 59
White, E. B., *One Man's Meat*, 590
White, E. B. and Thurber, James, 576
White, Walter, 286; *The Fire in the Flint*, 337–38, 570; *Flight*, 338, 573; *Rope and Faggott*, 338
Whitehead, Alfred North, 17–8
Whitfield, Raoul, *Death in a Bowl*, 237–38, 577
Whitman, Walt, 11–12, 24, 35, 174, 189; *A Backward Glance o'er Travel'd Roads*, 11–12; and modernism, 362, 445, 450; and Ole Rölvaag's work, 438; view of USA, 365–66
Wilder, Thornton, 230, 550; *The Bridge of San Luis Rey*, 574; *The Cabala*, 573; *Heaven's My Destination*, 230
Williams, Bert, 332
Williams, Dafydd Rhys, 431
Williams, William Carlos, 87, 356; *In the American Grain*, 171; *White Mule*, 228

Wilson, Edmund, 127, 134, 181, 194, 242; *American Jitters*, 190, 193, 250; *Axel's Castle*, 193, 198, 362; *I Thought of Daisy*, 154; *Patriotic Gore*, 93; *To the Finland Station*, 193; *Travels in Two Democracies*, 193

Wilson, Harry Leon, *Merton of the Movies*, 569

Winther, Sophus Keith, 440; *Mortgage Your Heart*, 585; *Take All To Nebraska*, 584; *This Passion Never Dies*, 586

Winthrop, John, 24

Winwar, Frances, 399

Wirth, Louis, 492

Wist, Johannes B., *The Home on the Prairie*, 435, 568; *Immigrant Scenes*, 435; *Jonasville*, 435, 569; *Newcomer Sketches*, 566

Wister, Owen, *The Pentecost of Calamity*, 562; *The Virginian*, 38, 53–54, 213

Wolfe, Thomas, 263–64, 515; *Of Time and the River*, 583; *Look Homeward, Angel*, 255, 262–63, 264, 576; *You Can't Go Home Again*, 263,588

Wolfert, Ira, *Tucker's People*, 227–28, 591

Wolff, David, 211

Wollstonecraft, Mary, *A Vindication of the Rights of Women*, 154

Woman's Home Companion, 165

women, black writers, 161; "domestic" novels, 213–14; feminization fear, **152–59**; in fiction, 32; landscape and female sexuality, 171; misogyny, 454; social fiction difficulties, 230–31; in Steinbeck's writing, 235; subjugation and repression, 204; suffrage, 154; and World War I, 95–96, 172; *see also* gender; sexuality

Wong, Jade Snow, 592

Woodward, C. Vann, 255

Works Progress Administration (US Government), 350, 388

World War I, 74–75, 173–74, 364; anti-German feeling, 95; and black Americans, 96–97; effect on language, 555; influence on writing, 89–01, 110; patriotism, 90–94; post-war

disillusionment, 97–01, 108, 110–12; return of detachment, 102–07; and the South, 251; women and, 95–96, 172

World War II, 364; atom bomb, 546–51; concentration camps, 539–43; internment after Pearl Harbor, 524–26; military build-up, 252, 515; modernism, 555–56; modernity, 539

WPA *see* Works Progress Administration

Wright, Harold, *The Winning of Barbara Worth*, 559

Wright, Richard, xix, 10, 199, 211, 242, **345–47**, 350; background, 492–93; breast imagery, 502; clock-time imagery, 491–93; and Communism, 517–18; compared with Zora Neale Hurston, 496–502; on Gertrude Stein, 377–78; on Hemingway, 467; influence of Eliot and Joyce, 495; modernity and racism, 498; in Southern Renaissance, 255; on wartime blood banks, 527; *American Hunger*, 378; *Black Boy*, 378, 390, 428, 496, 502, 592; *Lawd Today*, 345–46, 356, 490–91, 585; *Native Son*, 255, 10, 345, 346, 388, 454, 491–92, 493–95, 588; *The Outsider*, 537; *Savage Holiday*, 498; *Twelve Million Black Voices*, 190, 241, 243, 255, 496, 498; *Uncle Tom's Children*, 255, 198, 242, 346–47, 467, 500, 501–02, 586

Wyckoff, Walter, 40, 142

Yale Review, 153

Yamamoto, Hisaye, 389, 525–26, 595, 596

Yeats, W. B., 69

Yerby, Frank, 242, 498

Yezierska, Anzia, 170, 388; *Bread Givers*, 64, 572; *Hungry Hearts*, 363, 566; *Salome of the Tenements*, 363, 392–93, 407, 569

Yiddish-language writing, 431

Young, Stark, 268

Zafar, Rafia, xvii, xviii–xix

Zangwill, Israel, 362; *The Melting-Pot*, 412